Classic Devotionals by Jim Reimann

Evening by Evening: The Devotions of Charles Spurgeon
(expanded, indexed, and updated in today's language by Jim Reimann),
the companion volume to *Morning by Morning: The Devotions of Charles Spurgeon*

Morning by Morning: The Devotions of Charles Spurgeon
(expanded, indexed, and updated in today's language by Jim Reimann),
the companion volume to *Evening by Evening: The Devotions of Charles Spurgeon*

My Utmost for His Highest by Oswald Chambers
(updated by Jim Reimann)

Streams in the Desert: 366 Daily Devotional Readings by L. B. Cowman
(updated by Jim Reimann)

Streams for Teens by L. B. Cowman
(updated by Jim Reimann)

Streams in the Desert for Graduates by L. B. Cowman
(updated by Jim Reimann)

Morning by Morning

THE DEVOTIONS OF
CHARLES SPURGEON

EXPANDED, INDEXED & UPDATED EDITION IN TODAY'S LANGUAGE

JIM REIMANN

Editor of Updated Editions of *Streams in the Desert®*,
My Utmost for His Highest, and
Evening by Evening: The Devotions of Charles Spurgeon

ZONDERVAN®

ZONDERVAN.com/
AUTHORTRACKER
follow your favorite authors

ZONDERVAN

Morning by Morning: The Devotions of Charles Spurgeon
Copyright © 2008 by James G. Reimann

This title is also available as a Zondervan ebook.
Visit www.zondervan.com/ebooks.

Zondervan's edition formerly published as *Look Unto Me*

Requests for information should be addressed to:

Zondervan, *Grand Rapids, Michigan* 49530

Library of Congress Cataloging-in-Publication Data

Spurgeon, C. H. (Charles Haddon), 1834-1892.
    Morning by morning : the devotions of Charles Spurgeon : one of the best-loved devotionals of all
  time. — Expanded, indexed & updated in today's language /
Jim Reimann.
      p. cm.
    Originally published: Look unto me. c2008.
    Includes index.
    ISBN 978-0-310-32931-2 (softcover)
    1. Devotional calendars — Baptists. 2. Bible — Devotional literature. I. Reimann, James. II. Title.
  BV4811.   S6669 — 2010

  242'.2 — dc22   2010034212

Cover design: Michelle Lenger
Cover photography: Veer®
Interior design: Beth Shagene

Printed in the United States of America

The Sovereign LORD ... wakens me *morning by morning,*
wakens my ear to listen like one being taught.

Isaiah 50:4

The History behind *Morning by Morning*

The Sovereign Lord ... wakens me **morning by morning**,
wakens my ear to listen like one being taught.

Isaiah 50:4

"Sell all [the books] you have ... and buy Spurgeon"

These are the words of the noted twentieth-century German theologian Helmut Thielicke (1908 – 86). Including Spurgeon's 140 books and 25,000 sermons, he has some 25 million words in print, more than any other Christian author, living or dead.

Spurgeon's conversion

Charles Haddon Spurgeon (June 19, 1834 – January 31, 1892) finished writing *Morning by Morning* when he was only thirty-one years of age in 1865 — an amazing accomplishment for such a young man! By that time, however, he had been a pastor faithfully expositing God's Word fourteen years, for he was called to the ministry at the early age of seventeen. Ultimately, he would leave this earth at the age of fifty-seven, having spent forty years as a preacher, pastor, and author, as well as a founder of a pastor's college and an orphanage.

The Lord saved him at the age of fifteen on January 6, 1850. The following is his salvation account in his own words:

It pleased God in my childhood to convict me of my sin. I lived as a miserable creature, finding no hope or comfort; thinking, surely God would never save me. But I resolved to visit every place of worship in town to find the way of salvation. I was willing to do anything, and be anything, if God would only forgive me.

I set off, going to all the places of worship, and though I dearly venerate the men who occupy those pulpits now, and did so then, I must honestly say I never heard them once fully preach the gospel. I mean by that, they preached truth, great truths, many good truths that were fitting to many of their congregation — spiritually-minded people — but what I wanted to know was, "How can I get my sins forgiven?" And they never told me that. I wanted to hear how a poor sinner, under conviction of sin, might find peace with God.

At last, one snowy day — it snowed so much I could not go to the place I had determined to go — I was forced to stop along the road, and it was a blessed stop to me. I found an obscure street and on that street was a little chapel — a place I did not know. I entered and sat down, but no minister came. Finally, a very thin-looking man came to the pulpit and opened his Bible and read these words: "Look unto me, and be ye saved, all the ends of the earth" (Isa. 45:22 KJV). Then, setting his eyes upon me, as if he knew my heart, he said: "Young man, you are in trouble." Well, I was, sure enough. He continued, "You will never get out of it unless you look to Christ." And then, lifting up his hands, he cried out, "Look, look, look! It is only look!" I saw at once the way of salvation. Oh, how I did leap for joy at that moment! I don't know what else he said — I did not take much notice of it, for I was so possessed with that one thought. I had been waiting to do fifty things, but when I heard this word "Look!" what a charming word it seemed to me. Oh, I looked until I could almost have looked my eyes away! And in heaven I will look on still in my joy unspeakable.

I now think I am bound never to preach a sermon without preaching to sinners. I do think that a minister who can preach a sermon without addressing sinners does not know how to preach.

Thus began a life fully surrendered to the Lord and His Word.

Spurgeon's love of education

Although Spurgeon never finished college or attended seminary, it would be a mistake to consider him uneducated. His personal library consisted of more than 12,000 books, most, if not all, he had read, typically reading six books per week. He shares his lack of formal seminary training with the likes of Augustine (354 – 430), John Calvin (1509 – 64), Dwight L. Moody (1837 – 99), Arthur Pink (1886 – 1952), D. Martyn Lloyd-Jones (1899 – 1981), Billy Graham (1918-), and many other renowned preachers. Spurgeon's own writings have been so widely read and distributed that there are few pastors or seminarians around that world who do not own at least one of his books.

This is not intended to cast aspersions on formal theological training, for Spurgeon surely supported it — as long as it was biblically sound. Nevertheless, the church should remain open to Spurgeon's brand of training, or we may miss the next preacher with an exceptional insight into God's Word. In fact, Spurgeon spent much of his life training new candidates for the pastorate through the Pastor's College, which he founded in 1856, early in his career. He once described the professors of the college in these words: "The Lord has sent us tutors who are lovers of sound doctrine and zealous for the truth. Heresy in colleges means false doctrine throughout the churches, for to defile the fountain is to pollute the streams."

Why "From the pen of Jim Reimann" daily segments

Expanding and updating the writings of Charles Spurgeon is a humbling experience — something I readily admit. Yet my purpose is the same as my purpose in previously updating *My Utmost for His Highest* (Oswald Chambers) and *Streams in the Desert* (Lettie Cowman) — to make these great works from the nineteenth and early twentieth centuries accessible to today's readers.

In *Morning by Morning*, however, I also have added my own comments to supplement Spurgeon's thoughts. One purpose is to shed further light on the Scriptures based on my own life-long study of the Scriptures. The Lord called me to teach His Word more than twenty-seven years ago, and twelve years ago led me into a Bible-teaching ministry offering pilgrimages to Israel. Since then my wife Pam and I have been privileged to travel there more than twenty times, studying and teaching. Many of my comments have come from insights gleaned in what I consider to be the world's greatest seminary — Israel.

My primary purpose is to get people into God's Word itself, not simply another devotional book, for the true power lies there. You will soon discover that most of my comments consist of sharing additional verses of Scripture to consider, or giving the reader the context of Spurgeon's text. By design, one year in *Morning by Morning* will take the reader to every book of the Bible — a claim few devotionals can make.

Spurgeon's influence on Oswald Chambers and Lettie Cowman

There can be no doubt that the writers of the bestselling devotionals of all time, *My Utmost for His Highest* (Chambers) and *Streams in the Desert* (Cowman), were greatly influenced by the ministry of Charles Spurgeon. In fact, Oswald Chambers was saved as a fourteen-year-old teenager immediately after hearing Spurgeon preach at his church in London, while visiting there with his father, Clarence. Hannah, Oswald's mother, also was converted to Christ under the preaching of Spurgeon, and she and Oswald's father were both baptized by the great preacher. And Clarence Chambers was one of the first students to enroll in Spurgeon's Pastor's College. After spending many years reading *Morning by Morning, Evening by Evening* (also by Spurgeon), and *My Utmost for His Highest*, I can attest personally to the strong influence Spurgeon had on Oswald Chambers, as evidenced by his writings.

Lettie Cowman appears to have been greatly influenced by Spurgeon as well. Her *Streams in the Desert* is a compilation of more than 250 contributors who influenced her life, and Spurgeon is quoted thirty times, far more than any other contributor. And as I said in the introduction to the updated edition of *Streams in the Desert*, there is also a tie between Oswald Chambers and Lettie Cowman, because the Cowmans, who were missionaries to the Orient, once invited Oswald Chambers to minister with them in Japan.

There is thus a historic tie between all four of these enduring devotionals: *My Utmost for His Highest*, *Streams in the Desert*, *Morning by Morning*, and *Evening by Evening*.

Spurgeon's enduring legacy

Spurgeon once described his approach to preaching with these words: "I take my text and make a beeline to the cross" — making his message timeless! A personal friend of his once wrote:

> The work done by C. H. Spurgeon cannot die, for I once heard him say, "I beseech you to live not only for this age, but also for the next. I would fling my shadow through the eternal ages if I could." He has done it. His work is an imperishable as the truth of God. His memory shall not fade like a vanishing star, nor his works be forgotten like a dying echo. He will shine on, never ceasing to brighten human lives by the truth he preached, the work he accomplished, and the stainless life he lived.

Spurgeon has been called the greatest preacher since the apostle Paul and has come to be known as "the prince of preachers." My prayer is that you, the reader, will gain insight into God's Word through Spurgeon's work, expanded, indexed, and updated in *Morning by Morning*, and that new generations of readers will discover the timeless truths brought together by Spurgeon — God's uncompromising servant.

Like Abel, Charles Spurgeon "offered God a better sacrifice," and although he passed into glory 118 years ago, "by faith he still speaks, even though he is dead" (Heb. 11:4).

"May the glory of the Lord be praised in his dwelling place!" (Ezek. 3:12).

Jim Reimann
September 2010
(Reader's comments are welcome at *JimReimann.com*.)

Excerpt from Spurgeon's Original Preface, December 1865

Morning devotions have always been dear to enlightened, heaven-loving souls, and it has been their rule, never to see the face of man till they have first seen the face of God. Thus, the first fresh hour of every morning should be dedicated to the Lord, whose mercy gladdens it with golden light.

If you do not have time to read both the morning devotional and at least one chapter of Scripture, I earnestly entreat you to dispense with this book, for I would be greatly grieved to know that anyone read the Word of God less on my account. I have had it in my heart to lead my friends to search their Bibles more than ever, and therefore I have culled passages out of corners and nooks of Scripture, that curiosity might lead to a search for their context; I will be disappointed indeed, if, after all, I frustrate my own purpose by diverting one moment of time to the perusal of my remarks that ought to have been given to searching the Word of God itself.

With many prayers for Heaven's blessing upon this labor of love, and with earnest requests for the prayers of the faithful, this work is humbly dedicated to the honor of the Triune Jehovah, and respectfully presented to the Christian Church.

January

January 1

That year they ate of the produce of Canaan.

Joshua 5:12

From the pen of Charles Spurgeon:

Israel's weary wanderings were now at an end, and the rest that had been promised was at hand. There would be no more roving tents, poisonous snakes, fierce Amalekites, nor any howling wind-swept wilderness. They had come to the "land flowing with milk and honey" (Ex. 3:8) and were able to eat of the grain already growing there.

Dear Christian, perhaps this will be the case for you this year. This is a joyful prospect, and if our faith is active, it will yield pure unvarnished delight. For God's people to be given the blessing of resting in Jesus is an uplifting thought indeed, and to see the glory of it in this life is a double blessing. Unbelief may cause us to shudder at the Jordan that still separates us from the Prom-ised Land, but we may rest assured that this life has already caused us more pain and trials than death at its worst could inflict. So may we banish every fear and, instead, rejoice with exceedingly great joy at the prospect that this year we could actually begin our time to "be with the Lord for-ever" (1 Thess. 4:17).

Of course, a number of us will remain on earth this year in order to serve the Lord. If this is the case for us, there is still no reason why today's verse would not be true. "We who have believed enter that rest" (Heb. 4:3). "The prom-ised Holy Spirit ... is a deposit guaranteeing our inheritance" (Eph. 1:13 – 14), which has already been granted to us here below. Those above are secure in heaven just as we are secure in Christ Jesus; those in heaven are victorious and we ex-perience victories as well. The heavenly beings enjoy communion with the Lord, yet this is not denied to us; they rest in His love, and we have perfect peace in Him; and they sing His praises, a privilege we share in order to bless Him.

This year we will gather heavenly fruit on earthly ground where faith and hope have turned the desert into the Lord's garden. If "men ate the bread of angels" (Ps. 78:25) long ago, why not today?

May God grant us the grace to feed on Jesus and thereby eat of the fruit of the land of Canaan this year!

From the pen of Jim Reimann:

It seems we often approach a new year with mixed emotions, sometimes hesitant to let go of the past, even as difficult as our past year may have been. We tend to view the past with the idea that at least it is something known, while we view the future as a complete unknown. For believers, however, this should not be the case. Although we do not know the future in detail, we know the One who has made great promises to us as He guides us there.

"For I know the plans I have for you," declares the LORD, "plans to prosper you and not to harm you, plans to give you hope and a future. Then you will call upon me and come and pray to me, and I will listen to you. You will seek me and find me when you seek me with all your heart."

Jeremiah 29:11 – 13

Father, may we enter this new year in complete reliance and trust, knowing our steps into the unknown have been ordained by You. May our walk with You be one of dedi-cated obedience to Your Word and Your will, that You may be glorified in and through us.

JANUARY 2

Devote yourselves to prayer.

Colossians 4:2

From the pen of Charles Spurgeon:

It is interesting to note the large portion of God's sacred Word dedicated to the subject of prayer, either in delivering examples to follow, demanding obedience to its truth, or declaring promises regarding it. We can scarcely open the Bible before quickly reading, "At that time men began to call on the name of the LORD" (Gen. 4:26), and just before closing the Blessed Volume, the "Amen" (Rev. 22:21) of a purposeful petition reaches our ears.

Examples are plentiful. In this book we find a wrestling Jacob (Gen. 32:22 – 32), a Daniel who prayed three times a day (Dan. 6:10), and a David who called upon his God with all his heart (Ps. 55:16, 86:12). We see Elijah on a mountain (1 Kings 18:16 – 46) and Paul and Silas in a prison (Acts 16:16 – 40). We find multitudes of commands and myriads of promises.

What do these teach us, except the sacred importance and necessity of prayer? We can be certain that whatever God has made so prominent in His Word, He intends to be conspicuously evident in our lives. If He says so much about prayer, it is because He knows how much we need it. Our needs are so deep that we must not cease to pray until we are in heaven.

Do you feel you have no needs? Then I fear you do not know your true poverty. Do you have no desire or mercy to ask of God? Then may the Lord in His mercy show you your misery, for a prayer-less soul is a Christ-less soul! Prayer is the struggling speech of the believing infant, the war cry of the fighting believer, and the requiem of the dying saint falling asleep in the arms of Jesus. It is the breath, the password, the comfort, the strength, and the privilege of a Christian. So if you are a child of God, you will seek your Father's face and live in your Father's love.

Pray that this year you will be holy, humble, devoted, and diligent; that you will have closer communion with Christ, often entering the banquet room of His love. Pray that you will be an example and a blessing to others, and that you will live more and more for the glory of your Master.

May our motto this year be: "Devote yourselves to prayer."

From the pen of Jim Reimann:

If, as Spurgeon says, "A prayer-less soul is a Christ-less soul," how many of us go through our day without Him? How is it that we profess to know the Lord, claiming Him as our friend, yet spend so little time communing with Him in prayer?

Our Lord Jesus set a beautiful example for us in communing with His heavenly Father. "Very early in the morning, while it was still dark, Jesus got up, left the house and went off to a solitary place, where he prayed" (Mark 1:35). Our Lord prayed often — at the beginning of His day, before many of His miracles, before His meals, and before and during His crucifixion, just to name a few occasions. He prayed for the lost, for His disciples, for His enemies, for the world, and for Himself. Many of His prayers are recorded in His Word to teach us how to pray, when to pray, and for whom to pray.

If Jesus, the perfect Son of God, needed such times with His Father, how much more do we?

JANUARY 3

I ... will make you to be a
covenant for the people.

Isaiah 49:8

From the pen of Charles Spurgeon:

Jesus Christ is Himself the sum total of the covenant, and, as one of its gifts, He is the possession of every believer. Dear Christian, are you able to fathom what you have received in Him, "for in Christ all the fullness of the Deity lives in bodily form" (Col. 2:9)?

Consider the word *God* in all its infinite greatness, and then meditate on the beauty of "becom[ing] mature, attaining to the whole measure of the fullness of Christ" (Eph. 4:13). Remember, as God and man, all that Christ ever had or has is yours purely because of His favor. It has been freely bestowed on you and will be your inheritance forever.

Our blessed Jesus, as God, is omniscient, omnipresent, and omnipotent. Isn't it comforting to know that all of these glorious attributes are totally yours? Does He have the power you need? His power is yours in order to support and strengthen you, subdue your enemies, and sustain you forever.

Does He have the love you need? There is not a drop of love in His heart that is not yours, and you may dive into His immense ocean of love and say, "This is all mine!"

Does He have the justice you need? This may seem to be an unpleasant attribute, but even it is yours. And it is this very justice that will make sure everything promised in His covenant of grace will indeed be secured for you.

You also share in the Father's delight that was upon Him as a perfect man. He was accepted by the Most High God. Therefore, dear believer, God's acceptance of Christ is your acceptance as well. Do you not realize that the love the Father bestowed on the perfect Christ He now bestows on you?

All that Christ accomplished is yours. The perfect righteousness Jesus displayed is yours. Throughout His untarnished life He obeyed the law, made it honorable, and His righteousness is now imputed to you.

Through the covenant, Christ is yours!

My God, I am yours — what a comfort divine!
What a blessing to know that the Savior is
mine!
In heaven's pure Lamb, threefold happy I am,
And my heart does a dance at the sound of
His name.

Charles Wesley, 1707 – 1788

From the pen of Jim Reimann:

Yes, Christ is yours! And you have the assurance that the future of your inheritance doesn't depend upon you. You have "an inheritance that can never perish, spoil or fade — kept in heaven for you" (1 Peter 1:4).

Notice what this verse *doesn't* say, "Kept in heaven *by* you." No, it is kept *for* you! The passage goes on to say that you yourself "are shielded by God's power" (1 Peter 1:5). With that in mind, whom should we fear?

"So we say with confidence, 'The Lord is my helper; I will not be afraid. What can man do to me?'" (Heb. 13:6). And we pray along with the apostle Peter,

"Praise be to the God and Father of our Lord Jesus Christ! In his great mercy he has given us new birth into a living hope" (1 Peter 1:3).

January 4

Grow in the grace and knowledge
of our Lord and Savior Jesus Christ.

2 Peter 3:18

From the pen of Charles Spurgeon:

"Grow in grace" — not just in *some* grace — but in *all* grace. Grow in the root of all grace, which is faith. Believe God's promises more firmly than ever. Allow your faith to increase in its fullness, firmness, and simplicity.

Grow also in love. Ask God to stretch your love and make it more intense and practical, to the point of influencing your every thought, word, and action.

Grow in humility too. Seek to be unnoticed and to more fully recognize your own nothingness. Yet as you grow "downward" in humility, also seek to grow "upward," where you will have closer times with God through prayer and more intimate fellowship with Jesus.

May God the Holy Spirit enable you to grow in the "knowledge of our Lord and Savior." If you are not growing in the knowledge of Jesus, you are refusing to be blessed. To know Him is "eternal life" (John 17:3) and to grow in the knowledge of Him is to increase in happiness. If you do not long to know Christ more, then you do not yet know Him at all. If you have sipped of this wine, you will thirst for more. For although Christ certainly satisfies, He brings such a satisfaction that your appetite is not quenched but simply whetted.

If you know the love of Jesus, "as the deer pants for streams of water" (Ps. 42:1), so too your thirsty heart will pant for deeper drinks from the well of His love. If, however, you do not desire to know Him better, you do not love Him — for love always cries out, "Nearer! Nearer!"

The absence of Christ is hell — but the presence of Jesus is heaven. Never rest or be content until you have an ever-increasing intimacy with Jesus. Seek to know more of Him, to know more of His divine nature, His humanity, His finished work, His death, His resurrection, His ever-present glorious intercession on your behalf, and His future return as "King of kings" (Rev. 17:14).

Cling to the cross of Christ and search out the mysteries of His wounds. A growing love for Jesus and a more complete understanding of His love for us is one of the best tests of a life truly experiencing spiritual growth in grace.

From the pen of Jim Reimann:

Many professing Christians lack a passion to know Jesus intimately, and as Spurgeon says, "If you do not long to know Christ more, then you do not yet know Him at all." Paul said to us as believers, "I keep asking that the God of our Lord Jesus Christ, the glorious Father, may give you the Spirit of wisdom and revelation, *so that you may know him better*" (Eph. 1:17).

Spiritual health means being on a path to know Christ better, and one of the beautiful aspects of walking with Him is that we will be discovering the endless depths of His love and grace forever.

Paul says, in effect, *to know* something that is actually unknowable. "I pray that you … may have power … to grasp how wide and long and high and deep is the love of Christ, and *to know this love that surpasses knowledge* — that you may be filled to the measure of all the fullness of God" (Eph. 3:17 – 19).

Father, may I be filled with the wonderful knowledge of Your Son — yet not filled to my meager human standard of measure, but Your divine measure!

JANUARY 5

God saw that the light was good,
and he separated the light from the darkness.

Genesis 1:4

From the pen of Charles Spurgeon:

Light is good because it sprang from the decree of Goodness Himself: "Let there be light" (Gen. 1:3). Yet we who enjoy its benefits should be more grateful for it than we are and should see more of God in it and through it.

According to Solomon, physical "light is sweet" (Eccl. 11:7), but the light of the gospel is infinitely more precious, for it reveals eternal things and ministers to our immortal nature. When the Holy Spirit gives us this spiritual light and opens our eyes to behold the glory of God in the face of Jesus Christ, suddenly we see the stain of sin and our own helpless position. We see the Most Holy God as He reveals Himself, the plan of mercy He has set forth, and the world to come as His Word describes it.

Spiritual light shines with the rays of every color of a prism, but whether they are knowledge, joy, holiness, or life, they are all divinely good. Yet how much more glorious must be the light shining from His throne and the heavenly place where He reveals Himself!

O Lord, since Your light is so good, give us more — and more of Yourself, the true Light.

Of course, as soon as something good came into the world, a division became necessary. Light and darkness can have no fellowship. (See 2 Cor. 6:14.) Therefore, since God divided them, let's not confuse them. Children of light must not have fellowship with the deeds, doctrines, or deceits of darkness. They must be sober, honest, and bold in doing the Lord's work, leaving the works of darkness to those who will dwell in that darkness for eternity.

Our churches should exercise the discipline of dividing light from darkness, and we as believers — distinctly separated from the world — should do the same. Our judgment, our actions, our relationships, what we hear, what we teach — in all of these — we must discern between what is precious and what is vile. We must maintain the dramatic distinction the Lord made on the world's very first day.

O Lord Jesus, be our light through this entire day, for Your light is "the light of men" (John 1:4).

From the pen of Jim Reimann:

Light and darkness are distinct opposites and each displays its own unique properties. John 1:5 says, "The light shines in the darkness, but the darkness has not understood it." The NIV text note, however, gives this alternate translation of the Greek: "The light shines in the darkness, but the darkness has not *overcome*."

Darkness cannot overcome light. Consider this simple example: you open the door of your unlit closet while standing in your well-lit bedroom. What happens? Does the darkness spill over into the bedroom? Of course not. The light overcomes the darkness and you can now see into the once dark closet. Yet the light in the bedroom has not been diminished. Spiritual light has this same unique quality of physical light — it will always overcome darkness.

Lord, may Your light shine through me into a dark and dying world.

Day 5

January 6

Cast all your anxiety on him
because he cares for you.

1 Peter 5:7

From the pen of Charles Spurgeon:

There is no better way to soothe sorrow than to know, "He cares for me!" Dear believer, do not dishonor the Christian faith by always exhibiting a furrowed brow of worry. Instead, cast your burden upon your Lord. Why do you continue to stagger beneath a weight your Father would not even feel? What may seem to be a crushing burden to you would not amount to the weight of a speck of dust to Him. Nothing is as sweet as to:

> Lie passive in God's hands,
> And to know no will but His.
>
> William S. Plumer, 1802 – 1880

O child of suffering, be patient. Your sovereign God has not passed over or forgotten you. He who feeds the sparrows will also provide everything you need. Don't give up in despair — hope on! Hope forever! Use the weapons of faith against the seas of trouble and ultimately your foes will be defeated and your distress will come to an end.

There is One who cares for you. His eye is fixed upon you, His heart beats with pity for your suffering, and His omnipotent hand will not fail to provide you help. Even the darkest storm cloud will be scattered into showers of mercy and the darkest night will give way to the morning sun.

If you are a member of His family, He will bind your wounds and heal your broken heart. Never doubt His grace because of the troubles in your life, but believe He loves you just as much during the seasons of trouble as in times of happiness.

How quiet and peaceful your life would be if you would only leave the work of providing to the very God of providence! With "only a handful of flour in a jar and a little oil in a jug" (1 Kings 17:12), Elijah outlived the famine — and you will do the same.

If God cares for you, why should you care too? If you trust Him with your soul, can't you trust Him with your body? He has never refused to bear your burdens, nor has he ever fainted underneath their weight.

Come then, dear soul. Be done with fretting and worry — leave all your concerns in the hands of your gracious God.

From the pen of Jim Reimann:

Fear and worry are sins, yet we often think of them as simply inevitable and, therefore, tolerate them in our lives. Paul stated, "Everything that does not come from faith is sin" (Rom. 14:23). Yet from the Word we find that faith can coexist with some doubt. Consider the man who brought his son to Jesus for healing, who said, "I do believe; help me *overcome* my unbelief!" (Mark 9:24).

What a wonderful choice of words, for they were spoken to Him who said, "In this world you will have trouble. But take heart! *I have overcome the world*" (John 16:33).

> *Father, I thank You that "in all these things we are more than conquerors through him who loved us" (Rom. 8:37). Thank You that through You we who are Your people are an army of "overcomers" indeed!*

JANUARY 7

For to me, to live is Christ.

Philippians 1:21

From the pen of Charles Spurgeon:

No believer has ever lived his entire life for Christ. He began to do so only after God the Holy Spirit convicted him of sin and when by grace he was brought to see the dying Savior making a propitiation for his guilt — that is, becoming a sacrifice that satisfied the wrath of God for his sin. Only from that moment of new and heavenly birth did the new believer begin to live for Christ.

To believers, Jesus is the "one pearl of great price" (Matt. 13:46 KJV) for whom we are willing to forsake everything else we have. He has so completely become the love of our heart that it beats solely for Him. For His glory alone we live and we would willingly die to defend His gospel. He has become the pattern for our life and the model after which we sculpt our character.

Paul's words here mean more than most people think. Many believe he was implying that Christ was the purpose and objective of his life. No! Paul's life itself was Jesus. In the words of another ancient saint, "Paul ate, drank, and slept eternal life. Jesus was his very breath, the soul of his soul, the heart of his heart, and the life of his life."

As a professing Christian, can you say that you live up to this ideal? Can you honestly say that for you "to live is Christ"? Are your business dealings done for Christ or are they done for your own benefit or that of your family?

Have you asked yourself, "Is my primary purpose in life to live for Christ?" For a Christian it should be. If someone professes to live for Christ, how can he live for another purpose without committing spiritual adultery?

Many Christians live for Him to a certain degree, but who can claim to live wholly for Him as the apostle Paul did? Yet this alone is the true life of a Christian. It is its source, its sustenance, its pattern, its purpose, all brought together in one person — Christ Jesus.

Lord, accept me. Today I present myself to You, praying to live only in You and for You. May I be as the bull standing between the plow and the altar — whether to work or to be sacrificed.

May my motto be: "I'm ready for either!"

From the pen of Jim Reimann:

What an incredible standard Spurgeon lays down for us! He asks, "Who can claim to live wholly for [Christ] as the apostle Paul did?"

Yet remember, believer, Paul was simply flesh and blood. He struggled with the same temptations that lead us to the "spiritual adultery" Spurgeon warns against. Who of us, however, can say without reservation, as Paul did, "Whatever you have learned or received or heard from me, or seen in me — put it into practice"? (Phil. 4:9). What a bold statement!

Yes, Paul was only a man, but the same Holy Spirit that empowered him indwells every believer. Therefore, what we see in Paul truly can be "put ... into practice" in our lives through the power of the Spirit of God.

There is one thing, however, that we have to help us that Paul did not have as he began his walk with Christ — his letters that make up a major portion of the New Testament.

Why not read one of Paul's letters today?

JANUARY 8

It will be on Aaron's forehead,
and he will bear the guilt involved in the sacred gifts.

Exodus 28:38

From the pen of Charles Spurgeon:

What great meaning is unveiled and disclosed by these words! It would be profitable, yet humbling, to pause for a moment to consider this sad sight. The "guilt involved" in our public worship — its hypocrisy, formality, lukewarmness, irreverence, our wandering hearts, and our forgetfulness of God — is overwhelming! Our work for the Lord — its striving, selfishness, carelessness, laziness, and unbelief — is a rotting mass! Our private times of devotion — their laxness, coldness, neglectfulness, sleepiness, and vanity — are a mountain of dead earth! And if we looked even more carefully, we would find this guilt to be far greater than it appears at first blush.

Dr. Edward Payson (1783 – 1827), in a letter to his brother, wrote, "My parish, and my own heart, is much the same as the garden of a sluggard. What is worse, I find many of my desires to remedy either situation stem from my own pride, vanity, or laziness. I see weeds overtaking my garden and simply breathe out a wish that they were eradicated. But why? What prompts my wish? Perhaps it's so I may say to myself what an orderly garden I have. This is pride! Or maybe it's because I want my neighbors to look over the wall and say how wonderfully well my garden is flourishing. This is vanity! Perhaps I wish for the destruction of the weeds simply because I'm so tired of pulling them up. This is laziness!"

The truth here is that even our desires for holiness can be polluted by wrong motives. Even under the greenest grass, worms are hiding, and we don't need to look very long to discover them.

Yet how uplifting is the thought that when our High Priest bore "the guilt involved in the sacred gifts" He wore upon His forehead the words — "HOLINESS TO THE LORD" (v. 36 KJV). Even while Jesus was bearing our sin He did not present our unholiness before His Father's face — He presented His own holiness.

Oh, for the grace to view our great High Priest through the eye of faith!

From the pen of Jim Reimann:

Praise be to God that believers receive the holiness of Christ and are clothed in His righteousness — not ours — for "all our righteous acts are like filthy rags" (Isa. 64:6).

"I delight greatly in the LORD; my soul rejoices in my God. For he has clothed me with garments of salvation and arrayed me in a robe of righteousness" (Isa. 61:10).

Remember, believers, "You have come to God, the judge of all men, to the spirits of righteous men made perfect, to Jesus the mediator of a new covenant, and to the sprinkled blood that speaks a better word than the blood of Abel" (Heb. 12:23 – 24).

Heavenly Father, give us heavenly eyes to view our perfect Savior — the only One who "is able to save completely those who come to God through him, because he always lives to intercede for them. Such a high priest meets our need — one who is holy, blameless, pure, set apart from sinners, exalted above the heavens" (Heb. 7:25 – 26). Thank You for Him!

JANUARY 9

I will be their God.

Jeremiah 31:33

From the pen of Charles Spurgeon:

Dear Christian, what more could you possibly need? To be truly happy you desire something that will fully satisfy you. Is this promise not enough? If you could pour it into your own cup, would you not say, as David did, "'My cup overflows' (Ps. 23:5). I have more than I need"?

Once God fulfills this promise for you and becomes *your* God, will you not possess everything? Human desires are as insatiable as death itself, but He who is truly sufficient can fill them. Who can even measure the depth of human desire? Yet the immeasurable wealth of God can more than overflow it. I ask you, are you not complete when God is yours? Do you desire anything but Him? Isn't His all-sufficiency enough to satisfy you even when everything else fails?

Yet are you asking for more than just quiet satisfaction? Do you desire rapturous delight? Then come, dear soul, God is the maker of heaven itself, and music fit for heaven is your inheritance. Earthly music blown through the sweetest woodwinds or drawn from living strings could never produce a melody as sweet as this promise, "I will be their God."

In these words is a deep sea of blessings — a shoreless ocean of delight. Come, bathe your spirit in it — swim as long as you like — but you will find no shore. Dive into its depths for all eternity, but you will find no bottom.

"I will be their God." If this doesn't brighten your eyes and make your heart beat with utter happiness, then your soul must assuredly be in a very unhealthy state.

Do you desire something for the future as well — not just present joy? Does your heart crave something for which you may exercise hope? What more could you ever hope for than the perfect fulfillment of this great promise: "I will be their God"?

This is the masterpiece of all of God's promises. Truly recognizing it makes for a heaven on earth and a heaven above. Abide in the light of your Lord and always allow your soul to be ravished with His love.

Don't miss God's total provision for you in His promise, "I will be their God." Live up to your privileges and rejoice "with an inexpressible and glorious joy" (1 Peter 1:8). "My soul will be satisfied as with the richest of foods" (Ps. 63:5).

From the pen of Jim Reimann:

It seems the entire world is searching for happiness, love, and fulfillment. Yet so many of us search for these things everywhere except where they truly can be found — in God alone. Even as believers in Him, we as Christians often have a warped view of God, seeing Him as somewhat stingy, carefully doling out His blessings — a little here and a little there. Yet the apostle Paul wrote, "He who did not spare his own Son, but gave him up for us all — how will he not also, along with him, graciously give us all things?" (Rom. 8:32).

In essence, Paul is asking us this question, "Isn't it absurd to think that if God gave us the very life of His Son, that there is anything He would willingly withhold from us? After all, He has already given us the very best!"

Father, may I be content in You, and seek satisfaction — not in the things of the world, but in You alone.

JANUARY 10

There is in store for me the crown of righteousness.

2 Timothy 4:8

From the pen of Charles Spurgeon:

O doubting Christian, you have often said, "I'm afraid I'll never enter heaven." Fear not! *All* the people of God will enter.

I love the refreshing statement of a dying man who exclaimed, "I have no fear of going home. I've sent everything on ahead of me. God's finger is on the latch of my door and I'm ready for Him to enter."

Yet he was asked, "Are you not afraid you may miss your inheritance?"

"No," he responded, "there is one crown in heaven the angel Gabriel cannot wear. It will fit no one's head but mine. And there is one throne in heaven even the apostle Paul could not fill. It was made for me — and I will have it!"

O Christian, what a joyous thought! Your inheritance is secure: "There remains, then, a Sabbath-rest for the people of God" (Heb. 4:9). But do you still ask if it can be forfeited somehow? No! It is guaranteed to God's descendants. If I am a child of God I will never lose it, and it is securely mine as surely as if I were already there.

Come with me, believer. Let's sit atop Mount Nebo and view God's Promised Land — even Canaan. Do you see the river of death glistening in the sunlight? Yet across it do you see the spires of the eternal city? Do you see the thriving country-side with its joyful inhabitants?

Then know that if you could fly across to it, you would see written upon one of its many mansions these words: "This is reserved for someone special and is being held for him alone. Someday he will be caught up to dwell with God forever."

Poor doubting soul, look at your wonderful inheritance. It is yours — if you believe in the Lord Jesus, if you have repented of your sin, if your heart has been renewed. You are one of the Lord's people and there is a place reserved just for you. A crown has been stored up for you and a harp has been specially provided for you.

No one else will take what is yours, for it is reserved in heaven for you. And throughout eternity it will be yours, for there will be no vacant thrones in glory once all of God's chosen have been gathered in.

From the pen of Jim Reimann:

How many of us hope against hope for a heavenly inheritance! Yet our inheritance is more real and secure than anything here on earth! In fact, three times the apostle Paul tells us of its guarantee:

> He anointed us, set his seal of ownership on us, and put his Spirit in our hearts as a deposit, guaranteeing what is to come.
>
> 2 Corinthians 1:21 – 22

> Now it is God who has made us for this very purpose and has given us the Spirit as a deposit, guaranteeing what is to come. Therefore we are always confident ...
>
> 2 Corinthians 5:5 – 6

> Having believed, you were marked in him with a seal, the promised Holy Spirit, who is a deposit guaranteeing our inheritance until the redemption of those who are God's possession — to the praise of his glory.
>
> Ephesians 1:13 – 14

Father, thank You for "the deposit" of Your Holy Spirit — the very life of Jesus Christ in us — "the hope of glory" (Col. 1:27)!

January 11

They have no root.

Luke 8:13

From the pen of Charles Spurgeon:

My soul, examine yourself this morning by the light of this verse. You have received the Word with joy and your feelings have been stirred and awakened. Yet remember, receiving the Word into your ears is one thing, but receiving Jesus into your very soul is quite another. Superficial feelings are often linked to an inward hardness of heart, and stirred and awakened feelings typically don't last.

In this parable "some [seeds] fell on rock" (Luke 8:6) and probably were covered with a very thin layer of soil. When the seeds began to take root, their downward growth was hindered by the hard stone below. Therefore, they used all their strength to push the new green shoots as high as they could, but without enough moisture from the shallow soil to nourish the roots, they quickly withered away.

Is this my situation? Have I been making a good outward show in the flesh without having the corresponding inner life? True growth takes place upward and downward at the same time. Am I deeply rooted in sincere devotion, faithfulness, and love to Jesus? If my heart remains unsoftened and unfertilized by God's grace, the good seeds may germinate for a while, but they are ultimately doomed to wither, for they cannot flourish on a rocky, unbroken, and unsanctified heart.

May I dread a kind of godliness as rapid in growth but as lacking in endurance as Jonah's gourd. (See Jonah 4:5 – 11.) May I count the cost of being a follower of Jesus and, above all, experience the energy of His Holy Spirit, for then I will truly possess the abiding and enduring seeds of God's Word in my soul.

If, however, my mind remains as stubbornly resistant as it was by nature, the hot sunlight of trials will scorch the seeds. My hard heart will contribute to focusing the heat all the more harshly upon the shallow seeds and my faith will quickly die, creating terrible despair in my life.

Therefore, O Heavenly Sower, plow my heart before casting Your truth into it. Then allow me to yield a bountiful harvest for You.

From the pen of Jim Reimann:

In Israel the land is so rocky that the farmer is forced to remove huge amounts of rock before he even begins to sow the seed. The rocks are piled around the perimeter of the land, making a visible border for the farmer's property. It is probably with this image in mind that Jesus shared the parable of the sower in Luke 8:1 – 15. And it helps us understand how some of the seeds may fall upon the rocks, sprout quickly, but then just as quickly wither away due to a lack of moisture.

If you desire a deeper walk with Jesus, then new ground must be broken. Yet it is the first plowing that is always the most difficult. Yes, it's difficult, but it is typically the rich new ground that yields the best fruit and the most bountiful blessings.

"This is what the Lord says …, 'Break up your unplowed ground and do not sow among thorns'" (Jer. 4:3). "Sow for yourselves righteousness, reap the fruit of unfailing love, and break up your unplowed ground; for it is time to seek the Lord, until he comes and showers righteousness on you" (Hos. 10:12).

January 12

You are Christ's.

1 Corinthians 3:23 ESV

From the pen of Charles Spurgeon:

"You are Christ's." You are His because of a donation, for the Father gave you to His Son; His because He purchased you with His blood, paying the price for your redemption; His through dedication, for you have committed and consecrated yourself to Him; and His through a family relationship, for you have been named by His name, become one of His brothers or sisters, and made "co-heirs" (Rom. 8:17) with Him.

Endeavor to show the world you are the servant, the friend, and the bride of Jesus. When you are tempted to sin, respond by saying, "I can't do this terrible wickedness, for I am Christ's." Remember — eternal principles prohibit the friend of Christ to sin. So when ill-gotten wealth is set before you that can only be won through sin, say, "I am Christ's," and then refuse to touch it.

Are you facing difficulties and dangers? Stand firm in these evil days, remembering "you are Christ's." Do you find yourself sitting down with others, doing nothing? Then rise up to work with all your strength. And when the sweat beads up on your forehead and you are tempted to be idle again, cry out, "No, I can't stop, for I am Christ's! If I had not been purchased by His blood I might be like Issachar, 'lying down between two saddlebags' (Gen. 49:14), but I am Christ's and I can't linger." And when the siren song of pleasure tempts you from the path of righteousness, reply, "Your music can't attract me. I am Christ's."

Never betray your profession of faith in Christ. Always be a person whose walk is Christian, whose speech is like that of the Nazarene, whose conduct and conversation have such an aroma of heaven that everyone who sees you will know you belong to the Savior, recognizing in you His features of love and His countenance of holiness.

In ancient times, to say, "I am a Roman!" was a reason for integrity and pride. In a far greater way, then, let this proclamation be your argument for holiness — "I am Christ's!"

From the pen of Jim Reimann:

Continually reminding myself of whose I am helps me "take captive every thought to make it obedient to Christ" (2 Cor. 10:5). And personalizing Scripture is another means helping me be victorious over the temptations of life. For example, "Do [I] not know that [my] body is a temple of the Holy Spirit, who is in [me], whom [I] have received from God? [I am] not [my] own; [I was] bought at a price. Therefore [I will] honor God with [my] body" (1 Cor. 6:19 – 20).

As the Lord continues to sanctify us, making us more and more holy, we will indeed see victory even over sins with which we may have struggled for years. "For though we live in the world, we do not wage war as the world does. The weapons we fight with are not the weapons of the world. On the contrary, they have divine power to demolish strongholds. We demolish arguments and every pretension that sets itself up against the knowledge of God, and we take captive every thought to make it obedient to Christ" (2 Cor. 10:3 – 5).

"In all these things we are more than conquerors" (Rom. 8:37).

Dear Jesus, thank You that I am Yours, and that because I am in You, I am more than a conqueror.

January 13

Jehoshaphat built a fleet of trading ships to go to Ophir for gold,
but they never set sail — they were wrecked at Ezion Geber.

1 Kings 22:48

From the pen of Charles Spurgeon:

Solomon's ships had returned in safety (see 1 Kings 9:26 – 28), but Jehoshaphat's fleet never reached the land of gold. Our sovereign God may prosper one person while frustrating the desires of another, although both people may be in the same business and in the same place. Yet the Great Ruler is as good and wise in one case as in the other.

As we consider the above verse today, may the Lord grant us the grace to bless Him for ships "wrecked at Ezion Geber" as well as for fleets filled with earthly blessings. And may we not envy someone who is seemingly more successful, nor complain about our losses as though we were the only ones to ever experience a particular trial. Like Jehoshaphat, we are precious in the Lord's sight, although our plans may end in disappointment.

The hidden cause of Jehoshaphat's loss is worthy of note, for it is the root of much of the suffering of the Lord's people. The problem was his alliance with a sinful family, his fellowship with sinners. In 2 Chron. 20:37 we see that God sent Eliezer to prophesy against Jehoshaphat, "Because you have made an alliance with Ahaziah, the LORD will destroy what you have made." The verse then concludes with, "The ships were wrecked and were not able to set sail to trade."

This was a fatherly chastisement that apparently became a blessing to him, however, for in the verse following this morning's text, we see him refusing to allow his servants to sail in the same ships with those of the wicked ruler King Ahaziah. My prayer is that Jehoshaphat's experience may be a warning to the Lord's people to avoid being unequally "yoked together with unbelievers" (2 Cor. 6:14).

The destiny of believers who are willingly united in marriage, or any other way, with people of the world is typically a life of misery. Oh, may we have such a great love for Jesus that, like Him, we may be holy, harmless to others, pure and undefiled, and separate from sinners!

If this is not the case with us, we can often expect to hear, "The Lord will destroy what you have made."

From the pen of Jim Reimann:

How often have we seen believers marry unbelievers, thinking their experience will somehow defy God's truth, only to see their marriage end in divorce or survive in utter misery! "Do not be deceived: God cannot be mocked. A man reaps what he sows" (Gal. 6:7).

Often unmarried people are so consumed by their desire to be married, they are willing to compromise God's Word. This is dangerous ground to tread, for an unhappy or broken marriage is typically lonelier than the single life.

Whether married or single, we should look to our loving Savior to meet our needs. "My God will meet *all your needs* according to his glorious riches in Christ Jesus" (Phil. 4:19).

Father, help me submit my will to Yours alone. Thank You that I may trust You for the very best, for You have given me Your only Son!

JANUARY 14

... mighty to save.

Isaiah 63:1

From the pen of Charles Spurgeon:

Through the words *to save* we come to understand the great work of salvation, from our first holy desire to our complete sanctification. God's mercy is wrapped up in these words, for Christ is not *only* "mighty to save" those who repent but He is mighty to cause them to repent. Those who believe in Him, He will take to heaven; but more than that, through His might, He will give them new hearts and will work faith into their lives. He is mighty to cause the person who hates holiness to love it and to compel someone who despises His name to bend his knee before Him.

Yet these words are not fully defined even in all of this, for the Lord's divine power is equal in a person's life *after* the work of salvation has been accomplished. The life of a believer becomes an ongoing series of miracles performed by "the Mighty God" (Isa. 10:21). The bush continues to burn but is not consumed. After making His people holy, He is mighty to keep His people holy and also to preserve them in His reverence and love until He perfects and completes their spiritual existence in heaven.

Christ's mighty power does not lie in making someone a believer and then leaving him to fend for himself, for "he who [begins] a good work ... will carry it on to completion" (Phil. 1:6). He who imparts the first seed of life to a dead soul divinely continues that life, strengthening it until it completely bursts the bonds of every sin and until that soul leaps from earth perfected in glory.

O believer, what an encouragement this is! Are you praying for a dearly loved one? Don't give up — Christ is "mighty to save"! You are *power-less* to reclaim even one rebellious soul, but your Lord is *almighty*. So take hold of His mighty arm, stirring it to exhibit its strength.

Are you troubled about your own situation? Fear not! His strength "is sufficient for you" (2 Cor. 12:9). Whether Jesus is working salvation into another or continuing a work in you, He is "mighty to save." The best proof of this lies in the fact that He has saved *you*.

You can be thankful a thousand times over that He is not "mighty to destroy" — but He is "mighty to save"!

From the pen of Jim Reimann:

In Spurgeon's first paragraph today we see that salvation, sanctification, and repentance are all works of almighty God. We also see that even faith itself is a gift and is something He works into our lives.

Knowing that salvation, from that first wooing of the Holy Spirit to complete sanctification, is a work of the Father should give us an ever-increasing view of God's grace. And having the proper biblical view of salvation should bring Him glory, for we see that salvation is only of Him and from Him.

These truths should fill our hearts with gratitude for our loving God who "is mighty to save" and who is mighty to sanctify as well.

"May God himself, the God of peace, sanctify you through and through. May your whole spirit, soul and body be kept blameless at the coming of our Lord Jesus Christ. The one who calls you is faithful and he will do it" (1 Thess. 5:23 – 24).

January 15

LORD God,... do as you promised.
2 Samuel 7:25

From the pen of Charles Spurgeon:

God's promises were never meant to be cast aside like waste paper — He intends for us to use them. His gold is not the currency of a miser — He means for us to use it for trading. Nothing pleases our Lord more than to see us put His promises into circulation. He loves to see His children offering them up to Him while saying, "Lord God, do as you promised."

We glorify God when we earnestly plead His promises. Do you honestly believe God will be any poorer for giving you the riches He has promised? Do you actually suppose He will be any less holy for granting holiness to you? Do you somehow imagine He will be any less pure after cleansing you from your sins?

The Lord says, "Come now, let us reason together. Though your sins are like scarlet, they shall be as white as snow; though they are red as crimson, they shall be like wool" (Isa. 1:18). True faith takes hold of God's promise of pardon without delay and does not say, "This is a precious promise, I wonder if it's true." Instead, it takes the promise directly to God's throne and pleads, "Lord, here are your words. 'Do as you promised.'" Then He replies, "Be it done for you as you desire" (Matt. 15:28 ESV). When a Christian takes hold of a promise but does not take it to God, he dishonors Him. Yet when he immediately goes to God's throne of grace and cries out, "I have no basis to ask for this except that You have said it," then his desire will be granted.

Our heavenly Banker delights to cash His own checks, so never let His promises rust. Draw His Word of promise from its sheath and use it with an intense and holy force. Don't ever think God will be bothered or burdened when you remind Him of His promises. He loves to hear the loud outcries of needy souls, for it is His true delight to bestow His blessings on them.

In fact, He is always more ready to hear than we are to ask. In the same way the sun never grows weary of shining, nor a stream of flowing, it is God's nature to keep His promises. Therefore go immediately to His throne and say, "Do as you promised."

From the pen of Jim Reimann:

In order to take God's promises to Him in prayer, we must know those promises. Yet how many of us neglect His Word! How many of us, even longtime Christians, do not dig into His Word, mining those nuggets of gold that Spurgeon calls God's currency for trading? Digging deeper requires a strong commitment and ongoing discipline, and like everything else in our spiritual lives, it will not be easy. Yet it will pay eternal dividends of great worth.

You know with all your heart and soul that not one of all the good promises the LORD your God gave you has failed. Every promise has been fulfilled; not one has failed.
Joshua 23:14

Take to heart all the words I have solemnly declared to you this day.... They are not just idle words for you — they are your life.

Deuteronomy 32:46 – 47

Father, forgive me for neglecting Your Word. Since Your Word is my life, please deepen my desire for it today. "You open your hand and satisfy the desires of every living thing" (Ps. 145:16).

JANUARY 16

From the pen of Charles Spurgeon:

This morning may each of us hear the Lord Jesus speak to us, saying, "'I myself will help you.' It's a small thing for Me, as your God, to help you in your time of need, especially when you consider what I've done for you already. What! Not help you? I bought you with My blood. What! Not help you? I died for you, and if I've already done what is greater, will I now not do what is less? Help you? This is the very least I will ever do for you, for I have done much more for you in the past and will do much more for you in the future.

"Before the world began I chose you and made the covenant for you. I set My glory aside and became a man for you, and then I laid down My life for you. If I did all this, surely I will help you now. In helping you now, however, I'm only giving you what I've already bought for you. If you needed a thousand times more help, I would give it to you, for you require very little compared with what I am ready to give.

"Your need seems great to you, but it is nothing for me to bestow on you. Help you? Fear not! If you had a mere ant at the door of your granary asking for help, it wouldn't bankrupt you to give him a handful of your wheat. And yet, in comparison, you are not even a tiny insect when you stand at the door of My all-sufficiency. 'I myself will help you.'"

"O my soul" (Ps. 103:1), is this not enough for you? Or do you need more strength than the omnipotence of God's Holy Trinity? Do you want more wisdom than exists in the mind of the Father, more love than the Son displays, or more power than is manifested in the work of the Holy Spirit?

Bring the Lord your empty pitcher! Surely His well will fill it. Quickly gather your emptiness, your wants, your troubles, and your needs together. Remember — the river of God is your source of supply. What could you possibly desire that it cannot provide? Go forth, dear soul — in His might — knowing the eternal God is your helper!

"So do not fear, for I am with you; do not be dismayed, for I am your God. I will strengthen you and help you" (Isa. 41:10).

From the pen of Jim Reimann:

So often our god is too small. But this is not the infinite, all-powerful God of the Bible!

The God of the Bible is a gracious, giving, loving Father, "and we know that in *all things* God works for the good of those who love him, who have been called according to his purpose" (Rom. 8:28).

"If we are children, then we are heirs — heirs of God and co-heirs with Christ" (Rom. 8:17). The Lord calls us His child, not simply because of His love for us, but because there is one thing children do legally — they inherit! We share in Christ's inheritance as a member of His family. Remember His words? "Whoever does God's will is my brother and sister and mother" (Mark 3:35).

With an air of incredulity of believing otherwise, Paul declares: "He who did not spare his own Son, but gave him up for us all — *how will he not* also, along with him, graciously give us all things?" (Rom. 8:32).

Indeed, how will He not!

JANUARY 17

I looked, and there before me was the Lamb,
standing on Mount Zion.

Revelation 14:1

From the pen of Charles Spurgeon:

The apostle John was privileged to look within the gates of heaven itself. In describing what he saw he began by saying, "I looked, and there before me was the Lamb." This undoubtedly teaches us that the principal object of focus in that heavenly land is "the Lamb of God, who takes away the sin of the world!" (John 1:29). Nothing else drew the apostle's attention as much as the Divine Being who has redeemed us by His blood. And He is the subject of every song being sung by the glorified saints and the holy angels in heaven.

Dear Christian, this should be sheer joy for you, for you also have looked and have beheld the Lamb. Through your own tears you have seen the Lamb of God taking away your sins. So rejoice, for soon, once the tears have been wiped from your eyes, you will see that very same Lamb exalted on His throne.

The greatest joy of your heart is daily fellowship with Jesus, and you will have that same joy, yet to a greater degree, in heaven. And you will always see Him as you dwell in His presence forever.

"I looked, and there before me was the Lamb!" Actually, the Lamb *is* heaven Himself! As Samuel Rutherford (1600? – 1661), the Scottish Presbyterian preacher, said, "Heaven and Christ are the same thing." To be with Christ is to be in heaven, and to be in heaven is to be with Christ. Rutherford, that wonderful prisoner of the Lord, also said in one of his sweet and glowing letters, "O my Lord Jesus Christ, if I could be in heaven without you — heaven would be a hell; and if I could be in hell, but have you with me — hell would be heaven for me. You are all the heaven I desire!"

Isn't this true, dear Christian? Doesn't your soul agree?

> Not all the harps above
> Can make a heavenly place,
> If God His residence remove,
> Or but conceal His face.
>
> William Walker, 1809 – 1875

All you need to be blessed — incomparably blessed — is to "be with Christ" (Phil. 1:23).

From the pen of Jim Reimann:

The apostle John undoubtedly understood the ultimate blessing of dwelling with Christ. He wrote of how the Lord God chose to dwell with us now and in the life to come. Here is how John stated it at Jesus' first coming:

> The Word became flesh and made his dwelling among us.
>
> John 1:14

Later in his life, John described for us in the book of the Revelation where the Lord has chosen to live at His second coming:

> I saw the Holy City, the new Jerusalem, coming down out of heaven.…And I heard a loud voice from the throne saying, "Now the dwelling of God is with men, and he will live with them."
>
> Revelation 21:2 – 3

I praise You, Lord, for choosing to live with me throughout eternity and for allowing me to live with You.

JANUARY 18

There remains, then,
a Sabbath-rest for the people of God.

Hebrews 4:9

From the pen of Charles Spurgeon:

In heaven, how different will be the condition of the believer when compared to here! Here on earth he is born into fatiguing work and suffers weariness, but in the eternal land of the immortal, fatigue is never known. On earth, eager to serve his Master, he finds his strength not equal to the task or to his zeal, so his continual cry is, "Help me to serve You, O my God!" If he's an active Christian, he will have much work to do here on earth, not too much for his will, but more than enough for his strength. So he will cry out, "I'm not weary *of* the work — I'm weary *in* it."

O Christian, the long hot days of weariness will not last forever. The sun is nearing the horizon and will rise again on a brighter day than you have ever seen and upon a land where you will serve God day and night — yet with true rest from your labor. Rest on earth is incomplete, but there it is perfect. Here a Christian always feels unsettled as though he has not yet attained. But there, all are at rest, have attained the summit of the mountain, and have ascended to the sweet embrace of their God. They can go no higher.

O work-worn laborer, just think of when you will rest forever! Can you conceive of it? It is an eternal rest — a rest that "remains." Here my greatest joys grow dim, my fairest flowers fade, my finest teacups are drained to the dregs, the sweetest songbirds fall from Death's arrows, my most pleasant days always end with the coming shadows of night, and my floods of happiness subside into deserts of sorrow.

But there, everything is immortal. Harps play on without ever gathering rust, golden crowns never tarnish, eyes remain bright, voices are un-faltering, hearts unwavering, and every eternal being is filled with infinite delight.

Happy day! Truly happy! Mortality will be swallowed up by life, and the eternal Sabbath-rest will begin.

From the pen of Jim Reimann:

We live in a world full of stresses and strains, and we often hear of exhaustion or burnout, even among Christians. But compared to the apostle Paul, can we truly complain? Here is what he said:

> I have worked much harder, been in prison more frequently, been flogged more severely, and been exposed to death again and again. Five times I received from the Jews the forty lashes minus one. Three times I was beaten with rods, once I was stoned, three times I was shipwrecked, I spent a night and a day in the open sea, I have been constantly on the move. I have been in danger from rivers, in danger from bandits, in danger from my own countrymen, in danger from Gentiles; in danger in the city, in danger in the country, in danger at sea; and in danger from false brothers. I have labored and toiled and have often gone without sleep; I have known hunger and thirst and have often gone without food; I have been cold and naked. Besides everything else, I face daily the pressure of my concern for all the churches.... If I must boast, I will boast of the things that show my weakness.

2 Corinthians 11:23 – 28, 30

Dear Lord, "Let us not become weary in doing good, for at the proper time we will reap a harvest if we do not give up" (Gal. 6:9).

JANUARY 19

I looked for him but did not find him.

Song of Songs 3:1

From the pen of Charles Spurgeon:

Tell me exactly where you lost the fellowship of Christ and I will tell you the most likely place to rediscover Him. Did you lose Him in the closet, in what you considered to be unanswered prayer? Then your prayer closet is where you must seek Him. Did you lose fellowship with Christ through sin? Then the only way you will find Him is by giving up your sin and by seeking through the Holy Spirit to subdue any area of your life or body in which the lust for sin still abides. Did you lose Christ by neglecting the Scriptures? Then you must find Him in the Scriptures.

The saying "Look for something where you dropped it, for it is there" is also true here. So look for Christ where you left Him, for He has not gone away. Yet it is hard work to go back for Christ. John Bunyan (1628 – 1688) told us in *The Pilgrim's Progress* that Pilgrim discovered that the most difficult path he had ever traveled was the road back to the Arbor of Ease where he had lost his roll. To travel twenty miles ahead is always easier than to be required to travel even one mile back for something lost. Therefore be very careful once you rediscover your Master to cling to Him.

Again, how is it you lost fellowship with Christ? One would have thought you would never have parted ways with such a precious Friend, one whose very presence is so sweet, whose words are so comforting, and whose fellowship is so valued to you! How is it that you did not keep your eyes focused on Him every second, for fear of losing sight of Him?

Although you have let Him go, what a great mercy that you are now seeking Him even though you mournfully sigh, "If only I knew where to find Him!" Keep on seeking, for you know how dangerous it is to be without the fellowship of your Lord. Without Christ you are like a sheep without its shepherd, like a tree without water for its roots, or like a dry and withered leaf in a hurricane. You feel separated from the sustenance of the Tree of Life.

Seek Him with your whole heart and you will find Him. Remember to surrender yourself completely to the search and you will ultimately, surely, find Him to still be your true joy and delight.

From the pen of Jim Reimann:

A good example of Spurgeon's thoughts today is what the Lord told Israel through the prophet Jeremiah during their Babylonian captivity. But remember, of course, their captivity was the direct result of their disobedience.

"'I know the plans I have for you,' declares the LORD, 'plans to prosper you and not to harm you, plans to give you hope and a future. Then you will call upon me and come and pray to me, and I will listen to you. You will seek me and find me when you seek me with all your heart. I will be found by you,' declares the LORD" (Jer. 29:11 – 14).

What a gracious God we have! He is always ready to welcome His wayward children back — but we must return in humility and repentance.

"Because your heart was responsive and you humbled yourself before the LORD when you heard what I have spoken …and because you tore your robes and wept in my presence, I have heard you, declares the LORD" (2 Kings 22:19).

JANUARY 20

Abel kept flocks.

Genesis 4:2

From the pen of Charles Spurgeon:

As a shepherd Abel dedicated his work to the glory of God, offering a blood sacrifice on his altar. Therefore the Lord accepted Abel and his offering. This early example of a Christ-type is quite unmistakable and clear. Like the early morning's first ray of light barely illuminating the east at sunrise, it does not reveal everything, but it clearly demonstrates the great truth that the sun is rising.

As we see Abel, a shepherd *and* a priest, offering a sacrifice of sweet aroma unto God, we detect Christ, bringing before His Father a sacrifice that Jehovah eternally accepts. Without cause Abel was hated by his brother in the same way the Savior was hated. The natural and carnal man hated the Accepted Man, in whom the Spirit of grace was found, and refused to rest until His blood had been shed.

Abel fell, sprinkling his altar and his sacrifice with his own blood, foreshadowing the Lord Jesus' being slain by the hatred of mankind while serving as a priest before the Lord. "The good shepherd lays down his life for the sheep" (John 10:11). May we weep over Him as we see Him slain by the hatred of man, staining "the horns of [His] altar" (Ex. 29:12) with His own blood.

Abel's blood spoke to God, for "the LORD said to Cain, '… Your brother's blood cries out to me from the ground'" (Gen. 4:9 – 10). And the blood of Jesus has a powerful voice, yet the focus of its effective cry is not vengeance, it is mercy.

Standing at the altar of our good Shepherd is precious beyond all measure! To gaze upon Him bleeding as the slaughtered Priest and to hear His blood speaking peace to His flock — peace to our conscience, peace between Jew and Gentile, peace between mankind and their offended Maker, peace throughout ageless eternity for all blood-washed people — is precious beyond all preciousness.

Abel was the first shepherd in the chronology of time, but when it comes to the matter of excellence, Jesus will forever be first in our hearts.

O great Keeper of the sheep, "We your people, the sheep of your pasture, will praise you forever" (Ps. 79:13) *with our whole hearts as we see You slain for us.*

From the pen of Jim Reimann:

What a glorious picture we see today of the scarlet thread of redemption that is so beautifully woven through every book of the Bible! When we carefully read the Old Testament, we cannot help but see Jesus on every page. Time after time, it's as though our gracious heavenly Father is saying, "Don't miss this!" or "Here's another picture of Who is coming."

Let us join with the psalmist in prayer today, saying:

> "Blessed is he who comes in the name of the LORD. From the house of the LORD we bless you. The LORD is God, and he has made his light shine upon us. With boughs in hand, join in the festal procession up to the horns of the altar" (Ps. 118:26 – 27).

> Thank You, Father, that Christ "entered the Most Holy Place once for all by his own blood, having obtained eternal redemption" (Heb. 9:12).

January 21

And so all Israel will be saved.

Romans 11:26

From the pen of Charles Spurgeon:

In Exodus 15 we see Moses sing to the Lord by the Red Sea, for he rejoiced to know that Israel was safe. Not even a fine drop of mist fell from the huge wall of water until the last of the Israelites had safely planted his foot on the other side of the flood. Once the very last person was safely across, the waters roared back into their proper place — but not until then.

A portion of Moses' song was, "In your unfailing love you will lead the people you have redeemed" (Ex. 15:13). In the last days, when the elect of God will sing the song of Moses who was the servant of God and of the Lamb, the exultant claim of Jesus will be, "I have not lost one of those you gave me" (John 18:9). Not one throne in heaven will be vacant.

> For all the chosen race
> Shall meet around the throne,
> Shall bless the working of His grace,
> And make His glories known.
>
> Isaac Watts, 1674 – 1748

All whom God has chosen, all whom Christ has redeemed, all whom the Spirit has called, all who believe in Jesus will safely cross the dividing sea. Not all of us have safely reached land yet, for:

> Part of the host has crossed the flood,
> And part is crossing now.
>
> Watts

The front lines of the army have already reached the shore, while we are still marching through the depths, closely following our Leader into the heart of the sea. May our hearts be cheered, for soon the rear guard will stand where the front lines are today. Soon the last of God's chosen ones will have crossed the sea, and once all are safe and secure, a song of triumph will be heard.

Yet even if one soul was absent — yes! If just one in His chosen family was cast away, it would make for an eternal discord in the song of the redeemed. It would so severely cut the strings of the harps in heaven that music could never be drawn from them again.

From the pen of Jim Reimann:

Yes, believer, you *will* make it to the other side. "He who began a good work in you will carry it on to completion until the day of Christ Jesus" (Phil. 1:6).

Consider the progression from God's foreknowledge in eternity past to glorification in eternity future in the following passage:

> Those God foreknew he also predestined to be conformed to the likeness of his Son.... And those he predestined, he also called; those he called, he also justified; those he justified, he also glorified.
>
> Romans 8:29 – 30

And notice that the Lord sees us as already glorified (in the past tense), for He is faithful to complete what He starts — He is a covenant-keeping God!

"What, then, shall we say in response to this? If God is for us, who can be against us?" (Rom. 8:31).

JANUARY 22

Son of man, how is the wood of a vine better than
that of a branch on any of the trees in the forest?

Ezekiel 15:2

From the pen of Charles Spurgeon:

These words were meant to humble God's people. They are called God's vine, but in their own nature are they any better than others? Only through God's goodness have they become fruitful, having been replanted in good soil. The Lord has trained His vine along the walls of His sanctuary and they produce fruit for His glory, but what are they without their God? What are they without the continual influence of the Spirit who is the source of their fruitfulness?

Dear believer, learn to reject pride, seeing there is no basis for it in you. Whoever you are or whatever you have become you have done nothing over which to be proud. The more you have the more you are in debt to God, and you should never be proud over something that causes you to be a debtor.

Consider your beginning — look back to what you were. Consider what you would have been without God's divine grace. Then consider who you are now. If you are proud, doesn't your own conscience rebuke you? Don't your thousand past wanderings convict you, telling you that you are unworthy to be called His child? And if He has changed you, have you not been taught it is only His grace that has made you different?

O "great believer"! You would have been a great sinner if God had not made you different. And you who take such a courageous stand for truth, you would have been just as courageous for error if His grace had not taken hold of you.

Therefore, don't be proud. Although you may have a large spiritual estate — a wide domain of grace — you don't have even a single thing to call your own — except sin and misery.

Oh, what foolish infatuation to think that you, who has borrowed everything, should even think of exalting yourself! You are a poor dependent pensioner living on the generosity and riches of the Savior. You have a life that dies without the fresh streams of life flowing from Jesus.

And yet you are proud! Shame on you, O foolish heart!

From the pen of Jim Reimann:

It is a humbling exercise to consider the track of our lives before Christ saved us. Yet this is exactly what Paul encourages us to do in these verses:

Think of what you were when you were called. Not many of you were wise by human standards; not many were influential; not many were of noble birth. But God chose the foolish things of the world to shame the wise; God chose the weak things of the world to shame the strong. He chose the lowly things of this world and the despised things — and the things that are not — to nullify the things that are, so that no one may boast before him.

It is because of him that you are in Christ Jesus, who has become for us wisdom from God — that is, our righteousness, holiness and redemption. Therefore, as it is written: "Let him who boasts boast in the Lord."

1 Corinthians 1:26 – 31

Father, "May I never boast except in the cross of our Lord Jesus Christ, through which the world has been crucified to me, and I to the world" (Gal. 6:14).

JANUARY 23

I have exalted a young man from among the people.

Psalm 89:19

From the pen of Charles Spurgeon:

Why was Christ chosen "from among the people"? I will speak from my heart, for its thoughts are best. Wasn't He chosen "from among the people" in order to be our brother through the blessed bond of kindred blood? What a wonderful family relationship there is between Christ and believers! A believer can actually claim, "I have a Brother in heaven. I may be poor, but I have a Brother who is rich and who is a King. Will He allow me to be in need while He sits on His throne? No! He loves me — He is my Brother!"

Dear believer, wear this blessed thought like a diamond necklace around the neck of your memory. Slide it onto the finger of your remembrance as a golden ring and then use it as the King's own seal, stamping your petitions of faith with confidence of success. He is your Brother, born for adversity, so treat Him as such.

Also, Christ was chosen "from among the people" so He would know our needs and sympathize with us. "[He] has been tempted in every way, just as we are — yet was without sin" (Heb. 4:15). Therefore in all of our sorrows we have His sympathy. He knows them all — temptation, pain, disappointment, weakness, weariness, poverty — for He has felt them all.

Remember this, dear Christian, and allow it to comfort you. Despite how difficult and painful your path, it is marked with the footprints of your Savior. Even when you "walk through the valley of the shadow of death" (Ps. 23:4) or the deepest waters of a flooding Jordan River, you will find His footprints are there.

Wherever we may go, He has gone before us, and every burden we must carry has already been laid upon the shoulders of Immanuel.

His way was much rougher and darker than
  mine.
Did Christ, my dear Lord, suffer? Should I still
  whine?

John Newton, 1725 – 1807

Take courage! Royal feet have left a bloodstained trail upon your road and thereby consecrated the difficult path forever.

From the pen of Jim Reimann:

Jesus came to earth to identify with us in our humanity so we could identify with Him in His holiness. "He had to be made like his brothers in every way ... that he might make atonement for the sins of the people" (Heb. 2:17).

In other words, to "make atonement," He had to be one of us. "God sent his Son, born of a woman, born under law, to redeem those under law, that we might receive the full rights of sons" (Gal. 4:4 – 5).

Jesus Christ humbled Himself to become a man so you could not only become His friend but also a member of His family! And because He became a man, He can indeed sympathize with every struggle you will ever encounter.

Why not go to Him right now in prayer — knowing He cares? "Come to me, all you who are weary and burdened, and I will give you rest. Take my yoke upon you and learn from me, for I am gentle and humble in heart, and you will find rest for your souls" (Matt. 11:28 – 29).

JANUARY 24

Surely he will save you from the fowler's snare.
Psalm 91:3

From the pen of Charles Spurgeon:

God saves His people from "the fowler's snare" in two ways: "from" and "out of." First, He will often deliver them "from" the snare by not letting them enter it. Second, if they *do* get snared He delivers them "out of" it. Some people consider the first way more precious, while others cling to the second.

"He will save you from the fowler's snare." How? Trouble is often the means through which God delivers us. He knows our backsliding will ultimately end in our destruction, so in His mercy He sends His rod of correction. Then we ask, "Lord, why have you done this?" not even realizing our trouble has been His very means of delivering us from far greater evil. In this way many have been saved from ruin through their sorrows and the crosses they bear. These "birds" have been frightened "from" the fowler's net. At other times God keeps His people "from" the "fowler's snare" by giving them great spiritual strength. Then when they are tempted to do evil they say, "How then could I do such a wicked thing and sin against God?" (Gen. 39:9).

Yet what a blessed thought that when a believer *does* fall in an evil moment into the "fowler's snare," God will rescue him from it! O backslider, grieve—but don't despair. Although you have wandered from the truth, listen to what your Redeemer says, "'Turn, O backsliding children' (Jer. 3:14 KJV). I will have mercy on you." Do you respond, however, with, "I can't return. I'm a captive!" Then listen again to His promise: "Surely he will save you from the fowler's snare." Ultimately you will "surely" be saved "out of" all the evil into which you have fallen, and although you will never cease from needing to repent from sins you commit, He who has loved you will never cast you aside. He will receive you, giving you joy and delight, so that even the very bones He has broken may rejoice.

No bird of paradise will ever die in the "fowler's snare."

From the pen of Jim Reimann:

Consider for a moment the families you know. Think of the parents whose children are well disciplined, and then think of the parents who are lax in their discipline—those who are attempting to be more of a friend to their children than a parent. Which do you consider the better parents? Whose children would you rather be around? Of course, the answer is obvious. In the same way, our gracious Father is also our gracious Parent who disciplines us out of His great sense of love and care. What a joy to know that our loving God uses even the troubles produced by His rod of correction as a means of deliverance!

> God disciplines us for our good, that we may share in his holiness. No discipline seems pleasant at the time, but painful. Later on, however, it produces a harvest of righteousness and peace for those who have been trained by it. Therefore, strengthen your feeble arms and weak knees. "Make level paths for your feet," so that the lame may not be disabled, but rather healed.
> Hebrews 12:10–13

Dear Lord, thank You for the fact that even when I stumble and fall, needing correction, Your love is everlasting—and Your "rod of correction imparts wisdom" (Prov. 29:15).

JANUARY 25

I will tell of the kindnesses of the Lord, the deeds for which he is to be praised,
according to all the Lord has done for us.

Isaiah 63:7

From the pen of Charles Spurgeon:

Can you do this? Aren't there "kindnesses of the Lord" you have experienced? Although you may be sad and dejected now, can't you remember that blessed hour when Jesus met you and said, "Come to me" (Matt. 11:28)? Can't you remember that glorious moment when He snapped your shackles, cast your chains to the ground, and said, "I came to break your bonds and set you free"?

Even if your spiritual passion has faded, surely there must be a precious mile marker along the road of life that is not yet covered with moss — one on which you can still read a happy reminder of His mercy toward you.

What! Did you never have a sickness — perhaps like the one that you are now suffering — from which He did not restore you? Were you never poor that He did not supply your needs? Were you never in distressing circumstances that He did not deliver you?

Get up! Go to the river of your own experience, pull up a few bulrushes, weave them into an ark, and put your baby faith safely afloat. Don't forget what your God has done for you. Turn back the pages of the book of your memory and consider your past. Can you remember Mount Mizar? (See Ps. 42:5 – 6.) Did the Lord never meet with you at Mount Hermon? Have you never climbed these glorious mountains? Have you never been helped in your time of need?

No, I know you have! Think back a short time to the best memories of your life, and although everything may appear dark right now, illumine the lamps of the past. They will glisten through the darkness, and then you will trust in the Lord while you watch a new day dawn and see the shadows of night vanish.

"Remember, O Lord, your great mercy and love, for they are from of old" (Ps. 25:6).

From the pen of Jim Reimann:

Quite often the Scriptures admonish us to remember the past.

Remember those earlier days after you had received the light, when you stood your ground in a great contest in the face of suffering. Sometimes you were publicly exposed to insult and persecution; at other times you stood side by side with those who were so treated. You sympathized with those in prison and joyfully accepted the confiscation of your property, because you knew that you yourselves had better and lasting possessions. So do not throw away your confidence; it will be richly rewarded. You need to persevere so that when you have done the will of God, you will receive what he has promised.

Hebrews 10:32 – 36

I could never forget the day the Lord saved me, rescuing me from eternal destruction! Yet why do I often walk in a way that shows such a lack of trust in Him?

Dear Father, may I make a determination even now to "tell of the kindnesses of the Lord." "I will remember the deeds of the Lord; yes, I will remember your miracles of long ago" (Ps. 77:11).

"Remember the day you stood before the Lord your God" (Deut. 4:10).

JANUARY 26

Your heavenly Father ...
Matthew 6:26

From the pen of Charles Spurgeon:

God's people are doubly His children — they are His offspring through creation and they are His children through their adoption in Christ. Therefore, they are privileged to address Him by saying, "Our Father which art in heaven" (Matt. 6:9 KJV). *Father*. What a precious word!

The very word speaks authority. Yet, "If I am your Father, where is my honor? If you are my children, where is your obedience?" The term *Father* mingles affection with authority, an authority that does not evoke rebellion, but an authority demanding obedience that is cheerfully given and would not be withheld even when it could be. The obedience God's children render to Him must be a loving obedience.

Don't approach serving the Lord as a slave simply doing your taskmaster's work, but follow the path of His commands because it is your Father's path. "Offer the parts of your body to him as instruments of righteousness" (Rom. 6:13) because righteousness is your Father's will, and His will should also be the will of His child.

Father! The word denotes a kingly attribute. Yet it is so sweetly veiled in love that the King's crown is forgotten when viewing His face, and His scepter is not a rod of iron but a silver scepter of mercy. In fact, His scepter seems to be forgotten altogether in the tender hand of Him who wields it.

Father! In this term we find honor and love. How great is a father's love for his children! The word *friendship* will not do, nor will the term *kindness* come close to expressing what a father's heart and hands will do for his child. They are his offspring — he must bless them; they are his children — he must exhibit his strength in their defense. If an earthly father watches over his children with unceasing love and care, how much more does our heavenly Father display?

"*Abba*, Father" (Rom. 8:15)! Whoever can utter these words has expressed sweeter music than all the cherubim and seraphim could ever sing. Heaven is found in the depth of that word — *Father*! In that word is all I could ever ask, all my needs could ever demand, and all my heart could ever desire.

I have *all* of everything, throughout *all* of eternity, when I can say, "Father."

From the pen of Jim Reimann:

Unfortunately, too many people today have never experienced an earthly father or a heavenly one. We live in a time when a large percentage of babies are born to single women, a time that greatly undervalues the importance of having a father in the home. Yet relating to an earthly father is one of the primary ways we learn to relate to our heavenly Father.

Dear believer, whether or not you have the blessing of a close relationship with an earthly father — or no earthly father at all — there is a heavenly Father who is capable of being your "all in all" (1 Cor. 15:28), capable of meeting your every need. And this "Father knows what you need before you ask him" (Matt. 6:8).

Heavenly Father, I thank You for who You are and that You desire to have an intimate relationship with me. Deepen my desire to know You better, I pray.

"We pray this in order that you may live a life worthy of the Lord ... growing in the knowledge of God" (Col. 1:10).

JANUARY 27

From the fullness of his grace we have all received.

John 1:16

From the pen of Charles Spurgeon:

These words tell us there is a fullness in Christ. There is a fullness of His necessary Deity, "For in Christ all the fullness of the Deity lives in bodily form" (Col. 2:9). There is a fullness of His perfect manhood, for it was through Him "bodily" that the Deity was revealed. There is a fullness of the atoning effectiveness of His blood, for "the blood of Jesus, his Son, purifies us from all sin" (1 John 1:7). There is a fullness of justifying righteousness in His life, for "there is now no condemnation for those who are in Christ Jesus" (Rom. 8:1).

There is a fullness of the divine extensive scope of His prayers, for "he is able to save completely those who come to God through him, because he always lives to intercede for them" (Heb. 7:25). There is a fullness of victory in His death, for "by his death" He destroyed "him who holds the power of death — that is, the devil" (Heb. 2:14). There is a fullness of the effectiveness of His resurrection from the dead, for through it "he has given us new birth into a living hope" (1 Peter 1:3). There is a fullness of triumph in His ascension, for "when he ascended on high, he led captives in his train and gave gifts to men" (Eph. 4:8).

There is a fullness of blessings of every sort and shape — a fullness of grace to pardon, of grace to regenerate, of grace to sanctify, of grace to preserve, and of grace to perfect. And there is a fullness at all times — a fullness of comfort in times of affliction, and a fullness of guidance in times of prosperity. There is a fullness of every divine attribute — including a fullness of wisdom, of power, and of love. There is a fullness beyond our capacity to even comprehend, much less to fully explore.

"For God was pleased to have all his fullness dwell in him" (Col. 1:19). What a fullness this must be! And to think that we all receive! Indeed, what fullness there must be when the stream is always flowing, yet the well continues to spring up as free, as rich, and as full as ever.

Come, dear believer. Get all your needs supplied. Ask largely, and you will receive largely, for *this* fullness is inexhaustible and is stored where all needy souls may reach it.

It is found in Jesus — Immanuel — "God with us" (Matt. 1:23).

From the pen of Jim Reimann:

Yes, there is a fullness in Christ and, as Spurgeon says, "*This* fullness is inexhaustible." In fact, one of the most beautiful aspects of the divine fullness of each of His attributes is that His fullness overflows into the lives of His children, yet is never diminished.

My own human strength can only take me to a certain point before I grow weary and ultimately become exhausted. However, His strength through the power of the Holy Spirit is always available to me as I walk in obedience to Him.

Dear Father, may these words of Jesus be evident in my life today, and may others come to the fullness only He can provide:

"Whoever drinks the water I give him will never thirst. Indeed, the water I give him will become in him a spring of water welling up to eternal life" (John 4:14). "If anyone is thirsty, let him come to me and drink. Whoever believes in me … streams of living water will flow from within him" (John 7:37 – 38).

. . . perfect in Christ.
Colossians 1:28

From the pen of Charles Spurgeon:

When you search deeply within yourself, don't you find a lack of perfection? Doesn't every day of your life teach you that? Doesn't every tear that trickles from your eyes and every harsh word that proceeds from your lips mutter, "Imperfection." Too frequently you have had such a direct view into your own heart that it seems impossible to dream of even a moment of perfection in yourself.

Yet in the midst of this sad awareness of your own imperfection there is comfort for you — you are "perfect in Christ." In God's sight you are "complete in Christ" (Col. 1:28 NASB) — even now you are "accepted in the beloved" (Eph. 1:6 KJV).

Yet there is also a second perfection, still to come, which is guaranteed to all God's children. Isn't it a delight to look forward to the day when every stain of sin will be removed from believers — when we will be presented "without fault and with great joy" (Jude 24) before God's throne, "without stain or wrinkle or any other blemish, but holy and blameless" (Eph. 5:27). On that day Christ's church will be so pure, even the eye of Omniscience will not detect a spot or blemish in her — so holy and glorious it will not stretch the truth in the least to say of us:

> With my Savior's garments on,
> Holy as the Holy One.
> Samuel Hart, 1845 – ?

Only then will we know, taste, and feel the happiness of the fullness of this short phrase:

"Complete in Christ." Not till then will we fully comprehend the heights and depths of the salvation of Jesus. Doesn't your heart leap within you at this very thought? As dark as your soul may be, that day it will be "white as snow" (Isa. 1:18) — as filthy as you are, you will be clean.

What a miraculous salvation this is! Christ takes a mere worm and transforms it into an angel. He takes someone dark and deformed and makes him clean and matchless in His glory, without peer in His beauty, and fit to be the companion of seraphim.

"O my soul" (Ps. 103:1), stand and admire this blessed truth — "perfect in Christ."

From the pen of Jim Reimann:

Clean! If only we could see ourselves through the eyes of our precious Savior, who said, "You are already clean because of the word I have spoken to you" (John 15:3). Yet there *are* examples in the Scriptures of men who had the Lord's perspective. David declared, "The LORD has rewarded me according to my righteousness, according to my cleanness in his sight" (2 Sam. 22:25).

And Job once said, "My doctrine is pure, and I am clean in God's eyes" (Job 11:4 ESV), for the Lord had said of him, "There is no one on earth like him; he is blameless and upright, a man who fears God and shuns evil" (Job 1:8).

"Praise be to the God and Father of our Lord Jesus Christ.... For he chose us in him before the creation of the world to be holy and blameless in his sight" (Eph. 1:3 – 4).

JANUARY 29

... what is unseen.

2 Corinthians 4:18

From the pen of Charles Spurgeon:

In our Christian pilgrimage, generally it is best to be forward looking, for ahead lies our crown and onward is the goal. Whether we seek hope, joy, or consolation to further inspire our love, the future should, after all is said and done, be the primary object of the eye of faith. As we look into the future, we see death and "the body of sin ... done away with" (Rom. 6:6) and the soul made perfectly complete — fit to partake in the inheritance of the saints of light.

Looking further still, the believer's enlightened eye of faith can see that gloomy stream of death's river then forded and the attainment of the heights of the hills of light where shines that glorious celestial city. He sees himself within the pearly gates, hailed as more than a conqueror (see Rom. 8:37), crowned by Christ's own hands, embraced within the arms of Jesus, glorified with Him, and seated with Him on His throne — as He said, "To him who overcomes, I will give the right to sit with me on my throne, just as I overcame and sat down with my Father on his throne" (Rev. 3:21).

The very thought of such a glorious future should relieve the darkness of the past and the dreary gloom of the present. The joys of heaven will more than compensate for the sorrows of earth.

Hush then! O my doubts! Hush! Death is simply a narrow stream that quickly will be crossed. Time? How short! Eternity? How long! Death? How brief! Immortality? How endless!

Even now I can see myself eating of "the cluster of grapes" of "the Valley of Eshcol" (Num. 13:24) and sipping of the pure water of the well within its gate. The road is so very short! I will soon be there!

> When the world my heart is rending
> With its heaviest storm of care,
> My glad thoughts to heaven ascending,
> Find a refuge from despair.
> Faith's bright vision shall sustain me
> Till life's pilgrimage is past;
> Fears may vex and troubles pain me,
> *I shall reach my home at last.*
> William Hiley Bathurst, 1796 – 1877

From the pen of Jim Reimann:

It may seem counterintuitive, but isn't it true that the longer we live, the shorter we realize this life really is? Isn't it the older people among us who have the sense that every year seems shorter than the previous one? The apostle James declared, "What is your life? You are a mist that appears for a little while and then vanishes" (James 4:14).

> Lift up your eyes to the heavens, look at the earth beneath; the heavens will vanish like smoke, the earth will wear out like a garment and its inhabitants die like flies. But my salvation will last forever, my righteousness will never fail.

Isaiah 51:6

Help me, heavenly Father, to daily seek Your kingdom and Your righteousness, "for tomorrow will worry about itself" (Matt. 6:34).

JANUARY 30

As soon as you hear the sound of marching
in the tops of the balsam trees, move quickly.

2 Samuel 5:24

From the pen of Charles Spurgeon:

Members of Christ's church should be very prayerful, always seeking the anointing and power of the Holy One to rest upon their hearts so His kingdom may come and His "will be done on earth as it is in heaven" (Matt. 6:10). And as those times come when it appears God is especially favoring His army of Zion, they should be treated as "the sound of marching in the tops of the balsam trees."

It is then we should be doubly prayerful and earnest, wrestling before God's throne with more intensity than usual. Our actions should then be immediate and energetic, and because the tide is flowing, we should powerfully row for the shore. Oh, how we need the outpouring of the power of Pentecost and its resulting effective labor for Christ!

Dear Christian, there are times in your own life when "you hear the sound of marching in the tops of the balsam trees." At those times you have unmistakable power in prayer, the Spirit of God gives you deep joy and delight, the Scriptures appear fully open to you, God's promises are applied to your life, you walk in the light of God's countenance, you have a distinct and refreshing freedom and liberty in your quiet times of devotion, and you experience more intimate communion with Christ than usual.

Therefore, when those joyous times of hearing "the sound of the marching in the tops of the balsam trees" appear, stir yourself to action. It is time to rid yourself of any evil habit while "the

Spirit helps [you] in [y]our weakness" (Rom. 8:26). So spread your sail to the wind, but remember the words of this song:

> I can only spread the sail,
> But You must breathe the auspicious gale!
> Augustus Montague Toplady, 1740 – 1778

Just be sure to raise your sail, not missing the gale through a lack of preparation for it. Seek God's help that you may be all the more earnest in serving Him once your faith is strengthened, that you are especially devoted to prayer during those times of increased liberty before His throne, and that your conversation will be more and more holy while you experience these more intimate times with Christ.

From the pen of Jim Reimann:

The story of David in 2 Samuel 5:22 – 25 is an amazing story of hearing and trusting the Lord. Yet another king once had the opportunity to trust God to go before him into battle in an even greater way.

When three armies amassed against Israel, the Lord told Jehoshaphat, "The battle is not yours, but God's.... You will not have to fight this battle." Then, as God's people "began to sing and praise," the Lord defeated their enemies. "No one had escaped" (2 Chron. 20:15, 17, 22, 24).

*Father, I desire to know You so intimately
that I can hear Your army "in the tops of the
... trees." And grant me the faith to "sing and
praise" before the battle.*

JANUARY 31

He will be called: The LORD Our Righteousness.

Jeremiah 23:6

From the pen of Charles Spurgeon:

Thinking of the perfect righteousness of Christ will always give Christians the greatest sense of calm, quiet, ease, and peace. Yet how often the saints of God are sad and depressed! I don't think they should be and I don't believe they would be if they could always see their own perfection in Christ. Some Christians always talk about the corruption and depravity of the heart and the innate evil of the soul. Although this is certainly true, why not look a little further and remember that we are "perfect in Christ" (Col. 1:28)?

It is no wonder that those whose thoughts continually dwell on their own corruption have such downcast expressions on their faces. But if we would only call to mind that "Christ Jesus ... has become ... our righteousness" (1 Cor. 1:30), we would "be of good cheer" (John 16:33 KJV).

Whatever troubles afflict me, although Satan assaults me, and even though there may be many difficult experiences to endure before I go to heaven, each trial is provided for me within God's covenant of His divine grace. And there is nothing lacking in my Lord Jesus, for Christ has done it all. From His cross He said, "It is finished" (John 19:30), and if "it is finished," I am "complete in him" (Col. 2:10 KJV) and can rejoice "with an inexpressible and glorious joy" (1 Peter 1:8), "not having a righteousness of my own that comes from the law, but that which is through faith in Christ — the righteousness that comes from God and is by faith" (Phil. 3:9).

On this side of heaven you will never find a more holy people than those who have received the doctrine of Christ's righteousness into their hearts. When a believer says, "I live on Christ alone, solely rest on Him for salvation, and believe that however unworthy I may feel, I am forever saved in Jesus," then with a motive of gratitude arising within him, he begins to think, "Because this is true, should I not live for Christ? Should I not love Him and serve Him all the more since I am saved by His merits — not mine?"

"Christ's love compels us ... that those who live should no longer live for themselves but for him who died for them" (2 Cor. 5:14 – 15). Once we understand it is by His righteousness imputed to us that we are saved, then we will more greatly value that righteousness so graciously bestowed to us from His abundant supply.

From the pen of Jim Reimann:

Spurgeon speaks of Christ's "righteousness imputed to us." Imputation is an accounting term, meaning "to credit to an account." Christ's righteousness is credited (or imputed) to our sin account. Yet someone had to pay with His blood!

It has been said: "Christ came to pay a debt He did not owe, because we had a debt we could not pay." Because of that, and only that, His righteousness can be imputed to us. Our debt is forever canceled!

"When you were dead in your sins ... God made you alive with Christ. He forgave us all our sins, having canceled the written code ... that was against us;...he took it away, nailing it to the cross" (Col. 2:13 – 14).

"Abraham believed God, and it was *credited* to him as righteousness" (Rom. 4:3).

Lord, how amazing that "Christ Jesus ... has become ... [my] righteousness"!

February

FEBRUARY 1

May they sing of the ways of the LORD.

Psalm 138:5

From the pen of Charles Spurgeon:

Christians begin to "sing of the ways of the LORD" when they first lose their burden at the foot of the cross. Not even the songs of angels sound as sweet as that first song of rapture that gushes forth from the inner soul of a forgiven child of God. In *The Pilgrim's Progress*, John Bunyan (1628 – 1688) says that when poor Pilgrim left his burden at the cross, he made three giant leaps and then went on his way, singing:

Blessed cross! Blessed Tomb! Blessed rather be
The Man that there was put to shame for me!

Dear believer, do you remember the day your shackles fell away? Do you recall the place where Jesus met you and said, "I have loved you with an everlasting love" (Jer. 31:3); "I have swept away your offenses like a cloud, your sins like the morning mist" (Isa. 44:22); and "'None of the offenses [you have] committed will be remembered against [you]' (Ezek. 18:22) forever"?

Oh, what a sweet day it is when Jesus takes away the pain of sin! When the Lord first pardoned my sin, I was so joyful, I could barely refrain from dancing. On the way home from the house where I had been set free, I felt like telling even the stones on the street the story of my deliverance. My soul was so full of joy I wanted to tell every snowflake falling from heaven of the wondrous love of Jesus — He who had blotted out the sins of such a terrible rebel.

Yet it is not only at the onset of the Christian life that believers have reason to sing. As long as they live, they discover new reasons to "sing of the ways of the LORD." And as they experience His constant love they are led to proclaim, "I will extol the LORD at all times; his praise will always be on my lips" (Ps. 34:1).

O Christian, "Glorify the LORD with me" (Ps. 34:3) — today!

Long as we tread this desert land,
New mercies will new songs demand.
Philip Doddridge, 1702 – 1751

From the pen of Jim Reimann:

Certainly King David was not a new believer when he "danced before the LORD with all his might" (2 Sam. 6:14). He rejoiced because "the ark of the LORD was entering the City of David" (v. 16) after a long absence. And although his wife Michal "despised him in her heart" (v. 16) for it, he would not be deterred. He explained that his dancing was "before the LORD" and then went on to say, "*I will* celebrate before the LORD" (v. 21).

It was David who wrote our text verse today: "May they sing of the ways of the LORD." The same psalm says, "*I will* praise you, O LORD, *with all my heart* ... *I will* sing your praise. *I will* bow down toward your holy temple and *will* praise your name" (Ps. 138:1 – 2). Notice David's determination in these words.

Father, may the attitude of David be in me, to praise You "with all [my] might" and "with all my heart," regardless of what others may think.

I will "call to the LORD, who is worthy of praise" (Ps. 18:3).

Without the shedding of blood there is no forgiveness.

Hebrews 9:22

From the pen of Charles Spurgeon:

This is the voice of unchangeable truth. In Jewish ceremonies sins were never removed, even symbolically, without the actual shedding of blood. Without exception sin cannot be pardoned without that sin debt being satisfied through Christ's atonement — there is no other way. It should be clear then that there is no hope for me except for Christ, for no blood but His is worth even a second thought when it comes to atoning for sin.

Am I then trusting in Him alone? Is the blood of His atonement truly applied to my soul? All people are on an equal level in their need of Him. No matter how moral, generous, likable, or patriotic we may be, this truth will not be altered to make an exception for us. Sin will never yield to anything less powerful than the blood of Him whom God has sent to be our propitiation — the sacrifice that satisfies the wrath of God. What a blessing we have in this, the only path to forgiveness! Why should we seek another way?

People who simply practice the rituals of religion cannot understand how believers can rejoice that all our sins are forgiven for Christ's sake. Yet their works, prayers, and ceremonies give them very little comfort — and rightly so — for they are "ignor[ing] such a great salvation" (Heb. 2:3) — the one great and true salvation. They are seeking forgiveness "without the shedding of blood."

Dear soul, sit down and behold the justice of God that must punish sin and see that punishment being carried out on your Lord Jesus. Then fall before Him in humility and joy and kiss the dear feet of Him whose blood has atoned for your sin.

It is a vain exercise to find comfort in feeling sorry for your sin when your conscience has been pricked, for this is simply a habit we learned when we were in bondage in "Egypt." The only cure for a guilty conscience is to catch sight of Jesus suffering on the cross.

The Levitical law teaches, "The life of every creature is its blood" (Lev. 17:14). May we rest assured it is also the blood of Christ that is the life of faith, joy, and every other gift of God's holy grace.

> Oh! How sweet to view the flowing
> Of my Savior's precious blood;
> With divine assurance knowing
> He has made my peace with God.
>
> Richard Lee, 1780? – 18??

From the pen of Jim Reimann:

We often speak of "the precious blood of Christ" (1 Peter 1:19), but do we really comprehend the meaning of the word *precious*? Dictionaries define the term as meaning "of great value." But to truly know the value of something, don't we have to have something to compare it to?

Yet nothing in the universe compares to the blood of Jesus and its saving power! Thus, in this case the word *precious* must mean: beyond our ability to value it or place a price on it. His blood is worth far more than anyone could ever afford. After all, "what good will it be for a man if he gains the whole world, yet forfeits his soul? Or what can a man give in exchange for his soul?" (Matt. 16:26).

FEBRUARY 3

So then, brothers, we are debtors.

Romans 8:12 ESV

From the pen of Charles Spurgeon:

As people of God's creation we are all debtors to Him, owing Him obedience with our entire body, soul, and strength. And having broken His commandments, as each of us has, we are also debtors to His justice, therefore having a vast debt we are unable to repay.

For Christians, however, it can be said that we are not debtors to God's justice, for Christ has paid the debt His people owed. For this reason believers are all the more indebted to His love. I am a debtor to God's grace and His forgiving mercy, but in no way am I a debtor to His justice, for He will never accuse me of a debt that is already paid.

Christ said, "It is finished" (John 19:30), meaning that whatever His people owed was forever wiped away from His book of remembrance. Christ has utterly and completely satisfied divine justice; our account is settled; the final receipt, signed upon His cross, has been delivered. Therefore we are no longer debtors to God's justice. Yet, for the very reason we are no longer debtors to our Lord's justice, we are ten times more indebted to Him than we would have been otherwise.

Dear Christian, pause for a moment to ponder what a debtor you are to the Divine Sovereign! Think how much you owe to His unselfish love, for He gave His own Son to die for you. Consider how much you owe to His forgiving grace, for even after ten thousand offenses He loves you as infinitely as ever. Consider what you owe to His power — He has raised you from your death in sin, He has preserved your spiritual life, He has kept you from falling, and although a thousand enemies may have crossed your path, you have been empowered to continue on your way. And finally, consider what you owe to His unchangeable nature — though you have changed a thousand times, He has never changed even once.

You are as deeply in debt as you could possibly be to *every* attribute of God. Therefore you owe the Lord all that you are and all that you have. "Offer your bodies as living sacrifices, holy and pleasing to God — this is your spiritual act of worship" (Rom. 12:1).

From the pen of Jim Reimann:

We owe everything to Christ, for "he bought us with his own blood" (Acts 20:28). As a result, many may declare as Peter once did, "I will lay down my life for you" (John 13:37). Of course, he said this just before he denied Jesus three times! To be fair, Peter made this bold claim before the Holy Spirit was given.

Yet it is still easy to say, "I'm willing to die for you, Lord." The question is: How many of us are willing to *live* for Him? After all, Paul said to "offer your bodies as *living* sacrifices." Not *dead* sacrifices!

"For I take no pleasure in the death of anyone, declares the Sovereign Lord. Repent and live!" (Ezek. 18:32). "He is not the God of the dead, but of the living" (Luke 20:38). "For in him we live and move and have our being" (Acts 17:28).

"He died for all, that those who live should no longer live for themselves but for him who died for them and was raised again" (2 Cor. 5:15).

FEBRUARY 4

... the love of the Lord.

Hosea 3:1 KJV

From the pen of Charles Spurgeon:

Dear believer, look back over your life experience. Think of the way the Lord your God has led you through the wilderness and how He has fed and clothed you every day. Think of how He has put up with your bad manners, all your complaints, and your longings for the "pots of meat" (Ex. 16:3) back in Egypt. Think of how He has opened the rock to supply you with water and how He has fed you with manna that came down from heaven. Think of how His grace "is sufficient for you" (2 Cor. 12:9) in all your troubles, how His blood pardoned you for all your sins, and how His rod and His staff have comforted you (see Ps. 23:4).

Now that you have looked at "the love of the Lord" in your past, allow faith to survey His love in the future, for remember, Christ's covenant and His blood affect more than just your past. He who has loved you in the past will never cease to love and forgive you into the future as well. He is the "Alpha and the Omega" (Rev. 1:8); He is the first, and He will be the last.

Therefore remember, "Even though [you] walk through the valley of the shadow of death, [you should] fear no evil" (Ps. 23:4), for He will be with you. When you find yourself standing in the cold flooding water of the Jordan River, you need not fear, for death cannot separate you from His love. And when you finally find yourself standing before the mysteries of eternity, you need not tremble, "For I am convinced that neither death nor life, neither angels nor demons, neither the present nor the future, nor any powers, neither height nor depth, nor anything else in all creation, will be able to separate us from the love of God that is in Christ Jesus our Lord" (Rom. 8:38 – 39).

Dear soul, after reflecting on this, isn't your love refreshed? Doesn't this increase your love for Jesus? Doesn't a flight through the limitless heavens of His love rekindle your heart and compel you to "find your joy in the LORD" (Isa. 58:14)? Surely as we meditate on "the love of the Lord" we will feel "our hearts burning within us" (Luke 24:32) and we will long to love Him more.

From the pen of Jim Reimann:

When we remember the stories of the children of Israel who had recently been delivered from slavery in Egypt, we are amazed at how quickly they began to complain, saying, "It would have been better for us to serve the Egyptians than to die in the desert!" (Ex. 14:12). How could they have turned away from the Lord so quickly, especially after seeing so many of His miracles!

Not so fast! When I think back over my life, how many miracles has He performed for me? And how many times have I turned away from Him, looking with longing eyes to the wilderness of my past? "No one who puts his hand to the plow and looks back is fit for service in the kingdom of God" (Luke 9:62).

Dear Lord, forgive me when I forget Your loving mercies poured out so abundantly on me. Refresh and rekindle my love so my heart will overflow with love for You and for others. Help me walk in Your ways, always living in accordance with Your precious Word, which lovingly reminds me to "Love the LORD your God with all your heart and with all your soul and with all your strength" (Deut. 6:5).

FEBRUARY 5

The Father has sent his Son to be the Savior of the world.

1 John 4:14

From the pen of Charles Spurgeon:

It is a precious thought to think that Jesus Christ did not appear without His Father's permission, authority, consent, and assistance. He was sent by the Father to be the Savior of mankind, but we are much too prone to forget that fact. And while there are distinctions between the Persons of the Trinity, there are no distinctions as to the honor each deserves.

All too often we ascribe honor for our salvation more to Jesus Christ than we do to the Father, at least in terms of the depth of the gift itself. This is a serious mistake, for if Jesus came, didn't the Father send Him? If He spoke wonderful words, didn't the Father pour grace into His mouth so He would be a competent minister of the new covenant?

Someone who truly knows the Father, Son, and Holy Spirit as they should be known will never set one before the other when it comes to love. Instead he sees them at Bethlehem, Gethsemane, and Calvary, with each equally involved in the work of salvation.

Dear Christian, have you put your confidence in the Man Jesus Christ, solely relying upon Him? Are you united with Him? If so, then you should also know and believe you are united with the God of heaven. Since the Man Jesus Christ is your brother, with whom you share the most intimate of fellowship, you are thereby joined to God the eternal — "the Ancient of Days" (Dan. 7:9) — who is your Father and your friend.

Did you ever consider the depth of love in the heart of Jehovah when God the Father equipped His Son for His supreme mission of mercy? If not, let this thought be your meditation today: "The Father has sent his Son"!

Contemplate this. Think how Jesus works out the will of the Father. Consider the love of the great "I AM" (Ex. 3:14) in the wounds of the dying Savior. May your every thought of Jesus be forever connected with the eternal ever-blessed God, for "it was the LORD's will to crush him and cause him to suffer" (Isa. 53:10).

From the pen of Jim Reimann:

Indeed, we see the work of the Father, Son, and Holy Spirit throughout God's plan of redemption. The following verses are just a sampling of this truth:

> We ourselves, who have the firstfruits of the *Spirit*, groan inwardly as we wait eagerly for our adoption as sons, the *redemption* of our bodies.
>
> Romans 8:23

> It is because of [*God*] that you are in *Christ Jesus*, who has become for us wisdom from *God* — that is, our righteousness, holiness and *redemption*.
>
> 1 Corinthians 1:30

> Giving thanks to the *Father*, who has qualified you to share in the inheritance of the saints in the kingdom of light. For he has rescued us from the dominion of darkness and brought us into the kingdom of the *Son* he loves, in whom we have *redemption*.
>
> Colossians 1:12 – 14

Father, thank You for sending Your Son to die and for raising Him to life again through the power of Your Holy Spirit that I may enter Your eternal "kingdom of light." And may I be an agent of Your light to the dark world in which we live that others may enter Your kingdom as well.

FEBRUARY 6

Pray ... and always keep on praying.

Ephesians 6:18

From the pen of Charles Spurgeon:

What a great number of prayers we have uttered since the first moment we learned to pray. Our very first prayer was one for ourselves, asking God to have mercy upon us and to blot out our sin. Of course He heard that prayer, but once He had blotted out our sins like a cloud, we had more prayers for ourselves.

We have prayed for sanctifying grace, for the grace of self-control, for a renewed sense of assurance of faith, for God's promises to be applied to our lives, for deliverance in times of temptation, for power during times of spiritual warfare, and for help and relief during times of trial. We have been compelled to go to God as beggars for our souls' needs, constantly asking for everything.

Dear children of God, testify to the fact that you have never been able to get anything for your souls except from Him. All the bread your soul has eaten has come down to you from heaven, and all the spiritual water it has enjoyed has flowed from the living Rock — Christ Jesus the Lord. Your soul has never grown rich by itself but has always been dependent upon the daily bounty of God. As a result your prayers have risen to heaven for a range of spiritual blessings that is all but infinite.

Your wants were beyond being counted, yet God's supplies are infinitely vast. Your prayers have been as varied as His blessings have been countless. Don't you then have reason to say, "I love the Lord, 'for he has heard my cry for mercy'" (Ps. 28:6), for although your prayers have been numerous, so have God's answers to them been great as well? He has heard you "in the day of trouble" (Ps. 50:15) and He has strengthened you and helped you even when you have dishonored Him by trembling and doubting before His "mercy seat" (Ex. 25:17 KJV).

Remember that and let it fill your heart with gratitude to God, who has graciously heard your poor, weak prayers. "Praise the LORD, O my soul, and forget not all his benefits" (Ps. 103:2).

From the pen of Jim Reimann:

Our Lord is a generous God indeed, never stingily doling out His blessing, little by little, or withholding His greatest blessings for later. No, He lavishes His blessings on His children! Consider the many gifts "lavished on us" in just the two following verses:

> In him we have redemption through his blood, the forgiveness of sins, in accordance with the riches of God's grace that he lavished on us with all wisdom and understanding.
>
> Ephesians 1:7 – 8

> How great is the love the Father has lavished on us, that we should be called children of God!
>
> 1 John 3:1

Redemption, forgiveness, grace, wisdom, understanding, and love have all been "lavished on us"!

After all, "He who did not spare his own Son, but gave him up for us all — how will he not also, along with him, graciously give us all things?" (Rom. 8:32).

Lord, thank You for Your Son and for all the blessings that come from being in Him. May my heart be filled with gratitude as I consider Your generosity.

FEBRUARY 7

Arise and go.
Micah 2:10 ESV

From the pen of Charles Spurgeon:

The hour is approaching when the message will come to us as it ultimately comes to everyone — "'Arise and go' from the home in which you now live, and from the city where you have worked, from your family, and from your friends. Arise and take your last journey."

Yet what do we know of the journey or of the country where we are going? We have read a little bit about the future and some aspects have been revealed to us by the Holy Spirit, but how very little we actually know of the coming kingdom! We know there is a foreboding and stormy river to cross called "Death." God summons us to cross it, promising to be with us along the way, but what follows death?

What amazing world will dawn upon our astonished eyes? What scene of glory will unfold before us? Although no one has ever returned from there, we *do* know enough of that heavenly land to accept our summons from there with joy and delight. The journey through death may be dark, but we can face it fearlessly, knowing God is with us as we walk through that valley of gloom. Therefore we need "fear no evil" (Ps. 23:4).

We will be leaving everything we have known and loved here, but we will be going to our Father's house where Jesus is — to that royal "city with foundations, whose architect and builder is God" (Heb. 11:10). This will be the final time we will ever be dislocated, for we will dwell with Him forever, in the midst of His people — in the very presence of God.

Dear Christian, meditate often on heaven, for it will help you press on and forget the toil of this life. This valley of tears is simply the pathway to a better place. This world of woe is but a stepping-stone to a world of blessedness.

> Prepare us, Lord, by grace divine,
> For Your bright courts on high;
> Then bid our spirits rise, and join
> The chorus of the sky.
>
> Anne Steele, 1717 – 1778

From the pen of Jim Reimann:

"The LORD had said to Abram, 'Leave your country, your people and your father's household and go to the land I will show you.' So Abram left, as the LORD had told him" (Gen. 12:1, 4). Abram, later called Abraham, is a picture of what was to come. He became the Father of Faith because "By faith Abraham, when called to go to a place he would later receive as his inheritance, obeyed and went, even though he did not know where he was going" (Heb. 11:8).

Abraham was headed to an earthly land, but he knew where he was going was not the final Promised Land. And just as we should do, he kept heaven in his eyes, "for *he was looking forward* to the city with foundations, whose architect and builder is God" (Heb. 11:10).

Dear Lord, help me look forward with faith to the eternal city to come, and may I walk in obedience until You have fully prepared me to live there.

"And he carried me away … and showed me the Holy City, Jerusalem, coming down out of heaven from God" (Rev. 21:10).

FEBRUARY 8

You are to give him the name Jesus.
Matthew 1:21

From the pen of Charles Spurgeon:

When a person is very dear to us, everything connected with that person becomes dear to us as well. In this way the person of the Lord Jesus is deemed so precious by every true believer that everything about Him is considered precious beyond any price we could ever calculate. David said, "All your robes are fragrant with myrrh and aloes and cassia" (Ps. 45:8), as though the very garments of the Savior were so sweetened by His person, David could not help but love them.

We can be certain there is not a place where His holy feet have walked, not a word His blessed lips have uttered, nor even a thought His loving Word has revealed which is not precious to us beyond all price. This is also true of every name of Christ; they are all sweet to the ears of believers. Whether He is called the Husband of the Church, her Bridegroom, or her Friend — whether He is known as "the Lamb that was slain from the creation of the world" (Rev. 13:8), the King, the Prophet, or the Priest — whether our Master's title is Shiloh, Immanuel, Wonderful, or Mighty Counselor — each and every name is like honeycomb dripping with luscious drops of perfectly distilled honey.

But if there is one name sweeter than any other in the ears of believers, it is the name of Jesus. Jesus! The name that brings melody to the harps of heaven. Jesus! The life of all our joys. If there is one name more charming or more precious than any other, it is this name. It is the name woven into the very fabric of every psalm of praise. Many hymns begin with it, but very few that are any good end without it. It is the sum total of every delight, the music that rings the bells of heaven, a song in one word, and an ocean beyond all understanding.

Yet while it is only a mere drop of a word in that ocean when it comes to its length, it is a matchless oratorio in only two syllables and is a gathering chorus of the hallelujahs of all eternity in just five letters.

> Jesus, I love Your charming name,
> It's music to my ears.
>
> Philip Doddridge, 1702 – 1751

From the pen of Jim Reimann:

The name *Jesus* is precious to believers, yet sadly has become a curse word for many who don't know Him — even many who deny His existence. "Now to you who believe, this stone is precious. But to those who do not believe ... a stone that causes men to stumble and a rock that makes them fall" (1 Peter 2:7 – 8).

Speaking in spiritual terms today is acceptable in most cases as long as we do not invoke the name of Jesus. Even 2,000 years ago Peter and John were ordered more than once by the chief priest and other leaders "not to speak or teach at all in *the name* of Jesus" (Acts 4:18).

There is great power in "the name." "Everyone who calls on *the name* of the Lord will be saved" (Rom. 10:13). "For there is no other *name* under heaven given to men by which we must be saved" (Acts 4:12).

"Therefore God exalted him to the highest place and gave him *the name* that is above every name, that at *the name* of Jesus every knee should bow" (Phil. 2:9 – 10) — even those who today may deny His existence.

February 9

So David inquired of the LORD.
2 Samuel 5:23

From the pen of Charles Spurgeon:

When David made this inquiry he had just fought the Philistines, winning a significant victory. The Philistines had gone up "in full force" (v. 17), but with God's help David had easily put them to flight. It is important to note, however, that when the enemy came a second time, David did not immediately go to fight them, but he again "inquired of the LORD." After being victorious he might have said, as many others have, "I will be victorious again. Since I have conquered them once before, I can rest assured I will triumph again, so why should I take the time to seek help from the Lord's hands?"

Not so with David. He had triumphed in one battle through the strength of the Lord and would not venture into another battle until he was sure of God's continued help. So he "inquired of the LORD" again, asking if he should attack the Philistines. Then he waited until God's sign was given. Through this story we should learn from David to never take a step without the Lord.

Dear Christian, if you desire to know the path of service for your life, take God as your compass. If you want to be able to steer your ship through the darkest, highest waves, place the control of the rudder into the hands of the Almighty. Many a crushing rock might be escaped if we would only let our Father take the helm, and many a shoal or sandbar might be avoided if we would surrender ourselves to His sovereign will to choose and to command.

There is great truth in this saying of the Puritans: "To be sure, as soon as a Christian carves his own path he'll cut his own fingers." And an old saint of God's once said, "He who goes ahead of the cloud of God's providence goes on a fool's errand." Thus, we must be sure to take note of God's providence leading us, and if He lingers we must wait until He moves. He who runs ahead of God's providence will soon find himself very glad to run straight back to it.

"I will instruct you and teach you in the way you should go" (Ps. 32:8) is God's promise to His people. May we then take all our perplexing questions to Him, saying, "Lord, what would You have me do?" (See Acts 9:6.)

Do not leave your room this morning without inquiring of the Lord.

From the pen of Jim Reimann:

A wise friend once said, "You want to make God laugh? Then make plans!" Planning without seeking the Lord's counsel is not only unbiblical but also dangerous to our spiritual life, if not our physical life. We can only imagine what would have happened to David if he had not "inquired of the LORD."

We need to remember each of us has a "race marked out for us" (Heb. 12:1) by the Lord, and that is the race He intends for us to run. Yet my race is not yours and yours is not mine, which is why we need to seek the Lord's will for ourselves individually.

Solomon, the wisest man who ever lived, tells us: "Commit to the LORD whatever you do, and your plans will succeed" (Prov. 16:3). "In his heart a man plans his course, but the LORD determines his steps" (Prov. 16:9). And "Many are the plans in a man's heart, but it is the LORD's purpose that prevails" (Prov. 19:21).

Not our plans, "but the plans of the LORD stand firm forever" (Ps. 33:11).

FEBRUARY 10

I know what it is to have plenty.

Philippians 4:12

From the pen of Charles Spurgeon:

Many people who know "what it is to be in need" (v. 12) have never learned "what it is to have plenty." When they are placed on the mountaintop, they get dizzy and are about to fall. In fact, Christians disgrace their profession of faith in Christ much more often during times of prosperity than during adversity. Being prosperous is a dangerous thing and the crucible of adversity is a less severe trial for a Christian than "the refining pot" (Prov. 17:3 NASB) of prosperity.

Oh, what starvation of the soul and the neglecting of spiritual things have been brought about through the very blessings and bounty of God! Yet this is not necessary or inevitable, for the apostle Paul tells us, "I know what it is to have plenty." When he had plenty he knew how to use it, for God's abundant grace enabled him to handle God's abundant prosperity.

When the ship of Paul's life had full sails, he had plenty of ballast below deck to stabilize his boat so he could sail safely. It takes more human skill to handle a full cup of unrelenting joy without spilling it. Paul had learned that skill, for he declares, "I have learned the secret of being content in any and every situation, whether well fed or hungry" (Phil. 4:12). Knowing "the secret of being content" when "well fed" is a divine lesson, for God had once given the Israelites "what they craved. But ... even while it was still in their mouths, God's anger rose against them" (Ps. 78:29 – 31).

Many people have asked for blessings simply to satisfy the lust of their own hearts. Full stomachs have often led to a thirst for blood and a wanton disregard for godliness. When we have plenty of God's providential blessings, we often have little regard for God's grace, which leads to very little gratitude for the blessings we have received. When we are full, we forget God. Thus, being satisfied with earth, we are content to do without heaven.

Rest assured it is harder to know how to be well fed than it is to know how to be hungry due to the intense propensity of our human nature toward pride and forgetfulness of God. So be careful to pray, asking the Lord to teach you how to be "well fed."

> Let not the gifts Your love bestows
> Estrange our hearts from You.
>
> Lowell Mason, 1792 – 1872

From the pen of Jim Reimann:

All of us love mountaintop experiences, but it is a trap to always be expecting and looking forward to those times of exhilaration. And if we are truly honest, we will admit we have learned greater lessons from the Lord while in the valleys of life. Of course, our understanding of what God was doing typically comes much later. Kierkegaard, the Danish philosopher, once wrote, "Life can only be understood backwards, but it must be lived forwards."

When we compare the mountaintop to the valley, we realize that what sustains us — such as water, food, and fellowship — is found in the valley. And, the people who so desperately need our testimony of faith live there!

> Lord, may I honor You "in plenty or in want" (Phil. 4:12), and may I live victoriously in the valleys "that the world may know" You (John 17:23 KJV).

FEBRUARY 11

They took note that these men had been with Jesus.

Acts 4:13

From the pen of Charles Spurgeon:

A Christian should be a striking likeness of Jesus Christ. No doubt you have read books of the life of Christ that have been beautifully and eloquently written, but the best life of Christ is His living biography written in the words and actions of His people. If we were actually what we profess to be, and what we should be, we would be true pictures of Christ. We would bear such a striking likeness to Him that the world would not have to scrutinize us for long periods of time and then say, "Well, it looks *something* like Him."

No, immediately upon seeing us they would exclaim, "They have 'been with Jesus'! They have been taught by Him and are like Him. They are the embodiment of the holy Man of Nazareth, working out His life in their own lives and everyday actions."

As a Christian you should be courageous and bold like Christ, never blushing or being ashamed of your faith, for your profession of faith in Him will never disgrace you. So take care you never disgrace it. You should imitate Christ by exhibiting a loving spirit and by exercising kind thinking, speaking, and doing so people will say of you that you have "been with Jesus."

Imitate Christ in His holiness as well. Think of the zeal He had for His Master and then imitate your Master by always doing good, never wasting time, for time is too precious to waste. Did Christ deny Himself? Then do the same. Was He fervent in His devotion to His Father? Then be fervent in your prayers. Was He submissive to His Father's will? Then submit yourself to Him. Was He patient? Then learn to endure.

But to reflect Christ's greatest trait of all, endeavor to forgive your enemies just as He did. Let these glorious words of your Master forever ring in your ears: "Father, forgive them, for they do not know what they are doing" (Luke 23:34). Forgive as you hope to be forgiven (see Matt. 6:14) and "heap burning coals" (Prov. 25:22) on your enemy's head by extending kindness to him. Remember — to repay good for evil is godlike. (See Rom. 12:17.) So be godlike.

In every way, live your life so everyone may say of you that you have "been with Jesus."

From the pen of Jim Reimann:

A common trap is to say, "I just live my testimony." Yet often those who say this never speak of their faith, thinking it is enough to live a life of relative holiness. But Jesus was not only the Word — He proclaimed it!

My mouth will tell of your righteousness, of your salvation all day long, though I know not its measure. *I will* come and *proclaim* your mighty acts, O Sovereign Lord; *I will proclaim* your righteousness, yours alone. Since my youth, O God, you have taught me, and to this day *I declare* your marvelous deeds. Even when I am old and gray, do not forsake me, O God, till *I declare* your power to the next generation, your might to all who are to come.

Psalm 71:15 – 18

Father, I thank You that ultimately I will "be conformed to the likeness of [Your] Son" (Rom. 8:29), but may I never hesitate "to proclaim … the whole will of God" (Acts 20:27) and "proclaim … salvation day after day" (Ps. 96:2).

FEBRUARY 12

Just as the sufferings of Christ flow over into our lives,
so also through Christ our comfort overflows.

2 Corinthians 1:5

From the pen of Charles Spurgeon:

We see a blessed balance in this verse. The Ruler of Providence holds scales in His hand, putting His people's trials on one scale and placing their overflowing comfort on the other. When the scale of trials is light, the scale of comfort will be light as well, but when the scale of trials is full, the scale of comfort will be equally as heavy.

When clouds are their darkest, God's light is more brightly revealed. When night comes and the storm is raging, the Heavenly Captain is always the very closest to His crew. What a blessing to know that when we are the most downcast, we are the most sustained by the comfort of the Spirit of God!

One reason for this is that trials actually make more room for comfort. Thus, great hearts can only be made great through great troubles. The shovel of trouble digs the reservoir for comfort deeper, making even more room for it. When God comes into our heart, finding it full, He begins to break our comforts away, and as our heart empties, there is more room for grace. The more humble a person's life, the more comfort he will have because he will have a greater capacity to receive it.

Another reason why we are typically the happiest during times of trouble is because that is when we have our closest dealings with God. When our barns are full, we think we can live without God, and when our pockets are overflowing with gold, we tend to neglect our prayer life. But once our vine is taken away (see Jonah 4:6 – 11), we want God, and once the idols of our hearts are taken away, we are compelled to honor Jehovah.

"Out of the depths I cry to you, O LORD" (Ps. 130:1). There is no cry as good as one that comes from the very foot of the mountain, and no prayer as earnest as the one coming from the very depths of the soul through deep trials and suffering. Difficulties bring us closer to God and we are happier, for closeness to God *is* happiness.

Come, troubled believer, don't agonize over your heavy trials, for they are the messengers of God who announce and deliver His equally weighty blessings.

From the pen of Jim Reimann:

Corrie ten Boom, a Christian Holocaust survivor, shared a wonderful story of grace in her book *The Hiding Place.* As a small child she asked her father about sexual sin. Instead of answering, he asked Corrie to pick up his briefcase full of heavy watch parts from his repair shop. Tugging at it, she declared, "It's too heavy." Her father replied, "Yes, and some knowledge is too heavy for children. When you are older and stronger you can bear it. For now you must trust me to carry it for you."

When Corrie's family was caught protecting Jews, they were sent to a concentration camp where all the members of Corrie's family, except for her, died. We can only imagine the hard questions she asked the Lord, but she came to realize she had to entrust those answers to her heavenly Father's keeping. And she learned God's grace is always given in proportion to our need — never too little — never too much — and always on time!

FEBRUARY 13

How great is the love the Father has lavished on us,
that we should be called children of God! And that is what we are!
The reason the world does not know us is that it did not know him.
Dear friends, now we are children of God.

1 John 3:1 – 2

From the pen of Charles Spurgeon:

"How great is the love the Father has lavished on us!" Consider who we were — and how we feel about ourselves even now when sin is still so powerful in us — and you will be amazed we have been adopted. Yet we are called "children of God." What an exalted relationship, being a child, and what privileges it brings! Just think of the care and tenderness a child expects from his father and what love the father feels toward his child!

Yet all that — and more than that — we now have through Christ. Even the temporary drawback of this life — the suffering we share with our Older Brother — we accept as an honor. "The reason the world does not know us is that it did not know him." We are content to not be known as we share in His humiliation, for one day we will be exalted with Him.

"Dear friends, now we are children of God." Those words are easy to read but not quite as easy to feel. How do you feel deep within your heart this morning? Do you find yourself in the deepest depths of sorrow? Do past sins seem to be rising up within you, and does grace now seem like a mere spark long since trampled underfoot? Does your faith seem to be failing you? Don't be afraid. It is not by trusting in your gifts, talents, or feelings you are to live — you must live solely by faith in Christ. With all these things coming against us, whether we are in the very depths of sorrow or we find ourselves in the valley or even on the mountaintop, "Dear friends, now we are children of God."

Yet you say, "Just look at me! I'm a wreck! I'm not using my talents and my righteousness doesn't shine with God's glory at all." Then read on this morning, "What we will be has not yet been made known. But we know that when he appears, we shall be like him" (v. 2). The Holy Spirit will purify our minds and His divine power will perfect our bodies, and then: "We shall see him as he is" (v. 2).

From the pen of Jim Reimann:

Yes, when Jesus returns for us, "We shall see him as he is" — and — "We shall be like him"! Our loving Lord is in the process of perfecting or sanctifying us, but He desires we be actively involved, for Paul instructs us, "Continue to work out your salvation with fear and trembling"; but lest we begin to take credit for our ensuing holiness, he finishes his statement with: "for it is God who works in you to will and to act according to his good purpose" (Phil. 2:12 – 13).

The path to our complete sanctification is often difficult, but God finishes what He starts and tells us in His Word He has taken the burden of finishing the task upon Himself, for Paul said, "May God himself, the God of peace, sanctify you through and through. May your whole spirit, soul and body be kept blameless at the coming of our Lord Jesus Christ. The one who calls you is faithful and *he will do it*" (1 Thess. 5:23 – 24).

Father, "Open for me the gates of righteousness; I will enter and give thanks to the LORD" (Ps. 118:19).

FEBRUARY 14

Day by day the king gave Jehoiachin
a regular allowance as long as he lived.

2 Kings 25:30

From the pen of Charles Spurgeon:

Jehoiachin was not sent away from the king's palace with a supply of goods to last him for months, but was given his allotment "day by day." In this story he pictures for us the blessed position of all the Lord's people. A daily portion is really all we need. We do not need tomorrow's supply, for that day has not yet dawned and its needs are still unborn. The thirst we may experience in the month of June does not need to be quenched here in February, for we don't even feel it yet. As long as we have enough to meet our needs "day by day," as each day arrives, we will never be in need.

Each day's supply is all we can enjoy. We cannot eat or drink or wear more than each day's supply of food and clothing, not to mention the fact that having a surplus causes us the problem of finding a place to store it and having the anxiety of needing to protect it from a thief. One walking cane or stick helps a hiker, but trying to carry a bundle of them is a burden.

Having enough food is actually as good as a vast feast and in reality is all even the worst glutton can truly enjoy. This is all we should expect, and having a craving for more exposes our ungratefulness. When our Father does not give us more, we should be content with His daily allowance.

Jehoiachin's story is our story, for we too have a guaranteed supply given to us by our King. It is a perpetual and generous portion. Surely this is a great reason to be thankful.

Dear Christian reader, when it comes to the need for grace you simply need a daily supply.

Do you feel a lack of strength for this week? Then seek help "day by day" from above. What a sweet assurance it is to know you will be provided your daily portion! Through God's Word, ministry for Him, meditation, prayer, and waiting upon Him, your strength will be renewed. In Jesus everything you will ever need has been "stored up for you" (Col. 1:5).

So enjoy your "regular allowance." Never go hungry while the daily bread of grace is on God's table of mercy.

From the pen of Jim Reimann:

Due east of Jerusalem the landscape quickly and dramatically changes. Jerusalem is situated where it receives a good amount of moisture from the Mediterranean, but little makes it beyond the top of the Mount of Olives. Thus, desert conditions exist from its eastern slopes to the Dead Sea and beyond.

Bedouins there have learned to graze their sheep early in the morning. During the night enough moisture makes it over the mountains to generate little sprigs of grass, but only enough to feed them for one day. By afternoon "the grass withers" (Isa. 40:7) away.

David, the shepherd from Bethlehem, wrote, "He makes me lie down in green pastures" (Ps. 23:2), and since Bethlehem has much the same landscape, his "green pastures" were most likely these little daily sprigs of grass his Lord provided.

Heavenly Shepherd, thank You for Your faithfulness to "give us each day our daily bread" (Luke 11:3).

FEBRUARY 15

To him be glory both now and forever!
2 Peter 3:18

From the pen of Charles Spurgeon:

Heaven will be filled with the unceasing praise of Jesus. O eternity, your unending years will speed down their everlasting road — yet forever and forever "to him be glory!" Isn't Jesus "a priest forever, in the order of Melchizedek" (Ps. 110:4)? "To him be glory!" Isn't He "King for ever" (Ps. 10:16), "King of kings and Lord of lords" (1 Tim. 6:15), and the "Everlasting Father" (Isa. 9:6)? "To him be glory ... forever!"

His praise will never cease, for it arises from those bought by His blood, and thus — because of His shed blood — He is deserving of our praise throughout eternity. The glory of the cross must never be obscured and the radiance of His grave and resurrection never dimmed.

O Jesus, You will be forever praised! As long as immortal spirits live — as long as Your Father's throne endures — forever and forever unto You "be glory"!

Dear believer, you look forward with true anticipation to the time you will join the saints above in giving Jesus the glory due Him, but are you glorifying Him *now*? The apostle Peter's words are, "To him be glory both *now* and forever!"

Why not make this your prayer today:

"Lord, help me to glorify You. I am poor — help me to glorify You through contentment. I am sick — help me to honor You through patience. I have talents — help me to praise You by using them for You. I have time, Lord — help me to redeem it by using it to serve You. I have a heart to feel — let me feel no love but Yours, and let my heart glow with

no flame but my affection for You. I have a brain to think — help me to think of You.

"Lord, You have put me in this world for a reason — show me what that is and help me work out my life purpose. I can't do much, but as the widow put in her two mites — which was everything she had — I place my time and eternity into Your treasury. (See Luke 21:1 – 4.)

"Lord, I am Yours — take me and enable me to glorify You now in everything I say, in everything I do, and with all I have."

From the pen of Jim Reimann:

Even some Christians have said such things as, "If all we're going to do in heaven is stand around praising God, it will get boring." What a gross misunderstanding of heaven! Not only are they ignorant of the fact that we will have plenty to do there, but they fail to realize that praising the Lord is much, much more than singing and worship such as we do in church.

Praising the Lord will be a part of everything we do in heaven. If we have misunderstood that, then perhaps we need to be reminded as well that *whatever we do* in this life should bring praise and glory to Him. The following is a good reminder for each of us:

"Commit to the LORD *whatever you do*, and your plans will succeed" (Prov. 16:3). "So whether you eat or drink or *whatever you do*, do it all for the glory of God" (1 Cor. 10:31). "And *whatever you do*, whether in word or deed, do it all in the name of the Lord Jesus, giving thanks to God the Father through him. *Whatever you do*, work at it with all your heart, as working for the Lord, not for men" (Col. 3:17, 23).

FEBRUARY 16

I have learned to be content whatever the circumstances.
Philippians 4:11

From the pen of Charles Spurgeon:

This verse shows us that being content is not our natural propensity. Weeds naturally spring up in the same way covetousness, discontent, and complaining are as natural to us as thorns are to soil. We do not need to plant thistles and brambles — they come up naturally because they are native to earth — and we do not need to teach people to complain, for we complain quickly enough without ever being taught to do so.

In contrast, however, the most precious plants of earth must be cultivated. If we want wheat we must plow the earth and plant seeds, and if we want flowers we must dig a garden and give it continual care. Contentment is one of the precious flowers of heaven, and if we desire it, it must be cultivated. It will not grow in us naturally, for it is the new nature alone that can produce it. Yet even then we must be especially careful and vigilant to cultivate and maintain the grace God has sown in us.

Paul said, "I have *learned* to be content," indicating that at one time he did not know how to be content. There was a cost of great effort for him to attain the mystery of that wonderful lesson. No doubt there were times when he thought he had learned it but then he failed again. And when at last he had learned it and could finally say, "I have learned to be content whatever the circumstances," he was an old gray-haired man, living at the edge of his grave — a poor prisoner locked up in Nero's dungeon in Rome.

If we desire to attain this same degree of contentment, we must be willing to endure Paul's afflictions and to share the dark, cold dungeon with him. Never entertain the notion that you can learn contentment through knowledge alone — this lesson requires discipline. It is not a strength that comes naturally but a science to be acquired gradually over time — something we know from experience.

So, believer, hush your complaining, as natural as it may be, and continue to be a diligent student in the College of Contentment.

From the pen of Jim Reimann:

Paul is the ultimate example of suffering for followers of Christ. Consider what his school of contentment consisted of:

> I have ... been in prison ... frequently, been flogged ... severely, and been exposed to death again and again. Five times I received ... forty lashes minus one. Three times I was beaten with rods, once I was stoned, three times I was shipwrecked, I spent a night and a day in the open sea, I have been constantly on the move. I have been in danger from rivers, in danger from bandits, in danger from my own countrymen, in danger from Gentiles; in danger in the city, in danger in the country, in danger at sea; and in danger from false brothers. I have labored and toiled and have often gone without sleep; I have known hunger and thirst and have often gone without food; I have been cold and naked.
>
> 2 Corinthians 11:23 – 27

Take comfort in this: God gave Paul nothing that is not available to us! "I can do everything through him who gives me strength" (Phil. 4:13).

FEBRUARY 17

Isaac ... lived near Beer Lahai Roi.

Genesis 25:11

From the pen of Charles Spurgeon:

Hagar once found deliverance at this well and Ishmael drank from the water that God, who "looks down and sees all mankind" (Ps. 33:13), so graciously revealed. But Hagar and Ishmael's visit was merely a casual visit, the kind people extend to the Lord only during their times of need and only when it serves their purposes. They cry out to Him in times of trouble but forsake Him in times of prosperity.

Yet Isaac lived there and made this well of the living, all-seeing God his constant source of supply. The usual tone of a person's life, or the condition of his soul, is the evidence of his true nature. Perhaps it was the providential visit experienced by Hagar that led Isaac to revere this place, or perhaps it was its spiritual name — the well of the living One who sees me — that endeared it to him. His frequent times of evening meditation by its side made him familiar with the well, and the fact he met Rebecca there made his spirit feel at home by it. But best of all it was primarily that he enjoyed fellowship with the living God there that he selected this holy ground to be his home.

Let us learn to live in the presence of the living God and pray through the Holy Spirit that this and every day we may sense, "You are the God who sees me" (Gen. 16:13). May the Lord Jehovah be a well to us — delightful, comforting, unfailing — and "a spring of water welling up to eternal life" (John 4:14). As created beings our reservoir dries up and eventually cracks, but the well of the Creator never fails.

Happy is the person who lives by the well, having an abundant and constant supply close at hand. The Lord is a sure supply of help, for His name is El Shaddai — the all-sufficient, almighty God. Our hearts have often enjoyed the most delightful fellowship with Him and through Him our soul has found its glorious Husband, the Lord Jesus. "In him we live and move and have our being" (Acts 17:28). For this reason may we dwell in the closest fellowship with Him as possible.

Glorious Lord, may You cause us to never leave You, but to live by the well of the living God.

From the pen of Jim Reimann:

Beer Lahai Roi, or "the well of the living One who sees me," is deep in the Negev desert. Although it appears to be "godforsaken," it is the very place the Lord saw Hagar, pregnant and running away in fear. It was here He appeared to her, promising, "I will so increase your descendants that they will be too numerous to count" (Gen. 16:10).

The prophet Elijah also ran in fear "a day's journey into the desert ... and prayed that he might die. 'I have had enough, LORD,' he said. 'Take my life'" (1 Kings 19:4). Yet it was here in the desert he heard the Lord's "still small voice" (v. 12 KJV).

How often do we too run to the desert before hearing the Lord! Why is it that it often takes just that for our ears to be opened? Yet "we walk by faith, *not by sight*" (2 Cor. 5:7 KJV). "Whether you turn to the right or to the left, *your ears will hear* a voice behind you, saying, 'This is the way; walk in it'" (Isa. 30:21).

FEBRUARY 18

Tell me what charges you have against me.

Job 10:2

From the pen of Charles Spurgeon:

O tested soul, perhaps the Lord is dealing with you to develop your gifts. Some of your gifts would never be discovered, much less developed, if not for your trials. Don't you know your faith never looks as good in the warm weather of summer as it does during winter? Our love is all too often like that of a firefly whose light appears much stronger when surrounded by darkness. And hope itself is like a star whose light cannot be seen in the sunshine of prosperity but is only discovered during the dark night of adversity.

Afflictions are often the dark contrast in which God sets the jewels of His children's gifts in order to make them shine even brighter. Wasn't it just a little while ago you were on your knees praying, "Lord, I'm afraid I have no faith. Please let me know that I do"? Although perhaps not consciously done, wasn't this, in fact, a prayer for trials, for how will you ever know you have faith until your faith is exercised? You can depend upon the fact that God often sends trials in order for us to discover our gifts and to make us certain of their existence. Besides, the goal is not merely discovery of our gifts but is the real growth in God's grace that results from holy trials.

God often removes our comforts and our privileges in order to make us better Christians. He trains His soldiers, not in tents of ease and luxury, but by disciplining them through forced marches and difficult service. He makes them ford streams, swim across rivers, climb mountains, and walk many long miles with heavy knapsacks of sorrow on their backs.

Dear Christian, couldn't this account for the troubles you are now experiencing? Isn't the Lord revealing your gifts and causing them to grow? Isn't this His purpose in dealing with you?

Trials make the promise sweet,
Trials give new life to prayer,
Trials bring me to His feet,
Lay me low, and keep me there.
William Cowper, 1731 – 1800

From the pen of Jim Reimann:

Joseph is a great Old Testament example of suffering. Sold into slavery by his own brothers, he later experienced prison just as the apostle Paul did. Yet over time he saw God's hand at work and, when given the opportunity to take revenge on his brothers, he said, "You intended to harm me, but God intended it for good … the saving of many lives" (Gen. 50:20). He saw his leadership abilities and his position of power in Egypt as the result of being refined by affliction.

Paul learned the same lesson through suffering, for he wrote,

[The Lord] said to me, "My grace is sufficient for you, for my power is made perfect in weakness." Therefore I will boast all the more gladly about my weaknesses, so that Christ's power may rest on me. That is why, for Christ's sake, I delight in weaknesses, in insults, in hardships, in persecutions, in difficulties. For when I am weak, then I am strong.

2 Corinthians 12:9 – 10

"See, I have refined you.... I have tested you in the furnace of affliction" (Isa. 48:10).

FEBRUARY 19

This is what the Sovereign LORD says:
Once again I will yield to the plea of the house of Israel and do this for them.
Ezekiel 36:37

From the pen of Charles Spurgeon:

Prayer is the forerunner of mercy. If you look at biblical and church history, you will see that nearly every great blessing came from above only after times of supplication. I am sure you have found this true in your own life as well. God has favored you with blessings many times, yet fervent prayer has always been the prelude to any great blessing you have received.

When you first found peace with God through the blood of the cross, you had been earnestly praying, interceding with God that He would remove your doubts and deliver you from your troubles. Then came your assurance, which was the result of prayer. Every time you have been blessed with heavenly times of joy, you have felt compelled to look upon them as answers to your prayers. And when you have been delivered from severe trials and have experienced great help during times of great danger, you have been able to say, "I sought the LORD, and he answered me; he delivered me from all my fears" (Ps. 34:4).

Prayer is always the preface to blessings, going before them as their shadow. When the sunlight of God's mercy shines on our needs, it casts a shadow of prayer far across the landscape. Or, using another illustration, when God piles up His blessings, creating a large hill of them, He Himself shines across them. This casts a huge shadow of prayer across our spirit, so we may rest assured that if we are diligent in prayer, our pleadings are the shadows of His mercy. In this way prayer is connected with the blessing in order to show us the value of intercession.

If we received blessings without even asking, we would think of blessings as commonplace, but prayer makes those blessings more precious than diamonds. The things we ask for are precious, but we do not realize just how precious until we have sought them earnestly through prayer.

> Prayer makes the darkened cloud withdraw,
> Prayer climbs the ladder Jacob saw,
> Gives exercise to faith and love,
> Brings every blessing from above.
> William Cowper, 1731 – 1800

From the pen of Jim Reimann:

We often tend to forsake prayer until our circumstances turn tough. The psalmists were much the same, for they wrote: "In my anguish I cried to the LORD, and he answered" (Ps. 118:5). "The LORD has heard my weeping. The LORD has heard my cry for mercy; the LORD accepts my prayer" (Ps. 6:8 – 9).

Yet prayer is *moment-by-moment* access to God's throne of grace, whether in distress or not. "We have gained access by faith into this grace in which we now stand" (Rom. 5:2). Prayer is the very gateway to God, and our access to Him cost Him the death of His Son.

> *"Open for me the gates of righteousness; I will enter and give thanks to the LORD. This is the gate of the LORD through which the righteous may enter. I will give you thanks, for you answered me"* (Ps. 118:19 – 21).
> *"In the morning my prayer comes before you"* (Ps. 88:13).

FEBRUARY 20

God, who comforts the downcast, comforted us.

2 Corinthians 7:6

From the pen of Charles Spurgeon:

And who comforts like God? Just observe some poor, depressed, and troubled child of God who is told pleasant promises and who has had carefully chosen words of comfort whispered in his ear. His response is like that of a deaf cobra who ignores even the best tactics of the most talented snake charmers. After all, his life is full of bitterness right now and all the attempts of comfort in the world may only evoke a sigh or two of mournful resignation, not hallelujahs, joyful poems, or songs of praise.

Yet when God comes to His child, He lifts up his downcast countenance and the once tearful eyes suddenly glisten with hope. Can you hear his song?

> 'Tis paradise, if You are here;
> If You depart, 'tis hell.
>
> Author unknown

You could not have cheered him, but the Lord can do it, for He is "the God of all comfort" (2 Cor. 1:3). There is "no balm in Gilead" (Jer. 8:22), but there is healing in the Lord. There is no such physician among created beings, but the Creator is Jehovah-Rapha — the God who heals. Isn't it wonderful how one sweet word from God will translate into entire songs for Christians? One word from the Lord is like a piece of gold to a believer, who is like a jeweler, shaping and hammering out the promise for a number of weeks.

Consequently, poor troubled Christian, you do not have to give up in despair. Go to the Comforter and ask Him to grant consolation to you.

Perhaps you feel like a poor dry well, but surely you have heard that when a pump is dry, it must first be primed by pouring water through it. Only then will the water begin to flow. So, dear believer, when you are dry, go to God and ask Him to pour His joy into your heart that "your joy will be complete" (John 16:24, also see Rom. 5:5).

Do not go first to your earthly friends, for after all is said and done, you will find them to be like Job's "comforters." Instead, go first and foremost to your "God, who comforts the downcast." Then you will soon be prepared to say, "When anxiety was great within me, your consolation brought joy to my soul" (Ps. 94:19).

From the pen of Jim Reimann:

It seems the last thing we do when depressed is turn to God. But for believers, He should never be the place of "last resort." The psalmist understood the importance of turning to Him for consolation, for he wrote:

"Unless the LORD had given me help, I would soon have dwelt in the silence of death. When anxiety was great within me, *your consolation brought joy to my soul*" (Ps. 94:17, 19).

Jesus is the personification of that consolation. When He was dedicated as a baby at the temple, a man named Simeon was there. "He was waiting for the *consolation of Israel*," for "it had been revealed to him by the Holy Spirit that he would not die before he had seen the Lord's Christ" (Luke 2:25 – 26).

Take your depressed soul to Jesus today, for He *is* "the consolation of Israel."

FEBRUARY 21

God has said ...
Hebrews 13:5

From the pen of Charles Spurgeon:

If we would only grasp these words by faith, we would have an all-conquering weapon in our hands. What doubt could not be slain by this two-edged sword? What fear could there be that would not fall victim from a deadly wound inflicted by an arrow from the bow of God's promises?

Wouldn't the troubles of this life, the pain of death, our hidden secret sins, the traps of Satan, trials sent from above, and temptations sent from below all seem as "light and momentary troubles" (2 Cor. 4:17) when we hide ourselves beneath this fortress: "God has said"? Yes, whether for the purpose of joyful delight in times of quiet or for strength in conflict, we must find our daily refuge in the words: "God has said." May this teach us how important it is to "diligently study the Scriptures" (John 5:39).

In fact, there may be a promise in God's Word that exactly fits your situation, but if you do not know it, you will miss the comfort it could bring. At times you may be like a prisoner in a dungeon with a key chain full of keys, knowing one of the keys would unlock the door and bring you freedom. Yet you remain a prisoner because you refuse to look for the key, while all the time your liberty is so close at hand.

The perfect, powerful medicine for your cure may be in the vast pharmacy of Scripture, but you will remain sick unless you will examine and "diligently study the Scriptures" to discover what "God has said." Besides simply reading the Bible, shouldn't you be continually filling the memory banks of your mind with the promises of God? You can recall the sayings of great men and have committed to memory many verses of famous poets, but shouldn't you be proficient in your knowledge of the words of God? Shouldn't you be readily able to quote them when you have a difficulty to solve or when you need to overcome a doubt?

Since the phrase — "God has said" — is the source of all wisdom and the fountain of all comfort, determine to let it richly dwell in you as "a spring of water welling up to eternal life" (John 4:14). Then you will grow healthy, strong, and happy in your Christian life.

From the pen of Jim Reimann:

Many people do not realize the tremendous power there is in God's Word. "The Father ... does not change" (James 1:17), nor does His Word — but His Word changes lives! In fact, it is what gives us spiritual life, for "He chose to give us birth *through the word of truth*" (James 1:18).

"The word of God is living and active. Sharper than any double-edged sword, it penetrates even to dividing soul and spirit, joints and marrow; it judges the thoughts and attitudes of the heart" (Heb. 4:12). To access the power of the Word, however, we must know it. The Lord told Moses, "These commandments that I give you today are to be upon your hearts. Impress them on your children. Talk about them when you sit at home and when you walk along the road, when you lie down and when you get up. Tie them as symbols on your hands and bind them on your foreheads. Write them on the doorframes of your houses and on your gates" (Deut. 6:6 – 9). Yet the Lord promises His help as well:

"I will put my law in their minds and write it on their hearts" (Jer. 31:33).

FEBRUARY 22

His bow remained steady, his strong arms stayed limber,
because of the hand of the Mighty One of Jacob.

Genesis 49:24

From the pen of Charles Spurgeon:

The strength God gives His "Josephs" is real strength, not boastful fictional accounts of bravery that go up in smoke once the facts are known, but true divine strength. How was Joseph able to withstand such strong temptation? Because God helped him, for there is nothing we can do without the power of God. All true strength comes from "the Mighty One of Jacob."

Notice what a blessed and familiar way God gave His strength to Joseph: "His strong arms stayed limber, because of the hand of the Mighty One of Jacob." God placed His hands on the arms of Joseph. Just as a father teaches his children, the Lord teaches those who fear Him, laying His arms upon them.

What a wonderful act of humilation! God Almighty, the Eternal, and the Omnipotent stooped from His throne to lay His hand on His child's hand and stretched out His arm to place it upon Joseph's arm that He might be made strong! The strength He gave was also the strength of the covenant made with Jacob, for it was attributed to "the Mighty One of Jacob."

Thus, whenever you read of the God of Jacob in the Bible, remember God's covenant with him. Christians love to think of God's covenant, for all the power, grace, blessings, mercies, and comforts — in fact, everything we have — flow to us from "the Source of the Stream" through the covenant. If there were no covenant we would indeed fail, for all grace springs from it just as light and heat radiate from the sun. And no angels ascend or descend from heaven except on the ladder Jacob saw, which had a covenant God standing at its top.

Dear Christian, it may be the Enemy's ar-chers have painfully grieved you, wounding you with their arrows. Yet, like Joseph, your "bow remain[s] steady" and your arms strong. Be sure, therefore, to attribute all the glory for this strength to Jacob's God.

From the pen of Jim Reimann:

God also told Joshua to "be strong and courageous" (Josh. 1:6). But how do we obtain the strength we will need for battle in this life? "This is what the Sovereign Lord, the Holy One of Israel, says: 'In repentance and rest is your salvation, in quietness and trust is your strength'" (Isa. 30:15), and "The joy of the Lord is your strength" (Neh. 8:10). Also, "The Lord is my strength and my song; he has become my salvation" (Ex. 15:2); "The Lord is my strength and my shield; my heart trusts in him, and I am helped" (Ps. 28:7); "O my Strength, I sing praise to you; you, O God, are my fortress, my loving God" (Ps. 59:17); and "The Sovereign Lord is my strength; he makes my feet like the feet of a deer, he enables me to go on the heights" (Hab. 3:19).

Dear Lord, "In your unfailing love you will lead the people you have redeemed. In your strength you will guide them to your holy dwelling" (Ex. 15:13). "Summon your power, O God; show us your strength, O God, as you have done before" (Ps. 68:28). "Turn to me and have mercy on me; grant your strength to your servant" (Ps. 86:16).

"I love you, O Lord, my strength" (Ps. 18:1). "Be exalted, O Lord, in your strength; we will sing and praise your might" (Ps. 21:13).

FEBRUARY 23

Never will I leave you.

Hebrews 13:5

From the pen of Charles Spurgeon:

None of God's promises are private, as though they extend to only one person, for whatever God says to one of His saints, He says to all. When He opens up a well of water for one Christian, it is so all may drink. And when He opens the granary door to distribute food, one starving man may be the reason behind it, but nevertheless, all hungry saints may come and eat as well.

O believer, it makes no difference whether the promise originally came to Abraham or Moses, for He has given it to you as an heir of His covenant. There is no lofty blessing of God's too high for you, nor a vast mercy of His too wide for you. "Go up to the top of Pisgah and look west and north and south and east. Look at the land with your own eyes" (Deut. 3:27). View the full extent of God's divine promise, for all the land you see, you own — it is yours! There is not one brook of living water of which you may not drink. If it is "a land flowing with milk and honey" (Ex. 3:8), then eat the honey and drink the milk, for both are yours.

Be bold and believe "because God has said, 'Never will I leave you; never will I forsake you.'" Through this promise the Lord gives His people everything. "Never will I leave you." Due to this promise, no attribute of God can ever cease to be employed on our behalf. Is He mighty? He will "strengthen those whose hearts are fully committed to him" (2 Chron. 16:9). Is He love? Then He will crown "you with love and compassion" (Ps. 103:4). Whatever attributes comprise the character of God, each of them is employed to their fullest extent on our behalf.

To fully sum up this truth, there is nothing you could want, nothing you could ask for, nothing you could need in all of time or eternity, nothing living or dying, nothing in this world or the next, and nothing now, nothing on resurrection morning, or nothing in heaven that is not contained in this verse — "Never will I leave you; never will I forsake you."

From the pen of Jim Reimann:

The Lord said through Balaam, "God is not a man, that he should lie, nor a son of man, that he should change his mind. Does he speak and then not act? Does he promise and not fulfill?" (Num. 23:19). Later, Joshua's farewell to Israel's leaders answered Balaam's questions, "Now I am about to go the way of all the earth. You know with all your heart and soul that *not one of all the good promises the* LORD *your God gave you has failed.* Every promise has been fulfilled; not one has failed. But just as every good promise of the LORD your God has come true, so the LORD will bring on you all the evil he has threatened ... *if you violate the covenant* of the LORD your God" (Josh. 23:14 – 16).

Again, why did the children of Israel suffer so many difficulties? Because "they despised the pleasant land; *they did not believe his promise*" (Ps. 106:24). They should have been like David, who said, "I rejoice in your promise like one who finds great spoil" (Ps. 119:162).

"But the Scripture declares that the whole world is a prisoner of sin, *so that what was promised*, being given through faith in Jesus Christ, *might be given to those who believe*" (Gal. 3:22). "For no matter how many promises God has made, they are 'Yes' in Christ. And so through him the 'Amen' is spoken by us to the glory of God" (2 Cor. 1:20).

FEBRUARY 24

I will send down showers in season;
there will be showers of blessing.

Ezekiel 34:26

From the pen of Charles Spurgeon:

Here is a sure example of God's sovereign mercy: "I will send down showers in season." Isn't this a divine sovereign blessing, for who except God can say, "I will send down showers"? There is only one voice that can speak to the clouds and bring forth rain. Who "bestows rain on the earth; [who] sends water upon the countryside" (Job 5:10)? Isn't it only the Lord who can accomplish this?

"Grace ... is the gift of God" (Eph. 2:8) and although people need it, they are helpless to create it. In the same way, what would the ground do without showers? You could break up the hard clods of dirt, you may even sow your seeds, but what good would it do without the rain? Therefore the Lord's divine blessing becomes an absolute necessity. You would labor in vain unless God sent plenty of showers, sending salvation down. And He sends abundant grace. "I will send down showers." Notice He does not say, "I will send down a few drops," but He says "showers." So it is with grace as well.

When the Lord gives a blessing, He usually gives in such great measure "that you will not have room enough for it" (Mal. 3:10). Plentiful grace! Oh, how we need plenty of grace to keep us humble, prayerful, holy, and fervently devoted, to protect us through this life, and finally to take us to heaven! We cannot survive without the saturating showers of grace, but again, it is seasonal grace. "I will send down showers in season."

What season are you experiencing this morning? Is it a season of drought? Then it is also the season for showers. Is it a season of great difficulty with dark clouds? Then that too is the season for showers. God said, "Your strength will equal your days" (Deut. 33:25) and later offers another gracious benefit: "There will be showers of blessing." The word *showers* is in the plural, meaning the Lord will send all kinds of blessings. Also, all of His blessings go together like links in a golden chain. For example, if He gives grace for conversion He will also send grace for comfort. He will send "showers of blessing."

Thus, O parched plant, look up today, and then open your leaves and flowers to receive a heavenly watering.

From the pen of Jim Reimann:

Regarding seasons, God's Word says: "There is a time for everything, and a season for every activity under heaven: a time to be born and a time to die, a time to plant and a time to uproot, a time to kill and a time to heal, a time to tear down and a time to build, a time to weep and a time to laugh, a time to mourn and a time to dance, a time to scatter stones and a time to gather them, a time to embrace and a time to refrain, a time to search and a time to give up, a time to keep and a time to throw away, a time to tear and a time to mend, a time to be silent and a time to speak, a time to love and a time to hate, a time for war and a time for peace" (Eccl. 3:1 – 8).

And consider God's sovereignty in this: "He has made everything beautiful in its time. He has also set eternity in the hearts of men" (Eccl. 3:11).

FEBRUARY 25

... the coming wrath.

Matthew 3:7

From the pen of Charles Spurgeon:

It is quite pleasing to our senses to walk through the countryside shortly after a rainstorm to smell the freshness of the grass just after the rain has stopped and to observe the pure drops of rain glistening like clear diamonds in the sunlight. And that is the place of a Christian. He is traveling through a land where a storm has vented its fury upon the Savior's head, and if there are a few drops of sorrow still falling, they are distilling from clouds of mercy, while Jesus assures him the rain is not intended to bring about his destruction.

Yet how unnerving it is to witness a terrible storm approaching — to see the warning signs such as birds drooping their wings for protection, cattle keeping their heads low in fear, the sky growing black and blotting out the sun, and the heavens seemingly becoming sad and angry! How fearful it is to experience the approach of a tropical hurricane — to wait in terrible anticipation of the wind's full fury and force, powerful enough to rip trees up with their roots, force huge rocks from their foundations, and quickly destroy people's homes!

Sinners, that is your present position. No hot drops have yet fallen on you, but a shower of fire is coming. No fierce winds are yet howling around you, but God's tempest is gathering its fearful artillery. Thus far the floods of water have been dammed up by God's mercy, but soon the floodgates will be opened. God's thunderbolts are still in His storehouse, but beware! The fearful storm is coming and how awful will that first moment be once God, robed in vengeance, finally marches forth in fury!

Where — where — where, O sinner, will you hide yourself? Where will you flee? Oh, may the hand of God's mercy lead you even now to Christ! He has been freely set before you in the gospel — His pierced side is your rock of shelter. You know you need Him. So why not believe in Him and cast yourself upon Him?

Then the fury of the storm will be gone for eternity.

From the pen of Jim Reimann:

Nearly every unbeliever wants to focus on a God of love — not one of justice. "God *is* love" (1 John 4:8), but He is just as well and, therefore, sin must be judged. Thus, when Jesus returns, He will return as the Judge to make war. Here is how John described this future event:

> I saw heaven standing open and there before me was a white horse, whose rider is called Faithful and True. With justice he judges and makes war.... The armies of heaven were following him, riding on white horses and dressed in fine linen, white and clean. Out of his mouth comes a sharp sword with which to strike down the nations.
>
> Revelation 19:11, 14 – 15

And here is how Paul described it:

> God is just: He will pay back trouble to those who trouble you and give relief to you who are troubled, and to us as well. This will happen when the Lord Jesus is revealed from heaven in blazing fire with his powerful angels. He will punish those who do not know God and do not obey the gospel of our Lord Jesus. They will be punished with everlasting destruction and shut out from the presence of the Lord.
>
> 2 Thessalonians 1:6 – 9

FEBRUARY 26

Salvation comes from the LORD.

Jonah 2:9

From the pen of Charles Spurgeon:

Salvation is the work of God, for it is He alone who brings a soul to life, just as Paul said, "You were dead in your transgressions and sins. But because of his great love for us, God, who is rich in mercy, made us alive" (Eph. 2:1, 4 – 5). And it is also He alone who maintains a soul throughout its spiritual life, for He is "the Alpha and the Omega" (Rev. 1:8).

"Salvation comes from the LORD." So if I am prayerful, it is God who makes me prayerful. If I have been gifted, it is God who has granted those gifts to me. If I live a consistent life, it is because "the LORD upholds [me] with his hand" (Ps. 37:24). I do nothing whatsoever to accomplish my own preservation except what God Himself first does in and through me.

All the goodness I have within me is totally from the Lord alone. When I sin it is from me and is done on my own, but when I act righteously, it is wholly and completely of God. When I am victorious over a spiritual enemy, it is the Lord's strength that empowered my arms. If I live a life of devotion before others, it is not I for "I no longer live, but Christ lives in me" (Gal. 2:20). Have I been sanctified? If so I did not cleanse myself, for God's Holy Spirit sanctifies me. Have I been weaned from the things of the world? It is only accomplished through God's correction and discipline of me for my own good. Am I growing in knowledge? It is the great Instructor who teaches me.

Every jewel I have was fashioned by heaven's Hand. In God I find all I want and need, but in myself I find nothing but sin and misery. "He alone is my rock and my salvation" (Ps. 62:2). Do I get nourishment from God's Word? His Word would provide no nourishment at all unless the Lord made it food for my soul and enabled me to feed upon it. Do I live on the manna that comes down from heaven? What is that manna but the incarnate Jesus Christ Himself whose body and blood bring me nourishment. Is my strength continually being renewed? "Where does my help come from? My help comes from the LORD" (Ps. 121:1–2). I am helpless without Him. Jesus said, "No branch can bear fruit by itself; it must remain in the vine. Neither can you bear fruit unless you remain in me.…Apart from me you can do nothing" (John 15:4 – 5).

What Jonah learned in the depths of the sea may I learn this morning in my prayer closet: "Salvation comes from the LORD."

From the pen of Jim Reimann:

God is sovereign in everything, including salvation. Yet many people, even some Christians, believe they play a part in salvation, denying God's total sovereignty. Peter said this is shaky ground: "There will be false teachers among you. They will secretly introduce destructive heresies, *even denying the sovereign Lord*" (2 Peter 2:1).

David agrees with our text verse today by saying, "Our God is *a God who saves; from the Sovereign LORD comes escape from death*" (Ps. 68:20). Later Jude equates our Sovereign Lord with Jesus, when he calls Him "*our only Sovereign and Lord*" (Jude 4). Then John equates Him with God and eternal life itself by saying, "*Jesus Christ … is the true God and eternal life*" (1 John 5:20).

Sovereign Lord, thank You for giving me Jesus Christ, who is eternal life.

FEBRUARY 27

He who dwells in the shelter of the Most High will rest in the shadow of the Almighty.
If you make the Most High your dwelling — even the LORD, who is my refuge — then no harm
will befall you, no disaster will come near your tent.

Psalm 91:1, 9 – 10

From the pen of Charles Spurgeon:

The Israelites in the wilderness were continually exposed to change and were always moving from place to place. Whenever the "pillar of cloud" or the "pillar of fire" (Ex. 13:21) stopped moving, they pitched their tents. But the next day, once the sun had risen and the trumpet had sounded, "the ark of the covenant of the LORD went before them" (Num. 10:33), and the "pillar of fire" led them again through the mountains' narrow gorges, up hillsides or along the vast and arid wasteland of the wilderness. They barely had time to rest a little before they heard the call, "Get up …! For this is not your resting place" (Mic. 2:10). They never stayed long in one place and even wells of water or the shade of palm trees could not detain them.

Yet they had a constant and abiding home in their God. His "pillar of cloud" was their roof by day while His "pillar of fire" was their household light by night. They continued moving from place to place and, with the continual change, they never had time to settle in or to say, "Now we are secure. We will make our home in this place."

Just as Moses wrote, "Lord, you have been our dwelling place throughout all generations" (Ps. 90:1), Christians never experience change with regard to God. A believer may be rich today and poor tomorrow, he may be sick today and well tomorrow, he may be happy today and distressed tomorrow, but there is never a change in his relationship to God.

If God loved me yesterday He loves me today, for my unmoving mansion of rest is my blessed Lord. Even when my future prospects seem dim, my hopes are dashed, my joy has withered away, and all my possessions appear to be rusting and rotting away — even then I have lost nothing of what I have in God.

He is "my rock of refuge, to which I can always go" (Ps. 71:3). I am a pilgrim in this world but am always at home in my God. On this earth I may wander, but in Him I dwell in "a peaceful abode, a tent that will not be moved; its stakes will never be pulled up, nor any of its ropes broken" (Isa. 33:20).

From the pen of Jim Reimann:

So often we read familiar passages of Scripture too quickly, not taking time to allow the Lord to show us something new. Why not meditate on the following psalm this morning, asking God to speak to your heart? Then thank Him that you "will dwell" with Him forever!

The LORD is my shepherd, I shall not be in want. He makes me lie down in green pastures, he leads me beside quiet waters, he restores my soul. He guides me in paths of righteousness for his name's sake. Even though I walk through the valley of the shadow of death, I will fear no evil, for you are with me; your rod and your staff, they comfort me. You prepare a table before me in the presence of my enemies. You anoint my head with oil; my cup overflows. Surely goodness and love will follow me all the days of my life, and *I will dwell in the house of the LORD forever.*

Psalm 23:1 – 6

My hope comes from him.

Psalm 62:5

From the pen of Charles Spurgeon:

What a privilege for a believer to be able to say these words! If he is looking for something from this world, it is indeed a poor "hope." But if he looks to God to supply his needs, whether they are earthly or spiritual needs, his "hope" will not be in vain. He may continually make withdrawals from the bank of faith, getting his needs met from the riches of God's loving-kindness. This I know — I would rather have God as my banker than all the Rothschilds put together.

My Lord never fails to honor His promises, and when we take them to His throne He never sends them back unanswered. Therefore, I will wait only at His door, for He always opens it with His hands of generous grace. And I can try this afresh and anew at any hour.

Yet we also have "hopes" beyond this life. Soon we will die, but even then our "hope comes from him." Don't we hope and expect that when we are finally lying on our deathbed of sickness that He will send His angels to carry us to His side? (See Luke 16:22.) We hope through faith that when our pulse becomes faint and our heart struggles to beat that an angelic messenger will stand over us, looking with loving eyes upon us, and whisper, "Arise ... and come with me" (Song 2:10). Then as we approach the heavenly gate we hope to hear these words of welcome: "Come, you who are blessed by my Father; take your inheritance, the kingdom prepared for you since the creation of the world" (Matt. 25:34).

We hope for harps of gold and crowns of glory and soon to be among the multitude of shining souls before the throne of God. We look forward with longing for the time "we shall be like" our glorious Lord, "for we shall see him as he is" (1 John 3:2).

If these are your "hopes," "O my soul" (Ps. 103:1), then live for God. Live with the desire and determination to glorify Him who is your eternal supply and whose grace provided your election, redemption, and calling. And remember — it is only because of His grace you have any "hope" of the coming glory.

From the pen of Jim Reimann:

The Oxford dictionary defines *hope* as: "a desire [or wish] for a certain thing to happen." We say, "I *hope* you have a good day," meaning, "I *wish* you a good day," but hoping or wishing has no power to actually make it happen.

Yet biblical hope means much more. In fact, Paul equates *hope* with Jesus when he says, "God has chosen to make known among the Gentiles the glorious riches of this mystery, which is *Christ in you, the hope of glory*" (Col. 1:27).

Thus, *hope* should no longer be a wishy-washy term used so casually. Here is how Hebrews speaks of hope: "We who have fled to take hold of the hope offered to us may be greatly encouraged. *We have this hope as an anchor for the soul, firm and secure.* It enters the inner sanctuary behind the curtain, where Jesus, who went before us, has entered on our behalf" (Heb. 6:18 – 20).

This means a believer's hope is powerful and permanent — "an anchor ... firm and secure" — anchored "behind the curtain" to the very throne of God! Dear reader, in what — or whom — do you hope today?

February 29

I have drawn you with loving-kindness.

Jeremiah 31:3

From the pen of Charles Spurgeon:

The roaring thunder of the law and the fear of the terror of judgment are both used to bring us to Christ, but the final victory culminating in our salvation is won through God's loving-kindness. The prodigal son finally decided to return to his father's house out of his sense of need, "but while he was still a long way off, his father saw him and was filled with compassion for him; he ran to his son, threw his arms around him and kissed him" (Luke 15:20). Thus, his last few steps to his father's house were with that kiss still warm on his face and with his father's gracious welcome still resounding as music in his ears.

> Law and terror do but harden
> All the while they work alone,
> But a sense of blood-bought pardon
> Will dissolve a heart of stone.
>
> Joseph Hart, 1712 – 1768

The Master came one night and knocked on a man's door with the iron hand of the law. The door shook, trembling on its hinges, but the man piled every piece of furniture he had against the door and said to himself, "I will not let Him in." So the Master turned away, yet sometime later He returned, this time knocking with His own gentle hand. Using the very part of His hand the nail had pierced, He knocked again — oh, so very softly and tenderly.

This time the door did not shake, but strangely enough, it opened. And there on his knees was the once unwilling host now rejoicing to receive his guest. In humbleness he said, "Come in, come in, for Your knocking has turned my soul toward You. As You knocked I could not bear to think of Your pierced hand leaving the stain of Your precious blood on my door, and then of turning You away without a house in which to reside. I could not bear for You to have to say, 'Open to me.... My head is drenched with dew, my hair with the dampness of the night' (Song 5:2). I surrender! I surrender! Your love has won my heart."

Thus, in every case loving-kindness wins the day. What Moses' stone tablets of law could never do, Christ does with His pierced hands. This is what so aptly characterizes the doctrine of God's powerful and effectual calling. Can I say, however, that I understand this and have truly experienced it? Can I say:

> He drew me, and I followed on,
> Glad to confess the voice divine.
>
> Philip Doddridge, 1702 – 1751

If so, may He continue to draw me until at last I will sit down at "the wedding supper of the Lamb!" (Rev. 19:9).

From the pen of Jim Reimann:

How beautiful, and personal, is the call of God to His people! "This is what the Lord says — he who created you ...: 'Fear not, for I have redeemed you; I have summoned you by name; you are mine'" (Isa. 43:1). "You are precious and honored in my sight ... and ... I love you" (Isa. 43:4).

O Lord, how precious You are in my sight as well. Oh, how I love You!

March

MARCH 1

Awake, north wind, and come, south wind! Blow on my garden,
that its fragrance may spread abroad.

Song of Songs 4:16

From the pen of Charles Spurgeon:

Anything is better than the dead, quiet calm of indifference. Our souls may in fact wisely desire the cold "north wind" of trouble to blow, if that alone is what it will take to sanctify or to bring forth the "fragrance" of God's gracious gifts in our lives. As long as we don't have to say, "The LORD was not in the wind" (1 Kings 19:11), we should not run from even the most wintry "north wind" that ever blew on God's "garden" of grace.

In the above verse don't we see the bride humbly submitting herself to the rebuke of her beloved Husband, even encouraging Him to send forth His grace in some form, and placing no requirements on Him as to how to accomplish it? Didn't she, just as we do, become so utterly weary of the deathly unholy calm in her life that she longed for anything new that would stir her to action?

Yet she also desires the warm "south wind" of comfort as well — the smiles of divine love, and the joy of her Redeemer's presence, for these are often powerfully effective in arousing our stagnant and sluggish souls to life. Actually she desires either one or both so she somehow will be able to delight her beloved Husband with the "fragrance" of the spices in her "garden." The bride cannot tolerate being unproductive and neither can we.

And what an encouraging thought that Jesus — our beloved Husband — can find comfort in our lowly feeble gifts! Can this be, for it seems far too good to be true? May we then be willing to endure trials or even death itself if through these hardships we are assisted in bringing gladness to Immanuel's heart. Oh, that we would be willing for our hearts to be broken into tiny bits if only through that bruising our sweet Lord Jesus could be glorified!

Gifts unused are like fragrant perfume still sleeping deeply within our flowers' petals. But then the wisdom of the heavenly Gardener enters our lives to overrule any of our contrary desires only to produce His one desired result. Through both difficult trials and loving comfort He evokes from us, and from other fair flowers of His garden, grateful aromas of faith, love, patience, hope, obedience, and joy.

May each of us truly know through sweet experience what this means.

From the pen of Jim Reimann:

Many professing Christians run from troubles or try to "name and claim" them away. But what a beautiful thought that the Lord uses troubles in our lives, and even the comforts He sends us, to awaken our various unused gifts. May we never be satisfied with "the dead, quiet calm of indifference," as Spurgeon puts it today.

Another beautiful thought this morning is this: "Jesus — our beloved Husband — can find comfort in our lowly feeble gifts!" Thus, not only does Jesus receive glory from the use of our gifts but He also receives comfort from them. Have you ever considered serving the Lord, not just out of obedience, or even because it brings Him glory — but simply because it is comforting and refreshing to Him?

With Jesus all things are personal. He focuses His loving eyes on me, and asks, "Will *you* give me a drink?" (John 4:7).

March 2

So all Israel went down to the Philistines to have their plowshares,
mattocks, axes and sickles sharpened.

1 Samuel 13:20

From the pen of Charles Spurgeon:

We are engaged in an intense war with the "Philistines" of evil, and every weapon within our reach must be used. Preaching, teaching, praying, and giving must all be brought into the battle, and even our talents and gifts thought to be too meager to be of any use must now be employed. Every tool, including "plowshares, mattocks, axes and sickles," may all be useful in slaying "Philistines." Even rough dull tools can deliver hard blows, for the killing doesn't need to be fancy — just effective. Each moment of time, whether the optimum moment or not; each scrap of our ability, whether trained or not; each opportunity, whether favorable or not; must be used, for our foes are many and our forces are few.

Most of our tools need sharpening. We need ready discernment, tact, energy, promptness, and — in a word — complete *conformity* to the Lord's work. Practical common sense is actually very uncommon among people leading Christian endeavors. We should learn some lessons from our enemies and thereby make the "Philistines" sharpen our weapons.

This morning may we learn to sharpen our zeal for battle through the help of the Holy Spirit. We can even look at the energy of the Roman Catholics and how they will cross seas and continents to make one convert to their faith. Are they to be the only people to show great zeal? Then take note of the heathen and how their devotees endure horrific torture in the service of their idols! Are they to be the only ones who exhibit patience and self-sacrifice?

Finally, observe the Prince of Darkness. Note how he perseveres in his endeavors, how unfazed he is by failed attempts, how daring he is in his plans, how thoroughly he has thought through his plots, and how energetic he is in everything he does! His demons were united as one person in their infamous rebellion against God, while we believers in Jesus are often divided in our service for Him, rarely working with true unanimity.

Oh, that we may learn from Satan's hellish industriousness as he "prowls around like a roaring lion looking for someone to devour" (1 Peter 5:8). May we instead walk around like good Samaritans, looking for someone to bless!

From the pen of Jim Reimann:

The Lord gives every believer gifts to be used in His service — "gifts of the Holy Spirit distributed according to his will" (Heb. 2:4). We see from this that it is the Lord who determines which gift or gifts each of us will receive. And although "God's gifts and his call are irrevocable" (Rom. 11:29), they must, nevertheless, be sharpened or honed. Paul encourages us to *"try to excel* in gifts that build up the church" (1 Cor. 14:12).

Thus, we are to use our God-given gifts to serve our brothers and sisters in Christ, in fighting evil in the world, in sharing the gospel with the lost, and in helping anyone who needs a touch from the Lord through us. But we must be ready, and the only way to be ready is to use our gifts. It may seem awkward at first, but as we use them God will hone them — and we may even see our enemies being used as the sharpener!

MARCH 3

I have chosen thee in the furnace of affliction.

Isaiah 48:10 KJV

From the pen of Charles Spurgeon:

Dear tested and tried believer, comfort yourself with this thought: God said, "I have chosen thee in the furnace of affliction." Doesn't this verse fall on you like a soft rain shower, easing the intensity of the flames of the furnace? And doesn't it provide flameproof armor for us that fully protects us from the power of the heat? Then let afflictions come — God has chosen me. Poverty, you may walk through my door, but God is already in my house — He has chosen me. Sickness, you may intrude into my life, but I have a remedy close at hand — God has chosen me. Whatever may come my way as I walk through the valley of tears in this life, I know — He has chosen me.

Dear believer, if you still need greater comfort, remember you have the Son of God with you in the furnace. Even now in your quiet room Someone sits by your side — Someone you have not seen — Someone you love. And often, when you are unaware, He comes to your bed of affliction and smoothes your pillow for you. Perhaps you have a life of poverty, but within that life the Lord of life and glory is a frequent visitor. He loves to come to desolate places so He may visit you. He is "a friend who sticks closer than a brother" (Prov. 18:24).

You cannot see Him, but you can feel the gentle touch of His hand. And don't you hear His voice? "Even ... through the valley of the shadow of death" (Ps. 23:4) He says, "Do not fear, for I am with you; do not be dismayed, for I am your God" (Isa. 41:10). Remember the famous speech Caesar made to his army: "Fear not, for you carry Caesar and all his fortune with you." And, dear Christian, fear not, for Jesus is with you in an even greater way. In every fiery trial His presence is both your comfort and safety, and He will never leave someone He has chosen to be His own.

"Do not fear, for I am with you" is His secure word of promise to the ones He has chosen "in the furnace of affliction." Then won't you take a firm grasp on Christ and say:

> Through floods and flames,
> As Jesus leads,
> I'll follow where He goes.
>
> John Ryland, 1753 – 1825

From the pen of Jim Reimann:

May the faith and courage of Shadrach, Meshach, and Abednego be found in each of us when facing "the furnace of affliction." Consider their words as they refused to bow to King Nebuchadnezzar's golden idol: "If we are thrown into the blazing furnace, the God we serve is able to save us from it, and he will rescue us from your hand, O king" (Dan. 3:17). And consider their resolve in the following statement: "But *even if he does not [save us]*, we want you to know, O king, that *we will not serve your gods or worship the image of gold*" (Dan. 3:18).

God sent His preincarnate Son into the furnace to protect them and even the pagan king had to admit, "The fourth looks like a son of the gods," and then referred to the three men as "servants of the Most High God" (Dan. 3:25 – 26). The Lord will work miracles in our lives as well to reach the lost when we have faith!

MARCH 4

My grace is sufficient for you.
2 Corinthians 12:9

From the pen of Charles Spurgeon:

If we who are God's saints never experienced poverty or other trials, we would not have nearly the understanding of the comforts of His divine grace. When we come across a person who is homeless, who has nowhere to lay his head, yet who says, "I will still trust in the Lord"; when we see someone in abject poverty, who exists on nothing but bread and water but still glories in Jesus; when we see a bereaved widow overwhelmed with difficulties but whose faith in Christ remains strong; what great honor it reflects on the gospel!

God's grace is demonstrated and strengthened through poverty and other trials experienced by believers. True saints endure every burden of discouragement, believing "that in all things God works for the good of those who love him" (Rom. 8:28). They have faith that out of what may appear to be evil circumstances, a real blessing will ultimately arise. And they have the assurance their Lord will either deliver them quickly or He will sustain them through the trial for as long He desires to test them.

This kind of patience and perseverance proves the power of divine grace. It is like seeing a lighthouse that has been built far out in the sea. On a calm night I cannot tell if the lighthouse can withstand pounding waves, but once a storm begins to rage around it I will know if the structure will continue to stand. And so it is with the Spirit's work; if it were not for the many times of experiencing the storms of life I would never know for sure if His work was true and strong. If powerful winds never blew upon it, I would not know how firm and secure is the Spirit's work.

The most masterful works of God are those people who remain steadfast and unmovable even in the midst of severe difficulties.

> Calm amid bewildering cries,
> Confident of victory.
>
> Author unknown

A person who truly desires to glorify God must come to terms with the fact he will face many trials. No one can distinguish himself before the Lord unless he endures many conflicts. So if your journey through life follows a much-tested path, rejoice because your life will better exhibit the all-sufficient grace of God.

As to the idea the Lord may fail you — never even dream of it! Hate the thought. God who has been sufficient to this point should be trusted to the end.

From the pen of Jim Reimann:

Job is the greatest example of someone who severely suffered but who refused to "curse God and die," as his wife suggested (Job 2:9). He experienced great pain and loss, and although he expressed his desire "to argue [his] case with God" (Job 13:3), he maintained his trust, for he said, "Though he slay me, yet will I trust in him" (Job 13:15 KJV).

As Spurgeon says, suffering like this reflects great honor on the gospel. Yet it also performs a miracle in the person's life, for in the end Job said, "Surely I spoke of things I did not understand, things too wonderful for me to know.... My ears had heard of you but *now my eyes have seen you*" (Job 42:3, 5).

MARCH 5

Let us not be like others, who are asleep.

1 Thessalonians 5:6

From the pen of Charles Spurgeon:

There are many ways to encourage alertness among Christians. Allow me to strongly recommend one: believers should openly share with each other about the ways of the Lord. In *The Pilgrim's Progress* by John Bunyan (1628 – 1688) Christian and Hopeful say to each other as they travel toward the Celestial City, "To prevent drowsiness along the way, let's have a good conversation." Christian asks, "Brother, where should we begin?" And Hopeful answers, "Where God began with us." Then Christian sings this song:

> When saints do sleepy grow, let them come hither,
> And hear how these two pilgrims talk together;
> Yes, let them learn of them, in any wise,
> Thus to keep open their drowsy slumb'ring eyes.
> Saints' fellowship, if it be managed well,
> Keeps them awake, and that in spite of hell.

Christians who isolate themselves from others and walk through life alone are likely to be drowsy. But if you fellowship with other Christians you will stay wide-awake, will be refreshed and encouraged, and will make faster progress along the road to heaven. Yet as you meet with others to discuss the ways of God, take great care that the subject of your discussions remains the Lord Jesus. Let your eye of faith be continually focused upon Him, let your heart be full of Him, and let your lips always speak of His great worth.

Dear friend, if you live close to the cross, you will not sleep. Constantly strive to deepen your understanding of the true value of the place where you are going. If you remember your destination is heaven, you will not sleep along the road, and if you remind yourself that hell is behind you and that the Devil is pursuing you, you will not linger. Would a killer fall asleep, knowing his avenger is close behind him and that the city of refuge is just ahead?

Dear Christian, do you desire to sleep while the pearly gates of heaven are open before you, while the songs of angels await your voice, and while a crown of gold awaits your head? No! Instead, through saintly fellowship continue to "watch and pray so you will not fall into temptation" (Matt. 26:41).

From the pen of Jim Reimann:

Fellowship is the result of walking in the light and, conversely, isolation is the consequence of sinfulness, or walking in darkness. Here is how John stated this important truth: "If we walk in the light, as [God] is in the light, we have fellowship with one another" (1 John 1:7). The results of fellowship include encouragement, godliness, and spiritual growth. According to God's Word, fellowship is not optional.

When we fellowship with others, sharing how God is working in our life, we grow each other's faith. Thus, it becomes a means of encouragement, as we see from the following: "Let us consider how we may spur one another on toward love and good deeds. Let us not give up meeting together, as some are in the habit of doing, but let us encourage one another" (Heb. 10:24 – 25).

MARCH 6

You must be born again.

John 3:7

From the pen of Charles Spurgeon:

Regeneration is the subject forming the very foundation of salvation. Thus, we should be very diligent to know for sure we truly have been "born again," for there are many people who think they have been "born again" when they have not. Calling yourself a Christian doesn't give you the nature of a Christian, and being born in a so-called Christian country doesn't mean a thing. Even being recognized by others as professing the Christian faith is of no value whatsoever unless something is added to it — the experience of having been "born again." And this term — "born again" — is something so mysterious that human words cannot describe it.

"The wind blows wherever it pleases. You hear its sound, but you cannot tell where it comes from or where it is going. So it is with everyone born of the Spirit" (John 3:8). Nevertheless, it is a change that is known and felt; known by the works of holiness it produces, and felt through the awesome experience of grace. This great work of regeneration is supernatural, not something people can produce themselves. It is a new truth infused into a heart, which renews the soul and affects the entire person. It is not a name change, but a renewing of my nature so that I am not who I used to be, but instead have become a new person in Christ Jesus. To wash, embalm, and dress a corpse for burial is a far different thing than actually making it come alive. Man can do the former, but only God can do the latter.

Thus, if you have been "born again," your acknowledgment will be, "O Lord Jesus, the Everlasting Father, You are my spiritual Parent. Unless

Your Spirit had breathed the breath of a new, holy, and spiritual life into me, I would still be 'dead in [my] transgressions and sins' (Eph. 2:1) to this day. My heavenly life has been derived wholly from You, and to You only do I attribute it. My 'life is now hidden with Christ in God' (Col. 3:3), for 'I no longer live, but Christ lives in me'" (Gal. 2:20).

May the Lord enable us to have peaceful assurance on this vital subject of being "born again," for to be unregenerate is to be unsaved, unforgiven, "without hope and without God" (Eph. 2:12).

From the pen of Jim Reimann:

Some professing believers shy away from using the term "born-again Christian." But as we have seen today, Jesus said to Nicodemus, "You *must* be born again." Thus, it is impossible to be a Christian without being born again. Jesus, who is the incarnate Word of God, chose His words carefully, so it is no mistake He used this particular term.

One of the beautiful aspects of the term "born again" is that it not only relates to our salvation but that it also relates to the eternal nature of our salvation. Although a believer still sins and may backslide for some length of time, his salvation can never be taken away. In other words, he may appear to be lost at times, but since there is no such thing as reversing the birth process, he can never be "un-born." This truth, however, should never be used "to change the grace of our God into a license for immorality" (Jude 4), but should be an even greater motivation to walk in godliness and to serve the Lord faithfully.

MARCH 7

Have faith in God.

Mark 11:22

From the pen of Charles Spurgeon:

Faith is the foot of the soul that enables us to march along the road of the commandments. Love can make our feet move more quickly, but faith is what actually carries the soul. Faith is the oil that enables the wheels of holiness and devotion to roll freely, for without faith the wheels will ultimately come off our chariot and we will simply drag along the ground. With faith "I can do everything" (Phil. 4:13), but without it I will have neither the inclination nor the power to do anything in service to God.

If you are looking for people who will serve God the best, look for people with the most faith. Little faith can save a person, but little faith will never do great things for God. In *The Pilgrim's Progress* by John Bunyan (1628 – 1688) Little-faith could never have fought Apollyon — it took Christian to do that. Little-faith could never have slain Giant Despair — it required Great-heart's arm to knock down that monster. Little-faith most certainly will get to heaven, but often along the way will be forced to hide itself and thereby frequently loses all rewards except its crown of salvation.

Little-faith says, "This is a rough road, covered with the sharpest thorns and full of danger. I'm afraid to go." But Great-faith remembers the promise, "Thy shoes shall be iron and brass; and as thy days, so shall thy strength be" (Deut. 33:25 KJV), so Great-faith boldly ventures ahead. Little-faith waits in despondency, its tears mingling with the floodwaters it stands beside; but Great-faith sings, "When you pass through the waters, I will be with you; and when you pass through the rivers, they will not sweep over you" (Isa. 43:2); and then Great-faith fords the stream at once.

Do you desire to be comfortable and truly happy? Do you desire to enjoy your faith? Would you prefer a faith of cheerfulness as opposed to one of gloominess? Then "have faith in God" (Mark 11:22). But if you love darkness and are satisfied to live in misery and gloom, then convince yourself to be content with little faith.

If you love sunshine and would rather sing songs of rejoicing, then earnestly desire and seek the best gift: "great faith" (Matt 8:10).

From the pen of Jim Reimann:

Jesus used the words "great faith" only twice — neither in reference to the people of Israel. The first described a Roman centurion, someone hated by Israel, but a man with enough faith to ask Jesus to heal his servant. Upon this encounter Jesus said, "I have not found anyone in Israel with such great faith" (Matt. 8:10). The other reference was to a Canaanite woman who asked the Lord to deliver her daughter from demon possession. Jesus said to her, "Woman, you have great faith! Your request is granted" (Matt. 15:28).

What does this say about the exercise of faith of God's people today? As in days of old, we must be careful to follow the Lord in the inner heart of faith — not simply in our outward actions. In the Old Testament, God said of His people's unholy rituals, "They have become a burden to me; I am weary of bearing them" (Isa. 1:14). Thus, the church today as well must be careful not simply to have "a form of godliness [while] denying its power" (2 Tim. 3:5).

MARCH 8

We must go through many hardships to enter the kingdom of God.

Acts 14:22

From the pen of Charles Spurgeon:

Facing trials is a reality of God's sovereign design, for His people were "chosen ... in the furnace of affliction" (Isa. 48:10 KJV) — not chosen to worldly peace and earthly joy. Freedom from sickness and the pains accompanying mortality were never promised to them. In fact, when the Lord drew up His will, listing the privileges His people would inherit, He included chastisement, correction, and discipline.

Trials are part of our allotment in this life and they were predestined for us in Christ's inheritance. As surely as the stars were fashioned by His hands and the orbits of the planets were determined by Him, our trials are allotted to us. He has ordained their place, duration, intensity, and their effect on us.

Godly people must never expect to escape difficulties, for if they do they will be severely disappointed. Certainly none of their predecessors were able to avoid them. Look at "Job's perseverance" (James 5:11) through calamity, and remember Abraham and his trials and how through faith he endured them, ultimately becoming known as "the father of faith." If you fully consider the lives of all of the patriarchs of Israel as well as God's prophets, the apostles, and Christian martyrs, you will discover that all those whom God has chosen as His vessels of mercy were required to pass through "the furnace of affliction." Long ago God ordained that the cross of trials should be engraved on each and every vessel of His mercy as the royal mark denoting the King's vessels of honor.

Although tribulation is the path God's children must take, they can take comfort in knowing their Master has traveled that way before them. More than that, they have His presence with them, His sympathy to encourage them, His grace to support them, and His example to teach them how to endure. Then when they finally "enter the kingdom of God" it will more than make amends for the "many hardships" through which they have been required to pass to enter it.

From the pen of Jim Reimann:

Hebrews 11, often called "the roll call of faith," reiterates the necessity of suffering trials but also shows us their eternal value. After sharing various examples of the trials of many Old Testament saints, the writer continues:

> What more shall I say? I do not have time to tell about Gideon, Barak, Samson, Jephthah, David, Samuel and the prophets, who through faith conquered kingdoms, administered justice, and gained what was promised; who shut the mouths of lions, quenched the fury of the flames, and escaped the edge of the sword; whose weakness was turned to strength; and who became powerful in battle and routed foreign armies. Women received back their dead, raised to life again. Others were tortured and refused to be released, so that they might gain a better resurrection. Some faced jeers and flogging, while still others were chained and put in prison. They were stoned; they were sawed in two; they were put to death by the sword. They went about in sheepskins and goatskins, destitute, persecuted and mistreated — the world was not worthy of them.
>
> Hebrews 11:32 – 38

No, "the world was not worthy of them," but praise God — heaven is!

MARCH 9

He is altogether lovely.

Song of Songs 5:16

From the pen of Charles Spurgeon:

The unsurpassed beauty of Jesus is all-powerful in its attraction, yet it should not so much be admired as loved. He is more than superficially pleasing to look upon — He is truly lovely. Surely the lofty word *lovely* can be fully justified by the people of God, for He is the object of their warmest love, a love based upon the inherent excellence of who He is and the perfection of His nature.

O disciples of Jesus, look at your Master's lips. Can't you say, "His mouth is sweetness itself" (Song 5:16)? Don't His words cause you to say, "Were not our hearts burning within us while he talked with us on the road" (Luke 24:32)? You who worship Immanuel, look at His head of "much pure gold" (Ps. 19:10). Can't you say to Him, "How precious to me are your thoughts" (Ps. 139:17)? Isn't your adoration for Him sweetened as you humbly bow before Him whose "appearance is like Lebanon, choice as its cedars" (Song 5:15)? Isn't there an innate attraction to His every feature, and isn't His entire being fragrant "like perfume poured out" so that it's "no wonder the maidens love [Him]" (Song 1:3)!

Is there even one member of His glorious body that is not attractive, one part of His person that does not continually offer guidance for our souls, or one office He fills on our behalf that doesn't strongly bind Him to our hearts? Yet our love is not simply a seal binding us to His heart of love alone, but it also fastens us to His arm of power as well, for there is not a single part of Him that does not fasten itself to us. We anoint His entire being with the sweet perfume of our fervent love for Him.

We should imitate Him in the entirety of His life and His total character should be reflected by us. Every other person is lacking in some respect, but in Him we find complete perfection. Even the best of His chosen saints have stains on their garments and wrinkles upon their brows, yet He is nothing but loveliness. All earthly "suns" still have their sunspots, and even this world — as beautiful as it is — still has its wilderness. Thus, we find ourselves unable to love in its totality even the very loveliest of what this world has to offer.

Christ Jesus, however, is gold without impurities — light without darkness — glory without clouds. "He is altogether lovely"!

From the pen of Jim Reimann:

Although our Lord "is altogether lovely," Isaiah tells us: "He had no beauty or majesty to attract us to him, nothing in his appearance that we should desire him" (Isa. 53:2). What a glorious teaching that true beauty is inner beauty! Yet how many of us describe beauty only outwardly, and how many men today seek a spouse based primarily on outer appearance though God's Word says, "Beauty is fleeting; but a woman who fears the LORD is to be praised" (Prov. 31:30)?

Remember God's words to Samuel when he was sent to anoint Israel's next king and had one of David's brothers standing before him: "Do not consider his appearance or his height, for I have rejected him. The LORD does not look at the things man looks at. Man looks at the outward appearance, but the LORD looks at the heart" (1 Sam. 16:7).

"One thing I ask:... to gaze upon the beauty of the LORD" (Ps. 27:4). "Let the beauty of the LORD our God be upon us" (Ps. 90:17 KJV).

March 10

When I felt secure, I said, "I will never be shaken."
Psalm 30:6

From the pen of Charles Spurgeon:

"Moab has been at rest from youth, like wine left on its dregs, not poured from one jar to another — she has not gone into exile. So she tastes as she did, and her aroma is unchanged" (Jer. 48:11). In the same way, give a person wealth; let his ships come in, continually bringing him the richest freight from around the world; and even let the wind and waves appear to be his servants, safely carrying his ships across the mighty seas. Let his land always have an abundant yield and the weather always favor his crops, let uninterrupted success be his, and let him be unsurpassed as a successful merchant. Allow him constantly to enjoy good health and to march triumphantly through this world with nerves of steel and the sharpest eyes. Let him live in happiness, always with an energetic spirit and with a song on his lips, and let his eyes always sparkle with joy. Allow all of this — an incredibly easy life for anyone — and consider what the natural consequence will be. To think this person will be the best Christian who has ever breathed is sheer presumption!

Even David said, *"When I felt secure, I said, 'I will never be shaken.'"* And we are not better than David — not even half as good. Dear Christian, beware of the smooth places along the road of life, and when you encounter the rough places, thank God for them. If the Lord always rocked us in the cradle of prosperity, if we were constantly bounced on the knee of good fortune, if there were never any stain on the alabaster pillars of our life, if there were never a few clouds in our sky, and if there were not any bitter drops in the wine of this life, we would all become intoxicated with pleasure. And once intoxicated we might be-

lieve we are standing, and perhaps we would be. But it would be in a very dangerous place, like a man who has fallen asleep at the top of a ship's mast. He may be standing, but every second his life is in jeopardy.

Thus, we praise and thank God for afflictions and the changes in our lives. We glorify Him when we lose material possessions and other assets, for we know if He does not discipline us, we may become too secure. Remember this truth — constant worldly prosperity is actually a "painful trial" (1 Peter 4:12).

Afflictions, though they seem severe,
In mercy oft are sent.
John Newton, 1725 – 1807

From the pen of Jim Reimann:

As believers our attitude toward suffering and trials should be much different from that of the world. Spurgeon ends today's devotion with a brief two-word quote from Peter. As you read it in its context, notice his positive view:

Dear friends, do not be surprised at the *painful trial* you are suffering, as though something strange were happening to you. But rejoice that you participate in the sufferings of Christ, so that you may be overjoyed when his glory is revealed. If you are insulted because of the name of Christ, you are blessed, for the Spirit of glory and of God rests on you. If you suffer, it should not be as a murderer or thief or any other kind of criminal, or even as a meddler. However, if you suffer as a Christian, do not be ashamed, but praise God that you bear that name.
1 Peter 4:12 – 16

MARCH 11

Sin might become utterly sinful.

Romans 7:13

From the pen of Charles Spurgeon:

Beware of winking at sin or thinking too lightly of it. When we are first converted our conscience is so tender we are afraid of ignoring even the slightest sin. Young converts have a holy timidity or godly fear of offending the Lord. Unfortunately, the delicate blossom on this newly ripe fruit very soon falls off due to the rough handling of the surrounding world; the tender new plant of true devotion quickly turns into a willow that is too easily influenced.

Yes, sadly it is true that even a strong Christian may gradually become callous, where the sin that once alarmed him doesn't bother him in the least anymore. We become familiar with sin degree by degree until we come to the point of being like someone who has been exposed to the booming noise of a cannon so long he no longer even notices soft sounds. At first a little sin startles us, but soon we say, "Oh, it's just a little one." Then a larger sin comes along, followed by another, until by degrees we begin to think of them as only a minor problem. Soon our minds are filled with this unholy thinking: "True, we may have tripped a little and fallen into a little sin, but for the most part we've been righteous. We may have said one sinful word, but most of our conversation has been consistent with that of a Christian." Thus, we begin to gloss over our sin, throwing a coat over it to conceal it, and calling it cute and clever names.

Dear Christian, beware of taking sin too lightly. "Be careful that you don't fall" (1 Cor. 10:12) little by little. Sin? A little thing? Isn't it a poison? Who knows its deadliness? Sin? A little thing? Don't even "the *little* foxes … ruin the vineyards" (Song 2:15)? Doesn't the tiny coral ultimately build such a large rock it can shipwreck a navy? Don't small but steady strokes finally fell lofty oaks? Won't a slow but continual dripping of water ultimately erode huge rocks?

Sin? A little thing? It crowned the Redeemer's head with thorns and pierced His heart! It was the very reason He suffered anguish, heartbreak, and affliction. If you could measure even the least sin in the scales of eternity, you would flee from it as though it were a serpent and would abhor even the slightest appearance of evil.

Look at *each and every* sin as having crucified your Savior, and you will see sin as "utterly sinful."

From the pen of Jim Reimann:

No one likes to blush, but if nothing ever causes you to blush, you may have seared your conscience by thinking too lightly of your "little" sins. Jeremiah warned the people of his day, saying, "You have the brazen look of a prostitute; you refuse to blush with shame" (Jer. 3:3). Later he delivered this message of the Lord: "Are they ashamed of their loathsome conduct? No, they have no shame at all; they do not even know how to blush. So they will fall among the fallen; they will be brought down when I punish them" (Jer. 6:15).

Instead of becoming cold and hard, may we once again learn to blush. May our prayer today be in agreement with that of Ezra, who prayed:

"O my God, I am ashamed and blush to lift up my face to thee, my God: for our iniquities are increased over our head, and our trespass is grown up unto the heavens" (Ezra 9:6 KJV).

MARCH 12

Love your neighbor.

Matthew 5:43

From the pen of Charles Spurgeon:

"Love your neighbor." Perhaps he is rolling in money and you are poor, and you see yourself sleeping on your little cot right next to his elegant mansion where he holds the most elegant banquets using the finest linens. Do not forget, however, that God has given him these things. So do not covet his wealth or wish him ill will but be content with where God has placed you. And if you cannot better your position, do not look at your neighbor, wishing he would become like you. Instead, love him, for then you will not envy him.

On the other hand, perhaps you are rich and live next to the poor. Do not despise having to call them your neighbors but come to terms with the fact you are commanded to love them. The world thinks of them as their inferiors, but what makes them inferior? They are much more your equals than your inferiors, for "from one man [God] made every nation of men, that they should inhabit the whole earth" (Acts 17:26). Only your coat is better than theirs, but you are by no means better than they are. They are people — are you more than that? So be careful to "love your neighbor" even if he is dressed in rags and has fallen into the depths of poverty.

Yet perhaps you say, "I can't love my neighbors because even with all I do for them I only get ingratitude and contempt in return." That's all the more reason to exhibit the heroism of love! Do you want to be a "feather-bed-of-ease" warrior instead of warring the rough fight of love? He who risks the most will win the most, and if the path of love is rough, boldly march across it, still loving your neighbors through thick and thin.

"Heap burning coals on his head" (Prov. 25:22),

and if your neighbor is hard to please, don't seek to please him — seek to please your Master. And remember — if your neighbors spurn your love, your Master has not, for your kind deed is as acceptable to Him as though it had been acceptable to them.

"Love your neighbor," for in doing so you are following in the footsteps of Christ.

From the pen of Jim Reimann:

When Jesus was asked by "one of the teachers of the law": "Of all the commandments, which is the most important?" He replied, "The most important one is this: 'Hear, O Israel, the Lord our God, the Lord is one. Love the Lord your God with all your heart and with all your soul and with all your mind and with all your strength'" (Mark 12:28 – 30). This, of course, is a quote of Deuteronomy 6:4 – 5. Jesus then continued by quoting Leviticus 19:18, saying, "The second is this: 'Love your neighbor as yourself.' There is no commandment greater than these" (Mark 12:31).

What a beautiful teaching, for if we truly love the Lord we will not want to grieve Him by sinning. And if we love others, we will not desire to sin against them either. This is why Paul said,

Let no debt remain outstanding, except the continuing debt to love one another, for he who loves his fellowman has fulfilled the law. The commandments, "Do not commit adultery," "Do not murder," "Do not steal," "Do not covet," and whatever other commandment there may be, are summed up in this one rule: "Love your neighbor as yourself."

Romans 13:8 – 9

MARCH 13

Why stay here until we die?

2 Kings 7:3

From the pen of Charles Spurgeon:

Dear reader, this book was primarily intended for the edification of believers, but if you are still unsaved, my heart yearns for you to believe and I would like to share a few words I hope will be a blessing to you. Open your Bible and read the story of the lepers in 2 Kings 7 and consider that their position was much the same as yours today. If you stay where you are, you will perish for sure. If you go to Jesus, perhaps you will still die, but remember the old saying, "Nothing ventured — nothing gained." Isn't it true that in your case you have very little to risk? If you decide to remain in your place of hopeless despair, no one will pity you when you finally come to complete ruin. But if you were to die after truly seeking mercy — if that were actually possible — you would be the object of universal sympathy. No one who refuses to look to Jesus escapes destruction, and, in contrast, you probably have acquaintances who have believed in Him and are saved. So if some of your friends have received mercy, why not you?

The Ninevites said, "Who knows? God may yet relent and with compassion turn from his fierce anger so that we will not perish" (Jonah 3:9). Act upon that same hope and test the Lord's mercy. To perish is so horrific that even if there were only one last straw of an opportunity remaining, the instinct of self-preservation should cause you to stretch out your hand to grasp it.

To this point I have been sharing with you on the basis of your unbelief, but I now would like to assure you — as from the Lord — "if you seek him, he will be found by you" (1 Chron. 28:9). Jesus said, "Whoever comes to me I will never drive away" (John 6:37). If you would only trust him, you would never perish. On the contrary, you will find treasure far greater than the other poor lepers who remain huddled together in their deserted camp. May His Holy Spirit grant you the boldness to go at once to Him, knowing you will not believe in vain.

Then — once you are saved — spread the Good News. Like the lepers in 2 Kings 7 say, "This is a day of good news and we are keeping it to ourselves. If we wait until daylight, punishment will overtake us. Let's go at once and report this to the royal palace" (2 Kings 7:9). Share the news in order to unite yourself with the King's household. Inform your minister of your discovery as well and then proclaim the good news everywhere you go.

May the Lord save you before the sun sets today.

From the pen of Jim Reimann:

Some unbelievers laugh about going to hell, saying, "All my friends will be there, so we'll just have a big party!" But hell will be a horrific place. Have you ever burned a finger while cooking? If so, consider how much pain one little burn can cause. Yet it will be nothing compared to "those who suffer the punishment of eternal fire" (Jude 7). And though there will be fire, it also will be a place of "darkness, where there will be weeping and gnashing of teeth" (Matt. 8:12).

Isaiah, however, tells us of a God of grace who says to you: "In the time of my favor I will answer you, and in the day of salvation I will help you" (Isa. 49:8). Paul later, quoting the same passage, says that when it comes to salvation, time is of the essence: "I tell you, *now is the time of God's favor, now is the day of salvation*" (2 Cor. 6:2). Why not ask the Lord to save you today?

MARCH 14

If you think you are standing firm,
be careful that you don't fall!
1 Corinthians 10:12

From the pen of Charles Spurgeon:

It may sound strange to say, but it is true there is such a thing as being proud of the gifts God has provided to us by His grace. Consider the person who says, "I have great faith in God, so I won't fall. Those with small faith may fall, but I never will." Another person may say, "I have intense love for the Lord, so I will stand. There is no danger of my going astray."

Yet those who boast of the gifts of God's grace have little to boast about. People who boast like this believe the gifts they have received can keep them from sinning, not realizing the stream of God's gifts of grace must continually flow from the Source or else the brook will soon run dry. If an oil lamp does not have a constant flow of oil through its wick, it may burn brightly one day but will do nothing but smoke and put off noxious fumes the next.

Thus, beware to never glory in your gifts but always place your confidence in Christ and His strength, giving Him all the glory, for this is the only way to keep you from falling into sin. And remember to spend more time in prayer and worship and to be more earnest in reading the Scriptures, continually devoting time to them. Also watch your own life more carefully, being cautious to live more closely to God. Pattern your life after the most godly examples you know, and always let your conversation reflect that of heaven. And let your heart have the fragrance of true affection and love for the souls of others.

In other words, live in such a way others will "take note" you have "been with Jesus" (Acts 4:13) and have learned your ways from Him. Then when that glorious day arrives and He says

to you, "Friend, move up to a better place" (Luke 14:10), may you be joyously blessed to hear Him say, "[You] have fought the good fight, [you] have finished the race, [you] have kept the faith. Now there is in store for [you] the crown of righteousness" (2 Tim. 4:7 – 8) "that will never fade away" (1 Peter 5:4).

Onward, believer, but with carefulness and caution! Onward with holy "fear and trembling" (Phil. 2:12) and with faith and confidence in Jesus alone! May your constant prayer be: "Sustain me according to your promise" (Ps. 119:116). Remember — He alone "is able to keep you from falling and to present you before his glorious presence without fault and with great joy" (Jude 24).

From the pen of Jim Reimann:

Boasting, even over gifts of God, is nothing but pride, one of "seven [things] that are detestable to him" (Prov. 6:16). In fact, Solomon, who wrote Proverbs, lists "a proud look" as the first of the seven (v. 17 KJV) and then says, "Pride goes before destruction, a haughty spirit before a fall" (16:18).

Paul also had an interesting way of looking at boasting. He said, "If I must boast, I will boast of the things that show my weakness" (2 Cor. 11:30), and "I will not boast about myself, except about my weaknesses" (2 Cor. 12:5). After asking the Lord to take away his "thorn in [his] flesh" (v. 7), God said to him, "My grace is sufficient for you, for my power is made perfect in weakness," to which Paul beautifully responds, "Therefore I will boast all the more gladly about my weaknesses, so that Christ's power may rest on me" (v. 9).

MARCH 15

Be strong in the grace that is in Christ Jesus.

2 Timothy 2:1

From the pen of Charles Spurgeon:

In Christ is grace beyond measure, but He has not kept it to Himself. Just as a lake's reservoir is emptied through its pipes into the river, Christ has poured out His grace to His people. "From the fullness of his grace we have all received one blessing after another" (John 1:16). It's as though He has grace for only one purpose — to give it to us. He is like a continual fountain, always flowing, in order to supply His empty pitchers and to quench the thirsty lips that come to Him. He is like a tree that bears the sweetest fruit, not to hang beautifully on its limbs, but to be gathered and eaten by those who are in need.

His grace, whether used to pardon, to cleanse, to strengthen, to enlighten, to restore, or to make us alive in Him, is always freely available to us. Not only is there no cost to us for His grace, but there is not one work of His grace He has not bestowed on His people.

Just as the blood pumped by my heart belongs equally to every part of my body, the works of God's grace are the inheritance of every saint united with the Lamb. Because of this there is the closest and sweetest communion possible between Christ and His church, for they both receive and share the same grace. The oil of grace is first poured upon His head, but that same oil flows to the very hem of His robe. In this way even the very lowest saint has the same anointing power of that same costly oil that first poured onto His head.

True communion is experienced when the sap of grace flows from the stem to the branch, and when there is the recognition that the very nourishment that feeds the branch sustains even the stem itself. As we receive grace from Jesus day after day and begin to continually recognize it as coming from Him, we will truly discern the fact He is communing with us and will more fully enjoy that communion.

In light of this may we daily make full use of our riches in Him, always going to Him as our own covenant Lord. May we receive from Him who is our Source all we could ever need, but with the boldness and confidence people use to take money from their own pockets.

From the pen of Jim Reimann:

Our God gives liberally to His children, for we are heirs of Him who says, "Every animal of the forest is mine, and the cattle on a thousand hills.... The world is mine, and all that is in it" (Ps. 50:10, 12). May we meditate on the following verses this morning as we consider His greatness:

"You anoint my head with oil; my cup overflows" (Ps. 23:5). "I have come that they may have life, and have it to the full" (John 10:10). "How great is the love the Father has lavished on us, that we should be called children of God! And that is what we are!" (1 John 3:1). "I pray that out of his glorious riches he may strengthen you with power through his Spirit" (Eph. 3:16). "And my God will meet all your needs according to his glorious riches in Christ Jesus" (Phil. 4:19).

"Now to him who is able to do immeasurably more than all we ask or imagine, according to his power that is at work within us, to him be glory in the church and in Christ Jesus throughout all generations, for ever and ever! Amen" (Eph. 3:20 – 21).

MARCH 16

I dwell with you as an alien, a stranger.

Psalm 39:12

From the pen of Charles Spurgeon:

Yes, O Lord, I "dwell *with* you"—not "*near* You." All the alienation I had from You in my natural state has been removed by Your grace. And now, in true fellowship with You, I walk through this sinful world as a pilgrim in a foreign land. You as well are a stranger in Your own world, for people forget You, dishonor You, and enact new laws and practice customs without knowing or acknowledging You. When Your dear Son "came to that which was his own ... his own did not receive him" (John 1:11). "He was in the world, and though the world was made through him, the world did not recognize him" (John 1:10). There was never even a foreigner who was such "a fish out of water" among the citizens of any country as Your beloved Son was among His mother's own people.

Thus, it is no wonder that I who live the life of Jesus should be unknown and considered a stranger here on earth. In fact, Lord, I would never want to be a citizen in any land where Jesus is considered to be an alien. His pierced hands have loosened the ropes that once tied my soul to earth, and now I find that I myself am a stranger in this land.

My speech seems like a foreign language to "the Babylonians" among whom I live, and all my customs and ways seem strange to them as well. A crude Tartar would be far more at home in the slums of the city than I will ever be among the much-traveled paths of sinners.

Yet here is the sweetest part of my seeming predicament: I am a stranger "*with* you." You are my fellow-sufferer—my fellow-pilgrim. Oh, what a joy to wander this earth in such blessed company! My heart burns within me when He speaks with me along the road. (See Luke 24:32.) And though I am a wanderer, I am far more blessed than those who sit on thrones and far more at home than those who sit in their seemingly secure houses.

> To me remains no place, nor time,
> My country is in every clime:
> I can be calm and free from care
> On any shore, since God is there.
> While place we seek, or place we shun,
> The soul finds happiness in none:
> But with a God to guide our way,
> 'Tis equal joy to go or stay.
>
> William Cowper, 1731 – 1800

From the pen of Jim Reimann:

"'Tis equal joy to go or stay" or, as Paul said, "I am torn between the two" (Phil. 1:23). Believers have a God-given yearning for what lies ahead. "We ourselves ... groan inwardly as we wait eagerly for our adoption as sons, the redemption of our bodies" (Rom. 8:23). Yet Paul recognized he was being used to prepare others for glory—"I will continue with all of you for your progress and joy in the faith." Then he left the Philippians with this: "Whatever happens, conduct yourselves in a manner worthy of the gospel of Christ" (Phil. 1:25, 27).

What great advice! May we heed this advice today and always.

MARCH 17

Remember the poor.

Galatians 2:10

From the pen of Charles Spurgeon:

Why does God allow so many of His children to be poor? He could make all of them rich if He so desired by placing bags of gold at their doors or by simply providing them with a large annual income. He could continually spread abundant provisions around their houses just as He once provided for the Israelites and "brought them quail and satisfied them with the bread of heaven" (Ps. 105:40).

There is no reason for His children to be poor except that He sees it as best for them. "The cattle on a thousand hills" (Ps. 50:10) are His and He could provide for His children. He could even cause the richest and most powerful people on earth to give all their wealth and power to them, for the hearts of all people are in His control. However, He does not choose to do so but allows them to be in need, suffering poverty and obscurity.

Why is this? Actually there are many reasons, but the primary one is to give us who *have* been blessed with so many material blessings the opportunity of showing our love for Jesus by ministering to His poorer brothers and sisters. Yes, we show our love for Christ when we sing praises and pray to Him, but if none of His children were in need, we would lose one of our sweetest privileges and one of the best ways of publicly revealing our love for Him.

God has ordained we should prove our love for Him "not ... with words or tongue but with actions and in truth" (1 John 3:18). If we truly love Christ, we will care for those He loves and those who are precious to Him will be precious to us as well. May we then look upon it not as a duty but as a privilege to be used to ease the needs of the poor of the Lord's flock, remembering the words of the Lord Jesus, "Whatever you did for one of the least of these brothers of mine, you did for me" (Matt. 25:40).

Surely just knowing this sweet truth should be a strong enough motive to lead us to help our brothers and sisters in Christ with a willing hand and a loving heart — remembering that everything we do for His people is graciously accepted by Christ as having been done for Him.

From the pen of Jim Reimann:

The words of Jesus, "Whatever you did for one of the least of these brothers of mine, you did for me," is a reflection of this Old Testament truth: "He who is kind to the poor lends to the Lord, and he will reward him for what he has done" (Prov. 19:17). Throughout the Scriptures, especially in Proverbs, we are admonished to remember the poor. In fact, one of the character traits of the "Proverbs 31 Woman" is that "she opens her arms to the poor and extends her hands to the needy" (Prov. 31:20).

In the New Testament as well we see the early church involved in meeting the needs of the poor. As the church leaders made the decision of who would preach to the Gentiles and who would go to the Jews, Paul said, "All they asked was that we should continue to remember the poor, the very thing I was eager to do" (Gal. 2:10). Yet the spirit in which I "remember the poor" is critical, for as Paul also said, "If I give all I possess to the poor and surrender my body to the flames, but have not love, I gain nothing" (1 Cor. 13:3).

MARCH 18

You are all sons of God through faith in Christ Jesus.

Galatians 3:26

From the pen of Charles Spurgeon:

The fatherhood of God is a subject of common knowledge to all His children. Yet do you often find yourself saying, like Little-faith did in *The Pilgrim's Progress* by John Bunyan (1628 – 1688), "O if only I had the courage of Great-heart! I wish I could wield a sword as valiantly as he does. But, alas, I stumble at every turn and I'm even afraid of shadows."

Listen, Little-faith, Great-heart is God's child, but you are as well. And Great-heart is not one bit more His child than you are. Peter and Paul, apostles we think of as highly favored, were of the family of the Most High and so are you. In fact, a weak Christian is just as much a child of God as a strong one.

> This cov'nant stands secure,
> Though earth's old pillars bow;
> The strong, the feeble, and the weak,
> *Are one in Jesus now.*
>
> John Kent, 1766 – 1843

All our names are in the same family register. One of us may have been given more gifts of grace than another, but our heavenly Father has the same tender heart of love toward us all. One of us may do greater works for Him than another and, thus, may bring more glory to his Father, "yet he who is least in the kingdom of heaven" (Matt. 11:11) is just as much a child of His as one who stands amid the King's "mighty men" (2 Sam. 23:9). May this truth bring us joy and comfort when we "draw near to God" (Ps. 73:28 KJV) and say, "Our Father" (Matt. 6:9).

Yet while knowing this brings us comfort, may we never be content with weak faith, but may we ask as did the apostles, "Increase our faith!" (Luke 17:5). No matter how feeble our faith may be, if it is true faith in Christ, it will ultimately take us to heaven. But if it is weak, we will not bring much honor to our Master along the way and neither will we experience abundant joy and peace.

If you desire to live for Christ's glory and to be joyful in serving Him, then seek to be filled with "the Spirit of sonship" (Rom. 8:15) more and more completely until "perfect love drives out fear" (1 John 4:18).

From the pen of Jim Reimann:

Today Spurgeon reminds us of the blessing of being a member of the family of God but encourages us never to be content with weak faith. While considering our role in God's family, it would be wise to consider that it comes with certain responsibilities, accountability, and suffering. In fact, the following passage is the only use of the term "the family of God" in the entire Bible, and it is focused on the suffering, judgment, and godliness of believers:

> If you suffer as a Christian, do not be ashamed, but praise God that you bear that name. For it is time for judgment to begin with *the family of God.…* So then, those who suffer according to God's will should commit themselves to their faithful Creator and continue to do good.
>
> 1 Peter 4:16 – 17, 19

We praise You, Lord, that You have made us "heirs according to the promise" (Gal. 3:29) "that we might receive the full rights of sons" (Gal. 4:5).

MARCH 19

From the pen of Charles Spurgeon:

Dear Christian, take good care of your faith, always endeavoring to strengthen it. Remember — it is only through faith you can receive blessings, for if you desire the blessings of God, nothing can bring them down from heaven like faith. Prayer cannot obtain answers from God's throne unless it comes by way of earnest prayer from someone who believes. Faith is the angelic messenger between your soul and the Lord Jesus in glory, and if that "angel of faith" is not there, your prayer will not reach up to heaven, nor will the answer be sent down to earth.

Faith is the medium of communication that links heaven and earth. It is the link on which God's messages of love travel so fast that even "before [we] call [He] will answer; while [we] are still speaking [He] will hear" (Isa. 65:24).

But if that link is broken or disconnected, how can we receive His promise?

If I find myself in difficulty, I can secure help through faith. If the Enemy is attacking me, my soul can find refuge and rest in God through faith. But if faith is absent from my life, I will call out to Him in vain, for faith is the only road between my soul and heaven. Even in the dead of winter, faith is the road on which the vehicles of prayer may travel no matter how icy the road may be. Yet if that road is blocked by the absence of faith, how can I communicate with the Great King, for it is faith that links me with Him.

Faith clothes me with the power of God, engaging the omnipotence of Jehovah on my behalf, and it ensures every attribute of His is brought to my defense. It enters my fight to defy the hosts of hell and makes "my enemies turn their backs in flight" (Ps. 18:40).

Yet when I waver and have no faith, I am "like a wave of the sea" and "should not think [I] will receive anything from the Lord" (James 1:6 – 7)! Thus, dear Christian, pay close attention to your faith, for with it you can win all things no matter how materially poor you may be — but without it, you can obtain nothing.

"If you can [believe,] ... everything is possible for him who believes" (Mark 9:23).

From the pen of Jim Reimann:

James, the brother of our Lord and a leader in the early Jerusalem church, knew the prayer of faith was the only prayer that would be answered. Here is what he wrote regarding this vital practice of God's people:

> Is any one of you in trouble? He should pray. Is anyone happy? Let him sing songs of praise. Is any one of you sick? He should call the elders of the church to pray over him and anoint him with oil in the name of the Lord. And the prayer offered in faith will make the sick person well; the Lord will raise him up. If he has sinned, he will be forgiven. Therefore confess your sins to each other and pray for each other so that you may be healed. The prayer of a righteous man is powerful and effective.
>
> James 5:13 – 16

Lord, thank You for Your promise of answered prayer, for You have said, "They will call on my name and I will answer them; I will say, 'They are my people,' and they will say, 'The Lord is our God'" (Zech. 13:9).

MARCH 20

My beloved!
Song of Songs 2:8 ESV

From the pen of Charles Spurgeon:

"My beloved" was a precious name the early church often ascribed to the anointed of the Lord during its most joyful times. When it was the season for the singing of birds, the sweet voice of the turtledove could be heard in the land as she sang, "My beloved is mine, and I am his; he grazes among the lilies" (Song 2:16 ESV). Continually in her Song of Songs she calls Him by that wonderful name, "my beloved"! Even during Israel's long winter of sinfulness, when idolatry had withered the garden of the Lord, her prophets still found enough time to lay aside the burden of the Lord on occasion and to say, as Isaiah did, "Let me sing for my beloved my love song concerning his vineyard" (Isa. 5:1 ESV). And although the Old Testament saints had not seen His face, for He had not yet become "flesh and made his dwelling among us," nor had they "seen his glory" (John 1:14), He was nevertheless "the consolation of Israel" (Luke 2:25), the hope and joy of all God's chosen, and the "beloved" of all those who stand blameless before the Most High.

We who now live in the summer days of the church also love to speak of Christ as the most "beloved" of our souls, and He is very precious to us — the "outstanding among ten thousand" (Song 5:10) and "altogether lovely" (Song 5:16). It is so true the church loves Jesus and claims Him as her "beloved" that the apostle Paul defies the entire universe to "separate us from the love of Christ" and declares that neither "trouble or hardship or persecution or famine or nakedness or danger or sword" (Rom. 8:35) will be able to do so. In fact, he joyfully boasts, "In all these things we are more than conquerors through him who loved us" (Rom. 8:37).

O Lord, help us to know You better — You eternally precious One!

My sole possession is Your love;
In earth beneath, or heaven above,
I have no other store;
And though with fervent plea I pray,
And beseech You day after day,
I ask You nothing more.
Madame Jeanne-Marie Guyon, 1648 – 1717

Translated from French by William Cowper,
1731 – 1800

From the pen of Jim Reimann:

In the Old Testament, oil symbolizes the Holy Spirit. Thus, today believers speak of "the anointing of the Holy Spirit," just as David wrote: "You anoint my head with oil; my cup overflows" (Ps. 23:5). Paul in the following passage uses similar language to describe God's great love for us:

God has poured out his love into our hearts by the Holy Spirit, whom he has given us. You see, at just the right time, when we were still powerless, Christ died for the ungodly. Very rarely will anyone die for a righteous man, though for a good man someone might possibly dare to die. But God demonstrates his own love for us in this: While we were still sinners, Christ died for us.
Romans 5:5 – 8

"Greater love has no one than this" (John 15:13)!

MARCH 21

You will be scattered, each to his own home.
You will leave me all alone.

John 16:32

From the pen of Charles Spurgeon:

A select few were privy to Jesus' sorrows in Gethsemane, for the majority of His disciples were not sufficiently mature in grace to be allowed to behold the mysteries of His agony. With their minds still focused on the Passover feast, they represent the majority of people who live according to the letter of the law but who are mere babies when it comes to understanding the spirit of the gospel.

Only twelve — no, eleven — had the privilege of entering Gethsemane to see "this strange sight" (Ex. 3:3). And of the eleven, eight were left at a distance, having fellowship with the Master but not the intimate kind enjoyed by those who are greatly loved. Then only the three most highly favored disciples were allowed to approach the veil of our Lord's mysterious sorrow. Yet even they were kept at a distance, for Jesus "withdrew about a stone's throw beyond them" (Luke 22:41), not allowing them to intrude within the veil. Christ had to tread "the winepress alone" (Isa. 63:3), without anyone — disciple or not — with Him.

"Peter and the two sons of Zebedee" (Matt. 26:37), James and John, represent the few experienced and prominent saints. We think of them as fathers of our faith, for they transacted business on great and stormy seas. Thus, to some degree they understand the magnitude of the huge waves of the Redeemer's suffering. A select few souls are granted the opportunity, for the good of others and in order that they themselves will be strengthened for future service and tremendous conflict, to enter the inner circle and hear the pleading of the suffering High Priest. Through this they experience "the fellowship of sharing in his sufferings, becoming like him in his death" (Phil. 3:10).

Yet even these select few cannot penetrate the secret places of the Savior's suffering. A remarkable statement in Greek Orthodox liturgy refers to the Lord's agony as "Your unknown sufferings." Yes, there was an inner sanctum of our Master's grief totally closed to human knowledge and fellowship.

In that place Jesus was left "all alone." Yet it was there He was more than ever an "indescribable gift!" (2 Cor. 9:15). Wasn't the renowned hymnist Isaac Watts (1674 – 1748) correct when he wrote these words:

> And all the unknown joys he gives,
> Were bought with agonies unknown.

From the pen of Jim Reimann:

When Jesus taught "a hard teaching," "many of his disciples turned back and no longer followed him" (John 6:60, 66). Jesus then asked "the Twelve," "You do not want to leave too, do you?" (v. 67).

From this we learn Jesus had His "many," but within the many Jesus had His twelve, one of whom betrayed Him, leaving eleven. Of the eleven, only three were with Him on the Mount of Transfiguration and inside Gethsemane. Of the three, only one (John) referred to himself as "the disciple whom Jesus loved" (John 13:23). Hundreds to twelve to eleven to three to one!

Who of us desires to be "the one" if it requires suffering? May we have this view: "Rejoice that you participate in the sufferings of Christ" (1 Peter 4:13).

MARCH 22

Going a little farther,
he fell with his face to the ground and prayed.

Matthew 26:39

From the pen of Charles Spurgeon:

We can learn a great deal from the instructive characteristics of our Savior's prayer during this time of severe trial. The first thing to note is that it was "lonely prayer," for He withdrew from even His three most favored disciples. Dear believer, remember to practice solitary prayer quite often, especially during times of trial. Family prayer, public prayer, or prayer with other believers in the church will not suffice. All these are important, but the best beaten and broken incense will produce the most fragrant smoke in your censer in your private times of devotion where no ears will hear except God's.

Christ's prayer also was "humble prayer." Luke said, "He … knelt down" (Luke 22:41), but Matthew stated, "He fell with his face to the ground." If this is the Master's position, what should be yours as His humble servant? Shouldn't your head be covered with "dust and ashes" (Gen. 18:27)? Humility gives you a foothold in prayer, and there is no hope of prevailing with God in prayer unless you "Humble [yourself] … that he may lift you up in due time" (1 Peter 5:6).

His prayer also was "filial prayer," prayer befitting a son or a child of the Father. He prayed, "*Abba*, Father" (Mark 14:36). By pleading your adoption as His child, you will find a fortress of protection through your times of trial. If you were simply a subject of His, all your rights would long ago have been forfeited due to your treason, but nothing can forfeit a child's right to his father's protection. So do not be afraid to say, "My Father" (Matt. 26:39), "hear my cry … listen to my prayer" (Ps. 61:1).

Also notice Jesus' prayer was "persevering prayer." He prayed three times, so do not stop until you prevail. Be just as persistent as the widow in Jesus' parable, who because of "her continual coming" (Luke 18:5 ESV) gained what her first plea could not obtain. "Devote yourselves to prayer, being watchful and thankful" (Col. 4:2).

Lastly, it was "submissive prayer." He was resigned to do His Father's will, for He said, "Yet not as I will, but as you will" (Matt. 26:39). So yield to God's will, for He will determine what is best. Be content to leave your prayer in the hands of Him who knows when to give, how to give, what to give, and what to withhold.

Thus, those children of God who persevere in solitary prayer, yet with humility and submissiveness, will surely prevail.

From the pen of Jim Reimann:

What a wonderful example of prayer Jesus gave us in Gethsemane! It was there we see God the Son — He who had experienced nothing but unbroken perfect oneness and fellowship with His Father since eternity past — humbling Himself and beseeching God the Father. And if our Savior felt such a need for prayer, how much must we!

Because He was willing to drink the cup, about which He prayed in Gethsemane, we have access to the Father's throne through Him. If not for that prayer of His and its answer, our prayers would be meaningless!

O Lord, how blessed we are to know You and Your precious Son. Thank You for Him who suffered in Gethsemane and on the cross — for us!

MARCH 23

His sweat was like drops of blood falling to the ground.

Luke 22:44

From the pen of Charles Spurgeon:

The mental anguish resulting from our Lord's struggle with temptation in Gethsemane pushed Him to an untold emotional extreme, causing His pores to exude large "drops of blood falling to the ground." This proves the tremendously heavy weight of sin since it was able to crush the Savior to the point He sweated "drops of blood"!

It also demonstrates the mighty power of His love. Isaac Ambrose (Puritan author, 1602 – 1674) made the beautiful observation that sap exuding naturally from a camphor tree, without cutting it, is always the best. Jesus, the most precious "camphor tree" of all, yielded sweet spices from the wounds produced by the knotty whips and the piercing nails of the cross. But He gave forth the best spice in the garden without any whips, nails, or wounds.

This exhibits how voluntary His suffering was, for His blood freely flowed in Gethsemane without Him being pierced by a spear. There was no need for a physician to draw blood or cut Christ with a knife, for His blood flowed spontaneously in the garden. There was no need for the authorities to cry out, "Spring up, O well!" (Num. 21:17), for it flowed by itself in torrents of crimson.

When people suffer great mental pain and anguish, apparently their blood rushes to their hearts. Their faces become pale and, if the anguish is extreme enough, they will suffer a fainting spell, for their blood has gone inward as if to nourish the inner person during its severe trial.

Yet look at our Savior in His extreme agony — He was utterly oblivious to Himself. Instead of His blood being driven by His anguish to nourish His own heart, it rushed outward to the world to satisfy the earth's need for moisture. The agony of Christ that caused Him to be poured out upon the ground pictures perfectly for us the fullness of the offering He made for mankind.

Do we really perceive how intense His struggle in the garden must have been? Will we listen to His voice when He says to us, "In your struggle against sin, you have not yet resisted to the point of shedding your blood" (Heb. 12:4)?

Behold Jesus — the great Apostle and High Priest of our profession of faith! Then be willing to sweat blood rather than yield to the great Tempter of your soul.

From the pen of Jim Reimann:

Jesus suffered great agony in Gethsemane, praying, "My Father, if it is possible, may this cup be taken from me. Yet not as I will, but as you will" (Matt. 26:39). Our future as believers hung on the word *Yet,* or as the King James Version says, "*Nevertheless.*" Nevertheless — "as you will"! What a beautiful reflection and fulfillment of this prophecy:

> Yet it was the LORD's will to crush him and cause him to suffer, and though the LORD makes his life a guilt offering, he will see his offspring and prolong his days, and the will of the LORD will prosper in his hand. After the suffering of his soul, he will see the light of life and be satisfied; by his knowledge my righteous servant will justify many, and he will bear their iniquities. Therefore I will give him a portion among the great ... because he poured out his life unto death.
>
> Isaiah 53:10 – 12

MARCH 24

He ... was heard in that he feared.

Hebrews 5:7 KJV

From the pen of Charles Spurgeon:

Did this fear arise from the devilish suggestion that Jesus was utterly forsaken? There may be tougher trials in life, but being utterly forsaken is certainly one of the worst.

Satan says, "Look around — You don't have a friend anywhere! Your Father has closed His heart of compassion to You and not one angel in His courts will stretch out a hand to help You. All of heaven is alienated from You and you are completely alone. Just look at Your closest friends in whom You have confided the sweetest counsel. What good are they?

"Son of Mary, look over there at Your 'brother' James, Your 'beloved' disciple John, and Your 'bold' apostle Peter — see how the cowards sleep while You are experiencing such suffering! Look! You have no friends left in heaven or on earth and all of hell is against You. I have roused my demonic den from all regions, summoning every prince of darkness to come against You tonight. We will spare no weapons and will use all our devilish might to overwhelm You. What are You going to do? You are utterly alone!"

Perhaps this was Christ's trial. Apparently it was, for "an angel from heaven appeared to him and strengthened him" (Luke 22:43), removing the fear. "He was heard in that he feared." Thus, He was no longer alone, but heaven was with Him. Perhaps it is also the reason He went three times to His disciples.

> Backwards and forwards thrice He ran,
> As if He sought some help from man.
>
> Samuel Hart, 1845 – ?

By doing so, Jesus would see for Himself whether it was really true all had forsaken Him. Yes, He found His disciples asleep, but perhaps He gained some comfort from the fact that they were sleeping, not because of treason, but from sorrow. "The spirit is willing, but the body is weak" (Matt. 26:41).

In any case, "He was heard in that he feared." Jesus was heard during His deepest suffering. Dear soul, you will be heard as well!

From the pen of Jim Reimann:

Our verse today has a more accurate rendering in the NIV: "He was heard because of his reverent submission," as apposed to the KJV: "... in that he feared." Of course, Spurgeon had access to relatively few translations, or perhaps this particular devotion would be quite different. It should remind us of the importance of the underlying meaning of each and every word.

Jesus was fully God and fully man. As man He experienced the same temptations we do. But being afraid would indicate a lack of faith, and since "everything that does not come from faith is sin" (Rom. 14:23), as God, He could not have been afraid. He Himself said, "Don't be afraid; just believe" (Mark 5:36).

The word *fear* is used many times in God's Word to describe reverence and submission. For example: "Fear the Lord your God, serve him only ..." (Deut. 6:13). Jesus submitted to His Father's will, going to the cross on our behalf, and therefore, "He was heard because of his reverent submission." In the same way, the Lord hears our prayers when we reverently submit to Him.

MARCH 25

Are you betraying the Son of Man with a kiss?

Luke 22:48

From the pen of Charles Spurgeon:

My enemy's kisses are deceitful. Therefore I must be on guard when the world puts on its loving face, for whenever possible it will betray me just as it did my Master — with a kiss. Whenever someone is about to stab my faith in the back, he typically pretends to have great reverence for it. I must beware of the slick hypocrisy that is the armor-bearer of heresy and apostasy. Knowing how the ungodly love to deceive, I must be "as shrewd as snakes" (Matt. 10:16) in order to detect and thereby avoid the schemes of the Enemy.

May my soul graciously learn today from the "youth who lacked judgment" (Prov. 7:7) when tempted by the woman "with crafty intent" (v. 10). "She took hold of him and kissed him" (v. 13) and "with persuasive words ... led him astray; she seduced him with her smooth talk" (v. 21). May I never be seduced by the "smooth talk" of the world — may it have no effect on me whatsoever.

Holy Spirit, keep me — a poor frail son of man — from being betrayed "with a kiss"!

Yet what if I am guilty of the same cursed sin as Judas, "the one doomed to destruction" (John 17:12)? I have been "baptized into Christ Jesus" (Rom. 6:3), am a member of His visible church, and sit at His communion table, but are all these nothing but "kisses" on my lips? Am I truly sincere? If not, I am the lowest of traitors. Do I live as carelessly and worldly as unbelievers while professing to be a follower of Jesus? If so, I am exposing Christianity to ridicule and leading people to speak evil of the holy name by which I am called. If I live so inconsistently, surely I am a Judas and "it would be better for [me] if [I] had not been

born" (Mark 14:21). Do I hope to stay free and clear in this matter?

Then, dear Lord, keep me pure. Make me sincere and true and protect me from every false action. Never allow me to betray my Savior. Dear Jesus, I do love You, and although I often grieve You, my heart's desire is to be faithful "to the point of death" (Matt. 26:38). O God, may You keep me from being a smooth-talking hypocrite, simply professing Christ, but ultimately falling into "the fiery lake" (Rev. 19:20) because I betrayed my Master "with a kiss."

From the pen of Jim Reimann:

If we live the life of a hypocritical Christian, then in the world's eyes we are "crucifying the Son of God all over again and subjecting him to public disgrace" (Heb. 6:6). The things of the world should have no hold on us, for Paul said believers should "use the things of the world, as if not engrossed in them. For this world in its present form is passing away" (1 Cor. 7:31).

John contrasted Christians with the world by saying:

> The word of God lives in you, and you have overcome the evil one. Do not love the world or anything in the world. If anyone loves the world, the love of the Father is not in him.
>
> 1 John 2:14–15

"Anyone who chooses to be a friend of the world becomes an enemy of God" (James 4:4). But Jesus said, "I have called you friends, for everything that I learned from my Father I have made known to you" (John 15:15).

MARCH 26

"I told you that I am he," Jesus answered.
"If you are looking for me, then let these men go."

John 18:8

From the pen of Charles Spurgeon:

Dear soul, notice the care Jesus exhibited for His sheep even in the midst of His hour of trial! While submitting Himself to His enemies and facing death Himself, the controlling passion of His life remained constant and He graciously interceded on behalf of His disciples, speaking words of power to set them free. "As a sheep before her shearers is silent, so he did not open his mouth" (Isa. 53:7) for Himself, but He spoke with almighty power on behalf of His disciples.

"This is love" (1 John 4:10) — constant, selfless, faithful love. Yet isn't there far more here than meets the eye? Don't we hear the very soul and spirit of the atonement in His words? "The good shepherd lays down his life for the sheep" (John 10:11) and intercedes for their freedom. He became the security for their debt, and therefore justice demanded that those for whom He was a substitute should be set free.

In the midst of "Egypt's" grip of bondage, Jesus' voice rings out with mighty power, "Let these men go." It is from the slavery to sin and to Satan that the redeemed of God must emerge. In the dungeons of Despair, as in *The Pilgrim's Progress* by John Bunyan (1628 – 1688), these words echo through every cell: "Let these men go." Then Mr. Despondency and his daughter Much-afraid come forth. Satan hears the mighty voice of the Lord, which he knows well, and lifts his foot from the necks of the fallen. Death hears it as well and opens her graves, allowing the dead to rise.

The newly free now travel the path of progress, holiness, triumph, and glory, and no one will dare keep them from it. No ferocious lion or other ravenous animal will cross their way. "The morning buck" has drawn the aim of the cruel hunters upon Himself, and now even the most timid doe and fawn of the field may graze in perfect peace among the lilies with those they love. The thundercloud has burst over the cross of Calvary, and the pilgrims of Zion will never be struck by the lightning bolts of God's vengeance.

Come, dear heart, rejoice in the immunity your Redeemer has secured for you, and bless His name all day — every day.

From the pen of Jim Reimann:

An intercessor is someone who not only prays for you but is also someone willing to take your place. Thus, Jesus qualifies on both counts! He told Peter, "Satan has asked to sift you as wheat. But I have prayed for you" (Luke 22:31 – 32). Then He prayed for His disciples and for you by saying, "My prayer is not for them alone. I pray also for those who will believe in me through their message" (John 17:20). Of course, now He is seated "at the right hand of the throne of God" (Heb. 12:2) and "always lives to intercede for [you]" (Heb. 7:25).

He became the substitutionary sacrifice for you, as a believer, as well, taking your place on the cross.

> When you were dead in your sins … God made you alive with Christ. He forgave us all our sins, having canceled the written code;… he took it away, nailing it to the cross. And having disarmed the powers and authorities, he made a public spectacle of them, triumphing over them by the cross.
>
> Colossians 2:13 – 15

MARCH 27

Then all the disciples deserted him and fled.

Matthew 26:56

From the pen of Charles Spurgeon:

Jesus never deserted His disciples, but in their cowardly fear for their own lives they deserted Him at the very beginning of His sufferings. This is a great example of the frailty of us as believers if left to fend for ourselves, for at best we are sheep, and sheep flee when a wolf attacks. All the disciples had been warned of the coming danger, and yet each had promised to die rather than leave their Master. Still, when danger arrived, they were seized with sudden panic and took to their heels and ran.

Perhaps at the beginning of this day I have purposed in my mind to bear a trial for the sake of the Lord, and I feel certain I will exhibit perfect loyalty and faithfulness. Yet may I be careful to boast lest I have the same evil heart of unbelief and then depart from my Lord just as the apostles did. It is one thing to promise but quite another to actually perform. What an eternal honor it would have been for them to have stood by Jesus' side as men! Yet they fled the honor. *Lord, may I be kept from imitating them!*

Where else would they have been as safe as by their Master's side? At any moment He could have called down "more than twelve legions of angels" (Matt. 26:53). They fled from their only true safety. *O God, don't let me be such a fool as that, for Your divine grace can make even a coward brave.* "A smoldering wick he will not snuff out" (Isa. 42:3), for He can cause it to burst forth in flames on the altar whenever He wills. In fact, these very apostles who were as afraid and timid as a hare later grew to be as bold as a lion after the Holy Spirit descended upon them. In the same way, the Spirit can make my cowardly and unfaithful spirit brave so that I boldly confess my Lord and bear witness to His truth.

What anguish must have filled the Savior's soul as He watched the unfaithfulness of His friends! And this was but one bitter ingredient He saw when He looked in the cup (see Matt. 26:39), yet He drank it all. May I not put another drop in His cup. If I forsake my Lord, I crucify "the Son of God all over again and [subject] him to public disgrace" (Heb. 6:6).

Keep me, O blessed Spirit, from an end so shameful.

From the pen of Jim Reimann:

Sometimes we are tempted to be critical of certain Bible characters. We wonder how the disciples could be so shocked to learn one of them would betray Christ one minute, only to flee from and deny Him a few hours later. We see the children of Israel delivered from Egypt after witnessing miracle after miracle, such as the plagues and the parting of the Red Sea, simply to say so quickly, "If only we had died by the LORD's hand in Egypt!" (Ex. 16:3).

Rather than being so quick myself to condemn them, perhaps I should consider how many miracles the Lord has performed in my life and how often I have denied Him either in my words or my actions. Remember, as Spurgeon alludes to today, the disciples did not yet have the benefit of the Holy Spirit, and after He was sent in Acts 2, they were amazingly bold and fearless.

Father, thank You for the filling of Your Holy Spirit. May I keep on being filled, walking boldly and faithfully in Your truth, never denying You again.

MARCH 28

The love of Christ ... surpasses knowledge.

Ephesians 3:18 – 19

From the pen of Charles Spurgeon:

"The love of Christ" — in its sweetness, fullness, greatness, and faithfulness — "surpasses" all human comprehension. Where could language ever be found to describe His matchless and unparalleled love for the children of mankind? It is so vast and limitless that, just as a swallow swoops down to skim the surface without diving into the depths of the sea, all descriptive words for Christ's love barely touch the surface, leaving immeasurable depths untouched below. The poet may truly say:

O love, you fathomless abyss!

Johann Andreas Rothe, 1688 – 1758

for the love of Christ is indeed measureless and fathomless and fully beyond all human comprehension.

Yet to begin to understand His love, we must first understand His previous glory in its height of majesty relative to His incarnation on earth in all its depths of shame. But who can tell us the majesty of Christ? When He was enthroned in the highest heavens, He was "very God of very God" (The Nicene Creed) — God Himself — "for by him all things were created: things in heaven and on earth" (Col. 1:16). His almighty arm held the many spheres of the universe in their orbits, the praises of cherubim and seraphim perpetually surrounded Him, and a vast chorus of hallelujahs across the universe unceasingly flowed to the foot of His throne. He reigned supreme above all His creatures as God over all and blessed forever. Who then can fully explain the height of His glory? On the other hand, however, who can fully explain how low He descended?

To become a man was certainly humbling, but to become "a man of sorrows" (Isa. 53:3) was something far more. To bleed, to suffer, and to die were a lot to expect from the Son of God, but He suffered even more than that. He suffered the unparalleled agony of not only enduring a death of shame but also suffered desertion by His Father. This shows such a depth of Christ's humble love that even the most spiritual of minds miserably fails in attempting to fathom it.

"This is love" (1 John 4:10)! And it is truly a love that "surpasses knowledge." Oh, may this love — His love — fill our hearts with adoration and gratitude and lead us to practical demonstrations of its power in our lives.

From the pen of Jim Reimann:

In the first three chapters of Ephesians, Paul teaches the doctrine the Lord has given him and then follows those with three chapters of practical application of that doctrine. Our text today comes from the prayer toward the end of chapter three that is the interlude between these two sections.

That prayer reveals how overwhelmed Paul has become while considering that awe-inspiring theology, or the knowledge of God. He encourages us "to grasp how wide and long and high and deep is the love of Christ" (Eph. 3:18). Then in verse 19 he says something quite strange, encouraging us "to know *this love that surpasses knowledge.*" He is telling us to know something unknowable! Perhaps the infinite love of Christ is something finite mankind will spend eternity attempting "to grasp how wide and long and high and deep" it really is!

MARCH 29

Although he was a son, he learned obedience from what he suffered.

Hebrews 5:8

From the pen of Charles Spurgeon:

Is it any wonder that if the Captain of our salvation was "made perfect" (Heb. 5:9) through suffering that we who are sinful and far from perfect should be called to suffer as well? If the Head was crowned with thorns, should the other parts of the body continually be bounced on the lap of luxury and ease? If Christ had to walk through seas of His own blood to win the crown, should we easily walk to heaven with totally dry feet in soft silver slippers?

Certainly not! Our Master's experience teaches us suffering is necessary, and a truly born-again child of God must not escape it — and would not escape it, even if he could. But one very comforting thought in the fact that Christ was "made perfect" through suffering is that He now has complete sympathy with us. "For we do not have a high priest who is unable to sympathize with our weaknesses" (Heb. 4:15), and it is through His sympathy we find the power to sustain us when we suffer. In fact, one of the early Christian martyrs said, "I can bear it all, because Jesus suffered, and He suffers in me now. He sympathizes with me and this makes me strong."

Dear believer, take hold of that thought in your times of agony. Allow the thought of Jesus' sympathy to strengthen you as you follow in His steps. Find loving support in His sympathy, and remember: to suffer is an honorable thing, but to suffer for Christ is glory!

"The apostles left ... rejoicing because they had been counted worthy of suffering" (Acts 5:41). And as much as God gives us His grace to suffer *for* Christ, and *with* Christ, He equally graces us with honor. The jewels of a Christian are his afflictions, and the royal finery of the kings whom God has anointed is their troubles, sorrows, and heartbreaks.

Therefore, may we not shun being honored, nor turn away from being exalted, for troubles lift us up and sorrows exalt us. Remember — "If we suffer, we shall also reign with him" (2 Tim. 2:12 KJV).

From the pen of Jim Reimann:

Many in Christ's church today have an unbiblical view of suffering. One can only wonder how first-century Christians would react to our lives of relative ease and comfort. Perhaps *our* view needs to change. Rather than hopelessly attempting to "name and claim" our suffering away, we should adopt the apostles' view. They rejoiced "because they had been counted worthy of suffering"!

Suffering is a gift, a calling, and a blessing. And if, like Paul, we desire to know Christ, we will soon learn it will require the path of suffering. May the following truly become the prayer of our heart this morning:

I want to know Christ and the power of his resurrection and the fellowship of sharing in his sufferings, becoming like him in his death.... All of us who are mature should take such a view of things. And if on some point you think differently, that too God will make clear to you. Only let us live up to what we have already attained. Join with others in following my example, brothers, and take note of those who live according to the pattern we gave you.

Philippians 3:10, 15 – 17

MARCH 30

He ... was numbered with the transgressors.

Isaiah 53:12

From the pen of Charles Spurgeon:

Why do you think Jesus allowed Himself to be listed or "numbered" with sinners? This wonderful act of humbling Himself was justified for many powerful reasons. By humbling Himself, He could be a better advocate for sinners, "one who speaks to the Father in our defense" (1 John 2:1). Often an attorney identifies very strongly with his client and, in fact, the eye of the law views the two as one in a legal sense. So when a sinner is summoned to court, Jesus appears there in his stead and takes the stand Himself to answer the accusation. He points to His side, His hands, and His feet, and then challenges Justice to bring any charge against the sinner He represents. He pleads His own blood and does it so triumphantly — being "numbered with the transgressors" — that the Judge proclaims, "Let the defendant go. 'Spare him from going down to the pit; I have found a ransom for him'" (Job 33:24).

Also, Jesus "was numbered with the transgressors" in order that sinners may feel their hearts being drawn toward Him. Who could ever be afraid of someone whose name has been written on the same list with us? Surely we may come boldly to Him and confess our guilt, for He who is numbered with us cannot condemn us. Wasn't He listed with us sinners that we might be listed with the saints whose names have been written in His blood? Remember — He was holy and listed among the holy, while we were guilty and numbered with the guilty. But He transferred His name from the holy list to the dark list of indictment, and removed our names from the indictment and wrote them on the list of acceptance. In this way there was a complete transfer made between Jesus and His people.

Thus, Jesus has taken upon Himself our total state of misery and sin, and all He has comes to us. His righteousness, His blood, and everything He inherited from the Father He gives as the dowry to us who are known as His bride. So rejoice, dear believer, in your union with Him who "was numbered with the transgressors," and prove you are truly saved by living a life that makes it abundantly clear you are "numbered with" those who are "a new creation" (2 Cor. 5:17) in Him.

From the pen of Jim Reimann:

Jesus came to earth to identify with us that we may identify with Him in glory. God the Son humbled Himself to become man or, as John said, "The Word became flesh and made his dwelling among us" (John 1:14). Here is how the writer of Hebrews expressed this profound truth:

> Since the children have flesh and blood, he too shared in their humanity so that by his death he might destroy him who holds the power of death — that is, the devil — and free those who all their lives were held in slavery by their fear of death. For surely it is not angels he helps, but Abraham's descendants. For this reason he had to be made like his brothers in every way, in order that he might become a merciful and faithful high priest in service to God, and that he might make atonement for the sins of the people.

Hebrews 2:14 – 17

Lord, how grateful I am Jesus was willing to be "numbered with the transgressors" — even me! May my walk continually express my gratitude.

MARCH 31

By his wounds we are healed.

Isaiah 53:5

From the pen of Charles Spurgeon:

Pilate delivered our Lord over to his executioners to be scourged, and a Roman scourging whip was an incredibly dreadful instrument of torture. It was made of the tendons of oxen cut into straps, with sharp pieces of bone interspersed along each strap. So every time the straps hit the flesh, the pieces of bone inflicted horrible lacerations, literally ripping the flesh from the bones of the victim. There can be no doubt the Savior was tied to a pole and severely beaten in this way. He had been struck and beaten before, but this beating by the Roman executioners was probably the most severe of His beatings.

Dear believer, imagine this scene, then stand over Him, weeping for His poor stricken body. Can you gaze on Him without shedding tears as He lies before you as the perfect representation of agonizing love? At the same time He is as fair as a lily in His innocence and as red as a rose with the crimson color of His own blood. As you sense the certain and blessed healing "his wounds" have fashioned in you, doesn't your heart instantly melt with love and grief? If you have ever loved our Lord Jesus, surely now you must feel that affection for Him brightly glowing within your heart.

See how the patient Jesus stands,
Insulted in His lowest case!
Sinners have bound the Almighty's hands,
And spit in their Creator's face.
With thorns His temples gored and gashed
Send streams of blood from every part.

His back with knotted scourges lashed,
But sharper scourges tear His heart.

Samuel Hart, 1845 – ?

We would rather stay in our room this morning and weep, but our work calls us away. Before we leave, however, may we first pray that our beloved Savior imprint the image of His bleeding body upon the tablets of our heart all day long. Then at nightfall may we return to commune with Him, with true sorrow that our sin cost Him so dearly.

From the pen of Jim Reimann:

Redemption is defined as "freedom obtained through a price paid." Today we have considered that price, but who can fully calculate Jesus' pain and suffering or the value of even one drop of His blood!

We think of so-called precious metals as having great value, but the truth is they have no eternal value. In fact, since the word *precious* literally means "priceless or beyond the ability to value," metals such as silver and gold are not truly precious. And as we see from the following, they are indeed perishable:

For you know that it was not with perishable things such as silver or gold that you were redeemed from the empty way of life handed down to you from your forefathers, but with the precious blood of Christ, a lamb without blemish or defect.

1 Peter 1:18 – 19

April

APRIL 1

Let him kiss me with the kisses of his mouth.

Song of Songs 1:2

From the pen of Charles Spurgeon:

For several days now we have been dwelling on the Savior's passion, or suffering, and for a little longer we will continue to linger there. At the beginning of this new month may we seek to be filled with the same glowing desires exhibited in the heart of the one chosen to be the wife in the Song of Songs. See how she runs to her Beloved at once. There are no words of introduction and she does not even mention His name. Her heart is already centered on Him, for she speaks of Him as though He were the only person in the world. Look how bold her love is!

Contrast her boldness with the humble act of love by the repentant weeping woman who took "an expensive perfume,... poured it on Jesus' feet and wiped his feet with her hair" (John 12:3). It was also rich love that led the gentle Mary to sit "at the Lord's feet listening to what he said" (Luke 10:39) and learning from Him.

Yet here in the Song of Songs we see bold, fervent, and strong love that aspires to higher expressions of regard and closer signs of true fellowship. Esther trembled in the presence of her husband, King Xerxes, but a spouse who experiences the true joyful liberty of perfect love knows no fear. If we have received that same free spirit of love, we may expect the same kind of boldness.

And through the various "kisses" of Jesus we see the evidence of His affection that allows believers to truly enjoy His love. We have "the kiss of reconciliation," which we enjoyed at the moment of our conversion, and it was as sweet as honey dripping directly from the honeycomb. "The kiss of acceptance" is still warm on our face as we learn He has accepted us and our works

through His rich grace. There is "the kiss of daily, present communion" with Him, which we yearn for day after day, until it is changed into "the kiss of reception," which one day takes our soul from earth, and then ultimately yields to "the kiss of consummation," which fills us with the joy of heaven.

Our walk is by faith, but it is through true fellowship that reaches our emotions that we find rest. Faith is the road, but communion with Jesus is the deep well from which the pilgrims drink. O Lover of our souls, don't be estranged from us, but may the lips of Your blessing meet the lips of our asking, and may the lips of Your fullness touch the lips of our need. And may Your kiss quickly bear much fruit.

From the pen of Jim Reimann:

Spurgeon today mentions "the kiss of reconciliation." Jesus' mission on earth was to reconcile His chosen to His father. Thus, reconciliation is defined as "the ending of hostility and the establishing of peace between parties that are at odds with each other." Here is only a little of what Paul said of reconciliation:

> Once you were alienated from God and were enemies in your minds because of your evil behavior. But now he has reconciled you by Christ's physical body through death to present you holy in his sight, without blemish and free from accusation.
>
> Colossians 1:21 – 22

> Christ Jesus ... himself is our peace, who has made the two one and has destroyed the barrier, the dividing wall of hostility.
>
> Ephesians 2:13 – 14

APRIL 2

Jesus made no reply, not even to a single charge.
Matthew 27:14

From the pen of Charles Spurgeon:

Jesus had never been slow to speak when He could bless someone, but in order to save Himself, He would not say a single word. "'No one ever spoke the way this man does,' the guards declared" (John 7:46) — and no one was ever silent like He was! Was His exceptional silence the very sign of His perfect self-sacrifice? Did it show He would not utter one word to stop the slaughter of His sacred person, which He had dedicated as an offering for us? Had He so entirely surrendered Himself He would not intervene on His own behalf even to the slightest degree? Instead of intervening, was He willing to be bound and slain as an unstruggling and uncomplaining victim?

Was His silence designed to show us there was no defense for our sin? After all, what words could ever be said that could cover or excuse human guilt? Thus, He took the total weight of our sin upon Himself and stood speechless before His judge. Isn't patient silence the best reply to an accusing world that continually denies its own sin? And doesn't calm endurance answer some questions infinitely more conclusively than even the loftiest eloquence of words?

In fact, the best defenders of the faith in all of Christianity in the early years were its martyrs. An anvil can break a multitude of hammers by quietly enduring their blows. Didn't the silent Lamb of God provide for us a great example of wisdom? Every accusation against Him became a new opportunity for blasphemy, so He saw it as His responsibility not to offer any words to further fuel the flames of sin. Accusations that are ambiguous, false, petty, or have no basis in fact at all will soon disprove or refute themselves. Therefore the truth can afford to remain silent and then discovers there is wisdom in silence.

By His silence our Lord also provided a remarkable fulfillment of prophecy. A long defense of Himself would have been contrary to Isaiah's foretelling — "He was led like a lamb to the slaughter, and as a sheep before her shearers is silent, so he did not open his mouth" (Isa. 53:7). Thus, by His quiet submission He conclusively proved Himself to be the true Lamb of God.

Jesus, it is as the Lamb of God that we greet You this morning. Be with us today, and in the silence of our hearts may we hear the voice of Your love.

From the pen of Jim Reimann:

If Isaiah prophesied Jesus would "not open his mouth," how is it that when He stood trial before Pilate, He answered one of the governor's questions? Pilate asked, "Are you the king of the Jews?" to which Jesus replied, "Yes, it is as you say" (Matt. 27:11). This is not a contradiction, however, because Pilate asked a direct question as to who Jesus was. But when the chief priests and elders brought charges and accusations against Him, "Jesus made no reply, not even to a single charge — to the great amazement of the governor" (Matt. 27:14).

Why didn't He respond? He was standing in our place, and since we "are without excuse" (Rom. 1:20), no reply or defense could be made. Who could defend sinful man, when God's Word says, "Whoever keeps the whole law and yet stumbles at just one point is guilty of breaking all of it" (James 2:10)?

"This is love: not that we loved God, but that he loved us and sent his Son as an atoning sacrifice for our sins" (1 John 4:10).

APRIL 3

Finally Pilate handed him over to them to be crucified.
So the soldiers took charge of Jesus.

John 19:16

From the pen of Charles Spurgeon:

Jesus was in agony all night. He spent the early morning hours at the house of Caiaphas, then was hurried from Caiaphas to Pilate, from Pilate to Herod, and from Herod back to Pilate again. He was not allowed any food, drink, or rest, so by then He had little physical strength remaining. His enemies were eager for His blood and, thus, led Him out to die, forcing Him to carry His own cross. What a sorrowful procession! No wonder the "daughters of Jerusalem" (Luke 23:28) wept for Him. Dear soul, do you weep for Him as well?

What do we learn from this picture of our blessed Lord being led to His death? Do we recognize the truth foreshadowed by "the scapegoat" (Lev. 16:8)? Didn't the high priest "lay both hands on the head of the live goat and confess over it all the wickedness and rebellion of the Israelites — all their sins — and put them on the goat's head" (Lev. 16:21), removing the sins from the people? Wasn't the scapegoat then led "away into the desert in the care of a man appointed for the task" (v. 21), carrying away the sins of the people so that even if they were searched for they could not be found?

In the same way we now see Jesus brought before the priests and rulers who pronounce Him guilty. God Himself imputes our sins to Him, charging our sins to His account, for "the LORD has laid on him the iniquity of us all" (Isa. 53:6). "God made him who had no sin to be sin for us" (2 Cor. 5:21) as a substitute for our guilt. Upon His shoulders He bore our sins, represented by His cross, and the final great Scapegoat was led away by the appointed officers of justice.

Beloved soul, do you have the assurance He carried *your* sin? As you look at the cross upon His shoulders, does it represent *your* sin? There is one way by which you can be assured He carried your sin. If you have laid your hand upon His head, confessed your sin, and trusted in Him, then your sin no longer lies on you, but has all been transferred to Christ through blessed imputation. And He bears your sin on His shoulders as a weight heavier than His cross.

Don't let this picture fade from your mind until you have rejoiced in your own deliverance and then praised the loving Redeemer upon whom your iniquities were laid.

From the pen of Jim Reimann:

An ancient prison hewn out of the rock of Mount Zion is likely the place of the house of Caiaphas, the high priest, for it is there his sarcophagus, or stone coffin, was discovered. The site includes prison cells, a place of horrific beatings, and a deep pit to hold criminals overnight. Most likely Jesus was lowered into this cold, totally dark pit and held overnight, completely alone. It is therefore an amazing fulfillment of the following prophetic psalm:

I am counted among those who go down to the pit; I am like a man without strength.... You have taken from me my closest friends and have made me repulsive to them. I am confined and cannot escape.... Why, O LORD, do you reject me and hide your face from me?... You have taken my companions and loved ones from me; the darkness is my closest friend.

Psalm 88:4, 8, 14, 18

God made him who had no sin to be sin for us,
so that in him we might become the righteousness of God.

2 Corinthians 5:21

From the pen of Charles Spurgeon:

O grieving Christian! Why do you weep? Are you mourning over your own sinfulness? Then look to your perfect Lord and remember — you are complete in Him. In God's sight you are as perfect as if you had never sinned. In actual fact it is even better than that — "The LORD Our Righteousness" (Jer. 33:16) has clothed you in His divine garment so that you have more than the righteousness of man — you have "the righteousness of God."

Oh, you who mourn over your heredity of sin and depravity, remember that none of your sins can condemn you any longer. You have learned to hate sin, but you have also learned your sin is no longer yours — it was laid upon Christ's head. You don't stand before God on your own merits because you now stand in Christ by His work. Your acceptance is not in you, but lies in your Lord. Thus, you are as fully accepted before God today, with all of your sinfulness, as you will be when you stand before His throne free from all sin and depravity.

I plead with you to take hold of this precious thought — "Perfect in Christ" (Col. 1:28)? "In Him you have been made complete" (Col. 2:10 NASB). Clothed in your Savior's garment you are as holy as the Holy One Himself. "Who is he that condemns? Christ Jesus, who died — more than that, who was raised to life — is at the right hand of God and is also interceding for us" (Rom. 8:34).

Dear Christian, let your heart rejoice, for you are "accepted in the beloved" (Eph. 1:6 KJV). What do you have to fear? Let your face forever wear a smile, live near your Master, live in the suburbs of the Celestial City; for soon, when your time has come, you will rise up to where Jesus sits and will reign at His right hand.

All this because our Divine Lord, "who had no sin," was made "to be sin for us, so that in him we might become the righteousness of God."

From the pen of Jim Reimann:

The primary difference between Christianity and every other faith or religion is that our faith is truly the only faith-based, as opposed to works-based, religion. Thus, by definition, Christianity is the only *faith*. People of other religions totally misunderstand our beliefs, typically thinking our acceptance by God is earned by living up to His laws, with our good works ultimately outweighing our bad. But they don't understand this teaching of Paul: "No one will be declared righteous in his sight by observing the law; rather, through the law we become conscious of sin" (Rom. 3:20) — and our need of a savior. Paul later expounds on this truth, describing those who have been saved by Jesus:

> Therefore, there is now no condemnation for those who are in Christ Jesus, because through Christ Jesus the law of the Spirit of life set me free from the law of sin and death. For what the law was powerless to do ... God did by sending his own Son in the likeness of sinful man to be a sin offering. And so he condemned sin in sinful man, in order that the righteous requirements of the law might be fully met in us.
>
> Romans 8:1 – 4

If Jesus is *your* Savior, thank Him for this truth: "The LORD redeems his servants; no one will be condemned who takes refuge in him" (Ps. 34:22).

APRIL 5

They seized Simon from Cyrene ...
and put the cross on him and made him carry it behind Jesus.

Luke 23:26

From the pen of Charles Spurgeon:

Simon's carrying of the cross of Christ is an exact picture of the work of the church throughout time, for the church is the cross-bearer "behind Jesus." Mark this down, dear Christian, Jesus did not suffer to keep you from suffering. He bore His cross, not so you could escape it, but so you could endure it. Christ exempts you from sin — not sorrow — so remember that and expect to suffer.

Yet may we be comforted with this thought: in our case, just as it was in Simon's, *it is not our cross but is Christ's cross we carry.* Therefore, when you come under attack for your faith or when people mock you cruelly because of your faith, remember — it is not your cross, it is His. What an honor and a delight it is to carry the cross of our Lord Jesus!

You carry the cross "behind Jesus," so you have been blessed with great company, for your path is marked with the footprints of your Lord. And your heavy burden has been stained red by the blood of His shoulder. It is His cross and He goes before you as a shepherd goes before his sheep. So "take up [your] cross daily and follow [Him]" (Luke 9:23).

Remember this also: you bear the cross in partnership with Him. Some people have taught that Simon carried only one end of the cross and did not carry it by himself. It is quite possible Christ carried the heavier end, while Simon may have carried the lighter end. Certainly it is the same with you — you carry the light end of the cross, while Christ has already borne the heavier end.

And remember this: although Simon had to carry the cross for only a little time, it has given him lasting honor. And although we must carry the cross for a little while at most, we "will receive the crown of glory that will never fade away" (1 Peter 5:4).

Thus, truly we should love the cross and, instead of shrinking from its burden, we should consider it something precious — especially since we know "our light and momentary troubles are achieving for us an eternal glory that far outweighs them all" (2 Cor. 4:17).

From the pen of Jim Reimann:

What Simon of Cyrene was asked to do was in accordance with Roman law, for any civilian could be pressed into service to carry burdens up to one mile. This is why Jesus said, "If someone forces you to go one mile, go with him two miles" (Matt. 5:41). And the place of the Antonia Fortress, where Jesus stood before Pontius Pilate in the Old City of Jerusalem, is less than one mile from any of the possible crucifixion sites.

Simon's encounter with the Lord may have led him to trust Jesus as Savior. Mark 15:21 gives us more detail about Simon, referring to him as "the father of Alexander and Rufus," possibly the same Rufus whom Paul mentions in Romans 16:13 when he says, "Greet Rufus, chosen in the Lord, and his mother, who has been a mother to me, too."

Simon, like us, was chosen to carry the cross of Christ. Perhaps he then carried that cross, as a believer, for the rest of his life — much more than the one mile required by Roman law, but many miles as a true blessing of God!

APRIL 6

Let us, then, go to him outside the camp.

Hebrews 13:13

From the pen of Charles Spurgeon:

Jesus carried His cross "outside the camp" to suffer. And the reason a Christian goes "outside the camp" of the world's sin and religion is not because he loves to be different, but because it is what Jesus did, and a disciple must follow his Master. Christ was "not of the world" (John 17:14). In fact, His life and His testimony were a constant protest against conformity with the world. Never before was there such an overflowing love for people as was found in Him, yet He was separate from sinners. In the same way, Christ's people must "go to him," taking their position "outside the camp" as witnesses for the truth and must be prepared to tread the straight and narrow path. They must have bold, unflinching, lion-like hearts that love Christ first and His truth second — loving Him and His truth above everything else in the world.

Jesus desires that you as His child "go to him outside the camp" for your own sanctification, for you cannot grow in grace to any great degree if you remain conformed to the world. This life of separation through sanctification may be a path of sorrow, but it is a highway of safety. And although the separated life may cost you a great deal of pain and make every day a battle for you, it is still a life of abiding joy. In fact, no joy could ever exceed the joy of a soldier of Christ, for Jesus reveals Himself to him so graciously, continually providing such sweet refreshment, that His warriors experience more calm and peace in their daily fight than unbelievers do during their times of rest.

The highway of holiness is also the highway of communion and fellowship with Christ. And it is by following this highway we have the hope to "receive the crown of life" (James 1:12), but only once we are enabled by His divine grace to faithfully follow Christ "outside the camp."

This crown of glory comes to us *after* the cross of separation. Yet even a mere moment of shame will be well compensated with eternal honor, and a little time of bearing witness for Him will seem like nothing once we are "with the Lord forever" (1 Thess. 4:17).

From the pen of Jim Reimann:

Our text today commands believers to "go to [Jesus] outside the camp," and Spurgeon states we must love "*Him and His truth* above everything else in the world." And if Jesus is the Word incarnate — "The Word became flesh ... full of grace and truth" (John 1:14) — we cannot separate Him from His truth. In fact, He said, "I am ... the truth" (John 14:6) and prayed to His Father, "Your word is truth" (John 17:17). Thus, Jesus equals the Word, the Word equals truth, and truth equals Jesus; and if we truly love Him, we will love His Word and vice versa.

In light of this, each of us should examine our own hearts this morning and ask ourselves, "Do I love the Lord Jesus and His Word above everything else on earth?" But before we answer too quickly and superficially, let us consider how to measure our devotion to Him. Jesus said, "Where your treasure is, there your heart will be also" (Matt. 6:21).

I ask myself, "How do I invest my time? Is more of it invested in the treasure of God's Word or in the so-called treasures of the world? Can I say with the psalmist, 'Oh, how I love your law! I meditate on it all day long'" (Ps. 119:97)?

APRIL 7

How long, O men, will you turn my glory into shame?

Psalm 4:2

From the pen of Charles Spurgeon:

One inspired author once wrote a mournful list of the "honors" the blinded people of Israel awarded their long-awaited King. Here is his list:

1. They threw Him "a parade of honor" in which Roman soldiers, Jewish priests, and men and women took part, while He Himself carried His cross. This is the kind of triumphant award the world gave Him who came to overthrow their worst enemies. Derisive shouts were His only acclamations and cruel taunts were His only songs of praise.

2. They presented Him with "the wine of honor." But instead of it being a golden cup overflowing with wine, they offered Him the numbing death drink of a criminal, which He refused, choosing rather to fully experience the taste of death. Later, when He cried out, "I am thirsty," they gave Jesus "wine vinegar" (John 19:28–29) to drink, "mixed with gall" (Matt. 27:34), thrusting it to His mouth on a sponge. Oh, what wretched, detestable inhospitality to the King's Son!

3. He was provided with "an honor guard" who showed their great esteem for Him by gambling over His garments, which they stole from Him as their plunder. Such were the bodyguards of the Adored of heaven, men who were simply a gang of brutal gamblers.

4. "A throne of honor" was provided for Him — a blood-stained tree. These rebellious men would allow no better place of rest to their faithful Lord than a cross. In fact, the cross was the total expression of the world's feelings toward Him. It was as though the world was saying, "There, You Son of God, this is exactly how God Himself should be treated if we could get our hands on Him."

5. They gave Him "a title of honor" as "KING OF THE JEWS" (John 19:19). Yet this was given in name only, for the blinded nation's "chief priests ... protested to Pilate" (v. 21), quickly rejecting the title. And by desiring the release of Barabbas, and then placing Jesus between two thieves in such a shameful place, they showed they preferred the title "King of thieves."

In each of these humiliations, mankind turned Jesus' "glory into shame." Yet ultimately, through each of them, the eyes of all the saints and angels will be gladdened "for ever and ever! Amen" (Eph. 3:21).

From the pen of Jim Reimann:

Jesus' death was beautifully veiled with great symbolism and dramatic fulfillments of Scripture. For example, even the wood used to lift the sponge to Jesus was an amazing fulfillment of Passover. Notice what John 19:29 tells us: "A jar of wine vinegar was there, so they soaked a sponge in it, put the sponge on *a stalk of the hyssop plant*, and lifted it to Jesus' lips." Next notice God's instructions for the first Passover in Egypt: "*Take a bunch of hyssop*, dip it into the blood in the basin and put some of the blood on the top and on both sides of the doorframe" (Ex. 12:22). Thus, not only does hyssop tie the two events together but also the painting of blood on the door is tied to Jesus's being the Door of salvation through His shed blood on the cross. He said, "I am the door: by me if any man enter in, he shall be saved" (John 10:9 KJV).

Our loving Father gives us one beautiful picture after beautiful picture — one symbol and fulfillment after another — as if to say, "My child, don't miss this!"

APRIL 8

If men do these things when the tree is green,
what will happen when it is dry?

Luke 23:31

From the pen of Charles Spurgeon:

One very instructive interpretation of this thought-provoking question is this: If Jesus, the innocent substitute for sinners, suffered so horrifically, what will happen to a sinner — "the dry tree" — once he finds himself in the hands of an angry God? When God saw Jesus in the sinners' place, "He ... did not spare his own Son" (Rom. 8:32), and when He faces those who are unconverted and without Christ, He will not spare them either.

Dear sinner, in the same way Jesus was led away by His enemies, you will be dragged away by Satanic forces to the place appointed for you. Jesus was deserted by God, and if He was deserted — He who was considered a sinner only by virtue of the imputation of our sins to Him — how much more will you be?

What a terrible scream when "Jesus cried out in a loud voice, '*Eloi, Eloi, lama sabachthani?*'" (Mark 15:34). One day you too will cry out, "My God, my God, why have you forsaken me?" (v. 34). Then your answer will come, "Since you rejected me when I called,... since you ignored all my advice and would not accept my rebuke, I in turn will laugh at your disaster; I will mock when calamity overtakes you" (Prov. 1:24 – 26).

If God "did not spare his own Son," how much less will He spare you! What whips of burning steel will be yours when your conscience finally strikes you with all its terror. You who are the richest, the happiest, and the most self-righteous of sinners — who will take your place when God says to you, "'Awake, O sword' (Zech. 13:7), against this person who has rejected Me; strike him, and may he feel the pain forever"?

If "they spit on [Jesus]" (Matt. 27:30), dear sinner, what shame will be yours! It is impossible to express the massive sorrows that converged on the head of Jesus, who died for us. Thus, it is even more absurd to think we could fully explain what streams — No! What oceans — of grief will crash over *your* spirit if you die as you are. And you may die this way — you could even die right now.

I plead with you, therefore, on the basis of the agony of Christ, His wounds, and His blood, do not bring the coming wrath upon yourself! Trust in the Son of God, and you "will never die" (John 11:26).

From the pen of Jim Reimann:

The truth is, everyone deserves death, "for all have sinned and fall short of the glory of God" (Rom. 3:23). Perhaps you have heard the message of the gospel of Christ many times, but have never been saved and thereby still "fall short" of what you need for eternal life. "Therefore, since the promise of entering his rest still stands, let us be careful that none of you be found to have *fallen short* of it. For we also have had the gospel preached to us, just as they did; but the message they heard was of no value to them, because those who heard did not combine it with faith" (Heb. 4:1 – 2).

Why not combine the gospel message you have heard with faith this morning? "I tell you, now is the time of God's favor, now is the day of salvation" (2 Cor. 6:2). Ask Him to save you — to give you Jesus — and you will no longer "fall short of the glory of God," for He *is* "the glory of God"!

APRIL 9

A large number of people followed him,
including women who mourned and wailed for him.
Luke 23:27

From the pen of Charles Spurgeon:

Amid the mob who hounded the Redeemer to His doom were at least a few gracious souls whose bitter anguish was vented through their weeping and wailing — fitting music to accompany Jesus' march of woe. And when my mind's eye imagines the Savior bearing His cross to Calvary, I can see myself joining the godly women and weeping with them. There is true reason for grief, but one that lies much deeper than those mourning women ever thought.

The women bemoaned innocence mistreated, goodness persecuted, love bleeding, and meekness about to die, but my heart has a much deeper and bitter reason to mourn. My sins were the very scourges that lacerated the flesh of His blessed shoulders, and my sins were the thorns that crowned His bleeding brow. My sins cried, "Crucify him! Crucify him!" (Luke 23:21) and then laid the cross upon His gracious shoulders. His being led forth to die is enough sorrow for all of eternity to bear, but knowing I was His murderer is more grief — infinitely more — than one poor human fountain of tears can express.

Why the women loved Him and wept is not hard to imagine, but they could not have had any greater reasons for love and grief than my heart has. The widow of Nain saw her son restored to life (see Luke 7:11 – 17) — but I myself have been raised to "live a *new* life" (Rom. 6:4). Peter's mother-in-law was cured of a fever (see Matt. 8:14 – 15) — but I have been cured of the much greater plague of sin. Jesus "had driven seven demons" (Mark 16:9) out of Mary Magdalene — but He has cast an entire legion out of me. Mary and Martha were blessed with occasional visits from Him — but He dwells with me. His mother carried His body temporarily in her womb — but He has been born in me as "the hope of glory" (Col. 1:27).

When it comes to debt owed to Him, I lack nothing in comparison to those godly women. Thus, may I not lag behind them when it comes to my gratitude and grief.

> Love and grief my heart dividing,
> With my tears His feet I'll bathe.
> Constant still in heart abiding,
> Weep for Him who died to save.
>
> Original text by James Allan, 1734 – 1804;
> rewritten by Walter Shirley, 1725 – 1786

From the pen of Jim Reimann:

Spurgeon recognized the personal debt he owed the Lord, as all the saved of God should do. Recognition of this debt, along with recognition of Jesus' remedy for it on the cross, should motivate each of us to serve Him faithfully and with great gratitude in our hearts. With that said, let us take a moment to consider how God Himself views our sin debt, for He declared: "I will forgive their wickedness and will remember their sins no more" (Jer. 31:34).

Why not thank Him this morning that your sin debt not only has been paid in full, or forgiven, but also that it has been forgotten!

APRIL 10

When they were come to the place,
which is called Calvary, there they crucified him.
Luke 23:33 KJV

From the pen of Charles Spurgeon:

Calvary is the hill of comfort, while the wood of the cross is used to build the house of comfort. And Jesus, the Rock split in two by the spear that pierced His side, is the foundation of the temple of heavenly blessing. Thus, no scene in sacred history can gladden the soul like the tragic scene of Calvary.

> Is it not strange, the darkest hour
> That ever dawned on sinful earth,
> Should touch the heart with softer power,
> For comfort, than an angel's mirth?
> That to the cross the mourner's
>   eye should turn,
> Sooner than where the stars of Bethlehem
>   burn?
>
> John Keble, 1792 – 1866

A great Light shines from the midday midnight of Golgotha, and every lovely "flower of the field" (Isa. 40:6 KJV) blooms beneath the shadow of the once accursed tree. From Jesus' place of thirst, grace dug a fountain that forever gushes with water pure as crystal — each drop capable of alleviating the woes of man.

Dear believers, each of you has had your times of conflict, but you must confess it was not on the hill of the Mount of Olives, Mount Sinai, or Mount Tabor that you ever found comfort. No, it has been "Gethsemane" (Matt. 26:36), "Gabbatha" (John 19:13), and "Golgotha" (John 19:17) that have been used to comfort you. Often the bitter herbs of Gethsemane have taken away the bitterness of your life, the scourge of Gabbatha often has scourged away your worries, and the groans of Golgotha have produced unthinkably rich comfort for you. We would never have known the full height and depth of Christ's love if He had not died, nor would we have even been able to guess of the Father's deep affection if He had not given His Son to die.

The common everyday blessings of life we enjoy all sing of Christ's love, just as a seashell held to the ear whispers of the deep sea from which it came. Yet if we desire to hear "the ocean itself," we must not look at everyday blessings, but at the event of the crucifixion. One who truly desires to know love must go to Calvary and see the "man of sorrows" die (Isa. 53:3).

From the pen of Jim Reimann:

"The Old Rugged Cross" was written twenty-one years after Spurgeon's death, by George Bennard (1873 – 1958) in 1913. Yet with Spurgeon's preaching always so centered on the cross, surely he would have loved this beautiful hymn:

> On a hill far away stood an old rugged cross,
> The emblem of suffering and shame;
> And I love that old cross where the
>   dearest and best
> For a world of lost sinners was slain.

Father, "may I never boast except in the cross of our Lord Jesus Christ, through which the world has been crucified to me, and I to the world" (Gal. 6:14).

APRIL 11

I am poured out like water,
and all my bones are out of joint.
Psalm 22:14

From the pen of Charles Spurgeon:

Did earth or heaven ever behold a spectacle of suffering, grief, and woe more sad than that of the cross! In His soul and His body our Lord felt as weak as though He were "poured out like water" upon the ground. When His cross was lifted and then suddenly dropped into its hole in the ground, He was violently shaken. Every ligament in His body was strained, every nerve felt pain, "and all [His] bones [were] out of joint." Being pulled by His own weight, the majestic Sufferer felt the increasing strain each second of those six long hours. A sense of faintness and overall weakness was overpowering to Him, yet at the same time He was constantly aware of massive misery and pain.

When Daniel saw his "great vision," he described his sensations in this way: "I had no strength left, my face turned deathly pale and I was helpless" (Dan. 10:8). How much more weak and faint the greater Prophet must have been when He saw the dreadful vision of the wrath of God and then felt it being poured out on His own soul!

The excruciating pain and suffering our Lord experienced would have overcome each of us, and the blessing of unconsciousness would have come to our rescue. But in His case, "he was pierced" (Isa. 53:5) and felt the pain of the sword, and He drained the "cup" (Matt. 26:39), tasting *every* drop.

O King of Grief! (A title strange, yet true
To Thee of all kings only due)
O King of Wounds! How shall I grieve for Thee,

Who in grief gave Thyself for me!
George Herbert, 1593 – 1633

As we kneel before our now ascended Savior's throne, may we well remember the way in which He prepared His throne as a throne of grace for us. May we spiritually drink of His cup so we will be strengthened for our times of trial whenever they come. Every part of His physical body suffered, and it must be the same spiritually. Just as His body emerged uninjured from such great grief and suffering to unspeakable glory and power, His spiritual body will emerge from the fiery furnace with "no smell of fire" (Dan. 3:27) upon it.

From the pen of Jim Reimann:

Our text today speaks of being "poured out like water," an Old Testament prophecy of the coming Messiah's death. And Jesus, at the Last Supper, lifted His cup, saying, "This is my blood of the covenant, which is *poured out* for many for the forgiveness of sins" (Matt. 26:28). Then after His death on the cross "one of the soldiers pierced Jesus' side with a spear, bringing a sudden flow of blood and water" (John 19:34). What an amazingly accurate and detailed fulfillment!

Paul later used similar language in describing his approaching death: "I am already being *poured out* like a drink offering, and the time has come for my departure. I have fought the good fight, I have finished the race, I have kept the faith" (2 Tim. 4:6 – 7).

Father, may my life too be poured out to You as a blessed drink offering.

APRIL 12

My heart has turned to wax;
it has melted away within me.

Psalm 22:14

From the pen of Charles Spurgeon:

Our blessed Lord experienced a horrific sinking and melting feeling deep within His inner being. "A man's spirit sustains him in sickness, but a crushed spirit who can bear?" (Prov. 18:14). Deep depression of the spirit is the most oppressive and severe of all trials, making every other difficulty appear as nothing. For good reason our suffering Savior cried out to His God, "Do not be far from me" (Ps. 22:11), for the time when a person most senses his need for God is when his heart seems to be melting within him due to the heaviness of his circumstances.

Dear believer, draw near to the cross of Christ this morning. Humbly adore the King of glory who was taken far lower into mental distress and inward anguish than any one of us. Take notice of His qualifications to become our faithful High Priest, one who can truly be touched with, and sympathetic to, the feelings of our human weakness and infirmities. My prayer is that especially those of us whose sadness and depression are arising from a sense that the Father's love has been withdrawn from us may enter into a close and intimate communion with Jesus. May we never give way to despair, always remembering our Master has passed through this dark way before us.

At times our souls may come to the point of severe longing and anguish. We may thirst nearly to the point of fainting, simply to behold the light of the Lord's countenance. At these times may we steady ourselves, recalling the sweet fact of the sympathy of our great High Priest. And as our tears of sorrow are swallowed up and forgotten in His vast ocean of grief, how high should our love for Him soar!

Oh, strong and deep love of Jesus, come into me like the seas of a springtime flood. Overwhelm all my desires, drown all my sins, wash away all my cares, and raise my earthbound soul, floating it to the very point of my Lord's feet. There let me lie as a poor broken shell, washed to glory by Your love and having no virtue or value of my own. Then may I only venture to whisper to You that if You would only put Your ear to me, You will hear within my heart the faint echoes of the vast waves of Your own love — Your own love, which has brought me to the point where it is my delight to lie, even at Your feet, forever!

From the pen of Jim Reimann:

One of the well-known believers of Spurgeon's day was David Livingstone (1813 – 1873). He was a medical missionary with the London Missionary Society and an explorer in Africa. The first European to see Victoria Falls, he named it after the reigning Queen of England. He took a strong stance against slavery and explored Africa, consistently sharing the gospel. Upon his death his heart was buried in Africa, while his body was returned to London and interred in Westminster Abbey.

Our devotions the last several days have been focused on the cross of Christ, and Livingstone's life and message were centered on it and Christ's kingdom. He was once quoted as saying, "I will place no value on anything I have or may possess except in relation to the kingdom of Christ."

Lord Jesus, may this be true of my life as well — each and every day!

APRIL 13

My lover is to me a sachet of myrrh
resting between my breasts.
Song of Songs 1:13

From the pen of Charles Spurgeon:

In this verse, myrrh is chosen as "a type of [Christ] who was to come" (Rom. 5:14 ESV) because of its preciousness; its perfume; its pleasantness; its healing, preserving, and disinfecting qualities; and its association with sacrifice. But why is Jesus compared to "a sachet [or *pouch*, NASB] of myrrh"? It is due to His sufficiency, for He is not simply a drop of it, but a barrel full. He is not just a sprig or a blossom of it, but an entire bouquet. In Christ there is enough for all my needs, so may I not be slow to avail myself of Him.

Our beloved Savior is compared to a sachet or pouch of myrrh because of His depth and fullness, "for in Christ all the fullness of the Deity lives in bodily form" (Col. 2:9). He meets every variety of needs, not just one, for everything we need is found in Him. Just consider the wonderful variety of roles He fulfilled — Prophet, Priest, King, Husband, Friend, and Shepherd. Think of His life, death, resurrection, ascension, and His second coming. Then picture His goodness, gentleness, courage, self-denial, love, faithfulness, truth, and righteousness. Everywhere we look He is a treasure of sufficiency.

In fact, Jesus is referred to as "a sachet of myrrh" to convey the idea of something to be kept safe and guarded as a treasure. We must value Him as our greatest treasure, prizing His words and His precepts. We must keep our thoughts and knowledge of Him as though they were under lock and key in our hearts in order to keep the Devil from stealing anything from us.

Finally, Jesus is called "a sachet of myrrh" as a symbol representing His extraordinary distinguishing and discriminating grace, for "before the creation of the world" (Eph. 1:4) He was set apart and consecrated for His people. He gives His perfume only to those who understand how to enter into communion with Him — those who have an intimate fellowship with Him.

Oh, how blessed are those to whom the Lord has disclosed His secrets — those for whom He has been set apart! Oh, the joy of those who have been chosen and made to say, "My beloved 'is to me a sachet of myrrh'"!

From the pen of Jim Reimann:

Another significant mention of myrrh in the Bible is this from the Psalms: "Your throne, O God, will last for ever and ever; a scepter of justice will be the scepter of your kingdom. You love righteousness and hate wickedness; therefore God, your God, has set you above your companions by anointing you with the oil of joy. *All your robes are fragrant with myrrh* and aloes and cassia" (Ps. 45:6 – 8). This psalm is undoubtedly a prophecy of Christ, because it is quoted in Hebrews 1:8 – 9, beginning with the words: "About the Son he says … " Thus, we see the Messiah coming with the fragrance of myrrh.

The Magi, visiting Jesus as a child, "presented him with gifts of gold and of incense and of myrrh" (Matt. 2:11). On the cross He was "offered … wine mixed with myrrh, but he did not take it" (Mark 15:23). After His death "Nicodemus brought a mixture of myrrh and aloes" (John 19:39) to embalm Him.

Gold — a gift for our King! Incense — a gift for our High Priest! And myrrh — a precious perfume for our precious Savior upon His death!

APRIL 14

All who see me mock me; they hurl insults,
shaking their heads.

Psalm 22:7

From the pen of Charles Spurgeon:

Mockery was one of the primary ingredients in our Lord's suffering. Judas mocked Him in Gethsemane, the chief priests and scribes laughed at Him with contempt, Herod treated Him as worthless and despicable, the servants and soldiers derisively jeered Him and brutally insulted Him, Pilate and his guards ridiculed His royalty, and finally, on the tree all sorts of horrid indignities and hideous taunts were hurled at Him.

Ridicule is always hard to bear, but when we are in intense pain it is so heartless and cruel it cuts to our very soul. As you consider this, consider our Savior, tormented with severe anguish and pain far beyond human ability to even imagine or comprehend. Then picture that diverse multitude surrounding their poor suffering victim, each "shaking their heads" or shouting out the cruelest words of contempt!

There was so much more in the crucified One than this mingled mob could see. How else could such a large and varied crowd so unanimously "honor" Him with such contempt! Surely it was evil itself — in the very moment of its greatest apparent triumph — confessing that, after all was said and done, it could do nothing more than mock the victorious Goodness, which was reigning on the cross.

O dear Jesus — "despised and rejected by men" (Isa. 53:3) — how could You have died for people who treated You so cruelly? "This is love" (1 John 4:10) — divine love — love beyond measure. Yet we too once despised You in the days before You regenerated us. And even since our new birth we have often enthroned the world higher in our hearts than You. Even so, You bled to heal our wounds and died to give us life. Oh, that we could place You on a high and glorious throne in the hearts of everyone! We long to proclaim Your praises over land and sea till people everywhere come to universally adore You as much as they once unanimously rejected You.

Your creatures wrong You, O Thou sovereign
  Good!
You are not loved — because not understood.
This grieves me most, that vain pursuits
  beguile
Ungrateful ones, regardless of Your smile.
  Madame Jeanne-Marie Guyon, 1648 – 1717

Translated from French by William Cowper,
1731 – 1800

From the pen of Jim Reimann:

Show me a greater love than this!

"God is love. This is how God showed his love among us: He sent his one and only Son into the world that we might live through him. This is love: not that we loved God, but that he loved us and sent his Son as an atoning sacrifice for our sins" (1 John 4:8 – 10). "Because of his great love for us, God … made us alive with Christ even when we were dead in transgressions" (Eph. 2:4 – 5).

"*Greater love has no one than this*, that he lay down his life for his friends" (John 15:13).

APRIL 15

My God, my God, why have you forsaken me?

Psalm 22:1

From the pen of Charles Spurgeon:

In this verse we see the Savior in the depth of His sorrows. No other place shows us the grief of Christ as well as Calvary, and no other moment at Calvary is as full of agony as the moment Jesus' cry split the air — "My God, my God, why have you forsaken me?" (Matt. 27:46). At that moment His physical weakness was combined with the severe mental torture of the shame and dishonor through which He had to pass. What was even worse, and what marked the culmination of His grief, was the spiritual agony beyond all description He suffered as a result of the departure of His Father's presence from Him. This was the darkest midnight of Jesus' horror and the point He descended into the very abyss of suffering.

No mere human can fully comprehend the meaning of His words, although at times we find ourselves wanting to cry out, "My God, my God, why have you forsaken me?" There are seasons in our lives when the brightness of our Father's smile is obscured by "clouds and thick darkness" (Ps. 97:2), but may we remember God never really forsakes us. In our experience it only feels as though He has forsaken us, but in Christ's case He was actually forsaken. We distress over what feels like a slight turning away of our Father's love from us, but God actually did turn His face away from His Son. Who could even estimate the tremendous agony that caused Him! In our case our pain is often caused by our own unbelief, but in His case it was the cry of a dreadful fact — God had actually turned away from Him for a time.

O poor distressed soul — you who once lived in the sunshine of God's face but now find yourself in darkness, remember He has not actually forsaken you. God, obscured by clouds, is just as much our God as when He is shining in the full brilliance of His grace.

Yet, because even the mere thought that He may have forsaken us brings us great agony, we can only imagine the intense suffering of the Savior when He exclaimed, "My God, my God, why have you forsaken me?"

From the pen of Jim Reimann:

Surely he took up our infirmities and carried our sorrows, yet we considered him stricken by God, smitten by him, and afflicted. But he was pierced for our transgressions, he was crushed for our iniquities; the punishment that brought us peace was upon him, and by his wounds we are healed.

Isaiah 53:4 – 5

Oh, how often I catch myself distressing over the hardships of this life, when Jesus suffered so much more on my behalf! Over time I have learned the Lord is using even my meager hardships to conform me to the image of His Son, but still I often complain.

Father, change my thinking! Help me to consider the sufferings of my Lord Jesus when I am tempted to complain. May I truly see how blessed I am to be counted worthy of "the fellowship of sharing in his sufferings" (Phil. 3:10).

"He was oppressed and afflicted, *yet he did not open his mouth*; he was led like a lamb to the slaughter, and as a sheep before her shearers is silent, so *he did not open his mouth*" (Isa. 53:7).

APRIL 16

The precious blood of Christ.
1 Peter 1:19

From the pen of Charles Spurgeon:

When we stand at the foot of the cross we see Christ's hands, feet, and side, all dripping into crimson streams of His precious blood. It is "the precious blood" because of its redeeming and atoning effectiveness. Through it atonement is made for the sins of Christ's people, they are redeemed from under the law, and they are reconciled to God — made one with Him.

His blood also is precious due to its cleansing power: it "cleanses us from all sin" (1 John 1:7 ESV). "Though your sins are like scarlet, they shall be as white as snow" (Isa. 1:18). Through Jesus' blood no spot whatsoever is left on any believer. We are "without stain or wrinkle or any other blemish" (Eph. 5:27).

Oh, precious blood — that makes us clean, removing the stains of our countless sins, and permitting us to stand accepted in Jesus in spite of the many ways we have rebelled against our God!

The blood of Christ also is precious due to its preserving power, for under His sprinkled blood we are safe from the destroying angel. Remember — the actual reason we are spared is because God sees the blood. This should be comforting to us, for even when our eyes of faith grow dim, God's eyes remain strong.

His blood also is precious due to its sanctifying power and influence in our lives. The very same blood that justifies us by taking away our sin at salvation continues to work, bringing life to our new nature and moving us forward in suppressing sin and obeying the commands of God. There could never be a greater motivation to holiness than that which streamed from the veins of Jesus.

And, how precious — unspeakably precious — is His blood because it has overcoming power: "They overcame him by the blood of the Lamb" (Rev. 12:11). How could they do otherwise! Whoever fights using the precious blood of Jesus uses a weapon that can never know defeat.

The blood of Jesus! Sin dies in its presence and death ceases to be death, for it opens the gates of heaven. The blood of Jesus! We shall march on to victory, ever conquering, as long as we trust in its power!

From the pen of Jim Reimann:

Christ ... went through the greater and more perfect tabernacle that is not man-made.... He did not enter by means of the blood of goats and calves; but he entered the Most Holy Place once for all by his own blood, having obtained eternal redemption. The blood of goats and bulls and the ashes of a heifer sprinkled on those who are ceremonially unclean sanctify them so that they are outwardly clean. How much more, then, will the blood of Christ, who through the eternal Spirit offered himself unblemished to God, cleanse our consciences from acts that lead to death, so that we may serve the living God!

Hebrews 9:11 – 14

So why do I value the things of this world? They are nothing compared to the precious blood! May I continually "behold, the Lamb of God, who takes away the sin of the world!" (John 1:29 ESV) and "consider him who endured such opposition from sinful men, so that [I] will not grow weary and lose heart" (Heb. 12:3). And may I remember that "in [my] struggle against sin, [I] have not yet resisted to the point of shedding [my] blood" (Heb. 12:4).

He shed His blood for me!

APRIL 17

You have come ... to the sprinkled blood that speaks
a better word than the blood of Abel.

Hebrews 12:23 – 24

From the pen of Charles Spurgeon:

Dear reader, have you come to "the sprinkled blood"? The question is not whether you have come to the knowledge of a particular doctrine, the observance of some ceremony, or a certain experience; but have you come to the blood of Jesus?

The blood of Jesus is the very life and foundation of all godliness. If you have truly come to Jesus, we know how you came — the Holy Spirit graciously brought you to Him. You came to the sprinkled blood through no merit of your own.

Guilty, lost, and helpless you came to claim His blood, and His blood alone, as your everlasting hope. You came to the cross of Christ with a trembling and aching heart, and, oh, what a precious sound it was to hear the voice of the blood of Jesus! The dripping of His blood is like the music of heaven to the repentant children of earth.

We come full of sin, but our Savior invites us to lift our eyes to Him. Then as we gaze upon His bleeding wounds each drop of blood cries out as it falls, "'It is finished' (John 19:30). I have brought an end to sin. I have brought everlasting righteousness."

Oh, how sweet are the words of the precious blood of Jesus! And if you have come to that blood once, you will come continually. Your entire life will be one of "looking to Jesus" (Heb. 12:2 ESV). Your total behavior will not be characterized by the idea of looking back to your first experience of coming to Him, but a continual life of always coming to Him. If you have ever come to the sprinkled blood, you will feel the need to come to it every day. But he who has no desire to wash in it daily has never washed in it at all.

A true believer always feels the joy and acknowledges the privilege of partaking in a fountain that is always open. Living on past experiences is insufficient food for Christians, but a continual coming to Christ alone brings us joy and comfort.

This morning may we each sprinkle our doorposts with His blood, and then feast upon the Lamb with the assurance the destroying angel must pass us by.

From the pen of Jim Reimann:

Living on past spiritual experiences and successes is what so many of us do. Yet Christ came to be my Savior today — this very day! He desires I come to the cleansing stream of His blood each day. "Now is the time of God's favor, now is the day of salvation" (2 Cor. 6:2).

Forget the former things; do not dwell on the past. See, I am doing a new thing! Now it springs up; do you not perceive it? I am making a way in the desert and streams in the wasteland.

Isaiah 43:18 – 19

Father, thank You for the precious blood of Jesus shed for me. Thank You that He is the Door and that He was willing to apply His blood to that Door for me. I pray I will not be distracted by the past, but that I would come to that cleansing flood daily.

APRIL 18

She tied the scarlet cord in the window.

Joshua 2:21

From the pen of Charles Spurgeon:

For her survival Rahab depended on the promise given by the spies whom she recognized as the representatives of the God of Israel. Her faith was not only simple and resolute but also very obedient. Tying a scarlet cord in the window was a trivial thing, yet she dared not run the risk of neglecting it.

Dear soul, is there a lesson here for you? Have you been obedient to *all* of the Lord's will even though some of His commands seem nonessential? For example, have you thoroughly followed His example and instructions by partaking in the two ordinances of believers' baptism and the Lord's Supper? When these ordinances have been neglected, a case can be made that there is still a great deal of unloving disobedience in your heart. From this point forward, determine to be totally blameless in all things, even if it means tying a scarlet cord in your window if that is what God commands.

This action of Rahab also sets forth an even more serious lesson. Have I unquestioningly trusted in the precious blood of Jesus? Have I tied a scarlet cord in my window, so intricately and tightly, that my trust can never be removed? Or can I look through my window toward the Dead Sea of my sins or the Jerusalem of my hopes without even seeing the blood and all that is connected to its blessed power.

Can someone passing by my window see a cord hanging there that is so conspicuous and vibrant in color it cannot be missed? How blessed I am if my life makes the effectiveness of the atonement quite conspicuous to all onlookers. What is there to be ashamed of? May men or devils gaze at it if they wish, for the blood of Christ is my boast and my song!

Dear soul, there is One who surely will see the scarlet cord even when your faith is weak and you cannot see it yourself. Jehovah, the Avenger, will see it and pass over you. Jericho's walls fell flat, and although Rahab's house was on the wall, it stood intact.

Although my nature is built into the wall of humanity, when destruction smites mankind I will remain secure. So, my soul, retie the scarlet cord to the window and rest in peace.

From the pen of Jim Reimann:

What a beautiful story of forgiveness and trust! Rahab, a prostitute when the spies of Israel found her, expressed great faith in the true God of her city's enemy. And although once a prostitute, a Gentile, and a foreigner to Israel, she goes on to become the great-great-grandmother of Israel's King David from whose line the Messiah would come.

In light of this, never allow *your* past, which has been covered by the blood of Christ, to keep you from doing great things for Him. There is no sin beyond the reach of Christ's scarlet blood, and "though your sins are like scarlet, they shall be as white as snow" (Isa. 1:18).

The Holy Spirit also testifies to us about this. First he says: "This is the covenant I will make with them after that time, says the Lord. I will put my laws in their hearts, and I will write them on their minds." Then he adds: "Their sins and lawless acts I will remember no more."

Hebrews 10:15 – 17

APRIL 19

At that moment the curtain of the temple
was torn in two from top to bottom.
Matthew 27:51

From the pen of Charles Spurgeon:

No minor miracle was accomplished in the tearing of such a strong and thick curtain, yet it was not intended to be merely a display of God's power but was meant to teach us a number of truths. The old law was being put away like a worn-out priestly garment, torn and laid aside. When Jesus died, the sacrificial system was completely finished, finding its fulfillment in Him. Therefore, the very place those sacrifices were presented to God was marked with the evidence of the system's demise.

The tearing of the curtain also revealed the hidden things of the old system. The "mercy seat" (Ex. 25:17 KJV) could now be seen and the glory of God shone above it. Through the death of our Lord Jesus we have a clear revelation of God, for He was "not like Moses, who would put a veil over his face" (2 Cor. 3:13). Life and immortality are now brought to light and things that have been hidden since the foundation of the world have been uncovered.

The annual ceremony of the Day of Atonement was thereby abolished. The blood of atonement, which had each year been sprinkled within the curtain, had now been offered once for all by the great High Priest. Thus, the place of the symbolic ritual was no longer needed. Now the blood of bulls and lambs was of no importance, for Jesus has entered "behind the curtain" (Heb. 6:19) with "his own blood" (Heb. 9:12). Consequently, direct access to God is permitted and has become the great privilege of every believer in Christ Jesus. He did not simply poke a small hole into the curtain whereby we could catch a mere glimpse of the "mercy seat," but He completely tore it "from top to bottom." We may approach the heavenly throne of grace with boldness.

It is no error to think of His opening the way into the Holy of Holies in this miraculous manner with His last dying breath as a symbol of the opening of the gates of paradise for all the saints by virtue of His passion and death. Our bleeding Lord holds the keys to heaven, and what He opens no one can shut. Thus, may we enter with Him into heavenly places and sit with Him until our common enemies will be made His footstool. (See Ps. 110:1.)

From the pen of Jim Reimann:

Another lesson that comes to mind in the miracle of the tearing of the curtain of the Holy of Holies is that God was saying, in effect, "I will no longer make my dwelling in a building made of stone, but in human hearts made of flesh."

This is why the apostle Paul wrote, "We are the temple of the living God. As God has said: 'I will live with them and walk among them, and I will be their God, and they will be my people'" (2 Cor. 6:16), and "Do you not know that your body is a temple of the Holy Spirit, who is in you, whom you have received from God? You are not your own; you were bought at a price. Therefore honor God with your body" (1 Cor. 6:19 – 20).

Lord, thank You for not only giving me access to Your very throne but also for living Your life in and through me as Your temple. May I bring glory to You by honoring You with my body.

APRIL 20

... that by his death he might destroy
him who holds the power of death.

Hebrews 2:14

From the pen of Charles Spurgeon:

Dear child of God, death has lost its sting because the Devil's power over it has been destroyed. So stop your fear of dying. Ask God the Holy Spirit for the grace to be strengthened for that dreaded time through the intimate knowledge and firm belief of your Redeemer's death. If you live your life close to the cross of Calvary, you will view death with pleasure and welcome it with great delight when it comes. It is a precious thing to die in the Lord — a covenant blessing to sleep in Jesus. Death is no longer banishment but is a return from exile for the believer. It is a homegoing to the many mansions where our loved ones already dwell.

The distance between the glorified saints in heaven and the saints still serving here on earth seems great, but that is not true. We are not far from home, for in a mere moment we may be there. Our sails have already been raised to the wind and our souls have launched out upon the deep.

How long will our voyage be? How many wearying winds must beat upon our sails before we are safely moored in the port of peace? How long will our souls be tossed about by waves before we sail upon that sea that knows no storms?

Listen to the answer: "Away from the body and at home with the Lord" (2 Cor. 5:8 ESV). A distant ship has just departed but has already reached its safe haven. It just now spread its sail and was there. Consider that ancient boat upon the Lake of Galilee. A storm tossed it to and fro, but Jesus said, "Peace! Be still!" (Mark 4:39 ESV), "and immediately the boat reached the shore" (John 6:21).

Never think a long period ensues between the moment of death and the eternity of glory. When our eyes close on earth, they open in heaven. The "chariot of fire and horses of fire" (2 Kings 2:11) are not even an instant on the road.

Thus, dear child of God, what is there for you to fear in death, knowing that through the death of your Lord its curse and sting are destroyed? Death is now nothing more than a Jacob's ladder (see Gen. 28:12) whose feet are in a dark grave, but whose top reaches to glory everlasting.

From the pen of Jim Reimann:

"Behold, I am coming soon! My reward is with me, and I will give to everyone according to what he has done. I am the Alpha and the Omega, the First and the Last, the Beginning and the End" (Rev. 22:12 – 13).

Since "our citizenship is in heaven ... and we eagerly await a Savior from there, the Lord Jesus Christ" (Phil. 3:20), and because "God raised us up with Christ and seated us with him in the heavenly realms in Christ Jesus" (Eph. 2:6); this earthly realm is not my home. As Larry Norman once sang on his album "Only Visiting This Planet," "I'm just passin' through."

Lord, may my grip on this world be loose and may I keep heaven in my eyes. "Let us fix our eyes on Jesus, the author and perfecter of our faith, who for the joy set before him endured the cross, scorning its shame, and sat down at the right hand of the throne of God" (Heb. 12:2).

"He who testifies to these things says, 'Yes, I am coming soon.' Amen. Come, Lord Jesus" (Rev. 22:20).

APRIL 21

I know that my Redeemer lives.

Job 19:25

From the pen of Charles Spurgeon:

The foundation of Job's comfort lay in that one little word *my* — "*my* Redeemer" — and in the fact that the Redeemer truly lives. Oh, to take hold of the living Christ! We must have a claim to Him before we can enjoy Him.

What good is gold still in the mine? There are plenty of beggars in the gold regions of Peru and California. It is gold in their pockets, not in the mine, that will satisfy their necessities by purchasing the bread they need.

So it is with a redeemer who has not redeemed me or an avenger who will never fight for my life. Of what value are they? Therefore, never rest until by faith you can say, "Yes, I have cast myself upon my living Lord and He is mine."

Perhaps you find yourself today with a weak and feeble grasp on Him, thinking it presumptuous to say, "He lives as *my* Redeemer." Yet remember, "if you have faith as small as a mustard seed" (Matt. 17:20) you are entitled to say it.

Two additional words here also express Job's strong confidence — "*I know*." There are thousands of believers in Jesus who never go beyond saying, "I hope so" or "I believe so." But to experience true peace and comfort you must be able to say, "I know." And words such as *if, but,* and *perhaps* are sure murderers of that peace and comfort.

Doubts are nothing but gloomy clouds in times of sorrow. Like wasps they sting my soul! If I have any suspicion Christ is not mine, I experience the bitterness of "vinegar ... mingled with [the] gall" (Matt. 27:34 KJV) of death. But

if I know Jesus lives for *me*, darkness is no longer dark and light surrounds me even at night.

If Job could say, "I know," ages before the coming of Christ, we should never be less sure. And God forbid our positive statement should be presumption. May we see that our evidence is true lest we build our faith on false hope, and may we never be satisfied with stopping at the mere foundation, for it is from the upper floors we have the greatest view.

A living Redeemer who is truly mine is "inexpressible and glorious joy" (1 Peter 1:8).

From the pen of Jim Reimann:

It is evident throughout the Scriptures that the Lord wants us to have assurance of our faith and salvation. "I write these things to you who believe in the name of the Son of God *so that you may know* that you have eternal life" (1 John 5:13). "Let us draw near to God with a sincere heart in *full assurance of faith*" (Heb. 10:22).

The apostle Paul reminds us numerous times of the importance of the resurrection of Jesus, as if to say, "What good would it be to have a dead redeemer?" He proclaimed, "If Christ has not been raised, your faith is futile; you are still in your sins" (1 Cor. 15:17).

Father, thank You that "I know that my Redeemer lives" and intercedes with You on my behalf.

"He is able to save *completely* those who come to God through him, because *he always lives* to intercede for them" (Heb. 7:25).

APRIL 22

God exalted him.

Acts 5:31

From the pen of Charles Spurgeon:

Jesus our Lord, once crucified, dead, and buried, now sits on the throne of glory. The most exalted place heaven could grant is His by undisputed right. Yet how wonderful to remember that Christ's exaltation in heaven is one that is representative of each believer's exaltation as well! Jesus is exalted to the Father's right hand, and although as Jehovah God He has glorious attributes we as finite creatures cannot share, as our Mediator the various honors that clothe Him in heaven are also the inheritance of each and every saint.

What a delight to reflect on the intimate oneness of Christ with His people! We are truly one with Him and other members of His body. Therefore, His exaltation is our exaltation. Just as He has overcome all things and is seated with His Father on His throne, we will sit and reign with Him. He has a crown, so He gives us crowns as well. He has a throne but is not content having it solely to Himself, for His queen, arrayed in the "gold of Ophir" (Ps. 45:9), must be seated at His right hand. He cannot be glorified without His bride.

Dear believer, look up to Jesus now. Allow your eyes of faith to behold Him with many crowns on His head, and remember that someday you "shall be like him, [when you] shall see him as he is" (1 John 3:2). No, you will not be as great as Christ or be divine, but to a certain degree you will share the same honors, enjoy the same happiness, and possess the same dignity He possesses.

Until then, be content to live unknown, to walk the weary way through the fields of poverty or up the hills of affliction. For in just a little while we will "be priests of God and of Christ and will reign with him" (Rev. 20:6).

What a wonderful thought for the children of God! We have Christ as our glorious representative in heaven's courts even now, but soon He will come and receive us to Himself to be with Him there — not only to behold His glory but also to share His joy.

From the pen of Jim Reimann:

When times are tough, our greatest temptation is to give up. Each of us, however, should have heaven in our eyes. "I lift up my eyes to you, to you whose throne is in heaven" (Ps. 123:1).

Paul wrote of the entire creation being in the same condition we endure. All creation suffers as a result of the fall of mankind, yet he wrote the following as an encouragement to us:

> I consider that our present sufferings are not worth comparing with the glory that will be revealed in us.... The creation itself will be liberated from its bondage to decay and brought into the glorious freedom of the children of God. We know that the whole creation has been groaning as in the pains of childbirth right up to the present time. Not only so, but we ourselves ... groan inwardly as we wait eagerly for our adoption as sons, the redemption of our bodies. For in this hope we were saved. But hope that is seen is no hope at all. Who hopes for what he already has? But if we hope for what we do not yet have, we wait for it patiently.
>
> Romans 8:18, 21 – 25

Father, since we have Jesus in our hearts, may we keep heaven in our eyes, yet "wait for it patiently"!

APRIL 23

No, in all these things we are more than
conquerors through him who loved us.

Romans 8:37

From the pen of Charles Spurgeon:

We go to Christ for forgiveness, but then too
often go to the law seeking the power to fight our
sins. Paul rebukes us for this, "You foolish Galatians! Who has bewitched you [that ye should
not obey the truth (KJV)]? ... I would like to learn
just one thing from you: Did you receive the Spirit by observing the law, or by believing what you
heard? Are you so foolish? After beginning with
the Spirit, are you now trying to attain your goal
by human effort?" (Gal. 3:1 – 3).

Take your sins to the cross of Christ for the
old man can only be crucified there, for "our old
self was crucified with him" (Rom. 6:6). The only
weapon to fight sin is the spear that pierced the
side of Jesus.

Allow me to illustrate this. If you desire to overcome your angry temper, how can you go about it?
It is entirely possible you have never tried the only
correct way — going to Jesus with it.

How did I receive salvation? I went to Jesus
just as I was and trusted Him to save me. Thus,
I must put my angry temper to death the same
way. That is the only way to ever kill it. I must take
it to the cross and say to Jesus, "Lord, I trust You
to deliver me from it." There is no other way to
deliver it a deathblow.

Are you covetous? Are you entangled by "the
things of the world" (1 Cor. 7:31)? You can struggle
against various evils as long as you live, but if one of
them persistently entangles you, you will never be
delivered from it in any way whatsoever except by
the blood of Jesus. Take it to Christ and say, "Lord, I
have trusted You. Your name is Jesus 'because [You]
will save [Your] people from their sins' (Matt. 1:21).
Lord, this is one of my sins. Save me from it!"

The law is nothing without Christ as the
means to put our sins to death. All your prayers,
every time of repentance, and all of your tears
— all of them combined — are worth nothing
apart from Him.

No one except Jesus can do helpless sinners
any good — or helpless saints either. If you
desire to be a conqueror, you will be one only
"through him who loved [you]" (Rom. 8:37).
Your laurel crown must grow amid His olives in
Gethsemane.

From the pen of Jim Reimann:

I am as foolish as the Galatians to think my
works, which did not bring me salvation, can in
some way maintain that salvation for me. If that
were the case, my eternal salvation would be the
result of my work, not the work of Christ, and His
death would have been for nothing. Jesus Himself prayed, "My Father, if it is possible, may this
cup be taken from me" (Matt. 26:39). It was not
possible — He had to "drink" the cup of suffering
on the cross. There was no other way!

And if His death was only sufficient for my
sins committed before He saved me — and not
sufficient for my future sins — then He would
need to die again and again each time I sin. Consider these words from Hebrews:

"Nor did he enter heaven to offer himself
again and again, the way the high priest enters
the Most Holy Place every year.... Then Christ
would have had to suffer many times.... But now
he has appeared once for all at the end of the ages
to do away with sin by the sacrifice of himself"
(Heb. 9:25 – 26).

APRIL 24

Because of all this we make a firm covenant.

Nehemiah 9:38 ESV

From the pen of Charles Spurgeon:

There are many times in our walk with the Lord it is fitting and beneficial to renew our covenant with Him, such as after recovering from an illness, when like Hezekiah years have been added to our life. (See 2 Kings 20:1 – 11.) After being delivered from some trouble or distress, when our joy has been renewed, let us return to the foot of the cross and renew our consecration. And especially after we have sinned, grieving the Holy Spirit and bringing dishonor to the cause of God, let us look to the blood that can make us "whiter than snow" (Ps. 51:7) and once again offer ourselves to the Lord.

However, not only should times of trouble determine our reconfirmation of our dedication to God, but times of prosperity should do the same. When we encounter what could be considered crowning moments of mercy, then surely it is the Lord who has crowned us. We should return the honor, crowning Him anew with all the jewels of His divine regalia He has stored in the jewelry chest of our hearts. May our God sit on the throne of our love arrayed in His royal apparel.

If only we would learn the profitable lessons of our prosperity, we would not need so much adversity! If we could reap all the goodness conferred upon us in His kiss, we would not so often feel the pain of His rod of discipline.

Have we lately received a blessing we did not expect? Has the Lord expanded our sphere of influence? Can we sing of His multiplied mercies? Then this is the day to put our hand on "the horns of the altar" (Ps. 118:27) and say, "Bind me here with cords, my God, for ever and ever."

Just as we need the fulfillment of new promises from God, let us offer renewed prayers that our old vows remain honored in our lives. This morning may we make a "sure covenant" with Him, once again remembering the sufferings of Jesus with gratitude in our hearts.

From the pen of Jim Reimann:

How many times have we seen even believers unable to handle the blessings of God! Today's devotion should be a reminder to us it is important to handle trials and blessings in much the same way. After all, the Lord has promised to use "all things" for our good that we may "be conformed to the likeness of his Son" (Rom. 8:28 – 29).

What is the difference between the rainstorms of life and showers of blessing? Isn't it only the intensity of the rain? Therefore, wouldn't it be true that what enables us to withstand the showers of blessing would be the same root structure that enables us to withstand the storms?

The storms of life should drive us to the Word of God so our roots will grow deeply into Him. May the Lord convict our hearts that — even in good times — we need those roots to remain strong and to thrive.

Father, every day — whether a day of trial or blessing — may I be rooted in Your Word alone.

"They received the message with great eagerness and examined the Scriptures every day" (Acts 17:11).

APRIL 25

Arise, my darling, my beautiful one, and come with me.

Song of Songs 2:10

From the pen of Charles Spurgeon:

Listen! I hear "the voice of my beloved!" (Song 2:8 ESV). He speaks to me! Fair spring weather is smiling on the face of the earth, and He desires I not be spiritually asleep while all of nature around me is waking from her winter's rest. He bids me "Arise," and well He does, for long enough I have been lying among the weeds of worldliness.

"He is risen" (Matt. 28:6 KJV) and I am risen in Him. Then why should I cling to the dust? From lesser loves, desires, pursuits, and aspirations I desire to rise toward Him. He calls me by the sweet title, "my darling," and considers me beautiful. Is this not a good argument to "arise"!

If He has exalted me to this place and thinks of me as lovely, how can I linger in "the tents of Kedar" (Song 1:5) and seek my friends among "the children of mankind" (Ps. 31:19 ESV)? He bids, "Come with me." Further and further from everything selfish, lowly, worldly, and sinful He calls me. Yes, from the outwardly religious world that does not know Him, and which has no understanding of the mystery of the higher way, He calls me.

"Come with me." The call has no harsh sound to it in my ears. Yet what is there that holds me to this wilderness of vanity and sin?

O my Lord, I desire to come with You, but I am tangled among the thorns and cannot escape them as I would like. I desire, if it were possible, to have neither eyes, nor ears, nor a heart for sin. You call me to Yourself by saying, "Come with me," and it is a melodious call indeed. To come to You is to come home from

exile, to come to land after a raging storm, to come to rest after tremendous toil, to come to the goal of my desires and the summit of my wishes. But, Lord, how can a stone arise? How can a lump of clay come with You from deep within a horrible pit?

Raise me! Draw me! Your grace can do it. Send forth Your Holy Spirit to kindle the flames of love in my heart, and I will continue to rise until I leave life and time behind and indeed come to You.

From the pen of Jim Reimann:

Oh, how we are loved!

And so we know and rely on the love God has for us. God is love. Whoever lives in love lives in God, and God in him. In this way, love is made complete among us so that we will have confidence on the day of judgment, because in this world we are like him. There is no fear in love. But perfect love drives out fear, because fear has to do with punishment. The one who fears is not made perfect in love. We love because he first loved us.

1 John 4:16 – 19

Father, thank You for the love expressed in the death of Your Son to redeem me, for "greater love has no one than this, that he lay down his life for his friends" (John 15:13). Help me express Your love to others by being willing to give of myself in the way You have given to me — not sparingly, but generously; not selfishly, but selflessly.

"God has poured out his love into our hearts by the Holy Spirit, whom he has given us" (Rom. 5:5).

APRIL 26

Do this in remembrance of me.

1 Corinthians 11:24

From the pen of Charles Spurgeon:

Indeed, it seems Christians may forget Christ! There would be no need for this loving exhortation if there were not the fearsome presumption that our memories might prove disloyal. And this presumption does not lack substance, for alas, it is all too well confirmed by our experience — not as a mere possibility, but as a lamentable fact.

Yet it seems nearly impossible that those who have been redeemed by "the blood of the [dying] Lamb" (Rev. 12:11), and loved "with an everlasting love" (Jer. 31:3) by the eternal Son of God, could ever forget their gracious Savior. But as startling as that is to hear, it is, alas, too apparent to the eye to allow us to deny the crime.

Forget Him who never forgot us! Forget Him who poured out His blood for our sins! Forget Him who loved us even to the death! Can it be possible?

Yes, it is not only possible but our conscience must confess it is sadly a fault in each of us. We simply allow Him to be a traveler tarrying only for the night. He who should be made the abiding tenant in our memories is only a visitor there. The cross, where we would think our memory would linger and forgetfulness would be an unknown intruder, is desecrated by the feet of forgetfulness.

Doesn't your conscience confirm this is true? Don't you find yourself forgetful of Jesus? Some earthly person has captured your heart instead, and you remain unmindful of Him upon whom your affections should be placed. Your eyes are focused on some earthly business when you should fix your eyes steadily upon the cross. It is the constant turmoil of the world and the continual attraction of earthly things that turns a soul away from Christ. While your memory all too well recalls a poisonous weed, it allows the "rose of Sharon" (Song 2:1) to wither.

Let us challenge ourselves to tie a heavenly "forget-me-not" around our hearts for Jesus our Beloved — and, whatever else may slip from our memory, *let us hold fast to Him.*

From the pen of Jim Reimann:

Hold fast to Christ! What a powerful exhortation against forgetfulness as "the cares of this world" (Mark 4:19 KJV) creep into our lives, turning our focus from the Savior. Indeed, we can take hold of Him through the power of His Holy Spirit. Yet thankfully Jesus has first taken hold of us.

> I press on to take hold of that for which *Christ Jesus took hold of me.* Brothers, I do not consider myself yet to have taken hold of it. But one thing I do: Forgetting what is behind and straining toward what is ahead, I press on toward the goal to win the prize for which God has called me heavenward in Christ Jesus.
>
> Philippians 3:12 – 14

Yes, even the apostle Paul did not consider himself to have fully "taken hold," but he continued to "press on toward the goal."

Father, "Let us hold fast the confession of our hope without wavering, for he who promised is faithful" (Heb. 10:23 ESV). Let us hold fast to "Christ Jesus our hope" (1 Tim. 1:1).

APRIL 27

God, even our own God, shall bless us.

Psalm 67:6 KJV

From the pen of Charles Spurgeon:

It is strange how little we make use of the spiritual blessings God gives us, but even stranger how little we make use of God Himself. Although He is "our own God," we don't stay in continual contact with Him and we ask Him for very little. How seldom we seek counsel at the hands of the Lord! How often we simply go about our business without seeking His guidance! Even in our troubles we constantly strive to bear our burdens ourselves instead of casting them upon the Lord so He may sustain us! (See 1 Peter 5:7.)

This is not due to some prohibition against it, for the Lord Himself suggests to us, in essence, "I am yours, dear soul, come and make use of Me as you will. You may freely approach My spiritual storehouse, and the more often you come the more welcome you will be." So it is our own fault if we do not partake in the riches of our God.

Therefore, since you have such a Friend and He invites you to come, why not receive from Him daily? Never go without when you have a God to go to, and never fear or faint when God is there to help you. Go to your treasure and take whatever you need, for He has more than you could even want. Learn the divine skill of allowing God to be all things to you. He can supply everything you need, or better yet, He Himself can be all you need.

I urge you then to make use of your God. Make use of Him through prayer, going to Him often, for "he is your God" (Deut. 10:21). O believer, will you fail to use such a great privilege?

Flee to Him and tell Him all your wants. Use Him constantly "by faith" (Rom. 1:17) at all times.

If some evil darkness has clouded your life, use your God as the sun, and if some strong enemy has attacked you, find your shield in Jehovah, for "He is your shield" (Deut. 33:29) and your sun. If you have lost your way in the mazes of life, use Him as your guide, for He will direct you.

Whoever you may be and wherever you may be, remember — God is all you may ever want, is everywhere you need Him to be, and can do everything you could ever want Him to do.

From the pen of Jim Reimann:

Indeed, our Lord is a personal God who *lavishes* His riches on us. Yet as we grow in Him, maturing from newborn babies to seasoned saints, our requests of Him should mature as well.

He says, "If my people, who are called by my name, will humble themselves and pray and *seek my face* and turn from their wicked ways, then will I hear from heaven" (2 Chron. 7:14).

Notice how He says "seek my face" and not "seek my hand." When we seek His face we seek to know Him better, but when we seek His hand we seek only the things He can give us.

What would we rather have, "the things of the world" (1 Cor. 7:31) or "the love the Father has lavished on us" (1 John 3:1) and "God's grace that he lavished on us with all wisdom and understanding" (Eph. 1:7 – 8)?

Father, my prayer is that You would help me loosen my grasp on the meaningless "things of the world" and deepen my desire for You alone.

APRIL 28

Remember your word to your servant,
for you have given me hope.

Psalm 119:49

From the pen of Charles Spurgeon:

Whatever your special need may be, a promise may readily be found in the Bible to meet that need. Are you weak and weary because your road is rough? Then here is the promise: "He gives strength to the weary and increases the power of the weak" (Isa. 40:29). So when you read such a promise, take it to the great Promiser and ask Him to fulfill His own word.

Are you seeking after Christ and thirsting for closer communion with Him? If so, then this promise shines like a star upon you: "Blessed are those who hunger and thirst for righteousness, for they will be filled" (Matt. 5:6). Take that promise to the throne continually and do not plead for anything else. Just go to God over and over again with this: "Lord, You have promised; therefore, 'Do as you promised'" (2 Sam. 7:25).

Are you distressed due to sin in your life and burdened with the heavy load of your iniquities? Then listen to these words: "I, even I, am he who blots out your transgressions ... and remembers your sins no more" (Isa. 43:25). Since you have no merit of your own as a basis to plead His pardon, plead His written-down covenants and He will perform them.

Are you afraid of not being able to endure to the end after having thought of yourself as a child of God? Do you fear, even as a child of His, that ultimately you will be proven nothing but an outcast? If that is your fear, take this word of grace to His throne and plead it: "Though the mountains be shaken and the hills be removed, yet my unfailing love for you will not be shaken nor my covenant of peace be removed" (Isa. 54:10).

If you have lost the sweet sense of the Savior's presence and are seeking Him with a sorrowful heart, remember these promises: "Return to me, and I will return to you" (Mal. 3:7); and "For a brief moment I abandoned you, but with deep compassion I will bring you back" (Isa. 54:7).

Whatever your fears or wants, feast your faith on God's own words. Then return to the Bank of Faith with a check signed by your Father's own hand, saying to Him, "Remember your word to your servant, for you have given me hope."

From the pen of Jim Reimann:

Sometimes it may seem a little presumptuous on our part to stand before God's throne and say to Him, as King David did, "Do as you promised." It sounds presumptuous even for a king, doesn't it? And perhaps all the more outrageous for us!

Yet it is exactly what the Lord would have us do. His Word declares, "You do not have, because you do not ask God" (James 4:2 – 3); "Ask of me, and I will make the nations your inheritance, the ends of the earth your possession" (Ps. 2:8); and "You did not choose me, but I chose you and appointed you to go and bear fruit — fruit that will last. Then the Father will give you whatever you ask in my name" (John 15:16).

I thank You, Father, that You are not only a promise-making God, but also a promise-keeping God.

APRIL 29

You are my refuge in the day of disaster.

Jeremiah 17:17

From the pen of Charles Spurgeon:

The path of the Christian is not always bright with sunshine, for even believers have their seasons of darkness and storms. True, it is written in God's Word, referring to the ways of godly wisdom and understanding: "Her ways are pleasant ways, and all her paths are peace" (Prov. 3:17). It is also a great truth that the Christian faith has been designed by God to give believers happiness in this life as well as true bliss in heaven above. And despite the following truth that "The path of the righteous is like the first gleam of dawn, shining ever brighter till the full light of day" (Prov. 4:18), experience tells us that sometimes the sun is eclipsed. At times clouds will obscure the believer's sun, causing him to walk in darkness and making him unable to see the light.

There are many believers who have rejoiced in God's presence for a season. They have basked in the sunshine in the early phases of their Christian walk and have walked "in green pastures ... beside quiet waters" (Ps. 23:2). Then suddenly they find the once glorious sky is clouded, and instead of walking "the land of Goshen" (Josh. 11:16 ESV) they find themselves forced to tread the sandy desert; and instead of sweet quiet streams, they find troubled waters that are bitter to the taste. Then they say, "Surely if I were a child of God this would not have happened."

Oh, you who are walking in darkness, never say this! Even the best of God's saints must drink of the bitterness of "the wormwood and the gall" (Lam. 3:19 ESV), and the most precious of His children must bear their cross. No Christian has ever enjoyed perpetual prosperity, and no believer is continually able to keep his joyful harp away from the weeping willow. (See Ps. 137:1 – 2.)

Perhaps at the onset of your Christian walk the Lord assigned you a smooth, unclouded path because you were weak and fearful. He was simply protecting His newborn lamb from the harsh cold wind. But now that you are stronger in your spiritual life, you must enter the more mature and rougher experience of God's full-grown children.

We need harsh winds and storms to exercise our faith, to tear away the rotten limbs of self-dependence, and to root us more firmly in Christ. The difficult days of evil reveal to us the true value of our glorious hope.

From the pen of Jim Reimann:

Without trials we would often miss seeing God's miraculous power. Unless we step into the raging sea, we will not see the Lord make a dry path for us, and unless we walk through the dry and dangerous desert, we will never see the miracle of a desert stream.

After all, who but the Lord can make a dry place in the sea and a wet place in the desert! "This is what the LORD says — he who made a way through the sea, a path through the mighty waters ... See, I am doing a new thing! Now it springs up; do you not perceive it? I am making a way in the desert and streams in the wasteland" (Isa. 43:16, 19).

Thank You, sovereign Lord, for the difficult days. May I never miss even one of the miracles You have for me by shrinking from the difficulties of life. May You receive glory in my daily walk, wherever that walk may lead.

APRIL 30

All the Israelites grumbled.

Numbers 14:2

From the pen of Charles Spurgeon:

There are grumblers among Christians today just as there were grumblers in the Israelite camps of old. When the Lord deems it necessary to dispense His rod of correction, there are believers who cry out against it, saying, "Why am I so afflicted! What have I done to be disciplined in this way?"

Allow me to have a word with you, O grumbler! Why should you grumble against the correction dispensed by your heavenly Father? Is it even possible for Him to treat you more severely than you deserve? Consider what a rebel you once were — yet He has pardoned you! Surely, if in His wisdom He now sees fit to discipline you, you should not complain. After all, have you really been afflicted more strongly than your sins deserve? When you honestly consider the corruption in your heart, will you continue to question the level of correction needed to remove it?

Evaluate yourself, attempting to discern the great amount of dross mixed with your gold, and then tell me if the refiner's fire is too hot to purge such a large amount of dross? Doesn't your proud rebellious spirit prove your heart is not completely sanctified? Isn't your grumbling itself contrary to the holy, submissive nature of God's children? Don't you need the correction?

If you continue to complain against God's discipline, take heed, for it goes hard for grumblers. God always corrects His children twice if they do not patiently submit to His first attempt. But know this: "He does not willingly bring affliction or grief to the children of men" (Lam. 3:33). All His corrections are sent in love to purify you and to draw you closer to Himself.

Recognizing your Father's hand will most assuredly help you bear His discipline with the patient spirit of submission "because the Lord disciplines those he loves, and he punishes everyone he accepts as a son" (Heb. 12:6). If you "endure hardship as discipline; God is treating you as sons" (Heb. 12:7).

"Do not grumble, as some of them did — and were killed by the destroying angel" (1 Cor. 10:10).

From the pen of Jim Reimann:

Complaining is so common it is almost as though we have forgotten it is sin. We tolerate it in our lives and in the lives of those around us, but it still grieves the heart of God.

"Do not grieve the Holy Spirit of God, with whom you were sealed for the day of redemption. Get rid of all bitterness, rage and anger ... along with every form of malice" (Eph. 4:30 – 31). Doesn't complaining lead us to "bitterness, rage and anger"? Then, as Paul says, we are to "get rid" of it!

Of course, we will get rid of it — one way or the other. Either we will remove it from our lives ourselves or we will force the Lord to remove it through correction and discipline. So it comes down to this, which road would you rather travel? And which road will bring greater glory to God?

James tells us: "God opposes the proud but gives grace to the humble. Submit yourselves, then, to God" (James 4:6 – 7). But He goes on to say, in essence, that instead of grieving the Lord, we should "grieve, mourn, and wail" (v. 9) over our own sin.

May

MAY 1

His cheeks are as a bed of spices, as sweet flowers.

Song of Songs 5:13 KJV

From the pen of Charles Spurgeon:

Yes, the month of flowers is here! March winds and April showers have done their work, and the earth is now arrayed with beauty. Come, my soul, don your festive clothes and go forth to gather garlands of heavenly thoughts.

Believer, you know where to go, for the "bed of spices" is well known to you and you have often smelled the perfume of "sweet flowers." So you will go at once to your beloved and find nothing but loveliness and pure joy in Him. Those kind cheeks, once so rudely beaten, often wet with tears of sympathy, then defiled and spat upon, is the face that still smiles with mercy as a fragrant perfume to your heart.

O Lord Jesus, You did not hide Your face from shame and spitting, so I will find my dearest delight in praising You. Your cheeks, furrowed by the plow of grief and crimson from red lines of blood flowing from your thorn-crowned temples, display marks of love beyond all bounds, which thrills my soul far more than precious perfume.

If I could not see Jesus' entire face, it would be enough to see His cheeks, for the least glimpse of Him is amazingly refreshing to my spirit and yields abundant joys. In Him I do not find simply one fragrance, but "a bed of spices." I find not one flower, but all kinds of "sweet flowers." He is my rose, my lily, my violet, and my "cluster of henna blossoms" (Song 1:14). Because I have Him, I have May year round. My soul goes out each day to bathe its happy face in the morning dew of His grace and to find comfort in the singing of the birds of His promises.

Precious Lord Jesus, allow me to truly know the blessedness that dwells in abiding, unbroken fellowship with You. I am a poor and worthless soul, whose cheek You have humbled Yourself to kiss! O Lord, may I kiss You in return with the kisses of my lips.

From the pen of Jim Reimann:

Jesus is a precious flower. But for His godly fragrance to fill the earth, He had to be crushed, just as flowers are crushed to make perfume. And we should never forget "He was crushed for our iniquities" (Isa. 53:5).

Shortly before that crushing took place, however, we see this story:

"While he was in Bethany ... a woman came with an alabaster jar of very expensive perfume, made of pure nard. She broke the jar and poured the perfume on his head" (Mark 14:3). Notice how even the jar itself had to be broken before the perfume could be poured out. And it was not until the jar was broken that "the house was filled with the fragrance of the perfume" (John 12:3).

A pleasing fragrance is obviously important to God, for His Word mentions seventy-eight times that an offering made to the Lord in the proper way is "an aroma pleasing" (Lev. 1:9) to Him. But the proper way of making the offering came with the idea of sacrifice on the part of the one making the offering. With that in mind, may we sacrificially offer ourselves to the Lord.

Dear Jesus, may my life be crushed, broken, and poured out according to Your will. And may my daily walk be a "pleasing aroma" (Gen. 8:21) to You.

MAY 2

My prayer is not that you take them out of the world.
John 17:15

From the pen of Charles Spurgeon:

In God's timing a joyous and blessed event will be experienced by all believers — going home to be with Jesus. In a few short years the Lord's soldiers who are now fighting "the good fight of faith" (1 Tim. 6:12) will be through with the conflict and will have entered into "the joy of the LORD" (Neh. 8:10). Although Christ prays for His people to be with Him where He is eventually, note that He does not ask for them to be taken away from this world to heaven immediately. He desires they stay here for now.

Yet how often does a weary pilgrim toss up the prayer: "Oh, that I had the wings of a dove! I would fly away and be at rest" (Ps. 55:6). Christ, however, does not pray like that. He leaves us in His Father's hands until, like fully ripened sheaves of corn, we will each be gathered into our Master's storehouse. Jesus does not ask for our instantaneous removal through death because our abiding in these bodies is needed by those around us, if not profitable for ourselves. He asks His Father to "protect [us] from the evil one" (John 17:15), but He never asks for us to be admitted into our inheritance in glory until we are at our God-determined age.

Christians often want to die when they encounter trouble. When asked why, they will say, "Because I want to be with the Lord." I fear, however, it is not so much that they are longing to be with the Lord as it is that they desire to get rid of their troubles. If this were not true, then they would express the same wish for death when they are not experiencing such difficult trials. They desire to go home to heaven not so much for the company of the Savior as much as they desire to be at rest.

It is quite appropriate to desire to depart if we can do it in the same spirit Paul did, because to "be with Christ ... is better by far" (Phil. 1:23). But a desire to leave simply to escape trouble is a selfish one.

Instead, may your concern and desire be to glorify God by your life here as long as He pleases even though it may be in the midst of toil, conflict, and suffering. Leave it with Him to say, "It is enough" (1 Kings 19:4 ESV).

From the pen of Jim Reimann:

Even Elijah, that great prophet of God, came to a point of despair. "He ... went a day's journey into the desert. He came to a broom tree, sat down under it and prayed that he might die. 'I have had enough, LORD,' he said. 'Take my life; I am no better than my ancestors'" (1 Kings 19:4).

One of the greatest characteristics of God's Word is that we see the humanness of even the major characters. Indeed, "Elijah was a man just like us" (James 5:17), but look how God used him!

Dear believer, you may be experiencing some grievous trial today, but don't despair. Consider the words of the apostle Paul, who said:

> We do not want you to be uninformed, brothers, about the hardships we suffered.... We were under great pressure, far beyond our ability to endure, so that we despaired even of life. Indeed, in our hearts we felt the sentence of death. But this happened that we might not rely on ourselves but on God, who raises the dead.
>
> 2 Corinthians 1:8 – 9

MAY 3

In this world you will have trouble.

John 16:33

From the pen of Charles Spurgeon:

Dear believer, do you find yourself asking the reason for this? Look upward to your heavenly Father and behold His purity and holiness. Do you realize that someday you will be like Him? Do you believe, however, it will be easy to be conformed to His image? (See Rom. 8:29.) Will you not require much refining in "the furnace of affliction" (Isa. 48:10) to become pure? Will it be an easy process to rid you of your sinful impurities and make you "perfect ... as your heavenly Father is perfect" (Matt. 5:48)?

Next, dear Christian, turn your eyes downward. Do you realize what enemies you have beneath your feet? You were once a servant of Satan, and no king willingly loses his subjects. Do you really believe Satan will leave you alone? No, he will always harass you, for he "prowls around like a roaring lion looking for someone to devour" (1 Peter 5:8). Therefore, believer, expect trouble when you look beneath your feet.

Next, look around you. Do you realize where you are? You are in the enemy's country — "an alien and a stranger" in his land. The world is not your friend. If it is, then you are not God's friend, for whoever is "a friend of the world makes himself an enemy of God" (James 4:4 ESV). Be assured you will find enemies everywhere. When you sleep, remember you are only resting on the battlefield, and when you are walking, suspect an ambush from behind every hedge. Just as mosquitoes are said to bite strangers more than natives, the trials of this earth will be harsher to you.

Finally, look within yourself, into your own heart, and observe what is there. Sin and self are still within you. If you had no devil to tempt you, no enemies to fight you, and no world to ensnare you, you would still find enough evil within you to bring severe trouble to yourself, for "the heart is deceitful above all things, and desperately wicked" (Jer. 17:9 KJV).

Thus, expect trouble but do not despair because of it, for God is with you to help and to strengthen you. He has said, "I will be with [you] in trouble, I will deliver [you] and honor [you]" (Ps. 91:15).

From the pen of Jim Reimann:

David got it right! He knew his sinfulness, for he wrote, "I know my transgressions, and my sin is always before me" (Ps. 51:3). Yet he trusted God to "create in me a pure heart, O God, and renew a steadfast spirit within me" (Ps. 51:10).

And when it came to trouble, he got it right once again. Here is what he said:

> One thing I ask of the Lord, this is what I seek: that I may dwell in the house of the Lord.... For in the day of trouble he will keep me safe in his dwelling.... Then my head will be exalted above the enemies who surround me; at his tabernacle will I sacrifice with shouts of joy; I will sing and make music to the Lord. Hear my voice when I call, O Lord; be merciful to me and answer me. My heart says of you, "Seek his face!" Your face, Lord, I will seek.
>
> Psalm 27:4 – 8

Dear Father, I know "some trust in chariots and some in horses, but we trust in the name of the Lord our God" (Ps. 20:7).

May 4

Do men make their own gods?
Yes, but they are not gods!
Jeremiah 16:20

From the pen of Charles Spurgeon:

One of the most persistent and troubling sins of ancient Israel was idolatry, and we as spiritual Israel are subject to the same foolishness. "The star of … Rephan" (Acts 7:43) no longer shines, and women are no longer "mourning for Tammuz" (Ezek. 8:14), but the god of money still imposes his golden calf, and the shrines of pride are not forsaken.

Self in various forms struggles to subdue God's chosen ones under its dominion, and the flesh sets up its altars wherever it can find room for them. These "favorite children" are often the cause of much sin in believers, and the Lord is grieved when He sees us obsessively doting on them. If we continue to do so, they will become as great a curse to us as Absalom was to David.

It is true that "they are not gods," for these objects of our foolish love are very doubtful blessings. The comfort they bring us even now is dangerous, and what help they can render us in a time of trouble is very little indeed. Why then are we so captivated by these vanities of life? We pity the poor heathen who worships a god of stone, while we worship our god of money. And is our god of flesh really superior to one of wood?

In truth the foolishness of this sin is the same in either case. Yet in our case it is even more egregious because we have more light and we sin directly in God's face. Heathens bow to a false deity and have never known the true God; we commit two evils — we forsake the living God to turn away to idols.

May the Lord purge us from this grievous iniquity!

> The dearest idol I have known,
> Whate'er that idol be;
> Help me to tear it from Thy throne,
> And worship only Thee.
>
> William Cowper, 1731 – 1800

From the pen of Jim Reimann:

Believers and unbelievers alike often say, "Money can't buy happiness," yet it appears our actions attempt to prove otherwise. In fact, the gods of money, power, sex, and drugs seem to rule our culture. When will we finally recognize the fact that this is nothing less than idolatry!

Here is what the Lord says, "If you turn aside and forsake my statutes and my commandments that I have set before you, and go and serve other gods and worship them, then I will pluck you up from my land" (2 Chron. 7:19 – 20 ESV).

Never despair, however, for the believer's hope is found in obedience to the Lord and in submission to His will.

"If my people, who are called by my name, will humble themselves and pray and seek my face and turn from their wicked ways, then will I hear from heaven and will forgive their sin and will heal their land" (2 Chron. 7:14).

Father, I pray that You "might give [us] repentance and forgiveness" (Acts 5:31) for our sin of idolatry and "heal [our] land."

MAY 5

I will be their God, and they will be my people.

2 Corinthians 6:16

From the pen of Charles Spurgeon:

What a wonderful name: "My people"! What an uplifting revelation: "Their God"! There is a great deal of meaning — something very special — expressed in the two words "My people."

"To the LORD your God belong the heavens, even the highest heavens, the earth and everything in it" (Deut. 10:14), and He reigns among "the children of men" (Ps. 21:10 KJV). Yet it is only those whom He has chosen and purchased for Himself — and no one else — whom He calls "My people." These words signify the idea of ownership and a special relationship, "For the LORD's portion is his people, Jacob his allotted inheritance" (Deut. 32:9).

All the nations of the earth are His and the entire world is in His control, yet they are His people, His chosen. More than that, they are His possessions, for He has done more for them than anyone else, having "bought [them] with his own blood" (Acts 20:28). He has brought them to Himself and focused His heart of affection on them, for He has loved them "with an everlasting love" (Jer. 31:3) — a love "many waters cannot quench" (Song 8:7) and one the passage of time will never diminish even to the least degree.

Dear friend, can you, by faith, see yourself among His people? Can you look to heaven and say, "'My Lord and my God' (John 20:28). Mine because of the intimate relationship that entitles me to call You Father. Mine because of the holy fellowship I have with You, to my delight, when you are pleased to reveal Yourself to me, something You never do with those of the world"?

Can you read His inspired Word and find the certificate of your salvation? Can you read your name written in His precious blood? Can you, by humble faith, take hold of Jesus' robe and say, "My Christ"?

If you can, then God calls you and others like you "My people." For, if God is your God and Christ is your Christ, the Lord has a special individual affinity toward you. You are the object of His choosing and have been "accepted in [His] beloved" Son (Eph. 1:6 KJV).

From the pen of Jim Reimann:

Yes, we belong to Christ. Yet what seems even more amazing is that we have been made full-fledged members of His family. We are His children!

The Scriptures teach that believers are adopted children of Abraham. Thus, we are not God's physical children, but His spiritual children, for "it is not the natural children who are God's children, but it is the children of the promise who are regarded as Abraham's offspring" (Rom. 9:8). "Understand, then, that those who believe are children of Abraham" (Gal. 3:7).

"The Spirit himself testifies with our spirit that we are God's children. Now if we are children, then we are heirs — heirs of God and co-heirs with Christ, if indeed we share in his sufferings in order that we may also share in his glory" (Rom. 8:16 – 17).

As His child, "all things are yours, whether ... the world or life or death or the present or the future — all are yours, and you are Christ's, and Christ is God's" (1 Cor. 3:21 – 23 ESV).

What an amazing Savior is *ours*!

MAY 6

We live in him.

1 John 4:13

From the pen of Charles Spurgeon:

Do you want a house for your soul? But do you ask, "What is the purchase price?" The price is actually much less than our proud human nature would like to pay. It cannot be bought with money — no matter how much. Still, you say that at least you would like to pay a respectable rent. You would love to *do something* to have Christ. If that is the case, then you cannot have the house at all, for it is without a price.

Are you willing to take my Master's house along with its eternal lease while paying nothing for it — nothing but the ground lease of loving and serving Him forever? Will you take Jesus and "live in him"? His house is fully furnished with all you need and is filled with more riches than you could spend throughout eternity. And inside His house you can have intimate communion with Christ and feast on His love, for the tables are well stocked with enough food to last forever. Once inside you can find rest for your weariness in Jesus, and from its windows you can view heaven itself.

Will you take the house? If your soul is homeless you will say, "I would like to have the house, but may I really have it?" Yes, you may, if you have the key. And the key is this: Come to Jesus. Still you say, "But I am too shabbily dressed for such a house as this." Don't worry, there are beautiful new clothes for you inside.

If you feel guilty and condemned — come. And although the house is too good for you, Christ will make you good enough for it over time. He will wash and cleanse you until you are able to sing, "We live in him."

Dear believer, how thrilled you must be to have such a dwelling place! You are greatly privileged indeed, for you have a "rock of refuge" (Ps. 71:3) where you are forever safe. And by living in Him, not only do you have a perfect and totally secure house but also one that is everlasting. When this world has long since faded away like a dream, your house will live and stand more indestructible than marble and more solid than granite. Your house will be as self-existent as God, for it *is* God Himself.

"We live in him"!

From the pen of Jim Reimann:

The two words that best sum up the writings of the apostle Paul are "*in Christ.*" These words are used ninety-eight times in the NIV Bible, once by the writer of Hebrews, three times by Peter, once in Acts (referring to Paul's message), and ninety-three times by Paul himself in his epistles. He expressed it in ways such as, "You also were included *in Christ* when you heard the word of truth, the gospel of your salvation" (Eph. 1:13).

Yes, we "live in him," and although the apostle John didn't use those exact words, he certainly understood its truth, for he wrote:

"If anyone acknowledges that Jesus is the Son of God, God lives in him and he in God. And so we know and rely on the love God has for us. God is love. Whoever lives in love lives in God, and God in him" (1 John 4:15 – 16).

Thank You, Lord, that "surely goodness and love will follow me all the days of my life, and I will dwell in the house of the LORD forever" (Ps. 23:6).

MAY 7

Many followed him,
and he healed them all.

Matthew 12:15 ESV

From the pen of Charles Spurgeon:

What an amazing number of hideously disgusting sicknesses must have thrust themselves under the eyes of Jesus! Yet we never read He was disgusted but, instead, He patiently attended to every case. What an unprecedented variety of evils must have congregated at His feet! What smelly, sickening open sores He must have encountered! Yet He was always prepared for every new facet of evil and was victorious over evil regardless of its form.

Evil arrows could fly from wherever they will, but He always quenched their flaming power. Whether the heat of fever, the cold of poor circulation, the tremors of palsy, the raging of insanity, the filth of leprosy, or the darkness of blindness, all knew the power of His word and fled at His command. Regardless of the disease, He triumphed over evil and received honor from the captives He delivered.

He came, He saw, He conquered — everywhere. This is still true this morning. Whatever my specific problem may be, my beloved Physician can heal me. And regardless the condition of others whom I remember in prayer this moment, I can have hope in Jesus that He is able to heal them of their sins. Whether my child, my friend, or my dearest loved one, I can have hope for each and every one when I simply remember the healing power of my Lord.

Even when it comes to my own situation, however severe my struggle with sin and sickness, I can still "be of good cheer" (Matt. 9:2 KJV). He who once walked this earth, dispensing healing as He went, still dispenses His grace and works miracles among people today. Let me earnestly go to Him right now.

Let me praise Him this morning as I remember how He worked His spiritual cures that brought Him the most renown. He took our sicknesses upon Himself, for "by his wounds we are healed" (Isa. 53:5). The church here on earth is full of souls healed by our beloved Physician, and the inhabitants of heaven itself now confess, "He healed them all" (Matt. 12:15 ESV).

Come then, my soul, and tell the world of the goodness of His grace. Let it "be for the LORD's renown, for an everlasting sign, which will not be destroyed" (Isa. 55:13).

From the pen of Jim Reimann:

Each of us had a sickness unto death — the sickness of sin. Thankfully, the great Physician "came to seek and to save" sinners, as Jesus Himself said while visiting Zacchaeus, the hated tax collector. Ironically, it is in the story of Matthew, another tax collector, where Jesus equates a sick person's need of a doctor to a sinner's need of a savior.

While Jesus was having dinner at Matthew's house, many tax collectors and "sinners" came and ate with him and his disciples. When the Pharisees saw this, they asked his disciples, "Why does your teacher eat with tax collectors and 'sinners'?" On hearing this, Jesus said, "It is not the healthy who need a doctor, but the sick.... For I have not come to call the righteous, but sinners."

Matthew 9:10 – 13

I thank You, dear God, for Jesus — the "balm in Gilead" (Jer. 8:22) *and my great Physician.*

MAY 8

The man who was healed had no idea who it was.

John 5:13

From the pen of Charles Spurgeon:

Years pass quickly for those who are healthy and happy, but thirty-eight years must have dragged wearily along in the life of this poor paralyzed man. Thus, when Jesus healed him just by speaking a few words while he lay beside the Pool of Bethesda, he was immediately and happily aware of the change.

The same is true for sinners who, for weeks, months, or years, have been paralyzed with despair and have wearily longed for salvation. Once the Lord Jesus speaks a word of power, giving them joy and peace through the gift of belief, they are very conscious of the change. The evil taken away is too great to be removed without discerning it, the life imparted too amazing to be possessed and remain paralyzed, and the change in the life too miraculous not to be perceived. Yet this poor man was still ignorant of the architect of his cure. He knew nothing of the sacredness of the Person, the positions of authority He held, or the mission that had brought Him to mankind.

Much ignorance of Jesus can still remain in the hearts of those who have felt the miracle-working power of His blood. We should not quickly condemn people for their lack of knowledge, for when we see evidence of saving faith, we must believe salvation has been given. The Holy Spirit makes people repentant long before He makes them perfect, and he who believes what he knows will soon know more clearly what he believes.

Ignorance is still a problem, however, for this poor man was completely unable to cope with the harassment of the Pharisees. It is good to be able to answer those who oppose us, but we will be unable to do so if we do not have a clear understanding of who the Lord Jesus is.

Fortunately in this man's case, the cure for his ignorance soon followed the cure of his impairment, for he was confronted by the Lord Jesus Himself in the temple. After that gracious encounter, he would finally be able to testify "that it was Jesus who had made him well" (John 5:15).

Lord, if You have saved me, show me Yourself, so I may declare You to others.

From the pen of Jim Reimann:

It appears the paralyzed man who was cured in this story only came to a saving faith in Christ once "Jesus found him" in the temple (v. 14). In fact, the previous verse tells us: "The man who was healed *had no idea who it was*, for Jesus had slipped away into the crowd" (v. 13).

This man's story is convincing evidence that receiving a physical miracle from God does not necessarily make the recipient a believer. Our gracious, miracle-working "Father in heaven … causes his sun to rise on the evil and the good, and sends rain on the righteous and the unrighteous" (Matt. 5:45). Isn't a sunrise a miracle of God? Isn't rain? And, of course, whether a believer or an unbeliever, everyone experiences these miracles. Thus, a physical miracle is not equal to a spiritual one, especially the miracle of salvation. This paralyzed man, however, first received a physical miracle and then received one much better — eternal life!

Jesus, thank You for finding me and giving me the miraculous gift of faith.

MAY 9

Who has blessed us ... with every spiritual blessing....

Ephesians 1:3

From the pen of Charles Spurgeon:

Christ blesses His people with all the goodness of the past, the present, and the future. In the mysterious ages of the past, the Lord Jesus was His Father's first elect, and we share an interest in that election, "for he chose us *in him* before the creation of the world" (Eph. 1:4). From eternity past He had enjoyed all the privileges of Sonship as His Father's "only Begotten" (John 1:14 KJV) and well-beloved Son. And in "the riches of God's grace" (Eph. 1:7) by adoption and regeneration, He has also elevated us to sonship and has given us "the right to become children of God" (John 1:12).

The eternal covenant, based upon the obligation of its fulfillment and the fact that it is "guaranteed ... with an oath," is ours — ours for "strong encouragement" (Heb. 6:17 – 18 ESV) and complete security. In the eternal and solid foundation of predestinating wisdom and by omnipotent decree, the eyes of the Lord Jesus have forever been fixed upon us. And may we rest assured that throughout eternity to come, there is no opposing power that can stand against the interests of His redeemed.

The great marriage proposal of the Prince of Glory is ours, for it is to us He is engaged, which will soon be declared to the entire universe through sacred wedding vows. The miracle of the incarnation of the God of heaven, along with all the amazing submissiveness and humiliation that came with it, is ours. The effect of His bloody sweat, His scourging, and His cross are ours forever. All of the glorious consequences flowing from His perfect obedience and finished atonement as well as His resurrection, ascension, and intercession are ours because of His own gift.

He now wears our names on His breastplate, and with authority He intercedes on our behalf, remembering us by name and pleading our case before the throne. He employs His dominion over "the authorities" and "the powers" (Eph. 6:12) and His absolute majesty in heaven is for the benefit of those who trust in Him. His high estate is just as much for our benefit as was His humiliation. He who gave Himself for us in the depths of suffering and death does not withdraw the gift now that He sits enthroned in the highest heavens.

From the pen of Jim Reimann:

Not only is our Savior seated in the highest heavens but "God raised us up with Christ and seated us with him in the heavenly realms in Christ Jesus" (Eph. 2:6), and "our citizenship is in heaven" (Phil. 3:20).

Do you find yourself asking, however, "If that is true, why is my life so difficult? Why are my circumstances so tough?"

Could it be you are focusing your eyes on the wrong things? Our loving, sovereign Lord uses "all things ... for the good of those who love him" (Rom. 8:28) and commands us to "fix our eyes on Jesus" (Heb. 12:2). We should keep heaven in our eyes as "we eagerly await a Savior from there" (Phil. 3:20).

Lord Jesus, thank You for choosing me "before the creation of the world." Thank You for interceding on my behalf before the throne in heaven, and please help me remember my eternal citizenship is with You. Help me, I pray, to keep heaven in my eyes as I look for Your return with great expectancy.

But Christ has indeed been raised from the dead.

1 Corinthians 15:20

From the pen of Charles Spurgeon:

Our entire system of Christian faith rests on the fact that "Christ has indeed been raised from the dead," for "if Christ has not been raised, our preaching is useless and so is your faith," and "you are still in your sins" (1 Cor. 15:14, 17). The surest proof of Christ's divinity is His resurrection since He "was declared with power to be the Son of God by his resurrection from the dead" (Rom. 1:4). Therefore, if He had not risen, it would not be unreasonable to doubt His deity.

Christ's sovereignty is also dependent upon His resurrection, "for this very reason, Christ died and returned to life so that he might be the Lord of both the dead and the living" (Rom. 14:9). Our justification, one of the greatest blessings of the covenant, is linked to Christ's triumphant victory over death and the grave as well, for "He was delivered over to death for our sins and was raised to life for our justification" (Rom. 4:25). Indeed, even our very regeneration is tied to His resurrection, for "he has given us new birth into a living hope through the resurrection of Jesus Christ from the dead" (1 Peter 1:3).

Most importantly, our ultimate resurrection rests in His resurrection, for "if the Spirit of him who raised Jesus from the dead is living in you, he who raised Christ from the dead will also give life to your mortal bodies through his Spirit, who lives in you" (Rom. 8:11). If Christ has not risen, then we will not rise; but if "He has risen" (Matt. 28:6), then those who are asleep in Him have not perished, but "in [their] flesh" will surely "see God" (Job 19:26).

Consequently, the silver thread of the resurrection runs through each of the believer's blessings, from one's regeneration to one's ultimate eternal glorification, and secures them together. Thus, what could be more important for a believer than the glorious fact of Christ's resurrection! What could bring more rejoicing than this great truth established beyond doubt — "Christ has indeed been raised from the dead"!

> The promise is fulfilled,
> Redemption's work is done,
> Justice with mercy's reconciled,
> For God has raised His Son.
>
> Joseph Hart, 1712 – 1768

From the pen of Jim Reimann:

Another point to consider is that if Jesus had not been raised from the dead, He would have been a liar, for He said, "Destroy this temple, and I will raise it again in three days.... The temple he had spoken of was his body" (John 2:19, 21). If Jesus was a liar, He would not have been God, for "God is not a man, that he should lie" (Num. 23:19). And, if He was not God, He would not have qualified to be the sinless "Lamb of God, who takes away the sin of the world!" (John 1:29), for He would have inherited a sin nature like the rest of us.

It comes down to this: what you believe is important — especially when it comes to Jesus and who He is. If we are wrong about Him and His resurrection, and "if only for this life we have hope in Christ, we are to be pitied more than all men" (1 Cor. 15:19)!

MAY 11

Surely I am with you always.
Matthew 28:20

From the pen of Charles Spurgeon:

It is comforting to know there is Someone who is always the same and always with us— one stable Rock amid the crashing waves of the sea of life.

"O my soul" (Ps. 103:1), don't set your affections on rusting, moth-eaten, decaying treasures. Set your heart upon Him who is forever faithful to you. Don't build your house on the shifting sands of a deceitful world, but fix your hopes on this Rock, who even amid driving rain and raging floods will stand immovably secure. I challenge you, "my soul," to store your treasure in the only truly secure Safe — to store your jewels where you can never lose them.

Place your all in Christ. Fix your affections on His person, your hope on His worth, your trust in His atoning blood, and your joy on His presence, so you can laugh at loss and defy destruction. Remember, every flower in the world's garden will ultimately fade and wither away, and the day is coming when nothing will remain but the dark, cold earth. And the darkness of death will one day extinguish the candle in your body.

Yet how wonderful to have sunlight once the candle is gone! Death's dark flood will one day come between you and your possessions, so fix your heart on Him who "will never leave you" (Deut. 31:6). Trust yourself to Him who will go with you through the dark and stormy currents of death's stream — He who will safely take you to land upon the celestial shore and allow you to sit with Him in heavenly places forever.

Dear distressed soul, go to Him! Tell your secrets to the Friend "who sticks closer than a brother" (Prov. 18:24). Trust all your concerns to Him who can never be taken from you, to Him who "will never leave you," and to Him who will never let you leave Him.

"Jesus Christ ... the same yesterday and today and forever" (Heb. 13:8). "Surely I am with you always" is enough for my soul to live on! Let anyone else forsake me.

From the pen of Jim Reimann:

What if Jesus told you He was going to leave you? How would you feel?

That is exactly what He once told His disciples: "My children, I will be with you only a little longer.... Where I am going, you cannot come" (John 13:33).

Of course, this was quite troubling to the disciples. So Jesus told them,

> Do not let your hearts be troubled.... I am going ... to prepare a place for you.... I will come back and take you to be with me that you also may be where I am.... And I will ask the Father, and he will give you another Counselor to be with you forever — the Spirit of truth.
>
> John 14:1 – 3, 16 – 17

Jesus' departure did not sound like good news to His disciples, but He told them, "It is for your good that I am going away. Unless I go away, the Counselor will not come to you; but if I go, I will send him to you" (John 16:7).

Believers have the very life of Jesus within them through the power of His indwelling Holy Spirit. "He ... put his Spirit in our hearts as a deposit, guaranteeing what is to come" (2 Cor. 1:21 – 22).

I thank You, Lord, for Your Spirit living within me. Thank You for Him who guarantees not only the present with You but also the future!

MAY 12

I ... will ... show myself to him.

John 14:21

From the pen of Charles Spurgeon:

The Lord Jesus gives special revelations of Himself to His people. Even if Scripture did not tell us this, there are many believers who could testify to its truth from their own experience. They have had such amazing manifestations of their Lord and Savior that no mere retelling can equal it.

In the lives of some of God's prominent saints we find many instances when Jesus was pleased, in a very special way, to speak to their souls, to unfold for them the wonders of His person, or to immerse their souls in such happiness that they thought they were in heaven itself. And although they were not actually in heaven, they were just on its threshold, for when Jesus reveals Himself to His people, it is heaven on earth, it is paradise unveiled, it is divine happiness begun.

These special manifestations of Christ have a profound and holy influence on a believer's heart. One effect is humility. If someone says, "Look at what a great person I am, for I have had 'such-and-such' communication with the Lord," then he has never communicated with Jesus at all. For "the LORD ... looks upon the lowly, but the proud he knows from afar" (Ps. 138:6). He does not need to come near the proud to know them and will never give them any special visits of love.

Another effect will be happiness, for "you will fill me with joy in your presence, with eternal pleasures at your right hand" (Ps. 16:11).

And holiness will be sure to follow. Someone who exhibits no holiness has never had a special manifestation of Christ. Some people make a great many claims, but we should not believe anyone unless their actions align with their words. "Do not be deceived: God cannot be mocked" (Gal. 6:7). He will not bestow His gifts on the wicked, for "surely God does not reject a blameless man or strengthen the hands of evil-doers" (Job 8:20).

Thus, there will be three effects of closeness to Jesus — humility, happiness, and holiness. May God give them to you, dear Christian!

From the pen of Jim Reimann:

Today's devotion brings to mind a story from "The Anatomy of a Church," a sermon by John MacArthur:

> One man said that Jesus comes into his bathroom and puts His arm around him while he is shaving. I thought, "Do you keep shaving? If you can keep shaving, then it isn't Jesus. If holy God came into the bathroom while you were shaving, you would fall to the floor so hard that you would kill yourself!" It is an awesome thing to confront an infinitely holy God!*

Even the prophet Isaiah, when he saw the Lord, responded, "'Woe to me!' I cried. 'I am ruined! For I am a man of unclean lips ... and my eyes have seen the King, the LORD Almighty'" (Isa. 6:5). Next consider the apostle John: "When I saw him, I fell at his feet as though dead" (Rev. 1:17).

Yes, an encounter with Jesus will lead to humility, happiness, and holiness — but humility must be first!

---

* *Grace to You.* Copyright © 2006. All rights reserved. Used by permission of *www.gty.org.*

MAY 13

Weeping may remain for a night,
but rejoicing comes in the morning.

Psalm 30:5

From the pen of Charles Spurgeon:

Dear Christian, if you are enduring a night of trials, think of tomorrow! Let your heart be cheered by the thought of your coming Lord. Be patient, for:

> Lo! He comes with clouds descending.
>
> John Cennick, 1718 – 1755

Be patient! The heavenly Harvester waits to reap His harvest. Be patient, for you know who said, "Behold, I am coming soon! My reward is with me, and I will give to everyone according to what he has done" (Rev. 22:12). If you have never been as distressed as today, remember:

> A few more rolling suns, at most,
> Will land you on fair Canaan's coast.
>
> John André, 1750 – 1780

Your head may be crowned with thorny troubles right now, but someday soon it will wear a starry crown. Your hands may be filled with many cares today, but will soon strum the strings of heaven's harp. Now your garments may be stained with dust and dirt, but soon they will be white. Wait a little longer.

Yes, how contemptible our troubles and trials seem today! Now they appear overwhelming, but once we get to heaven we will:

> With transporting joys recount,
> The labors of our feet.
>
> Isaac Watts, 1674 – 1748

Then our trials will seem as "light and momentary troubles" (2 Cor. 4:17).

May we boldly continue, and even if the night has never seemed so dark, the morning comes! This is more than anyone who is imprisoned in the darkness of hell can say.

Do you know what it means to live looking to the future with expectancy — to anticipate heaven? Happy is the believer who has such assurance and such a comforting hope. There may be nothing but darkness now, but soon there will be light; there may be nothing but trials now, but soon there will be nothing but happiness.

What difference does it make that "weeping may remain for a night" when "rejoicing comes in the morning"!

From the pen of Jim Reimann:

Today Spurgeon quotes hymns by John Cennick, John André, and Isaac Watts, reminding us how hymns once greatly influenced people's theology. Watts wrote 750 hymns that had a greater influence than those of John Newton ("Amazing Grace") or John and Charles Wesley. Cennick, an evangelist who died at thirty-six, established more than forty churches. And André, a British military officer hanged at the age of thirty as a spy, wrote "My Hiding Place" (excerpted above) just two days before his execution. It was found in his pocket after he was hanged.

Once we consider the trials of others, perhaps our complaining will end.

MAY 14

... co-heirs with Christ.

Romans 8:17

From the pen of Charles Spurgeon:

The limitless realms of His Father's universe are Christ's by legal right. As "heir of all things" (Heb. 1:2), He is the sole owner of God's vast creation, but has allowed us to claim it in its entirety as our own as well, by virtue of the "co-heirs with Christ" (Rom. 8:17) deed of ownership the Lord has signed for His chosen people. Through the work of our blessed Lord, the golden streets of paradise, the pearly gates, the river of life, the incomparable happiness, and the unspeakable glory have been made our everlasting possessions. Everything that is His He shares with His people.

Christ has placed a royal crown upon the head of His church, appointing her "to be a kingdom" (Rev. 1:6) and calling her sons "a royal priesthood" (1 Peter 2:9). He uncrowned Himself so we may have a coronation of glory, and would not sit upon His own throne until He had secured a place on it for all who overcome by His blood. (See Rev. 3:21.)

When the head is crowned, the entire body shares the honor. It is the reward of every Christian conqueror! Christ's throne, crown, scepter, palace, treasure, robes, and heritage are all yours and are far superior to jealousy, selfishness, and greed, which share no benefit to those who participate in them. Christ does not consider His happiness complete until it is shared by His people. "I have given them the glory that you gave me" (John 17:22). "I have told you this so that my joy may be in you and that your joy may be complete" (John 15:11).

The smiles of His Father are all the sweeter to Him because His people share them. The honors of His kingdom are more pleasing to Him be-cause His people "appear with him in glory" (Col. 3:4). His conquests are more valuable to Him since they have taught His people to overcome.

Christ delights in His throne because there is a place for His people on it. He rejoices in His royal robes because they cover them as well. And He delights all the more in His joy because He calls His people to "enter into the joy of your master" (Matt. 25:21 NASB).

From the pen of Jim Reimann:

What an unselfish Lord we have! He deserves all He has inherited — we don't. So it seems even more amazing that He has more joy because we share in that joy. Yet isn't this indicative of His true nature, character, and attributes?

The Lord God is eternal, infinite, infallible, immutable, sovereign, holy, just, patient, loving, merciful, omniscient, omnipotent, and omnipresent, just to name a few of His attributes. Even more, He is personal! And the fact He is a personal God means we can refer to Him as *He*, not *It*. He is not simply a power or force behind nature but a person. Thus, as a person He thinks and wills and acts, although He always does so "according to his purpose" (Rom. 8:28).

In light of who God is, and in light of His limitlessness, isn't it all the more miraculous He has purposed to have a relationship with us!

Dear eternal and sovereign Lord, thank You for the cross. Thank You that through it I may share life in Your Son, who gave His all for me. Thank You that You are a personal God who desires a personal relationship with Your people — even me!

MAY 15

Everyone who believes is justified.

Acts 13:39

From the pen of Charles Spurgeon:

A believer in Christ receives immediate justification. Faith does not gradually produce this fruit over time, but produces it now. Because justification is the result of faith, it is given to a soul at the very moment he is saved by Christ and has accepted Him as his "all in all" (1 Cor. 15:28).

Are those who presently stand before the throne of God justified? Of course, but so are we! We are as truly and clearly justified as those dressed in white robes, as those who are even now singing melodious praises to the music of celestial harps. The thief on the cross was justified the very moment he turned eyes of faith to Jesus; the aging apostle Paul, after many years of service, was not *more* justified than was that thief who had no service at all.

Today we are "accepted in the beloved" (Eph. 1:6 KJV) and absolved from sin. *Today* we stand acquitted before God's court. What a soul-moving thought! Yes, there are some clusters of Eshcol's grapes we will not gather until we enter heaven itself, but this is one cluster hanging over heaven's wall. (See Num. 13:23.) This is not like "the produce of the land" (Josh. 5:11) we cannot eat until we cross the Jordan. It is not "the manna in the desert," but "the bread that comes down from heaven" (John 6:49–50) — part of our daily nourishment provided by God for our daily activities.

Now — even now — we are pardoned. *Now* our sins are removed; *now* we stand accepted in the eyes of God as though we had never been guilty. "Therefore, there is *now* no condemnation for those who are in Christ Jesus" (Rom. 8:1). Not one sin remains in God's Book — right now — against any one of His people. Who can dare

to bring even one charge against them? There is no "stain or wrinkle or any other blemish" (Eph. 5:27) on any believer when it comes to the matter of justification in the eyes of the Judge of all the earth.

May our present privilege awaken us to our present duty — now. While we remain in this life, may we spend it — and be spent — for our sweet Lord Jesus.

From the pen of Jim Reimann:

Justification is a deep, and lofty, theological term — one with great meaning for believers. Essentially it means to be declared righteous by God in spite of my sins. It is a once-for-all change in my legal status before the Lord and is what puts me into a right-standing relationship with Him. Very simply put, it means God has made me righteous, not because of my works, but because of Christ's work on the cross. Christ's righteousness has become mine!

"To the man who does not work but trusts God who justifies the wicked, his faith is credited as righteousness" (Rom. 4:5). "It is because of him that you are in Christ Jesus, who has become for us wisdom from God — that is, our righteousness, holiness and redemption" (1 Cor. 1:30).

"God made him who had no sin to be sin [or *a sin offering*] for us, so that in him we might become the righteousness of God" (2 Cor. 5:21).

Father, I thank You that I stand as righteous in Your sight and am no longer condemned in spite of all my sins. Help me, I pray, to offer my body as a living sacrifice, "holy and pleasing" to You, as my "spiritual act of worship" (Rom. 12:1).

MAY 16

God … richly provides us with everything for our enjoyment.

1 Timothy 6:17

From the pen of Charles Spurgeon:

Our Lord Jesus is always giving, never withdrawing His hand for one instant. As long as there is even one vessel of His grace not yet full, His oil will continue to flow. He is an ever-shining sun, He is manna always falling into the camp, and He is a rock in the desert, continually sending forth streams of life from His pierced side. The rain showers of His grace are always falling, the river of His bounteous blessings is forever flowing, and the wellspring of His love is continually overflowing. And just as our King can never die, His grace can never fail.

Daily we pluck His fruit, and daily His branches bend themselves toward our hand with a fresh supply of mercy. Every day of every week is a feast day, so as many days as there are in a year is how many banquets we celebrate each year.

Who has ever walked from His door unblessed? Who has ever left His table hungry? Who has ever left His embrace unchanged? "His mercies never come to an end; they are new every morning" (Lam. 3:22 – 23 ESV) and fresh every evening. Who can know the number of His benefits or count His blessings?

Every grain of sand falling through the hourglass of time is but His latest reminder of a myriad of His mercies. The wings of our hours are covered with the silver of His kindness and the gold of His affection. The river of time flows from the mountains of eternity, revealing the golden sand of His favor. And the countless stars are just the standard bearers of even more innumerable multitudes of His blessings.

Who can count the blessings He bestows on Jacob or number the endless mercies He extends to Israel, for they are more numerous than the specks of dust on earth. How can my soul offer Him the praise He is due, for He daily fills me with His blessings and crowns me with His loving-kindness.

Oh, that my praise would be as ceaseless as His blessings! Oh, my miserable tongue, how can you be silent? Wake up, I tell you, or you will never bring me glory, only shame.

"Awake, harp and lyre! I will awaken the dawn" (Ps. 108:2).

From the pen of Jim Reimann:

One of the most beautiful aspects of God's countless blessings is that although they continually flow, they never delete His supply. And, not only do they fill His children, they fill us to overflowing! As long as we walk in obedience to Him, He continues to pour forth His blessings into our lives, and they continually overflow to those around us.

"Whoever drinks the water I give him will never thirst. Indeed, the water I give him will become in him a spring of water welling up to eternal life" (John 4:14). "Whoever believes in me, as the Scripture has said, streams of living water will flow from within him" (John 7:38).

"The Lord will guide you always; he will satisfy your needs in a sun-scorched land and will strengthen your frame. You will be like a well-watered garden, like a spring whose waters never fail" (Isa. 58:11).

"How can I repay the Lord for all his goodness to me? I will lift up the cup of salvation and call on the name of the Lord" (Ps. 116:12 – 13).

MAY 17

Whoever claims to live in him must walk as Jesus did.

1 John 2:6

From the pen of Charles Spurgeon:

Why should Christians imitate Christ? They should do it for their own sakes. If they desire to be spiritually healthy, to escape the sickness of sin, and to enjoy the vitality of increasing grace, Jesus should be their model. For the sake of their own happiness, if they desire to drink deeply of His best wine, if they want to enjoy holy and happy communion and oneness with Jesus, and if they desire to be lifted from the cares and troubles of this world, they "must walk as Jesus did."

Nothing will be of greater assistance in having a godly walk toward heaven than wearing the image of Jesus on your heart, allowing Him to rule your emotions. You will be the happiest and will best exhibit His sonship when you walk with Jesus in His very footsteps, enabled by the power of His Holy Spirit. Walking far from Him, however, makes you feel unsafe and uneasy.

Next, strive to be like Jesus for the sake of the gospel. Oh, poor gospel, you have suffered cruel blows from your enemies but have been only half as severely wounded by your foes as your friends! Who made those wounds in that sweet hand of godliness? It was the professing believer who used the dagger of hypocrisy. And he who enters the sheepfold under false pretenses, who is simply a wolf "in sheep's clothing" (Matt. 7:15), disturbs the flock more than the lion outside. There is no weapon half as deadly as a "Judas-kiss." Inconsistent, professing believers injure the gospel more than the sneering critic or the atheist.

Finally, imitate Christ's example especially for the sake of Christ Himself. Dear Christian, do you love your Savior? Is His name precious to you? Is His cause truly important to you? Do you want to see the kingdoms of this world become His? Is it your desire He be glorified? Are you longing for souls to be won for Him?

If so, imitate Jesus! Be an epistle of Christ, "known and read by everybody" (2 Cor. 3:2).

From the pen of Jim Reimann:

We have all heard, "Imitation is the highest form of flattery." Could it then also be said, "Imitation is the highest form of giving glory to Christ"?

The Word of God clearly tells us what to — and what not to — imitate:

"When you enter the land the LORD your God is giving you, do not learn to *imitate* the detestable ways of the nations there" (Deut. 18:9). The application of this is that we as believers should not imitate the ways of unbelievers.

"*Imitate* those who through faith and patience inherit what has been promised" (Heb. 6:12).

"Remember your leaders, who spoke the word of God to you. Consider the outcome of their way of life and *imitate* their faith" (Heb. 13:7).

"Dear friend, do not *imitate* what is evil but what is good" (3 John 11).

The apostle Paul declared, "I urge you to *imitate* me" (1 Cor. 4:16). "Whatever you have learned or received or heard from me, or seen in me — put it into practice" (Phil. 4:9). And what was the passion of Paul's heart?

"I resolved to know nothing while I was with you except Jesus Christ and him crucified" (1 Cor. 2:2). "I want to know Christ..., *becoming like him*" (Phil. 3:10).

MAY 18

In Christ all the fullness of the Deity lives in bodily form,
and you have been given fullness in Christ.
Colossians 2:9–10

From the pen of Charles Spurgeon:

All the attributes of Christ as God and man are at our disposal. "All the fullness of the Deity," and everything that wonderful phrase includes, is ours to make us complete, giving us "fullness in Christ." He cannot endow us with the attributes of Deity, but short of that He has done everything that can be done, for He has made even His divine power and the fullness of the Godhead submissive to our salvation. His omnipotence, omniscience, omnipresence, immutability, and infallibility are all combined for our protection and defense.

So arise, believer, and behold the Lord Jesus harnessing the fullness of His divine Godhead to the chariot of salvation! The vastness of His grace, the firmness of His faithfulness, the steadfastness of His immutability, the infiniteness of His power, and the limitlessness of His knowledge have all been made pillars of the temple of salvation by the Lord Jesus. And without diminishing one attribute's infinite depth, He has covenanted each of them to us as our eternal inheritance.

Every drop of the fathomless love of the Savior's heart, every sinew in His mighty arm, and every jewel in His majestic crown are ours. The immensity of His divine knowledge as well as the sternness of His divine justice are ours and will be employed on our behalf. All of Christ in His entirety and in His exalted character as the Son of God has been richly provided for us to enjoy.

His wisdom is our direction, His knowledge our instruction, His power our protection, His justice our guarantee, His love our comfort, His mercy our assurance, and His immutability our

trust. He holds nothing back, but opens even the deep recesses of the Mount of God and bids us to dig in its mines for hidden treasures. "All! All! All are yours!" He says. "Enjoy and be filled with the favor, the fullness, and 'the goodness of the LORD'" (Ps. 27:13).

Oh, how wonderful to behold Jesus in His fullness! How wonderful to be able to call upon Him with confident certainty that when we seek the infusion of His love or power in our lives, we are simply asking for something He has already faithfully promised!

From the pen of Jim Reimann:

"You have been given fullness in Christ." Notice this verse does not say, "You *will be given*." No, it is already accomplished. So why don't we walk in this truth? Could it be we really don't believe it? Or is it that we believe the Lord holds His riches for us in heaven, only opening His storehouse to us in the next life?

The life Jesus gives He gives now — in this life. He said, "I have come that they may have life, and have it to the full" (John 10:10). Yet we have a tendency to believe that the Lord is like us — always saving the best for last. Consider, however, the story of Jesus changing water into wine. The master of the wedding, not knowing what had taken place, told the bridegroom, "Everyone brings out the choice wine first and then the cheaper wine after the guests have had too much to drink; but you have saved the best till *now*" (John 2:10).

Jesus gives us His best *now* — not later! "He who did not spare his own Son ... how will he not also ... graciously give us all things?" (Rom. 8:32).

MAY 19

I have seen slaves on horseback,
while princes go on foot like slaves.

Ecclesiastes 10:7

From the pen of Charles Spurgeon:

Upstarts often arrogantly usurp the most prominent places, while truly great people are often relegated to total obscurity. The reason behind this puzzling situation, still within God's providence, will someday gladden the hearts of the righteous. Yet this situation is such a common fact of life that none of us should complain when it falls to us.

Although our Lord is the "King of kings" (Rev. 17:14) of the earth, He walked earth's paths of weariness and service as the Servant of servants. Is it any wonder then that His followers, who are princes through His blood, should also be looked down upon as inferior and contemptible people? The world is upside down. Therefore, the first are last and the last first. (See Matt. 19:30.)

Just look how the willing sons of Satan lord their position over the earth! What a high horse they ride! How they lift their "horns against heaven" (Ps. 75:5)! Haman is in the king's court, while Mordecai sits outside the king's gate. (See Est. 5:9.) David wanders the wilderness mountains, while King Saul reigns in power. Elijah complains in a desert cave, while Queen Jezebel boasts in her palace.

Yet who of us would wish to trade places with the proud rebels? And who of them, on the other hand, might not envy the despised saints of God? As the wheels of time turn, those who are lowest rise and the highest sink. Patience then, dear believer, eternity will right the wrongs of time. So let us not fall to the error of allowing our worldly passions and carnal appetites to ride in triumph while our godly strengths crawl through the dust.

Grace must reign as our prince and make the parts of our bodies instruments of righteousness. The Holy Spirit loves order and therefore sets our various strengths and abilities in their proper place and rank, giving the highest priority and space to those spiritual powers that connect us to our great King.

We should not disturb His divine arrangement but ask for grace that we may "discipline [our bodies] and keep [them] under control" (1 Cor. 9:27 ESV). We were not made "a new creation" (2 Cor. 5:17) in order to allow our passions to rule over us, but that we, as kings, may reign in Christ Jesus over the threefold kingdom of spirit, soul, and body — to the glory of God the Father.

From the pen of Jim Reimann:

This world is indeed upside down, and often the things of God seem counterintuitive. Yet remember His words, "As the heavens are higher than the earth, so are my ways higher than your ways and my thoughts than your thoughts" (Isa. 55:9). His ways will not always make sense to us, but keep in mind, "The foolishness of God is wiser than man's wisdom" (1 Cor. 1:25).

Therefore, it comes down to a matter of trusting Him even when we may not have full understanding. It is also a matter of trusting His Word, which says, "He is the Rock, his works are perfect, and all his ways are just" (Deut. 32:4).

"Hear my cry, O God; listen to my prayer.
From the ends of the earth I call to you, I call
as my heart grows faint; lead me to the rock
that is higher than I" (Ps. 61:1 – 2).

MAY 20

From the pen of Charles Spurgeon:

When our gifts are truly given from the heart, we have given well, yet most often we fail at this. This is never true of our Master and Lord, however, for His gifts are always performed with the love of His heart. He never sends us cold meat and mere scraps of food from His table of luxury, but dips our every morsel in His own dish and seasons each portion with the spices of His fragrant affection. When He places the golden expressions of His grace in our hands, He accompanies the gift with such a warm squeeze of our hand that the manner in which He gives is as precious to us as the gift itself.

He enters our house as He carries out His acts of kindness, but He does not enter as some rich unfriendly guest entering a poor man's lowly cottage. No, He sits by our side, never looking down on our poverty or criticizing our weaknesses.

Beloved, He smiles as He speaks! What golden words flow from His gracious lips! What affectionate embraces He gives us! If He only had a penny to give, the way He gives it would make it as gold. Yet from His abundance His valuable gifts sit in a golden basket beside His beautiful carriage. And it is impossible to doubt the sincerity of His charity, for the emblem of His heart, bleeding for us, is stamped upon each and every gift. "God ... gives generously to all without finding fault" (James 1:5). There is not one hint we are a burden to Him, not one cold glance for His poor beneficiaries. He rejoices in His mercies and holds us tightly to Himself as He pours out His life for us.

There is a fragrance to His exquisite perfume that nothing but His heart could produce and a sweetness to His honeycomb that could never exist unless the very essence of His soul's affection were mixed with it.

Oh, the remarkable communion only His heart can produce! May we continually taste and know the blessedness of it!

From the pen of Jim Reimann:

What a generous example of giving the Lord God has exhibited by giving us His son! "He who did not spare his own Son, but gave him up for us all — how will he not also, along with him, graciously give us all things?" (Rom. 8:32). We are indeed commanded to follow His example, for Jesus said, "I have set you an example that you should do as I have done for you" (John 13:15).

The apostle Paul told us, "Remember this: Whoever sows sparingly will also reap sparingly, and whoever sows generously will also reap generously. Each man should give what he has decided in his heart to give, not reluctantly or under compulsion, for God loves a cheerful giver. And God is able to make all grace abound to you, so that in all things at all times, having all that you need, you will abound in every good work. As it is written: 'He has scattered abroad his gifts to the poor; his righteousness endures forever.' Now he who supplies seed to the sower and bread for food will also supply and increase your store of seed and will enlarge the harvest of your righteousness. You will be made rich in every way so that you can be generous on every occasion, and through us your generosity will result in thanksgiving to God" (2 Cor. 9:6 – 11).

Dear one, try it yourself! "*Taste and see* that the Lord is good" (Ps. 34:8).

"... if ... ye have tasted that the Lord is gracious."

1 Peter 2:3 KJV

From the pen of Charles Spurgeon:

"If" — then this is not to be taken for granted for every member of the human race. "If" — then there is a possibility, even a probability, some people have not "tasted that the Lord is gracious." "If" — then it is not a universal mercy, but a specific and special one, one where knowing if we have experienced His grace requires an inward examination. In fact, there is no spiritual blessing that is not a reason to search our hearts.

While this should be an earnest and prayerful search, no one should ever be totally content while any question remains or if there is an "if" about whether one has "tasted that the Lord is gracious" or not. A sense of self-distrust may cause a believer to question himself, but a continual questioning by a true believer would be evil indeed. Yet we must not rest, even if it means a desperate struggle, until we embrace the Savior in the arms of faith and can truly say, "I know whom I have believed, and am convinced that he is able to guard what I have entrusted to him" (2 Tim. 1:12).

So do not rest, O believer, until you have "full assurance" (Heb. 10:22) of your claim in Jesus. Allow nothing to satisfy you until, through the perfect witness of the Holy Spirit testifying with your spirit, it is confirmed you are a child of God.

This is not something to consider as trivial or to neglect! Do not allow "if," "perhaps," or "maybe" to attempt to satisfy your soul. Do not allow doubts here, but build on eternal certainties, and strongly build upon them.

Get for yourself the "sure blessings promised to David" (Acts 13:34). Let your "anchor for the soul ... [enter] the inner sanctuary behind the curtain" (Heb. 6:19), and make sure your soul is secured to that anchor by a cable that will never break. Move beyond these lifeless "ifs" and live no longer in the wilderness of doubts and fears. Cross the Jordan of distrust and enter the Canaan of peace — yes, where Canaanites still linger, but where the land never ceases to flow with milk and honey.

From the pen of Jim Reimann:

Unfortunately, a Christian can lack full assurance of faith. There is even a denomination that teaches we can never know for sure. When asked if they will be in heaven when they die, they will typically respond, "Oh, I hope so!"

How terribly sad! What a poor witness to a lost and dying world that even Christians can lack assurance. Jesus desires we know we belong to Him.

As Spurgeon alludes to today, in agreement with the apostle Paul, "The Spirit himself testifies with our spirit that *we are God's children*" (Rom. 8:16). And the apostle John declared, "I write these things to you who believe in the name of the Son of God *so that you may know* that you have eternal life" (1 John 5:13). In an earlier passage John tells us the evidence of knowing we are believers:

"Dear children, let us not love with words or tongue but with actions and in truth. *This then is how we know that we belong to the truth*, and how we set our hearts at rest in his presence.... This is his command: to believe in the name of his Son, Jesus Christ, and to love one another as he commanded us. Those who obey his commands live in him, and he in them. And *this is how we know that he lives in us: We know it by the Spirit he gave us* (1 John 3:18 – 19, 23 – 24).

MAY 22

He led them by a straight way.

Psalm 107:7

From the pen of Charles Spurgeon:

Change often leads an anxious believer to ask, "Why is this happening to me? 'I looked for light, then came darkness' (Job 30:26). '[I] hoped for peace … but there was only terror' (Jer. 8:15). I said in my heart, 'I will never be shaken. O LORD,… my mountain [will] stand firm; but when you hid your face, I was dismayed' (Ps. 30:6 – 7). Only yesterday I could clearly see the way, but today my path is dark and my hopes are shrouded by clouds. Yesterday I could climb 'to the top of Pisgah' (Deut. 34:1), view the vast landscape, and rejoice with confidence in my future inheritance. Today my spirit has no hope, only fear; no joy, only great distress. Is this part of God's plan for me? Is this really the way that God would have me travel to heaven?"

Yes, it is by this way. The obscuring of your faith, the darkness of your mind, the fading of your hope — all these are simply part of God's method of maturing you for the great inheritance you will soon enter. These trials are designed to test and to strengthen your faith. They are waves that will wash you again upon the Rock and further establish you there. They are the winds that will transport your ship more swiftly toward the desired haven.

As the psalmist David wrote, may it be said of you: "He guided them to their desired haven" (Ps. 107:30). "Through glory and dishonor, bad report and good report" (2 Cor. 6:8), through plenty and poverty, through joy or distress, through persecution or peace, through and by all these things the life of your soul is maintained, and by each of them you are helped along your way.

Never think, dear believer, your sorrows are not in God's plan — they are a necessary part of it. "We must go through many hardships to enter the kingdom of God" (Acts 14:22). Therefore, even learn to "consider it pure joy … whenever you face trials of many kinds" (James 1:2).

> O let my trembling soul be still,
> And wait Thy wise, Thy holy will!
> I cannot, Lord, Thy purpose see,
> Yet all is well since ruled by Thee.
> John Bowring, 1792 – 1872

From the pen of Jim Reimann:

There is no better example of Christian suffering than the apostle Paul. He wrote, "We do not want you to be uninformed, brothers, about the hardships we suffered.… We were under great pressure, far beyond our ability to endure, so that we despaired even of life" (2 Cor. 1:8). The humanity of the great apostle shines forth in this and should be an encouragement to us when we suffer.

Paul went on to say, "Indeed, in our hearts we felt the sentence of death," but he then quickly gives us the purpose for the suffering: "This happened that we might not rely on ourselves but on God, who raises the dead" (2 Cor. 1:9).

Yes, we have a God "who raises the dead"! Are you at the point of "despair[ing] even of life," just as Paul once did? Then remember, our God "raises the dead" and "will not forsake his faithful ones" (Ps. 37:28).

"He has delivered us" — in the past; "he will deliver us" — in the future; and "he will continue to deliver us" (2 Cor. 1:10) — in the present. He can be trusted!

MAY 23

The LORD will fulfill [his purpose] for me.
Psalm 138:8

From the pen of Charles Spurgeon:

Most assuredly the confidence the psalmist expresses here is a divine confidence. He did not say, "I am gifted enough to 'fulfill [his purpose] for me,'" as if to say, "My faith is so unshakable it will not waver, my love is so warm it will never grow cold, and my resolution is so firm nothing can move it." No, his dependence was on the Lord alone.

If we trust in anything not grounded on the Rock of Ages, our confidence is less than a dream. It will simply crumble on us, covering us in its ruins to our own sorrow and confusion. All that Nature weaves will ultimately unravel over time to the eternal confusion of those who have clothed themselves in it.

The psalmist, however, was wise and trusted in nothing short of the Lord's work. It is the Lord "who began a good work in [us]" and "will carry it on to completion" (Phil. 1:6). And if He doesn't finish it, it will never be complete. If even one stitch of the celestial garment of our righteousness must be sewn by us, then we are lost and hopeless. But this is our confidence: The Lord "who began ... will carry it on to completion." He *has* done it all, *must* do it all, and *will* do it all.

Our confidence must never be in what we have done or have resolved to do, but entirely in what the Lord will do. Unbelief deceives us, saying, "You will never be able to stand. Just look at your evil heart! You will never conquer sin. Remember your sinful pleasures and the temptations of the world that continually plague you? Undoubtedly you will be allured and led astray by them."

Yes, if left to our own strength, we would indeed perish! If left to navigate our frail vessels through such rough seas alone, we might as well give up our voyage in despair. "But thanks be to God!" (1 Cor. 15:57). He "will fulfill [his purpose] for [us]" and take us to His desired haven.

We can never be too confident if our confidence is based on Him alone. And we can never be overwhelmed by the storms of life when our trust is in Him.

From the pen of Jim Reimann:

The world today has great respect for people with confidence, but if that confidence is based on human strengths and talents, it will ultimately fail. And when it comes to believers, the Lord will not — and cannot — tolerate our trusting in ourselves. If we trust in our own strengths, no matter how developed they may be, the Lord will be forced to send brokenness in the very area where we have placed — or misplaced — our trust. Consider these words of the psalmist, encouraging confidence in the Lord — not man:

"The LORD is with me; I will not be afraid. What can man do to me? The LORD is with me; he is my helper. I will look in triumph on my enemies. It is better to take refuge in the LORD than to trust in man. It is better to take refuge in the LORD than to trust in princes" (Ps. 118:6 – 9).

Solomon declared, "The LORD will be your confidence and will keep your foot from being snared" (Prov. 3:26), while the writer of Hebrews added, "So do not throw away your confidence; it will be richly rewarded" (Heb. 10:35).

Father, I pray that even "though an army besiege me, my heart will not fear; though war break out against me, even then will I be confident" (Ps. 27:3).

MAY 24

Praise be to God, who has not rejected my prayer.

Psalm 66:20

From the pen of Charles Spurgeon:

Upon reviewing the content of our prayers, if we do so honestly, we should be filled with awe that God has ever answered them. There may be some people who think their prayers are worthy of acceptance — just as the Pharisees did — but a true Christian, more spiritually aware in their review, weeps over his prayers, and if it were possible for him to retrace his steps would desire to pray more earnestly.

Remember, dear Christian, how cold your prayers have been. When in your prayer closet you should have wrestled as Jacob did, but instead your petitions have been faint and few, far removed from that humble, believing, persevering faith that cries out, "I will not let you go unless you bless me" (Gen. 32:26). However, isn't it amazing that God has not only heard your prayers but has also answered them!

Reflect on how infrequently you have prayed unless you have been in some difficulty. At those times you often go to God's "mercy seat" (Ex. 25:17 KJV), but once He has delivered you, what happens to your continual, earnest supplication? Yet even though you have ceased to pray as before, God has not ceased to bless. When you have neglected His "mercy seat," He has not deserted it, for the bright light of His Shekinah glory has always remained visible between the wings of the cherubim.

Oh, how marvelous that the Lord even considers our intermittent, annoying spasms of prayer that come only when we have needs! What an amazing God He is to hear the prayers of those who come to Him when they have pressing needs and wants, but who neglect Him once they have received a blessing; those who approach Him only when they feel forced to do so, but nearly forget to speak with Him when their blessings are plentiful and their sorrows are few.

May His gracious kindness in hearing such prayers so touch our hearts that from this point forward we may continually "pray in the Spirit on all occasions with all kinds of prayers and requests" (Eph. 6:18).

From the pen of Jim Reimann:

The story of King Jehoshaphat is an amazing story of confidently crying out to God, expecting to be heard by Him. He prayed, "We will stand in your presence before this temple that bears your Name and will cry out to you in our distress, and *you will hear us* and save us.... For we have no power to face this vast army that is attacking us. We do not know what to do, but our eyes are upon you" (2 Chron. 20:9, 12). What followed was the greatest victory on the face of the whole earth! From a human standpoint the odds were "everyone" against "no one." In other words, God fought the battle for Israel and gave them victory.

"This is the confidence we have in approaching God: that if we ask anything according to his will, *he hears us*. And if we know that *he hears us* — whatever we ask — we know that we have what we asked of him" (1 John 5:14 – 15).

"O Lord, hear my prayer, listen to my cry for mercy; in your faithfulness and righteousness come to my relief" (Ps. 143:1).

MAY 25

O Lord, do not forsake me.

Psalm 38:21

From the pen of Charles Spurgeon:

Frequently we pray that God would not forsake us in our time of trial and temptation, but all too often we forget we have need of the above quoted prayer "at all times" (Job 27:10). There is not a moment of our lives, however holy that moment may be, in which we can make do without being upheld by His constant support. Whether in light or in darkness, whether in oneness with Him or being tempted to sin, we need the prayer: "O Lord, do not forsake me."

"Uphold me, and I will be delivered" (Ps. 119:117). While learning to walk, a little child always needs his parent's steady hand. And a ship without a captain at the helm immediately begins drifting from its course. We cannot do without constant aid from above, so today let your prayer be:

"Do not forsake me." Father, do not forsake Your child lest I fall to the hand of the enemy. Shepherd, do not forsake Your lamb lest I wander from the safety of the fold. Great Gardener, do not forsake Your plant lest I fade, wither, and die. "O Lord, do not forsake me" now or at any moment of my life. Do not forsake me in times of great joy lest that joy turn my heart from You; and do not forsake me in times of sorrow lest I complain against You. Do not forsake me when I repent of sin lest I lose hope of Your pardon and fall into despair; and do not forsake me at the times of my strongest faith lest my faith degenerate into presumption of forgiveness.

"Do not forsake me," for without You I am weak, but with You I am strong. Do not forsake me, for my path is dangerous and full of snares and I cannot live without Your guidance. The hen does not forsake her brood, so forever "cover [me] with [Your] feathers, and under [Your] wings [may I] find refuge" (Ps. 91:4). "Do not be far from me, for trouble is near and there is no one to help" (Ps. 22:11). "Do not reject me or forsake me, O God my Savior" (Ps. 27:9).

O ever in our cleansed breast,
Bid Thy Eternal Spirit rest;
And make our inner soul to be
A temple pure — worthy of Thee.

Reginald Heber, 1783 – 1826

From the pen of Jim Reimann:

Job asks the question of himself, "Does God listen to his cry when distress comes upon him? Will he find delight in the Almighty? Will he call upon God *at all times*?" (Job 27:9 – 10).

Christian friend, do you call upon God "at all times"? Or do you find yourself crying out to Him only when you feel you *really* need Him? The feeling of being able to "go it alone" during so-called good times is actually nothing short of pride, something the Lord hates. After all, "Pride goes before destruction, a haughty spirit before a fall" (Prov. 16:18). "So, if you think you are standing firm, be careful that you don't fall!" (1 Cor. 10:12).

Remember, "It is God who makes both us and you stand firm in Christ" (2 Cor. 1:21).

Father, may I rest in You alone. Thank You that You are the One who causes me to "stand firm in Christ," and may I trust in You "at all times."

MAY 26

Cast your cares on the LORD and he will sustain you.

Psalm 55:22

From the pen of Charles Spurgeon:

Care, even when shown to legitimate objects, has the nature of sin in it if carried to excess. The moral precept to avoid excessive anxiety and care was earnestly and persistently taught by our Savior again and again and was reiterated by the apostles. It is a teaching that cannot be neglected without becoming sin, for the very essence of anxious care reveals the idea that we think we are wiser than God and are putting ourselves in His place to do for Him what He has promised to do for us. We try to think of those things we believe He will forget and work to take upon ourselves all our burdens, as though He were unable or unwilling to take them for us.

This obvious disobedience to His clear directive, this unbelief of His Word, and this presumptive intrusion upon His providence is all sinful. Even more than that, anxious care often leads to sinful actions. Someone who cannot calmly leave his cares and concerns in God's hands, but carries his own burdens, is likely to be tempted to pursue sinful means to help himself. This sin will lead to forsaking God as his counselor and resorting instead to human wisdom. This is attempting to drink from "the pitcher [that] is shattered," instead of drinking from "the spring" (Eccl. 12:6) — the sin charged to Israel of old.

Anxiety causes us to doubt God's lovingkindness, which then leads our love for Him to grow cold. Our feelings of mistrust then grieve the Spirit of God so that our prayers are hindered, the consistency of our testimony tainted, and our life self-seeking. This lack of confidence in God leads us to wander far from Him. Yet if through simple faith in His promise we will cast each burden upon Him as it comes to us and will "not be anxious about anything" (Phil. 4:6) because He has promised to care for us, we will stay close to Him and will be greatly strengthened to withstand temptation.

"You will keep in perfect peace him whose mind is steadfast, because he trusts in you" (Isa. 26:3).

From the pen of Jim Reimann:

The world today is often over-stressed and filled with anxiety, and unfortunately God's people are not immune. Living like this, however, is something our Lord never intended for us, and is, in fact, something He gave His life to prevent. Thus, living in the world's continual whirlwind of stress, fear, worry, and anxiety is sin and shows a total lack of God's peace in our lives.

Jesus died, not just to give us life in heaven but also to provide abundant life today. He said, "I have come that they may have life, and have it to the full" (John 10:10). "Peace I leave with you; my peace I give you. I do not give to you as the world gives" (John 14:27).

No, Jesus does not give peace "as the world gives." And how does the world give peace? To this day, people in Israel use the greeting "Shalom!" — meaning peace. So Jesus said, in essence, "Unlike the world, which simply wishes you peace, I give you true inner peace. So, 'do not let your hearts be troubled and do not be afraid'" (John 14:27).

Lord, thank You for Jesus, who was sent "to guide our feet into the path of peace" (Luke 1:79).

Mephibosheth lived in Jerusalem, because he always ate at the king's table,
and he was crippled in both feet.

2 Samuel 9:13

From the pen of Charles Spurgeon:

Mephibosheth was no great adornment to the royal table, yet he had a permanent seat there because King David could see the features of his beloved Jonathan in his face. And like Mephibosheth, we may cry out to the King of Glory, "What is your servant, that you should notice a dead dog like me?" (2 Sam. 9:8). Yet the Lord still indulges us with the pleasure of His close fellowship because He sees in our countenance the features of His dearly beloved Jesus.

Thus, the Lord's people are dear to Him for someone else's sake, for this kind of love is that which the Father bestows on His "one and only Son" (John 3:16). For His Son's sake He raises His Son's lowly brothers from poverty and banishment to a place of kingly friendship, noble rank, and royal provision. And their deformity will never rob them of their privileges, for lameness is no barrier to sonship. In fact, a crippled person is as much an heir as though he were "as fleet-footed" (2 Sam. 2:18) as Asahel.

Our *right* as an heir will never limp, although our *might* may. The King's table is a noble hiding place for our lame legs, and at the feasting table of the gospel we learn to "boast ... about [our] weaknesses" because "Christ's power" rests on us (2 Cor. 12:5, 9).

A severe disability, however, may taint the character of even the best-loved saints in many eyes. For example, Mephibosheth feasted with David in spite of the fact he was so crippled in both feet he could not flee with the king when he fled the city. As a result of his inability to flee, he was wrongfully maligned and accused by his servant Ziba. (See 2 Sam. 16:1 – 4.)

In a spiritual sense, saints whose faith is crippled and weak and whose godly knowledge is limited are terrible losers. They are vulnerable to many enemies and cannot follow the King wherever He leads. Their crippling "disease" frequently is the result of falling to sin, which is typically brought about by lack of spiritual nourishment during their infancy as a believer. This often causes converts to fall into a despondency from which they never recover, or in other cases leads to sins resulting in spiritual "broken bones."

Lord, help "the lame leap like a deer" (Isa. 35:6) *and satisfy all Your people with the bread of Your table!*

From the pen of Jim Reimann:

In the Scriptures the spiritual life is compared to running a race. Yet we cannot run when spiritually disabled. And when we are handicapped, we are to blame, not the Lord, for He has provided all we need to run the race He has called us to run and never disqualifies us because we were once lame. As Spurgeon says today, sin is what creates our ongoing spiritual lameness, so "let us throw off everything that hinders and the sin that so easily entangles, and let us run with perseverance the race marked out for us" (Heb. 12:1).

Yes, God in His sovereignty not only tells us *where* to run by marking out our particular race but also tells us *how* to run:

"Do you not know that in a race all the runners run, but only one gets the prize? Run in such a way as to get the prize" (1 Cor. 9:24).

MAY 28

Those he justified, he also glorified.

Romans 8:30

From the pen of Charles Spurgeon:

This verse is a precious truth for you, dear believer. You may be poor, enduring suffering, or be relatively unknown, but be encouraged. Simply consider your calling and the benefits that flow from it, especially the one mentioned in this passage. As surely as you are a child of God today, then just as surely your trials will soon come to an end, and you will be rich in every way with great joy and happiness. Wait a little while and your weary head will be adorned with the crown of glory and your now laboring hands will grasp the palm branch of victory.

Do not lament your troubles, but rejoice that soon you will be where "there will be no more death or mourning or crying or pain" (Rev. 21:4). The "chariots of fire" (2 Kings 6:17) will soon be at your door and in a moment you will be transported to the place of the glorified. The eternal song is nearly on your lips and the gates of heaven stand open for you. Never doubt you will fail to enter this place of rest, for if the Lord has called you, nothing "will be able to separate [you] from the love of God" (Rom. 8:39). Suffering cannot break the bond, the fires of persecution cannot burn the cord, nor can the hammer of hell break the chain.

You are secure, for the Voice who called you at first will call you once again — from earth to heaven and from death's dark gloom to immortality's unspeakable splendor. Rest assured that the heart of Him who justified you beats with infinite love toward you. You will soon be with the glorified where your inheritance awaits you. You wait here only to be made ready for that inheritance, and once that is done, the wings of angels will lift you far away to the mountain of peace, joy, and blessedness, where:

> Far from a world of grief and sin,
> With God eternally shut in,
> Charles Wesley, 1707 – 1788

you will rest for ever and ever.

From the pen of Jim Reimann:

What our Lord starts He finishes. After all, He is "the Alpha and the Omega, the First and the Last, the Beginning and the End" (Rev. 22:13), and is "the author and perfecter [or completer] of our faith" (Heb. 12:2). Therefore, each and every believer can be "confident of this, that he who began a good work in you will carry it on to completion until the day of Christ Jesus" (Phil. 1:6).

Our verse today in its context says, "Those God foreknew he also predestined to be conformed to the likeness of his Son, that he might be the firstborn among many brothers. And those he predestined, he also called; those he called, he also justified; those he justified, he also glorified" (Rom. 8:29 – 30).

Consider the progression from foreknowledge, to predestination, to calling, to justification, and finally to glorification. As believers, we are saints in process — the process of sanctification. He is conforming us "to the likeness of his Son," and He will not stop until we reflect Him perfectly — until we are indeed glorified!

Thank You, Father, that "we, who with unveiled faces all reflect the Lord's glory, are being transformed into his likeness with ever-increasing glory, which comes from the Lord, who is the Spirit" (2 Cor. 3:18).

MAY 29

You ... hate wickedness.

Psalm 45:7

From the pen of Charles Spurgeon:

"Be angry and do not sin" (Eph. 4:26 ESV). There can hardly be any goodness in a person if he is not angry at sin, for he who loves truth must hate every evil. Oh, how our Lord Jesus hated it when temptation came to Him! Three times it attacked Him in different ways, but He always confronted it with: "Get thee behind me, Satan" (Luke 4:8 KJV). He hated it in others no less fervently, yet He showed His hate more often through tears of pity than through words of rebuke. What words could be more stern and "Elijah-like," however, than the statement, "Woe unto you, scribes and Pharisees, hypocrites! for [you] devour widows' houses, and for a pretence make long prayer" (Matt. 23:14 KJV).

Jesus hated wickedness so much that He shed His blood in order to wound it to the heart, He died that it would die, He was buried so He could bury it in His tomb, and He rose again that He could forever trample it beneath His feet. Christ is the gospel and that gospel is opposed to wickedness in every form. Wickedness adorns itself in beautiful garments and imitates the language of holiness; but the teachings of Jesus, like His "whip ... of cords" (John 2:15), chase it out of the temple and will not tolerate it in the church.

Thus, what a war also rages "between Christ and Belial" (2 Cor. 6:15) inside the heart where Jesus reigns! And when our Redeemer returns as Judge with the thundering words, "Away from me, all you evildoers!" (Luke 13:27), these very words will be nothing but a continuation of His earthly teaching concerning sin and will show His abhorrence of iniquity. As warm as His love is for sinners is how hot is His hatred of sin; and as perfect as is His righteousness is how complete will be the destruction of every kind of wickedness.

Oh, You glorious champion of right and destroyer of wrong! For this very cause "God, your God, has set you above your companions by anointing you with the oil of joy" (Heb. 1:9).

From the pen of Jim Reimann:

Some people criticize Christians who believe in the doctrine of grace known as the perseverance of the saints. They often say something along the lines of, "You only believe you are eternally secure in Christ so you can have a license to sin." This shows a total misunderstanding of the nature of a mature believer's heart, for a mature believer desires to walk in obedience, yet still struggles with the inner battle common to all of us. The Scriptures even warn us about "godless men, who change the grace of our God into a license for immorality and deny Jesus Christ our only Sovereign and Lord" (Jude 4).

Even the apostle Paul was a person like us who struggled with sin, for he wrote, "I do not understand what I do. For what I want to do I do not do, but what I hate I do.... I know that nothing good lives in me, that is, in my sinful nature. For I have the desire to do what is good, but I cannot carry it out. For what I do is not the good I want to do; no, the evil I do not want to do — this I keep on doing" (Rom. 7:15, 18 – 19). Just a few verses later he complained and asked, "What a wretched man I am! Who will rescue me from this body of death?" (v. 24). Then he gave us the glorious answer:

"Thanks be to God — through Jesus Christ our Lord!" (v. 25).

MAY 30

Catch for us the foxes,
the little foxes that ruin the vineyards.
Song of Songs 2:15

From the pen of Charles Spurgeon:

A small thorn can cause great pain. A little cloud can hide the sun. "Little foxes ... ruin the vineyards," and little sins do harm to a vulnerable heart. These little sins burrow into the soul and fill it with what is so hateful to Christ that He will no longer share His close fellowship and communion with us. Even big sins cannot destroy a Christian, yet even a little sin can make him miserable. Jesus will not walk with His people unless they force every known sin from their lives. He says, "If you obey my commands, you will remain in my love, just as I have obeyed my Father's commands and remain in his love" (John 15:10).

In fact, some Christians very seldom enjoy their Savior's presence. How can this be? Surely it is painful for a vulnerable child to be separated from his father. Are you a child of God, yet satisfied to continue living without seeing your Father's face? What! You are the bride of Christ, yet content without His companionship! You have fallen into a sad condition indeed, for the pure bride of Christ mourns like a dove without her mate when he has left her.

Ask yourself what has driven Christ from you? He hides His face behind your wall of sins, a wall built with little pebbles as easily as large stones. Great seas are made of small drops of water and huge rocks are made of small particles. In the same way, the sea that divides you from Christ may be filled with the small drops of your little sins, and the rock that has nearly sunk your ship may be the daily buildup of the tiny cells of a coral reef comprised of little sins.

If you desire to live with Christ, walk with Christ, see Christ, and have fellowship with Christ. Beware of "the little foxes that ruin the vineyards"—"for our vines have tender grapes" (Song 2:15 KJV). Jesus invites you to go with Him and "catch ... the foxes." With His great power, He will undoubtedly, like Samson, quickly and easily catch them.

Why not go with Him to the hunt?

From the pen of Jim Reimann:

Unfortunately, instead of repentance, sin's first work in our lives is to cause us to attempt to hide from the Lord. When Adam and Eve "heard the sound of the LORD God as he was walking in the garden in the cool of the day ... *they hid from the LORD God* among the trees of the garden" (Gen. 3:8).

Notice this verse does not say the Lord hid Himself from them. No, it was their sins that built the dividing wall between themselves and God. "Your iniquities have separated you from your God; your sins have hidden his face from you, so that he will not hear" (Isa. 59:2). Yet even in the garden of Eden, God in His sovereign grace sought out Adam—"But the LORD God called to the man, 'Where are you?'" (Gen. 3:9).

Believers need never suffer alienation from Him because "now in Christ Jesus you who once were far away have been brought near through the blood of Christ. For he himself is our peace, who has made the two one and has destroyed the barrier, the dividing wall of hostility" (Eph. 2:13–14).

Confess this morning those "little foxes" that have broken your fellowship with Christ who shed His blood for you!

MAY 31

The king also crossed the Kidron Valley.

2 Samuel 15:23

From the pen of Charles Spurgeon:

King David, along with his company of mourners, crossed this depressing valley when fleeing his traitorous son. Even the "man after [God's] own heart" (1 Sam. 13:14) was not exempt from trouble. In fact, his life was full of trials. He was not only the Lord's anointed but also the Lord's afflicted. Then why should we expect to escape hardship? At sorrow's gates even the noblest of humankind have waited with ashes on their heads, so why should we complain "as though something strange were happening to [us]" (1 Peter 4:12)?

"The King of kings" (1 Tim. 6:15) Himself was not shown favor with a more cheerful or royal road. He crossed the filthy ditch of Kidron, through which the filth of Jerusalem flowed. God had only one sinless Son, but not one child who did not suffer the rod of trials. What great comfort and confidence come from knowing that Jesus "has been tempted in every way, just as we are" (Heb. 4:15).

What is your Kidron Valley this morning? Is it an unsaved friend, the sad loss of a loved one, a slanderous offense, or some dark trial looming over you? Your King has passed through all of these. Is your Kidron bodily pain, poverty, persecution, or contempt? Your King has crossed each of these Kidrons before you. "In all their distress he too was distressed" (Isa. 63:9). The idea that we are experiencing "something strange" or unique must be banished from our minds once and for all, for He who is the Head of all saints knows from experience the grief we think is so unique to us.

All the citizens of Zion, of which Prince Immanuel is the Head and Captain, will someday be freed from the Honorable Company of Mourners, for in spite of David's humiliation he later returned in triumph to his city. And David's Lord arose from His grave victorious!

So let us "be of good courage" (Ps. 27:14 KJV), for we too will triumph. We will still joyfully draw water from the well of salvation, though for a season we must walk beside the noxious streams of sin and sorrow. "Be strong and take heart" (Ps. 31:24), you soldiers of the cross. Your King Himself triumphed after crossing the Kidron Valley, and so will you!

From the pen of Jim Reimann:

The Kidron Valley in Jerusalem is joined by two other valleys, the Tyropoeon (Greek for Cheesemakers) and the Hinnom (or Gehenna or Gehenom). The Hinnom, considered the destination of the wicked, was a place of lepers cast from society, a place of sewage, and a place of constantly burning garbage. It was in this valley the children of Israel turned away from the Lord, "built the high places of Baal" and "cause[d] their sons and their daughters to pass through the fire unto Molech" (Jer. 32:35 KJV) — human sacrifice that is an abomination to God. The sewage from the Cheesemakers and Hinnom Valleys flowed into the Kidron and finally emptied into the Dead Sea. Even the city gate by the Cheesemakers Valley was known as the Dung Gate, as it is to this day. (See Neh. 2:13.)

Although we must walk these filthy and dangerous valleys of this life — remember — our Lord has already walked them and walks them again with us.

I praise You, Father, that "even though I walk through the valley of the shadow of death, I will fear no evil, for you are with me" (Ps. 23:4).

June

JUNE 1

There was evening,
and there was morning — the first day.

Genesis 1:5

From the pen of Charles Spurgeon:

Was it truly this way even in the beginning, that darkness and light divided the domain of time the very first day? Then is it any wonder I also experience changes in my circumstances from the sunshine of prosperity to the midnight of adversity. When it comes to the concerns of my soul, there will not always be the blazing sun of noonday. I must expect times when I must mourn the absence of former joys and must seek "my beloved ... [in] the night" (Song 5:2 KJV). Nor am I alone in this, for all the Lord's beloved ones have had to sing songs mixed with judgment and mercy, trials and deliverance, and of mourning and rejoicing.

It is part of divine Providence's plan that "day and night will never cease" (Gen. 8:22), either in the natural or the spiritual realm, until we reach the land foretold in the Scriptures where "there will be no more night" (Rev. 22:5). And remember, what our heavenly Father ordains is wise and good.

What then, my soul, is best for me to do? I must first learn to be content with God's divine order of things and be willing, just as Job was, to "accept good from God, and ... trouble" (Job 2:10). Next, I must determine to have rejoicing flow from my life in the morning and the evening. I must praise the Lord for the sun of joy when it rises and for the gloom of evening as it falls. There is beauty in both the sunrise and sunset, so I should sing of it and glorify the Lord. Just as a nightingale does, I should sing at all hours and believe that the night is as useful as the day. The dew of God's grace falls most heavily during the night of sorrow, and His stars of promise shine most gloriously amid the darkness of grief.

I must continue serving through all the changes in life. My daytime watchword must be "to work" and at night "to watch." Each hour of the day and night has a special duty, so I must faithfully continue in my calling as the Lord's servant until He suddenly "comes in His glory" (Matt. 25:31).

My soul, your evening of old age and death draws near, but do not dread it, for it is part of the day. Remember, God's Word says, "The LORD ... shields him *all day long*" (Deut. 33:12).

From the pen of Jim Reimann:

Day and night are parts of the cycle of life. Yet our response to them is what makes all the difference. Walking in joy or gloom is our decision and should never be determined by our circumstances. We should learn, as Paul did, "to be content whatever the circumstances" (Phil. 4:11). In fact, he thought it was totally absurd to waste our time complaining: "I consider that our present sufferings are not worth comparing with the glory that will be revealed in us" (Rom. 8:18).

And Peter tells us we possess "a living hope ... into an inheritance that can never perish, spoil, or fade — kept in heaven for you" (1 Peter 1:3 – 4). Notice that the "keeping" of our inheritance is not up to us. It is not based on our works any more than our salvation is. No, God does the keeping, and it has nothing to do with our circumstances! Then, agreeing with Deuteronomy 33:12 quoted above, Peter states that we "are shielded by God's power" until the very end — "until the coming of the salvation that is ready to be revealed in the last time" (1 Peter 1:5).

So, my friend, if you and your inheritance are secured by God's power — not yours — why should you ever fear the dark times of life? Rejoice instead!

JUNE 2

The sinful nature desires what is contrary to the Spirit,
and the Spirit what is contrary to the sinful nature.

Galatians 5:17

From the pen of Charles Spurgeon:

In every believer's heart there is a constant struggle between the old nature and the new. The old nature is still very active and wastes no opportunity to employ all of its deadly weapons of war against newborn grace, while the new nature is constantly on watch to resist and destroy its enemy. Grace within us employs prayer, faith, hope, and love to cast out evil. It "put[s] on the full armor of God" (Eph. 6:11) and earnestly wrestles. And these two opposing natures will never cease to struggle as long as we are in this world.

In *The Pilgrim's Progress* by John Bunyan (1628 – 1688), the battle between Christian and Apollyon lasts only three hours, but the battle between Christian and himself lasts all the way from the Wicket Gate in the river Jordan. Our enemy is so securely entrenched within us that it can never be driven out while we remain in this body. Yet, even though we are severely attacked and often in great conflict, we have an almighty Helper — Jesus, the Captain of our salvation — who is always with us and who assures us that eventually we will be "more than conquerors through him" (Rom. 8:37). Thus, with such great assistance, the newborn nature is more than a match for its foes.

Are you fighting with your adversary today? Are Satan, the world, and the flesh all coming against you? Don't be discouraged or dismayed. Fight on! For God Himself is with you; Jehovah-Nissi "is [your] Banner" (Ex. 17:15) and Jehovah-Rapha is He "who heals" (Ex. 15:26) your wounds. So do not be fearful; you "will overcome" (Rev. 17:14), for who can defeat Omnipotence? Fight on, "fix[ing] [y]our eyes on Jesus" (Heb. 12:2). Although the conflict is long and hard, how sweet will be the victory and how glorious the promised reward!

> From "strength to strength" (Ps. 84:7) go on;
> Wrestle, and fight, and pray,
> Tread all the powers of darkness down,
> And win the well-fought day.
>
> Charles Wesley, 1707 – 1788

From the pen of Jim Reimann:

Sometimes the road ahead seems far too treacherous to continue, to the point we worry and obsess over what tomorrow may hold.

> Therefore, I tell you, do not worry about your life.... Who of you by worrying can add a single hour to his life? ... But seek first [God's] kingdom and his righteousness, and all these things will be given to you as well. Therefore, do not worry about tomorrow, for tomorrow will worry about itself.
>
> Matthew 6:25, 27, 33 – 34

And all too often the road we walk seems far too long. At those times, remember the admonition and encouragement of James, who wrote:

> Now listen, you who say, "Today or tomorrow we will go to this or that city, spend a year there, carry on business and make money." Why, you do not even know what will happen tomorrow. What is your life? *You are a mist that appears for a little while and then vanishes.*
>
> James 4:13 – 14

Lord, help me to "fix [my] eyes on Jesus" and to remember this life is but a vapor when compared to eternity that lies just beyond the horizon of today's trial.

JUNE 3

These were the potters, and those that dwelt among plants and hedges:
there they dwelt with the king for his work.

1 Chronicles 4:23 KJV

From the pen of Charles Spurgeon:

Potters weren't considered the highest class of workers, and the material they used was nothing but clay. The king needed them, however, so they were employed in royal work. We as well may be engaged in the most menial tasks for the Lord, but it is still a great privilege to do anything for the King. Thus, we will continue in our calling, with the hope that "Even while [we] sleep among the campfires, the wings of [our] dove are sheathed with silver, its feathers with shining gold" (Ps. 68:13).

Our text verse tells us of "those that dwelt among plants and hedges"—those living and working in rough and difficult conditions. Perhaps they desired to live in the city among the workings of society and places of refinement, but they stayed in the appointed places, for they were doing the king's work.

In the same way, the place of our calling is fixed and we are not to leave it due to some fleeting whim or mood. Instead, we are to serve the Lord where we are by being a blessing to those around us. These potters and gardeners had royal company, for "they dwelt with the king," and although they had to live "among plants and hedges," it was *there* "they dwelt with the king."

There is no place or occupation, however menial, that can prohibit us from communing with our divine Lord — as long as that place or occupation is of Him. Even when visiting the poor in their roach-infested shacks, factories, or jails, we can go with the King. In all our works of faith we can count on fellowship with Jesus, and it is when we are at His work we will encounter His smile.

You unknown servants who work for your Lord amid the dirt and wretchedness of the lowest of the lowest class, be of good cheer! Jewels have been found in the dunghills of life, ordinary clay pots have been filled with heavenly treasure, and ugly weeds have been transformed into beautiful flowers.

Continue to dwell with the King, doing His work, and when He writes His final chronicles your name will be recorded there.

From the pen of Jim Reimann:

It may sound trite to say, "Bloom where you're planted," but there is profound truth in this simple statement. Paul addressed this very issue by saying, "Each one should retain the place in life that the Lord assigned to him and to which God has called him. This is the rule I lay down in all the churches" (1 Cor. 7:17).

We need to come to the realization our Lord has many different roles and gifts He bestows on His people. "We have different gifts, according to the grace given us" (Rom. 12:6). Not only is it important for each of us to exercise *what* our gift entails, it is important we exercise it precisely *where* God would have us do so. And we need each other to be faithful to this so that we as God's church do not become unbalanced. We depend on each other.

Help me, Lord, to use my gifts for Your glory — where You have placed me. May I be grateful for my gifts and never complain about what You have called me to do and where You have determined I should serve You.

JUNE 4

The kindness and love of God our Savior appeared.

Titus 3:4

From the pen of Charles Spurgeon:

How wonderful it is to behold the Savior communing with His own beloved people! There can be nothing more delightful than to be led by His Divine Spirit into this fertile field of blessing. Allow yourself to consider for a moment the history of our Redeemer's love, and a thousand beautiful acts of affection will come to mind. Each of them has been designed to weave your heart into Christ and to intertwine the thoughts and emotions of your renewed soul with the mind of Jesus. When we truly meditate on His amazing love and behold the all-glorious Bridegroom of the church bestowing on us all His ancient wealth, our souls may soon faint with joy. After all, who of us can endure such great love? Even our partial understanding of His love, which the Holy Spirit is sometimes pleased to impart, is more than any soul can bear. How overwhelming a complete view of it must be!

Once our souls have complete discernment of all the Savior's gifts, the wisdom with which to fully value them, and enough time in which to meditate upon them — such as will only be available to us in the world to come — we will then commune with Jesus much more closely than today. Who can even imagine the wonder of such sweet fellowship? This must be one of the things that "no mind has conceived [t]hat God has prepared for those who love him" (1 Cor. 2:9).

Oh, to burst open the doors of our "Joseph's" storehouses and behold how much He has stored up for us! We will certainly be overwhelmed with love. Today by faith "we see but a poor reflection as in a mirror" (1 Cor. 13:12) the image of His endless treasures. But when we finally see these heavenly blessings themselves with our own eyes, how deep will be the streams of fellowship in which our souls will soak!

Until then our loudest psalms of praise will be reserved for our loving benefactor, Jesus Christ our Lord, whose "love for [us is] wonderful, more wonderful than that of women" (2 Sam. 1:26).

From the pen of Jim Reimann:

Yes, "God has poured out his love into our hearts by the Holy Spirit, whom he has given us" (Rom. 5:5). And He did not pour that love into us sparingly, for John wrote, "How great is the love the Father has *lavished* on us" (1 John 3:1). There is no question "God is love" (1 John 4:8), and John describes His love in this way: "This is love: not that we loved God, but that he loved us and sent his Son as an atoning sacrifice for our sins" (1 John 4:10). "Greater love has no one than this, that he lay down his life for his friends" (John 15:13). As believers, what do we do with so great a love as this? John answers that for us as well:

"Dear friends, since God so loved us, we also ought to love one another. No one has ever seen God; but if we love one another, God lives in us and his love is made complete in us" (1 John 4:11 – 12). And remember the words of Jesus, who said, "By this all men will know that you are my disciples, if you love one another" (John 13:35).

Finally, God's consistent message is echoed by Paul in the following admonishment: "Owe no man any thing, but to love one another" (Rom. 13:8 KJV).

Lord, may Your great love flow through me into the lives of others.

JUNE 5

The LORD shut him in.

Genesis 7:16

From the pen of Charles Spurgeon:

Noah was shut away from the world in the ark by the hand of divine Love. The door of "God's purpose in election" (Rom. 9:11) intervenes between us and the world that dwells with the wicked one. We "are not of the world any more than [Jesus was] of the world" (John 17:14). We cannot enter into the sins of the multitudes or play in the streets of Vanity Fair of *The Pilgrim's Progress* (John Bunyan, 1628 – 1688) with the children of darkness, for our heavenly Father has "shut [us] in." Noah was not just shut in *by* his God but also *with* his God. The Lord's invitation — "I will establish my covenant with you…. Enter the ark — you and your sons and your wife and your sons' wives with you" (Gen. 6:18) — clearly shows that God Himself intended to dwell in the ark with His servant.

In the same way, all God's chosen dwell in Him and He in them. How blessed we are to be included in the same circle that contains the three persons of the Trinity of God: Father, Son, and Spirit! May we never ignore His gracious appeal: "Go, my people, enter your rooms and shut the doors behind you; hide yourselves for a little while until his wrath has passed by" (Isa. 26:20). Noah was so shut in that "no harm [could] befall [him]" (Ps. 91:10). Even the flood did nothing but lift him heavenward and the wind only wafted him on his way. Everything outside the ark was in total ruin, but inside was only rest and peace.

Without Christ Jesus we perish, but in Him there is complete safety. Noah was so shut in that he would never desire to come out, and those who are in Christ Jesus are in Him forever. We will never come out from Him, for eternal Faithfulness has shut us in, and our evil enemy can never drag us from safety. The Prince of the house of David has shut the door that no man can open. And "once the owner of the house gets up and closes the door" in the last days, those who profess Him in name only "will stand outside knocking and pleading" in vain, "Sir, open the door for us" (Luke 13:25). The same door that shuts in the wise virgins will shut out the foolish ones forever. (See Matt. 25:1 – 13.)

Lord, shut me in by Your grace.

From the pen of Jim Reimann:

The story of Noah and the ark is so much more than a child's Sunday school story! It is the story of God's sovereign work of grace in choosing — or electing — Noah and his family for His eternal salvation. And it clearly teaches us that those eight people were saved, not because of their good works but simply because they were in the ark. God Himself closed the door, sealing Noah in the ark in the same way the Holy Spirit seals us in Jesus Christ.

"You also were included in Christ when you heard the word of truth, the gospel of your salvation. Having believed, you were marked in him with a seal, the promised Holy Spirit" (Eph. 1:13). The "seal" of the Holy Spirit has a twofold purpose: He is not only the one who permanently protects us in Christ but also our King's seal of ownership on us, just as an earthly king sealed his letters with his own name. And the seal of "the promised Holy Spirit" is sufficient to protect us in Christ until He returns, for the next verse says: "You were sealed for the day of redemption" (Eph. 4:30).

I give thanks that "you alone, O LORD, make me dwell in safety" (Ps. 4:8).

JUNE 6

Behold, I am vile.

Job 40:4 KJV

From the pen of Charles Spurgeon:

Poor, lost sinner, here is a cheerful thought for you! Do you think you cannot come to God because you are vile? You need to know there is not one saint on earth who has not been made to feel vile. If Job, Isaiah, and Paul were all obliged to say, "I am vile," then will you, poor sinner, be ashamed to join in the same confession? If divine grace does not eradicate all sin from believers, how can you expect to do it yourself? And if God loves His people while they are still vile, do you really think your vileness will prevent Him from loving you?

Believe on Jesus, you outcast of the world's society! Jesus calls *you* — and just as you are!

> Not the righteous, not the righteous;
> Sinners, Jesus came to call.
>
> Joseph Hart, 1712 – 1768

Declare these words to Him this moment, "Lord Jesus, You died for sinners, and I am a sinner. Sprinkle me with Your blood." If you confess your sin you will be pardoned. If you will say with all your heart, "'I am vile,' cleanse me," you will be immediately clean. If the Holy Spirit will enable you to cry out from your heart:

> Just as I am, without one plea
> But that Thy blood was shed for me,
> And that thou bidd'st me come to Thee,
> O Lamb of God, I come!
>
> Charlotte Elliott, 1789 – 1871

you will stand after this morning's devotion with all your sins pardoned. Although you awoke this morning with every sin known to man upon your head, you will rest tonight "accepted in the beloved" (Eph. 1:6 KJV). Though you were once regarded with contempt and were clothed in rags of sin, you will be adorned in a "robe of righteousness" (Isa. 61:10) and will appear as bright as an angel. "For ... now" — yes, now — "is the time of God's favor, *now* is the day of salvation" (2 Cor. 6:2).

If you trust "God who justifies the wicked" (Rom. 4:5), "you are saved" (1 Cor. 15:2). Oh, may the Holy Spirit give you saving faith in Him who receives even the vilest of sinners!

From the pen of Jim Reimann:

So often the lost think they need to clean themselves up to come to Jesus. What they do not realize, however, is that they are powerless to do so. If that were possible, Christ's death would have been in vain. He prayed, "My Father, *if it is possible*, may this cup be taken from me" (Matt. 26:39). But, it was not possible. There was no other way. He had to die for us to be made clean.

My friend, remember: "*While we were still sinners*, Christ died for us" (Rom. 5:8). Notice He died "*while* we were still sinners," not *after* we had forsaken all of our sins — something we are incapable of doing.

"Because of his great love for us, God, who is rich in mercy, made us alive with Christ even *when we were dead* in transgressions" (Eph. 2:4 – 5). Yes, "*when we were dead.*" And a dead man can do nothing — much less clean himself up!

JUNE 7

Let those who love the LORD hate evil.

Psalm 97:10

From the pen of Charles Spurgeon:

You have good reason to "hate evil." Consider the damage it has already caused you and what an abundance of disobedience it has brought into your heart! Sin once blinded you so you could not see the beauty of the Savior and made you deaf so you could not hear the Redeemer's tender invitation. Sin caused your feet to walk in the way of death and poured poison into the deepest fountain of your being. It polluted your heart and made it "deceitful above all things and beyond cure" (Jer. 17:9).

Oh, what a wretched creature you were when evil had done its worst in you, before God's divine grace intervened! As others are, you were once an heir of His wrath and "follow[ed] the crowd in doing wrong" (Ex. 23:2). This is how we all once were, but Paul reminds us: "You were washed, you were sanctified, you were justified in the name of the Lord Jesus Christ and by the Spirit of our God" (1 Cor. 6:11).

Yes, we have good reason for hating evil when we look back and retrace its deadly work. Sinfulness did such great evil to us that our souls would still be lost if God's omnipotent love had not intervened to redeem us. And even now it is an active enemy, always alert, hoping to do us harm and to drag us once again into wickedness.

Therefore, dear Christians, "hate evil" unless you desire more trouble. If you wish to litter your path with thorns and fill your death-pillow with needles, then neglect to "hate evil." But if you desire to live a happy life and die a peaceful death, then walk in "the Way of Holiness" (Isa. 35:8), hating evil unto the very end. If you truly love your Savior and wish to honor Him, then "hate evil."

There is no better cure for a Christian's love of evil than abundant fellowship with the Lord Jesus. If you spend your time with Him, it will be impossible for you to be at peace with sin.

> Order my footsteps by Thy Word,
> And make my heart sincere;
> Let sin have no dominion, Lord,
> But keep my conscience clear.
>
> Isaac Watts, 1674 – 1748

From the pen of Jim Reimann:

We should learn to hate what the Lord hates and love what He loves.

> There are six things the LORD hates, seven that are detestable to him: haughty eyes, a lying tongue, hands that shed innocent blood, a heart that devises wicked schemes, feet that are quick to rush into evil, a false witness who pours out lies and a man who stirs up dissension among brothers.
>
> Proverbs 6:16 – 19

"The LORD loves righteousness and justice" (Ps. 33:5). And the Lord loves His Son, for He said, "This is my Son, whom I love. Listen to him!" (Mark 9:7).

What great advice for believers who desire to honor the Lord: "Listen to him!" But may we follow our listening with obedience to what we hear, making this commitment to the Lord, "We will listen and obey" (Deut. 5:27).

JUNE 8

Many others fell slain,
because the battle was God's.
1 Chronicles 5:22

From the pen of Charles Spurgeon:

Dear Christian warrior fighting under the banner of the Lord Jesus, consider today's verse with holy joy, for the same is true today as in biblical days of old — if the battle is of God, victory is certain. "The Reubenites, the Gadites and the half-tribe of Manasseh had [only] 44,760 men ready for military service" (v. 18), yet in their war with the Hagarites, "they ... took one hundred thousand people captive and many others fell slain" (vv. 21–22). This happened "because they cried out to [God] during the battle [and] He answered their prayers, because they trusted in him" (v. 20).

Whether we have an army of many or few makes no difference — it is up to us to go forth in Jehovah's name. Deliverance will come with even a handful of men for "the LORD Almighty is with us" (Ps. 46:7) and is our Captain. Israel did not neglect to take their shields, swords, bows, and arrows with them, but they did not place their trust in weapons. We too should use the weapons at our disposal, but our confidence must rest in the Lord alone, for He is the sword and the shield of His people. The absolute reason for Israel's extraordinary success lay in the fact that "the battle was God's."

Dear beloved, as you wage war with sin within and without — whether with doctrinal error or practical living, with spiritual wickedness in high or low places, or with the Devil and his allies — you are waging Jehovah's war. And unless He Himself can be overpowered, you need never fear defeat. Do not cower at the sight of superior numbers, shrink from difficulties, or fear what may appear to be impossible. Never flinch at either battle wounds or death, but strike the enemy with the "double-edged" (Heb. 4:12) "sword of the Spirit" (Eph. 6:17) and the slain will fall in droves.

"The battle is the LORD's and he will give [His enemies] into our hands" (1 Sam. 17:47). With sure footedness, strong hands, undaunted heart, and flaming zeal, run to the conflict. The hosts of evil will fly away "like chaff before the wind" (Ps. 35:5).

> Stand up! Stand up for Jesus!
> The strife will not be long;
> This day the noise of battle,
> The next the victor's song.
> To those who vanquish evil
> A crown of life shall be;
> They with the King of glory
> Shall reign eternally.
> George Duffield, Jr., 1818–1888

From the pen of Jim Reimann:

"The battle is the LORD's," yet we are told: "Put on the full armor of God, so ... you may be able to stand your ground" (Eph. 6:13). But remember, "It is God who makes both us and you stand firm in Christ" (2 Cor. 1:21). "Do not throw away your confidence; it will be richly rewarded. You need to persevere.... We are not of those who shrink back ... but of those who believe and are saved" (Heb. 10:35–36, 39).

JUNE 9

The LORD has done great things for us,
and we are filled with joy.

Psalm 126:3

From the pen of Charles Spurgeon:

Sadly, some Christians are prone to look on the dark side of everything and to dwell more on past difficulties rather than on what God has done for them. When asked their view of the Christian life, they list their continual conflicts, their deepest problems, their sad adversities, and the sinful condition of their heart. Seldom will they even allude to the great mercies God has graciously given them.

Yet a Christian whose soul is healthy is joyful and will share along the lines: "I will not speak about myself except to God's honor. 'He lifted me out of the slimy pit, out of the mud and mire; he set my feet on a rock and gave me a firm place to stand. He put a new song in my mouth, a hymn of praise to our God' (Ps. 40:2 – 3). 'The LORD has done great things for [me], and [I am] filled with joy'" (Ps. 126:3).

This kind of brief summary of their experience is the very best any child of God could hope to exhibit. Yes, it is true we must endure trials, but it is just as true that the Lord delivers us out of them. It is true we all have our sinful shortcomings, which we all regret, but it is equally as true that we have an all-sufficient Savior who overcomes these shortcomings and delivers us from their power.

When we look back, it would be wrong to deny we were once in the Slough of Despond [the bog in The Pilgrim's Progress by John Bunyan (1628 – 1688) where Christian sinks under the weight of his sins and guilt] or that we have crept along the Valley of Humiliation [also from The Pilgrim's Progress]. It would be equally as wrong to forget that we went through them safely and profitably. We did not remain in them, thanks to our almighty Helper and Leader who "brought us to a place of abundance" (Ps. 66:12).

The deeper our troubles have been, the louder our thanks to God should be, for He led us through them all and has preserved us until now. Our grievous trials should not sour our hymns of praise, but should actually become the bass part of life's song:

"The LORD has done great things for us, and we are filled with joy."

From the pen of Jim Reimann:

No one enjoys believers who live as though they have been baptized in vinegar. They drain energy from us rather than motivate us to be better Christians. If you examine yourself and come to the realization this describes you, there is hope. But it involves being honest and being willing to change your thinking.

"Whatever is true, whatever is noble, whatever is right, whatever is pure, whatever is lovely, whatever is admirable — if anything is excellent or praiseworthy — think about such things" (Phil. 4:8). "Do not conform any longer to the pattern of this world, but be transformed by the renewing of your mind" (Rom. 12:2).

Our thinking is transformed as we discipline ourselves to spend time in the Scriptures. "We have the mind of Christ" (1 Cor. 2:16) — the Word of God!

JUNE 10

We live to the Lord.
Romans 14:8

From the pen of Charles Spurgeon:

If it were God's will, each of us might have gone straight to heaven at the moment of our conversion. It was not absolutely necessary for us to linger here to be fully prepared for immortality. It is certainly possible for someone to be taken to heaven, fully prepared to partake of his inheritance as a saint of light the moment he believes in Jesus. But our sanctification is a long, continual process, and we will not be perfected until we lay aside our bodies and enter "the inner sanctuary behind the curtain" (Heb. 6:19). Nevertheless, if the Lord had so willed it, He could have immediately changed us from imperfect to perfect and taken us to heaven.

Then why are we here? Would God keep His children out of paradise a single moment longer than necessary? Why is the army of the living God still on the battlefield when a single strike from heaven could give us victory? Why are His children still wandering here and there through a maze when one word from His lips would take us to the very center of our hopes in heaven?

The answer is that we are here so we may "live to the Lord" and lead others to know His love. We remain on earth to sow His good seed, to plow the unsown ground, and to proclaim the message of salvation. We are here as "the salt of the earth" (Matt. 5:13) to be a blessing to the world. We are here to glorify Christ in our daily life. We are here as workers for Him and "as God's fellow workers" (2 Cor. 6:1).

Let us live so our lives fulfill His purpose. Let us live committed, useful, holy lives "to the praise of his glorious grace" (Eph. 1:6). In the meantime we long to "be with the Lord forever" (1 Thess. 4:17) and sing each day:

> My heart is with Him on His throne,
> Scarce can I bear delay;
> Each moment listening for His voice,
> "Rise up … and come away" (Song 2:10
> KJV).
>
> Horatius Bonar, 1808 – 1889

From the pen of Jim Reimann:

Many Christians are quick to say, "I'm willing to die for the Lord!" Yet how many of us are willing to *live* for Him? Remember Paul's exhortation to us? "I urge you, brothers, in view of God's mercy, to offer your bodies as *living sacrifices*, holy and pleasing to God — this is your spiritual act of worship" (Rom. 12:1). "Living sacrifices" — not dead sacrifices! God has called us to His work until He calls us home. Here is how Paul describes our ministry and message as believers:

"All this is from God, who reconciled us to himself through Christ and gave us the ministry of reconciliation.… And he has committed to us the message of reconciliation. We are therefore Christ's ambassadors, as though God were making his appeal through us" (2 Cor. 5:18 – 20).

And we are to be a *living* memorial to Him, not a *dead* memorial. Peter said, "You also, like *living* stones, are being built into a spiritual house to be a holy priesthood, offering spiritual sacrifices acceptable to God through Jesus Christ" (1 Peter 2:5).

JUNE 11

We love him, because he first loved us.

1 John 4:19 KJV

From the pen of Charles Spurgeon:

Just as there is no light on earth except that which comes from the sun, there is no true love for Jesus in our hearts except that which comes from the Lord Jesus Himself. Our love for God must flow from the overflowing fountain of the infinite love of God. This is a great undeniable truth: "We love him" for no other reason than "he first loved us." Our love for Him is beautifully born of His love for us.

Anyone may have cold unemotional admiration for the works of God, but warm emotional love can only be kindled in our hearts by God's Spirit. The greatest wonder is that we, such as we are, have ever been brought to love Jesus at all! How miraculous that after having rebelled against Him, He was willing to seek to draw us back through a display of such amazing love!

No, we would never have had even a seed of love toward God without it being sown in our hearts by the sweet seed of His love for us! Thus, our love's parent is the love God "has poured out ... into our hearts" (Rom. 5:5). Then after being divinely born, this love must be divinely nourished. It is an exotic plant — not one that will naturally flourish in human soil, and one that must be watered from above. Love for Jesus is a delicate flower and would soon wither if the only nourishment it received came from the hard rocky soil of our hearts. Just as love comes from heaven, it must feed on heavenly bread. It cannot exist in the wilderness unless it is fed with manna from on high.

Love must feed on love, and the very soul and life of our love for God is His love for us.

I love thee, Lord, but with no love of mine,
For I have none to give;
I love thee, Lord; but all the love is thine,
For by thy love I live.
I am as nothing, and rejoice to be
Emptied, and lost, and swallowed up in thee.

Madame Jeanne-Marie Guyon, 1648 – 1717

Translated from French by
William Cowper, 1731 – 1800

From the pen of Jim Reimann:

Love is a gift of God. In fact, salvation and everything that accompanies it comes from Him — "All this is from God" (2 Cor. 5:18). This gift of love that accompanies our salvation is wonderful evidence of that salvation, because we were once God's enemy. But when Jesus saved us "he himself [became] our peace ... and ... destroyed the barrier, the dividing wall of hostility" (Eph. 2:14).

Yet the miracle of God's love comes with a responsibility, not only to "Love the Lord your God with all your heart and with all your soul and with all your strength and with all your mind," but also to "Love your neighbor as yourself" (Luke 10:27).

"Dear friends, let us love one another, for love comes from God. Everyone who loves has been born of God and knows God" (1 John 4:7).

Lord, thank You for Your gift of love. May it overflow to those around me.

JUNE 12

You have been weighed on the scales and found wanting.

Daniel 5:27

From the pen of Charles Spurgeon:

It is a good idea to weigh yourself frequently "on the scales" of God's Word. You will find it a holy exercise to read a psalm of David and, as you meditate on each verse, to ask yourself, "Can I say this? Have I ever felt as David did? Am I as ever heartbroken over sin as he was when he penned his psalms of repentance? Has my soul ever been filled with complete confidence in times of difficulty as was David's when he sang of God's mercies in 'the cave of Adullam' (1 Sam. 22:1) or 'the strongholds of En Gedi'? (1 Sam. 23:29). Do I 'lift up the cup of salvation and call on the name of the LORD'?" (Ps. 116:13).

Next turn to the life of Christ in your Bible and, as you read, ask yourself how far along you are in being "conformed to [His] likeness" (Rom. 8:29). Seek to discover whether you have the same meekness, humility, and the kind spirit continually instilled and displayed in Him.

Finally turn to the epistles of Paul and see whether your life is in agreement with his experience. Have you ever cried out as he did, "What a wretched man I am! Who will rescue me from this body of death" (Rom. 7:24)? Have you ever felt his self-abasement? Have you ever felt that you were "the worst" (1 Tim. 1:15) of sinners and "the least of all God's people" (Eph. 3:8)? Have you ever known anything close to his level of devotion to God? Can you join him in saying, "For to me, to live is Christ and to die is gain" (Phil. 1:21)?

If we will read God's Word as a test of our spiritual condition, we will find many reasons to stop and say, "Lord, I have never been here, but take me to this place! Give me true repentance — the kind I see in Your Word. Give me real faith and warmer zeal, ignite me with more fervent love, grant me the gift of meekness — make me more like Jesus. May I no longer be 'found wanting' when 'weighed on the scales' of Your sanctuary, lest I be 'found wanting' when 'weighed on the scales' of Your judgment."

We should judge ourselves so we will not be judged and "found wanting."

From the pen of Jim Reimann:

Many Christians tend to misunderstand Jesus' admonition: "Do not judge, or you too will be judged" (Matt. 7:1). He is not saying not to judge at all, but not to be hypocritical. We are to judge ourselves first before judging others. "You hypocrite, first take the plank out of your own eye, and then you will see clearly to remove the speck from your brother's eye" (Matt. 7:5).

The apostle Paul tells us to judge believers in our fellowship, but to leave the judging of unbelievers to the Lord. "What business is it of mine to judge those outside the church? Are you not to judge those inside? God will judge those outside" (1 Cor. 5:12 – 13). He goes on to say, "Do you not know that the saints will judge the world? And if you are to judge the world, are you not competent to judge trivial cases? Do you not know that we will judge angels? How much more the things of this life!" (1 Cor. 6:2 – 3).

The best policy, however, is always to search inwardly first. If we are honest with what the Lord exposes in us, we will most likely be too busy to judge others. After all, He can take care of others: "He will judge the world in righteousness and the peoples in his truth" (Ps. 96:13).

June 13

Come!... Whoever wishes,
let him take the free gift of the water of life.
Revelation 22:17

From the pen of Charles Spurgeon:

Jesus says, "Take the free gift." He asks for no payment or preparation. He doesn't require any strong feelings or emotions, for as long as you are willing, you may come! Do you lack faith and repentance? Come to Him and He will give them to you. Come just as you are and "take the free gift" without money or cost. He gives Himself to those who are needy.

Public drinking fountains are wonderful things — open to everyone — so we can hardly imagine a thirsty person foolish enough to stand by one, reaching for his wallet on a hot summer day, and then saying, "I can't drink from it because I don't have any money." However poor a person may be, he may drink and may do so just as he is. As thirsty people walk by, whether dressed in jeans or in the finest cashmere, they do not seek anyone's permission to drink, for the fact that the water fountain is there is permission enough to drink freely. Whether the refreshing water has been put there through the generosity of the landlord or someone else makes no difference — it is there, so ask no questions, and "take the free gift of the water." Perhaps the only people who will go thirsty when a public drinking fountain is nearby are the highest of society in all their finery. They may be thirsty, but would never think to stoop so slow and demean themselves by drinking from a common water fountain, so they walk on by with their parched lips.

In the same way, how many people are rich in their own good works and therefore cannot come to Christ! They say to themselves, "I will not be saved the same way a prostitute or degenerate is saved. What! Go to heaven the same way as the lowest of society? Isn't there a way to get to glory except the way taken by a thief? I will not be saved that way!"

Those with such pride and boasting due to their own achievements, possessions, or abilities must continue without the "living water" (John 4:10). But, *whoever wishes, let him take the free gift of the water of life."*

From the pen of Jim Reimann:

Jesus was once at "the Jewish Feast of Tabernacles" (John 7:2). At the highest point of the feast, the Festival of the Water Libation, the high priest would lead a procession to the Pool of Siloam, fill the silver vessel with water, and return to the temple. The primary aspect of the holiday is the command: "Be joyful" (Deut. 16:14). At this most joyful moment, as the high priest was pouring the water onto the altar, "Jesus stood and said in a loud voice, 'If anyone is thirsty, *let him come to me and drink.* Whoever believes in me, as the Scripture has said, streams of living water will flow from within him'" (John 7:37 – 38).

Some believed immediately, saying, "He is the Christ," while others refused to believe "the Christ [could] come from Galilee" (John 7:41). "Thus the people were divided because of Jesus" (John 7:43).

The message is so simple, a child can understand it: *"If anyone is thirsty, let him come to me and drink."* But we must humble ourselves, for "Anyone who will not receive the kingdom of God like a little child will never enter it" (Mark 10:15).

JUNE 14

Delight yourself in the LORD.

Psalm 37:4

From the pen of Charles Spurgeon:

This verse must seem very strange to those who know nothing of living a godly life, but to sincere believers it is simply the reinforcement of a recognized truth. It describes the life of a believer as one of "delight" in God, and as believers we are proof of the great fact that true faith overflows with happiness and joy. The ungodly, and those who merely profess to be Christians, never look at faith as something joyful, for they see it as nothing but service, duty, and necessity, never pleasure or delight. The only attention they will ever pay to faith is for what they may get from it or for fear of the consequences of not having any faith at all.

Delight as a part of faith is such a foreign concept to most people that no two words are further apart to them than *holiness* and *delight*. But those who truly know Christ understand delight and faith are so blessedly united that even "the gates of Hades will not overcome" (Matt. 16:18) or separate them. Those who love God with all their hearts discover His ways are full of pleasantness and all His paths are those of peace.

These overflowing blessings of complete joy and delight are what the saints of the Lord discover in Him. Thus, we do not serve Him out of habit or tradition, and we faithfully follow Him even though the rest of the world may speak His name as something evil. As believers, we do not fear or reverence God due to any compulsion, for our profession of faith is not a shackle of slavery. Neither are we dragged to holiness or driven to duty. No, our devotion is our pleasure, our hope is our happiness, and our duty is our delight.

True faith and delight are as united as a root is to its flower and as indivisible as truth is from the facts. They are, in actuality, two precious jewels glittering side by side in a setting of gold.

> 'Tis when we taste Your love,
> Our joys divinely grow,
> Unspeakable like those above,
> And heaven begins below.
>
> Isaac Watts, 1674 – 1748

From the pen of Jim Reimann:

Not only should you "delight yourself in the Lord," but you should also delight yourself in His Word. And since Jesus is the Word incarnate, delighting yourself in the Lord and in His Word are actually synonymous. Therefore, it stands to reason we are incapable of delighting in the Lord without spending quality time in His Word.

"Blessed is the man who does not walk in the counsel of the wicked or stand in the way of sinners or sit in the seat of mockers. But his delight is in the law of the LORD, and on his law he meditates day and night" (Ps. 1:1 – 2). "I delight to do thy will, O my God: yea, thy law is within my heart" (Ps. 40:8 KJV). "I delight in your decrees; I will not neglect your word" (Ps. 119:16). "Your statutes are my delight; they are my counselors" (Ps. 119:24). "In my inner being I delight in God's law" (Rom. 7:22).

Lord, may I not only delight in You and in Your Word, but may You also delight in me. May my walk with You bring You glory all my days!

JUNE 15

Sarah said, "God has brought me laughter,
and everyone who hears about this will laugh with me."

Genesis 21:6

From the pen of Charles Spurgeon:

For the elderly Sarah to be honored with a son was far beyond the power of nature and quite contrary to its laws. In the same way, it is beyond all the laws of nature that I, a poor, helpless, and doomed sinner, should be given the gracious gift of the indwelling Spirit of the Lord Jesus in my soul. I once was in despair, and for good reason, for my old nature was as dry, withered, barren, and cursed as the windswept wilderness. Yet even I have been made to produce the fruit of holiness.

May my mouth be filled with joyous laughter because of the extraordinary, surprising grace I have received from the Lord, for I have been found by Jesus, the promised seed, and He is mine forever. Today I will lift up psalms of triumph to the Lord "who remembered [me] in [my] low estate" (Ps. 136:23), for "my heart rejoices in the LORD; in the LORD my horn is lifted high. My mouth boasts over my enemies, for I delight in your deliverance" (1 Sam. 2:1).

I desire that all those who hear of my great deliverance from hell and my blessed salvation, which have "come to [me] from heaven" (Luke 1:78), would laugh for joy with me. I would love to surprise my family with my overwhelming peace, delight my friends with my ever-increasing happiness, and edify God's church with my grateful confessions of praise. I would even love to impress the unbelieving world with the cheerfulness of my daily conversation.

In *The Pilgrim's Progress* by John Bunyan (1628 – 1688), we are told the maiden Mercy laughed in her sleep, and no wonder, for she dreamed of Jesus. And my joy will be no less than hers as long as my beloved Savior is the theme of my daily thoughts. The Lord Jesus is a deep sea of joy, and it is into that Sea my soul will dive and be swallowed up in the delights of His fellowship.

Just as Sarah gazed lovingly at her son Isaac and laughed with rapturous joy with all her friends, you, my soul, look upon your Jesus and call heaven and earth to unite with you in your "inexpressible and glorious joy" (1 Peter 1:8)!

From the pen of Jim Reimann:

Our Lord has given us all we need in Jesus, and one of His greatest gifts is deep abiding joy, even during the most difficult of times. Perhaps that is why we are told: "The joy of the LORD is your strength" (Neh. 8:10). And once our trial has ended, that joy should increase even more. This brings to mind the "inexpressible and glorious joy" of the Israelites as they returned to Jerusalem from captivity. The following is "a song of ascent," sung by them as they ascended the mountains around Jerusalem and climbed the steps of the temple itself.

When the LORD brought back the captives to Zion, we were like men who dreamed. Our mouths were filled with laughter, our tongues with songs of joy. Then it was said among the nations, "The LORD has done great things for them." The LORD has done great things for us, and we are filled with joy. Restore our fortunes, O LORD, like streams in the Negev. Those who sow in tears will reap with songs of joy. He who goes out weeping, carrying seed to sow, will return with songs of joy, carrying sheaves with him.

Psalm 126

Father, may Your joy be truly evident in me and may it overflow to others.

JUNE 16

I give them eternal life, and they shall never perish.

John 10:28

From the pen of Charles Spurgeon:

A Christian should never think or speak with doubts and unbelief. For a child of God to mistrust God's love, truth, or faithfulness must be greatly displeasing to Him. How can we grieve Him by doubting His sustaining grace?

Christian, it is contrary to every promise of God's precious Word that He would ever forget you or let you perish! Otherwise, how could He be true to this promise: "Can a mother forget the baby at her breast and have no compassion on the child she has borne? Though she may forget, I will not forget you!" (Isa. 49:15). What value would there be in this promise: "'Though the mountains be shaken and the hills be removed, yet my unfailing love for you will not be shaken nor my covenant of peace be removed,' says the LORD, who has compassion on you" (Isa. 54:10)? And what truth would there be in these words of Christ: "I give them eternal life, and they shall never perish; no one can snatch them out of my hand. My Father, who has given them to me, is greater than all; no one can snatch them out of my Father's hand" (John 10:28 – 29)?

And what about the doctrines of grace? They would *all* be disproved if even one child of God should perish. What about God's truthfulness, His faithfulness, His honor, His power, His grace, His covenant, and His oath, if anyone for whom Christ died and who has put his trust in Him should nevertheless be cast away from Him?

Banish any unbelieving fears, for they bring great dishonor to God! Get up and shake off the dust from yourself and put on your beautiful "garments of salvation" (Isa. 61:10). Remember, it is sinful to doubt His Word in which He has promised you will "never perish."

May the eternal life within you express itself in confident rejoicing!

> The gospel bears my spirit up:
> A faithful and unchanging God
> Lays the foundation for my hope,
> In oaths, and promises, and blood.
>
> Isaac Watts, 1674 – 1748

From the pen of Jim Reimann:

What sets Christianity apart from the religions of the world is that it is based solely on belief — or faith — as opposed to works. Every other faith is works-based, teaching man can stand righteous before God *only* if his good works outweigh his bad. Let's consider together "what ... Abraham, our forefather, discovered in this matter? If, in fact, Abraham was justified by works, he had something to boast about — but not before God. What does the Scripture say? 'Abraham *believed* God, and *it* [his faith] was credited to him as righteousness'" (Rom. 4:1 – 3).

Jesus said, "He who *believes* has everlasting life" (John 6:47). Later John tells us, "Who is it that overcomes the world? *Only he who believes* that Jesus is the Son of God.... Anyone who believes in the Son of God has this testimony in his heart. Anyone who does *not believe* God has made him out to be a liar, because he has *not believed* the testimony God has given about his Son" (1 John 5:5, 10).

Lord, thank You for the gift of eternal life and faith that "overcomes."

JUNE 17

Help, Lord.
Psalm 12:1

From the pen of Charles Spurgeon:

This prayer itself is quite remarkable, for it is short, but timely, sincere, and typical of David. He was grieved over the lack of faithful people, so he lifted up his heart in earnest prayer. When the creature failed, David went immediately to the Creator. He evidently felt his own weakness or he would not have cried out for help. Yet at the same time he still intended to be actively involved for the cause of truth, for the word *help* makes no sense if we do nothing.

These two simple words of David's prayer are direct, clear, and distinct, much more so, in fact, than the long rambling outpourings of many professing Christians. The psalmist runs straight to his God with a well-considered prayer. He knows what he is seeking and where to find it.

Lord, teach us to pray in the same blessed manner.

There are frequent occasions for using this prayer, such as providential trials and afflictions where believers find all their helpers have abandoned them. Students of the Bible who encounter a difficult passage may often obtain help by lifting up the cry, "Help, Lord," to the Holy Spirit of Christ, the great Teacher. Believers in inner spiritual warfare may go to God's throne for reinforcements, and this simple prayer can be a pattern for their requests. God's people who are involved in strenuous work may use this prayer to "find grace to help us in our time of need" (Heb. 4:16). And sinners who are seeking help with doubts and fears may offer up the same compelling prayer. In all of these cases, at all times, and in all places, this little prayer will serve needy souls.

"Help, Lord" serves the living and the dying, the unemployed or the working, the rejoicing or the sorrowing. Our help is found in Him, so may we not be slow to cry out to Him.

The answer to the prayer is certain if it is sincerely offered through Jesus, for the Lord's very character assures us He will not forsake His people. His relationship to us as Father and Husband guarantees us His help, just as His gift of Jesus is a pledge of "every good thing" (Philem. 6). And His unwavering promise still stands:

"Do not fear; I will help you" (Isa. 41:13).

From the pen of Jim Reimann:

When a Canaanite woman with a demon-possessed daughter came face-to-face with Jesus, her first words were, "Lord, help me!" (Matt. 15:25). Although she was a Gentile, and Jesus' disciples wanted her sent away, the Lord answered her prayer because of her faith.

"Then Jesus answered, 'Woman, you have great faith! Your request is granted.' And her daughter was healed from that very hour" (Matt. 15:28). As Spurgeon says today, "The answer to the prayer is certain *if it is sincerely offered through Jesus*." "For there is one God and one mediator between God and men, the man Christ Jesus" (1 Tim. 2:5).

Yet our prayers must not only be offered by faith through Jesus but must also be within His will. "This is the confidence we have in approaching God: that if we ask anything *according to his will*, he hears us" (1 John 5:14).

"Come quickly to help me, O Lord my Savior" (Ps. 38:22).

JUNE 18

... your Redeemer.

Isaiah 54:5

From the pen of Charles Spurgeon:

Jesus, the Redeemer, is completely and eternally ours, and every position or office of authority He holds is held on our behalf. He is King for us, Priest for us, and Prophet for us, and whenever we come across another title of His in His Word, we should appropriate Him as "ours" with each of those titles. The Shepherd's staff, the Father's rod, the Captain's sword, the Priest's headdress, the Prince's scepter, and the Prophet's robe are all ours. Jesus uses all His majesty for our exaltation, and He has no privilege or entitlement He will not employ in our defense. His fullness in the Godhead is our unfailing, inexhaustible treasure-house.

His manhood, which he took upon Himself for us, is also ours in all its perfection. Our gracious Lord conveys the spotless virtue of His stainless character to us, just as He gives us His praiseworthy power and effectiveness for a life of devotion. He bestows on us the reward He won through His obedient submission and eternal service. He gives us the pure garment of His life for our beautiful covering, the brilliantly shining virtues of His character as our crowning jewels, and the supernatural meekness of His death as our boast and glory. He bequeaths His manger to us, so we will learn how God came down to man, and His cross to us, to teach us how man may go up to God.

All Jesus' thoughts, emotions, actions, words, miracles, and prayers were for us. He walked the road of sorrow on our behalf and has bestowed upon us His entire heavenly legacy — the complete results and inheritance of every work of His life. He is as much ours today as He has ever been or will ever be, and He would be ashamed not to portray Himself as "*our* Lord Jesus Christ" (Rom. 5:1), though He is "the blessed and only Ruler, the King of kings and Lord of lords" (1 Tim. 6:15). Everywhere and in every way Christ is our Christ "richly ... to enjoy" (1 Tim. 6:17 KJV) forever and ever.

"O my soul" (Ps. 103:1), through the power of the Holy Spirit declare Him this morning "your Redeemer"!

From the pen of Jim Reimann:

Job declared, "I know that my Redeemer lives, and that in the end he will stand upon the earth. And after my skin has been destroyed, yet in my flesh I will see God; I myself will see him with my own eyes — I, and not another. How my heart yearns within me!" (Job 19:25 – 27). In spite of all his suffering, Job trusted in the Lord, whom he referred to as "my Redeemer," and he looked forward to the day when Jesus would actually "stand upon the earth." In some respects Job was called upon to show greater faith than we are, for he looked forward in faith, whereas we look back to Jesus' first coming with a great amount of evidence to support the fact that He indeed walked this earth.

Yet whether I look back on Jesus' first coming or forward by faith to His second coming, He is eternally mine! And I am His! This glorious revelation that He is "my Redeemer," and that I am His, should evoke the following prayer within me:

"May the words of my mouth and the meditation of my heart be pleasing in your sight, O Lord, my Rock and my Redeemer" (Ps. 19:14).

JUNE 19

All of them were filled with the Holy Spirit.

Acts 2:4

From the pen of Charles Spurgeon:

The rich blessings of the day of Pentecost and the ultimate consequences of the sacred infilling of the Holy Spirit in Christian souls are impossible to overestimate. Indeed it is impossible to separate life, comfort, light, purity, power, peace, and many other precious blessings from the presence of the benevolent Spirit.

As sacred oil, the Holy Spirit anoints the head of believers, setting us apart to the priesthood of saints and gracing us with everything we need to execute our calling and position well. As the only truly purifying water, He cleanses us from the power of sin and sanctifies us unto holiness, working in us "to will and to act according to his good purpose" (Phil. 2:13). As the light, He first reveals to us our lost estate, and then continues to reveal the Lord Jesus to us and in us, and guides us in "the way of righteousness" (Matt. 21:32). Thus, enlightened by His pure celestial rays, we who "were once darkness" are now "light in the Lord" (Eph. 5:8). As fire, He not only purges the dross from us but also sets our consecrated nature ablaze. He is the flame of the altar of sacrifice upon which we are enabled to offer our entire beings as "living sacrifices ... to God" (Rom. 12:1). As heavenly dew, He removes our barrenness and fertilizes our lives. Oh, that He would fall in this way on us even this morning, for such early morning dew would be such a blessed start to our day!

As the dove, the Holy Spirit broods over His church and the souls of believers with wings of peaceful love, and as the Comforter He dispels the cares and doubts that disturb the peace of His beloved people. He descends on His chosen as He did upon the Lord Jesus at His baptism in the Jordan River (see Matt. 3:16), and He bears witness to our sonship by working a family spirit in us, by which we call out, "*Abba*, Father" (Gal. 4:6). As the wind, He brings "the breath of life" (Gen. 2:7) to people and "blows wherever [He] pleases" (John 3:8), performing life-giving miracles by which His spiritual creation is made alive and sustained.

My prayer to God is that we would sense His presence today and every day!

From the pen of Jim Reimann:

Another consequence, and beautiful benefit, of having the Holy Spirit is assurance: "This is how we know that [Jesus] lives in us: We know it by the Spirit he gave us" (1 John 3:24). "The Spirit himself testifies with our spirit that we are God's children" (Rom. 8:16).

Through the power of the Spirit the very life of Jesus is given to us. Thus, the Spirit is also known as "the Spirit of Christ" (Rom. 8:9). And, it is His Spirit who led the Old Testament prophets, as the following passage attests:

> Concerning this salvation, the prophets, who spoke of the grace that was to come to you, searched intently and with the greatest care, trying to find out the time and circumstances to which *the Spirit of Christ* in them was pointing when he predicted the sufferings of Christ and the glories that would follow. It was revealed to them ... by the Holy Spirit sent from heaven. Even angels long to look into these things.
>
> 1 Peter 1:10 – 12

JUNE 20

For I will give the command,
and I will shake the house of Israel among all the nations as grain is shaken in a sieve,
and not a pebble will reach the ground.

Amos 9:9

From the pen of Charles Spurgeon:

Every time of shaking in a sieve, or sifting, comes by God's divine command and permission. For example, Satan had to seek permission before laying even a finger on Job. Yet in a greater sense our siftings as believers are the direct work of heaven, for this verse says, "I will shake the house of Israel." Satan may hold the sieve, hoping to destroy the grain, but he is simply a servant to the overruling hand of the Master, and instead of destroying the grain, he actually becomes part of the process accomplishing its purification.

Dear precious — although much sifted — grain on the Lord's sifting floor, be comforted by the blessed fact that the Lord Himself directs both the threshing tool and the sieve for His own glory and to your eternal benefit. The Lord Jesus will surely employ "His winnowing fork ... in his hand" (Matt. 3:12), using it to divide His beloved from the vile. All the people of Israel are not true Israel, just as all the grain on the threshing floor is not pure grain; thus, His winnowing process must be performed. And the weight, or significance, of the grain is important, for the husks and chaff that are devoid of substance will be blown away by the wind, with only solid grain remaining.

Yet notice the complete safety of the Lord's wheat, for even the smallest grain of true wheat has been given the promise of preservation. Although God Himself does the sifting, and the work is often difficult and seemingly harsh and done in every area — "among all the nations" — He sifts us in the most effective way possible. In spite of His grain being "shaken in a sieve," not the smallest, lightest, or most withered of us will be permitted to fall or "reach the ground."

Every individual believer is "precious in the sight of the LORD" (Ps. 116:15). As a shepherd would not lose one sheep, a jeweler one diamond, a mother one child, or a man one limb of his body, neither will the Lord lose one of His redeemed people. However insignificant we may feel, if we are the Lord's, we can rejoice that we are protected and preserved in Christ Jesus.

From the pen of Jim Reimann:

Consistent with the truth that Satan must seek permission to sift us, Jesus told Simon Peter, "Satan has asked to sift you as wheat" (Luke 22:31). What a comfort to know that nothing can enter our lives except through the sovereign will of God!

Another comforting thought is what Jesus went on to say: "But I have prayed for you, Simon, that your faith may not fail" (v. 32). Imagine, Jesus had already prayed for Peter — even before his sifting had begun!

Finally, we learn the comforting truth that Jesus used the sifting not only in Peter's life but also in the lives of others, for Jesus also says, "When you have turned back, strengthen your brothers" (v. 32).

Dear believer, God's purposes are established through your sifting. And, remember, "He is able to save completely those who come to God through him, because *he always lives to intercede for them*" (Heb. 7:25). Learn to thank Him not only for His intercession but also for the sifting itself.

JUNE 21

From the pen of Charles Spurgeon:

The entire person of Jesus is like a flawless gem, with His life being many facets of that same gem. His life, however, is totally complete, with His several parts comprising one all-glorious whole. His character is not like a multitude of beautiful colors all mixed together in confusion nor like a pile of precious stones thrown carelessly together one upon the other, but He is a picture of absolute beauty and a gloriously beautiful breastplate. In Him, "whatever is admirable" (Phil. 4:8) is in its proper place and each brings beauty to the others. Not one feature of His glorious person attracts attention to itself at the expense of the others, for He is perfect and "altogether lovely" (Song 5:16).

O Jesus! Your power, Your grace, Your justice, Your tenderness, Your truth, Your majesty, and Your immutability comprised such a man — or rather such a God-man — neither heaven nor earth had ever seen. Your virgin birth, Your sufferings, Your triumphs, Your death, and Your eternal existence are all woven into one gorgeous tapestry without seam, tear, or flaw. You are music in perfect harmony, and although You have many facets and are all things, You are not confusing or divided. As every color blends into one majestic rainbow, so all the glories of heaven and earth converge in You and unite so wondrously that there is no one like You. All the most excellent virtues we could ever imagine being bound together could not rival You, for You are the image of perfection. You have been anointed with the holy oil of "myrrh and ... cassia" (Ps. 45:8) that Your God has reserved for You alone. And as for Your fragrance, it is holy perfume, the likes of which even the best perfumer of the fragrance industry could only dream to compose, for each oil is fragrant — but Your composition is divine!

Oh, sacred symmetry! Oh, rare connection
Of many perfects, to make one perfection!
Oh, heavenly music, where all parts do meet
In one sweet strain, to make one perfect sweet!

Author unknown

From the pen of Jim Reimann:

Even mankind's greatest poets fall far short in attempting to describe our Lord and His glory. And the truth is that as long as we remain in these bodies of flesh, we would be unable to behold His absolute glory and perfection and live.

The Lord said to Moses, "You cannot see my face, for no one may see me and live.... When my glory passes by, I will put you in a cleft in the rock and cover you with my hand until I have passed by. Then I will remove my hand and you will see my back; but my face must not be seen" (Ex. 33:20, 22 – 23). Yet even that experience made Moses' face so radiant that he wore a veil because "the Israelites ... were afraid to come near him" (Ex. 34:30).

Yet someday, "We shall be like him, for we shall see him as he is" (1 John 3:2). Even now, however, "We ... with unveiled faces all reflect the Lord's glory, [and] are being transformed into his likeness with ever-increasing glory" (2 Cor. 3:18)!

JUNE 22

It is [Solomon] who will build the temple of the LORD,
and he will be clothed with majesty.

Zechariah 6:13

From the pen of Charles Spurgeon:

Christ Himself is the builder of His spiritual temple, and He is building it on the mountains of His unchangeable love, His omnipotent grace, and His infallible truth. But as was the case with Solomon's temple, the materials must be made ready. The Lord has His spiritual "cedars of Lebanon" (Ps. 29:5), but they need to be prepared for construction, for they have not been cut down, shaped, and sawn into beautiful planks whose fragrant beauty will bring joy to His heavenly temple. He also has His rough stones for His building, but they must be quarried, squared, and chiseled into shape.

All this is Christ's work, for each individual believer is being prepared, polished, and made ready for his place in the heavenly temple by the prep-work of the Lord's own hand. Even our afflictions and difficulties will not do their work of sanctification without being used by Him for that purpose, nor will our prayers and good works make us ready for heaven apart from the work of His hand, which fashions our hearts into His godly design.

As in the building of Solomon's temple, "Only blocks dressed at the quarry were used, and no hammer, chisel or any other iron tool was heard at the temple site while it was being built" (1 Kings 6:7). Everything was perfected elsewhere and brought to the exact spot they were to occupy. In the same way, Jesus is perfecting His building materials here on earth. Once we reach heaven, there will be no more sanctifying us — no chiseling us with afflictions and no sawing us with suffering. No, we must be made ready

here, for Christ will do His work beforehand. And once He has finished, we will be ferried across the stream of death by His loving hand and taken directly to the heavenly Jerusalem where we will stand as eternal pillars in the temple of our Lord.

> Beneath His eye and care,
> The edifice shall rise,
> Majestic, strong, and fair,
> And shine above the skies.
>
> Philip Doddridge, 1702 – 1751

From the pen of Jim Reimann:

Many of us spend a great deal of time fighting the effects of aging on our bodies. We also devote vast amounts of money and effort to diet and exercise, to coloring our hair, or even to cosmetic surgery in attempts to maintain some vestige of our former youthfulness. Yet in spite of all our efforts, we are fighting a losing battle. And praise the Lord we are!

> Now we know that if the earthly tent we live in is destroyed, we have a building from God, an eternal house in heaven, not built by human hands.... For while we are in this tent, we groan and are burdened ... to be clothed with our heavenly dwelling, so that what is mortal may be swallowed up by life. Now it is God who has made us for this very purpose and has given us the Spirit as a deposit, guaranteeing what is to come.
>
> 2 Cor. 5:1, 4 – 5

Lord, although "I ... would prefer to be away from the body and at home with [You]" (2 Cor. 5:8), I commit the temple of my body today to Your work.

JUNE 23

Ephraim is a flat cake not turned over.

Hosea 7:8

From the pen of Charles Spurgeon:

A "cake not turned over" is uncooked on one side. Thus, in many respects Ephraim was untouched by God's divine grace. Though there was partial obedience, a great deal of rebelliousness remained.

Dear soul, I ask if this is true in your case as well? Are you thoroughly obedient in the things of God? Has His grace so permeated the very core of your being that it flows through and divinely affects all your strengths, your actions, your words, and your thoughts? Your goal and prayer should be to become fully sanctified in spirit, soul, and body. And although your sanctification may not yet be perfect, the process should be affecting every area of your life to equal degrees. There should not be the appearance of holiness in one area while sin continues to reign supreme in another, or else you too will be a "cake not turned over."

A "cake not turned over" is soon burned on the side nearest the flame, and although no one can have too much knowledge of God's Word, some people appear to have been charred on one side with bigoted zeal for one part of the truth they have received. Or they are burned to a cinder with inordinate Pharisaical pride and ostentatious spiritual rituals performed simply to please themselves. This presumptive air of superiority and self-righteousness is frequently accompanied by a total absence of true living godliness. A "saint" who is only one in public is a devil in private, dealing in flour by day and soot by night, for a cake that is burned on one side remains as dough on the other.

Lord, if this is true of me — turn me! Turn the side of my unsanctified nature toward the flame of Your love and let it feel Your

sacred glow. And allow my burned side to cool somewhat, while I discover my own weakness and lack of heat when I am removed from Your heavenly fire. May I not be found as "a double-minded man" (James 1:8), *but as one entirely under the powerful influence of Your reigning grace, for I know quite well that if I am a "cake not turned over," without both sides being subject to Your grace, I will be consumed forever amid eternal flames.*

From the pen of Jim Reimann:

Our verse today is but a small portion of the Lord's lament over Israel's sinfulness. God longed to "restore the fortunes of [His] people, [but] whenever [He] would heal Israel, the sins of Ephraim [were] exposed" (Hosea 6:11 – 7:1). He continues:

Israel's arrogance testifies against him, but despite all this he does not return to the LORD his God or search for him.... Woe to them, because they have strayed from me! Destruction to them, because they have rebelled against me! I long to redeem them but they speak lies against me. They do not cry out to me from their hearts.

Hosea 7:10, 13 – 14

Today's warning is for the "half-baked" — those having only a false religiosity that suits their needs. The Lord warned Ephraim, "I desire mercy, not sacrifice, and acknowledgment of God rather than burnt offerings" (6:6). He had earlier warned Saul through His prophet Samuel in much the same way: "Does the LORD delight in burnt offerings and sacrifices as much as in obeying the voice of the LORD? *To obey is better than sacrifice*" (1 Sam. 15:22)!

Day 175

JUNE 24

As Jesus was saying these things, a woman in the crowd called out,
"Blessed is the mother who gave you birth and nursed you." He replied,
"Blessed rather are those who hear the word of God and obey it."

Luke 11:27–28

From the pen of Charles Spurgeon:

There are some people who enjoy the notion that Mary, the mother of our Lord, had very special privileges because they presumed she had the benefit of looking into His very heart in a way we could never hope to do. Although this idea may appear to have some plausibility, there is not much. We are not told that Mary knew more than others, but that what she did know she "pondered … in her heart" (Luke 2:19). And from what we read in the Gospels, she does not appear to have been a better-instructed believer than any other of Christ's followers. In fact, everything she knew we may discover as well.

Are you surprised by these statements? Then here is a verse to prove them: "The LORD confides in those who fear him; he makes his covenant known to them" (Ps. 25:14). And remember the Master's words: "I no longer call you servants, because a servant does not know his master's business. Instead, I have called you friends, for everything that I learned from my Father I have made known to you" (John 15:15). The Divine Revealer of secrets tells us His heart and holds nothing back that would be profitable for us. His words of assurance are: "If it were not so, I would have told you" (John 14:2).

Doesn't Jesus even today reveal Himself to us but not to those in the world? Because this is true, we do not call out to Him in ignorance, "Blessed is the mother who gave you birth." On the contrary, *with knowledge* we bless God for the fact that as a result of obediently following the Word after He revealed it to us, we have just as much fellowship and oneness with the Savior as the Virgin Mary had. And we have as much knowledge of the intimate secrets of His heart as some believe only she obtained.

Oh, the blessing of being so privileged!

From the pen of Jim Reimann:

The angel Gabriel told Mary, "Greetings, you who are highly favored!" and again, "You have found favor with God" (Luke 1:28–29). Being shown favor by the Lord, however, does not mean Mary was perfect, as some faiths teach. In fact, Mary recognized her need of a Savior, for she proclaimed, "My soul glorifies the Lord and my spirit rejoices in God *my Savior*" (Luke 1:46–47).

The truth is, *every* believer has been shown favor, for it is only by God's grace that any of us stand before Him redeemed, forgiven, and righteous. The Old Testament tells us, "Whoever finds me finds life and receives favor from the LORD" (Prov. 8:35); "Surely, O LORD, you bless the righteous; you surround them with your favor as with a shield" (Ps. 5:12); and "The LORD God is a sun and shield; the LORD bestows favor and honor; no good thing does he withhold from those whose walk is blameless" (Ps. 84:11). Then Paul, quoting from Isaiah 49:8, tells us, "'In the time of my favor I heard you, and in the day of salvation I helped you.' I tell you, now is the time of God's favor, now is the day of salvation" (2 Cor. 6:2).

Father, "May the favor of the Lord our God rest upon us; establish the work of our hands for us — yes, establish the work of our hands" (Ps. 90:17).

JUNE 25

Go up on a high mountain.

Isaiah 40:9

From the pen of Charles Spurgeon:

Our knowledge of Christ is somewhat like climbing a "high mountain." When you are at the foot of the mountain you actually see very little and the mountain itself appears to be only half as high as it really is. And if confined to a little valley you scarcely discover anything except babbling brooks as they descend to the base of the mountain. Yet as you climb the first rising knoll and look back, you see the valley lengthen and widen beneath you. Then as you continue, higher you see the surrounding countryside for four or five miles around and are delighted with the widening perspective. As you continue, the scenery enlarges until at last, when you reach the summit, you can look north, south, east, and west for many more miles. Perhaps you can see a forest two hundred miles away, a shimmering river meandering through a valley, smoking chimneys of a manufacturing town, and the masts of ships in a busy seaport far below as you look in various directions. The view delights you as you declare, "I could never have imagined all this could be seen from this elevation!"

The Christian life is much the same, for when we first believe in Christ, we see very little of Him. The higher we climb, however, the more we discover His beautiful attributes. Yet who has ever reached the summit? Who has ever fully "grasp[ed] how … high and deep is the love of Christ … that surpasses knowledge" (Eph. 3:18 – 19)? Still, the apostle Paul, elderly and gray-haired and shivering in a dungeon in Rome, could say with greater conviction than we can, "I know whom I have believed" (2 Tim. 1:12). Each experience of his had been like climbing a hill, each trial like ascending another summit, and his approaching death like attaining the top of a "high mountain" from which he could see the totality of the love and faithfulness of God to whom he had committed his soul.

Dear friend, "Go up on a high mountain"!

From the pen of Jim Reimann:

Indeed, our knowledge of Christ increases as we climb the mountains of life with Him. Yet in this life we will never attain complete knowledge. In fact, it seems that the more we learn, the more we realize we don't know. Paul prayed we would be able "to grasp how wide and long and high and deep is the love of Christ" and "to know this love.…" But he continues, "To know this love *that surpasses knowledge*" (Eph. 3:18 – 19).

In other words, Paul prayed we will know something that is unknowable — at least in this life! As we attempt to come to terms with this thought, doesn't it make sense in the following respect: the love of Christ is infinite, but we and our minds are finite. Perhaps we will spend eternity discovering the depths of His infinite love.

"How great is God — beyond our understanding! The number of his years is past finding out" (Job 36:26). When Christ returns, however, this will change, for — "Now I know in part; then I shall know fully, even as I am fully known" (1 Cor. 13:12).

"O Sovereign Lord, you have begun to show to your servant your greatness and your strong hand. For what god is there in heaven or on earth who can do the deeds and mighty works you do?" (Deut. 3:24).

JUNE 26

The grave below ... will say ..., "You have become like us."

Isaiah 14:9 – 10

From the pen of Charles Spurgeon:

Imagine the doom of the apostate — one who once professed faith, then rejected it, but who never truly knew the Lord. What will it be like when his naked soul appears before God? How will he bear to hear: "'Depart from me, you who are cursed' (Matt. 25:41). You rejected Me, and I reject you. 'You have lived as a prostitute' (Jer. 3:1) and departed from Me, so I have also banished you from My presence forever and 'will not have mercy' (Isa. 27:11 KJV) on you."

What shame this wretched apostate will experience on "the great day of the LORD" (Zeph. 1:14) as he is unmasked before the multitudes! Imagine profane sinners who never professed faith at all lifting themselves from their beds of fire, pointing at him and saying in disgust, "There he is! I wonder if he will preach his gospel here in hell?" Imagine another saying, "He rebuked me for cursing but was a hypocrite himself!" And yet another saying, "Here comes that hymn-singing churchgoer! He was always at church and boasted of being sure of his eternal life, but here he is with us!" There will be no greater eagerness amid Satanic tormentors than on those days when devils drag a hypocrite's soul to hell.

In *The Pilgrim's Progress*, John Bunyan (1628 – 1688) describes an awful scene of a "back way to hell." He tells of a wretched soul being bound with cords by seven devils and being dragged from the road to heaven on which he had professed to walk, and then being thrown into hell through its back door.

Caution, you who profess faith! Remember, there is a back way to hell! "Examine yourselves to see whether you are in the faith" (2 Cor. 13:5). Closely investigate whether or not you are truly in Christ. And beware, for it is the easiest thing on earth to be lenient when it comes to judging yourself. Thus, especially when it comes to this, be honest. Always be just with everyone, but even more stringent with yourself in this matter. Keep in mind, if you are not building your "house on the rock," when it finally falls it will fall "with a great crash" (Matt. 7:24, 27).

May the Lord grant you sincerity, endurance, and firmness of faith. May you never see the day, however evil things may become, that you will be led astray.

From the pen of Jim Reimann:

Indeed, not all who profess faith are true believers, as illustrated by this parable of Jesus:

> The kingdom of heaven is like a man who sowed good seed in his field. But while everyone was sleeping, his enemy came and sowed weeds among the wheat.... When [they both] sprouted ... the owner's servants ... asked him, "Do you want us to go and pull them up?" "No," he answered, "because while you are pulling the weeds, you may root up the wheat with them. Let both grow together until the harvest. At that time I will tell the harvesters: First collect the weeds and tie them in bundles to be burned; then gather the wheat and bring it into my barn."
>
> Matthew 13:24 – 30

"I write these things ... that you may know that you have eternal life" (1 John 5:13).

JUNE 27

Pharaoh said, "I will let you go to offer sacrifices to the LORD
your God in the desert, but you must not go very far."

Exodus 8:28

From the pen of Charles Spurgeon:

This is a crafty statement from the lips of Pharaoh, the evil tyrant. If the poor Israelite slaves had to leave Egypt, he would bargain with them so they would "not go very far," keeping them within the reach of his terror and within sight of his spies. In the same manner, the world today hates the nonconformity and dissidence of Christians. It would like for us to be a little more compromising and not take our ideas to the extreme.

Ideas such as being dead to "the foolish things of the world" (1 Cor. 1:27) and being "buried with [Christ]" (Rom. 6:4) are ones that unbelievers' carnal minds treat with ridicule. Thus, God's Word teaches that these truths are nearly universally neglected — even condemned. Worldly wisdom promotes a path of compromise and speaks of moderation. According to this carnal thinking, purity is considered to be quite desirable as long as we do not take it too far. And truth is a prudent course to follow as long as we don't denounce error too harshly. The world declares, "Sure, be spiritual by all means, but don't deny yourself a little worldly fun now and then. After all, what's the point of criticizing something when it is so fashionable and everybody is doing it?"

Many confessing Christians have fallen to this cunning advice but have suffered eternal loss as a result. Once we commit to fully following the Lord, we must immediately go into the wilderness of separation, leaving the carnal world of Egypt behind. We must leave its "wisdom," its pleasures, and its religion as well, going far away to the place the Lord has called His sanctified ones.

When our city is on fire, our house cannot be too far from the flames. When a dangerous plague is spreading, we cannot be too far away from contamination. The farther from a deadly snake the better, and the further from worldly conformity the better. May the trumpet call be sounded to all true believers:

"Come out from them and be separate" (2 Cor. 6:17).

From the pen of Jim Reimann:

We should never be surprised when the world acts like the world! We should not expect them to accept our values and think highly of our standards. More and more the world views Christians as hateful, intolerant, and uncompromising. But this is nothing new, for Paul wrote, "We have become the scum of the earth, the refuse of the world" (1 Cor. 4:13). Earlier in the same chapter Paul says, "Who makes you different from anyone else? What do you have that you did not receive? And if you did receive it, why do you boast as though you did not?" (v. 7).

The idea behind his words is that the only thing making us different from the world is that God has saved us — and He did it all, we can take no credit for it. Thus, our response to the world is what's important, for Paul goes on to say, "When we are cursed, we bless; when we are persecuted, we endure it; when we are slandered, we answer kindly" (vv. 12 – 13).

"Therefore I endure everything for the sake of the elect, that they too may obtain the salvation that is in Christ Jesus, with eternal glory" (2 Tim. 2:10).

JUNE 28

Let us fix our eyes on Jesus.

Hebrews 12:2

From the pen of Charles Spurgeon:

It is the Holy Spirit's role to always turn our eyes to Jesus and away from ourselves, but Satan's role is exactly the opposite, for he is constantly trying to make us think of ourselves rather than Christ. Satan insinuates, "Your sins are too many to be forgiven, you have no faith, you don't repent enough, you will never be able to endure to the end, you don't have the joy of God's children, and your grasp on Jesus is weak and wavering." All these thoughts are about *self*, yet we will never find comfort or assurance by looking inside ourselves. The Holy Spirit turns our eyes away from *self*, telling us we are nothing — but that Christ is our "all in all" (1 Cor. 15:28).

Remember, it is not *your* hold on Christ that saves you — it is Christ; it is not *your* joy in Christ that saves you — it is Christ; it is not even *your* faith in Christ, although that is the means He uses — it is Christ's blood, work, and worthiness. Therefore, don't look at *your* own hand with which you are grasping Christ — look to Christ; don't look at *your* hope — look to Jesus, the source of your hope; don't look at *your* faith — look to Jesus, "the author and perfecter of [y]our faith" (Heb. 12:2).

We will never find happiness by looking at *our* prayers, *our* work, or *our* feelings. It is who Jesus is that gives rest to our soul — not who we are. Quickly overcoming Satan and finding peace with God comes only by "fix[ing] our eyes on Jesus." Fix your eyes only on Him. Keep *His* death, *His* suffering, *His* work, *His* worthiness, *His* glory, and *His* intercession foremost in your mind. When you wake up in the morning, look to Him, and when you lie down at night, look to Him.

Never allow your hopes and fears to come between you and Jesus. Follow hard after Him and He will never fail you.

> My hope is built on nothing less
> Than Jesus' blood and righteousness:
> I dare not trust the sweetest frame,
> But wholly lean on Jesus' name.
>
> Edward Mote, 1797 – 1874

From the pen of Jim Reimann:

Our eyes are what so often lead us into sin. When we are tempted by something we see and refuse to turn away, our thoughts then take over and ultimately temptation gives birth to sin. Here is how God's Word puts it:

> Each one is tempted when, by his own evil desire, he is dragged away and enticed. Then, after desire has conceived, it gives birth to sin; and sin, when it is full-grown, gives birth to death.
>
> James 1:14 – 15

Thus, determining in advance what we will allow our eyes to view is critical. Consider the words of David, who said, "I will set before my eyes no vile thing" (Ps. 101:3); and Job, who said, "I made a covenant with my eyes not to look lustfully at a girl" (Job 31:1).

Father, "I lift up my eyes to you, to you whose throne is in heaven. As the eyes of slaves look to the hand of their master, as the eyes of a maid look to the hand of her mistress, so our eyes look to the LORD our God, till he shows us his mercy" (Ps. 123:1 – 2).

JUNE 29

God will bring with Jesus those
who have fallen asleep in him.

1 Thessalonians 4:14

From the pen of Charles Spurgeon:

This verse should not lead us to believe that their souls sleep in some unconscious state after death, for the whisper of Christ to every dying saint is: "Today you will be with me in paradise" (Luke 23:43). Yes, they "have fallen asleep in him," but their souls "are before the throne of God and serve him day and night in his temple" (Rev. 7:15) and are singing hallelujahs to Him who washed them from their sins in His blood.

The body sleeps in its lonely bed of earth beneath its blanket of grass, but what does the word *sleep* mean here? In this context the Spirit of God conveys the idea of *rest*. Sleep makes every night a Sabbath, or time of rest, for the previous day. And sleep tightly shuts the door of the soul, causing all intruders to tarry for a while so that the life within may enter its summer garden of rest. The work-weary believer quietly sleeps like a tired baby resting on his mother's breast.

How happy and blessed are those who die in the Lord! They rest from their labors and their good works follow them, yet their quiet rest will not be broken until God raises them up and gives them their full reward. Guarded by angels and shrouded by eternal mysteries, they — the heirs of glory — sleep on until the fullness of time ultimately brings them the fullness of redemption. And what an awakening will be theirs!

Their bodies were laid to rest weary and worn, but that is not how they will rise. They went to their earthly beds of rest with furrowed brows, pale and spent, but they will wake up in beauty and glory. The withered seed, with lack of form and attractiveness, will rise from the dust of the earth a beautiful flower. The cold winter grave will give way to the spring of redemption and the summer of glory.

Blessed is physical death, therefore, since through it God's divine power removes our everyday work garments and clothes us with the wedding garments of incorruption. Blessed are "those who have fallen asleep in [Jesus]"!

From the pen of Jim Reimann:

Many people fear death, but it is something believers should never fear. Paul makes it seem as natural and easy as falling asleep, and the Old Testament tells us: "There is a time for everything ... a time to be born and a time to die" (Eccl. 3:1 – 2).

Others may say, "It's not being dead I'm afraid of — it's getting dead!" Yet not only is the timing of our death in God's hands but also how we will die. And whether it is a painful home-going or not, the Lord promises, "Never will I leave you; never will I forsake you" (Heb. 13:5). He is "the Father of compassion and the God of all comfort, who comforts us in all our troubles" (2 Cor. 1:3 – 4).

> I eagerly expect and hope that I will in no way be ashamed, but will have sufficient courage so that now as always Christ will be exalted in my body, whether by life or by death. For to me, to live is Christ and to die is gain.
>
> Philippians 1:20 – 21

May even our death bring glory to God, for Jesus once shared with Peter — "the kind of death by which Peter would glorify God" (John 21:19).

JUNE 30

I have given them the glory that you gave me.

John 17:22

From the pen of Charles Spurgeon:

Observe the unparalleled generosity of the Lord Jesus — He has given us His all! Even a tithe of His possessions could make an entire universe filled with angels rich beyond all measure, yet He was not content until He had given us all He has. His grace still would have been amazing if He had only allowed us to eat the crumbs beneath His bountiful table of mercy, but He does nothing halfway, for He invites us to sit with Him and share His feast. If He simply had given us a small pension from His royal treasury, we would have reason enough to love Him forever, but He has chosen to make His bride as rich as Himself, and He will not possess any glory or gift that she will not share with Him. He is not content with making us less than "co-heirs" (Rom. 8:17) with Himself, for He desires us to have equal possessions.

Our Lord has emptied His entire estate into the treasury of the church and shares its ownership with His redeemed. He does not withhold the key to even one room in His house from His people, but gives them total freedom to take all He has as their own. He loves for His people to take from His treasure and appropriate for themselves as much as they can possibly carry.

The boundless fullness of Christ's all-sufficiency is as free to believers as the air we breathe. He puts the glass of His love and grace to our lips and invites us to drink forever. We are welcome to try to drain it completely but would never be able to exhaust His supply. Thus, He invites us to drink abundantly, for it all belongs to us.

What greater proof of fellowship and oneness could heaven or earth extend!

> When I stand before the throne
> Dressed in beauty not my own;
> When I see Thee as Thou art,
> Love Thee with un-sinning heart;
> Then, Lord, shall I fully know —
> Not till then — how much I owe.
> Robert Murray McCheyne, 1813 – 1843

From the pen of Jim Reimann:

We are indeed "co-heirs with Christ," and when it comes to describing our inheritance, there are no better words than these:

> I keep asking that the God of our Lord Jesus Christ, the glorious Father, may give you the Spirit of wisdom and revelation, so that you may know him better. I pray also that the eyes of your heart may be enlightened in order that you may know the hope to which he has called you, the riches of his glorious inheritance in the saints, and his incomparably great power for us who believe. That power is like the working of his mighty strength, which he exerted in Christ when he raised him from the dead and seated him at his right hand in the heavenly realms, far above all rule and authority, power and dominion, and every title that can be given, not only in the present age but also in the one to come.

Ephesians 1:17 – 21

"To him be glory and power for ever and ever! Amen" (Rev. 1:6).

July

July 1

Water will flow out from Jerusalem ...
in summer and in winter.

Zechariah 14:8

From the pen of Charles Spurgeon:

The streams of living water flowing from Jerusalem will not be dried up by the oppressive heat of midsummer any more than they will be frozen by the fierce winds of winter. My soul can rejoice that I will never need to testify to a lack of God's faithfulness. Seasons change and I change, but my Lord is eternally the same, and the streams of His love are as deep and wide and full as ever. The heated stress of business concerns and scorching trials create in me the need for the cooling effects of the river of His grace. And my thirst may be immediately quenched from His inexhaustible fountain, for whether summer or winter, it continues to pour forth abundantly.

"Blessed be the name of the LORD" (Ps. 113:2 KJV), for His high mountain streams are never meager and His underground springs never cease to flow. Elijah saw the Kerith brook dry up, yet Jehovah was still the same sovereign God. (See 1 Kings 17:1 – 7.) And Job said, "My brothers are as undependable as intermittent streams" (Job 6:15), but he found his God to be an overflowing river of consolation. Egypt places great confidence in the Nile, whose floods are quite unpredictable, but our Lord is evermore the same. Cyrus conquered the city of Babylon by diverting the course of the Euphrates (see Isa. 44:27 – 45:1 for a prophecy of this more than 100 years in advance), but no power on earth, whether human or satanic, can divert the river of God's divine grace.

Ancient riverbeds have been found totally dry and desolate, but the streams that find their source on the mountains of the Lord's divine sovereignty and infinite love will eternally flow. Generations of time melt away, but the course of His grace is unaltered. The river of God will sing with greater resolve and truth than the brook in this poem:

> Men may come, and men may go,
> But I go on forever.
>
> Alfred, Lord Tennyson, 1809 – 1892

How blessed is my soul to be led "beside [such] still waters" (Ps. 23:2 KJV)!

Never wander to other streams, lest you hear the Lord's rebuke, "Why go to Egypt to drink water from the [muddy Nile]?" (Jer. 2:18).

From the pen of Jim Reimann:

Every believer will partake of the eternal river of God in heaven, but what about today? In this life that blessing is tied to our love of His Word.

> Blessed is the man who does not walk in the counsel of the wicked or stand in the way of sinners or sit in the seat of mockers. But *his delight is in the law of the LORD,* and on his law he meditates day and night. *He is like a tree planted by streams of water,* which yields its fruit in season and whose leaf does not wither. Whatever he does prospers.
>
> Psalm 1:1 – 3

As a result, the believer becomes a vessel of blessing to others, for Jesus said, "Whoever believes in me, as the Scripture has said, streams of living water will flow from within him" (John 7:38).

"Oh, how I love your law!" (Ps. 119:97).

JULY 2

In him our hearts rejoice.

Psalm 33:21

From the pen of Charles Spurgeon:

It is a blessed fact that Christians can rejoice even during the deepest distress. Although trouble may surround us, we can still sing, and like many birds, we sing best in our cages. Raging waves may roll over us, but our souls quickly resurface to see the light of God's countenance, for we have a buoyancy about us that keeps our heads above water and helps us sing amid the storm, "God is with me still" (Oliver Sansom, 1636–1710).

To whom shall the glory be given for this blessing? To Jesus! It is all accomplished by Jesus! Trouble may not necessarily be accompanied by consolation when initially coming upon believers, but the presence of the Son of God in "the blazing furnace" (Dan. 3:23) nevertheless fills our hearts with joy. We may experience sickness and suffering, but Jesus visits us and makes our bed more comfortable. Even if dying, with the cold water of the Jordan gradually rising to our neck, Jesus puts His arms around us and whispers, "Fear not, beloved, for to die is to be blessed. The waters of death find their source in heaven. They are not bitter but are as sweet as honey, for they flow from the throne of God."

As departing saints wade through the river with waves billowing around us and our heart and bodies failing us, the same voice sounds in our ears, "Do not fear, for I am with you; do not be dismayed, for I am your God" (Isa. 41:10). And as we near the border of the infinite unknown, with fear of what's ahead, Jesus says to us, "Do not be afraid, little flock, for your Father has been pleased to give you the kingdom" (Luke 12:32).

Thus, strengthened and consoled, believers are not afraid to die. In fact, we are willing and ready to depart, for since we have seen Jesus, "the bright Morning Star" (Rev. 22:16), we long to gaze on Him as we once gazed at the sun when our bodies were strong. Truly the presence of Jesus is all the heaven we desire. He is both:

> The glory of our brightest days;
> The comfort of our nights.
>
> Author unknown

From the pen of Jim Reimann:

Our Lord Jesus is the perfect example of abiding joy even in the midst of suffering. "*For the joy set before him* [He] endured the cross, scorning its shame, and sat down at the right hand of the throne of God" (Heb. 12:2). It is difficult for us to understand how joy and suffering can coexist, but they can and do.

Was dying on the cross a joyful thing? It was in this regard — Jesus was in the perfect center of His Father's will, for He said, "I have come down from heaven not to do my will but to do the will of him who sent me" (John 6:38). In the same way, there is no greater joy for you as a follower of His than knowing you are walking in His perfect will. And this is true regardless of how difficult your surrounding circumstances may be. "Consider him who endured such opposition from sinful men, so that you will not grow weary and lose heart" (Heb. 12:3).

"*I delight to do thy will, O my God*" (Ps. 40:8 KJV).

JULY 3

The cows that were ugly and gaunt
ate up the seven sleek, fat cows.

Genesis 41:4

From the pen of Charles Spurgeon:

This dream of Pharaoh has all too often been my actual experience while awake. My days of slothfulness have ruinously destroyed all I had previously achieved during my times of diligent hard work, my times of cold idleness have frozen the warm glow of all my periods of fervent zeal, and my forays into worldliness have thrown me back from advances in my spiritual life. I should beware of "gaunt" prayers, praise, duties, and experiences, for these will devour the "fat" of my comfort and peace. If I neglect prayer for even a short time, I lose the level of spirituality I had achieved, and if I draw no fresh supplies from heaven, the old grain in my storehouse will quickly be consumed by the famine raging in my soul.

When the slowly moving caterpillars of indifference, worldliness, and self-indulgence render my heart completely desolate and cause my soul to languish, all my past fruitfulness and growth in grace benefit me nothing whatsoever. I need never worry that my life will have no "gaunt" days or lean hours! As I journey toward the goal of my spiritual desires, unfortunately I will sometimes backslide, which will leave me far from the prize of my high calling in Christ and will rob me of the past gains I have worked so hard to accomplish. The only way all my days can be like the "sleek, fat cows" is to feed them in the proper pasture and to continually immerse them in the Lord — in His service, His fellowship, His reverence, and His will.

Why shouldn't each new year be richer than the past when it comes to love, usefulness, and joy? After all, I am closer to the hills of heaven, I have had more experience with my Lord, and I should be more like Him.

> O Lord, keep the curse of leanness of soul far from me. May I never need to cry, "I waste away, I waste away! Woe to me!" (Isa. 24:16). Instead, may I be well fed and nourished in Your house "that I may praise your name" (Ps. 142:7).

From the pen of Jim Reimann:

In a culture so weight conscious, it is hard to even consider needing to be like "the seven, sleek fat cows"! Yet when it comes to our spiritual lives, that is exactly what is needed.

When Israel was redeemed from Egypt, "they all ate the same spiritual food and drank the same spiritual drink; for they drank from the spiritual rock that accompanied them, and that rock was Christ" (1 Cor. 10:3 – 4). Yet they quickly sinned against Him.

The psalmist wrote: "We have sinned, even as our fathers did; we have done wrong and acted wickedly. When our fathers were in Egypt, they gave no thought to your miracles; they did not remember your many kindnesses, and they rebelled" (Ps. 106:6 – 7).

May this be a lesson to us, for they "lusted exceedingly in the wilderness, and tempted God in the desert. And *he gave them their request; but sent leanness into their soul*" (Ps. 106:14 – 15 KJV).

Beware! The Lord may just grant your request.

JULY 4

Sanctify them by the truth.
John 17:17

From the pen of Charles Spurgeon:

Sanctification begins at the point of regeneration. The Spirit of God instills into a person that new living truth by which he becomes a "new creation" (2 Cor. 5:17) in Christ. This work, which begins at new birth, is carried out in two ways — through mortification, or death, whereby "the desires of the sinful nature" (Gal. 5:16) are placed in submission; and vivification, or life, whereby the life God has placed within us is made into "a spring of water welling up to eternal life" (John 4:14).

This process then continues each day through what is called *perseverance*, by which Christians are continually preserved in a state of grace and are made to "abound in every good work" (2 Cor. 9:8) "to the praise of [God's] glory" (Eph. 1:14). Ultimately believers will come to perfection in "glory" when the soul, totally purified, will be "caught up" (1 Thess. 4:17) to dwell with holy beings at "the right hand of the Majesty in heaven" (Heb. 1:3).

While the Spirit of God is the author of sanctification, there is one visible agent at work that must not be forgotten. Jesus said, "Sanctify them by *the truth; your word is truth*." There are many passages of Scripture which prove that the very instrument of our sanctification is the Word of God itself. Here is how it works: The Spirit of God brings the precepts and doctrines of truth to our minds and then applies them through His power. These truths are heard by our ears and, once received in our hearts, they work in us "to will and to act according to his good purpose" (Phil. 2:13).

His truth is the sanctifier; therefore, if we do not hear or read the truth, we will not grow in sanctification. We only progress in sound living as we progress in sound understanding. "Your word is a lamp to my feet and a light for my path" (Ps. 119:105). Never indulge error that conflicts with Scripture as a mere "matter of opinion," for no one indulges an error in judgment, for example, without sooner or later tolerating an error in his actions.

"Hold fast" (2 Tim. 1:13 KJV) to the truth, for by holding on to it you will be "sanctified by the Holy Spirit" (Rom. 15:16).

From the pen of Jim Reimann:

In our Christian walk, especially during difficult trials, it seems it would be easier to simply die and go on to heaven. How many times have we prayed for the Lord to just take us home and leave all our troubles behind!

Yet only two verses before, Jesus prayed, "Sanctify them by the truth." He says, "*My prayer is not that you take them out of the world* but that you protect them from the evil one" (John 17:15). Then He prayed, "I pray also for those who will believe in me through their message" (John 17:20).

Dear believer, when times get tough, remember, Jesus prayed for those "who *will* believe," meaning those in the future, such as you. And He prayed you would be protected "from the evil one." So walk in faith, knowing He cares and that He is in the process of perfecting You to "reflect the Lord's glory" (2 Cor. 3:18).

Father, grant me the gift of contentment in this life. And may I have a greater passion for Your Word, which You are using to sanctify me.

JULY 5

Called to be saints.

Romans 1:7

From the pen of Charles Spurgeon:

We are quite apt to regard the apostolic saints of the first century as though they were saints in a more special way than other children of God. We tend to think of the apostles as extraordinary people, scarcely subject to the same weaknesses and temptations we have, yet everyone God called by His grace and sanctified by His Spirit are saints. In thinking this way, however, we forget the truth that the closer a man lives to God, the more intensely he will mourn over his own evil heart; and the more his Master honors him in His service, the more the evils of the flesh tempt and test him day by day.

The fact is that if we had personally known the apostle Paul, we would have thought him to be remarkably like the rest of us in God's chosen family. And after speaking with him we would have said, "His experience is much the same as ours. He is more faithful, more holy, and better taught in God's Word than we are, but he has much the same, if not greater, trials to endure." Thus, don't look upon the saints of old as being exempt from difficulties, weaknesses, or sins, and don't regard them with such mystical reverence that you nearly become an idolater. The level of holiness they attained is possible for us, for we are "called to be saints" by the very same Voice who called them to their lofty vocation.

It is actually every Christian's duty to work his way into the inner circle of sainthood, and if we find that the attainments of the saints of old were superior to ours — as they certainly were — let us follow their example, emulating their passion and holiness. We have the same light they had, and the same grace is accessible to us, so why should we ever be satisfied with anything less in heavenly character? They lived *with* Jesus, they lived *for* Jesus, and, thus, they became *like* Jesus.

As we live by the same Spirit, may we live in the same manner they did — "fix[ing] our eyes on Jesus" (Heb. 12:2). Then our sainthood will soon be apparent.

From the pen of Jim Reimann:

Not only do we tend to think of the apostles as more "saintly" than we are but we often have an elevated opinion of the Old Testament saints. Yet they too were actually common ordinary people whom the Lord used in extraordinary ways. For example, James tells us, "Elijah was a man just like us. He prayed earnestly that it would not rain, and it did not rain on the land for three and a half years" (James 5:17).

Even more encouraging is what the writer of Hebrews tells us about our Lord Jesus:

> Since the children have flesh and blood, he too shared in their humanity so that by his death he might destroy him who holds the power of death — that is, the devil — and free those who all their lives were held in slavery by their fear of death. For surely it is not angels he helps, but Abraham's descendants. For this reason *he had to be made like his brothers in every way*, in order that he might become a merciful and faithful high priest in service to God, and that he might make atonement for the sins of the people. *Because he himself suffered when he was tempted, he is able to help [us] who are being tempted.*
>
> Hebrews 2:14 – 18

JULY 6

Whoever listens to me will live in safety and be at ease,
without fear of harm.

Proverbs 1:33

From the pen of Charles Spurgeon:

God's divine love is more obvious and shines more brightly from the midst of His judgment. One lonely star is more beautiful as its light smiles through a break in the storm clouds, the blooms of the oasis are more vibrant in the midst of the desert sand, and love is more enchanting from the midst of anger.

When the Israelites provoked the Most High God with their continued idolatry, He punished them by withholding both dew and rain. Thus, they experienced a severe famine, but while God did this, He made sure His own chosen ones remained secure. When all the other brooks dried up, there was one reserved just for Elijah, and even when that one failed, the Lord preserved another place of sustenance for him. (See 1 Kings 17:1 – 9.) Not only is this true, but God was not limited to just one "Elijah," for He also had His remnant in accordance with His doctrine of election of grace. This remnant, who were hidden "in two caves, fifty in each" (1 Kings 18:4), were not only fed but were fed from King Ahab's table by God's faithful servant Obadiah while the entire country suffered from a famine.

We can glean from this that regardless of what may come our way, God's people are safe. Let the solid earth shake and let the skies be torn in two, yet even amid the destruction of the world, believers remain as secure as they are during their calmest times of rest. And if the Lord does not save His people *under* heaven, He will save them *in* heaven. If the world becomes too hot to hold them, then heaven itself will receive them and be their place of safety.

Therefore be confident when "you … hear of wars and rumors of wars" (Matt. 24:6). Allow no disturbance to distress you, but remain quiet "and be at ease, without fear of harm." Whatever may come upon the earth, Jehovah will keep you secure "under his wings" (Ps. 91:4). Stand upon His promises, rest in His faithfulness, and you can defy even the darkest future, for nothing can harm you. Your only concern should be to exhibit to the world the blessedness of obeying the Voice of wisdom.

From the pen of Jim Reimann:

Especially in this day of terrorism, many people live in fear. Yet this should never be the case for believers. We should recognize the fact that to fear is to sin, for Paul wrote, "Everything that does not come from faith is sin" (Rom. 14:23), and fear is the opposite of faith. Our Lord also admonished us against being fearful, for He declared, "*Do not be afraid* of those who kill the body but cannot kill the soul" (Matt. 10:28).

To change our plans due to the evilness of mankind is to put the evildoers in control, and that is nothing but a trap. Consider the words of Solomon: "Fear of man will prove to be a snare, but whoever trusts in the LORD is kept safe" (Prov. 29:25).

"For you did not receive a spirit that makes you a slave again to fear, but you received the Spirit of sonship. And by him we cry, '*Abba*, Father'" (Rom. 8:15).

JULY 7

Pray for us.
1 Thessalonians 5:25

From the pen of Charles Spurgeon:

This morning I wish to remind you of the importance of praying for ministers of the gospel. Our verse today is a fervent request from the apostle Paul — one which I echo and implore every Christian household to observe today.

Christian brothers and sisters, a minister's work is solemn and momentous, involving spiritual wellness or woe to thousands, for we "treat" souls for God, dealing in His eternal business, and our words are "the fragrance of life" to some or "the smell of death" (2 Cor. 2:16) to others. A very heavy responsibility rests upon us and it will be no small mercy if we are ultimately found "innocent of the blood of all men" (Acts 20:26). As officers in Christ's army, we are a special target of the hatred of men and demons, for they carefully watch for any slip on our part and work diligently to make us stumble.

Our calling brings with it temptations from which others are exempt, and that calling all too often draws us away from our personal enjoyment of God's truth and into a ministerial and official consideration of it instead. We deal with many complicated situations, sometimes coming to our wits' end or becoming confused ourselves. We observe very sad episodes of backsliding among our people, wounding our hearts; and we see millions perishing without the gospel, and our spirits sink as a result. We desire that you would profit from our preaching, that we would be a blessing to your children, and that we would be useful to saints and sinners alike for many years to come.

Therefore, dear friends, intercede for us with God. We would be miserable indeed without the help of your prayers, but are happy when we know of your intercession for us. Although you do not look to us, but to our Master, for spiritual blessings, consider how often He has given those blessings through His ministers. Pray again and again that we may be the earthen vessels into whom the Lord may place the treasure of the gospel. We — the entirety of ministers, missionaries, evangelists, and Bible students — implore you in the name of Jesus:

"Pray for us"!

From the pen of Jim Reimann:

The calling to be a minister is a special blessing, but it can often be frustrating. Many ministers become discouraged due to the lack of spiritual growth they see in people. We can only imagine how Jeremiah must have felt when the Lord told him, "When you tell them all this, they will not listen to you; when you call to them, they will not answer" (Jer. 7:27). And the people themselves were amazingly bold in their defiance, for they told Jeremiah, "We will not listen to the message you have spoken to us in the name of the LORD!" (Jer. 44:16).

Paul even asked, "Who is equal to such a task?" (2 Cor. 2:16). Yet he went on to say, "Unlike so many, we do not peddle the word of God for profit. On the contrary, in Christ we speak before God with sincerity, like men sent from God" (2 Cor. 2:17).

With so many preaching for personal gain today, those ministers speaking "with sincerity" need our prayers more than ever. Why not take time this morning to pray for the ministers who have given of themselves to you?

JULY 8

Tell me the secret of your great strength.

Judges 16:6

From the pen of Charles Spurgeon:

In light of this verse, let's consider where the secret of our faith's strength lies. It lies in the food our faith feeds on, for true faith nourishes itself on God's promises. Each of His promises is an emanation of divine grace — the overflow of the generous heart of God. Faith says, "If not for His love and grace, my God could never have given this promise. Therefore it is absolutely certain His Word will be fulfilled." Then faith thinks of Who gave the promise, focusing not as much on the greatness of the promise but on the greatness of Who authored it.

Faith remembers the author is "God, who does not lie" (Titus 1:2) — God omnipotent and unchanging. Thus, faith concludes the promise must be fulfilled and acts on this firm conviction. Faith remembers why the promise was given in the first place — namely, for God's glory — and is perfectly sure God's glory is safe, for He will never stain His own shield of character or tarnish the luster of His own kingly crown. His promise must and will stand.

Next, faith considers the amazing work of Christ as clear proof of the Father's intention to fulfill His Word. "He who did not spare his own Son, but gave him up for us all — how will he not also, along with him, graciously give us all things?" (Rom. 8:32). Faith also looks at past battles that have given it strength and past victories that have given it courage. Faith recalls that God has never failed even one of His children, calling to mind past dangers when deliverance came. Faith remembers those times of great need when strength was found and firmly declares, "I will

never be led to think God can change and forsake His servant. The Lord has been my help in times past, and He will help me now."

Therefore, true faith views each promise in its connection to the Promise-giver. As a result it can say with assurance, "Surely goodness and love will follow me all the days of my life" (Ps. 23:6).

From the pen of Jim Reimann:

Our text verse today is taken from the story of Samson and Delilah. Many of us have known this story since childhood, but there is nevertheless often a misunderstanding as to the source of Samson's strength. His strength came not from the length of his hair but from what his hair represented. It was the symbol of his "vow of separation to the LORD as a Nazirite" (Num. 6:2). Thus, his strength came from the Lord as a result of his obedience to his vow.

Samson's encounter with Delilah was not the beginning of his downfall. It began when he "went to Gaza, where he saw a prostitute" (Judg. 16:1) and defiled himself with her. Living with the enemy led to his relationship with Delilah, and this continual breaking of his vow ultimately led to the *visible* sign of violating his vow — cutting off his hair.

In the same way, the essence of what Spurgeon says today is that our faith's strength comes from trusting in and being obedient to the promises of God. The Lord will not — in fact, cannot — release His power through us when we are disobedient to Him.

"This is what the Sovereign LORD ... says: 'In repentance and rest is your salvation, in quietness and trust is your strength'" (Isa. 30:15).

JULY 9

Praise the LORD, O my soul,
and forget not all his benefits.

Psalm 103:2

From the pen of Charles Spurgeon:

It is a delightful and profitable exercise to recognize the sovereign hand of God in the lives of the ancient saints of old, to observe His goodness in delivering them, His mercy in forgiving them, and His faithfulness in keeping His covenant with them. However, wouldn't it be even more interesting and profitable for us to recognize the hand of God in our own lives? Shouldn't we notice that our own history is at least as full of God's goodness, truth, faithfulness, and righteousness as any of the lives of the saints who have gone before us?

We do our Lord an injustice when we presume He worked all His mighty acts and displayed His strength to those in ancient times, but no longer works miracles or shows His power to the saints now living on earth. If we would only review our own lives, surely we would discover a number of blessed occasions that would refresh our faith and bring glory to God. Haven't you had experiences where He has delivered you? Haven't you passed through deep rivers supported by His divine presence? Haven't you walked through various fiery trials unharmed? Haven't you seen His miracles in your life? Haven't you seen numerous blessings from Him?

Hasn't the same God who gave Solomon his "heart's desire" (2 Chron. 1:11) listened to you and answered your requests? Hasn't the lavish God of abundance of whom David sang, "Who satisfies your desires with good things" (Ps. 103:5), "filled [you] with ... bounty" (Jer. 31:14) as well? Hasn't He ever made you "lie down in green pastures" or led you "beside quiet waters"

(Ps. 23:2)? Surely the goodness of God has been the same to us as to the saints of old.

Thus, may we weave His mercies into songs of worship. May we use the pure gold of thankfulness and the jewels of praise and fashion them into another crown for Jesus' head. May music as sweet and as stirring as that which came from David's harp flow from our soul while we praise the Lord whose "love endures forever" (Ps. 106:1).

From the pen of Jim Reimann:

Why is it we have faith the Lord will work in others' lives while doubting He will answer our personal prayers? Is it that, knowing ourselves, we feel undeserving or unworthy? Believer, if this lack of faith describes you, remember, God did not save you and does not keep you because of your good works.

No! You were "without hope"! "Remember that at that time you were separate from Christ ... *without hope* and without God in the world. But now in Christ Jesus you who once were far away have been brought near through the blood of Christ" (Eph. 2:12 – 13). Notice you "have been brought," indicating *God* brought you to Christ — you had nothing to do with it!

Thus, never hesitate to trust God to answer your prayers for yourself. He answers His children, not on the basis of what we have done but on the basis of "the blood of Christ." His work alone has made us worthy of His answer. We stand worthy before Him because we are "in Christ," and "*it is because of him* that you are in Christ Jesus" (1 Cor. 1:30).

"I call on you, O God, for you will answer me" (Ps. 17:6).

JULY 10

You are ... fellow citizens with God's people.

Ephesians 2:19

From the pen of Charles Spurgeon:

What is the meaning of "our citizenship is in heaven" (Phil. 3:20)? It means we are subject to heaven's government; Christ, the King of heaven, reigns in our hearts; and our daily prayer is, "Your will be done on earth as it is in heaven" (Matt. 6:10). It means we freely receive the proclamations issued from God's throne of glory and we cheerfully obey the Great King's decrees.

Then, as citizens of the New Jerusalem, we share heaven's honors. The glory belonging to the saints already glorified belongs to us, for we are already sons of God, already in the royal bloodline, already clothed in the spotless robe of Jesus' righteousness. We already have angels as our servants, saints as our companions, Christ as our brother, God as our Father, and a crown of immortality as our reward. We share the honors of citizenship, for we "have come ... to the church of the firstborn, whose names are written in heaven" (Heb. 12:22 – 23). As citizens we have public rights to all the property of heaven. The gates of pearl and walls of chrysolite are ours; the sky blue light of the city, which itself needs no candles or light of the sun, is ours; "the river of the water of life" is ours; and the "twelve crops of fruit" planted "on each side of the river" (Rev. 22:1 – 2) are ours. There is nothing in heaven that does not belong to us. "Whether ... things present, or things to come; all are [ours]" (1 Cor. 3:22 KJV).

As citizens of heaven we also enjoy its delights. Isn't there "rejoicing in heaven over one sinner who repents" (Luke 15:7) and prodigals who have returned? Then we share in that rejoicing. Don't they sing the glories of triumphant grace? We do as well. Do "they lay their crowns" (Rev. 4:10) at Jesus' feet? We share this honor too. Are they graced with His smile? It is no less sweet to us here below. Do they look forward to His second coming? We also "[long] for his appearing" (2 Tim. 4:8).

Thus, since we are indeed citizens of heaven, may our walk and actions be consistent with our high nobility and heavenly status.

From the pen of Jim Reimann:

Spurgeon is saying, in essence, that we should walk in agreement with who we are, or as the saying goes: "walk our talk"! Paul also says this, not by accident, in the verses just before He wrote, "Our citizenship is in heaven." Here is how he stated it:

> I want to know Christ and the power of his resurrection and the fellowship of sharing in his sufferings, becoming like him in his death, and so, somehow, to attain to the resurrection from the dead. *Not that I have already obtained all this, or have already been made perfect, but I press on* to take hold of that for which Christ Jesus took hold of me. Brothers, I do not consider myself yet to have taken hold of it. But one thing I do: Forgetting what is behind and straining toward what is ahead, I press on toward the goal to win the prize for which God has called me heavenward in Christ Jesus.
>
> Philippians 3:10 – 14

Paul realized he was in the process of being "made perfect" — that he had not "arrived." Yet he goes on to admonish each of us: "Only let us live up to what we have already attained" (Phil. 3:16).

May this be our prayer to the Lord today!

JULY 11

The God of all grace..., after you have suffered a little while,
will himself restore you and make you strong, firm and steadfast.

1 Peter 5:10

From the pen of Charles Spurgeon:

We have all seen the "arch of heaven" as it spans the meadows of earth with its glorious colors and hues. It is beautiful, but, alas, within minutes it vanishes and is no more. The lovely colors give way to fluffy clouds and the sky is no longer brilliant with the various tints of heaven. It is not permanent. How can it be? It is a glorious display but made of only momentary sunbeams and passing raindrops, so how can it survive?

The gifts of Christian character, however, must not resemble the rainbow in its passing beauty. On the contrary, they must be "strong, firm, and steadfast." Believer, seek to solidly establish every gift you have. May your character not be as writing on the sand, but rather inscriptions chiseled into rock! May your faith not be like some ethereal veil of a vision, but made of building materials that would endure the fires of judgment that would easily consume the "wood, hay, or straw" (1 Cor. 3:12) of a hypocrite. May you be "rooted and established in love" (Eph. 3:17). May your convictions be deep, your love real, and your desires profound. May your entire life be so "firm and steadfast" that all the weapons of hell and all the storms of earth will never be able to move you.

Yet notice how this blessing of being "strengthened in the faith" (Col. 2:7) is accomplished. The apostle Paul points us to suffering as the means: "after you have suffered a little while." It is useless to hope of being well rooted without stormy winds blowing across us. The old gnarled roots of the oak and its strange twisted branches all speak of the many storms that have swept over it and are indicators of the depth into which its roots have forced their way. In the same manner, Christians are made strong and are firmly rooted by all the trials and storms of life.

So never shrink from the tempestuous winds of trials. Instead, take comfort, believing that through their difficult discipline God is fulfilling this benediction in you: May "God ... himself ... make you strong, firm and steadfast."

From the pen of Jim Reimann:

Yes, it is important for believers to be rooted, but in what are we to be rooted? Paul said, "Just as you received Christ Jesus as Lord, continue to live in him, *rooted and built up in him*" (Col. 2:6–7). Thus, we are to be rooted in Christ. In fact, the prophet Isaiah referred to the coming messiah as a *root* in the following verse: "*The Root of Jesse will stand as a banner for the peoples ... and his place of rest will be glorious*" (Isa. 11:10). Of course "the Root of Jesse" refers to Jesus, who will be the descendant of David, Jesse's son.

Then Jesus Himself said, "I am the Root and the Offspring of David, and the bright Morning Star" (Rev. 22:16). Previously He had told His disciples, "I am the vine; you are the branches. If a man remains in me and I in him, he will bear much fruit; apart from me you can do nothing" (John 15:5). And Paul told the Gentiles who had been "grafted in" to the Messiah, or the root of the olive tree of Israel, "You do not support the root, but the root supports you" (Rom. 11:17–18).

Father, I pray that I will be rooted in and "continue in [the] faith, established and firm, not moved from the hope held out in the gospel" (Col. 1:23).

JULY 12

... sanctified by God the Father...

Jude 1 KJV

... sanctified in Christ Jesus...

1 Corinthians 1:2

... sanctifying work of the Spirit...

1 Peter 1:2

From the pen of Charles Spurgeon:

We should always note the oneness of the three divine persons in each of their gracious works. Many believers unwisely prefer one above the other or make distinctions between them. For example, they think of Jesus as the embodiment of everything wonderful and gracious, but regard God the Father as severely just and devoid of kindness. Equally wrong are those who overly stress the commands of the Father and the atonement of the Son, while minimizing the work of the Spirit.

When it comes to works of grace, none of the persons of the Trinity act independently of the others, for they are as united in their works as in their essence. They are in total harmony in their love for their chosen ones and undivided in every other action that flows from their great central source.

We should take special note of this when it comes to sanctification. While it is not wrong to say sanctification is a work of the Spirit, we must be careful not to think the Father and Son have no part in it. To be fully correct, we should refer to sanctification as the work of the Father, Son, and Spirit. Jehovah's words still stand: "Let us make man in our image, in our likeness" (Gen. 1:26); thus, we continue to be "God's workmanship, created in Christ Jesus to do good works, which God prepared in advance for us to do" (Eph. 2:10). The Lord places great value on holiness since all three persons of the Trinity are working together to produce "a radiant church, without stain or wrinkle or any other blemish" (Eph. 5:27).

Therefore, as a follower of Christ you must place great value on holiness — on a life of purity, including godly speech. Value the blood of Christ as the foundation of your hope, but never speak disparagingly of the work of the Spirit or the Father, "who has qualified you to share in the inheritance of the saints in the kingdom of light" (Col. 1:12).

May our lives today exhibit the work of the Triune God.

From the pen of Jim Reimann:

The Trinity is a difficult concept, and though the word *trinity* is not in the Bible, it *is* biblical. A helpful way to consider the three persons of the one God is to think of the Father as "the Will of God," the Son as "the Word of God," and the Spirit as "the Power of God." All three persons are involved in each work of God.

Consider the birth of Jesus. Mary was told, "The Holy Spirit will come upon you.... So the holy one to be born will be called the Son of God" (Luke 1:35). John said of the Son, "The Word became flesh and made his dwelling among us" (John 1:14). Later he wrote of the Father, "God so loved the world that he gave his one and only Son" (John 3:16).

And all three were involved from the outset of Jesus' ministry: "As soon as Jesus was baptized, he went up out of the water. At that moment heaven was opened, and he saw the Spirit of God descending like a dove and lighting on him. And a voice from heaven said, 'This is my Son, whom I love; with him I am well pleased'" (Matt. 3:16 – 17).

JULY 13

God said to Jonah,
"Do you have a right to be angry?"
Jonah 4:9

From the pen of Charles Spurgeon:

Anger is not necessarily sinful in all cases, but it has such a tendency to get out of control that whenever it shows itself we should be quick to question its nature. We should ask ourselves, "Do you have a right to be angry?" Perhaps we can answer, "Yes," for sometimes it is Elijah's "fire from heaven" (2 Kings 1:10 KJV), yet often it is simply the sign of an out-of-control madman. To have anger over sin is a good thing because of the wrong sin commits against our good and gracious God. It is good to be angry with ourselves for remaining foolish after so much godly instruction or to be angry with others when the sole cause of our anger is the evil they are doing. Someone who is not angry over sinfulness is someone who is partaking in the sin, for sin is a loathsome, hateful thing and no renewed heart can patiently endure it. God Himself is angry with the wicked every day and His Word says, "Let those who love the LORD hate evil" (Ps. 97:10).

Far more frequently, however, our anger is not commendable or justifiable, so our answer must be, "No, I don't have a right to be angry." Why do we get so enraged with our children, exasperated with our employees, and irritated with our friends? Is this type of anger honorable to our Christian testimony or glorifying to God? Isn't this kind of anger evidence of our old evil heart seeking to regain control, and shouldn't we resist it with all the power of our newborn nature? Many professing Christians allow their tempers free rein, as though it were useless to resist. Yet believers should remember that we must "*in all these things* [be] more than conquerors" (Rom. 8:37) or else we cannot be crowned.

If we cannot control our temper, what has grace done for us? Someone once said that grace is often grafted into the most bitter crabapple tree stump. That may be true, but then its fruit will no longer be bitter. We must never use our natural weaknesses as an excuse for sin. Instead we must run to the cross and pray for the Lord to crucify our temper and renew in us the traits of gentleness and meekness that reflect His image.

From the pen of Jim Reimann:

The apostle Paul addresses the issue of anger in the context of the struggle between our old and new natures. He says,

> You were taught, with regard to your former way of life, to put off your old self, which is being corrupted by its deceitful desires; to be made new in the attitude of your minds; and to put on the new self, created to be like God in true righteousness and holiness.... *"In your anger do not sin": Do not let the sun go down while you are still angry,* and do not give the devil a foothold.
> Ephesians 4:22 – 24, 26 – 27

Then he reiterates his admonition regarding anger, lest we miss it:

> Do not grieve the Holy Spirit of God, with whom you were sealed for the day of redemption. *Get rid of all bitterness, rage and anger,* brawling and slander, along with every form of malice. Be kind and compassionate to one another, forgiving each other, just as in Christ God forgave you.
> Ephesians 4:30 – 32

Lord, forgive me for my anger toward others and toward You. May my anger be directed only toward sin, not others.

JULY 14

If you make an altar of stones for me, do not build it with dressed stones,
for you will defile it if you use a tool on it.

Exodus 20:25

From the pen of Charles Spurgeon:

God's altar was to be built of uncut stones without any trace of human workmanship upon them. Human wisdom loves to craft and position the doctrines of the cross into a hollow system more compatible with the depraved ideas of the fallen nature, but instead of improving the gospel, our carnal wisdom actually pollutes it until it becomes "a different gospel" (2 Cor. 11:4) and not the truth of God at all. Any alteration or amendment of the Lord's Word defiles and pollutes it.

Our prideful hearts are so anxious to have a role in the justification of our soul before God that we trust in our good works for Christ and in our times of humility and repentance, and then we boast of our natural talents and abilities in a vain attempt to lift these human tools to God's holy altar. But it would be well for sinners to remember that, far from perfecting the Savior's work, our carnal confidences only pollute and dishonor it. Our Lord alone must be exalted in the work of atonement, and not a single stroke of our chisel or hammer will be tolerated. There is an inherent blasphemy in seeking to add to what Christ Jesus, in His dying moments, declared to be finished or in attempting to improve on His work in which the Lord Jehovah finds perfect satisfaction.

Unstable sinner, away with your tools! Fall on your knees in humble prayer and supplication and accept the Lord Jesus as the altar of your atonement, resting in Him alone.

Many professing Christians should take today's verse as a warning against the doctrines they believe. Among believers there is far too much of an inclination to attempt to square and reconcile the truths of God's revelation. This is nothing but a form of irreverence and unbelief, so may we strive against it. May we receive truth just as we find it, rejoicing that the doctrines of God's Word are uncut stones and, as such, are all the more perfect to build an altar for the Lord.

From the pen of Jim Reimann:

Why is it many Christians believe they had something to do with their salvation? They may not state it that directly, but as we peel back the layers of their theology, we find they have a sense of acceptance due to something they did — which is works, not faith. They speak of "making a decision for Christ," yet John said we have become God's children, not born "of human decision ... but born of God" (John 1:13). Jesus said, "You did not choose me, but I chose you" (John 15:16). Paul said of becoming God's child, "It does not, therefore, depend on man's desire or effort, but on God's mercy" (Rom. 9:16). Finally, Solomon, referring to God's sovereign control, wrote, "Every decision is from the LORD" (Prov. 16:33).

Perhaps it is the fact that in nearly every area of society, whether at home, church, school, or work, we often experience performance-based acceptance. Yet God's Word says, "He [has] made us accepted in the beloved" (Eph. 1:6 KJV).

"Therefore, if anyone is in Christ, he is a new creation; the old has gone, the new has come! All this is from God" (2 Cor. 5:17 – 18).

JULY 15

The fire must be kept burning on the altar continuously;
it must not go out.

Leviticus 6:13

From the pen of Charles Spurgeon:

As in our verse today, we must keep the fire burning on the altar of our private prayers, for prayer is the very life of faith and devotion. The altars of the church and the family get their fire from individual believers' altars, so may these fires burn brightly. Times of private devotion are the very essence, evidence, and measure of a vital, growing faith.

It is in private devotion you should burn "the fat of [your] sacrifice" (Lev. 4:26 KJV). These "secret" times when you "go into your room, close the door and pray" (Matt. 6:6) should be regular, frequent, and undisturbed, if at all possible. And remember, "The prayer of a righteous man is powerful and effective" (James 5:16). Do you feel you have nothing to pray for? Here are some suggestions: the church, those in ministry, your own soul, your children, your other family members, your neighbors, your country, and the cause of Christ and His truth throughout the world.

We should examine ourselves on this important matter of prayer and devotion. Are our private times with the Lord lukewarm? Is the fire of devotion barely burning in our heart? Have the chariot wheels of our prayers become bogged down in the mud? If so, we should be alarmed at these signs of weakness and decay. We should go to the Lord in tears and ask for His Spirit of grace and prayer. We should also set aside special times for extraordinary prayer, for if this important fire gets smothered beneath the ashes of worldly conformity, it will dim the fire of the family altar, which in turn will lessen our influence in both the church and the world.

Today's verse should also be understood and applied in the context of the altar of the heart, for this is a golden altar indeed. God loves to see the hearts of His people "on fire" toward Him. May we give our hearts, ablaze with love, to Him. And may we seek His grace that the fire will never be quenched, for it will not continue to burn unless the Lord Himself keeps it burning. Many enemies will attempt to extinguish it, but if God's unseen hand continues to pour His sacred oil on it, the fire will continue to blaze brighter and brighter.

May we use passages of Scripture as the fuel to stoke the fires of our heart, for they are live coals; may we attend church and hear sermons; but above all else, may we often be alone with Jesus.

From the pen of Jim Reimann:

Jesus — the Son of God who enjoyed perfect oneness and fellowship with His Father since eternity past — this same Jesus spent time alone with His Father. How much more do we need personal time with Him!

Our Lord prayed often — at various times of the day and night. "He went up on a mountainside by himself to pray. When evening came, he was there alone" (Matt. 14:23). "He went out into a mountain to pray, and continued all night in prayer to God" (Luke 6:12 KJV). "Very early in the morning, while it was still dark, Jesus got up, left the house and went off to a solitary place, where he prayed" (Mark 1:35).

Time alone with God is a discipline — one every true disciple will master.

JULY 16

Each morning everyone gathered
as much [manna] as he needed.

Exodus 16:21

From the pen of Charles Spurgeon:

Work to maintain a sense of your entire dependence on the Lord's goodwill and generosity for the ongoing provision of your greatest blessings. Never try to live on old manna or attempt to find help in Egypt, for if Jesus is not your source, you will be continually defeated. Old anointings will never suffice to impart new power to your spirit. Your head must be anointed with fresh oil from the golden horn of God's sanctuary, for oil loses its effectiveness over time.

You may find yourself today on the summit of God's mountain, but He who placed you there must keep you there or you will slip from the heights more quickly than you ever dreamed. The mountain under your feet is firm footing only when the Lord keeps the mountain firmly in its place, and if He hides His face from you, trouble will soon follow. And if the Savior should see fit, there is not one window through which you presently see the light of heaven that He could not darken in an instant.

Joshua asked the sun to "stand still" (Josh. 10:12), but Jesus can shroud it in total darkness. He can withdraw the joy of your heart, the light of your eyes, and the strength of your life, for the blessings of life lie in His hand, and if it is in His will, they can depart from you. Our Lord desires you recognize and feel the need for this hourly dependence upon Him, for He only permits you to pray for "daily bread" (Matt. 6:11), and He only promises "your strength will equal your days" (Deut. 33:25).

Isn't it best for us this is true so we may often draw near His throne and constantly be reminded of His love? Oh, how rich God's grace that continually meets our needs and never holds

back even in light of our ingratitude! Golden rain showers never cease and the clouds of blessing linger evermore above our lives.

O Lord Jesus, we bow at Your feet, recognizing our utter inability to do anything without You! And for every blessing we are privileged to receive, we worship Your blessed name and acknowledge Your inexhaustible love.

From the pen of Jim Reimann:

Christians have been anointed by the Lord, for His Word says, "It is God who makes both us and you stand firm in Christ. *He anointed us ... and put his Spirit in our hearts*" (2 Cor. 1:21 – 22). Thus, the following psalm of David applies to us as God's anointed:

May he give you the desire of your heart and make all your plans succeed. We will shout for joy when you are victorious and will lift up our banners in the name of our God. May the LORD grant all your requests. *Now I know that the LORD saves his anointed*; he answers him from his holy heaven with the saving power of his right hand. Some trust in chariots and some in horses, but *we trust in the name of the LORD our God.* They are brought to their knees and fall, but we rise up and stand firm.

Psalm 20:4 – 8

"My salvation and my honor depend on God; he is my mighty rock" (Ps. 62:7). "In him our hearts rejoice, for we trust in his holy name" (Ps. 33:21).

"O LORD our God ... we rely on you" (2 Chron. 14:11).

JULY 17

We know, brothers loved by God,
that he has chosen you.

1 Thessalonians 1:4

From the pen of Charles Spurgeon:

Many people wish to know if they are among God's elect before they ever look to Christ. But we cannot learn of our election in this manner, for it can only be discovered by "fix[ing] our eyes on Jesus" (Heb. 12:2).

Dear sinner, if you desire to ascertain whether or not you are among God's elect, then do the following and your heart will have assurance before Him. If you feel you are a lost and guilty sinner, go directly to the cross of Christ and confess it to Jesus. Then tell Him you have read in the Bible: "Whoever comes to me I will never drive away" (John 6:37), and, "Here is a trustworthy saying that deserves full acceptance: Christ Jesus came into the world to save sinners" (1 Tim. 1:15). Look to Jesus and believe on Him and you will find proof of your election immediately, for as soon as you believe, you are one of the elect. If you give yourself completely to Christ and trust in Him, you are one of God's chosen ones; but if you stop and say, "First I want to know whether or not I am one of the elect," then you really don't understand what you are asking.

Regardless of the magnitude of your guilt, go to Jesus just as you are and leave the questions regarding your election behind. Go directly to Christ and hide yourself in His wounds, and you will know of your election. The assurance of the Holy Spirit will be given to you and you will be able to say, "I know whom I have believed, and am convinced that he is able to guard what I have entrusted to him" (2 Tim. 1:12). Christ was present at the council of the godhead in eternity past

and He can tell you whether you were chosen in Him or not — you cannot find out any other way.

Go to Jesus, put your trust in Him, and His answer will be: "I have loved you with an everlasting love; I have drawn you with loving-kindness" (Jer. 31:3). Thus, there will be no doubt about His having chosen you, once you have "chosen" Him.

> Sons we are through God's election,
> Who in Jesus Christ believe.
>
> Isaac Watts, 1674 – 1748

From the pen of Jim Reimann:

Election is a doctrine that even many long-time Christians reject, although it is taught throughout the Scriptures. In its essence, election has to do with God's total sovereignty in our salvation. As Spurgeon once said, "Some men hate the doctrine of divine Sovereignty; but those who are called by grace love it, for they feel, if it had not been for sovereignty they never would have been saved. Was there anything good in us that moved the heart of God to save us? God forbid that we should indulge the blasphemous thought. Tell me, you who deny divine sovereignty, how is it that the publicans and harlots enter the kingdom of heaven, while the self-righteous Pharisee is shut out?"

If you find yourself struggling with election and sovereignty, consider the words of Jesus: "No one can come to me *unless the Father who sent me draws him,*" and "I told you that no one can come to me *unless the Father has enabled him*" (John 6:44, 65).

JULY 18

The men assigned to the camp of Dan ...
set out last, under their standards.

Numbers 2:31

From the pen of Charles Spurgeon:

When the armies of Israel were on the march, "the camp of Dan" brought up the rear. Although their placement was the farthest back in the ranks, it made no difference, for they were just as much a part of Israel as were the tribes up front. They followed the same pillars of cloud and fire, ate the same manna, drank from the same spiritual rock, and journeyed to the same inheritance.

Thus, my heart, cheer up! Though I may be last and least, I am privileged to be in God's army and am as nourished as those who lead the troop. After all, someone must be last in honor and esteem. Someone must do menial work for Jesus. Why shouldn't I? Whether I serve in a poor country village among the uneducated lower class, or in a back street of the city among the vilest sinners, I will work on, "set[ting] out last, under [my] standards."

The tribe of Dan actually occupied a very useful place. Stragglers from other tribes had to be helped along and lost possessions had to be gathered from the field. Those with fiery spirits may rush headlong over unexplored paths to learn more truth and win more souls for Jesus, while those with a more reserved spirit will still be well employed, reminding the church of her ancient doctrines and renewing those whose faith has faltered. Every position has its duties, and even the slower-moving children of God will discover their unique role is one that will be a profound blessing to the entire multitude.

The rear guard is a place of danger, for there are enemies behind us as well as ahead of us, and attacks may come from any direction. For example, Amalek attacked Israel and "smote the hindmost" (Deut. 25:18 KJV), killing some of them. The more experienced Christian can always find many ways to employ his weapons in helping the poor, doubting, depressed, and wavering souls who are hindmost in their faith, knowledge, and joy. They must not be left unaided; thus, it becomes the role of some of the more mature saints to carry the banners of the rear guard.

My soul, are you tenderly watching to help those who find themselves stationed at the rear today?

From the pen of Jim Reimann:

If you have been a believer for many years and are one of the "up-front" Christians, beware —"Do not think of yourself more highly than you ought" (Rom. 12:3). Remember,

> God has arranged the parts in the body, every one of them, just as he wanted them to be.... Those parts of the body that seem to be weaker are indispensable, and the parts that we think are less honorable we treat with special honor.... God has combined the members of the body and has given greater honor to the parts that lacked it ... that its parts should have equal concern for each other.
>
> 1 Corinthians 12:18, 22–25

And,

> Just as each of us has one body with many members, and these members do not all have the same function, so in Christ we who are many form one body, and each member belongs to all the others.
>
> Romans 12:4–5

JULY 19

The LORD our God has shown us his glory.

Deuteronomy 5:24

From the pen of Charles Spurgeon:

God's great purpose in each of His works is the manifestation of His own glory, and any goal less than this would have been unworthy of Him. But how is the glory of God to be manifested in such fallen creatures as we are? Man's eyes are not single-focused, for we continually have a view toward our own glory and too high an estimate of our own power; thus, we are not qualified to behold the glory of the Lord. Therefore it is obvious we must step out of the way to make room for God to be exalted. This is the very reason He often brings His people into difficulties and trials, which He then uses to make them conscious of their own foolishness and weakness so they may be able to behold the majesty of God when He comes to deliver them.

Someone whose life is nothing but a smooth and easy path will see very little of the glory of the Lord, for he will have few opportunities for self-emptying and, as a result, will be unfit for being filled with the revelation of God. They who only navigate narrow streams and shallow creeks know little of the God of storms, but they who are "merchants on the mighty waters" see "his wonderful deeds in the deep" (Ps. 107:23 – 24). Among the huge Atlantic waves of bereavement, poverty, temptation, and reproach we learn the power of Jehovah because we sense the smallness of mankind.

Therefore, thank God if your road has been rough, for this is what has given you the experience of God's greatness and loving-kindness. Your troubles have enriched you with a wealth of knowledge not gained in any other way, for your trials have been the "cleft in the rock" where Jehovah has put you, just as He did with His servant Moses, that you too might behold His glory as it "passes by" (Ex. 33:22).

Praise God that you have not been left in the darkness and ignorance that continuing prosperity may have brought you. Instead, through the great "furnace of affliction" (Isa. 48:10) you have been given the capacity to behold the shining of His glory in His wonderful dealings with you.

From the pen of Jim Reimann:

Why are we so quick to complain when disaster strikes? Isaiah said, "The Lord gives you the bread of adversity and the water of affliction" (Isa. 30:20), while Jeremiah said, "Is it not from the mouth of the Most High that both calamities and good things come?" (Lam. 3:38).

> For men are not cast off by the Lord forever. Though he brings grief, he will show compassion, so great is his unfailing love. For he does not willingly bring affliction or grief to the children of men.
>
> Lamentations 3:31 – 33

May we realize the good that results through suffering. And may we come to know, like the believers who have gone before us, that "out of the most severe trial, their overflowing joy and their extreme poverty welled up in rich generosity" (2 Cor. 8:2). May we "be joyful in hope, patient in affliction, faithful in prayer" (Rom. 12:12).

"Father of compassion" (2 Cor. 1:3), help me walk in the truth that my "light and momentary troubles are achieving for [me] an eternal glory that far outweighs them all" (2 Cor. 4:17).

JULY 20

... a deposit guaranteeing our inheritance.
Ephesians 1:13 – 14

From the pen of Charles Spurgeon:

Oh, what enlightenment, joy, comfort, and delight is experienced in the hearts of those who have learned to feed solely on Jesus, and Him alone! In this life, however, the realization of Christ's preciousness is imperfect at best. One author once wrote, "Tis but a taste!" We "have tasted that the Lord is good" (1 Peter 2:3), but we do not yet know just how good He is. Yet what we do know of His sweetness causes us to long for more. We have enjoyed "the firstfruits of the Spirit," which have left us hungering and thirsting for the fullness of the heavenly bread and wine, so we "groan inwardly as we wait eagerly for our adoption as sons" (Rom. 8:23).

In this life we are like Israel in the wilderness, who had only "a single cluster of grapes" from "the Valley of Eshcol" (Num. 13:23). In heaven, however, we will be in the vineyard itself. Here "the manna [is] like coriander seed" (Num. 11:7) falling only in small pieces, but there we will eat "the bread of heaven" (Ps. 105:40) — the grain of God's kingdom. Today we are simply beginners in spiritual knowledge, for though we have learned the first letters of the alphabet, we cannot yet read words, much less put sentences together. But as someone once said, "He who has been in heaven only five minutes knows more than all the greatest theologians on earth combined." Today we have many unfulfilled desires, but soon our every wish will be satisfied and all our talents and gifts will be happily employed in the eternal world of joy.

Dear Christian, heaven is but a few years away. Within a very little time you will be rid of all your trials and troubles, and your eyes, now filled with tears, will weep no longer. Instead you will gaze in unspeakable rapture upon the splendor of "him who sits on the throne" (Rev. 5:13).

Even more, you will sit upon His throne! The triumph of His glory — His crown, His joy, His paradise — will be shared by you. These will all be yours, for you will be one of the "co-heirs with Christ" (Rom. 8:17) who is the "heir of all things" (Heb. 1:2).

From the pen of Jim Reimann:

Unfortunately complaining is part of human nature, but it should not be a part of a believer's life. In fact, we should recognize the truth that becoming "co-heirs with Christ" comes with certain responsibilities, and that in order to "share in his glory," we must "share in his sufferings." As Paul wrote in the following verse, your blessings come with an "if" — in other words, they are conditional: "If we are children, then we are heirs — heirs of God and co-heirs with Christ, *if indeed we share in his sufferings* in order that we may also share in his glory" (Rom. 8:17).

Today we have compared various aspects of this life with what is to come, but Paul goes on to say, "*Our present sufferings are not worth comparing with the glory that will be revealed in us*" (Rom. 8:18). Thus, we should remember this admonition when tempted to complain:

Do everything without complaining or arguing, so that you may become blameless and pure, children of God without fault in a crooked and depraved generation, in which you shine like stars in the universe.
Philippians 2:14 – 15

There are glorious, godly reasons for our suffering!

JULY 21

The Daughter of Jerusalem tosses her head as you flee.
Isaiah 37:22

From the pen of Charles Spurgeon:

Reassured by the Word of the Lord, the trembling citizens of Zion, or Jerusalem, became bold and mockingly tossed their heads at Sennacherib's boastful threats. Strong faith enables the servants of God to look with calm contempt on their most arrogant foes. As believers, we should remember our enemies are attempting things that are actually impossible. For example, they seek to destroy our eternal life, something which cannot die while Jesus lives. They seek to overthrow the fortress of God's kingdom, but "the gates of Hades will not overcome it" (Matt. 16:18). Our enemies "kick against the goads" (Acts 26:14), only wounding themselves, and they storm against those protected behind Jehovah's shield, to their own harm.

We know their weaknesses, for aren't they only men themselves? And what is "man ... but a maggot" (Job 25:6)? "They are wild waves of the sea, foaming up their shame" (Jude 13). When the Lord moves, they fly away "like chaff before the wind" (Ps. 35:5) and are consumed "like the crackling of thorns" (Eccl. 7:6). Their utter powerlessness to do damage to the cause of God and His truth can make even the weakest soldier in Zion's ranks laugh them to scorn.

Above all, we know "the LORD Almighty is with us" (Ps. 46:7), and when He wields His weapons, where are His enemies? When He comes forth from His throne, "the potsherds on the ground" will not long "[quarrel] with [their] Maker" (Isa. 45:9). His "iron scepter ... will dash them to pieces like pottery" (Ps. 2:9) and will "cut off the remembrance of them from the earth" (Ps. 34:16 KJV).

Thus, away with all fears, for the kingdom is safe in the King's hand! May we "shout for joy" (Ps. 35:27), for "the LORD reigns" (Ps. 97:1), and His foes "will be trampled under him as straw is trampled down in the manure" (Isa. 25:10).

> As true as God's own word is true;
> Nor earth, nor hell, with all their crew,
> Against us will prevail.
> A jest, and byword, are they grown;
> God is with us, we are his own,
> Our victory cannot fail.
>
> Gustavus Adolphus, 1594 – 1632
>
> Translated from German by
> Catherine Winkworth, 1827 – 1878

From the pen of Jim Reimann:

"Whenever the ark set out, Moses said, 'Rise up, O LORD! May your enemies be scattered; may your foes flee before you'" (Num. 10:35). Later David quoted the same victorious prayer in Psalm 68:1, saying of our conquering Lord, "When you ascended on high, you led captives in your train; you received gifts from men" (Ps. 68:18).

Yet when Jesus "ascended on high," fulfilling David's psalm, instead of "*receiv[ing]*" gifts from men," He "*gave* gifts to men" (Eph. 4:8). "Our God is a God who saves; from the Sovereign LORD comes escape from death" (Ps. 68:20).

Thank You, Father, for the gift of salvation through the gift of Your Son.

JULY 22

I am your husband.

Jeremiah 3:14

From the pen of Charles Spurgeon:

Christ Jesus is joined to His people through the bond of marriage. In love His church was promised "as a pure virgin to him" (2 Cor. 11:2) long before she fell under the "yoke of slavery" (Gal. 5:1). Filled with intense affection, He worked just as "Jacob served seven years to get Rachel" (Gen. 29:20) and paid the full price for her. Now, having sought her by His Spirit and having brought her to a place of knowing and loving Him, He awaits the glorious moment when their mutual happiness will be consummated at "the wedding supper of the Lamb" (Rev. 19:9). The promised bride has not yet been presented, complete and perfected, to the glorious Bridegroom before "the Majesty in heaven" (Heb. 1:3). She has not yet actually entered into the enjoyment of her privileges and honors as His wife and queen, for she is still a wanderer in a world of woe — one who still "live[s] among the tents of Kedar" (Ps. 120:5).

Yet even now she is the bride, the spouse of Jesus — dear to His heart, "precious in [His] sight" (Ps. 116:15), "engraved ... on the palms of [His] hands" (Isa. 49:16), and one with His person. On earth He extends to her all the appropriate affection as her Husband, richly providing for her needs, paying all her debts, allowing her to assume His name, and sharing all His wealth. Never will He act in any other way toward her. The word *divorce* He will never mention, for He has said, "I hate divorce" (Mal. 2:16). And although death severs the marital bond here on earth between even the most loving mortals, nothing can divide the bonds of this immortal marriage. In heaven "people will neither marry nor be given in marriage; they will be like the angels in heaven" (Matt. 22:30). There is one marvelous exception to the rule, however, for in heaven Christ and His church will celebrate their joyous wedding.

Earthly marriage is the closest example we have of this kind of love, but our heavenly marriage will be everlasting. No matter how pure and intense the love of an earthly husband, it is but a faint picture of the flame that burns in the heart of Jesus. Surpassing any human union is the miraculous unity that the church has with Christ, who left His Father in heaven to become one flesh with her.

From the pen of Jim Reimann:

Thankfully our relationship with the Lord is one of permanency, unlike many marriages today. Unfortunately divorce had become rampant as well during the time of Jesus. Referring to the prevalence of divorce, the Pharisees, in attempting to test Him, asked, "Is it lawful for a man to divorce his wife *for any and every reason*?" (Matt. 19:3). This sounds very much like today's "no-fault" divorces, or divorces based on the idea that "we've just grown apart over time."

Nearly every family today has been touched in one way or another by the pain of divorce, but isn't it wonderful to know that as the bride of Christ, He has said to us, "Never will I leave you; never will I forsake you" (Heb. 13:5).

"The angel said to me, 'Write: "Blessed are those who are invited to the wedding supper of the Lamb!"' And he added, 'These are the true words of God'" (Rev. 19:9).

Lord, I praise You, "For great is your love, reaching to the heavens; your faithfulness reaches to the skies" (Ps. 57:10).

JULY 23

Because of the violence against your brother Jacob ... you will be destroyed forever....
While strangers carried off his wealth ... you were like one of them.

Obadiah 10 – 11

From the pen of Charles Spurgeon:

Edom owed Israel some brotherly kindness in their time of need, but instead of helping, the men of Esau did nothing and, in effect, sided with Israel's enemies. Special emphasis should be placed on the word *you* in our passage today: "*You* were like one of them," as when Caesar cried out, "*You* too, Brutus!" A bad action can be made even worse due to the person who committed it. When *we* sin — *we* who are the chosen favorites of heaven — our sin is magnified and becomes a "crying" offense, like Brutus's sin, because of indulging ourselves so grievously and sinning against our brother.

If an angel of heaven were to lay his hand on us while we are engaged in sin, he would not need any rebuke other than: "What! *You* too? What are *you* doing here?" Shall we — much forgiven, delivered, instructed, enriched, and blessed — dare to reach out our hand to do evil? "God forbid" (Rom. 6:2 KJV)!

Dear reader, a few minutes of confession may be quite beneficial to you this morning. Have you ever sinned like those who are wicked? Have you laughed at an unclean joke at a dinner party? Did the joke not even offend you, as though you were one of the lost? When others maligned the ways of God, did you stand by bashfully silent and thus become as one of the maligners to onlookers? When those of the world drove unfair bargains and business deals, were you a party to the deal? When others greedily pursued this type of vanity, were you as greedy for gain as they were? Is there any discernible difference between you and them?

Are you any different? This hits very close to home, but be honest with your own soul, making sure you are a "new creation" (2 Cor. 5:17) in Christ Jesus. But once you have made sure, jealously guard your walk with Him lest anyone will be able to say, "You are one of them." You would never desire to share their eternal doom, so why be like them here? Don't enter into their secret sins lest you come to the same ruin.

Side with the suffering people of God — not with the world!

From the pen of Jim Reimann:

As believers, there is a big difference between witnessing or ministering to the world and being like the world. Paul warns us:

> Do not be yoked together with unbelievers. For what do righteousness and wickedness have in common? Or what fellowship can light have with darkness? What harmony is there between Christ and Belial? What does a believer have in common with an unbeliever? What agreement is there between the temple of God and idols? For we are the temple of the living God. As God has said: "I will live with them and walk among them, and I will be their God, and they will be my people.'"Therefore come out from them and be separate, says the Lord. Touch no unclean thing, and I will receive you."

2 Corinthians 6:14 – 17

Consistent with Paul's message, James wrote: "You adulterous people, don't you know that friendship with the world is hatred toward God? Anyone who chooses to be a friend of the world becomes an enemy of God" (James 4:4).

JULY 24

Stand firm and you will see
the deliverance the LORD will bring you today.
Exodus 14:13

From the pen of Charles Spurgeon:

This verse is God's command to you as a believer when you are in dire straits and extraordinary difficulties. When you cannot retreat or advance and are shut off to your right and to your left, what are you to do? The Master's word to you is, "Stand firm." At such times it would be wise for you to listen only to your Master's word, for some evil advisers will come to you with their suggestions. Despair will whisper, "Lie down and die. Give up!" But God would have you clothe yourself with cheerful courage and, even in the worst of times, to rejoice in His love and faithfulness. Cowardice will say, "Retreat! Go back to the world's ways. You can't be a successful Christian. It's too difficult, so relinquish your principles." Yet no matter how much Satan may urge you to follow this course, you cannot follow it if you are a child of God.

God's divine decree urges you to "go from strength to strength" (Ps. 84:7), and so you will, and neither death nor hell itself will be able to turn you from your course. So what if God commands you to "be still" (Ex. 14:14) for a while? It is designed to renew your strength for a greater advance in the near future. Urgency cries out to you, "Do something! Get busy. To 'be still' and wait is nothing but sheer laziness." Your tendency will be to do something yourself at once instead of looking to the Lord. Remember, however, He will do everything when you are in this situation. Presumption will boast, "If the sea is before you, march right into it and expect a miracle!" But Faith never listens to Presumption, Despair, Cowardice, or Urgency; but hears God say, "'Stand firm' and as immovable as a rock."

So "stand firm" — keep the posture of an upright soldier, ready for action and expecting further orders. Cheerfully and patiently await your Commander's voice, for it will not be long before God will say to you — as distinctly as He spoke to Moses and the people of Israel — "Move on" (Ex. 14:15).

From the pen of Jim Reimann:

One of the most difficult things to do in this busy day and age in which we live is to "be still." Yet if the people of old needed that encouragement, how much more do we need it today! Actually the words are more than an encouragement — they are a command: "Be still"! The following are two more passages where God commands stillness:

"Commune with your own heart upon your bed, and be still" (Ps. 4:4 KJV). And, "Be still, and know that I am God" (Ps. 46:10).

At times, we as believers may need Jesus to do for us exactly what He did on the Sea of Galilee: "He got up, rebuked the wind and said to the waves, 'Quiet! Be still!' Then the wind died down and it was completely calm" (Mark 4:39).

Perhaps we need to be rebuked as well when the "winds" of our busy lives are so much louder than the Lord's "still small voice" (1 Kings 19:12 KJV). Only then will we experience the calmness we so desperately need, enabling us to hear Him.

"The Sovereign LORD has opened my ears" (Isa. 50:5).

JULY 25

She caught him by his cloak and said, "Come to bed with me!"
But he left his cloak in her hand and ran out of the house.

Genesis 39:12

From the pen of Charles Spurgeon:

In dealing with certain sins, the only road to victory is a hasty escape. Some naturalists of old wrote of the basilisk, a mythical reptile with a deadly gaze. It was said of the creature that its eyes could fascinate their prey, rendering them easy victims. In like manner, even the mere gaze of wickedness puts us in serious danger. So he who wishes to be safe from acts of evil should be quick to run from any opportunities of it.

We should make "a covenant with [our] eyes" (Job 31:1) not to even look at what may cause temptation, for some sins only need a spark to ignite what quickly becomes a blazing fire. After all, who would knowingly enter a hospital ward where those with a contagious disease have been quarantined? Only someone foolish enough to desire the disease himself would take such a risk. If a sea captain knew how to avoid a storm, he would do anything rather than run the risk of weathering it. Cautious sailors have no desire to see how close to sandbars or a rocky coast they can sail without springing a leak. No, their goal is to stay as close as possible to the middle of a safe channel.

If I am exposed to great danger today, may I "be as shrewd as snakes" (Matt. 10:16) to get away and avoid it. The wings of a dove may be more useful to me today than the jaws of a lion. It is true I may appear to be a loser by refusing evil company, but it is better to leave my cloak than lose my character. It is not essential I be rich, but it is incumbent upon me to be pure. No ties of friendship, no desire for beauty, no display of talent, and no threat of ridicule should be able to turn me from the wise resolve to flee from sin. I am to "resist the devil, and *he will flee from [me]*"

(James 4:7), but I must flee "the lustful desires of sinful human nature" (2 Peter 2:18) or they will surely overcome me.

O God of holiness, preserve Your Josephs, protecting them from Madame Bubble [an enchanting witch in The Pilgrim's Progress by John Bunyan (1628–1688) based on the adulterous woman in Proverbs]. *May she not be able to bewitch them with her vile, sinful temptations. May the horrible trinity of the world, the flesh, and the devil never overpower us!*

From the pen of Jim Reimann:

Sometimes there will be a cost to fleeing sin. The cost for Joseph was ultimately being sent to prison as an innocent man. Yet that cost was much better than losing his character. Often people say there was no way out, so they fell to their temptation. But God's Word tells us: "When you are tempted, [God] will also provide a way out so that you can stand up under it" (1 Cor. 10:13).

Others say, "My temptation was too great for me," but the same verse says, "No temptation has seized you except what is common to man. And God is faithful; he will not let you be tempted beyond what you can bear." Still others say, "God doesn't understand my temptation," but "We do not have a high priest who is unable to sympathize with our weaknesses, but we have one who has been tempted in every way, just as we are — yet was without sin.

"Let us then approach the throne of grace with confidence, so that we may receive mercy and find grace to help us in our time of need" (Heb. 4:15–16).

Make every effort to add to your faith goodness; and to goodness, knowledge; and to knowledge,
self-control; and to self-control, perseverance; and to perseverance, godliness;
and to godliness, brotherly kindness; and to brotherly kindness, love.

2 Peter 1:5 – 7

From the pen of Charles Spurgeon:

If you desire to have the clear understanding of "full assurance of faith" (Heb. 10:22) as a gift of grace from God's blessed Holy Spirit, do what this Scripture tells you. "Make every effort" to see that your faith is the right kind — not merely a doctrinal belief, but a simple faith depending on Christ and on Christ alone. "Make every effort" to have courage. Ask God to give you the face of a lion, determination, and an awareness of God's righteousness so you may boldly persevere. "Diligently study the Scriptures" (John 5:39) to get knowledge, for the knowledge of doctrine will strongly confirm your faith. "Make every effort" to understand God's Word — "Let the word of Christ dwell in you richly" (Col. 3:16).

Once you have done these things, add "to knowledge, self-control." Be self-controlled without, in your body; and be self-controlled within, in your soul. Be self-controlled when it comes to your mouth, your thoughts, your heart, and your entire life. Then add "to self-control, perseverance," asking God through the power of His Holy Spirit for perseverance that can endure difficulties, and "when ... tested ... will come forth as gold" (Job 23:10). Clothe yourself with endurance so you will not be tempted to complain or become depressed in your sufferings.

Once perseverance is won, add godliness, but remember, godliness is much more than mere religion. Make glorifying God the goal of your life, living in His sight and seeking close fellowship with Him, and you will have godliness. Then add "to godliness, brotherly kindness; and to brotherly kindness, love." Show kindness and love to all God's saints, the type of kindness and love that opens its arms to all people and truly loves their souls.

When you are finally adorned with all these jewels, or heavenly virtues, in the proper proportion as you practice them, you will have the clearest evidence and knowledge of "your calling and election" (2 Peter 1:10). Thus, "make every effort" if you desire "full assurance," for being lukewarm and doubting go hand in hand.

From the pen of Jim Reimann:

God's Word has much to say about diligence, or "mak[ing] every effort." For example, "The diligent man prizes his possessions" (Prov. 12:27), and "The plans of the diligent lead to profit" (Prov. 21:5). Yet one of the greatest passages is this:

> Be very careful to keep the commandment and the law that Moses the servant of the LORD gave you: to love the LORD your God, to walk in all his ways, to obey his commands, to hold fast to him and to serve him with all your heart and all your soul.
>
> Joshua 22:5

So then, dear friends, since you are looking forward to this, make every effort to be found spotless, blameless and at peace with him.

2 Peter 3:14

Lord, help me add each of these virtues to my life so You may receive glory and others may know — You alone are God!

July 27

He has given us his very great and precious promises.

2 Peter 1:4

From the pen of Charles Spurgeon:

If you desire to truly experience "his very great and precious promises" and to enjoy them in your own heart, then meditate on them often. God's promises are like grapes in a winepress, for when you walk in them the juice begins to flow. Thus, meditating on them will often be the prelude to their fulfillment, and while you are pondering them, the blessing you are seeking will come to you without you even sensing it. Many Christians who have thirsted for a particular promise have discovered the divine blessing it promises being ever so gently distilled into their soul while they were still meditating on it. They have since rejoiced that they were led to meditate on the promise in their heart.

Besides meditating on God's promises, seek to receive them into your soul as His very words. Say to your soul, "If I were dealing with the promise of a man, I should carefully consider the character of the person and his ability to deliver on his promise. The same is true with the promises of God. My eyes should not be as focused on the greatness of His mercy, which astonishes me, as much as they are focused on the greatness of the Promiser, which will truly cheer me. My soul, it is 'God, your God' (Heb. 1:9) — 'God, who does not lie' (Titus 1:2) — who speaks to you. This promise of His that you are considering is as true as His very existence. He is the unchangeable God and will never alter the words that have come from His mouth, nor will He ever call back a single comforting sentence. Nor does He lack the power to fulfill His promise, for the same God who made 'the heavens and the earth' (Gen. 2:1) has spoken it. He also has perfect wisdom to bestow the blessing at the proper time or to with-

hold it, and His wisdom will never fail. Therefore, knowing that the Word of God is so true, unchangeable, powerful, and wise, I will — and must — believe His promise."

If we will meditate on God's promises in this way, focusing on the Promiser, we will truly experience their blessings and receive their fulfillment.

From the pen of Jim Reimann:

According to Jewish tradition the Shield of David physically represents the Hebrew word *amen*. The emblem is better known as the Star of David, but its actual name is the Shield of David, because Israel is not to "make … an idol in the form of anything in heaven above" (Ex. 20:4). It is two interlocking triangles, one pointing to earth and the other to heaven, symbolically meaning: "Your will be done on earth as it is in heaven" (Matt. 6:10).

With that in mind, consider the words of Paul: "*No matter how many promises God has made, they are 'Yes' in Christ. And so through him the 'Amen' is spoken by us to the glory of God*" (2 Cor. 1:20). Thus, God's promises will be fulfilled in the same way His will is done in heaven.

The Hebrew word *amen* is twice used as a noun in Isaiah 65:16, which says, "Whoever invokes a blessing in the land will do so by the God of truth; he who takes an oath in the land will swear by the God of truth." Instead of "the God of truth," the literal Hebrew is "the God of *amen*." And when Jesus says, "Verily, verily, I say unto you" (John 1:51 KJV) or "I tell you the truth" (NIV) — something He says twenty-six times in John — He is literally saying in Hebrew, "Amen, amen"!

In other words — it "will be done," for our God is *the God of amen*!

July 28

So foolish was I, and ignorant:
I was as a beast before thee.
Psalm 73:22 KJV

From the pen of Charles Spurgeon:

Remember, this is the confession of David, "a man after [God's] own heart" (1 Sam. 13:14), confessing his inner life by saying, "I was senseless and ignorant." [Editor's note: Actually this is a psalm of Asaph, but he was one of David's choir leaders who may have written this on behalf of David.] The word *foolish* here means more than its usual meaning, for earlier David says, "I was envious at the foolish, when I saw the prosperity of the wicked" (Ps. 73:3 KJV), which shows the foolishness he intended was connected to the sin of envy. And in our text today he not only puts himself down as being "foolish" but adds a word to intensify the meaning: "*So* foolish was I."

How foolish? He couldn't say, but it was a sinful foolishness that was not to be excused due to the simple frailty of man. It was to be condemned due to its perversity and its willful ignorance, for he was envious of "the prosperity of the wicked" and was forgetful of the dreadful end awaiting them.

Are we any better than David that we should consider ourselves wise? Do we profess to have attained perfection or to have been so punished by the rod of correction that all our willfulness toward sin is gone? This is pure pride! If David was foolish, how foolish are we! If only we could see ourselves as we are!

Dear believer, consider times past when you have doubted God while He has been so faithful to you. Think of your foolish outcry during affliction, "No, my Father!" when He was actually working to give you a greater blessing. How often during dark and difficult days have you misread His sovereignty, misinterpreted His hand at work, and have complained, "Everything is working against me!" when they are truly "work[ing] together for [your] good" (Rom. 8:28 KJV)! Consider how often you have chosen sin because of its pleasure, when in fact that pleasure became a root of bitterness in you!

Surely if we know our own heart, we must plead guilty to the indictment of sinful foolishness. Then, once fully conscious of our foolishness, we must make David's resulting resolve our own: "Guide me with your counsel" (Ps. 73:24).

From the pen of Jim Reimann:

Our warning today is the foolishness of thinking we have "attained perfection." As Spurgeon says, "Are we any better than David?" Nor are we better than Paul, who said: "Not that I have already obtained all this, or have already been made perfect" (Phil. 3:12), and, "If you think you are standing firm, be careful that you don't fall!" (1 Cor. 10:12).

God "chose us in [Christ] ... to be holy and blameless in his sight" (Eph. 1:4), and He sees us as such already, but it is because He views us "in Christ," not because we have attained perfection. Thus, Paul continues in Philippians:

I press on to take hold of that for which Christ Jesus took hold of me. Brothers, I do not consider myself yet to have taken hold of it. But one thing I do: Forgetting what is behind and straining toward what is ahead, I press on toward the goal to win the prize for which God has called me heavenward in Christ Jesus.

Philippians 3:12 – 14

JULY 29

Yet I am always with you.

Psalm 73:23

From the pen of Charles Spurgeon:

"*Yet*," as if to say, in spite of all the foolishness and ignorance that David had been confessing to God (in yesterday's devotion), he was not at all less certain he was saved and accepted, and that the blessings of being constantly in God's presence were undoubtedly his. Fully aware of his own sinful condition and the deceitfulness and vileness of his nature, he nevertheless sings through a glorious outburst of faith, "Yet I am always with you."

Believer, do you feel compelled to agree with Asaph, who composed this psalm for David? Do you agree with his confession and acknowledgment of sin and, in the same spirit, say, "Yet, since I belong to Christ I am continually with God"? By saying, "I am always with you," he meant, "I am continually on His mind and He is always thinking of my welfare. 'The eyes of the LORD are [constantly] on [me]' (Ps. 33:18), for 'he who watches over [me] will neither slumber nor sleep' (Ps. 121:4). I am continually in His hand and 'no one can snatch [me] out of my Father's hand' (John 10:29). My name is constantly on His heart as a memorial, just as the high priest constantly wore the breastplate bearing 'each of the names of the sons of Israel' (Ex. 39:14) over his heart."

You are always thinking of me, O God. Your deep love continually yearns for me, and Your sovereignty is always working for my good. You have set me "like a seal on your arm; for [Your] love is as strong as death.... Many waters cannot quench [Your] love; rivers cannot wash it away" (Song 8:6 – 7). What astonishing grace that You see me in Christ! And that in myself alone I would be abhorred by You, but that You see me clothed in Christ's garments and washed in His blood;

thus, I stand accepted in Your presence. Consequently, I am always in Your favor — "always with you."

In this is found true comfort for the tried and afflicted soul, who may appear calm on the outside but is vexed by an inner storm. "Yet." Say it in your heart and receive the peace it gives. "Yet I am always with you."

From the pen of Jim Reimann:

In several Scriptures our Lord promises to be with us, just as He said to Joshua, "I will be with you; I will never leave you nor forsake you" (Josh. 1:5). That doesn't mean, however, that a believer's life will be easy. If that were true, the Lord would not have said several times to Joshua, "Be strong and courageous" (Josh. 1:6). Then God gives him the prescription for success — success in His eyes, not the eyes of the world:

Be strong and very courageous. Be careful to obey all the law my servant Moses gave you; do not turn from it to the right or to the left, that you may be successful wherever you go. Do not let this Book of the Law depart from your mouth; meditate on it day and night, so that you may be careful to do everything written in it. Then you will be prosperous and successful. Have I not commanded you? Be strong and courageous. Do not be terrified; do not be discouraged, for the LORD your God will be with you wherever you go.

Joshua 1:7 – 9

Father, "even though I walk through the valley of the shadow of death, I will fear no evil, for you are with me" (Ps. 23:4).

JULY 30

He broke down and wept.

Mark 14:72

From the pen of Charles Spurgeon:

Many believe that as long as Peter lived, the fountain of his tears would flow whenever he remembered denying his Lord. This is likely true, for his sin was very great, and grace in him had later performed its "perfect work" (James 1:4 KJV). The same experience is common to all God's redeemed family to the degree the Spirit of God has removed their natural "heart of stone" (Ezek. 36:26). We remember, like Peter, our boastful promise: "Even if all fall away, I will not" (Mark 14:29). We then eat our own words with "bitter herbs" (Ex. 12:8) of repentance. When we compare what we vowed to be with what we have been, we may weep rain showers of grief. And when Peter thought of denying his Lord, he clearly remembered where it took place, the little excuse that led him to commit such a heinous sin, how he sought to confirm his falsehood "with an oath" (Matt. 26:72) and blasphemies, and his dreadful hardness of heart that drove him to "disown [Jesus] three times" (Mark 14:30).

When we are reminded of the grievous nature of our sins, can we remain unmoved and stubborn? If so we will turn our house into a "Bokim" and cry to the Lord for renewed assurances of His pardoning love. (See Judg. 2:1 – 5.) May we never look at our sin with dry eyes lest we soon experience a dry, parched tongue in the flames of hell.

Peter also recalled his Master's look of love, for the Lord followed the warning voice of the rooster's crowing with a look of sorrow, pity, and love as His sole admonition. And that glance of love was never out of Peter's mind as long as he lived and was far more effective than ten thousand sermons preached without the power of the Spirit. There can be no doubt the repentant apostle would always weep when recollecting the Savior's complete forgiveness that restored him to his former place. And to think of how we have offended such a kind and good Lord is more than sufficient reason for us to constantly weep.

Lord, strike our rocky hearts, and make the waters flow. (See Ex. 17:6.)

From the pen of Jim Reimann:

Peter denied Jesus three times, so it was likely no surprise when the Lord later asked him three times, "Simon son of John, do you love me?" (John 21:17). Yet Peter had the audacity to be "hurt because Jesus asked him the third time" and responded, "Lord, you know all things; you know that I love you" (v. 17).

To be fair, both of these events took place before Peter was "filled with the Holy Spirit," as related in Acts 2:4. Thus, after Pentecost we see Peter truly live up to his name, which means *rock*. We never see him deny the Lord again in spite of the constant threat of death and imprisonment. Instead we see him boldly proclaiming the gospel and following Jesus' command to "feed my sheep" (John 21:17).

Indeed, as we recall our times of denial of the Lord Jesus, we too should weep with godly sorrow just as Peter did. More than that, however, we should obey the words of Jesus who told Peter, "Follow me!" (John 21:19). Then only three verses later Jesus reiterated His command, saying:

"You *must* follow me" (v. 22).

JULY 31

I in them ...

John 17:23

From the pen of Charles Spurgeon:

If this verse describes the union that exists between our soul and the Lord, imagine how deep and wide is the river of our communion with Him! This union is no narrow pipe through which a tiny thread-like stream winds its way. No, it is a river of amazing depth and breadth with a flood of "living water" (John 7:38) flowing through its entire glorious length.

"See, [He has] placed before [us] an open door" (Rev. 3:8). May we not be slow to enter this city of communion with Him. The city has "twelve gates," with "each gate made of a single pearl" (Rev. 21:21), and each one is open wide so we may enter and be assured of being welcome. If the city had simply one loophole (a narrow slit for shooting arrows through ancient fortress walls) through which to talk with Jesus, it would be a blessing enough just to share one word of fellowship through the narrow hole. But how much more of a blessing to have an entrance so large and open!

If the Lord Jesus were far away from us, with many a stormy sea between, we would yearn to send a messenger to Him with our love and would long for the messenger's return, bringing us news from His Father's house. But look at His kindness — He has built His house next door to ours. Even more than that, He resides with us, making our poor humble hearts His tabernacle so He may have continual communion with us.

Oh, how foolish we are if we do not live in habitual communion with Him! When our road is long, dangerous, and difficult we need not worry how seldom friends see each other, for when they live together, will Jonathan forget his David?

When a husband travels, his wife may handle several days without speaking with him, but she could never endure being separated from him if she knew he were in one of the rooms of her own house.

So why, believer, do you not sit at the Lord's "banquet of wine" (Est. 5:6 KJV)? "Seek [your] LORD," for "he is near" (Isa. 55:6). Embrace Him, for He is your Brother. Hold Him securely, for He is your Husband, and press Him to your heart, for He is your own flesh and blood.

From the pen of Jim Reimann:

It is nearly impossible for us as humans to comprehend the amazing oneness we have with the Lord Jesus and His church. He Himself was perfectly one with His Father. He had eternally experienced this unity with the Father, never having had even one thought outside His Father's will, much less an action. And although it is difficult for us to comprehend that level of oneness, Jesus said, "I will remain in the world no longer, but they are still in the world, and I am coming to you. Holy Father, protect them by the power of your name — the name you gave me — so that they may be one as we are one" (John 17:11).

And Jesus, as a symbol of our oneness with Him, not only shares His powerful name with us but gives us another beautiful symbol of oneness with Him — His glory — for He went on to say, "I have given them the glory that you gave me, that they may be one as we are one" (John 17:22).

Lord, help us as we "make every effort to keep the unity of the Spirit through the bond of peace" (Eph. 4:3) — in this life as it will be in heaven.

August

AUGUST 1

Let me go to the fields and pick up the leftover grain.

Ruth 2:2

From the pen of Charles Spurgeon:

Depressed and troubled Christian, come and glean today in God's field of promise. Here you will find an abundance of precious promises that will precisely meet your needs. Take this one for example: "A bruised reed he will not break, and a smoldering wick he will not snuff out" (Isa. 42:3). Does that fit your situation? Are you a "bruised reed," helpless, insignificant, and weak; a reed that cannot produce any music — weaker than weakness itself? You may be a "bruised reed," but He will not "break" you. On the contrary, He will restore and strengthen you. Are you like a "smoldering wick," without light and warmth coming from you? If so "he will not snuff [you] out," but will blow His sweet breath of mercy on you till He fans you into a glowing flame.

Do you want to glean another "ear of grain"? How about: "Come to me, all you who are weary and burdened, and I will give you rest" (Matt. 11:28)? What soft and kind words! Your heart is fragile and the Master knows it, so He speaks ever so gently to you. Why don't you obey and go to Him even now? Take another "ear of grain": "'Do not be afraid, O worm Jacob, O little Israel, for I myself will help you,' declares the LORD, your Redeemer, the Holy One of Israel" (Isa. 41:14). How can you be afraid with such a wonderful assurance as this? And there are ten thousand golden "ears" like these for you to gather! Such as: "I have swept away your offenses like a cloud, your sins like the morning mist" (Isa. 44:22). Or this: "Though your sins are like scarlet, they shall be as white as snow; though they are red as crimson, they shall be like wool" (Isa. 1:18). And this: "The Spirit and the bride say, 'Come!' And let him

who hears say, 'Come!' Whoever is thirsty, let him come; and whoever wishes, let him take the free gift of the water of life" (Rev. 22:17).

Our Master's field is rich with "grain." Behold "the bundles" (Ruth 2:16)! See, poor and timid believer, they are lying there before you! Gather them and make them your own, for Jesus wants you to take them. Don't be afraid — only believe! Grasp His sweet promises, reap them with meditation, and then feed on them with joy.

From the pen of Jim Reimann:

The believer's true nourishment comes from the Word of God, but it is often sorely neglected. Yet the more time we spend in His Word the more we will love it and the stronger we will be. As Spurgeon says today, we are to feed on God's promises with joy. In fact, as we spend time with the Lord in His Word, our joy will increase, for David said, "You will fill me with joy in your presence, with eternal pleasures at your right hand" (Ps. 16:11). David loved God's Word and understood the benefits of knowing, obeying, and loving it, for later he wrote:

> Oh, how I love your law! I meditate on it all day long. Your commands make me wiser than my enemies, for they are ever with me. I have more insight than all my teachers, for I meditate on your statutes. I have more understanding than the elders, for I obey your precepts.
>
> Psalm 119:97 – 100

And David knew the blessing of reaping nourishment from the Word, for he continued, "How sweet are your words to my taste, sweeter than honey to my mouth!" (Ps. 119:103).

[God] works out everything
in conformity with the purpose of his will.

Ephesians 1:11

From the pen of Charles Spurgeon:

If we believe in God's wisdom, it follows we will believe He has a determined purpose and plan in the work of salvation. What would creation have been without His design behind it? Is there a fish of the sea or a bird of the air that was simply left to chance for its formation? No. Each of us as well has evidence of the presence of God working everything according to the design of His infinite wisdom in every bone, joint, muscle, tendon, gland, and blood vessel. And if God were present in creation, ruling over it all, would He not rule over grace? Would His new creation have the fickle "genius" of free will to rule it when His divine counsel rules the old creation?

Look at Providence Himself! Do you know that not one sparrow "will fall to the ground apart from the will of your Father" (Matt. 10:29)? "Even the very hairs of your head are all numbered" (Matt. 10:30). God weighs "the mountains [of our grief] on the scales and the hills [of our tribulation] in a balance" (Isa. 40:12). Shall we believe in a God of Providence in these but not when it comes to grace and salvation? Shall the husk be ordained by His wisdom but the seed inside be left to blind chance? No, for He knows "the end from the beginning" (Isa. 46:10).

When God views His temple, not only does He see the cornerstone that was laid in its appointed place in the glorious color of His dear Son's blood but He sees each chosen stone taken from earth's quarry and polished by His grace, with each in its ordained place as well. He sees the entire building, from cornerstone to cornice, from floor to roof, from foundation to pinnacle. The Lord already has a clear knowledge of every stone that will be placed in its prepared space, He knows exactly how large the edifice will be, and He has declared the exact moment "he will bring out the capstone to shouts of 'God bless it! God bless it!'" (Zech. 4:7).

Then at last it will be seen that Jehovah accomplished His perfect will in every chosen vessel of His mercy who are His, and that in every aspect of His work of grace He accomplished His purpose and glorified His name.

From the pen of Jim Reimann:

God is sovereign, and although nearly every Christian acknowledges this doctrine, many deny it in their other beliefs and actions. It has been said, "If you want to make God laugh, make plans!" Of course, planning and goal setting are not bad in and of themselves, but our plans will never thwart God's sovereignty, for He has said, "The Lord brings the counsel of the nations to nothing; he frustrates the plans of the peoples" (Ps. 33:10 ESV).

Solomon certainly grasped this truth, for he wrote, "In his heart a man plans his course, but the Lord determines his steps" (Prov. 16:9). And again from the Psalms we read: "The Lord does whatever pleases him, in the heavens and on the earth, in the seas and all their depths" (Ps. 135:6).

This is true in all things, including salvation! "Blessed are those you choose and bring near to live in your courts!" (Ps. 65:4). "Salvation comes from the Lord" (Jonah 2:9).

AUGUST 3

The Lamb is its lamp.
Revelation 21:23

From the pen of Charles Spurgeon:

Quietly contemplate the Lamb as the light of heaven. Light in the Scriptures is the symbol of joy. And the joy of the saints in heaven is comprised of the following: Jesus chose us, loved us, bought us, cleansed us, robed us, kept us, and glorified us. Thus, saints are there entirely because of the Lord Jesus, and each of these works of His should be like a "cluster of grapes" from "the Valley of Eshcol" (Num. 13:23) to us.

Light is also the cause of beauty, for nothing of beauty can be seen when there is no light. Without light there can be no radiant brilliance shining from a sapphire or a ray of peace glowing from a pearl. Thus, all the beauty of the saints above comes from Jesus. Like planets, those in heaven reflect the light of "the sun of righteousness" (Mal. 4:2) and live as sunbeams coming from the central sphere. If He withdrew from them they would die, and if His glory were veiled their glory would cease.

Light is also the symbol of knowledge. In heaven our knowledge will be perfect, but the Lord Jesus Himself will be the fountain of it. Dark mysteries of God never before understood will be clearly seen, and all that puzzles us today will become plain to us in the light of the Lamb. Oh, what understanding there will be and what praising will take place to the God of love!

Light also means revelation, for light reveals what is hidden. In this world we have not yet seen what we will be in heaven. God's people are a "hidden" people, but when Christ receives His people into heaven, He will touch them with the scepter of His love and change them into the image of His revealed glory. Once poor and wretched, what a transformation there will be! Once stained by sin, with only a touch of His finger we will be bright as the sun and clear as crystal.

Oh, what a revelation! What a transformation! And all this flows from the exalted Lamb. Whatever radiance and splendor there will be, Jesus will be the center and soul of it all. O the joy to be present and to see Him in His own light — "KING OF KINGS AND LORD OF LORDS" (Rev. 19:16).

From the pen of Jim Reimann:

No, as Spurgeon said, "We have not yet seen what we will be in heaven," but we do know this: "*Now* we are children of God, and what we will be has not yet been made known. But we know that when he appears, *we shall be like him*" (1 John 3:2).

"We shall be like him!" What a glorious thought! Even more than that, what a glorious truth! Paul taught we are "in Christ Jesus" (1 Cor. 1:30) and "Christ is in [us]" (Rom. 8:10), so it should come as no surprise we will be "like him." However, this is yet another glorious truth of our loving Lord that "surpasses knowledge" (Eph. 3:19) and human comprehension.

"*We*, who with unveiled faces all reflect the Lord's glory, *are being transformed into his likeness* with ever-increasing glory, which comes from the Lord, who is the Spirit" (2 Cor. 3:18).

God, until then may I perfectly reflect Your glory, may I bring You glory each day, and may people take "note that [I have] been with Jesus" (Acts 4:13).

The people who know their God
will firmly resist him [the king of the North].

Daniel 11:32

From the pen of Charles Spurgeon:

Every believer understands that to know God is the highest and best form of knowledge. This spiritual knowledge is a great source of strength for the Christian, for it strengthens one's faith. Believers are often described in the Scriptures as being enlightened and taught by the Lord and are said to have "an anointing from the Holy One" (1 John 2:20). In fact, it is the Spirit's unique role to "guide [us] into all truth" (John 16:13), and all this is designed to increase and strengthen our faith.

Spiritual knowledge strengthens love as well as faith, for knowledge opens the door, and then through that door we see our Savior. Or, using another analogy, knowledge paints a portrait of Jesus, and seeing Him leads to loving Him, for we cannot love a Christ we do not know at least to some degree. If we know very little of the wonderful qualities of Jesus, what He has done for us, and what He is doing now, we cannot love Him very much. But the more we know Him the more we will love Him.

Spiritual knowledge also strengthens hope, for how can we have hope for something if we do not even know of its existence? Hope may be the lens, but until we have knowledge through instruction, our ignorance blocks that lens and we see nothing whatsoever. Knowledge, however, removes that blockage of ignorance, and when we look through the bright lens, we discern the glory yet to be fully revealed and anticipate it with joyous confidence.

Spiritual knowledge also supplies us with reasons for patience, for how will we have patience until we know something of the sufferings of Christ? Until we can sympathize with Him through suffering, we will never understand the good that comes from it, nor will we understand the good that comes from the correction our heavenly Father sends us.

Plus, there is not a single gift of God's grace to the Christian which, through the Lord, will not be nurtured and ultimately brought to perfection by holy knowledge. Thus, how important it is that not only we should "grow in ... grace" but also in the "knowledge of our Lord and Savior Jesus Christ" (2 Peter 3:18)!

From the pen of Jim Reimann:

Many believers often shy away from the term *theology*. Yet theology simply means "the knowledge of God." Paul wrote of "the knowledge of the truth that leads to godliness" (Titus 1:1), and since Jesus said, "I am ... the truth" (John 14:6), we are speaking of "the knowledge of [Jesus] that leads to godliness."

As we attempt to lead a godly life, many of us tend to focus on a system of "do's and don'ts," but if this passage is trustworthy — and all Scripture is — then it is knowing Jesus "that leads to godliness." This is why Paul, a former Pharisee, no longer stressed the law, but stressed the fulfillment of the law — Jesus. The primary focus of his life was "to know Christ" (Phil. 3:10). And his prayer for other believers was unshakably consistent, for he wrote:

"I keep asking that the God of our Lord Jesus Christ, the glorious Father, may give you the Spirit of wisdom and revelation, *so that you may know him better*" (Eph. 1:17).

AUGUST 5

We know that in all things God works
for the good of those who love him.

Romans 8:28

From the pen of Charles Spurgeon:

A true believer is absolutely sure about some things. For example, he knows God is firmly ensconced in the stern of the boat when the storm is at its worst. He believes His invisible hand is always on the world's rudder and that wherever God's providence may allow it to drift, Jehovah steers the ship. That reassuring knowledge prepares him for everything, for he looks across the raging sea and sees Jesus walking on the waves, and then he hears a voice saying to him, "It is I. Don't be afraid" (Matt. 14:27).

A believer also knows God is eternally wise and, knowing this, he is confident there can be no accidents or mistakes and that nothing can occur that should not happen. He is able to say, "If God wills it, it is better for me to lose all I have, and I know that experiencing the worst calamity is the wisest and kindest thing if God ordains it."

"We know that in all things God works for the good of those who love him," and a true Christian does not merely ascribe to it as some theory but knows it as a matter of fact. "All things" have worked for good so far — the bitter medicine mixed in the proper proportions have worked their cure, and the sharp cuts of the scalpel have cut away the proud flesh, cleansed the wound, and facilitated healing. To date every event has brought about the most divinely blessed results, and thus, believing God rules over all; He governs wisely, and He brings good out of evil, the believ-

er's heart is reassured and enabled to calmly face each trial as it comes.

A believer can pray in the true spirit of acceptance, "Send me what You will, my God — as long as it comes from You — for no evil portion has ever come from Your table to any of Your children."

Say not my soul, "From whence
Can God relieve my care?"
Remember that Omnipotence
Has servants everywhere.
His method is sublime,
His heart profoundly kind;
God never is before His time,
And never is behind.

Thomas Toke Lynch, 1818 – 1871

From the pen of Jim Reimann:

If we pray, as Spurgeon says today, "Send me what You will, my God," we must be willing to take the bad with the good. Yet what we call "bad" is not bad if it's God's will, for He promised to work "all things ... for ... *good.*"

This is problematic for "name it — claim it" Christians who believe we should never suffer. Yet this is unbiblical, for Paul taught that God uses "all things" to conform us "to the image of his Son" (Rom. 8:29 KJV), and said, "I want to know ... the fellowship of sharing in his sufferings, becoming like him" (Phil. 3:10).

Should we desire anything less?

AUGUST 6

Watchman, what is left of the night?

Isaiah 21:11

From the pen of Charles Spurgeon:

What enemies do I face? Doctrinal errors are rampant, with new ones appearing hourly, so what will be the latest heresy against which I must be on my guard? When darkness reigns, sins creep from where they lurk. Thus, I must climb the watchtower myself, watching in prayer. Yet our heavenly Protector sees every attack about to be perpetrated upon us before it is launched, so when the evil designed for us is still nothing but a desire of Satan, the Lord prays for us that when we are sifted "as wheat ... [our] faith may not fail" (Luke 22:31 – 32). *Continue, O gracious Watchman, to forewarn us of our foes. "For Zion's sake ... [do] not keep silent"* (Isa. 62:1).

"Watchman, what is left of the night?" What "weather" is ahead for the church? Are dark clouds ahead or is the sky above clear and fair? We must care for God's church with watchful love, and with various heresies from the Pope and unbelief looming today, may we observe "the signs of the times" (Matt. 16:3) and prepare for conflict.

"Watchman, what is left of the night?" What stars are visible? Which of God's precious promises apply to our present situation? Watchman, sound the alarm but help us as well for Christ, our guiding Star, is ever fixed in the heavens and all the stars are secure in the right hand of their sovereign Lord.

Watchman, but when will morning come? "The bridegroom [is] a long time in coming" (Matt. 25:5). Is there any "sign of [His] coming" (Matt. 24:3) as "the sun of righteousness" (Mal. 4:2)? Hasn't "the bright Morning Star"

(Rev. 22:16) arisen as the promise of day? When will "the day break, and the shadows flee away" (Song 4:6 KJV)?

> *O Jesus, if You do not come in person to Your waiting church today, then come through Your Spirit to my longing heart and make it "sing for joy"* (Ps. 67:4).

Now all the earth is bright and glad
With the fresh morn;
But all my heart is cold, and dark and sad:
Sun of the soul, let me behold Your dawn!
Come, Jesus, Lord!
O quickly come, according to Your word!

Christian Friedrich Richter,
1676 – 1711

Translated from German by
Catherine Winkworth, 1827 – 1878)

From the pen of Jim Reimann:

Entire nations are concerned with security today. And many Christians are overly concerned with safety, while God is our Watchman. House alarms may be fine, but our security comes from the Lord. "Unless the LORD watches over the city, the watchmen stand guard in vain" (Ps. 127:1). Others trust in wealth, but "riches do not endure forever" (Prov. 27:24). Thus, "Let the beloved of the LORD rest secure in him, for he shields him all day long" (Deut. 33:12).

> *"O righteous God,... bring to an end the violence of the wicked and make the righteous secure"* (Ps. 7:9).

AUGUST 7

The upright love Thee.

Song of Songs 1:4 KJV

From the pen of Charles Spurgeon:

True believers love Jesus with a deeper affection than they dare give any other being. They would rather lose their father or mother than part with Christ. They hold all earthly comforts loosely in their hands but carry Him securely locked in their hearts. They voluntarily deny themselves for His sake, but they are not to be led to ever deny Him. Love is shallow if the fires of persecution can dry it up, for the true believer's love is a deeper stream than this. Enemies have diligently worked to separate the faithful from their Master, but their attempts have been fruitless in every period of history. Neither crowns of honor nor frowns of anger have been able to untie this bond that is stronger than a Gordian knot. [Editor's note: A legend from the mid-sixteenth century says that the king of Gordium (a city in Asia Minor, now northwestern Turkey) tied an intricate knot, prophesying that whoever untied it would become ruler of Asia. The legend further has it that Alexander the Great severed it with his sword.] This attachment is no common bond that the world's power can dissolve even over a great length of time. The Devil himself, nor any man, has been able to find a key to open this lock. Never has the craftiness of Satan been more useless than when he has used it seeking to sever the union of two divinely welded hearts.

The Scriptures say, "The upright love Thee," and nothing will blot out that sentence. The intensity of the upright's love, however, should not be judged as much by what we see of it but by their inner longings. It should be our daily lament that we do not love enough, yearning that our hearts were capable of more love and could

be reaching further. Like Samuel Rutherford (Scottish Presbyterian theologian, 1600? – 1661), we cry, "Oh, for enough love to encircle the earth and rise above heaven — yes, even over the heaven of heavens and ten thousand worlds — that I may place it all upon my beautiful Christ — and only Christ."

Alas, our longest reach is only a span of love, and our affection is but a drop in the bucket compared to what He deserves. Yet if our love were measured by our intentions, it would be great indeed, so we trust our Lord to be its judge. Oh, that we could give all the love in our hearts in one great bundle — a massive gathering of all believers' love — to Him who is "altogether lovely" (Song 5:16).

From the pen of Jim Reimann:

Many professing Christians only look to Jesus for "fire insurance," thinking it saves them from the fires of hell. Yet a true relationship with Jesus is just that — a relationship — not an insurance contract. And one of the major evidences of that relationship is love — love for God and others, especially other believers.

From the beginning we have been commanded: "Love the LORD your God with all your heart and with all your soul and with all your strength" (Deut. 6:5), and Jesus added: "A new command I give you: Love one another. As I have loved you, so you must love one another" (John 13:34). This love is not to be simply an external love, but a deep inner love, for Peter wrote, "Love one another deeply, from the heart" (1 Peter 1:22).

"This is how we know that we love the children of God: *by loving God* and carrying out his commands" (1 John 5:2).

AUGUST 8

They ... spin a spider's web.

Isaiah 59:5

From the pen of Charles Spurgeon:

A spider's web is the symbolic picture of a hypocrite's so-called faith. It is designed to catch his prey, so just as the spider fattens himself on flies, the hypocritical Pharisee gets his reward. Foolish people are easily entrapped by the loud declarations of false believers, and even the most discerning does not always escape. Philip baptized Simon the Sorcerer, whose false profession of faith was quickly exploded by the stern rebuke of Peter. (See Acts 8:9 – 24.) Tradition, reputation, praise, advancement, and other "flies" are the small prey hypocrites trap in their nets. Look at the spider's web and admire the cunning craftiness of the hunter, for the web is skillfully and wonderfully woven. Doesn't a deceiver's false faith appear equally wonderful?

How does he make such a bald-faced lie appear to be truth? How can he make his flimsy foil of an answer seem to be as pure as solid gold? The spider's web comes completely from within its own bowels as opposed to the bee that gathers its wax from flowers. The spider takes nothing from a flower yet spins out the material for its web to any length it needs. Likewise, hypocrites find their trust and hope only within themselves. Their anchor is forged on their own anvil and the anchor's chain is twisted into shape by their own hands. They lay their own foundation and fashion the pillars of their own house, rejecting with disgust the idea of being a debtor to the sovereign grace of God.

However, a spider's web is very fragile and frail. Yes, it is wonderfully formed, but it is not made to endure. It is not a match to someone's walking cane or even a janitor's broom. The hypocrite needs no battery of Armstrong artillery guns to blow his hope to pieces, for a mere puff of wind will do it. Hypocritical cobwebs will be quickly removed when the broom of destruction begins its purifying work, which brings up another thought, namely this: such cobwebs of deception will never be tolerated in the Lord's house. The Lord Himself will see to it that the cobwebs, along with those who spin them, will be destroyed forever.

"O my soul" (Ps. 103:2), rest on something better than a spider's web. May the Lord Jesus be your eternal hiding place.

From the pen of Jim Reimann:

If it were not easy to be deceived, Jesus would not have warned, "False Christs and false prophets will appear and perform great signs and miracles to deceive even the elect — if that were possible" (Matt. 24:24). Of course, total deception of the elect is not possible, but imagine the plight of the godless. Here is what the book of Job, also using the analogy of a spider's web, tells us:

> Such is the destiny of all who forget God;
> so perishes the hope of the godless. What
> he trusts in is fragile; what he relies on is a
> spider's web. He leans on his web, but it gives
> way; he clings to it, but it does not hold. He
> is like a well-watered plant in the sunshine,
> spreading its shoots over the garden; it entwines its roots around a pile of rocks and
> looks for a place among the stones. But when
> it is torn from its spot, that place disowns
> it and says, "I never saw you." Surely its life
> withers away.
>
> Job 8:13 – 19

O Lord, "You are my hiding place; you will protect me from trouble and surround me with songs of deliverance" (Ps. 32:7).

AUGUST 9

The city does not need the sun
or the moon to shine on it.

Revelation 21:23

From the pen of Charles Spurgeon:

Far away in heaven the inhabitants are free from our earthly creature comforts. They have no need of new clothing, for their white robes never wear out, nor will they ever get dirty or stained. They have no need of medicine to heal diseases, for "No one living in Zion will say, 'I am ill'" (Isa. 33:24). They do not need sleep to refresh their bodies; they rest neither day nor night, but untiringly praise the Lord in His temple. They do not need any social relationships to minister comfort to them, and whatever enjoyment they derive from their friends is not essential to their happiness, for their fellowship with the Lord is enough to meet their greatest desires. No doubt they discuss the things of God with one another, but they need no teachers, for the Lord Himself instructs them.

Today we receive alms at the King's gate, but they feast at the King's table itself. Here we lean on a friend's arm, but there they lean on their Beloved and Him alone. Here we must have the help of our friends, but there they find all they want in Christ Jesus. Here we look to meat that spoils for nourishment and to clothing that is eaten by moths for covering, but there they find everything in God. Here we use a bucket to fetch water from the well, but there they drink living water directly from the Source of the fountain. Angels bring us blessings here, but there they need no messengers from heaven. They need no Gabriels to bring them love notes from God, for there they see Him "face to face" (1 Cor. 13:12).

Oh, what a blessed time that will be when we will have risen above every meaningless earthly cause and will rest upon the arm of God alone! What a glorious hour it will be when God and not His creatures, when the Lord and not His works will be our daily joy! Only then will our souls have attained the perfection of happiness.

From the pen of Jim Reimann:

Today we have looked at the difference between our lives here on earth and the lives of the saints who have gone before us to heaven. But is there really any comparison? Can we really understand what awaits us in heaven? Is it possible for our finite minds to fully comprehend the infinity of eternity ahead?

Jesus said, "In my Father's house are many rooms; if it were not so, I would have told you. I am going there to prepare a place for you. And if I go and prepare a place for you, I will come back and take you to be with me that you also may be where I am" (John 14:2 – 3). Later Paul said, "No eye has seen, no ear has heard, no mind has conceived what God has prepared for those who love him" (1 Cor. 2:9). Yet the Lord has given us some insight into what's ahead, for Paul goes on to say, "But God has revealed it to us by his Spirit. The Spirit searches all things, even the deep things of God" (1 Cor. 2:10).

And, of course, others such as Daniel and John were taken to the future to offer glimpses of what we will someday see in person. Yet when it comes to comparing today with our eternal future, always keep in mind: "Our present sufferings are not worth comparing with the glory that will be revealed in us" (Rom. 8:18).

AUGUST 10

Christ ... is your life.

Colossians 3:4

From the pen of Charles Spurgeon:

Paul's beautifully rich words here indicate that Christ is the source of our life. "When you were dead in your sins ... God made you alive with Christ" (Col. 2:13). The same Voice who brought Lazarus from the tomb (see John 11:1 – 44) raised us to "live a new life" (Rom. 6:4). He is now the sum and substance of our spiritual life, for it is by His life we live. He is in us, "the hope of glory" (Col. 1:27), the power behind our actions, and the central thought that spurs every other thought. Christ is the nourishment for our life, for what can a Christian truly feed upon but Jesus' flesh and blood? He "is the bread that comes down from heaven, which a man may eat and not die" (John 6:50).

Oh, travel-weary pilgrims in this wilderness of sin, you will never find even a morsel to satisfy the hunger of your spirit unless you find it in Christ! He is the source of peace for our life and all true joy come from Him, and in times of trouble His presence is our comfort. There is nothing worth living for but Him, and His lovingkindness is better than life!

Christ is the object of our life, and as a ship speeds toward its port, so the believer wings his way toward the haven of his Savior's embrace. Just as an arrow hits its target, so the Christian flies toward the perfecting of his fellowship with Christ Jesus. As a soldier fights for his captain and glories in his captain's victory, so the believer contends for Christ and triumphs from the victories of His Master. "For [the Christian], to live is Christ" (Phil. 1:21). He is the perfect ideal for our life and if His life is within us, there will be, and

there must be, evidence of His life exhibiting itself through us to a great extent. If we live in close fellowship with the Lord Jesus, we will grow to be like Him. We will set Him before us as our divine example and will seek to walk in His footsteps until He becomes the crown of our life in glory.

Oh, how secure, how honored, how blessed is the believer, since "Christ ... is [our] life!

From the pen of Jim Reimann:

The following verses, showing the context of today's verse, shed a great deal of light on what it means to be "heavenly minded" while maintaining a godly walk in this life:

> Since, then, you have been raised with Christ, set your hearts on things above, where Christ is seated at the right hand of God. Set your minds on things above, not on earthly things. For you died, and your life is now hidden with Christ in God. When Christ, who is your life, appears, then you also will appear with him in glory.
>
> Put to death, therefore, whatever belongs to your earthly nature: sexual immorality, impurity, lust, evil desires and greed, which is idolatry. Because of these, the wrath of God is coming. You used to walk in these ways, in the life you once lived. But now you must rid yourselves of all such things as these: anger, rage, malice, slander, and filthy language from your lips. Do not lie to each other, since you have taken off your old self with its practices and have put on the new self, which is being renewed in knowledge in the image of its Creator.
>
> Colossians 3:1 – 10

AUGUST 11

How I long for the months gone by.

Job 29:2

From the pen of Charles Spurgeon:

Many Christians view their past with pleasure but are dissatisfied with the present. They look back on days gone by when their communion with the Lord was the sweetest and the best times they have ever known, but see the present as though it is clothed in a dark coat of gloom and dreariness. Once they lived close to Jesus but now feel they have wandered away from Him and find themselves saying, "How I long for the months gone by." They complain they have lost assurance of their faith, they have no peace of mind, they no longer find enjoyment in the ways of grace, their conscience has lost its tenderness, or they lack their former zeal to glorify God.

The causes of this sad condition are many. It can arise due to neglecting prayer, for a neglected prayer closet is the beginning of all spiritual decline. It can be the result of idolatry when the affections of the heart have been focused more on things on earth than on the things of heaven and God Himself. A "jealous God" (Ex. 20:5) will not ever be content with a divided heart, for He must be loved first and above all else. He will withdraw the sunshine of His presence from a cold wandering heart. Or we may find the cause to be self-confidence and self-righteousness, for when pride is at work in the heart, self is exalted instead of humbling itself at the foot of the cross.

Dear Christian, if you are not as you once were in "the months gone by," do not be satisfied with simply wishing for a return to your former happiness. Go at once to seek your Master and tell Him of your sad condition. Ask for His grace and strength to help you walk more closely with Him. "Humble [yourself] before the Lord, and he will lift you up" (James 4:10), and will once again allow you to enjoy the light of His countenance.

Do not sit down only to grieve and cry, for since the beloved Physician lives, there is hope — more than that — there is a certainty of recovery for even the worst cases.

From the pen of Jim Reimann:

One of the greatest examples of backsliding is the story of King David's sin with Bathsheba and his attempt to hide it. Yet this story is also one of the greatest examples of repentance and restoration. The following psalm, written by David when confronted with his sin by Nathan the prophet, is a wonderful pattern for us to follow when we are convicted of sin as well:

Have mercy on me, O God, according to your unfailing love; according to your great compassion blot out my transgressions. Wash away all my iniquity and cleanse me from my sin. For I know my transgressions, and my sin is always before me. Against you, you only, have I sinned and done what is evil in your sight, so that you are proved right when you speak and justified when you judge....

Cleanse me with hyssop, and I will be clean; wash me, and I will be whiter than snow. Let me hear joy and gladness; let the bones you have crushed rejoice. Hide your face from my sins and blot out all my iniquity. Create in me a pure heart, O God, and renew a steadfast spirit within me. Do not cast me from your presence or take your Holy Spirit from me. Restore to me the joy of your salvation and grant me a willing spirit, to sustain me.

Psalm 51:1 – 4, 7 – 12

Dear Lord, like David, grant me humility and repentance when I sin.

Day 224

AUGUST 12

The LORD reigns, let the earth be glad.

Psalm 97:1

From the pen of Charles Spurgeon:

As long as this verse is true, there is no reason for anxiety. On earth the Lord's power as readily controls the raging of the wicked as the raging of the seas, and His love as easily refreshes the poor with mercy as the land with showers. His majesty shines in flashes of fire even amid the horror of the storm, and His glory is seen in its full grandeur in the fall of empires and the collapse of thrones. Thus, in all our conflicts and tribulations, we too can behold the hand of our divine King.

> God is God; He sees and hears
> All our troubles, all our tears.
> Soul, forget not, 'mid your pains,
> God o'er all forever reigns.
>
> Johann Friedrich Zihn, 1650 – 1719
>
> Translated from German by
> Catherine Winkworth, 1827 – 1878

The evil spirits of hell must acknowledge, to their own misery, God's undoubted supremacy, and even when allowed to roam the earth, one ankle is chained, His rein is in the monster's mouth, and His fishhook is in leviathan's jaws. The darts of death are under His lock and key, and He is the divine Watchman, also controlling the prison of the grave. The fearsome vengeance of the Judge of all the earth causes demons to cower and tremble, as dogs fear the hunter's whip.

> Fear not death, nor Satan's thrusts,
> God defends who in Him trusts;
> Soul, remember, in your pains,
> God o'er all forever reigns.
>
> Zihn and Winkworth

In heaven no one denies the sovereignty of the King Eternal — they fall on their faces to honor Him. Angels are His attendants, the redeemed are His favorites, and everyone delights to serve Him day and night. May we soon reach the city of the great King!

> For this life's long night of sadness
> He will give us peace and gladness.
> Soul, remember, in your pains,
> God o'er all forever reigns.
>
> Zihn and Winkworth

From the pen of Jim Reimann:

Unbelievers, and even some believers, deny God's sovereignty over their lives. But a mature Christian is thankful He is in control and recognizes the truth of Romans 8:28: "We know that in all things God works for the good of those who love him, who have been called according to his purpose."

"Your word, O LORD, is eternal; it stands firm in the heavens. Your faithfulness continues through all generations; you established the earth, and it endures. Your laws endure to this day, for all things serve you" (Ps. 119:89 – 91).

AUGUST 15

[Isaac] went out to the field one evening to meditate.

Genesis 24:63

From the pen of Charles Spurgeon:

Isaac's meditation was a worthy use of his time. Those who spend a great deal of time in idleness with friends, light reading, or useless hobbies could learn wisdom from Isaac. They would find more profitable fellowship and use of their time in meditation than in the vain activities that now have greater appeal to them. We would all know more, live closer to God, and mature in grace more if we spent more time alone in meditation. Meditation "chews the cud," extracting the nutrients from the mental food gathered elsewhere. Thus, when Jesus is the focus of our meditation, it is indeed satisfying and useful. Remember, Isaac found Rebecca while engaged in personal meditation, just as many others have found their beloved mate.

Isaac's choice of the place to meditate is worthy of note as well. In the outdoors we see numerous things upon which to meditate, from tall cedars to small hyssop plants, from soaring eagles above to chirping grasshoppers below, and from the blue expanse of heaven to a drop of dew. All these things are ripe with teaching, and when our eyes are divinely opened, that teaching flashes into our minds far more vividly than knowledge from written books. The inside of our house is not nearly as healthy, pleasant, thought provoking, or inspiring as the great outdoors. We should think of nothing in creation as common or unclean, but recognize that all created things point to their Maker. Then the outdoors will immediately become a holy place to us.

Isaac's choice of the time of day to meditate is also worthy of note. He chose the time when sunset is drawing its veil over the day, the perfect time for calming the soul and allowing earthborn cares to yield to the joys of heavenly communion. The glory of the setting sun and the solemnity of approaching night awaken our sense of wonder and awe.

If your schedule allows it, dear reader, it would be quite worthwhile for you to spend an hour walking outdoors this evening. But if you are in the city, the Lord is there as well, and will meet you in your room or even in the crowded street. Wherever you may be, let your heart go forth to meet with Him today.

From the pen of Jim Reimann:

Meditation often carries a negative connotation, probably due to its practice by many cults. Yet meditation *is* a biblical concept. What's critical is the object of our meditation, and the Psalms gives us a good list to focus upon:

"O God, we meditate on your unfailing love" (48:9).

"I will meditate on all your works and consider all your mighty deeds" (77:12).

"I meditate on your precepts and consider your ways" (119:15).

"Your servant will meditate on your decrees" (119:23).

"I will meditate on your wonders" (119:27).

"Oh, how I love your law! I meditate on it all day long" (119:97).

"I meditate on your statutes" (119:99).

"I ... meditate on your promises" (119:148).

"May the words of my mouth and the meditation of my heart be pleasing in your sight, O LORD, my Rock and my Redeemer" (Ps. 19:14).

AUGUST 16

Ascribe to the Lord the glory due his name.

Psalm 29:2

From the pen of Charles Spurgeon:

God's glory is the result of His nature and His works. He is glorious in His character, for there is such an abundance of everything that is holy, good, and lovely in the Lord, He must be glorious. The actions that flow from His character are also glorious, but while He intends for them to reveal His goodness, mercy, and justice to those He created, He is equally concerned that the glory associated with His deeds be ascribed only to Himself. After all, there is nothing in ourselves in which we may glory, for He is the one who made us differ from one another. And what do we have that we did not receive from the God of all grace? Thus, how careful we should be "to walk humbly" (Micah 6:8) before the Lord!

Since there is room for only one true Glory in the universe, the moment we glorify ourselves, we set ourselves up as rivals to the Most High God. Shall an insect that lives but one hour glorify itself rather than the sun whose warmth brought it to life? Shall a piece of pottery exalt itself above the man who fashioned it upon his potter's wheel? Shall the dust of the desert compete with the whirlwind, or drops in the ocean contend with a storm?

"Ascribe to the Lord, O mighty ones, ascribe to the Lord glory and strength. Ascribe to the Lord the glory due his name" (Ps. 29:1 – 2). "Not to us, O Lord, not to us but to your name be the glory" (Ps. 115:1). Learning to apply these two verses is one of the most difficult struggles of a Christian's life. It is a lesson God is continually teaching us, and learning it often requires the most painful discipline. If a believer were to boast, "I can do everything," without adding "through him who gives me strength" (Phil. 4:13), then before long he will have to cry out in regret, "I can do nothing!"

When we do anything for the Lord and He is pleased to accept our service for Him, may we "lay [our] crowns" at His feet "before the throne" (Rev. 4:10) and say, "Not I, but the grace of God that was with me" (1 Cor. 15:10)!

From the pen of Jim Reimann:

The Lord alone is worthy of our praise and honor, and His Word tells us He is not only jealous but that *Jealous* is His name: "Do not worship any other god, for the Lord, *whose name is Jealous*, is a jealous God" (Ex. 34:14). As you can see, the thought is reiterated so we will not miss it. Later God said, "I am the Lord; that is my name! I will not give my glory to another" (Isa. 42:8).

The remarkable thing is that our "jealous God" is willing to share His glory with His children, for Jesus prayed, "*I have given them the glory that you gave me*, that they may be one as we are one" (John 17:22). And Paul said, "Now if we are children, then we are heirs — heirs of God and co-heirs with Christ, if indeed we share in his sufferings in order that *we may also share in his glory*" (Rom. 8:17). And although believers will share in His glory, we will continue to glorify Jesus throughout eternity. John described our future as follows:

"In a loud voice they sang: 'Worthy is the Lamb, who was slain, to receive power and wealth and wisdom and strength and honor and glory and praise!'" (Rev. 5:12).

AUGUST 17

I trust in the mercy of God for ever and ever.

Psalm 52:8 KJV

From the pen of Charles Spurgeon:

Let us meditate on the mercy of God.

His mercy is tender. With "tender mercy" (Luke 1:78) "He heals the brokenhearted and binds up their wounds" (Ps. 147:3). He is as gracious in His application of mercy as He is in the amount of mercy He bestows, for there is nothing small with God.

His mercy is infinite. Like God Himself, His mercy cannot be measured and is so great that it forgives great sins of great sinners, after great lengths of time, and then bestows great blessings and great privileges, and finally raises us up to great enjoyments in the great heaven of the great God.

His mercy is undeserved. Indeed true mercy must be, for mercy that is deserved is simply a misnomer for justice. There is no right a sinner has that makes him deserving of the loving consideration of the Most High God, for if the rebellious sinner had immediately been doomed to eternal fire, he would have fully deserved it. And if he is delivered from God's wrath, the Lord's sovereign love alone has determined the cause, for there was none in the sinner himself.

His mercy is effective. Some things are large but ineffective. God's mercy is an uplifting blessing to your sagging spirit, a golden salve to your bleeding wounds, a heavenly cast to your broken bones, a royal chariot for your weary feet, and a sweet embrace of love for your trembling heart.

His mercy is diverse. As John Bunyan (1628 – 1688) said in *The Pilgrim's Progress*, "All the flowers in God's garden are double." There is no single mercy. You may think you have only one, but when you examine your life, you will find a cluster of mercies.

His mercy is abundant. Millions have received it, yet it is far from being exhausted. In fact, it is as fresh, full, and free as ever.

His mercy is unfailing. It will "never ... leave you" (Heb. 13:5). If mercy is your friend, it will be with you when you are tempted not to yield to the Lord and when you are in deep trouble, to keep you from sinking. It will always be with you to be the light and life of your countenance and to be the joy of your soul when earthly comfort is quickly fading.

From the pen of Jim Reimann:

Today we have meditated upon the tender, infinite, undeserved, effective, diverse, abundant, and unfailing mercy of God. Yet the most used word to describe the Lord's mercy in the Scriptures is *everlasting*. For example, "The LORD is good; his mercy is everlasting" (Ps. 100:5 KJV), and "The mercy of the LORD is from everlasting to everlasting upon them that fear him, and his righteousness unto children's children" (Ps. 103:17 KJV).

The Virgin Mary affirmed this truth in her beautiful Magnificat: "My soul glorifies the Lord and my spirit rejoices in God my Savior, for he has been mindful of the humble state of his servant. From now on all generations will call me blessed, for the Mighty One has done great things for me — holy is his name" (Luke 1:46 – 49). She then continues, affirming the truth of Psalm 103:17, "His mercy extends to those who fear him, from generation to generation" (Luke 1:50).

Lord, I fear and reverence You. Thank You for Your mercy.

AUGUST 18

We are disgraced ... and shame covers our faces,
because foreigners have entered the holy places of the LORD's house.

Jeremiah 51:51

From the pen of Charles Spurgeon:

In this passage the faces of the Lord's people were covered with shame, for it was a terrible thing for men to intrude into "the Holy Place" (Ex. 26:33) reserved for the priests alone. And all around us, even today, we see a like cause for sorrow. Consider how many ungodly men are now being educated with the idea of entering the ministry! And what a crying sin is the lie being imposed on our entire population that they all are included, at least in some small way, in a National Church! [Editor's note: Spurgeon is referring to the fallacy of considering everyone in England Christian simply because they have a denomination known as the Church of England.]

How fearful it is that holy ordinances of the church should be forced upon the unconverted, and that even among the more enlightened churches of our land there is such a lack of discipline. If the many people who read this devotion would take this matter before the Lord Jesus today, He will intervene and avert the evil that will otherwise come upon His church. To adulterate the church is akin to polluting a well, pouring water on a stove, or planting stones in a fertile field. May we all have God's grace to properly maintain the purity of the church as a true assembly of believers — not a nation or an unsaved community of the unconverted.

Our zealous work, however, must begin at home. May we examine ourselves first as to our right to eat at the Lord's table. May we make sure we are "wearing wedding clothes" (Matt. 22:11) ourselves, lest we become intruders in the Lord's sanctuary. "For many are invited, but few are chosen" (Matt. 22:14), and "small is the gate and narrow the road that leads to life, and only a few find it" (Matt. 7:14).

Oh, for the grace to approach Jesus in the proper way — with the faith of God's elect. He who struck down "Uzzah because of his irreverent act" (2 Sam. 6:7) of touching the ark is very jealous of His two ordinances of baptism and the Lord's Supper. As a true believer I may approach them freely, but as a "foreigner" I must not touch them lest I die. It is the responsibility of each person to "examine himself" (1 Cor. 11:28), searching his own heart, before being baptized or coming to the Lord's table.

"Search me, O God, and know my heart; test me and know my anxious thoughts" (Ps. 139:23).

From the pen of Jim Reimann:

Not only are unbelievers not to partake of the holy ordinances, but believers as well are to approach God in the proper way. For example, "Aaron's sons ... offered unauthorized fire before the LORD.... So fire came out from the presence of the LORD and consumed them and they died" (Lev. 10:1 – 2).

"Therefore, brothers, since we have confidence to enter the Most Holy Place by the blood of Jesus ... and since we have a great priest over the house of God, let us draw near to God with a sincere heart in full assurance of faith, having our hearts sprinkled to cleanse us from a guilty conscience and having our bodies washed with pure water" (Heb. 10:19, 21 – 22).

AUGUST 19

He will stand and shepherd his flock
in the strength of the LORD.

Micah 5:4

From the pen of Charles Spurgeon:

This verse refers to Christ's reign in His church as our "Shepherd King." He has supremacy, but His superiority is that of a wise and tender shepherd over his needy and loving flock. He commands and receives obedience, but it is the willing obedience of well-cared-for sheep. They render their obedience joyfully to their beloved Shepherd, whose voice they know so well. He rules with the power of love and the energy of goodness.

Christ's reign is practical in its character. Our text verse says, "He will stand and shepherd," meaning the great Head of the church is actively engaged in providing for His people. He does not sit down upon the throne in idleness or simply hold His scepter without wielding it in governing His people. No, He stands and shepherds, and as a shepherd He does everything expected of a shepherd. He guides, watches, protects, restores, tends, and feeds.

Christ's reign is continual in its duration. Our verse says, "He will stand and shepherd" — not, "He will stand and shepherd now and then, often leaving His position," nor, "He will send revival one day, and the next day leave His church in barrenness." Christ "will neither slumber nor sleep" (Ps. 121:4), His hands never rest, His heart never ceases to beat with love, and His shoulders are never weary of carrying His people's burdens.

Christ's reign is powerfully effective in its action. "He will ... shepherd ... in the strength of the LORD" — the Lord Jehovah. Wherever Christ is, there is God; and whatever Christ does is an action of the Most High God. Oh, what a joyful truth to consider that He who stands today representing the interests of His people is "Very God of Very God" (Nicene Creed), to whom "every knee [will] bow" (Phil. 2:10).

Blessed are we who belong to such a shepherd, whose humanity fellowships with us, and whose divinity protects us. "Let us bow down in worship ... [as] ... the people of his pasture" (Ps. 95:6 – 7).

From the pen of Jim Reimann:

Jesus the Messiah not only "will *stand* and shepherd his flock" but "will *sit* as a refiner and purifier of silver" (Mal. 3:3). There is a beautiful analogy in this, for a jeweler sits as he refines precious metals, such as silver. He puts the silver in the crucible, puts the fire to it, but does not then walk away, leaving it on its own. No, he sits and watches it, being careful not to set the fire too hot, which may ruin the metal, nor set it too low, which will not allow the heat to do its work to burn away the dross and impurities. He sits, carefully watching the metal, all the while adjusting the fire to exactly the right temperature. And when does he know it is perfectly pure? The answer is simple — when the jeweler can see his face in the metal, for it reflects his likeness.

In the same way, the Lord sends the heat of suffering into our lives to burn away our impurities and to conform us "to the likeness of his Son" (Rom. 8:29). "We ... are being transformed into his likeness with ever-increasing glory" (2 Cor. 3:18). "Now we see but a poor reflection as in a mirror; then we shall see face to face" (1 Cor. 13:12).

AUGUST 20

... the sweet psalmist of Israel ...
2 Samuel 23:1 KJV

From the pen of Charles Spurgeon:

Of all the saints whose lives are recorded in the Word, David's life is the most varied in experience and the most striking and instructive in character. In his history we see trials and temptations not seen, for the most part, in the lives of other saints of old. Thus, he is all the more indicative of a type of our Lord.

David knew the trials of all classes and conditions of men. Kings have their troubles, and David wore a crown; peasants have their cares, and David once held a shepherd's staff; wanderers have many hardships, and David lived in the caves of En Gedi; and a warrior has his difficulties, and David found the "sons of Zeruiah ... too strong for [him]" (2 Sam. 3:39). The psalmist also suffered trials due to unfaithful friends, such as his counselor Ahithophel, who conspired against him. Thus, David wrote: "Even my close friend ... who shared my bread, has lifted up his heel against me" (Ps. 41:9). Yet his worst foes were those of his own household, for his children were his greatest affliction.

The temptations of poverty and wealth, honor and reproach, health and weakness all tested their power on David. He had temptations from without to disturb his peace and temptations from within to sour his joy. He no sooner escaped one trial before falling into another, no sooner emerged from one period of despondency and fear before being taken again to the lowest depths, with all God's waves breaking over him.

This is probably the very reason David's psalms are so universally the delight of experienced Christians. Whatever our frame of mind, whether elation or depression, he precisely described our emotions. He was a true master of the human heart because he had been tutored in the best school of all — the school of heartfelt personal experience. And as we are instructed in the same school, maturing in grace and in years, we increasingly appreciate David's psalms, finding them to be "green pastures" (Ps. 23:2).

My soul, may David's experience cheer and counsel you today.

From the pen of Jim Reimann:

One beautiful aspect of God's Word is that we see the frailties of many of the prominent characters. Knowing they were people like us gives us the ability to relate to them. It also helps us relate to the Lord who used them in mighty ways in spite of their frailties. Thus, we can confidently say, "He can use me as well!"

David, "a man after [God's] own heart" (1 Sam. 13:14), nevertheless became an adulterer and a murderer. Yet that is not the end of the story. Due to God's grace and forgiveness, the Lord promised: "One of your own sons ... will build a house for me, and I will establish his throne forever" (1 Chron. 17:11 – 12).

Paul said,

> Do you not know that the wicked will not inherit the kingdom of God? Do not be deceived: Neither the sexually immoral nor idolaters nor adulterers nor male prostitutes nor homosexual offenders nor thieves nor the greedy nor drunkards nor slanderers nor swindlers will inherit the kingdom of God.
>
> 1 Corinthians 6:9 – 10

Like David, "that is what some of [us] were. *But [we] were washed, [we] were sanctified, [we] were justified in the name of the Lord Jesus Christ*" (1 Cor. 6:11).

AUGUST 21

He who refreshes others will himself be refreshed.

Proverbs 11:25

From the pen of Charles Spurgeon:

This verse teaches us a great lesson: to receive, we must give; to accumulate, we must scatter; to make ourselves happy, we must make others happy; and to become spiritually strong, we must seek the spiritual good of others.

How is it that when we refresh others, we ourselves are refreshed? Our efforts to be useful actually bring out our abilities for usefulness. We all have latent talents and dormant skills that are brought to light through exercise. Our full strength is hidden even from ourselves until we venture out to fight the Lord's battles or to climb mountains of difficulty. We will never know what tender sympathy we possess until we attempt to dry a widow's tears or soothe an orphan's grief. We often discover that in attempting to teach others, we are taught. And what gracious lessons some of us have learned while visiting at the sickbeds of others!

We endeavor to teach the Scriptures and come away blushing that we know so little of them. In our conversations with poor saints we are taught the way of God more perfectly for ourselves and gain a deeper insight into God's divine truth. Thus, refreshing others brings humility. We discover how much grace there is in places we had never looked for it and learn just how far a poor saint may surpass us in knowledge. Our own comfort is increased as well by serving others. We endeavor to cheer them and the consolation gladdens our own heart. Like the two men recently trapped in the snow, one rubbed the other's limbs to keep him from dying, and in so doing saved his own life because the rubbing kept his own blood circulating. The poor widow of Zarephath gave from her meager means for the prophet Elijah's needs, and from that day forward was never in want again (see 1 Kings 17:7 – 24).

Therefore, "give, and it will be given to you. A good measure, pressed down, shaken together and running over" (Luke 6:38).

From the pen of Jim Reimann:

Some people refer to using their "God-given common sense." If by that they mean using their brains, along with godly wisdom — then great! But we must be careful using so-called common sense — a term found nowhere in the Scriptures. The Bible says: "The foolishness of God is wiser than man's wisdom" (1 Cor. 1:25), and "'My thoughts are not your thoughts, neither are your ways my ways,' declares the LORD. 'As the heavens are higher than the earth, so are my ways higher than your ways and my thoughts than your thoughts'" (Isa. 55:8 – 9).

We are taught that to receive, we must give — something the world will never understand. We are taught to "humble yourselves before the Lord, and he will lift you up" (James 4:10). Thus, the proper thing to do is often the exact opposite of our natural inclination, or what our "common sense" is telling us.

Yet the ultimate dichotomy is that to live, we must die! Jesus said,

> I tell you the truth, unless a kernel of wheat falls to the ground and dies, it remains only a single seed. But if it dies, it produces many seeds. The man who loves his life will lose it, while the man who hates his life in this world will keep it for eternal life.

John 12:24 – 25

AUGUST 22

O daughters of Jerusalem, I charge you — if you find my lover,
what will you tell him? Tell him I am faint with love.

Song of Songs 5:8

From the pen of Charles Spurgeon:

This verse is the sentiment of every believer who thirsts for close fellowship with Jesus; he is "faint with love," longing for his Lord. Believers' souls are never perfectly at peace unless they are in a condition of closeness to Christ, for when they are away from Him, they lose their peace. The closer to Him, the closer they are to the perfect calm of heaven. The closer to Him, the more their heart is filled not only with peace but also with life, strength, and joy, for each of these depends on continual fellowship with Jesus. What the sun is to the day, the moon is to the night, and what the dew is to the flower, Jesus Christ is to us. What bread is to the hungry, clothing is to the naked, and what the shadow of a large rock is to a traveler in the desert, Jesus Christ is to us.

Therefore, if we are not consciously one with Him, it is little wonder our spirit cries out in the words of the Song of Songs, "O daughters of Jerusalem, I charge you — if you find my lover ... tell him I am faint with love." This intense longing for Jesus has a blessing attached to it: "Blessed are those who hunger and thirst for righteousness" (Matt. 5:6), and, therefore, *supremely* blessed are they who thirst after the Righteous One Himself. And blessed is that "hunger and thirst" because it comes from God, and if I am not experiencing the blessing of being completely filled, I will eagerly continue to seek that blessing in my emptiness until I am filled with Christ. And if I could not feed on Jesus, the next best thing to that heavenly condition would be to "hunger and thirst" after Him.

There is a holiness about that hunger because it truly shines among the beatitudes of our Lord. But the blessing also includes a promise, for "those who hunger and thirst ... *will be filled*" (Matt. 5:6) with what they are desiring. Thus, if Christ causes us to long for Him, He will certainly satisfy those longings. And when He does come to us — and come He will — oh, how sweet it will be!

From the pen of Jim Reimann:

King David, "a man after [God's] own heart," wrote the following psalm when he was in the desert during the time his son Absalom was conspiring against him. What a great example of thirsting for God! May these words of David and the following prayer of Isaiah be our prayer this morning:

"O God, you are my God, earnestly I seek you; my soul thirsts for you, my body longs for you, in a dry and weary land where there is no water. I have seen you in the sanctuary and beheld your power and your glory. Because your love is better than life, my lips will glorify you. I will praise you as long as I live, and in your name I will lift up my hands. My soul will be satisfied as with the richest of foods; with singing lips my mouth will praise you. On my bed I remember you; I think of you through the watches of the night. Because you are my help, I sing in the shadow of your wings. My soul clings to you; your right hand upholds me" (Ps. 63:1 – 8).

"You will keep in perfect peace him whose mind is steadfast, because he trusts in you.... Yes, Lord, walking in the way of your laws, we wait for you; your name and renown are the desire of our hearts. My soul yearns for you in the night; in the morning my spirit longs for you" (Isa. 26:3, 8 – 9).

AUGUST 23

I will rejoice over Jerusalem and take delight in my people;
the sound of weeping and of crying will be heard in it no more.

Isaiah 65:19

From the pen of Charles Spurgeon:

In heaven the glorified will weep no more, for all causes of grief will be gone forever. There will be no broken friendships or damaged hopes, and poverty, famine, danger, persecution, and slander will be unknown. There will be no distressing pain, no thought of death, and no saddening grief. "The sound of weeping ... will be heard ... no more" for everyone there will be perfectly sanctified. No "sinful, unbelieving heart" will tempt anyone to turn "away from the living God" (Heb. 3:12), for they will be "without fault before the throne of God" (Rev. 14:5 KJV) and will be fully "conformed to the likeness of his Son" (Rom. 8:29). They will cease to grieve over sin, for they will have ceased to sin. They will weep no more because all fear of change will be gone. They will know they are eternally secure; sin will be shut out, and they will be shut in.

They will dwell within a city that will never experience a storm, they will bask in a sun that will never set, they will drink from a river that will never run dry, and they will pick fruit from a tree that will never wither. Countless yearly cycles may go by, but eternity will never be exhausted, and while eternity endures, their immortality and blessedness will perfectly co-exist with it. They "will be with the Lord forever" (1 Thess. 4:17). They will weep no more, because every desire will be fulfilled, and they will not even be able to wish for something they do not already possess. Eye and ear, heart and hand, judgment, imagination, hope, desire, and will — in fact, all their faculties — will be completely satisfied.

As imperfect as our present ideas are of "what God has prepared for those who love him" (1 Cor. 2:9), we know enough through the revelation of the Spirit that the saints above will be supremely blessed. The joy of Christ, which is an infinite fullness of true delight, will be in them, and they will bathe in the bottomless, shoreless sea of infinite happiness and blessings.

That same joyful rest awaits us as well and may not be that far away. Before long our weeping willow will be exchanged for the palm branch of victory, and sorrow's teardrops will be transformed into pearls of everlasting joy.

"Therefore encourage each other with these words" (1 Thess. 4:18).

From the pen of Jim Reimann:

May these words of Jesus encourage your believing heart this morning:

"In my Father's house are many rooms; if it were not so, I would have told you. I am going there to prepare a place for you. And if I go and prepare a place for you, I will come back and take you to be with me that you also may be where I am" (John 14:2 – 3).

> Since you have kept my command to endure patiently, I will also keep you from the hour of trial that is going to come upon the whole world to test those who live on the earth. I am coming soon. Hold on to what you have, so that no one will take your crown. Him who overcomes I will make a pillar in the temple of my God. Never again will he leave it. I will write on him the name of my God and the name of the city of my God, the new Jerusalem, which is coming down out of heaven from my God; and I will also write on him my new name. He who has an ear, let him hear what the Spirit says to the churches.

Revelation 3:10 – 13

AUGUST 24

One who breaks open the way will go up before them....
Their king will pass through before them, the LORD at their head.

Micah 2:13

From the pen of Charles Spurgeon:

Because Jesus has gone before us, things have not remained the same as though He had never passed that way. He has conquered every foe that obstructed the way, so cheer up, you faint-hearted warriors. Not only has Christ traveled your road but He has also slain your enemies. Do you dread sin? He has nailed it to His cross. Do you fear death? He became the death of Death. Are you afraid of hell? He has barred the entrance for each of His children, and they will never even glimpse the pit of eternal damnation.

Whatever foes may come against a Christian are all defeated. They may be lions, but their teeth are broken; they may be serpents, but their fangs have been extracted; they may be rivers, but they have been bridged or are shallow enough to cross; they may be flames, but we wear "matchless" garments that make us invulnerable to fire. The sword that has been forged against us has already been blunted, and every other instrument of war that the enemy is preparing for us has already lost its sharpness as well. Through the person of Christ, God has taken away any power of anything designed to hurt us.

Thus, the Lord's army may march safely on, and you may go joyously along your journey, for all your enemies have been conquered beforehand. What will you do but march on and take the prey? Your enemies are beaten; they are vanquished; all that is left for you to do is to divide the spoils. It is true you will often be engaged in combat, but your battle will be with a vanquished foe. His head is crushed (see Gen. 3:15) and although he may attempt to injure you, his strength will not be sufficient to carry out his malicious plans. Your victory will be easy and your treasure will be beyond calculation.

Proclaim aloud the Savior's fame,
Who bears the Breaker's wondrous name;
Sweet name, and it becomes Him well,
Who breaks down earth, sin, death, and hell.

Samuel Medley, 1738 – 1799

From the pen of Jim Reimann:

David certainly understood that God's people are "more than conquerors" (Rom. 8:37), for the Lord delivered him from his enemies over and over again. And because of his strong belief, he did not walk in fear, but in faith. Here is how he stated it:

The LORD is my light and my salvation — whom shall I fear? The LORD is the stronghold of my life — of whom shall I be afraid? When evil men advance against me to devour my flesh, when my enemies and my foes attack me, they will stumble and fall. Though an army besiege me, my heart will not fear; though war break out against me, even then will I be confident. One thing I ask of the LORD, this is what I seek: that I may dwell in the house of the LORD all the days of my life, to gaze upon the beauty of the LORD and to seek him in his temple. For in the day of trouble he will keep me safe in his dwelling; he will hide me in the shelter of his tabernacle and set me high upon a rock. Then my head will be exalted above the enemies who surround me.

Psalm 27:1 – 6

AUGUST 25

I delight to sit in his shade,
and his fruit is sweet to my taste.
Song of Songs 2:3

From the pen of Charles Spurgeon:

Faith is often spoken of in the Scriptures in relation to our senses. For example, sight: "Look unto me, and be ... saved" (Isa. 45:22 KJV). Hearing: "Hear me, that your soul may live" (Isa. 55:3). Smell: "All your robes are fragrant with myrrh and aloes and cassia" (Ps. 45:8), and "Pleasing is the fragrance of your perfumes; your name is like perfume poured out" (Song 1:3). Touch: By faith, "a woman who had been subject to bleeding for twelve years ... touched the edge of his cloak" (Matt. 9:20), and through the sense of touch we handle the things of the life of faith. Taste: "How sweet are your words to my taste, sweeter than honey to my mouth!" (Ps. 119:103), and as Christ said, "Unless you eat the flesh of the Son of Man and drink his blood, you have no life in you" (John 6:53).

The sense of taste is actually faith in one of its highest applications. But one of the first uses of faith is hearing, for we hear the voice of God, not just with our physical ears but also with our spiritual ears. When we hear God's Word and believe it to be true, that is the "hearing" of faith. Then our mind "looks" on the truth as it has been presented to us, and when we understand it, truly perceiving its meaning, that is the "seeing" of faith. Next we discover its preciousness, beginning to admire it and finding how fragrant it is, and that is the "smelling" of faith. Then we begin to appropriate the mercies of God that have been prepared for us in Christ, and that is the "touching" of faith. Following this comes the enjoyment of peace, joy, and fellowship, which is the "tasting" of faith.

Each of these senses of faith is indicative of saving faith. Hearing Christ's voice as certain as the voice of God in our soul will save us. But it is the "tasting" aspect of faith that brings us true enjoyment. Christ, through holy "taste," is received into us, and by inward and spiritual awareness of His sweetness and preciousness, He becomes food for our souls.

It is then "I delight to sit in his shade, and his fruit is sweet to my taste."

From the pen of Jim Reimann:

Isn't it wonderful we have a Savior who wants to know us and has made a way for us to know Him in a way that uses all our senses! Surely we are "fearfully and wonderfully made" (Ps. 139:14), as David said. So this morning, "Taste and see that the LORD is good" (Ps. 34:8).

Consider today just how blessed believers are! We can "taste" the Lord, feeding on Him for our spiritual growth. The only alternative would be to "taste" death, but He has done that on our behalf, saving us from eternal separation from Himself. "We see Jesus, who was made a little lower than the angels, now crowned with glory and honor because he suffered death, so that *by the grace of God he might taste death for everyone*" (Heb. 2:9).

And notice in the following passage how the Jews used the word *taste*: Jesus said,

> "I tell you the truth, if anyone keeps my word, he will never see death." At this the Jews exclaimed, "... Abraham died and so did the prophets, yet you say that if anyone keeps your word, *he will never taste death*."
> John 8:51 – 52

That's right! Believers "will never taste death"!

AUGUST 26

He ordained his covenant forever.

Psalm 111:9

From the pen of Charles Spurgeon:

The Lord's people delight in God's covenant itself. It is an unfailing source of consolation to them as the Holy Spirit leads them "to the banquet hall," waving "his banner over [them of] love" (Song 2:4). They delight to consider how ancient God's covenant is, remembering that even before the sun was placed in space or the planets began their orbits, the interests of the saints were made secure in Christ Jesus. It is particularly pleasing to them to remember the certainty of the covenant, while meditating on God's "faithful love promised to David" (Isa. 55:3). They also delight in celebrating that the covenant is "signed, sealed, and delivered." And it often makes their hearts swell with joy to think of its immutability; that neither time nor eternity, life nor death, will ever be able to nullify a covenant as old as eternity itself and as everlasting as the Rock of Ages.

They also rejoice in feasting on the fullness of the covenant, for in it they see all the blessings provided for them. They see God as their inheritance, Christ as their companion, the Spirit as their Comforter, earth as their temporary lodging, and heaven as their home. In the covenant they see an inheritance reserved and protected for every soul possessing an interest in its ancient and eternal deed of gifts. Their eyes sparkled when they first saw the covenant as a blessed treasure trove in the Bible. But, oh, how their souls were elated all the more when they realized this last will and testament of their divine family was bequeathed to them as well!

Beyond everything else it is the pleasure of God's people to consider the graciousness of God's covenant. They see that the law was made void because it was a covenant of works that de-

pended on their merit. They rightly perceive this covenant, however, enduring because of grace — grace as the only basis, grace as the only condition, grace as the entire agreement, grace as the protection, grace as the foundation, and grace as the capstone.

Thus, the covenant is a treasury of wealth, a warehouse of food, a "fountain of life" (Ps. 36:9), a storehouse of salvation, a charter of peace, and a haven of joy.

From the pen of Jim Reimann:

Zechariah, the father of John the Baptist, was a priest who served in the Lord's temple. After John's birth he prayed a beautiful prophecy concerning God's "holy covenant," as he called it. Here is what "Zechariah ... filled with the Holy Spirit ... prophesied":

> Praise be to the Lord, the God of Israel, because he has come and has redeemed his people. He has raised up a horn of salvation for us in the house of his servant David (as he said through his holy prophets of long ago), salvation from our enemies and from the hand of all who hate us — to show mercy to our fathers and *to remember his holy covenant*, the oath he swore to our father Abraham: to rescue us from the hand of our enemies, and to enable us to serve him without fear in holiness and righteousness before him all our days.

Luke 1:67 – 75

Father, I was once a "[foreigner] to the covenants of the promise, without hope" (Eph. 2:12). *Thank You for Jesus, who is my "hope of glory"* (Col. 1:27)!

AUGUST 27

How long will they refuse to believe in me?

Numbers 14:11

From the pen of Charles Spurgeon:

We should diligently strive to keep the monster of unbelief away. It so dishonors Christ that He will remove His visible presence if we insult Him by indulging it. Unbelief is a weed whose seeds we can never entirely extract from the soil; thus, we must aim at each root with zeal and perseverance. Of things we should hate, it should be the most abhorred, for by its nature unbelief is so venomous that those who exercise it, and those upon whom it is exercised, are both hurt by it.

In your case, dear believer, it is even more wicked! The mercies the Lord blessed you with in the past increase your guilt in doubting Him now. When you distrust the Lord Jesus, He could very well cry out, "Behold, I am pressed under you, as a cart is pressed that is full of sheaves" (Amos 2:13 KJV). This is like crowning His head with thorns of the sharpest kind. It is cruel for a well-loved wife to mistrust a kind and faithful husband, and although that sin is needless, foolish, and unwarranted, Jesus has never given even the slightest grounds for suspicion. In fact, because He is always affectionate and faithful, it should be all the more difficult for us to doubt Him. Jesus is the Son of the Most High and has unlimited wealth; thus, it is shameful to doubt Omnipotence and distrust His all-sufficiency. "The cattle on a thousand hills" (Ps. 50:10) will suffice for even our largest meal, and the granaries of heaven are not likely to be emptied when we eat.

If Christ were only a cistern of water we might quickly exhaust His fullness, but who can drain a fountain? Multitudes of souls have drawn from His supply and not one of them has ever been able to honestly complain of the insufficiency of His resources.

Away then with the lying traitor of unbelief, for his only purpose is to cut the bonds of fellowship with our Savior and then cause us to mourn the lack of His visible presence. As John Bunyan (1628 – 1688) says in *The Pilgrim's Progress*, unbelief, or Giant Despair as he calls it, has "as many lives as a cat." If that is true, may we kill one of unbelief's lives now and continue working until the entire nine are dead.

Down with you, unbelief! You traitor! My heart detests you.

From the pen of Jim Reimann:

When Jesus returned to Nazareth during His ministry, we are told: "He did not [do] many mighty works there because of their unbelief" (Matt. 13:58 KJV).

Imagine what those people missed because of their lack of faith! And they were the people who should have known Him best, because they were the people of His hometown.

So what is the message in this for us who have a relationship with Christ? What have we missed due to our lack of faith? Only God Himself knows!

Therefore, we should heed the valuable advice of King Jehoshaphat. Here is what he told Israel just *before* God destroyed all their enemies: "Have faith in the LORD your God and you will be upheld; have faith in his prophets and you will be successful" (2 Chron. 20:20).

AUGUST 28

...olive oil for the light.

Exodus 25:6

From the pen of Charles Spurgeon:

My soul, you greatly need this oil because your lamp will not burn long without it. The wick will smoke offensively when its flame goes out, but it will not relight once the oil is gone. There is no oil well springing up from within your human nature, therefore you must go to Him who can supply you with oil or you will be like the foolish virgins, who cried out, "Our lamps are going out" (Matt. 25:8)! Even the consecrated oil lamps of the temple in Jerusalem could not give light without oil. Though they shone in that holy building, they needed a constant supply of oil, and though no strong winds blew on them, their wicks needed to be trimmed. Your need is equally as great, for even under the happiest of circumstances you cannot give light for another hour unless the fresh oil of grace is given to you.

Yet not just any oil could be used in the Lord's service in the temple — not the petroleum that flows so plentifully from the earth, oil from fish, nor the oil extracted from various nuts. Only olive oil was selected and it had to be the very best. Likewise, no counterfeit grace arising from natural goodness, nor imaginary grace from God's priest or his spiritual ceremonies, will ever serve the true saint of God. He knows the Lord would not be pleased even with rivers of such oil. Instead, he must go to the olive press of Gethsemane and draw his supply from Him who was crushed in it.

The oil of true gospel grace is pure and free from dregs and other impurities; thus, the light it fuels is clear and bright. Our churches are the Savior's golden candelabra and if they are to be bright lights in this dark world, they need a great supply of holy oil. May we pray for ourselves and our ministers and churches that they will never lack oil for their light. The beams of this sacred light are truth, holiness, joy, knowledge, and love, but we cannot shine them forth unless, through private devotion, we receive the oil from God the Holy Spirit.

From the pen of Jim Reimann:

In this morning's devotion Spurgeon mentions the olive press of Gethsemane. Yet there is a difference between an olive press and an olive crush. The garden of Gethsemane is the place where the Jews of Jerusalem would take their olives to have them crushed. In fact, *Gethsemane* refers to an olive crush, and an ancient one was actually discovered in the garden of Gethsemane. It is a round stone hewn from solid rock with another stone that rolls on end around its top. It was used to crush the meat of the olive from the pit. Then the meat of the olives would be placed in an olive press to squeeze the oil from them.

Surely it is no coincidence Jesus went to the place of crushing to pray before He was arrested. "He was crushed for our iniquities" (Isa. 53:5). Not only was He crushed but He was also "pressed," for in Gethsemane "his sweat was like drops of blood falling to the ground" (Luke 22:44).

Another thing to know is that the oil in the temple had to come from only one place — the Mount of Olives, where the garden of Gethsemane is located. Jesus went there to be prepared to be the "oil" to light the temple of our lives.

"In the same way, let your light shine before men, that they may see your good deeds and praise your Father in heaven" (Matt. 5:16).

AUGUST 29

Have mercy on me, O God.

Psalm 51:1

From the pen of Charles Spurgeon:

When the missionary William Carey was suffering from a dangerous illness, he was asked, "If this sickness proves fatal, what Scripture would you select as the text for your funeral?" He replied, "Oh, I feel that such a poor, sinful creature is not worthy to have anything said about him, but if a funeral must be preached, let it be from the words, 'Have mercy on me, O God, according to your unfailing love; according to your great compassion blot out my transgressions'" (Ps. 51:1). In the same spirit of humility, he directed in his will that the following inscription, and nothing more, be engraved on his tombstone:

William Carey, Born August 17, 1761
Died —
A wretched, poor, and helpless worm
On Your kind arms I fall.

It is only on the foundation of grace that even the most experienced and most honored of all saints may approach their God. The best of men are conscious above all others that even at their best they are still only men. Empty boats float high in the water, while heavily laden vessels float low. Only false Christians can boast, but true children of God cry for mercy for their unworthiness. We need the Lord to have mercy even on our good works, prayers, sermons, and offerings — all our holiest things. The blood of the sacrifice was not only sprinkled on the doorposts of Israel's houses but also on the sanctuary, "the mercy seat" (Ex. 25:17 KJV), and the altar. This is because as sin intrudes into our holiest things, the blood of Jesus is needed to purify them from defilement. And if mercy is needed for our holiest of duties, what can be said of our sins?

How precious is the reminder that inexhaustible mercy is waiting to be gracious to us — to restore us from our backslidings and to make our broken bones rejoice!

From the pen of Jim Reimann:

William Carey was an English missionary and minister in India often considered "the father of modern missions." His most famous quote is: "Expect great things from God; attempt great things for God!" Although he never completed a grade school education, he nevertheless learned dozens of languages, including Hebrew and Greek, and translated all or parts of the Bible into some thirty-five languages before his death.

He was the most famous missionary of his time and is one of the most famous in the entire history of the church. He accomplished a great deal through great suffering, including lifelong sicknesses and the loss of two wives and two sons. Yet he remained humble and remarked late in life of "how little I have done for God." Perhaps he truly grasped this verse: "Blessed are the poor in spirit, for theirs is the kingdom of heaven" (Matt. 5:3).

Oh, and just in case you were wondering, he entered "the kingdom of heaven" June 9, 1834, at the age of seventy-two.

AUGUST 30

Wait for the LORD.
Psalm 27:14

From the pen of Charles Spurgeon:

It may seem like an easy thing to wait, but it is one discipline a Christian soldier learns only after years of training. Marching and quick-step marching are actually much easier for God's warriors than standing still. There may be many hours spent in bewilderment and confusion, when people who have a willing spirit and are anxiously desiring to serve the Lord do not know what role to play. What should we do? Become exasperated in despair? Turn back in cowardice, go to the left or right in fear, or rush forward in ignorance?

No, we should simply wait — but wait in prayer. We should call upon God and plead our case before Him, telling Him our difficulty and pleading His promise of help. When we are torn between one opportunity or another, it is best to be as humble as a child while waiting with simplicity of soul for the Lord. We can be confident all will go well with us when we recognize our own foolishness and are sincerely willing to be guided by the will of God.

We should wait — but wait in faith. We should express our unwavering confidence in Him, for waiting without faith and trust is nothing but an insult to the Lord. We should believe that even if He keeps us waiting until midnight, He will still come at exactly the right time. "For the revelation awaits an appointed time.... Though it linger, wait for it; it will certainly come and will not delay" (Hab. 2:3).

We should wait — but with quiet patience. We should not rebel because of suffering through a difficulty, but instead should bless God for it. We should not complain about unfounded reasons for our problem, as the children of Israel did against Moses, and should not wish we could go back to the world again. We should accept our situation as it is and simply place it with our entire heart — without any self-will — into the hands of our covenant God, saying:

> Lord, "not my will, but yours be done" (Luke 22:42). I don't know what to do and am at my wits' end. Nevertheless, I will wait until You divide the waters before me or drive back my foes. Even if I must wait many days, I will wait with "my heart...steadfast, O God" (Ps. 57:7), on You alone. My spirit waits for You with the full conviction that You will still be my joy and "my salvation" (Ps. 27:1), "my refuge...[and my] strong tower" (Ps. 61:3).

From the pen of Jim Reimann:

It is true that waiting is one of the most difficult things "to do." Even many Christians believe that waiting is a waste of time. But when it comes to spiritual things, being "unproductive" may actually be the best use of our time. This is especially true if being busy is only producing "wood, hay or straw" (1 Cor. 3:12). It is also true if being active makes us unable to hear God's "still small voice" (1 Kings 19:12 KJV), which may be attempting to nudge us in another direction. Could it also be the Lord is using a time of waiting to prepare for us greater service to Him?

Thus, "I wait for the LORD, my soul waits, and in his word I put my hope. My soul waits for the Lord more than watchmen wait for the morning, *more than watchmen wait for the morning*" (Ps. 130:5 – 6).

Notice how the psalmist echoes his final thought. Perhaps when it comes to waiting, we need to be reminded again — again!

AUGUST 31

The islands will look to me
and wait in hope for my arm.

Isaiah 51:5

From the pen of Charles Spurgeon:

In times of severe trials, a Christian has nothing on earth in which to trust and is therefore compelled to cast himself on his God alone. When his boat is about to break in two and sink, and no human deliverance is possible, he must simply and entirely trust himself to the sovereignty and care of God. What a blessed storm that dashes a man on a rock such as this! Oh, blessed hurricane that drives a soul to God and God alone!

Sometimes it is difficult to reach out to God because of having so many friends around us. But when a man is poor, friendless, and so helpless he has nowhere else to turn, he runs into his Father's arms — and is blessed in His embrace! When someone is burdened with troubles so stressful and out of the ordinary he cannot share them with anyone but his God, he can be thankful for them, for he will learn more about his Lord at that time than any other.

Oh, dear storm-tossed believer, troubles that drive you to your Father are a blessing! Now that you have only your God to trust, see to it that you put your full confidence in Him. Do not dishonor your Lord and Master with unworthy doubts and fears, but be strong in faith, giving glory to God. Show the world your God is worth ten thousand worlds to you. Show the materially rich just how rich you are in your poverty when the Lord God is your helper. Show strong men just how strong you are in your weakness when "underneath [you] are the everlasting arms" (Deut. 33:27).

Now is the time for great feats of faith and courageous exploits. "Be strong and very courageous" (Josh. 1:7) and the Lord your God will certainly — as surely as He "created the heavens and the earth" (Gen. 1:1) — glorify Himself in your weakness and magnify His might in the midst of your distress. The grandeur of the canopy of heaven would be spoiled if there were even one visible column supporting the sky. In the same way, your faith will lose its glory if it rests on anything discernible by the physical eyes of man.

On the last morning of this month, may the Holy Spirit grant you faith that rests in Jesus alone.

From the pen of Jim Reimann:

Instead of trusting in the Lord alone, our world is overly impressed with wealth and the ability of some to produce great wealth. They should know, however, "It is [the LORD] who gives you the ability to produce wealth" (Deut. 8:18). And the following is the biblical fallacy of trusting in wealth and ourselves:

Why should I fear when evil days come, when wicked deceivers surround me — those who trust in their wealth and boast of their great riches? ... For all can see that wise men die; the foolish and the senseless alike perish and leave their wealth to others.... This is the fate of those who trust in themselves, and of their followers, who approve their sayings.... Do not be overawed when a man grows rich, when the splendor of his house increases; for he will take nothing with him when he dies, his splendor will not descend with him.... *A man who has riches without understanding is like the beasts that perish.*

Psalm 49:5 – 6, 10, 13, 16 – 17, 20

"But I trust in you, O LORD; I say, 'You are my God'" (Ps. 31:14).

September

SEPTEMBER 1

You guide me with your counsel,
and afterward you will take me into glory.

Psalm 73:24

From the pen of Charles Spurgeon:

The psalmist Asaph felt a need for divine guidance. He had just been discovering the foolishness of his heart, saying, "I was senseless and ignorant" (Ps. 73:22). And lest he be constantly led astray by it, he resolved from that day forth that God's counsel would guide him. Having a sense of our own folly is a giant step toward becoming wise if it leads us to rely on the wisdom of the Lord. As a blind man grasps his friend's arm to reach home in safety, we too should trust completely in God's divine guidance, without any doubt and with the assurance that although we cannot see, it is always safe to trust the all-seeing God. "You guide me" is a blessed expression of confidence, for Asaph was sure the Lord would not decline the lowly task.

Dear believer, there is a word for you in this in which you may rest. You may be assured your God will be your counselor and friend and will guide you and "direct all [your] ways" (Isa. 45:13 KJV). This promise is fulfilled by His written Word, for Holy Scripture is His counsel to you. How blessed we are to have God's Word always there to guide us! What is a sailor without a compass? And what is a Christian without the Bible? It is a trustworthy map, depicting every possible sandbar and channel, from the quicksand of destruction to the haven of salvation, with each faithfully mapped and marked by the One who knows the way.

Blessed are You, O God, that we may trust You to guide us now — and even to the end! Asaph recognized this as well, for after being guided through this life, he anticipated his divine reception into eternity: "Afterward you will take me into glory." What a thought for you, believer! God Himself "will take [you] into glory"! Wandering, sinning, straying — yet at last He will take you

safe and sound to glory! This is your inheritance, so live in it today. And if confusion and questions swirl around you, go in the strength of this text straight to the throne of God.

From the pen of Jim Reimann:

Indeed, believers have the Word of God to guide us, and Jesus promised the Holy Spirit as our guide to that truth. Here is what He told us:

I have much more to say to you, more than you can now bear. But when he, the Spirit of truth, comes, *he will guide you into all truth.* He will not speak on his own; he will speak only what he hears, and he will tell you what is yet to come. He will bring glory to me by taking from what is mine and making it known to you. All that belongs to the Father is mine. That is why I said the Spirit will take from what is mine and make it known to you.

John 16:12 – 15

Thus, the only guidance we can truly trust comes from the Lord, through His Word by His Spirit. In addition to our text verse this morning, here is a promise of God's continuing guidance to His people:

The LORD will guide you always; he will satisfy your needs in a sun-scorched land and will strengthen your frame. You will be like a well-watered garden, like a spring whose waters never fail.

Isaiah 58:11

Father, I thank You for guidance through Your Word, Your Spirit, and Your Son, whom You sent "to guide our feet into the way of peace" (Luke 1:79 KJV).

September 2

Simon's mother-in-law was in bed with a fever,
and they told Jesus about her.

Mark 1:30

From the pen of Charles Spurgeon:

This small look into the apostle Peter's house is quite interesting. We quickly see that everyday household joys and tasks should be no hindrance whatsoever to ministry. In fact, we see Peter's hospitality furnishing the opportunity to personally witness the Lord's gracious work to his own family. This may have even been a better instructor to him as a future teacher himself than any other earthly discipline. Catholicism and other sects may denounce marriage for some, but true Christianity and household life are very compatible. Peter's house was probably a poor fisherman's hut, but the Lord of Glory entered it, slept in it, and performed a miracle in it.

Perhaps you are reading this devotional book today in some very humble cottage, but may Peter's experience encourage those of your household to seek the fellowship of King Jesus. God is actually found more often in little huts than in palaces. Jesus is looking around your room even now and is waiting to be gracious to you. A deadly fever had entered into Simon Peter's house, sending his mother-in-law to bed, but as soon as Jesus was told of her sad affliction, He hurried to her side.

Is there any sickness in your house this morning? Jesus is by far the best physician, so go to Him at once and tell Him all about it, immediately laying the case before Him. And because it concerns one of His people, it will not be a trivial matter to Him. Notice how the Savior restored the sick woman to health at once, for no one can heal as He does. The Lord may not instantly remove all sicknesses from those we love, but we can know that believing prayer for the sick is far more likely to be followed by restoration than anything else in the world. And when He does not heal, we must meekly submit to His will from which life and death are determined.

The tender heart of Jesus waits to hear our troubles. May we pour them into His patient ears.

From the pen of Jim Reimann:

It was not until the excavations of 1968 – 1986, long after the time of Spurgeon, that archaeologists believe they discovered the house of Peter in Capernaum. The house was venerated as early as the second century AD and has since had two churches built over it. One of those, from the middle of the fifth century, is octagonal in shape, perhaps to symbolize the eight beatitudes that were preached nearby.

As Spurgeon thought, Peter's home is small and unassuming. What a great reminder that the Lord uses "the nobodies" of the world to accomplish His greatest work! How many humble pastors and missionaries, whose names we will never know, will do great things for God today? How many of us, everyday believers in our everyday homes with our everyday hospitality, will entertain the Lord of the universe!

We should take this instruction to heart: "Keep on loving each other as brothers. Do not forget to entertain strangers, for by so doing some people have entertained angels without knowing it" (Heb. 13:1 – 2).

SEPTEMBER 3

You whom I love …

Song of Songs 1:7

From the pen of Charles Spurgeon:

It is good to be able to say of the Lord Jesus without any "ifs, ands, or buts" — "You whom I love." Many people can only say they "hope" they love Him or they "trust" they love Him, but only those with a poor shallow experience of Jesus would be content to stay there. No one should allow his spirit to rest until he is quite sure about a matter of such vital importance. We should never be satisfied with a superficial "hope" that Jesus loves us or with unfounded "trust" that we love Him. The saints of old did not generally speak with "ifs," "buts," "hopes," and "trusts" — they spoke with certainty and directness. For example, Paul said, "I know whom I have believed" (2 Tim. 1:12), and Job said, "I know that my Redeemer lives" (Job 19:25).

Thus, make certain of your love for Jesus and refuse to be satisfied until you can speak of your relationship with Him as a reality. This will be made sure by having received the witness of the Holy Spirit and His seal upon your soul by faith, for true love for Christ is in every case the work of the Spirit and must be created in the heart by Him. He is the effective cause of our love for Christ, but the logical reason for our love lies in Jesus Himself.

Why do we love Jesus? "Because he first loved us" (1 John 4:19). Why do we love Jesus? Because He "gave himself for us" (Titus 2:14). We have life through His death and peace through His blood. (See Eph. 2:13 – 15.) "Though he was rich, yet for [our] sakes he became poor" (2 Cor. 8:9). Why do we love Jesus? Because of the wonder of His person. We are filled with a sense of His beauty, admiration of His power, and awareness of His infinite perfection! His greatness, goodness, and loveliness — all in one brilliant ray — enchant our soul until it becomes so overjoyed it exclaims, "He is altogether lovely" (Song 5:16).

It is a blessed love that binds the heart with chains softer than silk, but is a love that is constant and unshakable!

From the pen of Jim Reimann:

Another proof of my love for Jesus is my obedience to Him. In His "Upper Room Discourse" Jesus said all of the following regarding obedience:

"I have set you an example that you should do as I have done for you. Now that you know these things, you will be blessed *if you do them*" (John 13:15, 17). "*If you love me, you will obey* what I command" (John 14:15). "*If anyone loves me, he will obey* my teaching. My Father will love him, and we will come to him and make our home with him. He who does not love me will not obey my teaching. These words you hear are not my own; they belong to the Father who sent me" (John 14:23 – 24). *If you obey my commands, you will remain in my love*, just as I have obeyed my Father's commands and remain in his love" (John 15:10).

As Jesus said, "These words … belong to the Father." Thus, His teaching on the importance of obedience was nothing new, for we see it throughout the Old Testament as well. Yet — remember — obedience always comes with God's blessing attached to it. For example, God said, "Obey me, and I will be your God and you will be my people. Walk in all the ways I command you, that it may go well with you" (Jer. 7:23).

SEPTEMBER 4

Filled with compassion, Jesus reached out his hand and touched the man.
"I am willing," he said. "Be clean!"

Mark 1:41

From the pen of Charles Spurgeon:

The darkness of eternity past heard the Almighty's decree: "Let there be light" and immediately "there was light" (Gen. 1:3). And the Lord Jesus' words here were equal in majesty to that ancient word of creation power. Redemption, like creation, takes place through the word of power, for Jesus speaks and it is done. Leprosy yielded to no human remedies but fled immediately at the Lord's words: "I am willing.... Be clean!" When He spoke these words, the disease did not show just some hopeful signs or hints of recovery, for nature contributed nothing to the healing. His word alone caused the entire work at once and forever.

A sinner is in a predicament more miserable than a leper. Thus, he should imitate the leper who "came to [Jesus] and begged him on his knees" (Mark 1:40). He should exercise what little faith he has even if it is nothing more than, "If you are willing, you can make me clean" (Mark 1:40). Once a sinner does this, there can be no doubt as to the result of applying his faith, for Jesus spiritually heals all who come, for He said, "Whoever comes to me I will never drive away" (John 6:37).

It is worth noting: "Jesus ... touched the man." Considered unclean by ceremonial law, he broke through the regulations of that law by coming to Jesus. Yet far from condemning him, Jesus broke through the law Himself to meet him. Although it cleansed the man, by touching him Jesus became unclean according to Levitical law. In the same way, "God made him who had no sin to be sin for us, so that in him we might become the righteousness of God" (2 Cor. 5:21).

Oh, that poor sinners would go to Jesus, believing in the power of His blessed substitutionary sacrifice, and quickly learn the power of His gracious touch! The hand that multiplied the loaves, saved Peter from sinking, upholds afflicted saints, and crowns believers is the same hand that will touch each seeking sinner and, in an instant, will make him clean.

The love of Jesus is the source of salvation. He loves, He looks, He touches us, and — we live!

From the pen of Jim Reimann:

The man with leprosy gives us a beautiful example of an appropriate prayer of supplication. First he recognized the importance of praying according to God's will by saying, "If you are willing." If this is how Jesus prayed — "Not my will, but yours be done" (Luke 22:42) — then how much more appropriate is it for us!

Next the leper's prayer shows us the importance of exercising faith by saying, "You *can* make me clean." In a later encounter Jesus told a sick boy's father, "Everything is possible for him who believes" (Mark 9:23).

Yet a word of caution is due here. This does not mean God heals everyone just because they ask in faith. Remember, it must be according to God's will, for often the Lord sees a greater purpose in not removing illness. Even the apostle Paul said, "Three times I pleaded with the Lord to take [a thorn in my flesh] away" (2 Cor. 12:8). But he came to understand God's greater purpose — "to keep me from becoming conceited" (2 Cor. 12:7).

SEPTEMBER 5

Woe to me that I dwell in Meshech,
that I live among the tents of Kedar!
Psalm 120:5

From the pen of Charles Spurgeon:

As a Christian you have to live in the midst of an ungodly world, and it is of little use for you to cry: "Woe is me!" Jesus did not pray for His Father to "take [us] out of the world" (John 17:15), and if He did not ask for that, it should not be your desire either. It is better by far to meet a difficulty in the Lord's strength and to glorify Him through it. Your enemy is continually watching to detect inconsistency in your conduct, therefore you must "be holy in all you do" (1 Peter 1:15). Remember that all eyes are upon you and that more is expected of you than unbelievers. Strive to give no occasion for blame, but let your goodness be the only "fault" they can discover in you. Like Daniel, compel others to say of you, "We will never find any basis for charges against this man Daniel unless it has something to do with the law of his God" (Dan. 6:5).

You should not only seek to be consistent but also useful. Perhaps you think: "If I were in a better position I would serve the Lord's cause, but I can't do anything where I am." However, the worse the people are who surround you, the more they need your efforts. If they are crooked, the more they need you to be used of God to help straighten them, and if they are depraved, the more they need you to be used to turn their proud hearts to the truth. (See Phil. 2:15.)

Where is the best place for a physician but where there are many sick? Where is the greatest honor to be won by a soldier but in the hottest fire of the battle? And when you become weary of the strife and sin confronting you from every side, consider that all the saints of God have endured the same trials. They were not floated on featherbeds of ease to heaven, and you must not expect to travel an easier road than theirs. They had to risk their lives to the death on the highest ground of the battlefield, and you will not be crowned until you have endured hardship as a good soldier of Jesus Christ.

Therefore, "stand firm in the faith; be men of courage; be strong" (1 Cor. 16:13).

From the pen of Jim Reimann:

It is understandable, especially in light of life's difficulties, to occasionally want Jesus to take you on to heaven. The apostle Paul himself struggled with this, for he wrote: "To live is Christ and to die is gain.... Yet what shall I choose? I do not know! I am torn between the two: I desire to depart and be with Christ, which is better by far" (Phil. 1:21 – 23).

In spite of Paul's struggle, however, he understood the importance of being in the center of God's will and knew what his ministry meant to those he served, for he continued by saying, "But it is more necessary for you that I remain in the body. Convinced of this, I know that I will remain, and I will continue with all of you for your progress and joy in the faith" (Phil. 1:24 – 25).

In another letter, Paul addressed the issue again:

> We are always confident and know that as long as we are at home in the body we are away from the Lord. We live by faith, not by sight. We are confident, I say, and would prefer to be away from the body and at home with the Lord. *So we make it our goal to please him, whether we are at home in the body or away from it.*

2 Corinthians 5:6 – 9

SEPTEMBER 6

Do everything without complaining or arguing, so that you may become blameless and pure,
children of God without fault in a crooked and depraved generation, in which you shine
like stars in the universe as you hold out the word of life.

Philippians 2:14–16

From the pen of Charles Spurgeon:

Light is used to reveal things. Thus, a Christian's light should shine so brightly that a person could not know him even one week without also knowing the gospel. A believer's conversation should be such that those around him should clearly perceive whose he is, whom he serves, and should see the image of Jesus reflected in his daily actions.

Light is used for guidance. We are to help those around us who are in the dark, holding forth the Word of life to them. We are to point sinners to the Savior and the weary to the divine place of rest. When people read the Bible but fail to understand it, we should be ready, like Philip, to instruct the inquirer of the meaning of God's Word, the way of salvation, and the life of godliness. (See Acts 8:26–39.)

Light is used for warning. Just as a lighthouse warns sailors of a rocky coast, Christians should know there are many false lights all around the world, and therefore the right light is needed as a warning. Satan's army of destruction is everywhere, tempting the ungodly to sin in the name of pleasure. They shine the wrong light; thus, it is our job to shine the true light on every dangerous rock. We must point out each sin and its consequences so we may be "innocent of the blood of all men" (Acts 20:26), shining as lights in the world.

Light has a cheering influence, and so must Christians. A believer should be a comforter, having kind words on his lips and sympathy in his heart. He should take sunshine wherever he goes and spread happiness all around.

> Gracious Spirit dwell with me;
> I myself would gracious be,
> And with words that help and heal
> Would Your life in mine reveal,
> And with actions bold and meek
> Would for Christ my Savior speak.
> Thomas Toke Lynch, 1818–1871

From the pen of Jim Reimann:

Jesus said, "*I am the light of the world.* Whoever follows me will never walk in darkness, but will have the light of life" (John 8:12), and "While I am in the world, I am the light of the world" (John 9:5). And He told Nicodemus, "Light has come into the world, but men loved darkness instead of light because their deeds were evil. But whoever lives by the truth comes into the light, so that it may be seen plainly that what he has done has been done through God" (John 3:19, 21).

The Lord, who is the light, also told His followers,

> *You are the light of the world.* A city on a hill cannot be hidden. Neither do people light a lamp and put it under a bowl. Instead they put it on its stand, and it gives light to everyone in the house. In the same way, *let your light shine before men, that they may see your good deeds and praise your Father in heaven.*
> Matthew 5:14–16

SEPTEMBER 7

Since they could not get him to Jesus because of the crowd, they made an opening in the roof above Jesus and, after digging through it, lowered the mat the paralyzed man was lying on.

Mark 2:4

From the pen of Charles Spurgeon:

Faith can be very creative. In today's verse the house was full and even the door was blocked, but faith found a way of getting to the Lord and placing the paralyzed man before Him. Thus, if we can't get sinners to Jesus by ordinary methods, we must use extraordinary ones. According to Luke 5:19 we are told the man was lowered "through the tiles," meaning tiles were removed, probably causing a great deal of dust and possibly endangering others from the risk of falling tiles. Therefore, if the situation is quite urgent, we must not mind taking some risks and shocking people's ideas of correctness. Jesus was there to heal, and so whatever might fall, faith dared to act so his poor paralyzed friend may have his sins forgiven. Oh, that the church had more of this daring faith!

Can we, dear reader, seek this kind of faith for ourselves and our fellow Christians this morning? Can we attempt to perform some daring act today for the love of souls and the glory of the Lord? The unbelieving world is always creative, and if that's the case, can't faith be creative as well and, perhaps in some new way, reach the lost who are perishing around us?

It was the presence of Jesus that kindled the victorious courage in the four men carrying the paralyzed man — and isn't the Lord among us now? Have we seen His face for ourselves this morning? Have we felt His healing power in our own souls? If so, we should then endeavor to go through any door, window, or roof and break through any barrier to bring needy souls to Jesus. Any means is good and appropriate when faith and love are truly focused on winning souls. If hunger for bread can cause someone to break through stone walls to find it, surely hunger for souls should not hinder our efforts.

O Lord, make us creative in methods of reaching Your needy, sin-sick ones and make us bold enough to follow those methods amid any dangers.

From the pen of Jim Reimann:

Spurgeon says today that "Jesus was there to heal," and, in that regard, there is an interesting phrase in Luke's account of the story: "The power of the Lord was *present* for him to heal the sick" (Luke 5:17). An alternative reading is that "the power of the Lord was 'with Him' to heal the sick." This is, of course, the power of the Holy Spirit, and one of the beautiful aspects of the Spirit's power is that even though it is exerted for various works, such as healing, it is never diminished.

As Jesus would heal others, the power of the Spirit would flow from Him to others. For example, "The people all tried to touch him, because power was coming from him and healing them all" (Luke 6:19), and "At once Jesus realized that power had gone out from him" (Mark 5:30). And as the Lord told His followers just before His ascension into heaven, "*You will receive power* when the Holy Spirit comes on you...." But notice the rest of the sentence, which gives us the purpose for His power coming upon us: "*You will be my witnesses* in Jerusalem, and in all Judea and Samaria, and to the ends of the earth" (Acts 1:8).

September 8

Your fruitfulness comes from me.

Hosea 14:8

From the pen of Charles Spurgeon:

Our fruit is a direct result of our union with God. And since the fruit of the branch is directly traceable to the root, when the connection is severed, the branch dies and no fruit is produced. By virtue of our union with Christ, we bring forth fruit, and just as each bunch of grapes began in the root, passed through the stem, flowed through the sap veins, and is finally fashioned into external fruit, every good work is first in Christ before being brought forth externally in us.

Dear Christian, greatly value your precious union to Christ, for it is the source of all the fruitfulness you can hope to know. If you were not joined to Jesus Christ, you would be an extremely barren branch.

Our fruit is a direct result of God's sovereignty. When the dew falls from heaven, when a cloud looks down from above and is about to distill its liquid treasure, and when the bright sun increases the fruit in a cluster, each heavenly blessing could whisper to the tree and say, "Your fruitfulness comes from me." Yes, the fruit owes much to the root, which is essential to its fruitfulness, but it also owes much to external influences. Thus, consider how much we owe to God's sovereign grace! It is His grace that constantly provides us with life, guidance, comfort, strength, and anything else we need. We owe all our usefulness and goodness to His grace.

Our fruit is a direct result of God's wise gardening. The gardener's pruning knife promotes the fruitfulness of the vine by thinning clusters and cutting off excess shoots. It is the same, dear Christian, with the pruning the Lord gives you. Jesus said, "I am the true vine, and my Father is the gardener. He cuts off every branch in me that bears no fruit, while every branch that does bear fruit he prunes so that it will be even more fruitful" (John 15:1 – 2).

Thus, since God is the author of all our spiritual gifts of grace, may we give Him all the glory of our salvation.

From the pen of Jim Reimann:

Remember the words of Jesus, who said, "No branch can bear fruit by itself.... Neither can you bear fruit unless you remain in me. I am the vine; you are the branches.... Apart from me you can do nothing" (John 15:4 – 5). And when Spurgeon says, "May we give [God] all the glory of our salvation," he is not referring to just the moment the Lord saved our soul but is referring to our ongoing salvation, growth, and fruitfulness in Jesus Christ as well. Here is how Jesus put it, "This is to my Father's glory, that you bear much fruit, showing yourselves to be my disciples" (John 15:8).

As confirmation of these thoughts, here is the context of our text verse today, along with the Lord's final admonition given through Hosea:

> I will be like the dew to Israel; he will blossom like a lily. Like a cedar of Lebanon he will send down his roots; his young shoots will grow. His splendor will be like an olive tree, his fragrance like a cedar of Lebanon. Men will dwell again in his shade. He will flourish like the grain. He will blossom like a vine, and his fame will be like the wine from Lebanon.... Who is wise? He will realize these things. Who is discerning? He will understand them. The ways of the LORD are right; the righteous walk in them, but the rebellious stumble in them.

> Hosea 14:5 – 7, 9

SEPTEMBER 9

Call to me and I will answer you
and tell you great and unsearchable things you do not know.

Jeremiah 33:3

From the pen of Charles Spurgeon:

One translation renders this verse, "I will tell you great and fortified things," while another says "great and reserved things." The idea is that there are certain things reserved for Christians, and yet every believer does not easily attain some of the higher things of the spiritual life. Of course there are some things the entire Christian family enjoys, such as repentance, faith, joy, and hope; but there is an upper realm of rapture of communion with Christ and awareness of Him that is far from being the common dwelling place of believers. Everyone does not have the privilege of John of "leaning back against Jesus" (John 13:25), nor of Paul who was "caught up to the third heaven" (2 Cor. 12:2). There are heights of experiential knowledge of the things of God that even those with an eagle's eye for learning and philosophy have never seen. God alone can take us there, but the chariot He uses to uplift us and the "horses of fire" (2 Kings 2:11) by which the chariot is pulled is powerful, prevailing prayer.

Prevailing prayer is victorious over the God of mercy — "As a man [Jacob] struggled with God. He struggled with the angel and overcame him; he wept and begged for his favor. He found him at Bethel and talked with him there" (Hos. 12:3 – 4). Prevailing prayer takes a Christian to the top of Mount Carmel and enables him to cover the heavens with clouds of blessing and the earth with floods of mercy. (See 1 Kings 18:42 – 45.) Prevailing prayer lifts a Christian to Mount Nebo and shows him the inheritance reserved for him. (See Deut. 34:1 – 4.) It elevates him to Mount Tabor and transfigures him so he reflects the likeness of his Lord to this world. (See Luke 9:28 – 36.) [Editor's note: Mount Tabor is the traditional site of the Transfiguration. Yet Mount Hermon is the more likely site, for in each of the three gospel accounts the preceding story took place at Caesarea Philippi near Mount Hermon, Israel's highest mountain.]

If you desire to reach something higher than an ordinary, lowly existence, look to the Rock who is higher than you and gaze with eyes of faith through the window of persistent prayer. Once you unlock the window on your side of heaven, you will find it unlocked on the other side as well.

From the pen of Jim Reimann:

Consider how David's prevailing prayer moved omnipotent God:

In my distress I called to the LORD; I cried to my God for help. From his temple he heard my voice; my cry came before him, into his ears. The earth trembled and quaked, and the foundations of the mountains shook; they trembled because he was angry. Smoke rose from his nostrils; consuming fire came from his mouth, burning coals blazed out of it. He parted the heavens and came down; dark clouds were under his feet. He mounted the cherubim and flew; he soared on the wings of the wind. He made darkness his covering, his canopy around him — the dark rain clouds of the sky. Out of the brightness of his presence clouds advanced, with hailstones and bolts of lightning. The LORD thundered from heaven; the voice of the Most High resounded.... The valleys of the sea were exposed and the foundations of the earth laid bare at [His] rebuke.... He rescued me from my powerful enemy ... who [was] too strong for me.

Psalm 18:6 – 13, 15, 17

SEPTEMBER 10

Jesus went up on a mountainside and called to him
those he wanted, and they came to him.

Mark 3:13

From the pen of Charles Spurgeon:

This is an example of God's sovereignty. Impatient souls may fret and fume because they are not called to the highest places of ministry, but dear reader, let your heart rejoice that Jesus calls whom He wills. If He asks you to be only "a doorkeeper in [His] house" (Ps. 84:10), cheerfully bless Him for His grace in allowing you to do anything in His service.

The call of Christ's servants comes from above. Jesus stands on His mountain, eternally higher than the world in holiness, sincerity, love, and power. Those whom He calls must go up the mountain to Him and must seek to rise to His level by living in constant communion with Him. They may not be able to rise to the highest positions of all or attain the greatest level of knowledge, but like Moses, they must climb "the mountain of God" (Ex. 24:13) and have intimate communion with the unseen God or else they will never be fit to proclaim "the gospel of peace" (Eph. 6:15). Jesus "went up on a mountainside by himself" (Matt. 14:23) to have holy fellowship with the Father, and we must enter into the same divine companionship if we hope to be a blessing to our fellow man. No wonder the apostles were clothed with power as soon as they returned from the mountain where Jesus was. (See Matt. 28:16 – 20.)

This morning we must endeavor to ascend the mountain of communion so we may be ordained for the calling for which we have been set apart by God. May we not see the face of another person today until we have seen Jesus, for time spent with Him is the most blessed use of our time. We too will cast out demons and work miracles if we descend to the world strengthened with the divine power that only Christ can give. There is no use to even go to the Lord's battle until we are armed with heavenly weapons. It is essential we see Jesus. We must linger at His "mercy seat" (Ex. 25:17 KJV) until He reveals Himself to us in ways He does not reveal Himself to the world and until we can truthfully say, "We were with him on the sacred mountain" (2 Peter 1:18).

From the pen of Jim Reimann:

Everyone loves the view from the mountaintop, and in the Scriptures mountains are often connected to the very presence of God and time alone with Him. Many major biblical events took place on mountains, but unless we are careful we will revere the mountain itself, rather than God. Notice that nearly every time Israel turned away from God they set up "high places" with altars to pagan gods, but the Lord warned, "If you do not listen to me … I will destroy your high places" (Lev. 26:27, 30).

And consider Jesus' conversation with the woman at the well:

> Jesus declared, "Believe me, woman, a time is coming when you will worship the Father neither on this mountain nor in Jerusalem.… A time is coming and has now come when the true worshipers will worship the Father in spirit and truth, for they are the kind of worshipers the Father seeks. *God is spirit, and his worshipers must worship in spirit and in truth.*"
>
> John 4:21, 23 – 24

Lord, may my heart long for daily time with You on Your mountain, and may I faithfully serve and worship You in the calling You gave me while there.

SEPTEMBER 11

Be separate.

2 Corinthians 6:17

From the pen of Charles Spurgeon:

As a Christian, you are "still in the world" (John 17:11) but are not to be "of the world" (John 17:14). What should set you apart is the object of your life. For you "to live" should be "Christ" (Phil. 1:21). "So whether you eat or drink or whatever you do, do it all for the glory of God" (1 Cor. 10:31). You may store up treasure but store it up "in heaven, where moth and rust do not destroy, and where thieves do not break in and steal" (Matt. 6:20). You may strive to be rich but let your ambition be to be "rich in faith" (James 2:5) and "good deeds" (1 Tim. 6:18). You may enjoy yourself, but when you are happy, "Speak to one another with psalms, hymns and spiritual songs. Sing and make music in your heart to the Lord" (Eph. 5:19).

You should differ from the world in your goals and in your spirit. You prove you are of a heavenly race by walking humbly before God, always being aware of His presence, delighting in communing with Him, and seeking to know His will. You should also differ from the world in your actions. Even if something is considered right, if you lose by doing it, it must not be done; and if something is definitely wrong, although you would gain by doing it, you must shun the sin for your Master's sake. You must have no "fellowship … with darkness" (2 Cor. 6:14) and its unfruitful works, but instead should reject them. Walk worthy of your high calling and position.

Remember, believer, you are a child of the "KING OF KINGS" (Rev. 19:16). Therefore keep yourself untarnished by the world. Don't dirty your fingers, which will soon be strumming celestial strings. Don't allow your eyes, which will soon see the King in His beauty, to become windows of lust. Don't let your feet, that will soon be walking streets of gold, to become mired in filth. And don't allow your heart to be filled with pride and bitterness, for that same heart will soon be filled with heaven itself and will overflow with rapturous joy.

> Then rise my soul! and soar away,
> Above the thoughtless crowd;
> Above the pleasures of the day,
> And splendors of the proud;
> Up where eternal beauties bloom,
> And pleasures all divine;
> Where wealth, that never can consume,
> And endless glories shine.
> Henry Moore, 1732 – 1802

From the pen of Jim Reimann:

Our text is from the following passage, and is worthy of review:

> Do not be yoked together with unbelievers. For what do righteousness and wickedness have in common? Or what fellowship can light have with darkness? What harmony is there between Christ and Belial? What does a believer have in common with an unbeliever? What agreement is there between the temple of God and idols? *For we are the temple of the living God.* As God has said: "I will live with them and walk among them, and I will be their God, and they will be my people. Therefore come out from them and *be separate.*"
> 2 Corinthians 6:14 – 17

SEPTEMBER 12

The LORD is a jealous ... God.

Nahum 1:2

From the pen of Charles Spurgeon:

Your Lord is very jealous for your love, dear believer. Did He choose you? Then He cannot bear for you to choose another. Did He buy you with His own blood? Then He cannot endure for you to think you are "your own" (1 Cor. 6:19) or that you belong to this world. He loved you with such great love that He would not live forever in heaven without you, and He would sooner die than allow you to perish. Thus, He cannot endure for anything to come between your heart's love and Himself.

Your Lord is very jealous for your trust. He will not permit you to trust in an "arm of flesh" (2 Chron. 32:8). He cannot bear to watch you digging in dried-out wells when His overflowing fountain is always free to you. He is glad when we lean on Him, but when we transfer our dependence to another, when we rely on our own wisdom or the wisdom of a friend, or — worst of all — when we trust in any works of our own, He is displeased and will discipline us in order to bring us back to Himself.

Your Lord is very jealous of your relationships. There should be no one with whom you converse as much as Jesus. To abide in Him alone shows true love, but to commune with the world, to find satisfaction in worldly comforts, or even to prefer the fellowship of fellow Christians above private communion with Him grieves your jealous Lord. He is pleased when we abide in Him, enjoying constant fellowship with Him, and many of the trials He sends us are intended to wean our hearts from the created and then refocus them more closely upon the Creator Himself.

May our Lord's jealousy, which is designed to keep us close to Christ, be a true comfort to us. For if He loves us so deeply, enough to care this much about our love for Him, we should be confident He will allow nothing to harm us and will protect us from all our enemies.

Oh, that we may have the grace today to keep our hearts in sacred fidelity for our Beloved alone, and may we with sacred jealousy close our eyes to all the enticements of the world!

From the pen of Jim Reimann:

Why is God a jealous God? Why is jealousy okay for Him, but not for us? It all comes down to the nature of the Lord, versus our nature. God is jealous for our love because of His nature to be absolutely faithful, while if we are jealous we would be hypocritical, for we often walk in unfaithfulness to Him. We allow many things to come between us and our fellowship with our faithful God.

The apostle Paul said to the young pastor Timothy, "If we are faithless, he will remain faithful, for he cannot disown himself" (2 Tim. 2:13). When Paul said, "He cannot disown himself," he means the Lord cannot violate His nature, and one of His attributes is His faithfulness. Thus, since He cannot be unfaithful, He alone can be righteously jealous.

We can take comfort in the fact, however, that although we walk in unfaithfulness from time to time, He has covered us with the righteousness of Christ and "chose us in him before the creation of the world to be holy and blameless in his sight" (Eph. 1:4).

SEPTEMBER 13

As they pass through the Valley of Baca,
they make it a place of springs; the autumn rains also cover it with pools.

Psalm 84:6

From the pen of Charles Spurgeon:

This verse teaches that the blessings obtained by one person often prove to be of service to others, just as these springs would provide refreshing water for those who followed. For example, a particular book may provide great comfort to others and to you, like Jonathan's staff "dipped … into the honeycomb" (1 Sam. 14:27), which provided honey for sustenance and brightened his eyes.

Suddenly we realize someone has been here before us and not only dug a well for himself but also for us. Books such as *Night of Weeping — Words for the Suffering Family of God* (by Horatius Bonar, 1808 – 1889), *Midnight Harmonies* (by Octavius Winslow, 1808 – 1878), *A Crook in the Lot* (by Thomas Boston, 1676 – 1732), and *Comfort for Mourners* (by Henry Law, 1797 – 1884), as well as the hymn "Eternal Day" (by Charles Wesley, 1707 – 1788), have all been wells dug by a fellow pilgrim for himself but also have proved to be just as useful to others.

We especially see this in the Psalms such as: "Why are you downcast, O my soul?" (Ps. 42:5). Travelers are always delighted to see the footprints of others on the barren shore ahead, and we love to see the evidence of fellow pilgrims while passing through the valley of tears. These pilgrims may dig the well, but strangely enough, it gets filled from the top, not the bottom. We may use the well, but the blessing does not spring from it, for it is heaven that fills it with rain. A warhorse may be prepared for battle, but safety is of the Lord. The means may be connected to the end, but the means does not produce the end itself. As in our text verse today, the rain fills the pools so that they become useful reservoirs for the water. The labor to dig the wells was important, but it would have been useless without God's divine work in sending the rain.

Grace is a good comparison to the rain for its purity, for its refreshing and revitalizing work, for the fact it is sent from above, and for the truth that it is a work of God's sovereignty in either being given or withheld. May you, dear reader, have showers of blessing, and may the wells you have dug be filled with water! Consider what your efforts would be without the smile of heaven! They would be like clouds without rain and pools without water.

O God of love, open the windows of heaven and pour us out a blessing!

From the pen of Jim Reimann:

Charles Spurgeon himself truly exemplifies today's devotion. He "dug the well" of these devotions, originally published in 1865, and today we are able to continue to drink from that well. Yet what would these devotions be without the Lord who poured the "rain" of insight and understanding into the life of Spurgeon? And what would they be without a life fully submitted to God and His Word?

Today Spurgeon mentions a number books, some written by his contemporaries and others from the previous century. As is often the case, men of God have reached back to the saints of old for instruction. Perhaps we should think of these saints reaching forward to us by the hand of God, lovingly teaching us by the power of the Holy Spirit and guiding us "into all truth" (John 16:13).

SEPTEMBER 14

There were also other boats with him.

Mark 4:36

From the pen of Charles Spurgeon:

Jesus was the Lord High Admiral of the sea that night and His presence preserved the entire fleet. It is good to sail with Jesus even if you are in a small boat. When we sail in Christ's fleet it does not necessarily mean fair weather for us, for huge storms may toss the ship carrying the Lord Himself. Thus, we should not expect to find the sea less rough around our little boat. If we travel with Jesus we must be content to fare as He fares and know that when the waves are rough for Him, they will be rough for us. It is through the tempest and tossing that we will reach the shore, just as He did before us. When the storm swept over Galilee's dark lake, all the faces there were dark as well and all the hearts dreaded shipwreck.

Yet when all creature help was useless, the slumbering Creator arose and, with a word, transformed the riotous storm into the deep quiet of pure calm. Then not only was the vessel that carried the Lord at rest but the others that were with Him on the lake were as well. Jesus is the Star of the sea, and although there may be sorrow on the sea, when He is present, joy abides there.

May our hearts make Jesus their anchor, rudder, lighthouse, lifeboat, and harbor. His church is the Admiral's flagship, so may we well attend to her movements and cheer her officers with our presence. Christ Himself is our great attraction, so may we ever follow in His wake, pay close attention to His signals, steer by His chart, and never fear while He is within earshot of our prayers. Not one ship in His fleet will suffer shipwreck, for the great Commodore will steer each one in safety to the desired haven.

By faith we will unmoor our boat for another day's cruise and sail forth with Jesus into a sea of tribulation. Winds and waves will not spare us, but they all obey Him. Therefore, whatever squalls may blow without, faith will feel a blessed calm within. The Lord is always in the midst of the weather-beaten fleet, so may we rejoice in Him. His ship has reached the haven, and so will ours.

From the pen of Jim Reimann:

The preceding verse of our text says, "When evening came, [Jesus] said to his disciples, "Let us go over to the other side" (Mark 4:35). Notice He did not say, "Let's go to the middle of the lake and drown." Of course, we know a storm came, Jesus rebuked it, and they ultimately made it to the other side.

After rebuking the wind and the waves, however, Jesus rebuked His disciples for their total lack of faith. He did not say to them, "Why do you have so *little* faith?" He said, instead, "Why are you so afraid? Do you still have *no* faith?" With faith they could have trusted in three things:

The promise of Jesus. He said, "Let us go over to the other side."

The presence of Jesus. He was in their boat — even through the storm.

The power of Jesus — to either transform the storm or to transform them.

It is worth noting that during the storm the disciples were afraid, but after the winds and waves were "completely calm" (v. 39), "they were terrified and asked each other, 'Who is this? Even the wind and the waves obey him!'" (v. 41). Storms may lead us as well to say, as Paul did on the Damascus Road, "Who are You, Lord?" (Acts 9:5). May we seek to "know him better" (Eph. 1:17)!

SEPTEMBER 15

A righteous man ... will have no fear of bad news.
Psalm 112:6–7

From the pen of Charles Spurgeon:

Dear Christian, you should never dread the arrival of bad news, and if you are someone who becomes distressed by it, consider what you have that others do not. Others do not have your God to run to and have never proved His faithfulness as you have done. Is it any wonder then that they cower in fear? You, however, profess to have a different spirit, for you have been "given ... new birth into a living hope" (1 Peter 1:3). Your heart lives in heaven and should not be swayed by "earthly things" (Phil. 3:19). If the world sees you as distressed as they are after receiving bad news, what is the value of the grace you profess to have received, and where is the worthiness of the new nature you claim to possess?

To reiterate, if you are filled with as much alarm as others, you would no doubt be led into sins common to them under trying circumstances. When the ungodly are overwhelmed by bad news they rebel against God, complaining and believing He has dealt too harshly with them. Will you fall into that same sin? Will you do as they do and "provoke the LORD to anger" (2 Kings 17:11 KJV)?

Additionally, the unconverted often run to the wrong things in order to escape their difficulties, and you will be sure to do the same if you allow your mind to yield to the current pressures. "Trust in the LORD" (Prov. 3:5) and "wait patiently for him" (Ps. 37:7). Your wisest course is to do as Moses did at the Red Sea: "Stand firm and you will see the deliverance the LORD will bring you today" (Ex. 14:13). If you give in to fear when you hear bad news, you will be unable to face the trial with the calm composure that strengthens you for service and that sustains you during adversity. How can you glorify God if you act like a coward? Many saints have often sung God's highest praises amid the fires of adversity, but do you believe your doubting and despondency, as though you had no one to help you, will bring glory to the Most High God?

Then have courage, and while relying in unwavering confidence on the faithfulness of your covenant God, "Do not let your hearts be troubled and do not be afraid" (John 14:27).

From the pen of Jim Reimann:

Fear is tied to sin in the Scriptures, for fear is the opposite of faith, and "everything that does not come from faith is sin" (Rom. 14:23). In fact, the very first mention of fear is immediately after Adam and Eve committed their first act of disobedience. When God called to Adam in the garden after he sinned, Adam told Him, "I was afraid because I was naked; so I hid" (Gen. 3:10). And the first admonition against fear is when "the word of the LORD came to Abram in a vision: 'Do not be afraid, Abram. I am your shield, your very great reward'" (Gen. 15:1).

Thus, fear is the result of sin. But notice that the first warning against fear came when the Lord confirmed His covenant with Abraham, in effect saying, "I am making a way for sin, and fear, to be taken away!"

"So we say with confidence, 'The Lord is my helper; I will not be afraid. What can man do to me?'" (Heb. 13:6).

Father, forgive me for my many fears.
Help me to walk in faith with You.

You may participate in the divine nature.

2 Peter 1:4

From the pen of Charles Spurgeon:

Of course, to "participate in the divine nature" is not to become God. That cannot happen, for the essence of Deity is not to be participated in by the creature. Between the creature and the Creator there will always be "a great chasm" (Luke 16:26) in respect to the essence of godhood. Yet just as the first man, Adam, was created "in the image of God" (Gen. 1:27), we too by the renewal of the Holy Spirit, in an even more divine sense, are made in the image of the Most High God and "participate in the divine nature."

We have been made in God's image by grace. Since "God is love" (1 John 4:8) we have become love — "Everyone who loves has been born of God" (1 John 4:7). God is truth; thus, we have become true and we love that which is true. God is good and He makes us good by His grace so that we become "the pure in heart" who "will see God" (Matt. 5:8).

In addition, we "participate in the divine nature" in even a higher sense than this — in fact, in as lofty a sense as can be conceived short of our becoming absolutely divine. Don't we become members of the body of the divine person of Christ? Yes, and the same blood that flows in the head flows in the hand, and the same life that makes Christ alive gives life to His people, "for you died, and your life is now hidden with Christ in God" (Col. 3:3). And if this were not enough, we are married to Christ. He has betrothed, or pledged, us to Himself in righteousness and faithfulness, and we who are joined to the Lord are one in spirit with Him.

What a miraculous mystery! One with Jesus! We study it, but who can fully understand it? We are so perfectly one with Him that as the branch is one with the vine, we are just as much a part of our Lord, Savior, and Redeemer! While we rejoice in this, may we remember that those who "participate in the divine nature" will reveal their high and holy relationship in their dealings with others, and may we make it evident by our daily walk and conversation that we have escaped the corruption that is in the world through the lust of the flesh.

Oh, that we may have more divine holiness of life!

From the pen of Jim Reimann:

What an amazing thing that our Lord allows us to participate in His nature! Rather than becoming proud over this, however, we should approach the Lord with great humility, as David did in the following psalm. May this be our prayer today:

"O Lord, our Lord, how majestic is your name in all the earth! You have set your glory above the heavens. From the lips of children and infants you have ordained praise because of your enemies, to silence the foe and the avenger. When I consider your heavens, the work of your fingers, the moon and the stars, which you have set in place, what is man that you are mindful of him, the son of man that you care for him? You made him a little lower than the heavenly beings and crowned him with glory and honor. You made him ruler over the works of your hands; you put everything under his feet: all flocks and herds, and the beasts of the field, the birds of the air, and the fish of the sea, all that swim the paths of the seas. O Lord, our Lord, how majestic is your name in all the earth!" (Ps. 8:1 – 9).

Bring the boy to me.

Mark 9:19

From the pen of Charles Spurgeon:

The poor disappointed father turned away in despair from the disciples to their Master. The man's son was in the worst possible condition and everything he tried had failed, but the suffering child was quickly delivered from the Evil One when, in faith, the father obeyed the Lord Jesus' words: "Bring the boy to me." Children are a precious gift and "heritage from the LORD" (Ps. 127:3), but a great deal of anxiety comes with them. They may bring great joy or great misery to their parents, and they may be filled with the Spirit of God or possessed by the spirit of evil. Yet in every case the Word of God gives us one remedy for the cure of all their troubles, "Bring [them] to me."

Oh, that we would agonize in prayer on their behalf while they are still babies! Their sin nature is there, so may our prayers begin to attack sin early. Our cries in prayer for our children should precede the crying we will endure upon their actual first steps into the world of sin. When our children are teenagers, we may see sad signs of that "deaf and dumb" spirit causing them to refuse to pray or hear the voice of God in their soul, but Jesus still commands, "Bring [them] to me." And once they become adults, they may still wallow in sin and rage with hostility toward God. Yet even then, when our hearts are breaking, we should remember the great Physician's words, "Bring [them] to me." We must never cease to pray for them until they cease to breathe, for no case is hopeless while Jesus lives.

Sometimes the Lord allows His people to be forced into a corner so they may truly learn from experience how vital He is to them. And ungodly children, especially when they reveal our own powerlessness against the depravity of their hearts, force us to run to our Lord for strength, which is a great blessing to us.

Whatever your need may be this morning, may it be a strong river taking you to the ocean of God's divine love. Jesus can quickly remove your sorrow, for He delights to comfort you. May you quickly run to Him while He waits to meet with you.

From the pen of Jim Reimann:

Have you ever noticed how children do not need to be taught to be selfish, to lie, to take from others, or to use words such as *I, me, my,* or *mine*? What could be greater proof that we are all born with original sin? Here is how God's Word puts it: "Surely I was sinful at birth, sinful from the time my mother conceived me" (Ps. 51:5). "Even from birth the wicked go astray; from the womb they are wayward and speak lies" (Ps. 58:3). "Folly is bound up in the heart of a child, but the rod of discipline will drive it far from him" (Prov. 22:15). "You have neither heard nor understood; from of old your ear has not been open. Well do I know how treacherous you are; you were called a rebel from birth" (Isa. 48:8).

All this points to exactly why we need a Savior and why as parents we must run to Him for help. Jesus said, "Let the little children come to me, and do not hinder them" (Mark 10:14). And not only should we "not hinder them" but we must be proactive, and as the Lord also said, "*Bring* [them] to me."

Godly parents will take their children to Jesus through prayer continually and will "bring them up in the training and instruction of the Lord" (Eph. 6:4).

SEPTEMBER 18

Since we live by the Spirit,
let us keep in step with the Spirit.

Galatians 5:25

From the pen of Charles Spurgeon:

The two most important things in our holy religion are the life of faith and the walk of faith. If you understand these, you are not far from mastering theology, at least from an experiential point of view, for they are vital points for a Christian. You will never find true faith apart from true godliness, and, conversely, you will never discover a truly holy life whose root is not a living faith based on the righteousness of Christ. And woe to those who seek one without the other!

There are some people who cultivate faith while forgetting holiness. Their professed beliefs may be high in orthodoxy, but they will be deep in condemnation, for they profess the truth but walk in unrighteousness. Then there are others who strive to live a holy life while denying the faith. They are akin to the Pharisees of old whom the Master said were like "whitewashed tombs" (Matt. 23:27).

We must have faith, for it is the foundation; and we must have a holy life, for it is the structure above the foundation. What good is a mere foundation of a building to a man weathering a storm? Can he hide himself in the foundation and be protected? No, he needs a house to cover himself as well as a foundation for the house. In the same way, we need the structure of a holy spiritual life if we are to have comfort in a time of doubt. But we should never seek a holy life without faith, for that would be to erect a house that can offer no permanent shelter because its foundation is not built "upon a rock" (Ps. 27:5).

Faith and a holy life must go together. Then, like two bridge abutments, they make our arch of spiritual devotion strong and enduring. Like light and heat streaming from one and the same sun, they are full of blessings. Like the "two pillars" (2 Chron. 3:15) of the temple, faith and holiness are for glory and beauty. They are two streams flowing from the fountain of grace, two lamps lit with holy fire, and two olive trees watered by heavenly care.

Lord, give us life within today, and may it reveal itself without to Your glory.

From the pen of Jim Reimann:

Spurgeon uses the word *religion* today, referring to "the two most important things in our holy *religion*." Today, however, the word *religion* has come to mean a works-based method of attempting to obtain salvation, which is why believers will often say, "Christianity is not a religion, it's a relationship." Yet both the King James and the New International Versions of the Bible, as well as many others today, still use the word *religion* in regard to Christianity.

As you read the following words of James from the NIV, notice his emphasis on purity: "If anyone considers himself religious and yet does not keep a tight rein on his tongue, he deceives himself and his religion is worthless. Religion that God our Father accepts as pure and faultless is this: to look after orphans and widows in their distress and to keep oneself from being polluted by the world" (James 1:26–27).

Thus, when it comes to our "religion," may Jesus never have to say, "Woe to you ... you hypocrites!" (Matt. 23:27).

SEPTEMBER 19

It is for freedom that Christ has set us free.

Galatians 5:1

From the pen of Charles Spurgeon:

This freedom we have makes us a party to heaven's constitution — the Bible. Dear believer, here is a blessed passage for you: "When you pass through the waters, I will be with you" (Isa. 43:2). You have freedom to partake of this promise. Here is another: "Though the mountains be shaken and the hills be removed, yet my unfailing love for you will not be shaken nor my covenant of peace be removed" (Isa. 54:10). You have freedom in that as well, for you are a welcome guest at the table of the promises of God. Scripture is a never-failing treasury filled with a limitless abundance of grace. It is the bank of heaven from which you may draw as much as you please without any obstruction or restriction whatsoever.

Come in faith and you are welcome to all the covenant blessings. Not one promise in the Word will be withheld. When you are in the depths of tribulation let this freedom comfort you, when you are amid the waves of distress let it cheer you, and when sorrows surround you let it be your solace. This is your Father's symbol of love, and you are free to partake at any time.

You also have the freedom to "approach the throne of grace" (Heb. 4:16). (Also see Eph. 3:12.) As a believer, it is your privilege to have access at all times to your heavenly Father. Whatever your desires, difficulties, or needs, you have the liberty to place them all before him. No matter how much we have sinned, we may ask for and expect His pardon. Regardless of how poor we are, we may plead His promise that He will provide everything we need. We have permission to approach His throne at all times, whether at midnight's darkest hour or during midday's most burning heat.

Therefore, exercise your right, dear believer, and live up to your privilege. You are free to partake of all the treasures of Christ — wisdom, righteousness, sanctification, and redemption. Whatever your need, there is a full supply in Christ awaiting you.

Oh, what freedom is yours! Freedom from condemnation, freedom to partake in God's promises, freedom to approach the throne of grace, and finally — freedom to enter heaven!

From the pen of Jim Reimann:

Jesus once quoted an Old Testament prophecy of Himself regarding freedom, which says, "The Spirit of the Sovereign LORD is on me, because *the LORD has anointed me to ... proclaim freedom for the captives and release from darkness for the prisoners*" (Isa. 61:1). And who are the captives and prisoners he came to free? The answer is, as Hebrews puts it: "the children God has given [Jesus]," for it goes on to say, "Since the children have flesh and blood, he too shared in their humanity so that by his death he might destroy him who holds the power of death — that is, the devil — and *free those who all their lives were held in slavery*" (Heb. 2:13 – 15).

Thus, as a child of God, may my prayer be the same as the psalmist:

> "*May your unfailing love come to me, O LORD, your salvation according to your promise. I will walk about in freedom, for I have sought out your precepts*" (Ps. 119:41, 45).

SEPTEMBER 20

A sword for the LORD and for Gideon!
Judges 7:20

From the pen of Charles Spurgeon:

Gideon ordered his men to do two things: At his signal they were to break jars with torches inside, allowing the light to shine. He also ordered, "When I and all who are with me blow our trumpets, then from all around the camp blow yours and shout, 'For the LORD and for Gideon'" (Judg. 7:18).

This is precisely what all Christians must do. First, you must shine, breaking the jar that hides your light, removing the bowl that has been hiding it. "Let your light shine before men" (Matt. 5:16). Let your good deeds be such that others will take "note that [you have] been with Jesus" (Acts 4:13).

Then you must blow the trumpet. There must be intentional efforts to bring sinners into the kingdom by proclaiming "Christ crucified" (1 Cor. 1:23). Take the gospel to them, carrying it to their door, placing it in their way, not allowing them to escape it, blowing the trumpet in their ears.

Yet remember that the true war cry of the church is Gideon's watchword: "A sword for the LORD and for Gideon!" God must do it. It is His work. But we are not to be idle; we are to be a vessel to be used. It is "A sword for the LORD"—and—"for Gideon!" If we only shout, "A sword for the LORD," we will be guilty of idle presumption; and if we shout, "A sword for Gideon!" alone, we will reveal an idolatrous reliance on "only the arm of flesh" (2 Chron. 32:8). We must balance the two in effective harmony: "A sword for the LORD and for Gideon!"

We can do nothing by ourselves, but we can do everything through the help of our God.

May we be determined, therefore, to go out in His name, personally serving with the flaming torch of a holy example and with trumpet notes of earnest proclamation and testimony. God will be with us, Midian will be thrown into confusion (see Judg. 7:22), and the Lord of hosts "will reign for ever and ever" (Rev. 11:15).

From the pen of Jim Reimann:

The story of Gideon is another example of how the Lord uses the "nobodies" of the world to His glory. Before Gideon became the commander of the Lord's army, he was a coward, "threshing wheat in a winepress to keep it from the Midianites" (Judg. 6:11) because he was afraid. Yet "the angel of the LORD appeared to him" and said, "The LORD is with you, mighty warrior. Go in the strength you have and save Israel out of Midian's hand" (Judg. 6:12, 14).

Gideon did not feel like a "mighty warrior," however, for he responded, "But Lord, how can I save Israel? My clan is the weakest in Manasseh, and I am the least in my family" (Judg. 6:15). The tribe of Manasseh was considered by many to be somewhat of a laughingstock in Israel and, of course, Israel had been told: "The LORD did not set his affection on you and choose you because you were more numerous than other peoples, for *you were the fewest of all peoples*" (Deut. 7:7).

Thus, in effect, Gideon was the least in his family, his family was the least in his tribe, Manasseh was the least tribe of Israel, and Israel was the least of all nations. He was indeed "the least of the least of the least of the least"!

Now that is someone the Lord can use—someone who can bring Him great glory!

SEPTEMBER 21

I will rejoice in doing them good.

Jeremiah 32:41

From the pen of Charles Spurgeon:

How encouraging for believers to know that God rejoices in His saints! We cannot see any reason in ourselves for the Lord to take pleasure in us. And we cannot take delight in ourselves, for we recognize and are burdened with our sinfulness, thus deploring our own unfaithfulness to Him. We also fear that God's people cannot delight in us, for surely they discern many of our imperfections and foolish actions. In fact, they are more apt to mourn our weaknesses than admire our talents and strengths. Due to this, we love to dwell on this incomparable truth — this glorious mystery — that just as a bridegroom rejoices over his bride, the Lord rejoices over us.

Nowhere in the Scriptures do we read that God rejoices in cloud-capped mountains or sparkling stars, but we do read that He delights in places where His people are found, and that He rejoices in His people themselves. Nor do we see anywhere in God's Word where even angels bring His soul delight, for nowhere does He say, concerning cherubim and seraphim: "You will be called Hephzibah,... for the LORD will take delight in you" (Isa. 62:4). But He does say that to us — poor, fallen creatures, debased and depraved by sin — yet saved, exalted, and glorified by His grace.

How strongly God expresses His delight in His people! Who could have even conceived of the eternal One bursting forth into song? Yet His Word tells us: "He will take great delight in you, he will quiet you with his love, he will rejoice over you with singing" (Zeph. 3:17). As the Lord looked upon the world He had created, He said, "It was very good" (Gen. 1:31). But when He beheld those who were purchased by the blood of Jesus, His own chosen ones, it seems as though the great heart of the Infinite could no longer restrain itself, for it overflowed in divine exclamations of joy.

In light of this, we should declare our grateful response to the Lord's miraculous declaration of His love for us and sing to Him: "I will rejoice in the LORD, I will be joyful in God my Savior" (Hab. 3:18).

From the pen of Jim Reimann:

Speaking of rejoicing, we as believers can rejoice over what the Lord has prepared for His people, for He has said:

Behold, I will create new heavens and a new earth. The former things will not be remembered, nor will they come to mind. But *be glad and rejoice forever in what I will create, for I will create Jerusalem to be a delight and its people a joy. I will rejoice over Jerusalem and take delight in my people;* the sound of weeping and of crying will be heard in it no more.... They will build houses and dwell in them; they will plant vineyards and eat their fruit. No longer will they build houses and others live in them, or plant and others eat. For as the days of a tree, so will be the days of my people; my chosen ones will long enjoy the works of their hands. They will not toil in vain or bear children doomed to misfortune; for they will be a people blessed by the LORD, they and their descendants with them. Before they call I will answer; while they are still speaking I will hear.

Isaiah 65:17 – 19, 21 – 24

Father, how amazing that You rejoice in me! I rejoice in You today!

Let Israel rejoice in their Maker.

Psalm 149:2

From the pen of Charles Spurgeon:

Rejoice in your heart, dear believer, but remember that the source of your gladness is the Lord Himself. You have great reason for gladness in your God, so you can sing with the psalmist, "God, my joy and my delight" (Ps. 43:4). Be glad that the Lord reigns — that Jehovah is King! Rejoice that He sits upon the throne and rules all things! Every attribute of God should be like a bright ray in the sunlight of our gladness, and the fact that He is wise should make us glad, especially since we know our own foolishness so well.

That He is mighty should cause us, who tremble at our own weakness, to rejoice. That the Lord is everlasting should always be a theme of joy because we know "people are grass" and "the grass withers" (Isa. 40:7 – 8). That He is unchanging should forever cause us to sing, since we change every hour. That He is full of grace — in fact, overflowing with grace — and that His grace has been given to us through His covenant, that it is ours for cleansing, ours to preserve us, ours to sanctify us, ours to perfect us, and ours to ultimately take us to glory should make us rejoice in Him.

Our gladness in God is like a deep river, yet thus far we have only touched the river's edge. We know a little of its clear, fresh heavenly streams, but further ahead its depth is greater and its current more swift and powerful in its joy. What a joyful thing that Christians may rejoice not only in who God is, but also in all God has done in the past. The Psalms reveal that God's people of old were accustomed to meditate on God's actions and to have a song preserving the memory of each of them.

May God's people today remember the works of the Lord! May we tell of His mighty acts and "sing to the LORD, for he is highly exalted" (Ex. 15:1). May we "[sing] to the LORD every day" (2 Chron. 30:21), for as new mercies flow to us day by day, so should our gladness for the Lord's loving, sovereign acts of grace manifest itself in continual thanksgiving to Him.

"Be glad, O people of Zion, rejoice in the LORD your God" (Joel 2:23).

From the pen of Jim Reimann:

Paul began his "Epistle of Joy" to the church at Philippi with: "I thank my God every time I remember you. In all my prayers for all of you, I always pray with joy" (Phil. 1:3 – 4). Later he says, "Finally, my brothers, rejoice in the Lord!" (Phil. 3:1), but he was not yet finished exhorting us to rejoice, for in the last chapter he reiterates the thought with these other important instructions to us as believers:

Rejoice in the Lord always. I will say it again: Rejoice! Let your gentleness be evident to all. The Lord is near. Do not be anxious about anything, but in everything, by prayer and petition, with thanksgiving, present your requests to God. And the peace of God, which transcends all understanding, will guard your hearts and your minds in Christ Jesus.

Finally, brothers, whatever is true, whatever is noble, whatever is right, whatever is pure, whatever is lovely, whatever is admirable — if anything is excellent or praiseworthy — think about such things. Whatever you have learned or received or heard from me, or seen in me — *put it into practice.*

Philippians 4:4 – 9

SEPTEMBER 23

...accepted in the beloved.

Ephesians 1:6 KJV

From the pen of Charles Spurgeon:

Accepted! What a privilege! Being accepted includes our justification before God, but the term *acceptance* in the Greek means even more than that. It signifies we are also the objects of God's divine pleasure and delight. How miraculous that we — mere mortals and contemptible sinners — could be the objects of divine love! Yet it is only because we are "in the beloved."

Some Christians live as though they are "accepted in their own experience." At least that is their perception. When their spirits are upbeat and their hopes are bright, they think God accepts them. At those times they feel so elated and heavenly minded, they seem to float above the earth! But when their spirits are down and their souls seem to be trudging through the mud, they become victims of the fear that they are no longer accepted.

If only they could see that their highest joys do not exalt them in their Father's eyes, and that their lowest times of depression do not lessen them in His sight! If only they could understand they stand accepted in One who never changes, in One who is always "the beloved" of God, and in One who is always perfect — "without stain or wrinkle or any other blemish" (Eph. 5:27) — how much happier they would be and how much more they would honor the Savior!

Thus, dear believer, rejoice in this: You are "accepted in the beloved." Don't look at yourself, for you will have to say, "I see nothing acceptable here!" Instead, look at Christ and see that everything is acceptable there. If your past sins trouble you, remember: God has cast your sins behind His back, and you are accepted in the Righteous

One. Although you must continue to battle sinfulness and wrestle with temptation, you are already accepted in Him who has overcome the power of evil. The Devil will tempt you "but take heart" (John 16:33), he cannot destroy you, for you are accepted in Him who has crushed Satan's head. (See Gen. 3:15.)

"In full assurance of faith" (Heb. 10:22), know your glorious standing. Even the glorified souls already in heaven are not more accepted than you. Even there they are accepted only because they are "in the beloved."

You are accepted in Christ in the same way — and you are accepted now!

From the pen of Jim Reimann:

Our text verse today comes from Ephesians, chapter one. Notice Paul's message, reiterated for our benefit in just the first few verses of his letter:

"To the...faithful *in Christ Jesus*..." (Eph. 1:1).

"God...has blessed us...with every spiritual blessing *in Christ*" (v. 3).

"He chose us *in him* before the creation of the world" (v. 4).

"His glorious grace ... he has freely given *in the One he loves*" (v. 6).

"*In him* we have redemption through his blood" (v. 7).

"He made known ... the mystery of his will ... *in Christ*" (v. 9).

"*In him* we were also chosen" (v. 11).

"We, who were the first to hope *in Christ* ..." (v. 12).

"You also were included *in Christ*" (v. 13).

> Lord, I thank You that "my beloved is mine, and I am his" (Song 2:16 KJV).

September 24

I was ashamed to ask the king for soldiers and horsemen to protect us from enemies on the road,
because we had told the king, "The gracious hand of our God is on everyone who looks to him,
but his great anger is against all who forsake him."

From the pen of Charles Spurgeon:

A security entourage would be a desirable thing for some travelers, but a holy concern of being shamed and embarrassed would not allow Ezra to ask for one. He was afraid the heathen king would think his declarations of faith in God would be perceived as mere hypocrisy, or that the king would believe the God of Israel was unable to preserve His own worshipers. Ezra would not allow even his mind to lean on an "arm of flesh" (2 Chron. 32:8) in a matter so evidently of the Lord. Therefore his caravan set out without any visible protection, but guarded by Him who is the sword and shield of His people.

What a shame that so few believers have such a holy jealousy for God as Ezra, even those who in some respects walk by faith, but who occasionally mar the luster of their testimony by craving help from man! It is the most blessed thing to have no safety fallback position or, in other words, to "work without a net" — standing upright and firm on the Rock of Ages, upheld by the Lord alone.

Would any believers really want government financial aid for their church if they remembered that the Lord is dishonored by asking for Caesar's help, as though God could not supply for the needs of His own cause! Would we be so quick to run to friends and family for assistance if we remembered that the Lord is glorified by our absolute reliance on His arm alone?

"My soul, wait ... only upon God" (Ps. 62:5 KJV). Someone may ask, "But aren't we to use everything at our disposal?" Of course we are, but our error seldom lies in neglecting to use whatever means we have, but far more frequently in foolishly believing in our means rather than believing in God. Few of us err in neglecting to use the help of others, but many of us sin in making too much of it.

Believer, learn to glorify the Lord by neglecting to use your own means or the help of others, if by using them you would dishonor the name of the Lord.

From the pen of Jim Reimann:

Indeed, we should honor the Lord by trusting solely in Him. If, however, you walk in fear of "going it alone," heed these words of the psalmist:

In my anguish I cried to the LORD, and he answered by setting me free. The LORD is with me; I will not be afraid. What can man do to me? The LORD is with me; he is my helper. I will look in triumph on my enemies. It is better to take refuge in the LORD than to trust in man. It is better to take refuge in the LORD than to trust in princes.

Psalm 118:5–9

Ezra certainly understood this truth, as did the apostle Paul, who on one of his missionary journeys went alone to Corinth, one of the most evil cities of the Roman Empire. Yet he was not alone, for "one night the Lord spoke to Paul in a vision: 'Do not be afraid; keep on speaking, do not be silent. For I am with you, and no one is going to attack and harm you'" (Acts 18:9–10).

Fear is sin and brings the opposite of safety, for "Fear of man will prove to be a snare, but whoever trusts in the LORD is kept safe" (Prov. 29:25).

SEPTEMBER 25

[God is] just and the one who justifies
those who have faith in Jesus.

Romans 3:26

From the pen of Charles Spurgeon:

"Since we have been justified through faith, we have peace with God" (Rom. 5:1), and even our consciences no longer accuse us. (See Rom. 2:15.) Judgment and justice now find in favor of the sinner instead of against him. Our memories look back on past sins with deep sorrow but without any dread of penalty to come, for Christ has paid the debt of His people to "the smallest letter" and "the least stroke of a pen" (Matt. 5:18). He has obtained a paid-in-full receipt, and unless God were so unjust as to demand double payment for the same debt, no soul for whom Jesus died as a substitute can ever be cast into hell.

One of the primary beliefs of our new nature is that God is just. At first this belief brings us great fear, but isn't it wonderful that this same belief in God's justice later becomes the very pillar of our confidence and peace! If God is just, a sinner without a substitutionary sacrifice must be punished, but Jesus stood in my place and has been punished for me. And now, if God is just, I — a sinner who stands in Christ — can never be punished. In fact, God would have to change His nature before one soul for whom Jesus died could suffer even one lash of the law.

Thus, since Jesus has taken the place of the believer — having received the full penalty for God's divine wrath and having suffered all that His people should have suffered as a result of their sin — believers can shout in glorious triumph, "Who will bring any charge against those whom God has chosen?" (Rom. 8:33). Certainly not God, for He has justified believers. Certainly not Christ, for He died to pay the price — and "He has risen from the dead" (Matt. 28:7).

My hope is alive not because I am not a sinner but because I am a sinner for whom Christ died. My trust lives not because I am holy but because, being unholy, He is my righteousness. My faith rests not on what I am or will be, or on what I feel or know, but on who Christ is, on what He has done, and on what He is still doing for me.

The fair maiden of hope rides as a queen on the lion of justice.

From the pen of Jim Reimann:

The verse preceding today's text is: "God presented [Jesus] as a sacrifice of atonement, through faith in his blood" (Rom. 3:25). Some other translations use the word *propitiation* instead of "sacrifice of atonement." This theological term means "the sacrifice that fully satisfies the wrath of God." Since God is holy and just, sin had to be judged. Thus, the verse continues:

> He did this to demonstrate his justice, because in his forbearance he had left the sins committed beforehand unpunished — he did it to demonstrate his justice at the present time, so as to be just and the one who justifies those who have faith in Jesus.
>
> Romans 3:25 – 26

This means God had to judge sin "to demonstrate his justice" and "to be just" — or *to remain just*. God "does not change" (James 1:17) and "cannot disown himself" (2 Tim. 2:13). Therefore, the Lord cannot disown His nature to be just.

"This is love … he loved us and sent his Son to be the propitiation for our sins" (1 John 4:10 ESV).

SEPTEMBER 26

During the night I had a vision — and there before me was a man riding a red horse!
He was standing among the myrtle trees in a ravine.

Zechariah 1:8

From the pen of Charles Spurgeon:

Zechariah's vision describes the condition of Israel in his day but may also be interpreted as prophecy describing God's church today. The church is described as flourishing "myrtle trees in a ravine." The trees, by virtue of being "in a ravine," were hidden, unseen, and thus, were not seeking any honor for themselves or attracting any attention from a casual observer. The church, like Jesus her head, has glory, but it is concealed today from human eyes, for the time of the church being revealed in all her splendor has not yet come.

The vision also suggests the idea of tranquil security, for the myrtle trees lie in the calm, peaceful ravine, while storms sweep across mountain summits. Violent winds bear down on the craggy peaks of the Alps, but down below "there is a river whose streams make glad the city of God" (Ps. 46:4). The myrtles flourish "beside quiet waters" (Ps. 23:2), unshaken by the raging wind.

Thus, how great is the inner tranquility of God's church! Even when opposed and persecuted, she has a "peace … not … as the world gives" (John 14:27) and, thus, which the world cannot take away. It is "the peace of God, which transcends all understanding" and which "will guard [the] hearts and … minds" (Phil. 4:7) of God's people.

The vision strongly portrays the peaceful, yet perpetual, growth of God's saints. Just as the myrtle does not shed its leaves, the church is "evergreen," and even in the most difficult times the church continues to have the blessed green lushness of grace about her. In fact, she appears to be the greenest during times of "winter" when the contrast of color is the sharpest, and she has prospered the most when her adversities have been the most severe.

Consequently the vision hints of victory as well, for not only is the myrtle a symbol of peace but it is also a strong symbol of triumph. In days of old, conquerors were crowned with wreaths of myrtle and laurel, and isn't the church eternally victorious? Aren't all believers "more than conquerors through him who loved us" (Rom. 8:37)? Thus, living in peace, the saints of God ultimately fall asleep in the arms of victory.

From the pen of Jim Reimann:

Our text today of Zechariah's vision, of a man on a red horse standing among myrtle trees in a ravine, continues with the following:

> Behind him were red, brown and white horses. I asked, "What are these, my lord?" The angel who was talking with me answered, "I will show you what they are." Then the man standing among the myrtle trees explained, "They are the ones the LORD has sent to go throughout the earth." And they reported to the angel of the LORD, who was standing among the myrtle trees, "We have gone throughout the earth and found the whole world at rest and in peace."
>
> Zechariah 1:8 – 11

Obviously, this refers to the future to come of everlasting peace. Yet, as believers, isn't that exactly what the Lord has promised for this life, for He said, "In me you may have peace. In this world you will have trouble. But take heart! I have overcome the world" (John 16:33).

SEPTEMBER 27

Blessed are you, O Israel! Who is like you, a people saved by the LORD?

Deuteronomy 33:29

From the pen of Charles Spurgeon:

Someone who believes Christianity makes people miserable is a complete stranger to it. Our faith would be strange indeed if it made us miserable, for consider the position to which we have been exalted — we are children of God! Do you believe God would reserve happiness for His enemies and only send mourning to His family? Should His foes have gladness and joy, while His own children inherit sorrow and misery? Should a sinner who has no part in Christ be rich in happiness, while we must mourn as though we were penniless beggars?

No! We will "rejoice in the Lord always" (Phil. 4:4) and glory in our inheritance, "for [we] did not receive a spirit that makes [us] a slave again to fear, but [we] received the Spirit of sonship. And by him we cry, 'Abba, Father'" (Rom. 8:15). As His children, "the rod of discipline" (Prov. 22:15) will rest on us when we deserve it, but it will also work in us the comforts of "the fruit of righteousness" (Phil. 1:11). As a result, through the aid of the divine Comforter, we — "a people saved by the LORD" — will rejoice in "God our Savior" (Ps. 68:19).

We are pledged to marriage with Christ, so can you imagine our loving Bridegroom allowing His bride to linger in constant grief? Our hearts are woven together with His and we are members of His body, and although we may suffer for a while, as our Head once suffered, we are even now blessed with heavenly blessings in Him. We have been given all the comforts of the Spirit, which are neither few nor small, along with the Spirit Himself who is the "deposit guaranteeing our inheritance" (Eph. 1:14). Thus, we are heirs of eternal joy and have already been given a foretaste of that inheritance. Even now we experience rays of the sunlight of joy as a prelude to our eternal sunrise.

Our everlasting riches lie beyond the sea; the eternal city with firm foundations lies on the other side of the river, and yet today, gleams of glory from the spiritual world ahead cheer our hearts and urge us onward. Truly this has been said of us: "Blessed are you, O Israel! Who is like you, a people saved by the LORD?"

From the pen of Jim Reimann:

Spurgeon briefly quotes from Romans 8 today. This beautiful chapter addresses the fact that we have already inherited God's blessings and the idea that we should be looking to Christ's return with eager, yet patient, anticipation. Here is how Paul said it:

> If we are children, then we are heirs — heirs of God and co-heirs with Christ, if indeed we share in his sufferings in order that we may also share in his glory. I consider that our present sufferings are not worth comparing with the glory that will be revealed in us. We know that the whole creation has been groaning as in the pains of childbirth right up to the present time....We ourselves ... groan inwardly as we wait eagerly for our adoption as sons, the redemption of our bodies. For in this hope we were saved. But hope that is seen is no hope at all. *Who hopes for what he already has? But if we hope for what we do not yet have, we wait for it patiently.*
>
> Romans 8:17 – 18, 22 – 25

SEPTEMBER 28

From heaven the LORD looks down and sees all mankind.

Psalm 33:13

From the pen of Charles Spurgeon:

Perhaps nothing describes our Lord with more grace than when He is shown as humbly stooping from His throne, descending from heaven to attend to the needs and woes of mankind. We love Him who would not destroy the wicked cities of Sodom and Gomorrah until He had personally visited them. (See Gen. 19.) We cannot help but pour out love to Him who inclines His ear from the highest glory, listening to the lips of a dying sinner whose failing heart longs for reconciliation with God. How can we not love Him when we know "the very hairs of [our] head[s] are all numbered" (Matt. 10:30), "the race [is] marked out for us" (Heb. 12:1), and our "steps ... are ordered by the LORD" (Ps. 37:23 KJV)?

As we consider how attentive He is to us, another great truth is that He is not merely focused on the temporal needs of His people but also on our spiritual concerns. And although there is a vast distance between the infinite Creator and us as His finite creatures, there are bonds uniting us with Him. For instance, when you shed a tear, never think God does not see, for "as a father has compassion on his children, so the LORD has compassion on those who fear him" (Ps. 103:13). Even your sigh is able to move the heart of Jehovah, your whisper can incline His ear toward you, your prayer can stop His hand, and your faith can move His arm.

Never think God is enthroned on high, paying no attention to you. Remember — no matter how "poor and needy" you may be, "the Lord think[s] of [you]" (Ps. 40:17). "For the eyes of the LORD range throughout the earth to strengthen those whose hearts are fully committed to him" (2 Chron. 16:9).

> Oh! Then repeat the truth that never tires;
> No God is like the God my soul desires;
> He at whose voice heaven trembles, even He,
> Great as He is, knows how to stoop to me.
> Madame Jeanne-Marie Guyon, 1648 – 1717

From the pen of Jim Reimann:

Our Lord Jesus left His throne, humbling Himself to become man. He identified with us as man so we may identify with Him in His glory. And Paul says we are to identify with Him in His humility as well:

> Your attitude should be the same as that of Christ Jesus: Who, being in very nature God, did not consider equality with God something to be grasped, but made himself nothing, taking the very nature of a servant, being made in human likeness. And being found in appearance as a man, he humbled himself and became obedient to death — even death on a cross! Therefore God exalted him to the highest place and gave him the name that is above every name, that at the name of Jesus every knee should bow, in heaven and on earth and under the earth, and every tongue confess that Jesus Christ is Lord, to the glory of God the Father.
> Philippians 2:5 – 11

God, thank You for our humble Savior — the "LORD OF LORDS" (Rev. 19:16)!

September 29

If the disease has covered his whole body,
he shall pronounce that person clean.

Leviticus 13:13

From the pen of Charles Spurgeon:

This regulation from Leviticus seems strange to us, yet there is wisdom in it. If someone could overcome a disease at this stage, it proved there was still strength and health in the body. But what is the application of such an unusual teaching for us this morning?

We are spiritual lepers and can apply this law for lepers to ourselves. It is only when someone sees himself as totally lost and ruined — completely covered with the defilement of sin with nothing free from its pollution, renouncing any claim of righteousness of his own, and pleading his guilt before the Lord — that he is clean by the blood of Jesus and the grace of God. Hidden, unfelt, and unconfessed sinfulness is the true leprosy, but once sin is acknowledged and felt, it has received its deathblow and the Lord looks with eyes of mercy on the soul afflicted with it. Nothing is more deadly than self-righteousness or more hopeful than sorrowful remorse.

We must confess that we are covered with sin, for no confession short of this will be the whole truth. If the Holy Spirit is truly at work in us, convicting us of sin, we will have no problem making such an admission. In fact, it will flow spontaneously from our lips.

What a great comfort our text affords those who are under a deep sense of their sin! Sin mourned and confessed, no matter how dark and foul, will never shut out someone from the Lord Jesus. "Whoever comes to me I will never drive away" (John 6:37). Although as dishonest as a thief, as unchaste as the "woman caught in adultery" (John 8:3), as sinister as Saul of Tarsus (Acts 9:11), as cruel as Manasseh (see 2 Kings 21:1 – 18), and as rebellious as the prodigal son (see Luke 15:11 – 32), the great heart of Love will look upon the person who sees nothing but sickness within himself and "shall pronounce that person clean" when he trusts in Jesus crucified.

"Come to me, all you who are weary and burdened [with sin]" (Matt. 11:28).

> Come needy, come guilty, come loathsome and bare;
> You can't come too filthy — come just as you are.
>
> Joseph Hart, 1712 – 1768

From the pen of Jim Reimann:

Acknowledgment of sin is the first step to spiritual health, for until we recognize our need, we will never go to the only One who can truly cleanse us. This is why believers are told:

> If we walk in the light, as he is in the light, we have fellowship with one another, and the blood of Jesus, his Son, purifies us from all sin. If we claim to be without sin, we deceive ourselves and the truth is not in us. *If we confess our sins, he is faithful and just and will forgive us our sins and purify us from all unrighteousness.* If we claim we have not sinned, we make him out to be a liar and his word has no place in our lives.
>
> 1 John 1:7 – 10

And to "walk in the light" of spiritual health, His Word *must* have its proper "place in our lives."

SEPTEMBER 30

Sing the glory of his name;
make his praise glorious!

Psalm 66:2

From the pen of Charles Spurgeon:

Whether to praise God is not an option we determine. Praise is the Lord's most rightful entitlement, and every Christian as a recipient of His grace is obligated to praise God day after day. Although it is true there is no authoritative legal requirement demanding our praise, and no commandment prescribing certain times each day for songs and thanksgiving, the law written on our hearts teaches us it is the right thing to do. And that mandate comes to us with as much force as though it had been written on tablets of stone and handed to us from the top of a thundering Mount Sinai.

Yes, it is a Christian's duty to praise God. It is not just a pleasurable exercise but is the absolute obligation of life. And if you think you are exempt from praising because of numerous times of mourning in your life, think again. You cannot fulfill your duty to your God without songs of praise. By the bonds of His love you are obligated to bless His name as long as you live, and "his praise [should] always be on [your] lips" (Ps. 34:1). You are blessed in order for you to bless Him — "The people I formed for myself that they may proclaim my praise" (Isa. 43:21). If you do not praise God, you are not bringing forth the fruit that He, as the Divine Gardener, has a right to expect.

Do not allow your harp to hang silently from the weeping willows (see Ps. 137:2), but take it down and, with a grateful heart, do your best to make beautiful music. Arise and sing His praise as each morning dawns, lifting up your notes of thanksgiving. And may your songs follow each day's setting sun as well. Encircle the earth with your praises, surrounding it with an atmosphere of melody, and God Himself will hear from heaven and will accept your music.

> E'en so I love You, and will love,
> And in Your praise will sing,
> Because You are my loving God,
> And my redeeming King.
>
> Francis Xavier, 1506 – 1552

From the pen of Jim Reimann:

It has often been said that we had better get used to praising the Lord here because we will be doing plenty of it in heaven. Although this is a true statement, it makes it seem as though lifting praise to God is a hardship or an unpleasant burden. Yet what John saw as he looked into heaven did not seem burdensome to those around God's throne. May the fact that God is worthy of our praise be our watchword today!

> Then I looked and heard the voice of many angels, numbering thousands upon thousands, and ten thousand times ten thousand. They encircled the throne and the living creatures and the elders. In a loud voice they sang: *"Worthy is the Lamb, who was slain, to receive power and wealth and wisdom and strength and honor and glory and praise!"* Then I heard every creature in heaven and on earth and under the earth and on the sea, and all that is in them, singing: "To him who sits on the throne and to the Lamb be praise and honor and glory and power, for ever and ever!" The four living creatures said, "Amen," and the elders fell down and worshiped.
>
> Revelation 5:11 – 14

October

OCTOBER 1

At our door is every delicacy, both new and old,
that I have stored up for you, my lover.

Song of Songs 7:13

From the pen of Charles Spurgeon:

The woman in today's text desires to give her lover all that she produces. Our hearts as well have "every delicacy, both new and old" fruits, that are "stored up for [our] lover." And now that we are into autumn, the richest season for fruit, may we consider what's in our storehouse.

We have "new" fruits. We have the desire to experience new life, new joys, and new gratitude. We desire to make new resolutions and carry them out through new efforts. Our heart blossoms with new prayers and our soul pledges itself to new endeavors.

We have some "old" fruits as well. There is our "first love" (Rev. 2:4), a choice fruit and one in which Jesus delights. There is our "first faith" (1 Tim. 5:12 KJV), that simple childlike faith by which, having nothing, we became possessors of all things. There is the joy of when we first met the Lord — may we revive it! We have our old remembrances of God's promises — how faithful He has been! In sickness, how soft He made our bed! In deep water, how peacefully He kept us afloat! In "the blazing furnace" (Dan. 3:17), how graciously He delivered us!

Indeed, we have many old fruits, for God's mercies have been more than the number of hairs on our head. And we have old sins, which we must regret, but we also have experienced many times of repentance. And it is through the Lord's gift of repentance to us that we have wept our way to the cross and learned the amazing worthiness of His blood.

Yes, we have many fruits this morning, "both new and old," but here is the main point: they are all "stored up" for Jesus. Surely the very best fruit is the service we do where Jesus is the solitary aim of our soul and where His glory is the focus of all our efforts. May our many fruits be "stored up" only for our beloved Lord. May we display them when He is with us for His glory alone — not to be seen by others.

Jesus, I unlock the door of my garden this morning. May no one enter to rob You of even one good fruit from the soil You watered with Your precious bloody sweat. My all is Yours and Yours alone, blessed Jesus, my Beloved!

From the pen of Jim Reimann:

It is interesting that Paul lists for us "the *acts* of the sinful nature," and then contrasts them to "the *fruit* of the Spirit" (Gal. 5:19, 22). Obviously he did not want to use the term *fruit* for things that are evil in nature. As we consider this, we must also be careful not to take credit for the fruit our lives produce, even as we dedicate that fruit to the Lord. In fact, immediately after Paul lists "the fruit of the Spirit" (Gal. 5:22), he gives us a warning: "Let us not become conceited" (Gal. 5:26). May our lives truly exhibit "the fruit of the Spirit," but may we remember — it is "the fruit *of the Spirit.*"

The acts of the sinful nature are obvious: sexual immorality, impurity and debauchery; idolatry and witchcraft; hatred, discord, jealousy, fits of rage, selfish ambition, dissensions, factions and envy; drunkenness, orgies, and the like.... But the fruit of the Spirit is love, joy, peace, patience, kindness, goodness, faithfulness, gentleness and self-control.

Galatians 5:19 – 23

OCTOBER 2

... the hope that is stored up for you in heaven.

Colossians 1:5

From the pen of Charles Spurgeon:

Our hope in Christ for our future in heaven is the foundation and driving force behind our joy here. It inspires our hearts to think often of heaven, for all we could ever desire is promised there. Here we are weary and worn from our work, but beyond is the land of rest where the sweat of labor will no longer bead upon the worker's brow and where fatigue will be forever banished. And for those who are weary, feeling totally spent, the word *rest* conveys a sense of heaven and its fullness to come.

Here we are always on the field of battle, being tempted within and continually attacked by foes without, to the point we experience little or no peace. But in heaven we will enjoy the victory, the banner will be waved high in triumph, the sword will be returned to its sheath, and we will hear our Captain say, "Well done, good and faithful servant" (Matt. 25:21). Here we suffer bereavement after bereavement, but we are headed to the land of the immortal where graves are unknown things. Here sin is a constant misery and grief to us, but there we will be perfectly holy, for nothing will ever be able to enter that kingdom that could cause any defilement whatsoever. No poisonous hemlock will ever be found in the furrows of celestial fields.

Oh, what joy! We are not banished to dwell in this wilderness forever but will soon inherit the heavenly Canaan. Yet may it never be said of us that we continually dream of the future while forgetting the present. Instead, may the future sanctify the present for the highest possible purposes. Through the Spirit of God, the hope of heaven is the most powerful force for producing godly character, the fountain or source of joyful service, and the cornerstone of cheerful holiness.

The person who has the hope of heaven goes about his work with passion and determination, "for the joy of the LORD is [his] strength" (Neh. 8:10). He strenuously fights temptation, for the hope of the next world "extinguish[es] all the flaming arrows of the evil one" (Eph. 6:16). And he can work diligently without present reward, for he looks for his reward in the world to come.

From the pen of Jim Reimann:

In the context of our verse today, Paul says God's gifts of "faith and love" spring from "the hope that is stored up for you in heaven." Of course, Paul thought of hope as much more than an attribute. He saw it as something personified by Jesus Himself, for he continued: "God has chosen to make known among the Gentiles the glorious riches of this mystery, which is *Christ in you, the hope of glory.* We proclaim him, admonishing and teaching everyone with all wisdom, so that we may present everyone perfect in Christ. To this end I labor, struggling with all his energy, which so powerfully works in me" (Col. 1:27 – 29).

Paul wrote much about hope, including these prayers: "May *the God of hope* fill you with all joy and peace as you trust in him, *so that you may overflow with hope* by the power of the Holy Spirit" (Rom. 15:13). "I pray also that the eyes of your heart may be enlightened *in order that you may know the hope to which he has called you*, the riches of his glorious inheritance in the saints" (Eph. 1:18).

Why not make these your prayers today?

OCTOBER 3

Are not all angels ministering spirits sent
to serve those who will inherit salvation?
Hebrews 1:14

From the pen of Charles Spurgeon:

Angels are the invisible servants of the saints of God, for they "lift [us] up in their hands, so that [we] will not strike [our] foot against a stone" (Ps. 91:12). Loyalty to their Lord leads angels to take a deep interest in the children of His love. They rejoice over the return of the prodigal to his father's house on earth below (see Luke 15:24) and also welcome the home-going of the believer to the King's palace in heaven above. (See Luke 15:10.)

In biblical days of old, the sons of God were blessed with the visible appearance of angels, and still today, although they are unseen by us, heaven is open and "the angels of God [are] ascending and descending" (Gen. 28:12) on the Son of man, so they may visit "those who will inherit salvation." Seraphim still fly with "live coal[s] ... from the altar" (Isa. 6:6) to touch the lips of God's greatly beloved. If God were to open our spiritual eyes, we would see "horses and chariots of fire" (2 Kings 6:17) surrounding the servants of the Lord, for we are encircled by "thousands upon thousands of angels in joyful assembly" (Heb. 12:22), sent to protect His royal seed. Thus, these lines from Spenser's hymn are not poetic fiction:

> How oft do they with golden feathers cleave
> The flitting skies, like flying attendants
> Against foul fiends to aid us militant!
> Edmund Spenser, 1552? – 1599

What an amazing level of dignity God's chosen enjoy when we consider that the radiant attendants of heaven have become our willing servants! To what level of communion have we been elevated when we realize we abide with spotless heavenly beings! How well are we defended, knowing "the chariots of God are tens of thousands" (Ps. 68:17), and knowing they are armed for our deliverance! To whom do we owe this great blessing?

May the Lord Jesus Christ be forever endeared to us, for through Him, God has "seated us ... in the heavenly realms" (Eph. 2:6) "far above all rule and authority, power and dominion" (Eph. 1:21). It is He whose "angel ... encamps around those who fear him" (Ps. 34:7). He is the true Michael who "fought against the dragon" (Rev. 12:7).

Hail, Jesus, angel of Jehovah's presence! To You I offer my daily vows.

From the pen of Jim Reimann:

What a blessing to know God created His angels to be "ministering spirits," and that they are here to serve His children! Their ministry even continues after this life, for we are told of the poor man who died "and the angels carried him to Abraham's side" (Luke 16:22). And from Joel we learn of the vastness of God's angelic hosts: "The LORD thunders at the head of his army; his forces are beyond number, and mighty are those who obey his command" (Joel 2:11).

Believer, take comfort from these truths this morning. May the Lord's ministry to us by His angels inspire us to serve Him with greater confidence.

OCTOBER 4

When evening comes, there will be light.

Zechariah 14:7

From the pen of Charles Spurgeon:

We often look ahead to old age with fear and trembling, forgetting that "when evening comes, there will be light." Yet for many saints, old age is the best season of their lives. A more pleasant tropical breeze warms the mariner's face as he nears the shore of immortality. Fewer waves ripple his sea, and quiet reigns — deep, peaceful, and majestic. From the altar of age, the fiery flashes of youth may be gone, but the more steady flame of true and sincere feeling remains. These older pilgrims have reached "Beulah" (Isa. 62:4), that blessed country where each day is like heaven on earth. Angels visit there, heavenly breezes blow across it, flowers of paradise grow on it, and its air is filled with the music of seraphim. Some people dwell here for years, while others reach it only a few hours before their departure. It is the closest thing to Eden on earth.

We may very well yearn for that time when we will rest in its shady groves and be satisfied with hope until the ultimate time of fruition arrives. The setting sun seems larger than when it is high in the sky, and a splendor of glory paints all the clouds surrounding it with tinges of color as it sets. Even pain does not break the calm of the sweet twilight of age, for "power ... made perfect in weakness" (2 Cor. 12:9) endures with patience through it all. The ripe fruit of blessed experience is gathered as a sumptuous meal of life's evening as the soul prepares itself for rest.

The Lord's people will enjoy His light at the hour of death. Will unbelief lament life and ask, "Are shadows falling, is night ahead, is existence facing an end?" "No!" faith will respond. "The night is far from over, for the true day has just arrived. The 'light has come' (Isa. 60:1) — the light of immortality, the light of the Father's countenance. Prepare to rise from your bed. See the angels waiting to escort you away! Farewell, beloved one, for you are leaving as you wave your hand good-bye. Then suddenly — all is light! The pearly gates of heaven are open and the streets of gold shine with the brilliance of jasper. (See Rev. 21:11.) You shield your eyes as you see the unseen for the very first time. Adieu, dear brother, you have light 'when evening comes' — light greater than you have ever seen!"

From the pen of Jim Reimann:

So many Christians fear death, but in truth a believer never really dies. Otherwise, eternal life would not be eternal. And if we think about it, do we really want to live forever in these earthly bodies, facing continual weakening, decline, and decay? Perhaps our thinking needs to be transformed regarding these worldly shells we call bodies. May we comfort each other with these words of Paul:

"The dead will be raised imperishable, and we will be changed. For the perishable must clothe itself with the imperishable, and the mortal with immortality. When the perishable has been clothed with the imperishable, and the mortal with immortality, then the saying that is written will come true: 'Death has been swallowed up in victory.' 'Where, O death, is your victory? Where, O death, is your sting?'" (1 Cor. 15:52 – 55).

So he got up and ate and drank.
Strengthened by that food, he traveled forty days and forty nights.

1 Kings 19:8

From the pen of Charles Spurgeon:

All the strength our gracious God supplies for us is meant to be used for service, not wanton behavior or boasting. When the prophet Elijah, as he lay under the broom tree, found "by his head" the "cake of bread baked over hot coals, and a jar of water" (1 Kings 19:6), he was no gentleman to be gratified with fancy fare so he might simply stretch out in ease. Much to the contrary, he was being commissioned to travel "forty days and forty nights" by its strength "until he reached Horeb, the mountain of God" (1 Kings 19:8).

In the same light, consider what happened when the Master invited the disciples to "Come and have breakfast" (John 21:12) with Him after His resurrection. When the meal was concluded, Jesus said to Peter, "Feed my sheep," and then added, "Follow me" (John 21:17, 19). It is meant to be the same with us. We eat "the bread of heaven" (Ps. 105:40) so the strength we gain from it may be spent in the Master's service. We are told to come to Passover to eat of the Paschal Lamb [Editor's note: from *paschalis,* Latin for Passover] "with your cloak tucked into your belt, your sandals on your feet and your staff in your hand" (Ex. 12:11) so we may leave at once after our hunger has been satisfied.

Some Christians are all for living *on* Christ but are not nearly as eager to live *for* Christ. Earth is simply preparation for heaven, and heaven will be where the saints will feast the most but will also serve the most. We will sit at the table of our Lord and will serve Him day and night in His temple, eating heavenly food and rendering perfect service.

Believer, in the strength you gain each day from Christ, work for Him. Some of us still have much to learn about the Lord's purpose in giving us His grace. We are not to simply hold onto the precious grains of God's truth as Egyptian mummies held onto grains of wheat for ages to come without ever giving it an opportunity to grow. No, we must sow the seed and water it.

Why do you think the Lord sends down rain upon the thirsty earth and then provides warm sunshine? Isn't it to help the fruits of the earth to yield their food for mankind? In the same way, the Lord feeds and refreshes our soul so we may then use our renewed strength to promote His glory.

From the pen of Jim Reimann:

Eating is one of the favorite pastimes of Christians, and many church meetings of believers take place around a table of food. But just as continual eating without proper exercise will make us physically overweight, continually taking in spiritually without ever serving others will make us spiritually fat. And what we eat is important as well, which is why the writer of Hebrews was so frustrated with his audience. He expressed his displeasure with the fact that they were still living on "milk, not solid food!" (Heb. 5:12).

He then continues, "Solid food is for the mature, who by constant use have trained themselves to distinguish good from evil. Therefore let us leave the elementary teachings about Christ and go on to maturity" (Heb. 5:14 – 6:1).

If we truly desire to live for God's glory, we *must* "go on to maturity"! "Perseverance must finish its work so that you may be mature" (James 1:4).

OCTOBER 6

Whoever drinks the water I give him will never thirst.

John 4:14

From the pen of Charles Spurgeon:

A believer in Jesus finds enough in his Lord to satisfy him now and forevermore. A true believer is not someone whose days are tiresome for lack of comfort and whose nights seem extremely long due to the absence of heart-cheering thoughts, for in his faith he finds such a spring of joy and such a fountain of comfort that he is content and happy. Place him in a dungeon and he will find fellowship; place him in a barren wilderness and he will eat "the bread of heaven" (Ps. 105:40); or drive him away from every earthly friendship and he will meet the "friend who sticks closer than a brother" (Prov. 18:24). Wither all his vines (see Jonah 4:7) and he will find shade beneath the Rock of Ages, or sap the source of his earthly hopes and his heart will remain fixed, trusting in his Lord.

The human heart is as insatiable as the grave until Jesus enters it, but then it becomes a cup full to overflowing. There is such fullness in Christ that He alone is the believer's "all in all" (1 Cor. 15:28). A true saint is so completely satisfied with the all-sufficiency of Jesus that he thirsts no more, except for a deeper drink from the living fountain. In that same sweet way, dear believer, you will thirst. Yet it will not be a painful thirst but one of loving desire, and you will find it to be a glorious thing to be panting after a fuller enjoyment of Jesus' love. Someone long ago said, "I have been sinking my bucket into the well quite often, but now my thirst for Jesus has become so insatiable that I long to put the well itself to my lips and continually drink."

Believer, does this describe the longing of your heart today? Do you feel that all your desires are satisfied in Jesus, and that you have no more needs except your longing to know more of Him and to have closer fellowship with Him? If so, then continually come and "drink without cost from the spring of the water of life" (Rev. 21:6). Jesus will never accuse you of taking too much but will always welcome you, saying, "Drink your fill, O lovers" (Song 5:1).

From the pen of Jim Reimann:

To this day, as in biblical times, water is more important to Israel than oil. Perhaps this is why the Old and the New Testaments are replete with passages using water as the symbol for spiritual life and salvation. Jesus told the woman at the well,

> If you knew the gift of God and who it is that asks you for a drink, you would have asked him and he would have given you living water.... Everyone who drinks this water [from this well] will be thirsty again, but whoever drinks the water I give him will never thirst. Indeed, the water I give him will become in him a spring of water welling up to eternal life.

> John 4:10, 13 – 14

A thousand years earlier, foreshadowing the coming Christ, David wrote: "The LORD is my shepherd, I shall not be in want. He makes me lie down in green pastures, he leads me beside quiet waters, he restores my soul" (Ps. 23:1 – 3). And seven hundred years before Jesus, Isaiah prophesized, "'God will come ... to save you.' ... Water will gush forth in the wilderness and streams in the desert. The burning sand will become a pool, the thirsty ground bubbling springs" (Isa. 35:4, 6 – 7).

Father, thank You for Your living water that has given me eternal life!

OCTOBER 7

He asked the LORD,
"Why have you brought this trouble on your servant?"
Numbers 11:11

From the pen of Charles Spurgeon:

Our heavenly Father sends us frequent troubles to try our faith, and if our faith has any value it will stand the test. Thin gold leaf fears the fire, but gold nuggets easily withstand it; and imitation gems of paste dread to be tested by diamonds, but genuine jewels never fear the test. Poor faith only trusts God when friends are faithful, the body is healthy, and business is profitable; but true faith continues to trust in the Lord's faithfulness when friends are gone, the body is sick, emotions are depressed, and the light of our Father's countenance is hidden. True, heaven-born faith is faith that can say, even amid the most severe trouble, "Though he slay me, yet will I hope in him" (Job 13:15).

The Lord afflicts His servants to glorify Himself, for He is greatly glorified in the gifts of His people, which are all actually His own handiwork. When "suffering produces perseverance; perseverance, character; and character, hope" (Rom. 5:3–4), the Lord is honored by these growing virtues.

We would never know the music of a harp if the strings were left untouched, enjoy the juice of grapes if they were not trodden in a winepress, discover the sweet scent of cinnamon if it were not pressed and beaten, nor feel the warmth of a fire if the logs were not burned. The wisdom and power of the great Artisan are discovered due to the trials through which His vessels of mercy are permitted to pass. And our present afflictions also tend to heighten our future joy just as a painting must have various levels of darker shades to reveal the beauty of the light.

Could we expect to be so supremely blessed in heaven if we had never known the curse of sin and the sorrow of earth? Isn't peace much sweeter after conflict and rest much more welcome after hard work? Won't the remembrance of past suffering enhance the happiness of the glorified?

There are many additional answers of comfort to the question: "Why have you brought this trouble on your servant?" Why not consider them all day long today?

From the pen of Jim Reimann:

Many people have difficulty believing the Lord sends trouble into the lives of His children. Yet our text today, as well as many others, suggests otherwise. For example, Isaiah wrote: "The Lord gives you the bread of adversity and the water of affliction" (Isa. 30:20). However, as we read the passage in its context, it reveals God's graceful and loving purpose in sending these trials.

The LORD longs to be gracious to you; he rises to show you compassion. For the LORD is a God of justice. Blessed are all who wait for him! O people of Zion, who live in Jerusalem, you will weep no more. How gracious he will be when you cry for help! As soon as he hears, he will answer you. Although the Lord gives you the bread of adversity and the water of affliction, your teachers will be hidden no more; with your own eyes you will see them. Whether you turn to the right or to the left, your ears will hear a voice behind you, saying, "This is the way; walk in it."
Isaiah 30:18–21

"Though I walk in the midst of trouble, you preserve my life" (Ps. 138:7).

OCTOBER 8

Put out into deep water,
and let down the nets for a catch.

Luke 5:4

From the pen of Charles Spurgeon:

We can learn from this passage the importance of human involvement. The catch of fish was miraculous indeed, but neither the fisherman, his boat, nor his fishing gear was ignored; they were all used to catch the fish. And while God's system of grace will stand, the Lord uses particular methods, such as preaching, in the saving of souls. "God was pleased through the foolishness of what was preached to save those who believe" (1 Cor. 1:21). When God works without using us as vessels, He is glorified, but He Himself has selected the plan of using instruments of His grace as being the way by which He is the most glorified on earth. Yet the instruments left alone will always end in utter failure.

Simon Peter said to the Lord, "Master, we've worked hard all night and haven't caught anything" (Luke 5:5). What was the reason for this? Weren't they experienced fishermen plying their special calling and trade? Truly they were not new to the profession and they understood their work, so were they doing the work without skill? No, they were well trained. Then did they lack diligence and perseverance? No, they had worked hard, laboring all through the night. Was there a lack of fish in the sea? Certainly not, for as soon as the Master arrived, schools of fish swam straight into the net. Then what is the reason?

It is because there is no power in the means by themselves apart from the presence of Jesus, who said, "Apart from me you can do nothing" (John 15:5). But we "can do everything through him" (Phil. 4:13). Christ's presence itself bestows success. He sat in Peter's boat and by the mysterious power of His will drew the fish to the net. And when Jesus is lifted up in His church, His very presence is the church's power, for the promise of a King is in the church's midst: "I, when I am lifted up from the earth, will draw all men to myself" (John 12:32).

May we leave our homes this morning for our work of fishing for souls, looking up in faith and all around us in earnest expectation. May we work until night comes and may our labor not be in vain, for He who bids us to let down our net will fill it with fish.

From the pen of Jim Reimann:

There is probably not a child alive today who enjoys hearing this response from one of his parents: "Because I said so." Yet due to children's lack of experience, maturity, and ability to understand certain truths, sometimes those "hated" words are exactly the right answer.

Simon Peter, who often made mistakes due to his impetuousness, nevertheless in today's story did just as Jesus instructed him. His initial response was, "Master, we've worked hard all night and haven't caught anything," yet consider the very next words that came from his lips, "But because you say so, I will let down the nets" (Luke 5:5). In Scripture, and in life, success in God's eyes will only follow obedience.

Remember what Mary told the servants at the wedding in Cana, just before Jesus changed the water into wine: "Do whatever he tells you" (John 2:5).

What great advice! "Do whatever [Jesus] tells you"! Why? Because He said so. That alone is reason enough!

Lord, help me obey whatever You tell me
— simply because You said so!

OCTOBER 9

To him who is able to keep you from falling...

Jude 24

From the pen of Charles Spurgeon:

In one sense the path to heaven is very safe, but in others there is no road so dangerous. It is plagued with difficulties. One misstep — an easy thing if grace is absent — and down we go. What a slippery path some of us must tread! How often do we have to exclaim with the psalmist, "My feet had almost slipped; I had nearly lost my foothold" (Ps. 73:2)! If we were all strong, sure-footed mountaineers, this wouldn't matter as much, but how weak we are in ourselves! Even on the best roads and the smoothest paths we quickly falter and stumble. These feeble knees of ours can barely support our unstable weight. A piece of straw may trip us and a pebble may bruise us, for we are mere children unsteadily taking our first steps in our walk of faith. If it were not for our heavenly Father holding us by the arm, we would quickly fall.

Since we are kept from falling, oh, how we should praise the patient Power who watches over us day by day! Think how prone we are to sin, how prone we are to choose a path of danger, and how strong our tendencies are even to trip ourselves. These thoughts should cause us to sing more sweetly than ever, Glory "to him who is able to keep [us] from falling"!

In this life we will encounter many foes trying to push us down. The road is rough and we are weak, but in addition, enemies lurk in an attempt to ambush us, jumping out when we least expect it. They work to trip us up or throw us down from the nearest precipice. Only the Almighty's arm can preserve us from these unseen foes seeking to destroy us. His arm is employed for our defense, "for he who promised is faithful" (Heb. 10:23) and "is able to keep [us] from falling."

Thus, with a deep sense of our utter weakness, may we gratefully cherish a firm belief in our complete safety, saying with joyful confidence:

> Against me earth and hell combine,
> But on my side is power divine;
> Jesus is all, and He is mine!
>
> John Newton, 1725 – 1807

From the pen of Jim Reimann:

The enemy who tempted Jesus still "prowls around like a roaring lion looking for someone to devour" (1 Peter 5:8). Quoting Psalm 91:12, Satan said to our Lord, "If you are the Son of God ... throw yourself down. For it is written: 'He will command his angels concerning you, and they will lift you up in their hands, so that you will not strike your foot against a stone'" (Matt. 4:6). But Jesus turned the tables on the Devil, saying, "It is also written: 'Do not put the Lord your God to the test'" (Matt. 4:7), a quote of Deuteronomy 6:16. May this be a lesson to us that our enemy may appear as "a roaring lion," sounding quite spiritual at times, which is why Peter warned in the same verse to be "self-controlled and alert."

Remember, however, that although the devil may portray himself as a "roaring lion," he is an impostor. Jesus alone is the victorious lion, as we see here: "Do not weep! See, the Lion of the tribe of Judah, the Root of David, has triumphed" (Rev. 5:5). And since we are "in Christ," we too are victorious and kept by Him. Surely a God who is great enough to save us is great enough to keep us!

To him who is able ... to present you
before his glorious presence without fault ...

Jude 24

From the pen of Charles Spurgeon:

Roll those wondrous words around in your mind: "without fault"! Today we are far from faultless, but since our Lord never stops short of perfection in His works of love, one day we too will reach perfection. The Savior who will keep His people to the very end will also finally "present her to himself as a radiant church, without stain or wrinkle or any other blemish, but holy and blameless" (Eph. 5:27).

All the jewels of the Savior's crown are of the highest quality, being the most transparent and without a single flaw. All the maids of honor who attend us, as the Lamb's bride, are pure virgins also "without stain ... or any other blemish." But how will Jesus make us faultless? He will cleanse us from our sins with His own blood until we are as pure and fair as God's holiest angel, and then He will clothe us in His own righteousness, making us saints who are absolutely without fault — yes, absolutely perfect in His sight.

We will be completely above reproach in God's eyes. His law will not only be able to bring no charge against us, but it will actually be glorified in us. Furthermore, the work of the Holy Spirit within us will be totally complete, for He will make us so perfectly holy that we will no longer have any lingering tendency toward sin. Our judgment, memory, and will — indeed, every power and passion in us — will be liberated from the captivity of evil. We will be holy even as God is holy and we will dwell in His presence forever. And His saints will not be out of place in heaven, for their beauty will be as great as that of the place prepared for them.

Oh, the rapturous joy of that moment when the eternal doors will be raised, and we, having been made ready for our inheritance, will dwell with the saints in everlasting light! Sin will be gone, Satan will be shut out, temptation will be forever past, and we will be faultless before God — this will be heaven indeed!

May we be joyful now as we rehearse the song of eternal praise that will soon roll forth in full chorus from the blood-cleansed hosts of heaven. May we imitate David's jubilation before the ark of the covenant as a prelude to our glorious joy before God's throne. (See 2 Sam. 6:14 – 15.)

From the pen of Jim Reimann:

Yes, someday believers will be "without fault," "present[ed] before [God's] glorious presence." Here is John's description of our future:

> There before me was a great multitude that no one could count, from every nation, tribe, people and language, standing before the throne and in front of the Lamb. They were wearing white robes and were holding palm branches in their hands. And they cried out in a loud voice: "Salvation belongs to our God, who sits on the throne, and to the Lamb."

Revelation 7:9 – 10

Our "white robes" will be the wedding clothes of the righteousness of Christ who "has become ... our righteousness" (1 Cor. 1:30). In that day "Jerusalem will live in safety [and] it will be called: The LORD Our Righteousness" (Jer. 33:16). "I saw the Holy City, the new Jerusalem, coming down out of heaven from God, prepared as a bride beautifully dressed for her husband" (Rev. 21:2).

OCTOBER 11

Let us lift up our hearts and
our hands to God in heaven.

Lamentations 3:41

From the pen of Charles Spurgeon:

Prayer is an undertaking that actually teaches us our unworthiness, a very beneficial lesson for such proud beings as we are. If God favored us with blessings without requiring us to pray for them, we would never know how poor we really are. But true prayer forces us to inventory our wants and needs, which unveils our hidden poverty. Prayer is the believer's way of applying for God's divine wealth and is thus a confession of human emptiness.

In fact, the healthiest state for a Christian is always to be empty of self, while constantly depending upon the Lord for supply; always to be poor in self and rich in Jesus; and weak as water personally, but mighty through God to do great things for Him. The use of prayer, therefore, because it gives adoration to the Lord, places the human creature exactly where he should be — in the very dust. Thus, prayer, in and of itself, is a great benefit to Christians — apart from the answer it brings. Just as a runner gains strength for an upcoming race through daily exercise, we acquire energy for the great race of life through the holy work of prayer. Prayer feathers the wings of God's young eaglets so they may learn to soar above the clouds. Prayer shields the bodies of God's warriors and sends them forth into combat with their tendons firm and their muscles strong.

An earnest prayer warrior exits his prayer closet just as the sun rises from the east, rejoicing like a strong runner fully prepared to run his race. Prayer is the uplifted hands of Moses routing the Amalekites more than it is the sword of Joshua (see Ex. 17:8 – 13), and it is the arrow shot from Elisha's room predicting the defeat of the Arameans (see 2 Kings 13:14 – 19). Prayer enshrouds human weakness with divine strength, turns human foolishness into heavenly wisdom, and gives troubled mortals the peace of God. The truth is — we really do not know what prayer cannot do!

We thank You, O great God, for Your "mercy seat" (Ex. 25:17 KJV) — an amazing proof of Your miraculous loving-kindness. Help us to approach it properly by prayer throughout this day!

From the pen of Jim Reimann:

One of the major reasons for prayer is this: our heavenly Father desires our fellowship. Jeremiah wrote: "The LORD appeared to us in the past, saying: 'I have loved you with an everlasting love; I have drawn you with loving-kindness'" (Jer. 31:3). Later he went on to say, "This is what the LORD says, he who made the earth, the LORD who formed it and established it — the LORD is his name: 'Call to me and I will answer you and tell you great and unsearchable things you do not know'" (Jer. 33:2 – 3).

The very God of the universe desires to commune with us! And if we truly love Him, we will reciprocate from a heart filled with love. Many mistakenly use the following verse to indicate Jesus is knocking on the door of an unbeliever's heart, but these words were written to the church:

"Here I am! I stand at the door and knock. If anyone hears my voice and opens the door, I will come in and eat with him, and he with me" (Rev. 3:20).

Will I keep Him waiting or will I open the door through prayer right now?

OCTOBER 12

I meditate on your precepts.

Psalm 119:15

From the pen of Charles Spurgeon:

There are times when solitude is better than fellowship and when silence is wiser than speech. We would be better Christians if we spent more time alone, waiting on God and finding spiritual strength for service to Him by meditating on His Word. We should ponder the things of God because only then will we get real nutrition from them.

Truth is like a cluster of grapes on a vine: if you want wine from it, you must bruise and crush the grapes, pressing and squeezing them many times. Your feet must come joyfully down on the clusters or else the juice will not flow, and you must completely tread the grapes or much of the precious juice will be wasted. In like manner, we must tread the clusters of God's truth through meditation if we desire to glean the wine of comfort from them.

Simply taking food into our mouths does not nourish our bodies, for it is the full process of digestion that supplies nutrients to muscles, nerves, sinews, and bones. And it is through spiritual "digestion" that outward food is assimilated into our inner life. Our souls are not nourished merely by listening for a while to this, then to that, and later to another portion of divine truth. Hearing, reading, examining, and learning all require inward digestion to complete their usefulness, and that inner digesting of the truth takes place primarily by meditating on it.

Why is it that some Christians make such slow progress in their spiritual life in spite of hearing many sermons? It is because they neglect time alone in their prayer closet meditating on God's Word. They love bread but are not willing to grind the wheat; they would like some corn but are unwilling to go into the field to gather it; the fruit hangs low on the tree, but they will not pluck it; and the water flows at their feet, but they will not stoop down to drink.

O Lord, deliver me from such foolishness. May this be my resolve this morning: "I will meditate on your precepts" (Ps. 119:78).

From the pen of Jim Reimann:

The Word of God uses the word *meditate* fourteen times, twelve of which are in the Psalms, with eight of those in Psalm 119 alone. We are told once to meditate on God's "unfailing love" (Ps. 48:9), four times on His wonders or works, but a full seven times to meditate on His Word — mentioned as His law, precepts, decrees, statutes, and promises.

The psalmist prays, "Let me understand the teaching of your precepts" in Psalm 119:27, but goes on to say in verse 99: "I have more insight than all my teachers, for I meditate on your statutes." Obviously, the answer to spiritual wisdom and understanding is tied to God's Word. To truly work it into our lives, we must take time to read it, pray over it, and meditate upon it. And to be successful in God's eyes, we must follow His command to Joshua: "Do not let this Book of the Law depart from your mouth; meditate on it day and night, so that you may be careful to do everything written in it. Then you will be prosperous and successful" (Josh. 1:8).

Why not take a few minutes to read Psalm 119 this morning? As you read, ask the Lord to give you a deep love for His Word, such as the psalmist proclaims: "Oh, how I love your law! I meditate on it all day long" (Ps. 119:97).

OCTOBER 13

Godly sorrow brings repentance.

2 Corinthians 7:10

From the pen of Charles Spurgeon:

Genuine spiritual mourning over sin is the work of the Spirit of God. Repentance is too high quality a flower to grow naturally in nature's garden. Pearls form naturally in oysters, but repentance is never found in sinners unless God's divine grace has worked it into them. If you have even a hint of a real hatred of sin, the Lord must have given it to you, for human nature's thorns have never produced as much as a single fig. "Flesh gives birth to flesh" (John 3:6).

True repentance has a distinct tie to our Savior. When we truly repent of sin, we will have one eye on sin and another on the cross, or, better still, we will fix both eyes on Christ and see our transgressions only through the light of His love.

True sorrow over sin is very practical, for no one can truly hate sin while living in it. Repentance makes us see the evil of sin, not merely in theory but experientially, as a child who has been burned now fears fire. We should be just as afraid of sin as someone who recently has been robbed is afraid of thieves. And we should shun it — shun it in everything — not only in big things but also in little things, just as people shun small vipers as well as huge snakes. True mourning over sin will also make us very careful over our tongue, lest we say even one wrong word. It will make us watchful over our daily actions, lest we sin in anything, and will lead us to close each day with the painful confessions of our shortcomings. Then it will lead us to open each day with diligent prayers, asking the Lord to uphold us that we may not sin against Him today.

Sincere repentance is also continuous, for believers will repent until their dying day. It is a continual flowing stream. Every other sorrow fades over time, but sorrow over sin grows as we mature. Thus, it is a bittersweet blessing, but one for which we should thank God, that He has permitted us to enjoy and to suffer repentance until we enter our eternal rest.

From the pen of Jim Reimann:

The complete verse from which our text is derived today is as follows: "Godly sorrow brings repentance that leads to salvation and leaves no regret, but worldly sorrow brings death." As this passage indicates, there is a vast difference between "godly sorrow" and "worldly sorrow."

More often than not, what we see in today's society is worldly sorrow, which is simply being sorry for getting caught. It is not true sorrow over having committed the sin in the first place, but sorrow for having to suffer the consequences of sinful actions. And one of these consequences is having the ongoing burden of living with guilt and regrets. Yet with godly sorrow, which "brings repentance," there is no lingering guilt. The most important difference between godly sorrow and worldly sorrow, however, is the end result: the former "leads to salvation," or life, while the latter "brings death."

Paul taught Timothy that repentance is a gift of God. May our prayer today for the lost include his words to the young pastor:

> Lord, we pray for the lost that You would "grant them repentance leading them to a knowledge of the truth, and that they will come to their senses and escape from the trap of the devil, who has taken them captive to do his will" (2 Tim. 2:25 – 26).

OCTOBER 14

I consider everything a loss compared
to the surpassing greatness of knowing Christ Jesus my Lord.

Philippians 3:8

From the pen of Charles Spurgeon:

Spiritual knowledge of Christ is a *personal* knowledge. I cannot know Jesus through someone else's acquaintance with Him. No, I must know Him myself — on my own account.

It is also an *intelligent* knowledge. I must know *Him* — not some illusive vision of Him — but as the Word reveals Him. I must know of His two natures: divine and human. I must know of His positions of authority, His attributes, His works, His shame, and His glory. I must meditate upon Him until I "have power, together with all the saints, to grasp how wide and long and high and deep is the love of Christ, and to know this love that surpasses knowledge" (Eph. 3:18 – 19).

Our knowledge of Him will be an *affectionate* knowledge, for if I know Him at all, I must love Him. And an ounce of heart knowledge is worth a ton of head knowledge.

It will be a *satisfying* knowledge. When I know the Savior as my own, my mind will be full to overflowing and will feel I have that which my spirit has always longed to know. He is "the bread of life" and whoever eats of that bread "will never go hungry" (John 6:35).

Spiritual knowledge of Christ is an *exciting* knowledge, for the more I know of my Beloved, the more I will want to know. The knowledge I glean by climbing even loftier summits will invite my eager footsteps to continue. The more I learn of Him, the more I will want. Like a miser with his treasure, my spiritual gold will make me yearn for more.

In conclusion, this knowledge of Christ Jesus will be the most *blessed* knowledge I can imagine. In fact, it will be so uplifting that often it will completely carry me above all trials, doubts, and sorrows. And while I enjoy this knowledge, it will be working in me to make me more than "man born of woman [who] is of few days and full of trouble" (Job 14:1), for it will clothe me in the immortality of the ever-living Savior and wrap me in His eternal joy.

Come, my soul, sit at Jesus' feet and learn of Him throughout today.

From the pen of Jim Reimann:

What is the goal of your life? Paul had a single-minded focus when it came to this question, for he said, "I want to know Christ" (Phil. 3:10). Obviously he was a believer and had a relationship with Christ, but he desired more. In the same way, he prayed for the believers in Ephesus, saying, "I keep asking that the God of our Lord Jesus Christ, the glorious Father, may give you the Spirit of wisdom and revelation, *so that you may know him better*" (Eph. 1:17).

May we apply these words of Paul to our hearts this morning:

[My determined purpose is] that I may know Him [that I may progressively become more deeply and intimately acquainted with Him, perceiving and recognizing and understanding the wonders of His Person more strongly and more clearly], and that I may in that same way come to know the power outflowing from His resurrection [which it exerts over believers], and that I may so share His sufferings as to be continually transformed [in spirit into His likeness even] to His death.

Philippians 3:10 AMPLIFIED

OCTOBER 15

Who can endure the day of his coming?

Malachi 3:2

From the pen of Charles Spurgeon:

Christ's first coming was without external pomp or show of power, yet in reality very few could withstand its testing might. Herod and all of Jerusalem with him were stirred at the news of His wondrous birth, and even those who professed to be looking for His coming exposed the fallacy of their shallow profession by rejecting Him when He arrived. His life on earth was a winnowing fork that sifted the huge pile of religious profession and very few withstood the process.

But what will His second coming bring? What sinner can even stand to think of it? "He will strike the earth with the rod of his mouth; with the breath of his lips he will slay the wicked" (Isa. 11:4). Consider the soldiers who humiliated Christ by arresting Him. "When Jesus said, 'I am he,' they drew back and fell to the ground" (John 18:6). Imagine the terror of His enemies at His second coming when He will more fully reveal Himself as the "I AM" (Ex. 3:14)!

Jesus' death shook the earth and darkened heaven, so imagine the dreadful splendor of that day when, as the *living* Savior, He will summon "the living and the dead" (Acts 10:42) to stand before Him as their judge. Oh, that the coming terror of the Lord would persuade people to forsake their sins and "kiss the Son, lest he be angry" (Ps. 2:12)!

Although Jesus is the Lamb, He is still "the Lion of the tribe of Judah," able to tear His prey into pieces (Rev. 5:5). And though "a bruised reed he will not break" (Isa. 42:3), He will break His enemies with an "iron scepter;... dash[ing] them to pieces like pottery" (Ps. 2:9). None of His foes will be able to stand against the winds of His wrath or hide from the boundless hail of His indignation.

Yet Christ's beloved blood-washed people look forward to His coming with joy and hope to observe it without fear. To them He already "sit[s] as a refiner" (Mal. 3:3), but "when he has tested [them], [they] will come forth as gold" (Job 23:10).

May we examine ourselves this morning "to make [our] calling and election sure" (2 Peter 1:10) so that the coming of the Lord will cause no dark foreboding or apprehension in our minds. Oh, for God's grace to cast away all hypocrisy and to be found by Him to be sincere and without rebuke on the day of "his appearing" (2 Tim. 4:1)!

From the pen of Jim Reimann:

Believers can indeed look to Christ's second coming without fear, which is why Spurgeon encourages us with the words of Peter "to make [our] calling and election sure." Nothing will be more devastating on "the day of the Lord" (1 Thess. 5:2) than to hear Him say, "I never knew you. Away from me" (Matt. 7:23). Paul also encourages us to check out our salvation with these words: "Examine yourselves to see whether you are in the faith; test yourselves" (2 Cor. 13:5). Once this is done we may joyfully declare:

"Now there is in store for me the crown of righteousness, which the Lord, the righteous Judge, will award to me on that day — and not only to me, but also to all who have longed for his appearing" (2 Tim. 4:8).

OCTOBER 16

Jesus [said] unto them, "Come and dine."

John 21:12 KJV

From the pen of Charles Spurgeon:

Through these words believers are invited to a holy closeness to Jesus. "Come and dine" implies eating at the same table and eating the same food and sometimes means sitting by His side and resting our head on Him. It is being taken into the banquet hall where the banner of redeeming love hangs.

The invitation, "Come and dine," also gives us a vision of oneness with Jesus because the only food we can feast upon when we dine with Jesus is the Lord Himself. And oh, what a union it is! It has amazing depth and is something reason cannot fathom — that we feed on Jesus! "Whoever eats my flesh and drinks my blood remains in me, and I in him" (John 6:56).

It is also an invitation to enjoy fellowship with other saints. Christians may differ on a variety of points, but we all have one spiritual appetite, and although we may not all *feel* alike, we can all *feed* alike on "the bread of life" that has "come down from heaven" (John 6:35, 38). At Jesus' table of fellowship we are one bread and one cup with each other, and as the loving cup is passed, we are joined in spirit to one another. As you get closer to Jesus, you will find yourself linked more and more closely with others who are nourished by the same heavenly manna. Thus, as you move closer to Jesus, you move closer to others as well.

The words of this invitation are also a source of strength for every Christian. Looking to Christ brings life, but for the strength to serve Him we must "Come and dine." We often labor with so much unnecessary weakness because we have neglected this invitation of the Master. This is one diet that does not need to be low in calories. On the contrary, we should fatten ourselves on "the richest ... foods" (Ps. 63:5) of the gospel so we may gain strength from it and then fully employ that strength in the Master's service.

In summary, if you desire closeness to Jesus, oneness with Him, love for His people, and strength from Him — then "Come and dine" with Jesus by faith.

From the pen of Jim Reimann:

Jesus invitation to "Come and dine" is a beautiful fulfillment of the following prophetic invitation given through Isaiah to the saved of the Lord:

> Come, all you who are thirsty, come to the waters; and you who have no money, come, buy and eat! Come, buy wine and milk without money and without cost. Why spend money on what is not bread, and your labor on what does not satisfy? Listen, listen to me, and eat what is good, and your soul will delight in the richest of fare. Give ear and come to me; hear me, that your soul may live. I will make an everlasting covenant with you, my faithful love promised to David.
>
> Isaiah 55:1 – 3

Later John the apostle was shown another fulfillment of the prophecy:

> He said to me: "It is done. I am the Alpha and the Omega, the Beginning and the End. To him who is thirsty I will give to drink without cost from the spring of the water of life. He who overcomes will inherit all this, and I will be his God and he will be my son."
>
> Revelation 21:6 – 7

Lord, how blessed we are to be invited to dine with You! May we look forward with great expectation to "the wedding supper of the Lamb" (Rev. 19:9)!

OCTOBER 17

David thought to himself,
"One of these days I will be destroyed by the hand of Saul."
1 Samuel 27:1

From the pen of Charles Spurgeon:

This thought of David's heart was false because he certainly had no grounds for thinking God's anointing of him by Samuel was an empty, meaningless act. Not even on one occasion had the Lord deserted His servant David. Quite often he had been placed in perilous positions, but not one instance had occurred in which God's divine intervention had not delivered him. The trials to which David had been subjected were quite varied, yet in every case He who had sent the trial had also graciously ordained a way of escape. David could not point to any particular entry in his journal and say, "Here is the evidence that the Lord will forsake me," for his entire past experience proved exactly the opposite. Instead of doubting, David should have argued that God would continue to defend him based on what the Lord had done previously.

But don't we doubt God's help in the same way? And isn't it distrust without cause? Like David, have we ever had even a shadow of a reason to doubt the Father's goodness? Hasn't His loving-kindness toward us been wonderful? Has He ever failed one time to warrant our trust?

No! Our God has never forsaken us. We have had dark nights, but His star of love has shone forth amid the darkness. We have faced difficult conflicts, but the Lord has always held a shield above us in our defense. We have endured many trials but always to our advantage — never to our detriment. Thus, from our past experience, we can conclude that He who has been with us through six difficulties will not forsake us during the seventh. What we have experienced in the past from our faithful God proves He will keep us to the very end.

Therefore, may we never allow thoughts contrary to the evidence. How can we ever be so self-absorbed as to doubt our God?

Lord, throw down the Jezebel of our unbelief. May the dogs devour it. (See 2 Kings 9:33 – 37.)

From the pen of Jim Reimann:

Trust is as simple as believing the promises of God. Shortly before Moses died, he told the Israelites, "The LORD your God goes with you; he will never leave you nor forsake you" (Deut. 31:6). Soon thereafter the Lord said to Joshua, "I will be with you; I will never leave you nor forsake you" (Josh. 1:5). Hundreds of years later, David said to his son Solomon, "The LORD God, my God, is with you. He will not fail you or forsake you" (1 Chron. 28:20).

Do you see a common theme here? God, through His Word, has gone on record. Thus, His very integrity is at stake were He to break this promise. Yet, as Paul told Timothy, "If we are faithless, he will remain faithful, for he cannot disown himself" (2 Tim. 2:13). Still, there is nothing wrong with reminding the Lord of His promises if it is done in faith. In fact, David prayed: "Fulfill your promise to your servant" (Ps. 119:38).

Finally, don't forget these words reiterated to us as Christians:

"God has said, 'Never will I leave you; never will I forsake you.' So we say with confidence, 'The Lord is my helper; I will not be afraid. What can man do to me?'" (Heb. 13:5 – 6).

OCTOBER 18

Your paths drip with abundance.

Psalm 65:11 NKJV

From the pen of Charles Spurgeon:

There are many paths of the Lord that "drip with abundance," but one of the most special is the path of prayer. No believer who spends a great deal of time in his prayer closet will ever have the occasion to cry out, "I waste away, I waste! Woe to me!" (Isa. 24:16). Thus, souls who are starving live a distance from God's "mercy seat" (Ex. 25:17 KJV) and become like parched fields in times of drought. Wrestling with God through prevailing prayer is sure to make a believer strong — if not happy. And the closest place to the gate of heaven is the throne of grace. If you spend a great deal of time alone with Jesus through prayer, you have great assurance of faith, but if you spend very little time, your faith will be shallow, polluted with many doubts and fears, and will lack the effervescent joy of the Lord.

Since the soul-enriching path of prayer is open even to the weakest saint, since no high achievements are required, since we are not invited to come because we are some superior saint but are invited simply because we are a saint, then, dear reader, make sure you are often found on that path of prayer. Be on your knees often in the same way Elijah brought rain to the famished fields of Israel with "his face between his knees" (1 Kings 18:42).

Another special path "drip[ping] with abundance" for those who walk upon it is the secret path of communion. Oh, the amazing delights of fellowship with Jesus! Earth has no words to fully express the holy peace of a soul held in His sweet embrace. In fact, very few Christians understand it, for they live in the valley and have seldom "climbed Mount Nebo" (Deut. 34:1). They live in the temple's outer court and never "enter the Most Holy Place" (Heb. 10:19) to take advantage of their privilege of priesthood. Thus, they only see the sacrifice from afar, never sitting down to enjoy the fat of the burnt offering with their High Priest.

But you, dear reader, determine to sit continually in the shadow of Jesus. Come up to that palm tree and take hold of the branches. Allow your Beloved to be as an apple tree among the forest to you, and your "soul will be satisfied as with the richest of foods" (Ps. 63:5).

O Jesus, "visit me with thy salvation" (Ps. 106:4 KJV)!

From the pen of Jim Reimann:

As David's psalm says in our text today, the paths of the Lord "drip with abundance." What is even more wonderful is that our heavenly Father is sovereign and graciously guides us to the proper path. Solomon wrote: "In his heart a man plans his course, but the Lord determines his steps" (Prov. 16:9). Then Isaiah tells us, "Whether you turn to the right or to the left, your ears will hear a voice behind you, saying, 'This is the way; walk in it'" (Isa. 30:21). And the writer of Hebrews encourages us to "throw off everything that hinders and the sin that so easily entangles, and let us run with perseverance the race marked out for us" (Heb. 12:1).

What a loving gracious Father we have! He not only marks out the path we are to follow but when darkness seems to surround us, He also gives us the perfect solution for our problem:

"Your word is a lamp to my feet and a light for my path" (Ps. 119:105).

OCTOBER 19

... mere infants in Christ.

1 Corinthians 3:1

From the pen of Charles Spurgeon:

Are you grieved, dear believer, because you are weak in your spiritual life, because your faith is so small and your love so feeble? Cheer up, for you have reasons for gratitude! Remember, in some ways you are equal to the strongest and most mature Christian. The same "precious blood of Christ" (1 Peter 1:19) has redeemed you and you are as much an adopted child of God as any other believer. An infant is as much a child of his parents as is a full-grown man. You are as completely justified as any other believer, for justification is not measured by degrees. You are fully justified, for your faith has made you totally clean.

You also have as much right to the precious things of the covenant as the most advanced believer, for your right to covenant mercies does not depend on your level of growth, but upon the covenant itself. Nor is your faith in Jesus the measure, because your faith is actually the evidence of your inheritance in Him. You are as rich as the richest believer in actual possession, if not enjoyment. Even the smallest shining star is set in heaven and its faintest ray of light is akin to our sun, the greatest globe and source of light in our sky.

In the family registry in glory, "the small and the great" (Job 3:19) are written with the same pen, and you are as dear to your Father's heart as the greatest in the family. Jesus is very tender and loving toward you, for you are like the "smoldering wick" to Him. A less tender person would say, "Put out that 'smoldering wick.' It is filling the room with an offensive odor!" But "a smoldering wick he will not snuff out" (Isa. 42:3). And you are like "a bruised reed" to Jesus. A less gentle hand than that of the Chief Musician would simply throw you away or pluck you from the ground and trample you underfoot. But "a bruised reed he will not break" (Isa. 42:3).

Thus, instead of being down or depressed because of what I am, I should "triumph in Christ" (2 Cor. 2:14 KJV). Am I only somewhat in spiritual Israel? No, I am "seated ... with him in the heavenly realms" (Eph. 2:6). Am I poor in faith? Nevertheless, in Him I am "heir of all things" (Heb. 1:2). Although I may be "worthless and less than nothing" (Isa. 40:17), I can boast in Him. Yet if the determination is left to me, "I will rejoice in the LORD, I will be joyful in God my Savior" (Hab. 3:18).

From the pen of Jim Reimann:

It is true we all begin the Christian walk as "mere infants in Christ" and that being a new believer is nothing for which to be ashamed. However, we should never be content to stay a spiritual infant. It is in this regard that the writer of Hebrews shares some frustration with the recipients of his letter by saying:

> You are slow to learn. In fact, though by this time you ought to be teachers, you need someone to teach you the elementary truths of God's word all over again. You need milk, not solid food! Anyone who lives on milk, being still an infant, is not acquainted with the teaching about righteousness. But solid food is for the mature, who by constant use have trained themselves to distinguish good from evil. *Therefore let us leave the elementary teachings about Christ and go on to maturity.*
>
> Hebrews 5:11 – 6:1

OCTOBER 20

In all things grow up into him.

Ephesians 4:15

From the pen of Charles Spurgeon:

Many Christians are stagnant and stunted in their spiritual growth, so much so they appear to be the same year after year. And many of them seem to lack any desire to advance or grow more knowledgeable. They simply exist but do not "in all things grow up into him." But should we ever be content to remain only a green sprout when we have the opportunity to develop a crop and to eventually ripen into a full-grown ear of corn? Should we be satisfied merely to believe in Christ and say, "I'm safe," but without the desire to experience more of the fullness that may be found in Him?

No! It should never be this way, for as good "traders" in heaven's market we should yearn to be enriched in the knowledge of Jesus. It is fine to work in someone else's vineyard, but we must not neglect our own spiritual growth and maturity. Why should it always be winter in our hearts? Yes, we all need a time of seeding in the spring, but we should move on to a summer season, which will then give us the hope of an early harvest.

If we truly desire to "ripen" in grace, we must be close to Jesus, living in His presence and becoming ripened in the sunshine of His smiles. We must have sweet fellowship with Him as well, no longer being satisfied with a long-distance view of His face but coming close to Him as John did when he "lean[ed] back against Jesus" (John 13:25) at the table. Only then will we find ourselves advancing in holiness, love, faith, and hope — indeed, in every precious gift.

Just as the rising sun first casts its golden beams across the mountaintops, giving passing travelers spectacular views, one of the most beautiful sights on earth is the glow of the Spirit's light upon the head of a godly saint who has grown in spiritual stature, as Saul once stood "a head taller than any of the others" (1 Sam. 9:2). What a glorious sight to watch a saint mature to the point of becoming like a mighty Alp — snow-capped, chosen of God, and magnificently reflecting the bright rays of "the sun of righteousness" (Mal. 4:2) and His radiance, lifting Christ up for all to see the glory of His Father who is in heaven.

From the pen of Jim Reimann:

Continuing on his theme from yesterday, Spurgeon encourages us to never be content with remaining "mere infants in Christ" (1 Cor. 3:1). Our text today, however, is taken from another epistle of Paul's whereby he explains that the Lord desires we "be built up ... and become mature." Here is how he said it:

> It was [Christ] who gave some to be apostles, some to be prophets, some to be evangelists, and some to be pastors and teachers, to prepare God's people for works of service, so that the body of Christ may be built up until we all reach unity in the faith and in the knowledge of the Son of God and become mature, attaining to the whole measure of the fullness of Christ. Then we will no longer be infants, tossed back and forth by the waves, and blown here and there by every wind of teaching and by the cunning and craftiness of men in their deceitful scheming. Instead, speaking the truth in love, we will in all things grow up into him who is the Head, that is, Christ.
>
> Ephesians 4:11 – 15

OCTOBER 21

Christ's love compels us.

2 Corinthians 5:14

From the pen of Charles Spurgeon:

How much do you owe the Lord? Has He ever done anything for you? Has He forgiven your sins? Has He "covered [you] with [a] robe of righteousness" (Isa. 61:10 KJV)? Has He "set [your] feet on a rock and [given you] a firm place to stand" (Ps. 40:2)? Has He prepared heaven for you and prepared you for heaven? Has He written your name in "the book of life" (Phil. 4:3)? Has He given you countless blessings? Has He "stored up for you in heaven" (Col. 1:5) wondrous mercies that "no eye has seen, no ear has heard" (1 Cor. 2:9)?

If so, then do something for Jesus worthy of His love, but don't merely give the Redeemer who died for you an offering of empty words. How will you feel when your Master returns if you have to confess you did nothing for Him, that you kept your love inside like a stagnant pool instead of pouring it out on the poor or into the Lord's work?

Away with love like that! Most people would prefer an open rebuke than that kind of secret love that never results in action. After all, who would accept a love so weak it never prompts a single act of devotion, self-denial, generosity, or heroism.

Think how Jesus has loved you and given Himself for you! Do you know the power of His love? Let it be "like the blowing of a violent wind" (Acts 2:2) to your soul, clearing away the clouds of your worldliness and the mists of your sin. "For Christ's sake" (2 Cor. 12:10), may the power of one of the "tongues of fire" (Acts 2:3) rest upon you. "For Christ's sake," may His power bring you His divine passion and heavenly creativity that

will lift you from earth. May His Spirit make you "as bold as a lion" (Prov. 28:1) and cause you to "soar on wings like eagles" (Isa. 40:31) in service to your Lord.

Love will give wings to our feet of service to the Lord and strength to our arms for His work. May we truly exhibit a determined love for Jesus that is fixed on Him with a faithfulness that will not be shaken, that is resolved to honor Him with a steadfastness that can never be swayed, and that presses ahead with a passion that will not grow weary.

May the divine Lodestone draw us heavenward toward Himself.

From the pen of Jim Reimann:

Spurgeon ends today's devotion with a word seldom used today: *lodestone*. He refers to Jesus as the Lodestone, defined by Merriam-Webster as "magnetite possessing polarity" or "something that strongly attracts."

Consider this in light of today's text: "Christ's love compels us." What an amazing Savior we have! And what amazing love—a love that "strongly attracts" us to Him! "We love him, because he first loved us" (1 John 4:19 KJV). And although "he had no beauty or majesty to attract us to him, nothing in his appearance that we should desire him" (Isa. 53:2), He nevertheless draws us to Himself. He has called His chosen to come to Him, attracting us to His light.

"You are a chosen people, a royal priesthood, a holy nation, a people belonging to God, that you may declare the praises of him *who called you out of darkness into his wonderful light*" (1 Peter 2:9).

OCTOBER 22

I will ... love them freely.

Hosea 14:4

From the pen of Charles Spurgeon:

This verse is the complete doctrine of God in miniature. Whoever understands its meaning is a true theologian, and he who can fully plumb its depths is a true master of Israel. The verse is a summary of the glorious message of salvation that was delivered to us through Christ Jesus our Redeemer, but its meaning hinges on the word *freely.*

Freely is the glorious, fitting, and divine way by which God's love flows from heaven to earth. It is a spontaneous love freely flowing to those who neither deserve it, purchase it, nor seek after it. Indeed, this is the only way in which God can love people such as we are. Today's verse — "I will ... love them freely" — is a deathblow to any sense of His love being deserved by us, for if there were any deservedness in us, His love would not be "freely" given. Any merit whatsoever would be, at the very least, a dilution and a drawback to the freeness of it. Thus, the verse will stand: "I will ... love them freely."

We complain, "Lord, my heart is so hard." He answers, "I will ... love [you] freely." We continue, "But I don't even feel my need for Christ as much as I should." He responds, "I don't love you because you feel a need for Me. 'I will ... love [you] freely.'" We argue, "I don't even feel a softening of my spirit that I should desire." Remember, a softening of your spirit is not a condition to your experiencing God's covenant of grace, for He has attached no conditions whatsoever. Thus, without any merit or conditions, we may trust this promise from God given to us through Christ Jesus: "Whoever believes in him is not condemned" (John 3:18).

What a blessing to know the grace of God is always free to us — without preparation or merit on our part and totally without a price for us to pay! "I will ... love them freely." These words are an invitation for backsliders to return. In fact, the first phrase of Hosea 14:4 reads: "I will heal their waywardness and love them freely."

Dear backslider! Surely the gracious generosity of this promise will break your heart, yet at the same time cause you to return, and as you do, to seek your dishonored Father's face.

From the pen of Jim Reimann:

God's love is indeed free to us and He loves us freely. Yet this does not mean He extends His love without cost, for it cost God His Son. Redemption is defined as: freedom obtained through a price paid. And God's Word tells us the Lord determined before creation He would send His Son to die to pay the price for our freedom. Here is how Peter stated it:

> You know that it was not with perishable things such as silver or gold that you were redeemed from the empty way of life handed down to you from your forefathers, but with the precious blood of Christ, a lamb without blemish or defect. He was chosen before the creation of the world, but was revealed in these last times for your sake.
>
> 1 Peter 1:18 – 20

Thus, because of God's great love for us, "The Spirit and the bride say, 'Come!' And let him who hears say, 'Come!' Whoever is thirsty, let him come; and whoever wishes, *let him take the free gift of the water of life*" (Rev. 22:17).

OCTOBER 23

"You do not want to leave too, do you?" Jesus asked.

John 6:67

From the pen of Charles Spurgeon:

Many people have forsaken Christ, not walking with Him any longer. But what reason do *you* have to make a change? Has there ever been a reason in the past? Hasn't Jesus proven Himself to be your all-sufficient Lord? He appeals to you this morning, asking, "Have I been a desert to [you]?" (Jer. 2:31). When your soul has placed simple trust in Jesus, have you ever been disappointed? To date, haven't you found your Lord to be a compassionate and generous friend, and hasn't your simple faith in Him given you all the peace your spirit could desire? Can you even dream of a better friend than He has been to you? Then why would you change the old tried and true for the new and false?

Can anything in the present compel you to leave Christ? When we find ourselves besieged by the troubles of this world or by the even more difficult trials within the church, it is one of the greatest blessings to find ourselves within the sweet embrace of our Savior, placing our head upon His shoulder. This is the joy we have *today* — that we are saved in Him — and since this joy is so satisfying, why would we ever think of changing?

Who would be foolish enough to trade pure gold for worthless dross? We would never renounce and forgo the sun until we find a better light; nor would we leave our Lord, hoping for a better one to appear. And since this can never happen, we will hold onto Him with an everlasting grasp and will place His name "like a seal on [our] arm" (Song 8:6).

As for the future, can you think of anything that could arise that would render it necessary for you to commit mutiny or desert your old flag to serve another captain? Surely not! Whether our life is long or short, Jesus never changes. If we are poor, who better to have than Christ who can make us rich? When we are sick, what more could we desire than to have Jesus attend our bed of sickness? Even when we face death, isn't it written that "neither death nor life,... neither the present nor the future,... will be able to separate us from the love of God that is in Christ Jesus our Lord" (Rom. 8:38–39)?

Thus, we can respond with Peter, "Lord, to whom shall we go?" (John 6:68).

From the pen of Jim Reimann:

Peter, who was quick to put his foot in his mouth at times, nevertheless answered the Lord's question on this particular occasion with one of the most glorious responses in all of Scripture: "Lord, to whom shall we go? You have the words of eternal life" (John 6:68). It's as though Peter is saying, "You *alone* are the source of eternal life!"

Let each of us consider what our answer would be to Peter's penetrating question, if for some foolish reason we decided to walk away from the Lord. "To whom shall we go?" May the words of this psalm be ours today and always:

> When you are on your beds, search your hearts and be silent. Offer right sacrifices and trust in the LORD. Many are asking, "Who can show us any good?" *Let the light of your face shine upon us, O LORD. You have filled my heart with greater joy than when their grain and new wine abound. I will lie down and sleep in peace, for you alone, O LORD, make me dwell in safety.*

Psalm 4:4–8

OCTOBER 24

The trees of the LORD are full of sap.
Psalm 104:16 KJV

From the pen of Charles Spurgeon:

Without sap a tree cannot exist, much less flourish. Life is essential to Christians, and for life to exist it must be infused into us by God the Holy Spirit or else we cannot be trees of the Lord. Being a Christian in name only is dead, for we must be filled with God's divine life, which is something quite mysterious. Just as we do not fully see how the sap of a tree circulates or by what power it rises and falls in the tree, neither do we fully understand the sacred mystery of the life within us. Regeneration is a work of the Holy Spirit who enters a person and becomes his life. This divine life in a believer then feeds upon the flesh and blood of Christ and is therefore sustained by God's divine food, but where it comes from or where it goes, who can explain to us? What a secret thing is this divine "sap"!

The roots of trees search deep into the soil, sending out their tiny tentacles, but we cannot see them extract the various nutrients or see how they transform them into fruit, for their work is done in secret. Likewise, our root is Christ Jesus and "[our] life is now hidden with Christ in God" (Col. 3:3), which is the secret of the Lord. The origin of the Christian life is as secret as that of life itself.

As the sap of a cedar is constantly active, so is the divine life always at work in Christians, not always in producing fruit but in inner purposes as well. A believer's gifts of grace are not always being exhibited and used, but his life never ceases to have an inner palpitation. He is not always at work for God, but his heart is always drawing its life from Him. And as the sap reveals itself in producing the foliage and fruit of the tree, so it is with a truly healthy Christian, for God's gift of grace is externally revealed through his walk and conversation. If you talk with a believer, he cannot help speaking about Jesus, and if you look at his actions you will take "note that [he has] been with Jesus" (Acts 4:13). He will have so much "sap" within, it will completely fill his conduct and conversation with life.

From the pen of Jim Reimann:

God always does things in a big way, and when He gives life, He does not do so sparingly. Jesus said, "I am come that they might have life, and that they might have it more abundantly" (John 10:10 KJV). As believers, we are to pour our lives into the lives of others, but the life we pour out is God's life. Jesus described it as a never-ending well, or fountain. He said, "Whoever drinks the water I give him will never thirst. Indeed, the water I give him will become in him a spring of water welling up to eternal life" (John 4:14), and "Whoever believes in me, as the Scripture has said, streams of living water will flow from within him" (John 7:38).

Paul then spoke of God's overflowing abundance by saying:

> He who supplies seed to the sower and bread for food will also supply and increase your store of seed and will enlarge the harvest of your righteousness. You will be made rich in every way so that you can be generous on every occasion, and through us your generosity will result in thanksgiving to God. This service that you perform is not only supplying the needs of God's people but is also overflowing in many expressions of thanks to God.
>
> 2 Corinthians 9:10 – 12

OCTOBER 25

Because of the truth,
which lives in us and will be with us forever ...

2 John 2

From the pen of Charles Spurgeon:

Once the truth of God makes an entrance into the human heart and subdues the complete person to its power, no human power on earth or demonic power from hell can dislodge it. We entertain God's truth, not as a guest in us but as the master of the house.

This is a Christian necessity, for someone who does not believe this is not a Christian. Those who feel the living power of the gospel and who know the power of the Holy Spirit as He teaches, applies, and seals the Lord's Word in them would sooner be torn to pieces than be torn away from "the gospel of [their] salvation" (Eph. 1:13). A thousand godly blessings are bundled together with the assurance that the truth will be with us forever, and that it will be our living support, our dying comfort, our rising song, and our eternal glory!

This is a Christian privilege, for without these gifts of mercy our faith would have little value. Some earthly rudimentary truths are simply lessons for beginners we ultimately outgrow and leave behind, but we must not treat God's divine truth in the same way, for although it may be sweet food for babies, it is also powerful meat for adults in the highest sense imaginable. The truth that we are sinners is always painfully with us to make us humble and vigilant, while the more blessed truth that "everyone who calls on the name of the Lord will be saved" (Rom. 10:13) is continually with us as our hope and joy.

The experiences of life, rather than loosening our hold on the doctrines of grace, instead have bound them to us more and more firmly. Our motives and reasons for believing have only been strengthened and are more numerous than ever. And we have reason to expect that will continue until, in death, we will finally embrace the Savior in our arms.

Once this abiding love of truth is discovered in us, we are then obligated to exercise that love. And the circle of our gracious sympathy must not be narrow, for the loving communion of our hearts should flow far and wide, extending as widely as God's gift of election. As the truth we share is received by others, we must realize they may mix it with a great deal of error. Thus, may we make war on the error while still loving our brother for whatever level of truth we have seen in him. Above all, may we love others while dedicating ourselves to spread God's truth.

From the pen of Jim Reimann:

Spurgeon ends today's devotion with an admonition reminiscent of Paul's encouragement to speak "the truth in love" (Eph. 4:15). If we are mature, seasoned believers, we will have more discernment than new Christians because we will have been trained through the "constant use" of God's Word "to distinguish good from evil" (Heb. 5:14). While we must never tolerate error, we must be careful not to alienate baby Christians, remembering we were once as they are.

Make time this morning to read Ephesians 4:11 – 16. Take careful note that God's ultimate goal is that we be "prepare[d] ... for works of service," "built up," "reach unity," "become mature," "attaining ... the fullness of Christ."

OCTOBER 26

"You expected much, but see, it turned out to be little.
What you brought home, I blew away. Why?" declares the LORD Almighty.
"Because of my house, which remains a ruin, while each of you is busy with his own house."

Haggai 1:9

From the pen of Charles Spurgeon:

Uncharitable people scrimp on their donations to church ministries and missionary organizations and then call such savings good economizing. Little do they know, however, they are only impoverishing themselves. Their excuse is that they must care for their own families, while forgetting that to neglect the house of God is the surest way to bring ruin upon their own houses. Our God's sovereign ways can cause our endeavors to succeed beyond our wildest expectations or they can defeat our plans to our own dismay and confusion. With a simple touch of His hand, God can steer our vessel into a profitable channel or He can run it aground in poverty and bankruptcy. The Scriptures teach us that the Lord enriches the generous but leaves the miserly to discover that withholding their money only leads to poverty.

Over a very wide range of observation, I have noticed that the most generous Christians I have known have always been the happiest and, almost invariably, the most prosperous as well. I have seen generous givers rise to wealth they never would have dreamed of, and I have just as often seen ungenerous misers descend into poverty by the very tightfistedness by which they thought they would rise. Just as people will trust good stewards of wealth with larger and larger sums, so it is quite frequently with the Lord. He gives truckloads to those who give by the bushels, and even when He does not bestow great wealth, the Lord makes a little go further. He also gives a contentment the sanctified heart will experience in proportion to how their tithe has been dedicated to the Lord.

Selfishness will always look first to its own home, but godliness will "seek first [God's] kingdom and his righteousness" (Matt. 6:33). In the long run, selfishness is loss while godliness is great gain. It requires faith to act toward our God with open hands, but surely He deserves that from us. Even doing all we can is still a very poor acknowledgment of our amazing indebtedness to His goodness.

From the pen of Jim Reimann:

Spurgeon mentions today that some Christians blame their lack of giving on the fact they need to care for their families. Yet Jesus encountered the exact opposite problem. The Jewish leaders of Jesus' time were refusing to take care of their families, as commanded by God, by saying all of their money was "Corban (that is, a gift devoted to God)" (Mark 7:11). Jesus told them, "You nullify the word of God by your tradition that you have handed down" (Mark 7:13). Most likely the Jews who were twisting God's Word to justify their lack of honoring their parents with their wealth were not using the savings to honor the Lord either.

The truth is, we are commanded to give to the Lord's ministry while still honoring and caring for our families. In both areas, an attitude of stinginess is something the Lord will not — and cannot — bless. It has been said we cannot out-give God, but how blessed we would be if we tried!

Seek first his kingdom and his righteousness, and all these things will be given to you as well.

Matthew 6:33

OCTOBER 27

Here is a trustworthy saying.

2 Timothy 2:11

From the pen of Charles Spurgeon:

Paul made four of these "trustworthy saying[s]." The first is 1 Timothy 1:15: "Here is a trustworthy saying that deserves full acceptance: Christ Jesus came into the world to save sinners." The second is 1 Timothy 4:8 – 9: "Godliness has value for all things, holding promise for both the present life and the life to come. This is a trustworthy saying that deserves full acceptance." The third is 2 Timothy 2:11 – 12: "Here is a trustworthy saying: If we died with him, we will also live with him; if we endure, we will also reign with him." And the fourth is Titus 3:8: "This is a trustworthy saying ... that those who have trusted in God may be careful to devote themselves to doing what is good."

And a connection between these four passages can be made. The first "trustworthy saying" lays the foundation of our eternal salvation through the free grace of God as revealed to us by the mission of the great Redeemer. The second passage affirms the double blessing we obtain through this salvation — the blessings of earthly and heavenly springs, or of time and eternity. The third shows one of the duties to which the chosen are called: it is ordained by God that we are to suffer for Christ with the promise that "if we endure, we will also reign with him." The fourth and final passage sets forth the admonition of Christian service, calling us to diligence in maintaining good works.

Thus, we have the root of salvation in free grace; next, the privileges of that salvation in our present life and in that to come; and we have the two great teachings regarding our suffering with Christ and our serving with Him, both filled with the blessings of the Spirit. May we treasure these "trustworthy saying[s]" and may they guide our life, our comfort, and our instruction. Paul, the Apostle to the Gentiles, proved their trustworthiness, and they are still trustworthy today. Not one word of God's will ever fall to the ground. They are worthy of our acceptance, so may we fully accept them now and prove their trustworthiness.

May these four "trustworthy saying[s]" be written on the four corners of *my* house.

From the pen of Jim Reimann:

When we consider the number of biblical prophecies already fulfilled, we shouldn't need a reminder that God's Word can be trusted. Yet mankind is forgetful, although we shouldn't be, for the Lord says to us, "Who are you that ... you forget the LORD your Maker" (Isa. 51:12 – 13).

Nevertheless, in light of our forgetfulness, may the following passages remind us of the trustworthiness of God's Word:

"O Sovereign LORD, you are God! Your words are trustworthy" (2 Sam. 7:28). "The law of the LORD is perfect, reviving the soul. The statutes of the LORD are trustworthy, making wise the simple" (Ps. 19:7). "O LORD,... the statutes you have laid down are righteous; they are fully trustworthy" (Ps. 119:137 – 138).

And as we look to God's promises yet to be fulfilled, remember the words of the angel to John: "These words are trustworthy and true. The Lord, the God of the spirits of the prophets, sent his angel to show his servants the things that must soon take place" (Rev. 22:6).

OCTOBER 28

I have chosen you out of the world.

John 15:19

From the pen of Charles Spurgeon:

Today's verse shows God's distinctive grace and discriminating regard, for only some have been chosen to be the objects of His divine affection. Don't be afraid to ponder this lofty doctrine of election. When you feel the most down and depressed, you will find it to be the most uplifting medicine possible. Those who don't believe the doctrines of grace or who cast them in a bad light miss the richest "cluster of grapes" from the "Valley of Eshcol" (Num. 13:23) and "the best of meats and the finest of wines" (Isa. 25:6). There is no "balm in Gilead" (Jer. 8:22) comparable to them. If the honey from the woods caused Jonathan's eyes to brighten, this is honey that will truly enlighten your heart to learn and to love the mysteries of the kingdom of God. (See 1 Sam. 14:27.) It is the best of foods but food you need not fear eating too much of, nor worry it is too rich, for meat from this King's table will never hurt any of His servants.

Desire to have your mind enlarged so you can comprehend more of the eternal, everlasting, and discriminating love of God. And once you have climbed as high as election, linger on its sister mountain — the covenant of grace. Covenant agreements are the protective munitions of massive rock behind which we lie entrenched. Covenant promises, along with the deposit of Christ Jesus as their guarantee, are the quiet resting places of trembling souls.

His oath, His covenant, His blood,
Support me in the raging flood;
When every earthly prop gives way,

He still is all my strength and stay.

Edward Mote, 1797 – 1874

If Jesus worked to take you to glory, and if the Father promised He would give you to the Son as part of the infinite reward of the suffering of His soul, then until God Himself is unfaithful or Jesus ceases to be the truth — you are safe. When David danced before the ark of the covenant, he told his wife Michal it was election that made him do so — because the Lord had chosen him. (See 2 Sam. 6:21.)

Rejoice before the God of grace and "leap for joy" (Luke 6:23) in your heart.

From the pen of Jim Reimann:

Spurgeon mentions the covenant of grace today, which in covenant theology follows two others. The first, the covenant of redemption, says the Father, Son, and Holy Spirit made a covenant in eternity past to provide redemption. The second, the covenant of works, is a covenant made with man. The Westminster Confession says, "Life was promised to Adam ... upon condition of perfect obedience" — or works, and goes on to say, "Man, by his fall, ... made himself incapable of life by that covenant" and "the Lord was pleased to make ... The Covenant of Grace; wherein He freely offer[ed] unto sinners life and salvation by Jesus Christ ... promising to give unto all those that are ordained unto eternal life His Holy Spirit, to make them willing, and able to believe."

We all deserve death. May we praise Him that He chose to save some!

OCTOBER 29

This, then, is how you should pray:
"Our Father in heaven, hallowed be your name ... "
Matthew 6:9

From the pen of Charles Spurgeon:

The Lord's Prayer begins where all true prayer should begin — with the spirit of adoption: "Our Father." No prayer is acceptable until we can say, "I will arise and go to my father" (Luke 15:18 KJV). This childlike spirit will then soon perceive the grandeur of the Father "in heaven" and ascend to the devout adoration of "hallowed be your name." The childish mouthing of "*Abba*, Father" (Rom. 8:15) quickly grows into the angelic cry, "Holy, holy, holy" (Isa. 6:3).

Then there is only one step from rapturous worship to a radiant missionary spirit, which is the certain outgrowth of devoted love and reverent adoration — "your kingdom come, your will be done on earth as it is in heaven" (Matt. 6:10). Next follows the heartfelt expression of dependence upon God: "Give us today our daily bread" (Matt. 6:11). Further illumination led by the Spirit takes us to the discovery that we are not only dependent but also sinful. Hence the plea for mercy: "Forgive us our debts, as we also have forgiven our debtors" (Matt. 6:12). Once we have been pardoned, having the righteousness of Christ imputed to us and knowing we have been accepted by God, we humbly plead for holy perseverance: "Lead us not into temptation" (Matt. 6:13).

Someone who is truly forgiven is eager not to offend again, for possessing justification leads one to a strong desire for sanctification. The phrase — "Forgive us our debts" — is justification, while — "lead us not into temptation, but deliver us from the evil one" — is sanctification, stated in a negative and a positive way. Finally, as a result of all this, a triumphant attribution of praise flows forth: "yours is the kingdom and the power and the glory forever. Amen" (Matt. 6:13, NIV verse note). We rejoice that our King reigns in sovereignty and shall reign in grace "from the River to the ends of the earth" (Ps. 72:8), and that "his kingdom will never end" (Luke 1:33).

In summary, from a sense of adoption that ultimately rises to the level of fellowship with our reigning Lord, this short model of prayer guides our soul.

"Lord, teach us to pray" (Luke 11:1).

From the pen of Jim Reimann:

A beautiful complement to the Lord's Prayer is Jesus' prayer in John 17. In this High Priestly Prayer, He again discloses the truth of election in praying for His followers: "I pray for them. I am not praying for the world, but for those you have given me" (v. 9). And He also prayed for His followers yet to come: "I pray also for those who will believe in me through their message" (v. 20).

During our most difficult times, we may wish to be taken on to heaven so we no longer have to deal with our problems, but Jesus prayed, "My prayer is not that you take them out of the world but that you protect them from the evil one" (v. 15), which is consistent with the Lord's Prayer.

Jesus prayed for our unity as well: "May they be brought to complete unity" (v. 23), and shared the idea of His indwelling life: "I have made you known to them ... that I myself may be in them" (v. 26). Perhaps best of all, He gave us the following glorious definition: "Now this is eternal life: that they may know you, the only true God, and Jesus Christ, whom you have sent" (v. 3).

I will praise you, O LORD.

Psalm 9:1

From the pen of Charles Spurgeon:

Praise should always follow answered prayer like the mist of earth's gratitude rises when the sun of heaven's love warms the ground. Has the Lord been gracious to you and "turned his ear" (Ps. 116:2) to hear your earnest plea of prayer? Then praise Him as long as you live. Allow the ripe fruit to fall upon the fertile soil from which it drew its life. Never deny a song of praise to Him who has answered your prayer and who has "give[n] you the desires of your heart" (Ps. 37:4). To remain silent over God's merciful gifts is to commit the sin of ingratitude, being as ungrateful as the nine lepers who, after being cured of leprosy by Jesus, did not return to give Him thanks. (See Luke 17:11 – 19.)

In fact, to forget to praise God is to refuse to benefit ourselves, for praise, like prayer, is one of the greatest means of fostering spiritual growth. Praise helps lift our burdens, strengthen our hope, and increase our faith. It is a healthy, invigorating exercise that quickens the pulse of believers, preparing us for new ventures in our Master's service. Blessing God for the mercies we have received is also a way to benefit our fellowman, for "the afflicted [will] hear and rejoice" (Ps. 34:2). Others who have experienced similar circumstances will take comfort if we can say, "Glorify the LORD with me; let us exalt his name together.... This poor man called, and the LORD heard him" (Ps. 34:3, 6). Weak hearts will be strengthened and downcast saints will be revived as they listen to our "songs of deliverance" (Ps. 32:7). Their doubts and fears will be rebuked as we "teach and admonish one another with ... psalms, hymns and spiritual songs" (Col. 3:16). They too will "sing of the ways of the LORD" (Ps. 138:5) when they hear us magnify His holy name.

Praise is the most heavenly of Christian duties. Angels do not pray, but they never cease to praise God both day and night. And the redeemed, "wearing white robes and ... holding palm branches in their hands" (Rev. 7:9), never weary of singing "a new song: ... 'Worthy is the Lamb'" (Rev. 5:9, 12).

From the pen of Jim Reimann:

David — shepherd, warrior, king, but also poet and musician — is our greatest example of someone who understood the power of praising God. The following is only a portion of the beautiful song he sang "when the LORD delivered him ... from the hand of Saul" (2 Sam. 22:1):

The LORD is my rock, my fortress and my deliverer; my God is my rock, in whom I take refuge, my shield and the horn of my salvation. He is my stronghold, my refuge and my savior — from violent men you save me. I call to the LORD, who is worthy of praise, and I am saved from my enemies.... In my distress I called to the LORD; I called out to my God. From his temple he heard my voice; my cry came to his ears.... He reached down from on high and took hold of me; he drew me out of deep waters. He rescued me from my powerful enemy, from my foes, who were too strong for me. They confronted me in the day of my disaster, but the LORD was my support. He brought me out into a spacious place; he rescued me because he delighted in me.... Therefore I will praise you, O LORD, among the nations; I will sing praises to your name.

2 Samuel 22:2 – 4, 7, 17 – 20, 50

OCTOBER 31

Renew a steadfast spirit within me.
Psalm 51:10

From the pen of Charles Spurgeon:

A backslider, if there is even a spark of life remaining in him, will look back after being restored and groan. A work of God's grace is required in renewal just as in conversion, for we needed repentance then and we certainly need it now. We lacked faith in order to come to Christ at first, and only a work of grace like that can take us to Jesus now. We needed a word from the Most High — a word from the lips of the loving One — to end our fears then, and as we will quickly discover under the conviction of our present sin, we need it now. No one can be renewed without as real a manifestation of the Holy Spirit's power that he needed at first, because the work of renewal is as great, and our flesh and blood are as much in the way as ever.

May your personal weakness, dear Christian, be an argument causing you to pray earnestly to your Lord for help. Remember, when David felt powerless, he did not fold his arms and keep quiet, but he ran to God's "mercy seat" (Ex. 25:17 KJV) and cried, "Renew a steadfast spirit within me." Never let the teaching that alone "you can do nothing" (John 15:5) put you to sleep, but instead let it prod you forward with an awe-inspiring earnestness to approach Israel's strong Helper. May you have the grace to plead with God as though you were pleading for your very life, "Lord, 'renew a steadfast spirit within me.'" He who sincerely prays for God to do this proves his honesty by using the very means through which God works. So "pray continually" (1 Thess. 5:17), placing yourself wholly on the Word of God. Put the lusts that have driven you from your Lord to death, and be vigilant, watching for sin to raise its head again.

The Lord has appointed His own specific ways of working, so sit in His path and you will be ready when He passes by. Continue to follow His blessed prescribed ways, and they will nourish you forever. Thus, knowing all spiritual power comes from Him, never cease to cry, "Renew a steadfast spirit within me."

From the pen of Jim Reimann:

David prayed Psalm 51 after being confronted with his sin by Nathan, the prophet of God. Not only had he committed adultery with Bathsheba but he also committed murder by killing her husband, Uriah, in an effort to cover up his sin. (See 1 Sam. 11:1 – 12:25.) Oh, if only we could truly grasp this truth: "You may be sure that your sin will find you out" (Num. 32:23)!

Thankfully, we have a God who desires that we be restored to cleanliness and righteousness and who has made a way for it. And we as His people are to get involved in the process, for we are told: "Brothers, if someone is caught in a sin, you who are spiritual should restore him gently. But watch yourself, or you also may be tempted. Carry each other's burdens, and in this way you will fulfill the law of Christ" (Gal. 6:1 – 2). We should always remember God's goal for us is restoration, not condemnation, for "there is now no condemnation for those who are in Christ Jesus" (Rom. 8:1).

Believer, are you struggling with the conviction of sin, perhaps believing you have done something so grievous it could never be forgiven? Remember this: God forgave David of adultery and murder, and "the blood of Jesus, his Son, purifies us from *all sin*" (1 John 1:7) — not *some*.

November

NOVEMBER 1

To the church that meets in your home...

Philemon 2

From the pen of Charles Spurgeon:

Since believers comprise the church, is there a "church" in your house? If so, is everyone who spends time in your house a member, including the parents, children, friends, and household servants, if any? Or are some still unconverted? Take a moment and let the question sink in, and then ask yourself, "Am I a member of the church in my own house?" Oh, how a Christian father's heart would leap for joy and a Christian mother's eyes fill with holy tears if everyone from the oldest to the youngest in the family were saved! May we pray for this great blessing until the Lord grants it to us.

It was probably one of Philemon's greatest desires that his entire household be saved, but it was not completely granted to him initially. He had a wicked servant, Onesimus, who had wronged him and run away from his master's service. But Philemon's prayers went with him, and finally, according to God's will, Onesimus was led to hear Paul preach. The Lord then touched his heart and he returned to Philemon, not only to be a faithful servant but also a beloved brother and the newest member of the church in Philemon's house.

Is there an unconverted child missing from your home this morning? If so, intercede for him in prayer that he will return home with the joyous good news of what God's grace has done. And if there is a believing child in the home, encourage him to join you in your intercession.

If there is a church that meets in your house, you have a greater responsibility to keep your house in good spiritual order, and every member of the household should remember all their actions are in the sight of God. May even the ordinary things of life be done with a determined sense of holiness, diligence, kindness, and integrity. More is expected of a church than a typical household. Thus, family worship should be more enthusiastic and devout, the love inside the home should be more warm and unbroken, and the actions outside the home should be more sanctified and Christlike.

Small home churches need never fear being unimportant, for the Holy Spirit has given us this beautiful reminder in His book of remembrance of the family church that met in Philemon's house. Whether our church is large or small, may we draw near to the great Head of God's universal church, and may we petition Him for the grace to shine before others to the glory of His name.

From the pen of Jim Reimann:

Onesimus's story is a beautiful one. Here is what Paul wrote about him:

I appeal to you for my son Onesimus, who became my son while I was in chains. Formerly he was useless to you, but now he has become useful both to you and to me. I am sending him — who is my very heart — back to you. I would have liked to keep him with me so that he could take your place in helping me while I am in chains for the gospel. But I did not want to do anything without your consent, so that any favor you do will be spontaneous and not forced. Perhaps the reason he was separated from you for a little while was that you might have him back for good — no longer as a slave, but better than a slave, as a dear brother. He is very dear to me but even dearer to you, both as a man and as a brother in the Lord.

Philemon 10 – 16

NOVEMBER 2

I the LORD do not change.

Malachi 3:6

From the pen of Charles Spurgeon:

Amid all the changeableness of life, it is good to know there is One whom change does not, and cannot, affect; One whose heart will never change; and One whose brow the changes of life will never furrow. Everything else in the universe changes, for even the sun itself eventually will grow dim with age and "the earth will wear out like a garment" (Isa. 51:6). The rolling up of them "like a [worn-out] robe" (Heb. 1:12) has already commenced; soon "heaven and earth will pass away" (Matt. 24:35); and "they will perish,... they will all wear out like a garment" (Ps. 102:26). But there is One who has immortality, One whose years will never end, and One whose character will never change.

The delight a sailor feels when setting foot on solid ground after having been tossed by the waves for many days is the security a Christian has amid all the changes of this trouble-filled life, when he sets his foot of faith upon this truth: "I the LORD do not change." The stability an anchor gives a ship in the harbor is like the stability a Christian's hope provides him when it is fixed upon this glorious truth: "The Father of the heavenly lights ... does not change like shifting shadows" (James 1:17).

The attributes of God in days of old are still His today. His power, wisdom, justice, and truth are all unchanged. He has always been "a refuge in times of trouble" (Nah. 1:7) for His people, and He is still their helper. His love has never changed, for He has loved His people "with an everlasting love" (Jer. 31:3). He loves us as much now as He ever did, and when everything on earth has melted away in the final flaming inferno, His love will still be adorned with "the dew of [its] youth" (Ps. 110:3).

How precious is the assurance that "the LORD do[es] not change"! Yes, the wheel of His sovereignty still turns, but its axle is eternal love.

> Death and change are busy ever,
> Man decays, and ages move;
> But His mercy waneth never;
> God is wisdom, God is love.
>
> John Bowring, 1792 – 1872

From the pen of Jim Reimann:

"God is not a man, that he should lie, nor a son of man, that he should change his mind. Does he speak and then not act? Does he promise and not fulfill?" (Num. 23:19). Thus, in light of the truth of today's devotion that "the LORD do[es] not change," we see that He does not change His mind either. What a blessing that is!

Imagine if that were not true. What if the Lord reneged on His promises, such as: "Whoever comes to me I will never drive away" (John 6:37) and "Never will I leave you; never will I forsake you" (Heb. 13:5)?

Although there may be times when we desire to change God's mind, we should understand that His sovereignty will always stand and His way is always best. Remember His words: "As the heavens are higher than the earth, so are my ways higher than your ways and my thoughts than your thoughts" (Isa. 55:9).

"Jesus Christ is the same yesterday and today and forever" (Heb. 13:8).

NOVEMBER 3

He is praying.

Acts 9:11

From the pen of Charles Spurgeon:

Prayers are instantly noticed in heaven. The moment Saul (soon to be Paul) began to pray, the Lord heard him. This should be a comfort to the distressed, though praying, soul. Often a poor brokenhearted soul bends his knees in prayer but can only utter his cries in the language of sighing and tears. Yet His groaning has made all the harps of heaven burst into song, and his falling tears have been caught by God and placed as treasure in the teardrop bottle of heaven. "You ... put my tears in your bottle" (Ps. 56:8 ESV) implies the tears are caught as soon as they flow. The petitioner whose fears prevent his words from flowing will be well understood by the Most High. He may only be able to look heavenward with misty eyes, but "prayer is the falling of a tear" (Joseph Parker, 1830 – 1902). Tears are the diamonds of heaven, sighs are part of the music of Jehovah's kingly court, and both are counted with "the sublimest strains that reach the Majesty on high" (James Montgomery, 1771 – 1854).

Never think your prayer, no matter how weak or trembling, will be disregarded. Jacob's ladder or stairway is lofty, but our prayers rest upon the Angel of the covenant and thus climb to the heights of the starry hosts. (See Gen. 28:12.) Our God not only hears our prayers but also loves to hear them. "He does not ignore the cry of the afflicted" (Ps. 9:12). Yes, it's true He doesn't give heed to prideful looks and lofty words, He doesn't care for the pomp and pageantry of kings, He doesn't listen to the loud blare of warlike music, nor is He impressed by the triumph and pride of mankind.

Yet wherever there is a heart swollen with sorrow, or a lip quivering in agony, or deep groans, or repentant sighs; then the heart of Jehovah is open. He registers each one in the journal of His memory, putting our prayers like rose petals between the pages of His book of remembrance. And when that book is finally opened, a precious fragrance will arise from it.

> Faith asks no signal from the skies,
> To show that prayers accepted rise,
> Our Priest is in His holy place,
> And answers from the throne of grace.
>
> Josiah Conder, 1789 – 1859

From the pen of Jim Reimann:

Today Spurgeon quotes Joseph Parker, one of his contemporaries and a minister in London. Here is the beautiful quote in its context:

Prayer is the uplifting of an eye, prayer is the falling of a tear, prayer is the outdarting of an arm as if it would snatch a blessing from on high. You do not need long sentences, intricate expressions, elaborate and innumerable phrases; a *look* may be a battle half won. According to "thy faith: be it unto thee" (Matt. 15:28 KJV). You may pray now, or in the crowded street, or in the busiest scene — you can always have a word with God — you can always wing a whisper to the skies. "Pray without ceasing" (1 Thess. 5:17 KJV). Live in the spirit of prayer, let your life be one grand desire, Godward and heavenward, then use as many words or as few as you please, your heart is itself a prayer, and your look a holy expectation.

The People's Bible: Discourses upon Holy Scripture

My power is made perfect in weakness.

2 Corinthians 12:9

From the pen of Charles Spurgeon:

A primary qualification for serving God with any degree of success and for doing His work well and triumphantly is a sense of our own weakness. When the Lord's warrior marches forth to battle, strong in his own might, or when he boasts, "I know I will be victorious, for my own mighty arm and conquering sword will give me the victory," defeat is not far away. God will not go forward with the person who marches ahead in his own strength. He who has counted on victory in this fashion has counted wrongly, for "'Not by might nor by power, but by my Spirit,' says the LORD Almighty" (Zech. 4:6). Those who enter the battle boasting of their own prowess will return with their victory banners dragging through the dust and their armor stained with disgrace.

Those who serve the Lord must serve Him in His way and His strength or He will never accept their service. Whatever mankind does unaided by God's divine strength, He will never accept as His work. He throws mere fruit of the earth away and will only reap fruit produced from seed sown from heaven, watered by grace, and ripened by the sun of His divine love.

God will empty you of yourself before He will put His resources in you, cleaning out your granary before filling it with the finest of His wheat. The river of the Lord is full of water, but not one drop of it flows from earthly springs. He will never allow any strength to be used in His battles except that which He Himself imparts.

Believer, are you mourning your own weakness? Take courage, for you must have an awareness of your own weakness before the Lord will

give you victory. Your emptiness is the necessary preparation for being filled, and being cast down is simply preparing you to be lifted up.

> When I am weak then am I strong,
> Grace is my shield and Christ my song.
> Isaac Watts, 1674 – 1748

From the pen of Jim Reimann:

When it comes to spiritual things, human weakness — or human strength, for that matter — is meaningless. Although God has chosen to work through His people in many ways, He is not dependent upon us, or on our human power, to accomplish His purpose. The Lord has said, "I make known the end from the beginning, from ancient times, what is still to come. I say: My purpose will stand, and I will do all that I please" (Isa. 46:10).

Paul certainly understood that God's purpose indeed "will stand" and that His "power is made perfect in [our] weakness." This is why he went on to say, after our text verse today, that instead of boasting in his own power, "I will boast all the more gladly about my weaknesses, so that Christ's power may rest on me. That is why, for Christ's sake, I delight in weaknesses, in insults, in hardships, in persecutions, in difficulties. For when I am weak, then I am strong" (2 Cor. 12:9 – 10).

Father, as "the power of the LORD came upon Elijah" (1 Kings 18:46), may Your power be mine today. May I trust solely in Your strength, be faithful to Your calling, and do Your will in Your way and in Your timing.

NOVEMBER 5

No weapon forged against you will prevail.

Isaiah 54:17

From the pen of Charles Spurgeon:

November 5 is a notable date in English history due to two great events of God's deliverance. On this day in 1605 the plot of Guy Fawkes and other Roman Catholics to destroy England's Houses of Parliament was uncovered and defeated.

> While for our princes they prepare,
> In caverns deep a burning snare,
> He shot from heaven a piercing ray,
> And the dark treachery brought to day.
>
> Author unknown

Today is also the anniversary of the landing of William III at Torbay, England, in 1688. He crossed England, gathering support to quash the idea of having a Roman Catholic on the English throne, and religious liberty was secured.

Thus, today should be celebrated, not with the wild revelry of pagans but with the songs of the saints. Our Puritan forefathers were quite devout in making today a special time of thanksgiving. In fact, a record of Matthew Henry's sermons preached in celebration of this day still exists. Our Protestant sense and our love of liberty should make us regard this anniversary with holy gratitude. May our hearts and mouths exclaim, *"We have heard with our ears, O God; our fathers have told us what you did in their days, in days long ago"* (Ps. 44:1).

Lord, You have made our nation the home of the gospel, and when the enemy has risen against it, You have shielded it. Help us to offer repeated songs to You for Your many works of deliverance. Grant us a greater and greater hatred of anything that is anti-Christ, and hasten the day of the extinction of all heresies. Until then and forever may we believe Your promise, "No weapon forged against you will prevail."

May the heart of everyone who loves the gospel of Jesus be burdened today to plead for the destruction of false doctrines and the advancement of God's truth. And may each of us search for any Roman Catholic planks of self-righteousness — doctrines of works-based salvation — that may be concealed within our hearts and remove them at once.

From the pen of Jim Reimann:

In the nearly 150 years since Spurgeon wrote these devotions, much has changed. In fact, within twenty-two years of their publication, on October 28, 1887, Spurgeon withdrew from the Baptist Union over what was known as the Down-Grade Controversy. He wrote in "The Sword and the Trowel," regarding many pastors and their preaching: "Natural theology frequently took the place that the great truths of the Gospel ought to have held, and the sermons became more and more Christ-less. Corresponding results in the character and life, first of the preachers and then of the people, were only too plainly apparent."

Pastors were questioning the authority of Scripture, and Spurgeon declared war on this heresy. And like Paul he preached God's inspired Word in its simplicity: "For I resolved to know nothing while I was with you except Jesus Christ and him crucified" (1 Cor. 2:2). May we too take a stand for God's truth!

NOVEMBER 6

I will pour water on the thirsty land.

Isaiah 44:3

From the pen of Charles Spurgeon:

When believers fall into a sad, depressed state, they often try to lift themselves from it by bombarding themselves with even more dark and depressing fears. Yet doing so is not the way to rise from the dust but is only a way to continue in it. Instead they should chain their depression and doubt to "wings like eagles" (Isa. 40:31) and thereby increase their sense of God's grace. It is not the law but the gospel that initially saves a seeking soul, and it is not legal bondage but gospel liberty that can restore a believer's fainting heart after salvation. Submission to legalistic fear will not restore a backslider to God, but the wooing of God's love to return to Jesus' sweet embrace will.

Believer, are you thirsty this morning for the living God and unhappy because He is no longer the delight of your heart? Have you lost the joy of your faith and has your prayer become: "Restore to me the joy of your salvation" (Ps. 51:12)? Are you also aware that you are as barren and dry as "the thirsty land," that you are not bearing as much fruit for God that He has a right to expect from you, and that you are not as useful in the church or in the world as your heart desires to be?

If so, then here is the exact promise you need: "I will pour water on the thirsty land." You will receive enough grace for each of your needs, enough to fully satisfy each and every one. Just as water refreshes the thirsty, you will be spiritually refreshed and your desires will be fulfilled. Just as water brings drooping plants back to life, your life will be enlivened by fresh grace. Water causes the buds of plants to swell and causes their fruit to ripen. And God's fruit-bearing grace will make you fruitful in His ways so you will enjoy every good quality of divine grace to the full once again. You will receive all the riches of God's grace in abundance as though you were drenched in it. You will be like meadows flooded by overflowing rivers and fields that are turned into pools. Your "thirsty land" will become "flowing streams" (Isa. 44:4).

From the pen of Jim Reimann:

Isaiah wrote that the children of Israel often were like a "desert and ... parched land" (Isa. 35:1). Thus, we see the recurring theme of the need for God's living water of grace for refreshment and restoration. Yet he prophesied of a day when salvation would bring great change. Here is his description:

> Water will gush forth in the wilderness and streams in the desert. The burning sand will become a pool, the thirsty ground bubbling springs.... The ransomed of the LORD will return. They will enter Zion with singing; everlasting joy will crown their heads. Gladness and joy will overtake them, and sorrow and sighing will flee away.
>
> Isaiah 35:6 – 7, 10

The need for restoration is often true of the Lord's church today as well. When we are sad and depressed, may we also recall these words of Jeremiah:

> My soul is downcast within me. Yet this I call to mind and therefore I have hope: Because of the LORD's great love we are not consumed, for his compassions never fail. They are new every morning; great is your faithfulness. I say to myself, "The LORD is my portion; therefore I will wait for him." The LORD is good to those whose hope is in him, to the one who seeks him.
>
> Lamentations 3:20 – 25

NOVEMBER 7

See, I have engraved you on the palms of my hands.

Isaiah 49:16

From the pen of Charles Spurgeon:

Part of the wonder of today's verse has to do with the emphatic word *See*, which is the Lord's response to Zion's lamentation of unbelief: "The LORD has forsaken me, the Lord has forgotten me" (Isa. 49:14). God appears to be amazed at this wicked lack of belief. In fact, what could be more astounding than the Lord's favored people expressing unfounded doubts and fears! His loving words of rebuke should make us blush, for it is as though He is crying, "How could I have forgotten you when 'I have engraved you on the palms of my hands'? How dare you doubt my constant remembrance of you when the reminder is etched in my very flesh!"

Oh, unbelief, what a strange phenomenon you are! What is more incredible to us: the faithfulness of God or the unbelief of His people? He keeps His promise to us a thousand times, and yet the very next trial leads us to doubt Him. The Lord never fails, for He is never a dry well, a setting sun, a passing meteor, or a disappearing vapor. In spite of this, however, we are continually troubled with anxieties, obsessed with suspicions, and disturbed with fears as though our God were some mere mirage in the desert.

"See," in this context, is a word intended to elicit admiration. Especially in this case we have a reason for awe and wonder. Indeed, heaven and earth should be amazed that such rebellious people are so close to the heart of infinite Love that they are written upon the palms of His hands. Notice that the Lord says, "I have engraved *you*," not "I have engraved your *name*." Yes, your name is there, but that is not all. "I have engraved *you*." Notice the completeness of this! "I have engraved your person, your image, your situation, your circumstances, your sins, your temptations, your weaknesses, your wants, your works; I have engraved *you*, everything about you, and all that concerns you on the palms of my hands."

In light of this, will you ever say again that your God has forsaken you when He has engraved you on the very palms of His hands?

From the pen of Jim Reimann:

The Lord loves His children so much He has not only engraved Himself with us but has also marked *us* with His name. In the Old Testament, Isaiah says, "you be called by a new name that the mouth of the LORD will bestow" (Isa. 62:2). Then in the New Testament we are told:

> Him who overcomes I will make a pillar in the temple of my God. Never again will he leave it. I will write on him the name of my God and the name of the city of my God, the new Jerusalem, which is coming down out of heaven from my God; and I will also write on him my new name.
>
> Revelation 3:12

As Paul said, our heavenly Father has also "set his seal of ownership on us, and put his Spirit in our hearts as a deposit, guaranteeing what is to come" (2 Cor. 1:22). In another of his epistles Paul reiterated this truth by saying, "Having believed, you were marked in him with a seal, the promised Holy Spirit, who is a deposit guaranteeing our inheritance" (Eph. 1:13 – 14).

Lord, how privileged we are to know You, to be Yours, and to be called by Your name! May our lives bring You glory and clearly exhibit we are Yours.

November 8

As you received Christ Jesus the Lord ...
Colossians 2:6 ESV

From the pen of Charles Spurgeon:

The life of faith is described here as *receiving*, which implies the exact opposite of things such as merit or works. Faith is simply the acceptance of a gift. Just as the earth drinks in the rain, the sea receives the streams, and night accepts light from the stars, we, without doing or giving anything, freely partake of the grace of God. By nature God's saints are neither flowing wells nor streams, but are cisterns into which the "living water" (John 4:10) flows; we are empty vessels into which God pours His salvation. The idea of receiving implies a sense of the realization of what the Lord has done. Someone cannot very well receive a shadow but must receive something substantial. And so it is in the life of faith — Christ becomes real to us — a reality. Before we have faith, Jesus is merely a name — a person who lived a long time ago — so long ago that His life is only history to us! But through an act of faith, Jesus becomes a real person in the consciousness of our heart.

Yet *receiving* also means "to take hold of" or to "gain possession of." Thus, what I receive becomes my own; whatever has been given to me I appropriate for myself. When I receive Jesus, He becomes *my* Savior — so much mine "that neither death nor life ... will be able to separate" (Rom. 8:38 – 39) Him from me. All this is what it means to receive Christ — to take Him as God's free gift, to realize He is in my heart, and to appropriate Him as my own.

Salvation has been described as the blind receiving sight, the deaf receiving hearing, and the dead receiving life, but we not only have received these blessings we also have received Christ Jesus Himself. It is true He has given us life from the dead, has pardoned us from sin, and has imputed His righteousness to us. While these are all precious gifts, we should not be content with them alone, for we have received Christ Himself. The Son of God has been poured into us, we have received Him, and we have appropriated Him as ours.

How our hearts must be filled, for heaven itself cannot contain Him!

From the pen of Jim Reimann:

Spurgeon ends today's devotion by pointing us to the infinite nature of Christ. We are told that "by him all things were created: things in heaven and on earth ... all things were created by him and for him" (Col. 1:16). Thus, it only stands to reason that if He created everything, He must be greater than His creation.

How amazing is it that the Creator of the universe has poured His very life into us and desires fellowship with us! May the following be our prayer to Him this morning:

"O Lord, our Lord, how majestic is your name in all the earth! You have set your glory above the heavens.... When I consider your heavens, the work of your fingers, the moon and the stars, which you have set in place, what is man that you are mindful of him, the son of man that you care for him? You made him a little lower than the heavenly beings and crowned him with glory and honor. You made him ruler over the works of your hands; you put everything under his feet.... O Lord, our Lord, how majestic is your name in all the earth!" (Ps. 8:1, 3 – 6, 9).

NOVEMBER 9

So walk in him.

Colossians 2:6 ESV

From the pen of Charles Spurgeon:

If we have received Christ Himself in our inmost hearts, our new life will reveal its intimate relationship *with* Him by a walk of faith *in* Him. Walking implies *action*. Thus, our faith is not to be confined only to our prayer closet but we also must apply our beliefs outwardly in every practical way possible. If someone walks in Christ, he will act as Christ would act. If Christ is in him, his hopes, love, and joy — his complete life — will reflect the image of Jesus, and others will say of him, "He is like his Master; he lives like Jesus Christ."

Walking also signifies *progress*. "So walk in him" — grow from grace to grace, moving straight ahead until you reach the highest level of knowledge of our Beloved that a person can attain. Walking implies *continuance*, for a true believer must have a perpetual abiding in Christ. How many Christians think they should spend time with Jesus in the morning and evening but may then give their hearts to the world the rest of the day? That, however, is a meager existence, for we should always be with Him, walking in His steps and doing His will. Walking also implies *habit* or *routine*. When we refer to a person's walk and conversation, we mean his habits and the general tenor of his life. If we enjoy Christ at times and then forget Him, if we call Him our own at times but quickly loosen our hold on Him, then that is not a habit and we do not "walk in him." We must stay close to Him, cling to Him, never let go of Him — "live and move and have our being" (Acts 17:28) in Him.

"As you received Christ Jesus the Lord, so walk in him" (Col. 2:6 ESV). Persevere in the same way in which you began your walk, when Christ Jesus was the only focus of your faith, the source of your life, the motive behind your actions, and the joy of your soul. May He be the same to you until your life ends, when you "walk through the valley of the shadow of death" (Ps. 23:4) and ultimately "share your master's happiness" (Matt. 25:23), entering into the "Sabbath-rest for the people of God" (Heb. 4:9).

O Holy Spirit, enable us to obey this heavenly precept.

From the pen of Jim Reimann:

In God's Word we are often reminded to *walk* in godliness and that His blessings are tied to our walk. For example: "What does the LORD your God ask of you but to fear the LORD your God, to walk in all his ways, to love him, to serve the LORD your God with all your heart and with all your soul, and to observe the LORD's commands and decrees that I am giving you today for your own good?" (Deut. 10:12 – 13); "Blessed are all who fear the LORD, who walk in his ways" (Ps. 128:1); and "This is what the LORD says: 'Stand at the crossroads and look; ask for the ancient paths, ask where the good way is, and walk in it, and you will find rest for your souls'" (Jer. 6:16).

The Lord commands His people to walk in His ways, but in His grace He also promises to guide us when we veer onto the wrong path, for He said, "Whether you turn to the right or to the left, your ears will hear a voice behind you, saying, 'This is the way; walk in it'" (Isa. 30:21). Later Jesus, who is the ultimate extension of God's grace, said, "I am the light of the world. Whoever follows me will never walk in darkness, but will have the light of life" (John 8:12).

NOVEMBER 10

The eternal God is your refuge.
Deuteronomy 33:27

From the pen of Charles Spurgeon:

The word *refuge* can also be translated *mansion* or *abiding place*, which offers the idea of God being our home. There is a beautiful fullness in this metaphor, for home is always dear to our hearts, whether it is the humblest of cabins or the smallest of attic rooms. Even more dear to us, however, is our blessed God in whom "we live and move and have our being" (Acts 17:28).

It is at home we feel safe, where we shut out the world and dwell in quiet, peaceful security. And when we are with our God we "fear no evil" (Ps. 23:4), for He is our shelter and retreat — our abiding refuge. Home is where we rest and relax after the tiring labor of the day. Likewise, our hearts find rest in God and our soul dwells in peace; when wearied by life's conflicts we turn to Him. At home we can let our guard down, not fearing we will be misunderstood or that our words will be twisted or misconstrued. And when we are with God we can freely communicate with Him, completely laying open all our hidden desires. If "the LORD confides in those who fear him" (Ps. 25:14), then certainly the secrets of His children should and must be entrusted to Him. Home is also the place of our truest and purest happiness, and it is in God our hearts find their deepest delight, for our joy in Him far surpasses any other joy in life.

It is for our home we work at our jobs. Thoughts of our home and family give us strength to handle our daily burdens and motivate us to perform our tasks more quickly. In this same sense, we relate to God as our home. Love for Him strengthens us, and as we think of Him in the person of His beloved Son, catching a glimpse of the suffering face of our Redeemer, we are compelled to work for His cause. We become more motivated in our service to Him, for there are people yet to be saved, and we will desire to fill our Father's heart with joy by bringing His wandering sons home. In fact, we will yearn to fill with holy joy the hearts of our entire sacred family with whom we dwell.

"Blessed is he whose help [or refuge] is the God of Jacob" (Ps. 146:5)!

From the pen of Jim Reimann:

David, who spent years running from King Saul, certainly understood the importance of places of refuge. Even more importantly, however, he came to realize there is no such thing as a place of total safety in this world, and that the only unshakeable refuge is the Lord Himself. Here is how he expressed this important truth in two of his psalms:

> Find rest, O my soul, in God alone; my hope comes from him. He alone is my rock and my salvation; he is my fortress, I will not be shaken. My salvation and my honor depend on God; he is my mighty rock, my refuge. Trust in him at all times, O people; pour out your hearts to him, for God is our refuge.
>
> Psalm 62:5 – 8

> In you, O LORD, I have taken refuge; let me never be put to shame. Rescue me and deliver me in your righteousness; turn your ear to me and save me. Be my rock of refuge, to which I can always go; give the command to save me, for you are my rock and my fortress. Deliver me, O my God, from the hand of the wicked.
>
> Psalm 71:1 – 4

NOVEMBER 11

Underneath are the everlasting arms.

Deuteronomy 33:27

From the pen of Charles Spurgeon:

God — "The eternal God" (Deut. 33:27) — is Himself our support at all times, especially when we are sinking into deep trouble. There are seasons in a Christian's life when he sinks quite low in humiliation. Under a profound sense of his own great sinfulness and because he feels so worthless in his own eyes, he is humbled before the Lord until he scarcely knows how to pray.

Dear child of God, remember at times like these, even when you are at your very worst and lowest, "underneath [you] are the everlasting arms." However low sin may drag you, Christ's great atonement is still fully under you. Perhaps you have descended to the depths of the ocean, but you cannot have fallen beyond the reach of His salvation, for "he is able to save completely" (Heb. 7:25). And sometimes a Christian will sink very low again due to some severe trial from without, one where every earthly prop seems to be pulled away. What will happen then? Even then — "underneath [him] are the everlasting arms." A believer cannot fall so deep into distress and affliction that the covenant grace of our ever-faithful God will be unable to encircle him. A Christian may also be sinking due to troubles from within, but regardless of how fierce the conflict, he cannot fall so low as to be beyond the reach of "the everlasting arms." They are still underneath him and as long as they sustain him, Satan's efforts to harm will come to no avail.

This assurance of God's support should be a true comfort to every weary, but earnest, servant in His service. It implies the Lord's promise of strength for each day, grace for each need, and power for each duty. And even when death comes to us, His promise still holds true. When we are crossing over Jordan, we will be able to say with David, "I will fear no evil, for you are with me" (Ps. 23:4). We will descend to the grave through death, but we will go no lower, for the eternal arms will prevent our fall. Throughout this life and even at its close, we will be upheld by "the everlasting arms" — arms that neither tire nor lose their strength, for "the LORD is the everlasting God.... He will not grow tired or weary" (Isa. 40:28).

From the pen of Jim Reimann:

Today we revisit yesterday's theme of the Lord Himself being our protection. We are to trust Him completely to be our refuge and our defender. Once again may we meditate on one of the Psalms. Yet as we do, notice God's promises are conditional, applying only to those who are His own.

If you make the Most High your dwelling — even the LORD, who is my refuge — then no harm will befall you, no disaster will come near your tent. For he will command his angels concerning you to guard you in all your ways; they will lift you up in their hands, so that you will not strike your foot against a stone. You will tread upon the lion and the cobra; you will trample the great lion and the serpent. "Because he loves me," says the LORD, "I will rescue him; I will protect him, for he acknowledges my name. He will call upon me, and I will answer him; I will be with him in trouble, I will deliver him and honor him. With long life will I satisfy him and show him my salvation."

Psalm 91:9 – 16

Lord, "I will not be afraid. What can man do to me?" (Ps. 56:11).

NOVEMBER 12

The trial of your faith ...
1 Peter 1:7 KJV

From the pen of Charles Spurgeon:

Untested faith may be real faith, but no doubt it will be "little faith" (Matt. 6:30) and will likely remain stunted in its growth as long as it has no trials. Faith never prospers better than when everything comes against it, for storms are its trainers and lightning its illuminator. When calm reigns on the sea, you can spread your ship's sails if you wish, but she will not move toward the desired harbor, for when the ocean slumbers the ship's keel sleeps as well. Yet when winds begin to howl and waves begin to rise, the ship may rock from side to side, her deck may be washed with waves, and her mast may creak under the pressure of the full and swelling sails, but it is only then she makes great headway toward her desired haven.

No flowers are adorned with a more lovely shade of blue than those growing at the very foot of a frozen glacier, no stars shine more brightly than those glistening in a cold polar sky, no water tastes as sweet as that springing up from desert sand, and no faith is as precious as that which lives and triumphs in adversity.

Testing is a learning experience. You would never have known or believed your own weakness if you had never been compelled to pass through rivers, and you would never have known God's strength if you had never been supported amid their raging torrents. Faith solidifies through tribulations and grows in assurance and intensity the more it is exercised. Faith is precious and its trial is precious too.

This truth, however, should not discourage those of you who are young in your faith. You will have plenty of trials in your life without seeking them, for a full portion will be measured out to you in due time. Meanwhile, although you cannot yet claim the results of a long Christian experience, you can still thank God for what grace you have and can praise Him for whatever level of holy confidence you have attained thus far. If you will walk according to this advice, you will experience more and more of the blessing of God until you have "a faith that can move mountains" (1 Cor. 13:2) and conquer any impossibility.

From the pen of Jim Reimann:

No one begs the Lord for increased adversity, yet a mature believer understands adversity is actually a gift of God's grace and love designed to strengthen His child. Isaiah says, "The Lord gives you the bread of adversity and the water of affliction" (Isa. 30:20), and Paul says, "It has been granted to you on behalf of Christ ... to suffer for him" (Phil. 1:29). Thus, adversity, affliction, and suffering are gifts, but gifts that fulfill the purposes of the Giver.

The Lord scattered the people of Israel due to their sin, and in His love made them "pass through the sea of trouble," but His purpose was soon revealed: "'I will strengthen them in the LORD and in his name they will walk,' declares the LORD" (Zech. 10:11 – 12).

Therefore, new believer, "Consider it pure joy ... whenever you face trials of many kinds, because you know that the testing of your faith develops perseverance. Perseverance must finish its work so that you may be mature and complete, not lacking anything" (James 1:2 – 4).

November 13

No branch can bear fruit by itself.

John 15:4

From the pen of Charles Spurgeon:

When and how did you begin to bear fruit? It was when you came to Jesus and cast yourself on His great atonement and then rested on His finished righteousness. Oh, what fruit you had then! Do you remember those early days when "the vines had budded [and] the pomegranates were in bloom" (Song 6:11), the "tender grapes" (Song 2:15 KJV) appeared, and "the beds of spices" (Song 6:2) sent forth their lovely fragrance? Has your fruit declined since then? If so, remember "your first love" — "Repent and do the things you did at first" (Rev. 2:4 – 5). Focus on the things in your past experience that have proven to draw you closer to Christ because it is from Him all of your fruit will come, and any holy exercise that takes you closer to Him will help you bear more fruit. The sun no doubt works great wonders of fruit creation among the trees of the orchard, and Jesus the Son does even more among the trees of His garden of grace.

So when have you been the most fruitless? Hasn't it been when you lived the furthest from the Lord Jesus Christ, when you neglected prayer, when you departed from the simplicity of your faith, when you were engrossed with your own strength and gifts rather than focusing your attention on your Lord? Hasn't this been when your fruit production ceased?

We must ultimately understand we can produce nothing apart from Christ, which requires severe humility of heart before the Lord. Once we realize the utter barrenness and death that come from our own power, we will cry in anguish, "All my fruit must come from Christ, for no fruit can ever come from me." Our past experience should teach us that the more simply we depend upon the grace of God in Christ and wait upon the Holy Spirit, the more fruit for God we will produce.

Oh, may we fully trust Jesus for fruit as well as for life!

From the pen of Jim Reimann:

The context of our verse today teaches another principle regarding the production of fruit. Not only do we learn from John 15 that "no branch can bear fruit by itself" but we also learn the importance of God's pruning, for "every branch that does bear fruit he prunes so that it will be even more fruitful" (John 15:2). Yet pruning involves cutting, and spiritual pruning involves spiritual cutting — something unpleasant, but necessary.

The beautiful thing about it, however, is that our "Father is the gardener" (John 15:1). And as our omniscient heavenly Gardener, He knows who will bear fruit and who won't, and He desires that those who do "bear fruit … will be even more fruitful." The lesson is similar to that of the parable of the talents in that the Lord invests more in His children who walk with Him in a way that produces a great amount of fruit. In the parable, the master calls the unproductive servant, "You wicked, lazy servant!" (Matt. 25:26), and goes on to say, "Take the talent from him and give it to the one who has the ten talents" (Matt. 25:28).

Father, may each of us "bear fruit — fruit that will last" (John 15:16) and may we remember: "The righteous … will still bear fruit in old age" (Ps. 92:12, 14).

NOVEMBER 14

I will cut off ... those who bow down
and swear by the LORD and who also swear by Molech.

Zephaniah 1:4 – 5

From the pen of Charles Spurgeon:

The people referred to in these verses thought they were safe because they were pandering to both sides; they went along with the followers of Jehovah while also bowing down to Molech. But duplicity is an abomination to God, and His soul hates hypocrisy. An idolater who completely gives himself to his false god is not as great a sinner as someone who takes his defiled and detestable sacrifice to the temple of the Lord while his heart is consumed with the world and its sins. To pretend to live with the hares but run with the hounds is a despicable practice. A double-minded person is despised in any area of life, but in the area of faith he is repulsive to the nth degree. And the penalty the Lord decreed in our text is terrible but well deserved, for how can God's divine justice spare a sinner who knows what is right, approving it and professing to follow it, but all the while loving evil and allowing it to rule his heart instead?

Dear soul, search yourself this morning to see if you are guilty of double-dealing. If you profess to be a follower of Jesus, do you truly love Him? Is your heart right with God? Are you of the family of old Father Honest or a relative of Mr. By-ends? [Editor's note: Both of these are characters in *The Pilgrim's Progress* by John Bunyan, (1628 – 1688).] Professing to live by a godly name is of little value if I am indeed "dead in ... transgressions and sins" (Eph. 2:1). Having one foot in the land of truth and another on the sea of falsehood ultimately leads to a terrible downfall and total ruin, for Christ demands all or nothing. God fills the entire universe; thus, there is no room for another god. If He reigns in your heart, there is no room for any other power to reign.

Do I trust solely in Jesus crucified and live for Him alone? Is He truly the desire of my heart? If so, blessed be His mighty grace that has led me to salvation!

If this is not true of me, O Lord, forgive my grievous offense, grant me unity of heart, and cause me to fear Your name.

From the pen of Jim Reimann:

Today double-mindedness is politically correct in our modern society where all standards have been abandoned, especially the standard of the Bible. But God abhors it, as did the psalmist who said, "I hate double-minded men, but I love your law" (Ps. 119:113). Listen to what Jesus said to the church of Laodicea:

I know your deeds, that you are neither cold nor hot. I wish you were either one or the other! So, because you are lukewarm — neither hot nor cold — I am about to spit you out of my mouth. You say, "I am rich; I have acquired wealth and do not need a thing." But you do not realize that you are wretched, pitiful, poor, blind and naked. I counsel you to buy from me gold refined in the fire, so you can become rich; and white clothes to wear, so you can cover your shameful nakedness; and salve to put on your eyes, so you can see. Those whom I love I rebuke and discipline. So be earnest, and repent.

Revelation 3:15 – 19

And in the following, we see James in full agreement:

Submit yourselves, then, to God. Resist the devil, and he will flee from you. Come near to God and he will come near to you. Wash your hands, you sinners, and purify your hearts, you double-minded.

James 4:7 – 8

NOVEMBER 15

For the LORD's portion is his people.

Deuteronomy 32:9

From the pen of Charles Spurgeon:

How did "his people" become His? We are His by God's own sovereign *choice*. He chose us and "set his affection on [us]" (Deut. 7:7) completely apart from any goodness in us at the time or any future goodness He saw in us. He said, "I will have mercy on whom I will have mercy" (Ex. 33:19) and ordained a chosen group for eternal life. Therefore, we are the Lord's by His purposeful election.

We are not only His by *choice* but also by *purchase*. He has bought and paid for us to the utmost farthing; thus, there can be no dispute about His ownership. [Editor's note: A farthing is a former coin of England worth one quarter of a penny.] "It was not with perishable things such as silver or gold ... but with the precious blood of Christ" (1 Peter 1:18 – 19) that "the LORD's portion" has been fully redeemed. There is no mortgage on His estate and no one can place a lien against it, for the price was paid in open court and the church is the Lord's, free and clear forever. Those who are His are marked by His blood, which is invisible to the human eye but seen by Christ, for "the Lord knows those who are his" (2 Tim. 2:19). He will never forget those He has "purchased from among men" (Rev. 14:4). He counts the sheep for whom He "laid down His life" (1 John 3:16), and He has total remembrance of the church for which He gave Himself.

We are also His by *conquest*. What a battle He faced in us before we would be won by Him! Oh, how long He laid siege to our hearts! How often He sent us terms of surrender only to see us bar the gates and reinforce our walls against Him! Don't we remember the glorious hour when He ultimately won our hearts by storm, when He placed His cross against the wall and scaled our ramparts, and when He finally raised the blood-red flag of His omnipotent mercy from our stronghold? We are indeed the conquered captives of His omnipotent love.

Thus, in summary, we are chosen, purchased, and subdued by Him, and His rights as our divine possessor are absolute. We rejoice we never can be our own, and we desire to do His will and exhibit His glory day by day.

From the pen of Jim Reimann:

The word *portion* conveys the idea of inheritance, and in that sense, "the LORD's portion is his people." As we will see in tomorrow's reading as well, thankfully the converse is also true, for the Psalms say: "God is the strength of my heart and my portion forever" (Ps. 73:26); "You are my portion, O LORD; I have promised to obey your words" (Ps. 119:57); and "You are my refuge, my portion in the land of the living" (Ps. 142:5). Thus, we are His — but He is ours as well!

The Old Testament declares that "the LORD set apart the tribe of Levi ... to minister.... That is why the Levites have no share or inheritance among their brothers; *the LORD is their inheritance*" (Deut. 10:8 – 9). Yet the priestly tribe of Levi is not the only priesthood, for long ago God said His people "will be for me a kingdom of priests and a holy nation" (Ex. 19:6). And Peter, showing the fulfillment of this prophecy, said the Lord's church is "being built into a spiritual house to be a holy priesthood" (1 Peter 2:5).

O Lord, "your chosen ones ... join your inheritance in giving praise" (Ps. 106:5). "We pray ... joyfully giving thanks to the Father, who has qualified [us] to share in the inheritance of the saints in the kingdom of light" (Col. 1:10 – 12).

NOVEMBER 16

I say to myself, "The LORD is my portion."

Lamentations 3:24

From the pen of Charles Spurgeon:

Notice this verse does not say, "The LORD is *partly* my portion" nor "The Lord is *in* my portion." No, He Himself makes up the sum total of my soul's inheritance, for within His circumference lies all we possess or desire. "The LORD is my portion"—not merely His grace, His love, nor His covenant, but Jehovah Himself. He has chosen us for His portion, and we have chosen Him for ours, although it is true He had to first choose our inheritance for us or else we would never have been able to choose it for ourselves. But if we are really "called according to his purpose" (Rom. 8:28), of electing love we can sing:

Loved of my God for Him again
With love intense I burn;
Chosen of Him ere time began,
I choose Him in return.

Augustus Montague Toplady,
1740 – 1778

The Lord is our all-sufficient portion, for since God fills Himself and is all-sufficient in Himself, He is all-sufficient for us. And it is not easy to satisfy our desires because when we think we are satisfied, we will soon have the feeling there is something yet to be fulfilled. "The leech" in our heart soon begs for more, crying, "Give! Give!" (Prov. 30:15). But all we could ever wish for is found in our divine portion so we may declare, "Whom have I in heaven but you? And earth has nothing I desire besides you" (Ps. 73:25).

Therefore, may we "delight [ourselves] in the LORD" (Ps. 37:4), who causes us to "drink from [His] river of delights" (Ps. 36:8). Our faith "will soar on wings like eagles" (Isa. 40:31) into the heaven of God's divine love as its proper dwelling place. "The boundary lines have fallen for [us] in pleasant places; surely [we] have a delightful inheritance" (Ps. 16:6). Let us "rejoice in the Lord always" (Phil. 4:4) and may we show the world we are a happy and blessed people, causing them to exclaim, "Let us go with you, because we have heard that God is with you" (Zech. 8:23).

From the pen of Jim Reimann:

The Lord is indeed our portion, or inheritance, and He loves to bless His people who find their delight in Him. Today Spurgeon quotes a portion of the following verse, expressing that truth: "Delight yourself in the LORD and he will give you the desires of your heart." This passage has a two-fold meaning.

Most people understand that the Lord wants to fulfill "the desires of [their] heart," and that is true. Yet many people miss the fact that He not only fulfills those desires but He gives us the desires in the first place. Notice the specific wording: "He will give you the desires of your heart." Thus, our gracious Lord not only fulfills our desires but He has placed those very desires within us!

Believer, do you understand how this brings Him great glory? He is the originator of the desire—and its fulfillment. It is all about Him and His greatness. This then helps us understand why certain of our desires may not be fulfilled, for they may not be of Him, or perhaps He is teaching us the importance of waiting on His timing. Therefore, may we seek contentment in Him alone as our portion!

NOVEMBER 17

To him be the glory forever! Amen.

Romans 11:36

From the pen of Charles Spurgeon:

"To him be the glory forever!" This should be the foremost desire of every Christian, for every other desire must point to and be subservient to this. A believer may have a desire for prosperity in his business, but it should only go as far as to promote this: "To him be the glory forever!" He may desire to attain more talents and gifts, but it should only be in order that "To him be the glory forever!" You are not behaving properly if you are motivated by any motive other than bringing your Lord glory.

As a Christian, you are a child *of* God and *through* God, so live *to* God. Never allow anything to cause your heart to beat more strongly than it does from your love for Him. Let this ambition be the fire of your soul, the foundation of every endeavor you begin, and your sustaining motivation whenever your zeal for Him starts to cool. Make God the only object of your life and depend upon that, for focusing on yourself is the beginning of sorrow. Yet if God is your supreme delight and the only object of your life, you can say:

To me 'tis equal whether love ordain
My life or death — appoint me ease or pain.
Madame Jeanne-Marie Guyon, 1648 – 1717

Translated from French by
William Cowper, 1731 – 1800

Your desire for God's glory should be a growing desire as well. If you blessed Him in your youth, never be content with the same level of praise you brought Him then. Has He prospered you in business? If so, then give Him more as He has given you more. Has God given you experiences to grow your faith? Then praise Him with stronger faith than you exercised at first. Has your knowledge of Him grown? Then sing to Him more sweetly. Do you enjoy better times than you once had? Have you been restored from sickness and has your sorrow been turned into peace and joy? Then sing more songs to Him, putting more coals and sweet frankincense into the censer of your praise.

In every practical way, may your life give Him honor. May you put the "Amen" of this doxology today in its proper place by giving your great and gracious Lord the glory He is due through your own individual service to Him and through an increasingly holy walk with Him.

From the pen of Jim Reimann:

Is God's glory truly the foremost desire of your heart? Take a moment and reflect on your deepest desires. If after being honest with yourself you discover this is lacking in your life, reflect on what we considered in yesterday's devotion: that the Lord is the one who places godly desires within us in the first place. Then ask Him to give you the desire to bring Him greater glory. David said, "I sought the LORD, and he answered me" (Ps. 34:4).

Next, make a determination to follow through in your life and your walk. In the same psalm David shows his determination by saying, "I will extol the LORD at all times; his praise will always be on my lips. Glorify the LORD with me; let us exalt his name together" (Ps. 34:1, 3).

NOVEMBER 18

You are a spring enclosed, a sealed fountain.

Song of Songs 4:12

From the pen of Charles Spurgeon:

This verse symbolizes the inner life and very plainly shows the idea of *secrecy*. It mentions a spring that is *enclosed*. In the Middle East, springs would often have some sort of covering or enclosure over them in order to protect them from people other than those who knew where the secret entrance was located. In the same way, there is a mysterious life no human power can touch in a believer's heart that has been renewed by God's grace. It is so mysterious and secretive that no one can truly know it. In fact, even the one possessing it cannot share it with another person.

Today's verse not only shows the idea of *secrecy* but also *separation*. The spring is not one from which every passerby may drink but is protected and preserved. It is a "sealed fountain" bearing the King's royal seal, a particular mark indicating it is special and intentionally separated from all others. It is the same with the spiritual life, for God's chosen were separated by His eternal decree, separated by Him "for the day of redemption" (Eph. 4:30), and separated to possess a life others don't have. Thus, it is impossible for them to feel at home in the world or to delight in its pleasures.

There is also the idea of *sacredness*. An enclosed and sealed spring indicates it is reserved for some special person, just as a Christian's heart is a spring kept for Jesus. Every believer should feel he has God's seal upon him and should be able to say with Paul, "Let no one cause me trouble, for I bear on my body the marks of Jesus" (Gal. 6:17).

Finally, there is another prominent idea, one of *security*. Oh, how safe and secure is the inner life of a believer! Even if all the powers of earth and hell come against it, God's immortal principle will still prevail, for He who gave it pledged His life for its preservation. And "if God is for us, who can be against us?" (Rom. 8:31).

From the pen of Jim Reimann:

"God said, 'Let us make man in our image, in our likeness'" (Gen. 1:26), and He followed through in many ways. In today's text the Lord refers to us as a spring, which is also how He refers to Himself in the following verse: "My people have committed two sins: They have forsaken me, *the spring of living water*, and have dug their own cisterns, broken cisterns that cannot hold water" (Jer. 2:13).

Jesus spoke of a spring as well when He told the woman at the well, "Whoever drinks the water I give him will never thirst. Indeed, the water I give him will become in him *a spring of water* welling up to eternal life" (John 4:14). Later in Jerusalem, during the Feast of Tabernacles, "on the last and greatest day of the Feast, Jesus stood and said in a loud voice, 'If anyone is thirsty, let him come to me and drink. Whoever believes in me, as the Scripture has said, streams of living water will flow from within him'" (John 7:37 – 38).

In agreement with these truths, David wrote, "You give [men] drink from your river of delights. For with you is the fountain of life" (Ps. 36:8 – 9).

Jesus, may Your living water freely flow from within me to a dry and thirsty world. May I trust in Your provision alone, O Lord, and may You help me remember: "All my fountains are in you" (Ps. 87:7).

Avoid foolish controversies.

Titus 3:9

From the pen of Charles Spurgeon:

Our days are few and are much better spent doing good than in disputing matters that are at best of little importance. So-called men of learning years ago did the world a great disservice by their incessant debating of subjects of no practical importance, and our church today greatly suffers from such petty warring over obscure ideas and unimportant issues. And once everything has been said that can be said, neither side is any wiser. This type of discussion no more promotes knowledge than it does love; thus, it is foolish to sow our time in its barren field. Arguing issues where Scripture is silent, discussing mysteries that belong to God alone, debating prophecies of doubtful interpretation, and disputing mere modes of observing the sacraments are all foolish, and the truly wise will avoid them. Our concern should not be to ask or to answer foolish questions but to avoid them altogether. If we would obey Paul's teaching in the preceding verse to our text to "be careful to devote [ourselves] to doing what is good" (Titus 3:8), we will find ourselves much too busy with profitable activities to waste our time with unworthy and needless contentions.

There are, however, some questions that are the exact opposite of foolishness, topics that should not be avoided but must be faced honestly and directly. They include such questions as: Do I believe in the Lord Jesus Christ? Am I being "transformed by the renewing of [my] mind" (Rom. 12:2)? Am I walking "according to the Spirit" rather than "the sinful nature" (Rom. 8:4)? Am I "grow[ing] in ... grace" (2 Peter 3:18)? Does my conversation exalt the doctrine of God my Savior? Am I looking forward to "the coming of the Lord" (1 Thess. 4:15), and am I continually watching as a servant who is expecting his Master? Is there more I can do for Jesus?

Questions such as these demand our urgent attention and, if we are currently involved in petty issues, let us turn our thoughts to things much more profitable. May we be peacemakers and endeavor to lead others to "avoid foolish controversies" not only by our thinking but also by our example.

From the pen of Jim Reimann:

As believers we must choose our battles wisely and, as we have seen, "avoid foolish controversies." Paul, who wrote our text verse, also encourages Christians not to "[pass] judgment on disputable matters" (Rom. 14:1).

Paul's letters to Timothy and Titus, known as "the pastoral epistles," were focused, instead, on the importance of sound doctrine. What Christians should be prepared to debate are the foundational truths, or the fundamentals, of our faith. Here is what Paul told these two young ministers: "The time will come when men will not put up with sound doctrine" (2 Tim. 4:3). "An overseer ... must hold firmly to the trustworthy message as it has been taught, so that he can encourage others by sound doctrine and refute those who oppose it" (Titus 1:7, 9). "You must teach what is in accord with sound doctrine" (Titus 2:1).

Although God has kept some things secret, He nevertheless holds His children accountable to the sound doctrine He has revealed. "The secret things belong to the LORD our God, but the things revealed belong to us and to our children forever, *that we may follow all the words of this law*" (Deut. 29:29).

O Lord, you took up my case;
you redeemed my life.
Lamentations 3:58

From the pen of Charles Spurgeon:

Notice with what assurance the prophet Jeremiah speaks in this verse, for He doesn't say, "I hope," "I trust," or "I sometimes think the Lord 'took up my case.'" No, he speaks as a matter of fact not to be disputed, saying, "You took up my case." In the same way may each of us, with the help of our gracious Comforter, shake off all the doubts and fears that so disrupt our peace and comfort. May it be our prayer to be finished with the shaky voice of doubt and suspicion and instead to be able to speak with the clear melodious voice of full assurance.

Next, notice how gratefully Jeremiah speaks, ascribing all the glory to God alone! His focus is on the Lord, not his own pleadings, for he does not attribute his deliverance in any measure to any man, much less himself or his own merit. On the contrary, he says, "O Lord, *you* took up my case; *you* redeemed my life." Christians should cultivate this kind of grateful spirit, singing our praises to Him especially when He delivers us from trouble. Earth should be a temple filled with the songs of grateful saints and every day should be a censer smoking with the sweet incense of thanksgiving.

Also notice how joyful Jeremiah appears to be as he records the Lord's mercy. How triumphantly he lifts his song to the Lord! He has been in the lowest of dungeons, and even at this point is still "the weeping prophet," and the very book of our text verse is known as *Lamentations*. Yet the voice of Jeremiah is as cheerful as the song of Miriam when she "took a tambourine in her hand" (Ex. 15:20) and sang to the Lord, and as thrilling as the song of victory of Deborah and Barak (Judg. 5). His voice of praise rises to heaven saying, "O Lord, you took up my case; you redeemed my life."

O children of God, seek after a living experience of the Lord's loving-kindness. Then once you experience it, speak positively of it, sing gratefully, and shout triumphantly.

From the pen of Jim Reimann:

As Jeremiah said, the Lord took up his case, something Jesus continues to do for His children, for John wrote, "My dear children, I write this to you so that you will not sin. But if anybody does sin, we have one who speaks to the Father in our defense — Jesus Christ, the Righteous One" (1 John 2:1). Who better to plead our case than the One who paid the price for our redemption! May we then gratefully "tell of his works with songs of joy" (Ps. 107:22).

"Great is the Lord and most worthy of praise; his greatness no one can fathom. One generation will commend your works to another; they will tell of your mighty acts. They will speak of the glorious splendor of your majesty, and I will meditate on your wonderful works. They will tell of the power of your awesome works, and I will proclaim your great deeds. They will celebrate your abundant goodness and joyfully sing of your righteousness" (Ps. 145:3 – 7).

"I will praise you, O Lord, with all my heart; I will tell of all your wonders. I will be glad and rejoice in you; I will sing praise to your name, O Most High" (Ps. 9:1 – 2).

Do not grieve the Holy Spirit of God.

Ephesians 4:30

From the pen of Charles Spurgeon:

All that you have as a believer comes from Christ, but it comes solely through the channel of the Spirit of grace. In addition, just as all blessings flow to you through the Holy Spirit, nothing good can flow out of you, such as holy thinking, devout worship, or any gracious action, apart from the sanctifying operation of that same Spirit. Even if the "good seed" (Matt. 13:24) has been sown in you, it will lie dormant unless He "works in you to will and to act according to his good purpose" (Phil. 2:13). Do you aspire to speak for Jesus? How can you unless the Holy Spirit touches your tongue? Do you desire to pray? Oh, what tedious work it would be unless "the Spirit himself intercedes for us"! Do you long for holiness and to subdue sin in your life? Do you desire to imitate your Master? Do you hope to rise to lofty heights of spirituality, wanting to be made like the angels of God, full of eagerness and zeal for your Master's cause? You can't without the Spirit — "Apart from me you can do nothing" (John 15:5).

Dear branch of the vine, you cannot produce any fruit without the sap of the vine! O child of God, you have no life within you apart from the life God gave you through His Spirit! Thus, may we not grieve Him or provoke Him to anger by our sin. May we be sensitive to even His faintest touch, follow His every suggestion, and be ready to obey His every prompting.

If the Holy Spirit is indeed so powerful, may we never attempt anything without Him. May we begin no project, run no enterprise, or conclude any transaction without imploring His blessing. May we give Him His due honor by recognizing our complete weakness apart from Him and then depend upon Him alone. And may this be our prayer:

> Lord, open my entire heart and soul to Your infilling, and uphold me with Your Spirit once I have received the fullness of that Spirit in my inmost being.

From the pen of Jim Reimann:

The Holy Spirit is also known as the Spirit of God and the Spirit of Christ, which is what Paul called the Spirit in the following verse: "You, however, are controlled not by the sinful nature but by the Spirit, if the *Spirit of God* lives in you. And if anyone does not have the *Spirit of Christ*, he does not belong to Christ" (Rom. 8:9). And the life of Christ we live as believers, we live through the power of His indwelling Spirit, for as Paul said, "I no longer live, but Christ lives in me" (Gal. 2:20).

Spurgeon today quotes one partial verse of John 15, but here is more of the passage to consider. As you meditate on these words of Jesus, remember it is His Spirit — "the Spirit of Christ" — who lives within you:

> I am the true vine, and my Father is the gardener. He cuts off every branch in me that bears no fruit, while every branch that does bear fruit he prunes so that it will be even more fruitful. You are already clean because of the word I have spoken to you. Remain in me, and I will remain in you. *No branch can bear fruit by itself,* it must remain in the vine. Neither can you bear fruit unless you remain in me. I am the vine; you are the branches. If a man remains in me and I in him, he will bear much fruit; *apart from me you can do nothing.*

John 15:1 – 5

NOVEMBER 22

Israel [or Jacob] served to get a wife,
and to pay for her he tended sheep.

Hosea 12:12

From the pen of Charles Spurgeon:

"Jacob was angry and took Laban to task," saying, "I have been with you for twenty years now.... I did not bring you animals torn by wild beasts; I bore the loss myself. And you demanded payment from me for whatever was stolen by day or night. This was my situation: The heat consumed me in the daytime and the cold at night, and sleep fled from my eyes" (Gen. 31:36, 38–40).

Yet even more wearisome was the life of our Savior here on earth. Like Jacob, He watched over His sheep and ultimately gave us this account: "I have not lost one of those you gave me" (John 18:9). His hair was wet with dew and "sleep fled from [His] eyes" as well, for He spent an entire night in prayer wrestling for His people. One moment Peter needed His pleadings, and soon thereafter another of His children claimed His tearful intercession.

No shepherd sitting beneath the cold skies and looking up at the stars could ever utter more legitimate complaints due to the difficulty of his tiresome labor than Jesus Christ. He certainly had reason to complain if He had chosen to do so, based on the extreme severity of His mission to redeem His bride.

> Cold mountains and the midnight air,
> Witnessed the fervor of His prayer;
> The desert His temptations knew,
> His conflict and His victory too.
>
> Isaac Watts, 1674–1748

It is interesting to consider the spiritual parallel of Laban requiring all the sheep from Jacob.

If the sheep were "torn by wild beasts" and killed, he had to pay Laban for them, and he always stood as the pledge or security for them, guaranteeing a complete flock. And wasn't the mission of Jesus for His church the work of one who was under His Father's legal obligation to bring every believer safely into the hand of Him who had committed them to His care? When we see Jacob laboring so diligently, we see a type of Him who was to come — Him of whom Isaiah said, "He tends his flock like a shepherd" (Isa. 40:11).

From the pen of Jim Reimann:

If we view the Old Testament with spiritual eyes, it is impossible not to see Jesus on every page. Over and over again we see stories prefiguring the coming Messiah, such as in today's devotion with the story of Jacob and Laban. Yet these are but a shadow of our precious Savior.

For example, Paul wrote of feasts and observances required in the books of the law, saying, "Do not let anyone judge you by what you eat or drink, or with regard to a religious festival, a New Moon celebration or a Sabbath day. *These are a shadow of the things that were to come; the reality, however, is found in Christ*" (Col. 2:16–17). And the writer of Hebrews said, "*The law is only a shadow of the good things that are coming — not the realities themselves....* Therefore, when Christ came into the world, he said: ...'Here I am — *it is written about me in the scroll* — I have come to do your will, O God'" (Heb. 10:1, 5, 7).

Look for Jesus as you read your Bible. You will find Him on every page.

… fellowship with him …
1 John 1:6

From the pen of Charles Spurgeon:

When we were united with Christ by faith, we were brought into such complete fellowship with Him that we were made one with Him, and His interests and ours became mutual and identical. We have fellowship with Christ in His love. What He loves, we love. He loves the saints — so do we; He loves sinners — so do we. He loves the poor perishing race of mankind and yearns to see earth's "wastelands" transformed into "the garden of the Lord" (Isa. 51:3) — so do we.

We also have fellowship with Him in His desires. He desires the glory of God — we work for the same purpose. He desires for the saints to be with Him where He is — we long to be there as well. He desires to drive sin away — we fight under His banner with the same goal. He desires His Father's name to be loved and adored by all His creatures — we pray daily, "Your kingdom come, your will be done on earth as it is in heaven" (Matt. 6:10).

We have fellowship with Christ in His sufferings as well. We are not nailed to the cross, nor do we die a cruel death, but when He suffers reproach, so do we. Yet what a blessed thing it is to be accused for His sake, to be despised for following the Master, and to have the world against us. "A student is not above his teacher, nor a servant above his master" (Matt. 10:24).

We also fellowship with Him in His work, ministering to others through "the word of truth" (2 Tim. 2:15) and by deeds of love. "[Our] food," like His, "is to do the will of him who sent [Him] and to finish his work" (John 4:34).

Finally, we have fellowship with Christ in His joy. We are happy in His happiness and rejoice in His exaltation. Dear believer, have you ever tasted His joy? There can be nothing more refreshing or thrilling this side of heaven than having Christ's joy fulfilled in us — "to make our joy complete" (1 John 1:4).

His glory awaits us and will ultimately complete our fellowship, for His church will sit with Him upon His throne as His well-beloved bride and queen.

From the pen of Jim Reimann:

What an amazing thing, that the Lord and Creator of the entire universe desires to fellowship with us! David, in amazement of this truth, proclaimed, "O Lord, what is man that you care for him, the son of man that you think of him? Man is like a breath; his days are like a fleeting shadow" (Ps. 144:3 – 4). In the following psalm David reiterates this truth, all the while praising his creator:

O Lord, our Lord, how majestic is your name in all the earth! You have set your glory above the heavens. From the lips of children and infants you have ordained praise because of your enemies, to silence the foe and the avenger. When I consider your heavens, the work of your fingers, the moon and the stars, which you have set in place, *what is man that you are mindful of him, the son of man that you care for him?* You made him a little lower than the heavenly beings and crowned him with glory and honor. You made him ruler over the works of your hands; you put everything under his feet: all flocks and herds, and the beasts of the field, the birds of the air, and the fish of the sea, all that swim the paths of the seas. O Lord, our Lord, how majestic is your name in all the earth!

Psalm 8:1 – 9

NOVEMBER 24

There the LORD will be our Mighty One.
It will be like a place of broad rivers and streams.

Isaiah 33:21

From the pen of Charles Spurgeon:

"Broad rivers and streams" produce fertility and abundance, and the nearby land is remarkable for its variety of plants and plentiful harvests. And that is what God is to His church, for because we have Him, the church has abundance. What can we ask for that the Lord will not give us? What need can we mention that He will not supply? "On this mountain the LORD Almighty will prepare a feast of rich food for all peoples" (Isa. 25:6). Do you need "the bread of life" (John 6:35)? It will drop like manna from the sky. Do you need a refreshing stream? The rock from which the stream flows follows you, and that Rock is Christ. If you suffer from any lack or need, it is your own fault, for if you are impoverished, you are not impoverished in Him but in your own heart.

"Broad rivers and streams" also suggest a place of commerce. Our glorious Lord is a place of heavenly "merchandise" to us. Through our Redeemer we have the affluence of commerce from the past, for we have the wealth of Calvary, the treasures of the covenant, the riches of our election "before the creation of the world" (Eph. 1:4), and all His eternal possessions. All these flow to us down the "broad rivers and streams" of our gracious Lord. But we also have the affluence of commerce from the future. What amazing ships loaded with His treasures to the water's edge come to us from His millennial kingdom! What visions we enjoy of the days of heaven upon earth! Indeed, through our glorious Lord we transact commerce with angels and share communion with the shining saints washed in His blood who sing before the throne. And better still, we have fellowship with the infinite One.

"Broad rivers and streams" suggest the idea of security. In days of old, rivers provided great security from the enemy. O beloved, what a great defense God is to His church! Even the Devil cannot cross this broad river of God. Oh, how he wishes he could redirect the river's flow, but fear not — God remains immutably the same! Satan may harass us, but he cannot destroy us. "No galley with oars will ride them, no mighty ship will sail them" (Isa. 33:21).

From the pen of Jim Reimann:

Isaiah refers to the Lord several times as a stream, and especially in the arid Middle East, the significance of this was not lost on God's people. For thousands of years, even up to the present age, wars in the area have been fought over water. And oftentimes, when the Lord's chosen people were disobedient to Him, He withheld the rain.

Thus, streams represent the blessing of the Lord, and Isaiah tied the streams more than once directly to the coming Messiah. He said,

> "Be strong, do not fear; your God will come, he will come with vengeance; with divine retribution he will come to save you." Then will the eyes of the blind be opened and the ears of the deaf unstopped. Then will the lame leap like a deer, and the mute tongue shout for joy. Water will gush forth in the wilderness and streams in the desert. The burning sand will become a pool, the thirsty ground bubbling springs.

Isaiah 35:4 – 7

> See, I am doing a new thing! Now it springs up; do you not perceive it? I am making a way in the desert and streams in the wasteland.

Isaiah 43:19

Day 329

NOVEMBER 25

He has sent me to proclaim freedom for the prisoners.

Luke 4:18

From the pen of Charles Spurgeon:

No one but Jesus can give true liberty to prisoners, for real freedom comes only from Him. It is a freedom *righteously bestowed*, for the Son who is "heir of all things" (Heb. 1:2) has a right to make men free. Saints then should honor the justice of God that secures their salvation.

It is a freedom that has been *dearly purchased*. Christ speaks freedom by His power, but He bought it at the great cost of His blood. He makes me free, but it is through His own chains. I go free because He bore my burden; I have freedom because He suffered in my place.

Though dearly purchased, it is freedom *freely given*. Jesus asks nothing of me as preparation for this liberty. He finds me sitting in "sackcloth and ashes" (Est. 4:3) and invites me to clothe myself instead in His beautiful garment of freedom. He saves me precisely as I am, all without my help or merit.

When Jesus sets me free, the freedom is also *eternally done*, for no chain can ever shackle me again. Once the Master says to me, "Prisoner, I have freed you," it is done forever. Satan may plot to enslave me, but "if God is for [me], who can be against [me]?" (Rom. 8:31) — "Whom shall I fear?" (Ps. 27:1). The world with its temptations may seek to ensnare me, but "greater is he" (1 John 4:4 KJV) who is for me than all those combined who are against me. The scheming of my own deceitful heart may harass and annoy me, but "he who began a good work in [me] will carry it on to completion" (Phil. 1:6). The foes of God and the enemies of man may gather their considerable armies together, coming against me with all their powerful fury, but if the Lord acquits, "who is he that condemns?" (Rom. 8:34).

Even an eagle that soars to his aerie high atop a rocky cliff and then outsoars the clouds is not more free than a soul whom Christ has freed.

Thus, since I am no longer under the law and am freed from its curse, may my freedom be *practically exhibited* in serving God with gratitude and joy.

"O LORD, truly I am your servant; I am your servant, the son of your maidservant; you have freed me from my chains" (Ps. 116:16). "Lord, what do You want me to do?" (Acts 9:6 NKJV).

From the pen of Jim Reimann:

Spurgeon says today that we as saints "should honor the justice of God." The way we do that is by walking in the freedom Christ purchased for us, not allowing ourselves to live like slaves again. We "used to be slaves to sin" (Rom. 6:17) and were condemned by the law "that stood opposed to us" (Col. 2:14), but Paul says, now that we are believers, "Sin shall not be your master" (Rom. 6:14). And he gives this warning: "It is for freedom that Christ has set us free. Stand firm, then, and do not let yourselves be burdened again by a yoke of slavery" (Gal. 5:1). Previously he said, "Christ redeemed us from the curse of the law by becoming a curse for us" (Gal. 3:13). Jesus took our sin debt that "stood opposed to us," stamped it PAID IN FULL, and redeemed us by "nailing it to the cross" (Col. 2:14) with His own body. Thus, let us follow his advice:

You, my brothers, were called to be free. But do not use your freedom to indulge the sinful nature; rather, serve one another in love.

Galatians 5:13

NOVEMBER 26

Whatever your hand finds to do,
do it with all your might.
Ecclesiastes 9:10

From the pen of Charles Spurgeon:

"Whatever your hand finds to do" refers to works that are possible for us, yet there are many things our heart can find to do that we will never do. It's fine to have an idea in our heart, but it would be much more useful if, instead of just being content to have an idea or talking about doing something, we would actually do it — do "whatever your hand finds to do." One good deed is worth far more than a thousand brilliant ideas never done. We should never simply sit and wait for big opportunities or for a different kind of work to come along. We should, each and every day, do the things our "hand finds to do."

We have no time in which to live but the present, for the past is gone and the future has not yet come. So do not wait until your life experience has ripened into maturity before you attempt to serve God. Endeavor to bring forth fruit now. Serve Him now but be careful how you do what "your hand finds to do," for you should "do it with all your might." Do it promptly, not frittering your life away, thinking of what you intend to do tomorrow as if that could compensate for your idleness today. No one ever served God by doing things tomorrow. It is what we do today that generates blessings and brings honor to Christ. And whatever you do for Him, throw your entire soul into it. Don't give Christ a little halfhearted work done every now and then, but when you serve Him do it "with all your heart and with all your soul and with all your strength" (Deut. 6:5).

Yet where is the might or power of a Christian to be found? It is certainly not in himself, for he is "perfect...weakness" (2 Cor. 12:9). No, a Christian's might lies in the Lord Almighty so let us seek His help and move forth in prayer and with faith. And once we have done what our "hand finds to do," let us "wait upon the LORD" (Ps. 123:2 KJV) for His blessing. Then what we do for Him will be done well and our service will never fail in its effectiveness.

From the pen of Jim Reimann:

Diligence and endurance have become nearly lost commodities today. Yet as Christians we should be motivated by our love for God to serve Him well. Paul told Timothy to "set an example for the believers in speech, in life, in love, in faith and in purity," and then stressed to "be diligent in these matters; give yourself wholly to them, so that everyone may see your progress" (1 Tim. 4:12, 15). And in another place Paul echoed our text verse from Ecclesiastes, teaching the principle of serving the Lord wholeheartedly. As you read this passage this morning, apply it to your vocation and place of service to the Lord:

> Slaves, obey your earthly masters in everything; and do it, not only when their eye is on you and to win their favor, but with sincerity of heart and reverence for the Lord. *Whatever you do, work at it with all your heart, as working for the Lord*, not for men, since you know that you will receive an inheritance from the Lord as a reward. It is the Lord Christ you are serving.
> Colossians 3:22 – 24

If I truly love Jesus, I will pour my total being into His work and someday I will hear Him say, "Well done, good and faithful servant! You have been faithful with a few things; I will put you in charge of many things. Come and share your master's happiness!" (Matt. 25:21). What could be more glorious than that!

NOVEMBER 27

He showed me Joshua the high priest
standing before the angel of the LORD.

Zechariah 3:1

From the pen of Charles Spurgeon:

In this verse Joshua the high priest is a picture of each child of God. We stand before the Lord because of the blood of Christ, having been taught to minister in holy things, and we enter into the "Most Holy Place behind the curtain" (Lev. 16:2). Jesus has made us priests and kings unto God, and even here on earth we exercise the priestly duties of consecrated living and holy service.

In today's verse notice the position of the high priest. He is standing — "*standing* before the angel of the LORD" — meaning he is in a position ready to minister. And this should be the continual position of every true believer. We should think of everywhere we are as God's temple and, as such, we can truly serve Him in our daily work as though we were in His very house. We are to minister continually, offering "a sacrifice of praise" (Heb. 13:15) and prayer and presenting ourselves to Him as "living sacrifices" (Rom. 12:1).

Next notice where Joshua stands to minister — it is "*before* the angel of the LORD" Jehovah. Thus, it is only through a mediator that we poor defiled ones can ever become priests unto God. I present my sacrifice before God's messenger, the angel of the covenant — the Lord Jesus. My prayers find acceptance only by being wrapped in His prayers, and my praises are made fragrant only as they are combined with bundles of "myrrh and aloes and cassia" (Ps. 45:8) from Christ's own garden. If all I can bring Him are my tears, He will place them with His tears in His own bottle, for He once wept as well. If all I can bring Him are my groans and sighs, He will accept them as an acceptable sacrifice, for He once was brokenhearted and His soul sighed heavily too.

I myself, standing in Christ, am "accepted in the beloved" (Eph. 1:6 KJV), and all my polluted works, though they are in and of themselves simply objects of God's divine loathing, are through Him received in such a way they become a "pleasing aroma" (Gen. 8:21) to God. He is content in my "sacrifice of praise" and prayer and I am blessed.

Finally, therefore, notice the position of the Christian — a "priest standing before the angel of the LORD."

From the pen of Jim Reimann:

Three months after the Lord delivered His children from Egypt, He told them through Moses, "Now if you obey me fully and keep my covenant, then out of all nations you will be my treasured possession. Although the whole earth is mine, *you will be for me a kingdom of priests and a holy nation*" (Ex. 19:5 – 6).

Consider the awesomeness of God's Word and His faithfulness as you read of the fulfillment of this prophecy in Christ's church more than 1,500 years later! Here is how Peter describes our Lord Jesus and us as His followers:

As you come to him, the living Stone — rejected by men but chosen by God and precious to him — you also, like living stones, are being built into a spiritual house to be a *holy priesthood*, offering spiritual sacrifices acceptable to God through Jesus Christ.... But you are a chosen people, *a royal priesthood, a holy nation*, a people belonging to God, that you may declare the praises of him who called you out of darkness into his wonderful light.

1 Peter 2:4 – 5, 9

NOVEMBER 28

It gave me great joy to have some brothers come and tell
about your faithfulness to the truth and how you continue to walk in the truth.

3 John 3

From the pen of Charles Spurgeon:

John addressed his letter: "To my dear friend Gaius, whom I love in the truth" (3 John 1). The truth was in Gaius and Gaius walked in the truth. And if the first part of that were not true, the second part could never have occurred; and if the second part could not be said of him, the first part would have been a mere pretense. Truth must enter into the soul, penetrating and saturating it, or else it is of no value. Doctrine accepted simply as a matter of a system of belief is like bread in one's hand, providing no nourishment to the body whatsoever. But doctrine accepted by the heart is like digested food that through assimilation sustains and builds up the body.

Truth must be a living force, an active energy and indwelling reality in us, a part of the underlying structure of our being. And if the truth is *in* us, we cannot lose it in the future. A person can lose a garment or even one of his limbs, but his inner parts are vital and cannot be torn away without complete loss of life. A true Christian can die physically, but he cannot deny the truth.

It is a natural law that the inner parts affect the outer body just as light shines from the center of a lantern through the glass. Therefore, in the same way, when the truth is kindled within us, its brightness shines forth in our outer life and conversation. Just as the food of certain worms colors the silk cocoons they spin, the nutrients upon which mankind's inner nature lives colors every word and action proceeding from within him.

Walking in the truth, therefore, leads to a life of integrity, holiness, faithfulness, and simplicity. It is the natural by-product of the principles of truth the gospel teaches and which the Spirit of God enables us to receive. Thus, we are able to judge the secrets of a person's soul by the manifestation of the truth in their life and conversation.

May it be mine today, O gracious Spirit, to be ruled and governed by Your divine authority, so that nothing false or sinful may reign in my heart lest it extend its deadly influence to my daily walk before others.

From the pen of Jim Reimann:

Whether in his gospel account or in his epistles, the primary focus of John's writing was truth. Of course, it was in John 14:6 where Jesus was equated with truth itself, for He said, "I am the way and *the truth* and the life. No one comes to the Father except through me." Thus, since He is the truth, it would be appropriate to say, in essence, "No one comes to the Father except through [the Truth]." In fact, James says, "He chose to give us birth through the word of truth" (James 1:18).

Furthermore, we could say that walking in the truth is equal to walking with Jesus Himself. This emphasis on the importance of our walk is quite evident in John's letters. In 2 John 4 he said, "It has given me great joy to find some of your children walking in the truth, just as the Father commanded us." And later in 3 John 4 he reiterated that thought by saying, "I have no greater joy than to hear that my children are walking in the truth."

Father, may I bring You great joy as I walk in the truth of Your Son.

NOVEMBER 29

Do not go about spreading slander among your people....
Rebuke your neighbor frankly so you will not share in his guilt.

Leviticus 19:16 – 17

From the pen of Charles Spurgeon:

Malicious gossip emits a threefold poison, for it injures the speaker, the hearer, and the person who is the subject of the accusation. Whether the report is true or not, God's Word forbids us to spread it. The reputations of the Lord's people should be very precious in our sight, and we should consider it shameful to help the Devil dishonor the church and the name of the Lord. Some tongues need a bridle, not a spur, for a number of people take pride in pulling down their brothers as though it lifts themselves higher.

Noah's sons Shem and Japheth wisely "took a garment ... and covered their father's nakedness" (Gen. 9:23), but Ham spoke of his father's nakedness and earned a horrible curse as a result. We too may have a dark day ahead, one in which we would appreciate self-restraint and silence from our family in Christ. Thus, let us cheerfully offer the same courtesy to those who need it now. May this be our family rule and personal pledge: "Slander no one" (Titus 3:2)!

The Holy Spirit, however, permits us to criticize sin but prescribes exactly how we are to do so. We are to rebuke our brother to his face rather than complain behind his back. This useful method carries God's blessing and is therefore brotherly, Christlike, and powerful. Our flesh will shrink from this approach, but we should consider the greater stress upon our conscience if we refuse to do the right thing. By ignoring the problem we allow our friend to continue in sin, and then we ourselves actually become participants in it.

Many people have been saved from shameful sinfulness through the timely, wise, and affectionate warnings of faithful ministers and friends. And our Lord Jesus Himself has set a gracious example for us in dealing with erring friends. We see His warning to Peter regarding his boastful statement of support being preceded by prayer and delivered with gentleness.

From the pen of Jim Reimann:

At the Last Supper, Jesus' disciples "began to question ... who would [betray Him]. Also a dispute arose among them as to which of them was considered to be greatest" (Luke 22:23 – 24). Peter even boasted, "Lord, I am ready to go with you to prison and to death" (v. 33). This type of prideful speech and boasting was something Jesus would not tolerate in His followers.

Yet even before Peter's boast, Jesus had told him, "Satan has asked to sift you as wheat. But I have prayed for you" (vv. 31 – 32). Especially notice the words, "*But I have prayed for you*," and the fact that Jesus' prayer preceded this rebuke: "Peter, before the rooster crows today, you will deny three times that you know me" (v. 34). This is the example Jesus gave us, for a rebuke of another believer first must be bathed in prayer and must be gentle. "If someone is caught in a sin, you who are spiritual should restore him gently" (Gal. 6:1).

Ultimately Peter learned the importance of controlling his tongue, for he later wrote,

> Do not repay evil with evil or insult with insult, but with blessing, because to this you were called so that you may inherit a blessing. For, "Whoever would love life and see good days must keep his tongue from evil and his lips from deceitful speech."
>
> 1 Peter 3:9 – 10

Amaziah asked the man of God,
"But what about the hundred talents I paid for these Israelite troops?"
The man of God replied, "The LORD can give you much more than that."

2 Chronicles 25:9

From the pen of Charles Spurgeon:

This question was important to Amaziah, King of Judah, but perhaps is even more important to a tested and tempted Christian. Losing money is never pleasant, and even when it involves a matter of principle, our flesh is not always ready to sacrifice. We ask ourselves, "Why must I lose this money that could be used so well somewhere else? Why am I being required to pay such a high price? What am I supposed to do without this money? What about my children and the fact that my income is so low already?" These questions and a thousand more may tempt a Christian with unrighteous gain or may keep him from following through on his deeply held convictions if it may lead to serious loss. Unbelievers cannot consider these matters in the light of faith, but even with followers of Jesus the thought, "We have to live," carries a lot of weight.

"The LORD can give you much more than that" is a satisfactory answer to our anxiety over money. Our Father holds the purse strings and whatever we lose for His sake He can repay a thousandfold. Our role is simply to obey His will, and then we can rest assured He will provide, for our Lord will be a debtor to no one. A true saint knows that even what appears to be a small blessing from Him can have more value than a ton of gold. Someone with a threadbare coat who wraps that coat around a clear conscience has gained spiritual wealth far more desirable than whatever was lost financially. Even if living in a dungeon, God's smile is enough for a pure heart.

If your bad situation becomes worse, let the money go — you have not lost your treasure, for that is above, where Christ is seated "at the right hand of God" (Rom. 8:34). Meanwhile — right now — the Lord causes "the meek ... [to] inherit the earth" (Matt. 5:5) and "no good thing does he withhold from those whose walk is blameless" (Ps. 84:11).

From the pen of Jim Reimann:

We live in a world where virtually everything is measured by money. Yet it is a trap to measure success by the world's standard. Even churches often measure their success by their financial numbers and reports. Monday morning staff meetings tend to be more about how much money was collected in the offering plates Sunday morning than asking the question, "Were we obedient to what the Lord called us to do yesterday?"

The world ties success with financial prosperity, but the Lord never has — and never will! Notice the separation of them in this verse: "Do not let this Book of the Law depart from your mouth; meditate on it day and night, so that you may be careful to do everything written in it. *Then you will be prosperous and successful*" (Josh. 1:8). Another translation puts it this way: "Then you will make your way prosperous, and then you will have good success" (ESV). And the underlying meaning here is that prosperity itself is not just financial.

We would do well to remember the words of David, who said, "I have never seen the righteous forsaken or their children begging bread" (Ps. 37:25).

December

DECEMBER 1

You made both summer and winter.

Psalm 74:17

From the pen of Charles Spurgeon:

Dear soul, begin this wintry month with your God. Let the cold snow and piercing wind remind you He keeps His covenant with you day and night. And let that give you the assurance He will also keep the glorious covenant He made with you in the person of Christ Jesus. He who is true to His Word in the cycle of the seasons of this poor sin-polluted world will not then prove to be unfaithful in His dealings with His own well-beloved Son.

Winter in the soul can be an uncomfortable season as well. If it is something you are experiencing right now, consider this word of comfort, namely, that the Lord has sent it. He sends the cold blasts of adversity to nip the buds of our expectations. "He ... scatters the frost like ashes" over the once green meadows of our joy and "hurls down his hail like pebbles" (Ps. 147:16 – 17), freezing the streams of our delight. He does it all, for He is the King of Winter, ruling even the realms of frost. Therefore, we should not complain, for losses, crosses, weariness, sickness, poverty, and a thousand other difficulties are sent by the Lord and come to us through His wise purpose. Remember, frost also kills deadly insects, stemming agonizing diseases. It softens the hardness of the soil as well and sweetens our soul. Oh, that such good results would always follow our winters of affliction!

Oh, how we enjoy the warm cheerful glow of a roaring fire on the hearth on a cold wintry day! In the same manner, may we treasure our Lord who is the constant source of warmth and comfort in every time of trouble. May we "come near to God"

(James 4:8) and find our joy and peace through faith in Him. May we wrap ourselves in the warm garments of His promises and go forth to service appropriate to the season, never being like "the sluggard [who] will not plow by reason of the [winter] cold; therefore shall he beg in [the summer] harvest, and have nothing" (Prov. 20:4 KJV).

From the pen of Jim Reimann:

Today Spurgeon mentions God's covenant with day and night. What He is referring to is this: "As long as the earth endures, seedtime and harvest, cold and heat, summer and winter, day and night will never cease" (Gen. 8:22). In a world seemingly obsessed over climate change and the possibility of global warming, what a comfort to know the Lord is the one in control! And if we can trust His sovereignty over the sun, the moon, the planets, and the seasons, surely we can trust Him when it comes to the seasons of our own soul.

Spurgeon, like many people today, suffered occasional bouts of depression. Yet from today's devotion we see he understood that even those were sent to him with a purpose from his heavenly Father. If you can relate, may the experiences of Paul and David bring you comfort. Paul was once at the point where he "despaired even of life" and said, "Indeed, in our hearts we felt the sentence of death." Yet he saw God's purpose in it, for he went on to say, "But this happened that we might not rely on ourselves but on God, who raises the dead" (2 Cor. 1:8 – 9). And David went from times of great elation to times of despair, yet prayed, "If I go up to the heavens, you are there; if I make my bed in the depths, you are there" (Ps. 139:8).

DECEMBER 2

All beautiful you are, my darling.
Song of Songs 4:7

From the pen of Charles Spurgeon:

The Lord's affection for His church is quite wonderful, and His description of her beauty is very glowing. He doesn't merely speak of His bride as beautiful, but "all beautiful." He sees her as being in Himself, washed in His sin-atoning blood, and clothed in His legally won righteousness. He considers her pleasing to look upon and, in fact, full of beauty. Yet this is not surprising since it is actually His own perfect qualities He is admiring, for the church's holiness, glory, and perfection are His own glorious garments in which He has clothed His well-beloved spouse. She is not simply pure—she is positively lovely and beautiful!

She also has true merit! Her deformities due to sin have been removed, but even more, through her Lord she obtained a legally won righteousness by which her true beauty has been conferred upon her. Believers have an absolute righteousness given to them when they are "accepted in the beloved" (Eph. 1:6 KJV).

Again, the Lord doesn't see His church as barely lovely but "all beautiful," for He also refers to her as the "most beautiful of women" (Song 5:9). She has true worth and excellence that cannot be rivaled by all the nobility and royalty of the world. If Jesus could exchange His elect bride for all the queens and empresses on earth, or even for the angels in heaven, He would not do so, for she is His priority and the "most beautiful of women." Like the moon, she outshines the stars, and this is not an opinion He is ashamed of, for He wants all people to hear Him. In Song of Songs 4:1, He doesn't simply say, "How beautiful!" but "*Oh*, how beautiful!" drawing even more attention to it. And in that verse He reiterates the thought, saying, "How beautiful you are, my darling! Oh, how beautiful!"

Even now our Lord proclaims His glorious opinion of His bride. And one day, from the throne of His glory, He will reconfirm this truth before the assembled multitudes of the universe. His solemn affirmation of the beauty of His elect will be the words: "Come, you who are blessed by my Father" (Matt. 25:34).

From the pen of Jim Reimann:

Today's devotion is a glorious reminder of the power of God's grace to transform His people. Paul asked, "Do you not know that the wicked will not inherit the kingdom of God? Do not be deceived: Neither the sexually immoral nor idolaters nor adulterers nor male prostitutes nor homosexual offenders nor thieves nor the greedy nor drunkards nor slanderers nor swindlers will inherit the kingdom of God. And that is what some of you were" (1 Cor. 6:9–11).

And that is what some of *us* were! Yet the power of God's amazing grace is revealed as Paul continues in verse 11: "But you were washed, you were sanctified, you were justified in the name of the Lord Jesus Christ and by the Spirit of our God." Paul also said, "Therefore, if anyone is in Christ, he is a new creation; the old has gone, the new has come!" (2 Cor. 5:17), and "He chose us in him before the creation of the world to be holy and blameless in his sight" (Eph. 1:4)—not to mention beautiful.

And as Solomon said in another of his books, "He has made everything beautiful in its time" (Eccl. 3:11)—even us!

December 3

My darling, there is no flaw in you.

Song of Songs 4:7

From the pen of Charles Spurgeon:

Yesterday we considered how the Lord sees His church as full of beauty, and today we see Him confirm His praise of His beloved through the use of a precious negative: "There is *no* flaw in you." It's as though the thought may have occurred to the Bridegroom that our accusing world would insinuate He had mentioned only the beautiful parts of His bride, purposely omitting any features that are deformed or defiled. Thus, He sums up His description of her by saying she is completely beautiful and devoid of any flaw whatsoever. A tiny flaw could be covered easily and would not detract from her beauty in the least, but the Lord has removed every tiny flaw of each believer.

If He had said there is no hideous scar, no horrible deformity, or no deadly tumor in His bride, we might have been astonished. But when He declares she is free from even the slightest flaw, the depth of our astonishment is greatly deepened. Even if He had promised simply to remove all flaws eventually we would have had reason for eternal joy, but when He says it is already done, who can suppress their emotions of the most intense satisfaction and delight? O dear believer, here is "the richest of foods" (Ps. 63:5), so eat till your soul is fully satisfied with "delicacies fit for a king" (Gen. 49:20)!

Christ Jesus has no quarrel with His bride, and although she often wanders from Him and may often "grieve [His] Holy Spirit" (Eph. 4:30), He does not allow her faults to affect His love. Sometimes He rebukes her but always in the most tender of ways and with the kindest of intentions, for even then He refers to her as "My darling."

He has no remembrance of our foolishness and does not harbor bad thoughts of us; instead He pardons us and loves us as much after we sin as before the offense. What a wonderful thing this is. For if Jesus harbored hurts like we are so prone to do, how could He fellowship with us? Believers may be upset with the Lord for some work of His sovereignty in our lives we don't like, but our precious Husband knows our foolish hearts all too well to take any offense by our bad manners.

From the pen of Jim Reimann:

Although believers are still undergoing sanctification, when it comes to our forgiving Savior, we are even now "holy and blameless in his sight" (Eph. 1:4). And in the same book as that quote we are told, "Christ loved the church and gave himself up for her to make her holy, cleansing her by the washing with water through the word, and to present her to himself as a radiant church, without stain or wrinkle or any other blemish, but holy and blameless" (Eph. 5:25 – 27).

Spurgeon today refers to Jesus as "our precious Husband." Thus, it is our heavenly Spouse who says, "I, even I, am he who blots out your transgressions, for my own sake, and remembers your sins no more" (Isa. 43:25). Unfortunately we remember our sins, but thankfully our Savior does not. Perhaps we should adopt His view, for whose view is actually "the *true* truth," as some may ask for emphasis? Once again, thankfully it is His view that counts for eternity!

"Praise the LORD, O my soul, and forget not all his benefits — who forgives all [my] sins" (Ps. 103:2 – 3), *and who sees me as "holy and blameless"!*

DECEMBER 4

I have many people in this city.
Acts 18:10

From the pen of Charles Spurgeon:

This verse should be a great encouragement for us to do God's work, since among the vilest of the vile, the most depraved and degenerate, and the most drugged and drunken people, the Lord has His elect people who must be saved. When you take God's Word to them, you do so because He has sovereignly ordained you to be the messenger of life to their souls, and they must receive it, for this is how the decree of predestination works. They are as much redeemed by Christ's blood as the saints now standing before His eternal throne. They are His property and, although they may now be lovers of bars and alcohol and haters of holiness, if Jesus Christ purchased them, He *will* have them. God is faithful to remember the price His Son has paid for His elect, and He will not allow Christ's substitutionary sacrifice to be an ineffective, dead thing for any of them. Multitudes of redeemed souls are not yet regenerated, but regenerated they must and will be. This is the comfort and assurance we have when we go forth to take God's life-giving Word to them.

Furthermore, these ungodly souls have been prayed for by Christ before the throne of God, for the great Intercessor said, "My prayer is not for [My disciples] alone. I pray also for those who will believe in me through their message" (John 17:20). Poor ignorant souls know nothing about praying for themselves, but Jesus prays for them. Their names are written on His breastplate, and before long they will bend their stubborn knees to Him and will finally breathe a repentant sigh before His throne of grace.

"The time of figs [is] not yet" (Mark 11:13 KJV). The predestined moment has not yet struck for many, but when it comes they will obey. "As soon as they hear me, they obey me" (Ps. 18:44), for God will have those who are His. They must come to Him, for the Spirit cannot be ignored when He comes forth in the fullness of His power; they must become willing servants of the living God. "Thy people shall be willing in the day of thy power" (Ps. 110:3 KJV).

"After the suffering of his soul ... my righteous servant will justify many.... I will give him a portion among the great, and he will divide the spoils with the strong" (Isa. 53:11 – 12).

From the pen of Jim Reimann:

Today we see God's absolute sovereignty in salvation. Paul said, "If anyone is in Christ, he is a new creation; the old has gone, the new has come! *All this is from God*, who reconciled us to himself through Christ" (2 Cor. 5:17 – 18). The Lord, however, has chosen to involve His people in spreading the gospel. As Spurgeon said today, Jesus prayed for those who would later "believe in [Him] through their message."

Paul continues in 2 Corinthians 5 by saying, "God ... gave us the ministry of reconciliation.... And he has committed to us the message of reconciliation. We are therefore Christ's ambassadors, as though God were making his appeal through us" (2 Cor. 5:18 – 20). May we remember what transpired when Paul preached the gospel: "When the Gentiles heard this, they were glad and honored the word of the Lord; and *all who were appointed for eternal life believed*" (Acts 13:48).

DECEMBER 5

Ask and it will be given to you.

Matthew 7:7

From the pen of Charles Spurgeon:

There is a place that still exists in England where a handout of bread is given to every passerby who asks for it. Whoever the traveler may be, he only has to knock on the door of St. Cross Hospital and he will be given an allotment of bread. Jesus Christ also has built a "St. Cross Hospital" so that whenever a sinner is hungry, he only has to knock to have his needs fulfilled. In fact, He has done even better; He has added a bath to His Hospital of the Cross so that a dark and filthy soul only has to go there to be cleaned. And the bath is always full and always effective, for no sinner ever entered it and found it could not wash away the stains of sin. The stains have all disappeared, for "though your sins are like scarlet [or crimson], they shall be as white as snow" (Isa. 1:18).

If this were not enough, attached to the Hospital of the Cross is a fully stocked closet, and a sinner who applies, simply as a sinner, may be clothed from head to toe. If he desires to be a soldier, he will not be given ordinary street clothes but will be covered from the sole of his foot to the top of his head with armor. If he asks for a sword and a shield, those will be given to him as well, for nothing good for him will be denied. He will have spending money for as long as he lives and will have an eternal heritage of glorious treasure when he enters into "the joy of the LORD" (Neh. 8:10).

O dear soul, if all these things can be yours merely by knocking at mercy's door, then knock loudly this morning and ask great things of your generous Lord. Don't leave the throne of grace until all your needs have been laid before the Lord and until by faith you have the comfortable assurance they will all be supplied. Your bashfulness need not inhibit you when Jesus invites you to come. No unbelief should hinder you when Jesus promises. And no coldheartedness should restrain you when such blessings are yours for the asking.

From the pen of Jim Reimann:

Today Spurgeon mentions St. Cross Hospital in England. Yes, it is still in existence today just as it was in his day. In fact, it was originally established between 1132 and 1136 by William the Conqueror's grandson Henri du Blois. It is the oldest charitable poorhouse in England, located near Winchester, and now includes St. Cross Church as well. It served as a wayside stop for pilgrims en route to Canterbury, and during the Crusades the crusaders would spend their last night there before sailing from Southhampton. The tradition of giving bread to passersby is still practiced today. All a visitor need do is stop at the Porter's Gate and ask. One wonders how many go hungry when all they need do is ask.

One wonders as well how often we as believers go without because we don't ask. Perhaps we don't ask because we forget the provision is not based on our works but on Christ's work, for the Scriptures say, "Since we have a great high priest who has gone through the heavens, Jesus the Son of God, let us hold firmly to the faith we profess. For we do not have a high priest who is unable to sympathize with our weaknesses, but we have one who has been tempted in every way, just as we are — yet was without sin. *Let us then approach the throne of grace with confidence, so that we may receive mercy and find grace to help us in our time of need*" (Heb. 4:14 – 16).

DECEMBER 6

As is the man from heaven,
so also are those who are of heaven.

1 Corinthians 15:48

From the pen of Charles Spurgeon:

Jesus as the head of the church and believers as members of His body have the same nature, unlike the monstrous statue Nebuchadnezzar saw in his dream. "The head of the statue was made of pure gold, its chest and arms of silver, its belly and thighs of bronze, its legs of iron, its feet partly of iron and partly of baked clay" (Dan. 2:32 – 33). Yet Christ's spiritual body is not comprised of such absurd opposites. The members of His body were mortal, therefore Jesus died; the glorified Lord as head of the body is immortal, therefore the body is immortal as well. For the Scripture still stands: "Because I live, you also will live" (John 14:19). Thus, every single member of the body is like our loving Head. We have a chosen Head and chosen members, an accepted Head and accepted members, and a living Head and living members. Since the Head is of pure gold, the parts of His body are of pure gold. In order to bring the closest possible oneness, God worked a miraculous union of the infinite with the finite.

Dear reader, pause here for a moment and contemplate how the infinite Son of God humbled Himself and thereby exalted you from your state of complete wretchedness into a blessed union with Him and His glory. Can you even consider this without being in utter amazement? As a finite mortal person, you were once so low and ordinary you could have viewed corruption as your father and a mere worm as a member of your family. But in Christ you have been so honored that you can say to the Almighty, "Abba, Father" (Rom. 8:15), and to the incarnate Son of God, "You are my brother and my husband."

Thus, if being related to ancient families and nobility causes people to think highly of themselves, then we have a much greater reason to glory far above them all. May the poorest and most despised believer take hold of this privilege and not allow a spirit of senseless laziness to cause him to neglect to trace his spiritual lineage. And may he never allow any foolish attachment to worldly things to so occupy his thoughts that it blocks recognition of this glorious heavenly honor of his union with Christ.

From the pen of Jim Reimann:

Paul referred to Jesus as "God, the blessed and only Ruler, the King of kings and Lord of lords, who alone is immortal" (1 Tim. 6:15 – 16). But Paul also gave us this promise: "The dead will be raised imperishable, and we will be changed. For the perishable must clothe itself with the imperishable, and the mortal with immortality" (1 Cor. 15:52 – 53).

This is exactly what Spurgeon is referring to today when he says, "The glorified Lord as head of the body is immortal, therefore the body is immortal." What an amazing miracle! And it is in complete agreement with these words of John: "What we will be has not yet been made known. But we know that when he appears, we shall be like him, for we shall see him as he is" (1 John 3:2).

Start your morning today with this glorious thought: "When the perishable has been clothed with the imperishable, and the mortal with immortality, then the saying that is written will come true: 'Death has been swallowed up in victory'" (1 Cor. 15:54).

December 7

He chose the lowly things of this world.

1 Corinthians 1:28

From the pen of Charles Spurgeon:

If you dare to walk city streets by moonlight, you will see sinners. When the night is dark and the wind is howling, you will see sinners lurking in doorways. If you go to the city jail and walk through the wards, you will see sinners there as well, men with deep-set eyes and furrowed brows — men you would not want to face alone at night. Go to a juvenile reformatory and notice teens who have displayed unbridled delinquency, and you will see sinners. Cross the seas and go to the deepest, darkest jungle where ancient tribes still practice cannibalism, and you will find sinners there. Go wherever you choose, yet you need not comb the entire earth, for sinners are very common. You will find them on every street and lane of every city, town, village, and hamlet.

It is for people such as these that Jesus died. Even if you find for me the worst and lowest specimen of humanity, as long as he is "born of woman" (Job 14:1) I still will have hope for him because Jesus Christ "came to seek and to save" (Luke 19:10) *sinners*. God's electing love has chosen some of the worst to be changed into the best. His grace turns the most common of pebbles in the stream into jewels for His royal crown, and He can transform even worthless dross into pure gold. His redeeming love has set apart many of the worst of mankind to be the reward of the Savior's passion. God's effective grace calls many of the vilest of the vile to sit at His table of mercy. Therefore, none of us should ever despair for the lost.

I implore you, dear reader, consider the love coming from Jesus' tearful eyes; the faithful, strong, pure, just, and abiding love also flowing from His bleeding wounds; and the amazing depth of the Savior's compassion. Do not turn away as though it is nothing to you. Instead, "be-lieve in the Lord Jesus, and you will be saved" (Acts 16:31). Trust your soul to Him and He will take you to His Father's right hand in glory everlasting.

From the pen of Jim Reimann:

Some people believe it would be wonderful for the Lord to save famous people who could then use their fame, reputation, and platform to spread the gospel. Indeed, it would be great for them to be saved, but the truth is — God doesn't need their platform! Could He use it? Sure. But does He need it? No!

Think about what would bring God the most glory: using a "nobody" whom He has saved and changed into His messenger and whom He has given His platform, or the famous person who already has his own platform. If you look carefully at God's Word, you will find it to be the story of "the nobodies" whom He has transformed into "the somebodies."

Consider the story of David, when Samuel was sent to his father's home to anoint Israel's next king. David's father, Jesse, didn't even think enough of David to line him up with his brothers. Yet David became Israel's greatest king and was given this promise by the Lord Himself:

I took you from the pasture and from following the flock to be ruler over my people Israel.... Now I will make your name great, like the names of the greatest men of the earth.... Your house and your kingdom will endure forever before me; your throne will be established forever.

2 Samuel 7:8 – 9, 16

Only God can do that, for He chooses "the lowly"!

DECEMBER 8

Yet you have a few people in Sardis who have not soiled their clothes.
They will walk with me, dressed in white, for they are worthy.

Revelation 3:4

From the pen of Charles Spurgeon:

This verse refers to the justification of believers. "They will walk ... in white"— meaning they will enjoy a constant sense of their justification by faith, they will have the understanding that Christ's righteousness has been imputed to them, and they will know they have been washed whiter than newly fallen snow.

It also refers to joy and gladness, for the Jews wore white robes during their holidays. They who wear undefiled garments will always have bright faces and will understand what Solomon meant when he said, "Go, eat your food with gladness, and drink your wine with a joyful heart, for it is now that God favors what you do. Always be clothed in white" (Eccl. 9:7 – 8). Everyone who is accepted by God will wear white garments of joy and gladness while walking in sweet communion with the Lord Jesus. Then why are there so many doubts and so much misery and mourning among believers? It is because so many of us defile our garments with sin and error and therefore lose "the joy of [our] salvation" (Ps. 51:12) and the intimate fellowship of the Lord Jesus. It is because we do not "walk ... in white."

This promise also refers to "walk[ing] ... in white" before the throne of God. Those "who have not soiled their clothes" here on earth will certainly "walk ... in white" in heaven, where the white-robed hosts sing perpetual hallelujahs to the "Most High" (Gen. 14:18). They will be filled with joy beyond belief, happiness beyond their wildest imagination or dream, and blessedness beyond their deepest desire. "They whose ways are blameless" (Ps. 119:1) will have all this, not through their own merit or works but by grace.

"They will walk with [Christ] ... in white, for [He has made them] worthy." In His sweet fellowship they will drink from "springs of living water" (Rev. 7:17).

From the pen of Jim Reimann:

After Solomon's temple was destroyed, the time finally came for a new one to be erected, and it must have been beautiful as well, for the Lord said this regarding it, "The glory of this present house will be greater than the glory of the former house" (Hag. 2:9). Yet the people had defiled themselves by their sinfulness, causing God to say, "So it is with this people and this nation in my sight. Whatever they do and whatever they offer there is defiled" (v. 14).

The second temple was replaced by Herod the Great, a man considered great not because he was a great king but because he was a great builder. In fact, the sages of Israel praised his temple by saying, "Whoever has never seen Herod's Temple, has never beheld a beautiful building in his life." But even Herod's Temple will pale in comparison to the heavenly temple yet to be revealed, where all God's children will "walk ... in white." It is well beyond our imagination, for John, who had the future revealed to him by Jesus Himself, says this of it:

I did not see a temple in the city, because *the Lord God Almighty and the Lamb are its temple.*... On no day will its gates ever be shut, for there will be no night there....Nothing impure will ever enter it, nor will anyone who does what is shameful or deceitful, but only those whose names are written in the Lamb's book of life.

Revelation 21:22, 25, 27

DECEMBER 9

The Lord waits to be gracious to you.
Isaiah 30:18 ESV

From the pen of Charles Spurgeon:

God often delays in answering prayer, and there are several instances of this in sacred Scripture. For example, Jacob had to wait all night for a blessing from the Lord, for God "wrestled with him till daybreak" (Gen. 32:24). Jesus did not immediately answer the plea of the woman of Syrian Phoenicia "whose little daughter was possessed by an evil spirit" (Mark 7:25). "Three times [Paul] pleaded with the Lord to take ... away" his "thorn in [the] flesh" (2 Cor. 12:7–8), but never received any assurance it would happen. Instead, he was given this promise from the Lord: "My grace is sufficient for you" (v. 9).

If you have been knocking at God's gate of mercy but have not received an answer, do you believe I can tell you why the all-powerful Creator has not opened the door and let you enter? I cannot, for our Father has reasons for keeping us waiting that are all His own. Sometimes it is to demonstrate His power and sovereignty so people will know Jehovah has a right to give and to withhold. Yet more often than not it is for our own benefit. Perhaps you have been kept waiting in order that your desires would become more passionate. God knows His delay will enliven and increase your desire, and that if He keeps you waiting, you will see your needs more clearly and will seek an answer more earnestly, and that ultimately you will value His mercy even more after having waited for it. There may also be some error in you needing to be removed before "the joy of the Lord" (Neh. 8:10) is given to you. Perhaps your understanding of the gospel plan is confused, or perhaps you have been relying too much on yourself instead of trusting simply and completely on the Lord Jesus. Or finally, perhaps God is requiring you to wait awhile so He may more fully "show [you] the incomparable riches of his grace" (Eph. 2:7). All your prayers are filed in heaven, and although they may not be answered immediately, they are not forgotten, for in just a little while they will be fulfilled to your complete delight and satisfaction. Therefore, never allow despair to cause you to become silent but remain earnest and "faithful in prayer" (Rom. 12:12).

From the pen of Jim Reimann:

In today's society we have been ingrained with the idea of doing; thus, waiting is one of the most difficult things we are asked to do. Ask us to do anything but wait! Yet waiting is a discipline every disciple of Jesus must learn.

Remember the words of Habakkuk, a prophet of God who understood the concept of waiting:

I will stand at my watch and station myself on the ramparts; I will look to see what he will say to me, and what answer I am to give to this complaint. Then the LORD replied: "Write down the revelation and make it plain on tablets so that a herald may run with it. *For the revelation awaits an appointed time; it speaks of the end and will not prove false. Though it linger, wait for it; it will certainly come and will not delay."*
Habakkuk 2:1–3

Before you begin your day of "doing," take time to consider these words of David, another man who knew what it meant to wait:

I am still confident of this: I will see the goodness of the LORD in the land of the living. Wait for the LORD; be strong and take heart and wait for the LORD.
Psalm 27:13–14

December 10

So we will be with the Lord forever.

1 Thessalonians 4:17

From the pen of Charles Spurgeon:

Even our sweetest times with Christ seem so short and fleeting! One moment our eyes see Him and we rejoice with "inexpressible and glorious joy" (1 Peter 1:8), but so quickly we don't see Him, for our beloved withdraws from us. Like a young deer He leaps across a ridge of mountains separating us from Him; He is gone to the higher land of spices and no longer feeds among the lilies.

> If today He stoops to bless us
> With a sense of pardoned sin,
> He tomorrow may distress us,
> Make us feel the plague within.
>
> John Kent, 1766 – 1843

Oh, how sweet to consider the time when we will not behold Him from a distance, but "shall see [Him] face to face" (1 Cor. 13:12) — when He will not be as a constant traveler only tarrying for the night, but will eternally embrace us with His glory! For a short season we will not see Him, but:

> Millions of years our wondering eyes,
> Shall o'er our Savior's beauties rove;
> And myriad ages we'll adore,
> The wonders of His love.
>
> Author unknown

In heaven we will have no interruptions from unmet needs or sin, no weeping will blur our eyes, no earthly business will distract our happy thoughts, and nothing will hinder us from gazing forever with unwearied eyes on "the sun of righteousness" (Mal. 4:2). If it is so sweet to see Him now and again here, imagine how wonderful it will be to gaze on His blessed face forever, to never have even a cloud come between us, and never have to turn our eyes away to look on a world of weariness and woe!

Blessed day, when will you dawn? Rise, O never-setting sun! Earthly joys may leave us when they will, for this day will make glorious amends. If dying is simply entering into uninterrupted communion with Jesus, then indeed "to die is gain" (Phil. 1:21) and the darkness of "death has been swallowed up in victory" (1 Cor. 15:54).

From the pen of Jim Reimann:

It is so easy to complain about the difficulties of this life, but Paul said, "I consider that our present sufferings are not worth comparing with the glory that will be revealed in us" (Rom. 8:18). Think about these amazing words!

Paul had been blessed with a glimpse of heaven unlike anything we have ever seen. He described his experience as having seen "visions and revelations from the Lord" (2 Cor. 12:1); as having been "caught up to the third heaven" (v. 2); as being "caught up to paradise" and having "heard inexpressible things" (v. 4); and finally, as having been given "surpassingly great revelations" (v. 7).

Remember! This man — who saw and heard all this — said, "Our present sufferings are not worth comparing with the glory that will be revealed in us"!

DECEMBER 11

The one who calls you is faithful and he will do it.

1 Thessalonians 5:24

From the pen of Charles Spurgeon:

Heaven is a place where we will never sin and where we will finally be able to let down our constant guard against our determined enemy. The tempter will not be there to ensnare our feet, the wicked will no longer trouble us, and the weary of the Lord will be at rest. Heaven is the ultimate inheritance, for it is the place of perfect holiness and is therefore the place of complete security.

Yet don't the saints here on earth occasionally taste the joys of blessed security? The teaching of God's Word is that all who are in union with the Lamb are safe and secure, that all the righteous will remain on their path, and that those who have committed their souls to the keeping of Christ will find Him to be a faithful and immutable protector and preserver. This doctrine sustains us so we can enjoy security even on earth. Not that this supreme and glorious security renders us free from every stumble, but it comes with the sure promise of Jesus "that whoever believes in him shall not perish" (John 3:16) and will be with Him wherever He is. Thus, may we often reflect with joy on this doctrine of the perseverance of the saints and honor the faithfulness of our God by displaying a holy confidence in Him.

Dear believer, may our God grant you a sense of your security in Christ Jesus! May He assure you by saying, "I have engraved you on the palms of my hands" (Isa. 49:16), and may He whisper this promise in your ear, "Do not be afraid, for I am with you" (Isa. 43:5). Look upon Him, the great "guarantee of a better covenant" (Heb. 7:22), "[who] ... is called Faithful and True" (Rev. 19:11) and who is therefore fully occupied and obligated to present you, the weakest of the family, along with all the other chosen ones, before the throne of God. As you wait in sweet contemplation, may He give you His "spiced wine to drink, the nectar of [His] pomegranates" (Song 8:2), and may you taste the luscious fruits of paradise. You will enjoy an appetizer of the enjoyments that are even now delighting the souls of the perfected saints in glory if you believe, with unwavering faith, that "the one who calls you is faithful and he will do it."

From the pen of Jim Reimann:

This morning Spurgeon shares the truth of the process of sanctification and the fact that Jesus came to give us abundant life in this life as well as the next. Christ said, "I have come that they may have life, and have it to the full" (John 10:10). Sanctification is defined as the ongoing process in the life of a believer that leads to more holy living. Paul encourages us to get involved in the process when he says, "Continue to work out your salvation with fear and trembling" (Phil. 2:12). Some people confuse this verse with the salvation of the soul, but Paul is referring to our ongoing eternal salvation, or sanctification, for he continues, "For it is God who works in you to will and to act according to his good purpose" (v. 13).

Today's verse in its context confirms that the Lord has taken it upon Himself to perfect us through what we call sanctification. Paul says:

May God himself, the God of peace, sanctify you through and through. May your whole spirit, soul and body be kept blameless at the coming of our Lord Jesus Christ. *The one who calls you is faithful and he will do it.*"

1 Thessalonians 5:23 – 24

DECEMBER 12

His ways are eternal.

Habakkuk 3:6

From the pen of Charles Spurgeon:

How God worked in the past is how He will work in the future. Man's ways change, but God's ways are everlasting. There are many reasons for this great comforting truth, including these: the Lord's ways are the result of His unwavering wisdom, and He directs all things according to the counsel of His own will. Human actions are often the result of a fleeting compulsion or fear and are followed by regrets and changes. But nothing takes the Almighty by surprise or happens other than what He has planned. God's ways are the outgrowth of His immutable character and in His ways we clearly see His determined, unchangeable attributes. The eternal Himself cannot undergo change. Therefore His ways, which are simply God in action, must remain eternally the same.

Is the Lord eternally just, gracious, faithful, wise, and loving? Then His ways also must forever be described by the same unchangeable attributes. All beings act according to their nature. Thus, when their nature changes, their conduct also will change. But since God cannot "change like shifting shadows" (James 1:17), His ways will abide everlastingly the same. In addition, there is no outside force that could reverse His divine ways since they are the embodiment of His irresistible might and power. Habakkuk said of the Lord:

> You split the earth with rivers; the mountains saw you and writhed.... The deep roared and lifted its waves on high. Sun and moon stood still.... In wrath you strode through the earth.... You came out to deliver your people.
>
> Habakkuk 3:9 – 13

No one can hold back his hand or say to him: "What have you done?"

Daniel 4:35

Yet it is not God's power alone that gives stability to His ways, for they are the revelation of His eternal principles of right and justice as well, and therefore they can never pass away. Wrong breeds decay and leads to ruin, but justice, truth, and goodness have a vitality that the ages can never diminish.

May we go to our heavenly Father with confidence this morning, remembering: "Jesus Christ is the same yesterday and today and forever" (Heb. 13:8), and in Jesus Christ, the Lord is eternally gracious to His people.

From the pen of Jim Reimann:

We can never separate knowing God from knowing His ways, which is why knowing the Scriptures is vitally important. Studying the Word is the best way — much more trustworthy than examining our own experiences — to learn of God's character and His ways. This leads us to unshakable faith, such as Habakkuk displayed even when disaster was on the doorstep of Israel. Although enemies were threatening and everything seemed to be going against him, he wrote:

> Though the fig tree does not bud and there are no grapes on the vines, though the olive crop fails and the fields produce no food, though there are no sheep in the pen and no cattle in the stalls, yet I will rejoice in the LORD, I will be joyful in God my Savior. The Sovereign LORD is my strength.
>
> Habakkuk 3:17 – 19

God, I thank You that You have said, "I the LORD do not change" (Mal. 3:6).

DECEMBER 13

... salt without limit.

Ezra 7:22

From the pen of Charles Spurgeon:

Israel was to "add salt to all [their] offerings" (Lev. 2:13) and, due to its preserving and purifying properties, it became the natural symbol of God's divine grace for the soul. Thus, it is worth noting that when King Artaxerxes gave salt to Ezra the priest, he set no limit on the quantity, and we may be certain that when the "King of kings" (Rev. 17:14) distributes His grace among His "royal priesthood" (1 Peter 2:9) He does not skimp on the supply. We may find grace lacking in ourselves but never in the Lord, for in Him "each one [may] gather as much [manna] as he needs" (Ex. 16:16). There is no famine in spiritual Jerusalem, so its citizens may eat their bread and drink their water "without limit." Some things in God's economy, however, are measured. For example, "gall ... and ... vinegar" (Ps. 69:21) are precisely measured so we will never have one drop too much. But when it comes to the salt of grace, no restriction is made, for you may "ask whatever you wish, and it will be given you" (John 15:7).

Parents must often hide the candy and cookie jars from their children, but there is never a need to put salt under lock and key, for few children would eat too much of it. A person may have too much money or too much honor, but one can never have too much grace. When "Jeshurun grew fat," he "kicked" (Deut. 32:15) against God. But there is no fear of someone having too much grace because an excess of grace is impossible. Greater wealth brings more responsibilities and worries, but more grace brings greater joy. "With much wisdom comes much sorrow" (Eccl. 1:18), but an abundance of the Spirit brings the "fulness of joy" (Ps. 16:11 KJV).

Dear believer, go to God's throne for an abundant supply of heavenly salt. It will season your afflictions, which are "tasteless ... without salt" (Job 6:6), and it will preserve your heart, which becomes corrupt when salt is lacking. And just as salt will kill snails, it will kill your sins. You need much of the "salt" of God's grace; therefore seek much and receive much.

From the pen of Jim Reimann:

Paul opens his letter to the church in Ephesus with the salutation: "Grace and peace to you from God our Father and the Lord Jesus Christ" (Eph. 1:2). He then continues with the theme of God's grace, but notice how he describes it as you read the following:

> In love he predestined us to be adopted as his sons through Jesus Christ, in accordance with his pleasure and will — to the praise of *his glorious grace*, which he has *freely given* us in the One he loves. In him we have redemption through his blood, the forgiveness of sins, in accordance with *the riches of God's grace that he lavished on us* with all wisdom and understanding.
>
> Ephesians 1:4 – 8

Later he told Timothy, "The grace of our Lord was poured out on me *abundantly*, along with the faith and love that are in Christ Jesus" (1 Tim. 1:14). Finally, he gives us the proper response to God's grace when he says, "All this is for your benefit, so that the grace that is reaching more and more people may cause thanksgiving to overflow to the glory of God" (2 Cor. 4:15).

Lord, my heart overflows in thanksgiving for Your gift of "glorious grace"!

DECEMBER 14

They go from strength to strength.

Psalm 84:7

From the pen of Charles Spurgeon:

There are various renderings of these words in different Bible translations, but all of them convey the idea of progress. "They go from strength to strength" means they grow stronger and stronger. Typically when walking, for example, we go from strength to weakness. We start fresh and strong for our journey, but when the road gets rough and the sun beats down, we begin to tire and then must painfully continue upon our weary way. Yet a Christian pilgrim continuously receives fresh supplies of grace and is as vigorous after many years of toilsome travel and difficulties as when he first began. He may not appear as zealous or as spontaneous in his zeal as he once was, but he is much stronger in the things that constitute true power, and although he may travel more slowly, he travels far more steadily.

Some gray-haired veterans are as strong in their grasp of the truth and as zealous in sharing it as they were in their younger days. Regrettably, often that is not the case, for the love of many grows cold and sin abounds in their life. This, however, is their own fault — not the fault of this promise of God that still holds true: "Even youths grow tired and weary, and young men stumble and fall; but those who hope in the LORD will renew their strength. They will soar on wings like eagles; they will run and not grow weary, they will walk and not be faint" (Isa. 40:30 – 31).

Other Christians sit around worrying and troubling themselves about the future, saying, "We only go from affliction to affliction." That may be true, "You of little faith" (Matt. 14:31), but you also "go from strength to strength," for you will never find a bundle of affliction that does not have sufficient grace tied to it. And God will always give you strength equal to the burden your shoulders must bear.

From the pen of Jim Reimann:

One of the beautiful aspects of the Christian life is that we never have to rely on our own strength. So-called "good deeds" done in our strength do not have the blessing of God upon them and do not bring Him glory. In fact, these works done only in our own power are simply works of the flesh. This means they are actually sinful deeds and will ultimately burn as "wood, hay or straw" (1 Cor. 3:12). Our role is simply to be a vessel through which the Lord can work regardless of the level of our personal physical strength. This is precisely why the Lord told Paul, "My grace is sufficient for you, for my power is made perfect in weakness," to which Paul responded, "Therefore I will boast all the more gladly about my weaknesses, so that Christ's power may rest on me. That is why, for Christ's sake, I delight in weaknesses, in insults, in hardships, in persecutions, in difficulties. For when I am weak, then I am strong" (2 Cor. 12:9 – 10).

Meditate on the following promises today, trusting in the Lord who is your strength: "The LORD is my rock, and my fortress, and my deliverer; my God, my strength, in whom I will trust" (Ps. 18:2 KJV). "The LORD, is my strength and my song; he has become my salvation" (Isa. 12:2). "Trust ... in the LORD for ever: for in the LORD JEHOVAH is everlasting strength" (Isa. 26:4 KJV).

Father, grant me the attitude of John the Baptist, who declared, "[Christ] must become greater; I must become less" (John 3:30).

DECEMBER 15

Orpah kissed her mother-in-law good-by,
but Ruth clung to her.

Ruth 1:14

From the pen of Charles Spurgeon:

Both of Naomi's daughters-in-law, Orpah and Ruth, loved Naomi and therefore set out with her upon her return to the land of Judah. But then the time of testing came when Naomi quite unselfishly laid out before them the trials ahead, urging them to return to their friends in Moab for the sake of their own ease and comfort. Initially both of them declared they would return with her to the Lord's people, but upon further consideration Orpah "wept again" and then "kissed her mother-in-law good-by" (Ruth 1:14), returning to her idolatrous friends. Ruth, however, followed through on her commitment and with all her heart submitted herself to the God of her mother-in-law.

It is one thing to love the ways of the Lord when times are easy but quite another to cling to them during all kinds of discouragements and difficulties. The kiss of an outward profession is easy, yet worthless. Actually clinging to the Lord, which reveals itself through a holy decision for truth and holiness, is no small matter.

What about us? Is our heart fixed on Jesus? Is our "sacrifice [bound] with cords, even unto the horns of the altar" (Ps. 118:27 KJV)? Have we counted the cost and are we sincerely ready to suffer all worldly loss for the sake of the Master? The future eternal gain will be abundant compensation, for "the treasures of Egypt" (Heb. 11:26) "are not worth comparing with the glory that will be revealed in us" (Rom. 8:18).

Orpah is never heard from again, for her life melts away through worldly ease and idolatrous pleasure into the gloom of death. In great contrast, however, Ruth lives today in history and in heaven, for God's grace placed her in the royal lineage from which came the "King of kings" (Rev. 17:14). "Blessed ... among women" (Luke 1:42) are those who for Christ's sake renounce all things, but forgotten — or even worse than forgotten — are those who in a time of temptation sear their conscience and return to the world.

May we never be content with having only the form or pretense of devotion, which may be no better than Orpah's kiss. Instead, may the Holy Spirit do such a work in us that we will cling with our whole heart to our Lord Jesus.

From the pen of Jim Reimann:

The story of Naomi's daughter-in-law Orpah is much like the sad account of Lot. Abram gave Lot the first choice of the land where he would settle by saying, "If you go to the left, I'll go to the right; if you go to the right, I'll go to the left" (Gen. 13:9). Of course, Lot chose what he considered the best land, but we are told he "pitched his tents near Sodom. Now the men of Sodom were wicked and were sinning greatly against the LORD" (vv. 12 – 13).

The fact that Lot "pitched his tents near Sodom," which was well known for its wickedness, should be a red flag to us. Attempting to pitch our tents at the edge of the world's wickedness will never work out well for us either.

Lord, help me remember: "The world has been crucified to me, and I to the world" (Gal. 6:14). Help me walk in that glorious truth, and may I never have simply the "form of godliness" while "denying its power" in my life" (2 Tim. 3:5).

DECEMBER 16

Come to me.

Matthew 11:28

From the pen of Charles Spurgeon:

The call of the Christian faith is the gentle word "Come." Conversely, the Jewish law harshly said, in effect, "Carefully guard your steps and the path in which you walk. Break the commandments and you will perish, but keep them and you will live." The law was administered with terror, driving people to follow it through the threat of scouring punishment, but the gospel draws people with cords of love. Jesus is "the good shepherd" (John 10:11) leading His sheep, bidding them to follow Him, and always directing them onward with the sweet word "Come." The law drives people away, but the gospel attracts; the law reveals the distance between God and man, while the gospel bridges that awful chasm and delivers sinners across it.

From the very first moment of your spiritual life until you are ushered into glory, Christ's words to you will be: "Come to me." Just as a mother holds out her arms, urging her child to walk by saying, "Come," Jesus does the same. He will always be ahead, bidding you to follow Him as a soldier follows his general. He will forever walk before you, paving your way and clearing your path, and you will hear His life-giving voice calling you to follow throughout your days. Even at your solemn hour of death, His sweet words ushering you into His heavenly world will be: "Come, you who are blessed by my Father" (Matt. 25:34).

Furthermore, if you are a believer, "Come" is not only Christ's call to you but it will be your call to Him as well. You will be longing for His second coming and saying, "Come quickly. Amen. Even so, come, Lord Jesus" (Rev. 22:20 KJV). You will be yearning for closer and closer communion with Him, and as He bids you "Come," your response to Him will be, "Come, Lord, and abide with me.

Come and be the sole, unrivaled sovereign reigning on the throne of my heart, and consecrate me entirely to Your service."

From the pen of Jim Reimann:

Jesus says, "Come to me," and then simply adds, "Follow me" (John 21:19). In truth, it is actually a gracious act of His to lead rather than commanding us to do so. Not only does He lead but He has a particular "race marked out for us" (Heb. 12:1) and graciously lights the way ahead, for "[His] word is a lamp to my feet and a light for my path" (Ps. 119:105).

It is all very simply stated, but how we over-complicate His will! He even said, "This is the will of him who sent me, that I shall lose none of all that he has given me, but raise them up at the last day" (John 6:39). Thus, He has taken it upon Himself to lead us, and we have His very Word as calm assurance we will ultimately arrive at His eternal home. We also have the assurance that the law is no longer a burden to us because of Him. Here is how Paul stated it:

What the law was powerless to do in that it was weakened by the sinful nature, God did by sending his own Son in the likeness of sinful man to be a sin offering. And so he condemned sin in sinful man, in order that the righteous requirements of the law might be fully met in us, who do not live according to the sinful nature but according to the Spirit.... The mind of sinful man is death, but the mind controlled by the Spirit is life and peace.

Romans 8:3 – 4, 6

Father, thank You for "the freedom we have in Christ Jesus" (Gal. 2:4).

DECEMBER 17

I remember the devotion of your youth.

Jeremiah 2:2

From the pen of Charles Spurgeon:

It is worth noting that Christ delights to think of His church and to look upon her beauty. Just as a bird returns often to its nest and a traveler hurries back home, the mind continually dwells on the choice object of its affection. We can never look too often on the face of a loved one, for we desire to have our precious things continually in our sight. And so it is with our Lord Jesus, for from eternity He has been "delighting in mankind" (Prov. 8:31). Since before time began His thoughts looked forward to the time when His elect would be born into the world, and He viewed them through the window of His foreknowledge. Through David, God said, "All the days ordained for me were written in your book before one of them came to be" (Ps. 139:16). "For the foundations of the earth are the LORD's; upon them he has set the world" (1 Sam. 2:8), and "he set up boundaries for the peoples according to the number of the sons of Israel" (Deut. 32:8).

Before Jesus' incarnation He actually descended to earth many times in the likeness of man. Examples of the Son of Man visiting His people are found in the stories of Abraham at Mamre near Sodom and Gomorrah (Gen. 18); Jacob wrestling with God at the Jabbok stream (Gen. 32:22 – 32); Joshua at the walls of Jericho (Josh. 5:13 – 6:5); and the story of Shadrach, Meshach, and Abednego in the fiery furnace of Babylon (Dan. 3). Because the Lord's soul delighted in them, He could not stay away, for His heart longed for them. They were never absent from His heart and He even "engraved [them] on the palms of [His] hands" (Isa. 49:16). Just as the breastplate bearing the names of the tribes of Israel was the most beautiful ornament worn by the high priest (see Ex. 28:29), so the names of Christ's elect are His most precious jewels, glittering over His heart.

We may often forget to meditate upon the perfections of our Lord, but He never ceases to remember us. Therefore, let us admonish ourselves for our past forgetfulness and pray for the grace to keep Him in our fondest remembrance forever.

Lord, paint upon the eyes of my soul the image of Your Son.

From the pen of Jim Reimann:

One beautiful aspect of being a Christian is having the New Testament as a lens through which we may view and interpret the Old Testament. Through that lens we see Christ on every page, not simply in the passages Spurgeon mentions today. For example, Genesis says, "In the beginning God created the heavens and the earth" (Gen. 1:1), and the New Testament tells us Jesus Himself is the Creator. Think of our sweet Savior as your Creator as you consider these verses:

By him all things were created: things in heaven and on earth, visible and invisible, whether thrones or powers or rulers or authorities; all things were created by him and for him.

Colossians 1:16

In these last days he has spoken to us by his Son, whom he appointed heir of all things, and through whom he made the universe.

Hebrews 1:2

DECEMBER 18

Rend your heart and not your garments.

Joel 2:13

From the pen of Charles Spurgeon:

Rending of garments and other outward signs of religious fervor are easily displayed but are frequently hypocritical. Demonstrating true repentance is far more difficult and thus is far less common. People will follow a host of detailed ceremonial rituals, for such things are pleasing to the flesh; but true faith is all too humbling, heart-searching, and thorough for the likes of carnal people. These sinful people prefer, instead, something more ostentatious, flimsy, and worldly. Outward rituals bring temporary comfort, for they are pleasing to eyes and ears, the ego is fed, and self-righteousness is inflated; but they are ultimately misleading, for when it comes to the time of death and the day of judgment, the soul needs something more substantial than ceremonies and rituals upon which to lean. Apart from essential godliness, all religion is utterly useless. Every form of worship lacking sincerity of the heart is nothing but a solemn sham and an impudent mockery of the Majesty in heaven.

Rending of the heart, on the other hand, is a divine work of God and is felt deeply. It is a secret hidden grief that is personally experienced, not merely in form and ritual but as a soul-moving work of the Holy Spirit on the inmost heart of a true believer. It is not something simply to be discussed or something we simply acknowledge mentally, but something that is strongly and deeply felt in every loving child of God. It is powerfully humbling and completely sin-purging, yet it sweetly prepares the soul for gifts of God's grace that proud unyielding spirits are completely unable to receive. It is also distinctly discriminating, for it belongs solely to the elect of God — and to them alone.

Today's verse commands us to rend our hearts, but the human heart is by nature as hard as stone. Since this is true, how can this be done? We must take our hearts to Calvary where our dying Savior's voice once broke the rocks in two — knowing His voice is just as powerful today.

O blessed Spirit, may we truly hear the death cry of Jesus, and may our hearts be torn as people once tore their garments during times of mourning.

From the pen of Jim Reimann:

Job's story is a perfect example of true heart-rending repentance. At the end of his difficult ordeal he finally said, "Surely I spoke of things I did not understand, things too wonderful for me to know.... My ears had heard of you but now my eyes have seen you. Therefore I despise myself and repent in dust and ashes" (Job 42:3, 5 – 6). Notice how his experience caused him to see the Lord as He is, further leading him to humble himself in repentance. Finally, only after his repentance do we read: "And the Lord accepted Job's prayer" (v. 9).

David as well understood the difference between outward signs of repentance and the rending of the heart. After being confronted with his sin by the prophet Nathan, he prayed, "You do not delight in sacrifice, or I would bring it; you do not take pleasure in burnt offerings. The sacrifices of God are a broken spirit; a broken and contrite heart, O God, you will not despise" (Ps. 51:16 – 17).

I praise You, Lord, for You have said, "I will give you a new heart and put a new spirit in you; I will remove from you your heart of stone and give you a heart of flesh" (Ezek. 36:26).

DECEMBER 19

The lot is cast into the lap,
but its every decision is from the LORD.

Proverbs 16:33

From the pen of Charles Spurgeon:

If the Lord controls "the lot cast into the lap," what about our lives in total? If He guides even the simple casting of a lot, imagine how much more He must guide the events of our entire life, especially in light of our blessed Savior's words: "Not one [sparrow] will fall to the ground apart from the will of your Father. And even the very hairs of your head are all numbered" (Matt. 10:29 – 30).

Believer, always remembering this will bring a holy calm to your mind. It will so relieve you from anxiety, you will be better enabled to walk in patience, quiet, and cheerfulness as all Christians should. When you are anxious you cannot pray in faith, and when you are troubled by the things of the world you cannot serve your Master, for your thoughts are only of serving yourself. Yet if you would "seek first his kingdom and his righteousness,… all these things will be given to you as well" (Matt. 6:33). When you worry about your circumstances and lot in life, you are meddling in Christ's business and neglecting your own. This is nothing but attempting to provide what only God can provide while forgetting your role is only to obey. Thus, be wise and focus on obeying and let Christ handle the providing.

Go to your Father's storehouse and ask if He will really let you starve when it is overflowing with abundance. Examine His heart of mercy and see if it can ever prove to be unkind! Look at His unfathomable wisdom and see if it can ever be in error. Yet above all, look to Jesus Christ, your In-tercessor who pleads your case, and ask yourself: "Can my Father ever be ungracious toward me?"

If He remembers even a sparrow, will He ever forget one of "the least" (Matt. 25:45) of His poor children? "Cast your cares on the LORD and he will sustain you; he will never let the righteous fall" (Ps. 55:22).

> My soul, rest happy in thy low estate,
> Nor hope nor wish to be esteemed or great;
> To take the imprint of the Will Divine,
> Be that thy glory, and those riches thine.
> Madame Jeanne-Marie Guyon, 1648 – 1717
>
> Translated from French by
> William Cowper, 1731 – 1800

From the pen of Jim Reimann:

"His Eye Is on the Sparrow," the hymn written in 1905 by Civilla D. Martin (1866 – 1948) and Charles H. Gabriel (1856 – 1932), wonderfully complements Spurgeon's thoughts today:

> Why should I feel discouraged,
>   why should the shadows fall,
> Why should my heart be troubled,
>   when all but hope is gone?
> When Jesus is my fortress;
>   my constant friend is He.
> His eye is on the Sparrow,
>   and I know He watches me.
> I sing because I'm happy,
>   I sing because I'm free,
> For His eye is on the sparrow,
>   and I know He watches me.

DECEMBER 20

I have loved you with an everlasting love.

Jeremiah 31:3

From the pen of Charles Spurgeon:

Jesus often expresses His love to His church. Ralph Erskine (Scottish preacher and hymn writer, 1685 – 1752) described it well in these words from one of his sermons:

Jesus does not think it is enough to express His love to His church behind her back, but in her very presence He says, "All beautiful you are, my darling" (Song 4:7). Although this is true, it is not His typical method, for He is a wise lover, knowing when to hold back the expression of His love and when to share it. Yet there are times when He makes no secret of it — times when He makes it plain beyond dispute to the souls of His people.

The Holy Spirit is often pleased in the most gracious way to witness to our spirit of the love of Jesus. He takes of the things of Christ and reveals them to us, and though we hear no voice from the clouds and see no vision in the night, we have a testimony more certain than either of these. Even if an angel flew from heaven to inform a saint personally of the Savior's love for him, the evidence would not be one bit more satisfactory than that produced in the heart by the Holy Spirit. Ask the most spiritual of the Lord's people, those who live closest to the very gates of heaven, and they will tell you they have experienced times in their life when the love of Christ toward them has been such a clear and certain fact that they could no more doubt His love for them than question their own existence.

Yes, beloved, both you and I have experienced times of refreshment in the presence of the Lord, times when our faith has soared to the utmost heights of assurance. We have had the loving confidence to lean our heads against our Lord, just as John was blessed to do, and have had no more reason to question our Master's affection for us than John himself. In fact, we have even less cause to question His love, for even John asked, "Is it I [who will betray You]?" (Mark 14:19 KJV), and that dark question has been taken far from us. He has kissed us with His lips, and has put our doubts to death by the closeness of His embrace. Thus, Jesus' love has been sweeter to our souls than wine.

From the pen of Jim Reimann:

Four times in his gospel John refers to himself as "the disciple whom Jesus loved" (John 13:23, 20:2, 21:7, 21:20). This may lead us to pose the following question: Did Jesus love John more than the others? The obvious answer to this is: of course not! And Peter confirms this answer by telling us, "I now realize how true it is that God does not show favoritism" (Acts 10:34). In this verse Peter is referring to how the Lord "accepts men from every nation" (Acts 10:35) for salvation, but a strong case also can be made that Jesus loves everyone equally, "for God so loved the world" (John 3:16).

If Jesus loves everyone equally, then why did John refer to himself as "the disciple whom Jesus loved"? Perhaps it is due to the personal way the Lord loves His own. He loves each of us deeply, intimately, and individually, meeting each of us at our own point of need. In light of this, as a believer in Him, each of us should feel as though we are "the disciple whom Jesus loved"!

Remember — Jesus also expressed great love for Lazarus after his friend's death, for "the Jews said, 'See how he loved him!'" (John 11:36).

DECEMBER 21

Has he not made with me an everlasting covenant?

2 Samuel 23:5

From the pen of Charles Spurgeon:

First notice that the covenant mentioned here is of divine origin. "Has *HE* not made with me an everlasting covenant?" Oh, that great word *He*! Be still, my soul, for God, the everlasting Father, has made a covenant with me. Yes, the God who spoke the world into existence by His Word, stooping from His majesty, took hold of my hand and made a covenant with me. This isn't just any deed but a stupendous condescension that would enrapture our hearts forever if we could fully understand it. "Has *HE* not made with me an everlasting covenant?" He isn't simply a king — as great as that would be — but the "KING OF KINGS" (Rev. 19:16); El Shaddai, or God Almighty, who is the all-sufficient Lord; the Jehovah of the ages; the everlasting Elohim. "Has *HE* not made with me an everlasting covenant?"

Next notice the definite object of the covenant: "Has he not made with *ME* an everlasting covenant?" In this lies the true preciousness for every believer, for He made peace with the world for ME! It is one thing that He made a covenant but quite another that He has made a covenant *with ME*. What blessed assurance — the covenant is with ME! If God the Holy Spirit has given me that assurance, then His salvation is mine, His heart is mine, He Himself is mine — "He is my God" (Ex. 15:2).

Finally notice that the covenant is everlasting in its duration. An everlasting covenant is one that has no beginning and one that will never end. Amid all the uncertainties of life, how precious to know that "God's solid foundation stands firm" (2 Tim. 2:19) and to have the Lord's own promise: "I will not violate my covenant or alter what my lips have uttered" (Ps. 89:34).

Like King David as he was dying, I will sing of this: "Is not my house right with God? Has he not made with me an everlasting covenant?" (2 Sam. 23:5).

From the pen of Jim Reimann:

God's covenant of grace is revealed in various covenants in the Scriptures, such as this covenant with David, referred to in today's text:

> When your days are over and you rest with your fathers, I will raise up your offspring to succeed you, who will come from your own body, and I will establish his kingdom. He is the one who will build a house for my Name, and I will establish the throne of his kingdom forever. I will be his father, and he will be my son. When he does wrong, I will punish him with the rod of men.... But my love will never be taken away from him, as I took it away from Saul, whom I removed from before you. Your house and your kingdom will endure forever before me; your throne will be established forever.
>
> 2 Sam. 7:12 – 16

Later we are given David's beautiful last words:

> The Spirit of the LORD spoke through me; his word was on my tongue. The God of Israel spoke, the Rock of Israel said to me: "When one rules over men in righteousness, when he rules in the fear of God, he is like the light of morning at sunrise on a cloudless morning, like the brightness after rain that brings the grass from the earth." Is not my house right with God? Has he not made with me an everlasting covenant, arranged and secured in every part? Will he not bring to fruition my salvation and grant me my every desire?
>
> 2 Samuel 23:2 – 5

DECEMBER 22

I will strengthen you.
Isaiah 41:10

From the pen of Charles Spurgeon:

God has a full reserve of power with which to fulfill today's promise, for He is able to do all things. Dear believer, until you can drain the ocean of God's omnipotence dry, or until you can break the towering mountains of His almighty strength into pieces, you need never fear. Never think that man's strength will ever be able to overcome the power of God. As long as the earth's huge pillars still stand, you have reason enough to stand firm in your faith. The same God who directs the earth in its orbit, who fuels the burning furnace of the sun, and who lights the starry lamps of heaven has promised to supply you with daily strength. Since He is fully able to sustain the universe, never even imagine He will prove unable to fulfill His own promises.

Remember what He did in days of old, in the former generations. Remember how He spoke and it was done, how He commanded and creation came to be. Will He who created the world now grow weary? Will He who hung the world on nothing suddenly be unable to support His children? Will He be unfaithful to His Word for lack of power? Who is it that controls the storms, for "He makes the clouds his chariot and rides on the wings of the wind" (Ps. 104:3) and holds the oceans "in the hollow of his hand" (Isa. 40:12)? How can He fail you? When He has placed such a faithful promise as this in His Word, will you believe for even a moment that He may have "out-promised" Himself, going beyond His power to fulfill? No, doubt no longer!

O my God and my strength, I believe Your promise will be fulfilled, for the boundless reservoir of Your grace can never be exhausted, and the overflowing storehouse of Your strength can never be emptied by Your friends or stolen by Your enemies.

Now let the feeble all be strong,
And make Jehovah's arm their song.
Philip Doddridge, 1702 – 1751

From the pen of Jim Reimann:

Today Spurgeon focuses our attention on our sovereign, omnipotent God — "The LORD [who] is faithful to all his promises and loving toward all he has made" (Ps. 145:13). Why not spend the remainder of your devotional time this morning reflecting on two of today's Scriptures in their following contexts:

Praise the LORD, O my soul. O LORD my God, you are very great; you are clothed with splendor and majesty. He wraps himself in light as with a garment; he stretches out the heavens like a tent and lays the beams of his upper chambers on their waters. He makes the clouds his chariot and rides on the wings of the wind. He makes winds his messengers, flames of fire his servants. He set the earth on its foundations; it can never be moved.

Psalm 104:1 – 5

Who has measured the waters in the hollow of his hand, or with the breadth of his hand marked off the heavens? Who has held the dust of the earth in a basket, or weighed the mountains on the scales and the hills in a balance?

Isaiah 40:12

And always remember — "The grass withers and the flowers fall, but *the word of our God stands forever*" (Isa. 40:8).

DECEMBER 23

Friend, move up to a better place.

Luke 14:10

From the pen of Charles Spurgeon:

When the life of grace first begins in the soul, we do indeed draw closer to God, but it is with great fear and trembling. A soul who has become aware of his guilt, and who truly has been humbled by it, is overwhelmed by the sacredness of his new position in God's grace and is brought down to earth by an awareness of the grandeur of Jehovah in whose presence he now stands. Thus, with true humility, the soul seeks the lowest, or most humble, place.

Although true believers will never forget the sacredness of their new position and will never lose the sense of holy awe surrounding it, the ongoing walk with Christ causes the earlier feelings of fear and terror to subside. As a Christian grows in grace, the fear of being in the very presence of the God who can create or destroy becomes more of a holy reverence and is no longer an overshadowing dread. As believers mature, they are called "to a better place" — a place of greater access to God in Christ Jesus. As they begin their walk amid the glorious splendor of Deity as well as amid the blood and righteousness of Jesus Christ, they veil their faces like heavenly cherubim do with their wings. As they reverently and submissively approach the Lord's throne, they see a God of love, goodness, and mercy and more fully realize the covenant character of God. Rather than cowering in fear before the absolute Deity, they recognize more of God's goodness as opposed to His greatness, and more of His love as opposed to His majesty.

At this point of Christian maturity, the soul, while still humbly bowing and continuing to prostrate itself before the glory of the infinite God, will enjoy a more sacred liberty of intercession and will be sustained by the refreshing awareness of being in the presence of limitless mercy, infinite love, and total acceptance "in the beloved" (Eph. 1:6 KJV).

Thus, the believer is invited "to a better place" and is enabled to exercise the privilege of rejoicing in God and drawing closer to Him in holy confidence, while saying, "*Abba*, Father" (Rom. 8:15).

> So may we go from strength to strength,
> And daily grow in grace,
> Till in Your image raised at length,
> We see You face to face.
>
> Author unknown

From the pen of Jim Reimann:

The words of today's poem, "So may we go from strength to strength," are based on Psalm 84, which beautifully describes the believer's pilgrimage that ultimately leads to the very throne of God. May these words be our prayer this morning:

> "*Blessed are those who dwell in your house; they are ever praising you. Blessed are those whose strength is in you, who have set their hearts on pilgrimage.... They go from strength to strength, till each appears before God in Zion.... Better is one day in your courts than a thousand elsewhere; I would rather be a doorkeeper in the house of my God than dwell in the tents of the wicked*" (Ps. 84:4 – 5, 7, 10).

Though he was rich, yet for your sakes he became poor.

2 Corinthians 8:9

From the pen of Charles Spurgeon:

The Lord Jesus was eternally rich, glorious, and exalted, but "though he was rich, yet for your sakes he became poor." Just as a rich saint cannot have true oneness with his poor brothers unless he ministers to their needs from his substance, the same is true of the head and its members. In other words, it would have been impossible for our Divine Lord to have fellowship with us unless He gave of His own abundant wealth and became poor to make us rich. If He had remained upon His throne of glory and we had continued in the ruins of mankind's fall without receiving His salvation, communion would have been impossible for both sides. Except through God's covenant of grace, it is as impossible for fallen man to communicate with God as it is to have "harmony ... between Christ and Belial" (2 Cor. 6:15).

Thus, in order for communion to be provided, it was necessary for our rich Brother to bestow His estate upon His poor relatives, and because our righteous Savior gave His sinful brothers of His own perfection, we who are the poor and guilty have received "from the fullness of his grace ... one blessing after another" (John 1:16). The result of this giving and receiving, with One descending from the heights of heaven and others ascending from the depths of earth, is the ability to embrace one another in genuine heartfelt fellowship. Our poverty must be enriched by Christ, in whom are found infinite treasures, before we can experience true communion. And our guilt must lose itself in Christ's imputed and imparted righteousness before our soul can walk in fellowship and purity. Jesus must clothe His people in His own garments or He cannot allow them to enter His palace in heaven, and He must wash them in His own blood or else they will remain too defiled for the embrace of His fellowship.

O believer, "this is love" (1 John 4:10)! "For your sakes [the Lord Jesus] became poor" that He might lift you up into communion with Himself.

From the pen of Jim Reimann:

The context of today's verse has to do with Paul encouraging the church in Corinth to generously give to the Lord's work. The verse preceding our text says, "I want to test the sincerity of your love by comparing it with the earnestness of others" (2 Cor. 8:8). Yet the obvious comparison they are to make is not with others in their church but with the generosity of the Lord, for Paul continues, "For you know the grace of our Lord Jesus Christ, that though he was rich, yet for your sakes he became poor, so that you through his poverty might become rich" (v. 9). Who of us fares well in that comparison!

Yet Paul keeps on encouraging us by later saying,

Whoever sows sparingly will also reap sparingly, and whoever sows generously will also reap generously. Each man should give what he has decided in his heart to give, not reluctantly or under compulsion, for God loves a cheerful giver. And God is able to make all grace abound to you, so that in all things at all times, having all that you need, you will abound in every good work. As it is written: "He has scattered abroad his gifts to the poor; his righteousness endures forever."

2 Corinthians 9:6 – 9

Lord, thank You for Jesus who became poor "to make grace abound"!

DECEMBER 25

The virgin will be with child and will give birth to a son,
and will call him Immanuel.

Isaiah 7:14

From the pen of Charles Spurgeon:

Let us go down to Bethlehem today with the wondering shepherds and adoring Magi, and let us see Him "who has been born king of the Jews" (Matt. 2:2). By faith we may lay claim to Him and may sing, "To *us* a child is born, to *us* a son is given" (Isa. 9:6). Jesus is Jehovah incarnate, our Lord and our God, yet is also our brother and friend.

Therefore, let us adore and admire Him, but first, let us remember His miraculous conception. It was an event unheard of before and unparalleled since — that a "virgin will be with child and will give birth to a son." The first promise of His coming mentioned the offspring of the woman, not the offspring of the man. (See Gen. 3:15.) Since it was the woman who led the way into sin that lost paradise for mankind, it was she, and she alone, who would usher in the One to regain that paradise once lost. Although our Savior was truly man, when it came to His human nature He was "the Holy One of God" (Mark 1:24). Let us reverently bow before the holy Child whose innocence restores for mankind his ancient, former glory, and let us pray that "Christ [may be] formed in [us]" (Gal. 4:19) — "the hope of glory" (Col. 1:27).

Next let us remember His humble parentage. His mother has been described simply as "the virgin" — not a princess, or a prophetess, or the matriarch of a large estate. It's true that the blood of kings ran in her veins, that her mind was strong, and that she was well taught, for she sang one of the sweetest songs of praise ever sung. Yet consider her humble state, how poor was the man to whom she was engaged, and how miserable the accommodations provided for the newborn King!

"'They will call him Immanuel' — which means, 'God with us'" (Matt. 1:23). "God with us" — in our nature, in our sorrow, in our life's work, in our punishment, and in our death. "God with us" *now* — or actually we with Him — in His resurrection, ascension, triumph, and the splendor of His second coming.

From the pen of Jim Reimann:

Our present-day view of the nativity has been shaped more by tradition than fact. To this day in the Middle East the typical sheepfold is a cave with only one doorway. The shepherd puts his sheep in the cave for the night and then lies across the doorway, literally protecting his sheep with his life. This is why Jesus said, "I am the gate for the sheep.... Whoever enters through me will be saved. He will come in and go out, and find pasture.... I am the good shepherd. The good shepherd lays down his life for the sheep" (John 10:7, 9, 11).

The typical manger was not what we see in modern nativity displays, but was a basin hewn from a large rock. The shepherd places the grain for the animals in one and water in another. What a humble, but appropriate, place for the Son of God to be placed after His birth, for He would later say, "I am the bread that came down from heaven" (John 6:41), and "If anyone is thirsty, let him come to me and drink" (John 7:37).

What a beautiful picture of a beautiful Savior — "Look, the Lamb of God, who takes away the sin of the world!" (John 1:29).

The last Adam . . .
1 Corinthians 15:45

From the pen of Charles Spurgeon:

Jesus is the covenant head of His elect. Just as every heir of flesh and blood has a personal stake in Adam because he is the covenant head and representative of the race that is under the law of works, so every redeemed soul is one with the Lord from heaven under the law of grace because He is the second or "the last Adam"— the Representative and Substitute of the elect in "a new covenant" (Heb. 12:24) of love. The writer of Hebrews taught that "when Melchizedek met Abraham, Levi was still in the body of his ancestor" (Heb. 7:10). Thus, it is a certainty that the believer was in the body of Jesus Christ, the Mediator, when during eternity past the covenant agreements of grace were decreed, ratified, and guaranteed forever.

Consequently, everything Christ has done He has done for the entire body of His church. We were crucified in Him and "buried with Him" (see Col. 2:10–13), yet even more wonderful, we were "raised . . . up with Christ and seated . . . with him in the heavenly realms" (Eph. 2:6). It is through Him, therefore, that the church "fully met" the "righteous requirements of the law" (Rom. 8:4) and is "accepted in the beloved" (Eph. 1:6 KJV). Because of Him the law has been satisfied and the church now stands justified before a just Jehovah, for He views her in Jesus, never seeing her separate from her covenant Head.

As the anointed Redeemer of Israel, Christ Jesus lays claim to nothing distinct from His church, for all He possesses He holds for her. Adam's righteousness was ours as long as he maintained it, but his sin became ours the moment he committed it. In the same manner, all that "the last Adam" is or does is as much ours as His because He is our representative.

This truth is the very foundation of the covenant of grace and the gospel of our salvation. It is this gracious system of representation and substitution that moved Justin Martyr (AD 100–165) to proclaim, "O blessed change! O sweet permutation!" Thus, it should be received with strong faith and rapturous joy.

From the pen of Jim Reimann:

Today's devotion brings to mind the doctrine of imputation, an accounting term that means to charge to an account. For example, if someone makes a credit card purchase with their card on your behalf, then your purchase is *imputed* to their account. With that in mind, here are the three imputations in the Scriptures:

Adam's sin to all mankind: "Sin entered the world through one man, and death through sin, and in this way death came to all men, because all sinned" (Rom. 5:12).

The sins of the elect to Christ: "The Lord has laid on him the iniquity of us all" (Isa. 53:6). "He himself bore our sins in his body on the tree" (1 Peter 2:24).

The righteousness of Christ to all believers: "A righteousness from God, apart from law, has been made known. . . . This righteousness from God comes through faith in Jesus Christ to all who believe" (Rom. 3:21–22).

"My soul rejoices in [You] my God. For [You have] clothed me with garments of salvation and arrayed me in a robe of righteousness" (Isa. 61:10).

DECEMBER 27

Can reeds thrive without water?

Job 8:11

From the pen of Charles Spurgeon:

A reed is spongy and hollow, like a hypocrite who has no substance or stability. It shakes to and fro in the wind, much like people more concerned with legalism and the form of worship than with any inner significance and who therefore yield to every outside influence. This is the reason a reed is not broken by a storm and why hypocrites are never troubled by persecution. While most of us would not willingly be a deceiver or be deceived, our text verse today is perhaps a good test to determine whether we are hypocrites. For example, a reed by nature lives in water and owes its very existence to the mud and moisture where it has taken root, but if the mud dries out, the reed quickly withers. Its greenness is absolutely dependent upon its circumstances, for an abundance of water causes it to flourish, while a drought destroys it.

Is this my case? Do I serve God only when good people surround me or when my faith is profitable and respected? Do I love the Lord only when worldly comforts come from His hands? If so, I am nothing but a shameful hypocrite and, like a withering reed, I will perish when death deprives me of outward joys. Can I honestly say that when bodily comforts have been few and my surroundings have been hostile to my walk of grace that my integrity has been maintained? If so, then I have hope of a genuine living godliness in me.

A reed cannot grow without moisture, but plants of "the LORD's right hand" (Ps. 118:15) can and do flourish, even in a year of drought. In fact, a godly man often grows best when his worldly circumstances decay. He who follows Christ for His moneybag is nothing but a Judas (see John 13:29), and they who follow Him for loaves of bread and fish are children of the Devil. But they who follow Him due to their genuine love for Him are His beloved ones.

Lord, let me find my life in You — not in the muck and mire of this world's favor or gain.

From the pen of Jim Reimann:

Paul warns against hypocrisy by describing people who have "a form of godliness" while "denying its power" (2 Tim. 3:5). In light of this and today's teaching, consider these words from Jeremiah:

Cursed is the one who trusts in man, who depends on flesh for his strength and whose heart turns away from the LORD. He will be like a bush in the wastelands; he will not see prosperity when it comes. He will dwell in the parched places of the desert, in a salt land where no one lives. But blessed is the man who trusts in the LORD, whose confidence is in him. He will be like a tree planted by the water that sends out its roots by the stream. It does not fear when heat comes; its leaves are always green. It has no worries in a year of drought and never fails to bear fruit.

Jeremiah 17:5 – 8

In contrast to the reed that is so dependent on its environment, here is what the future holds for those who truly love the Lord:

The righteous will flourish like a palm tree, they will grow like a cedar of Lebanon; planted in the house of the LORD, they will flourish in the courts of our God. They will still bear fruit in old age, they will stay fresh and green.

Psalm 92:12 – 14

DECEMBER 28

The life I live in the body,
I live by faith in the Son of God.
Galatians 2:20

From the pen of Charles Spurgeon:

When the Lord in His mercy passed by and saw us in our flesh and blood, the first thing He did was say, "Live." He did this first because life is essential when it comes to spiritual matters, for until it is bestowed we are incapable of partaking in things of the kingdom. And the life that God's grace bestowed at the moment of a saint's spiritual quickening is none other than the life of Christ. His life, like sap flowing through a stem, runs into us who are the branches and establishes a living connection between our souls and Jesus. The faith that follows is then the first gift of God's grace and is what enables us to perceive our union with Christ. It is the "firstfruits" and the neck that joins the body of the church to its all-glorious Head.

> O Faith! You bond of union with the Lord,
> Is not this office yours, and your fit name?
> In the economy of gospel types,
> And symbols suitable — the church's neck;
> Identifying her in will and work
> With Him ascended?
> Author unknown

Faith takes hold of the Lord Jesus with a firm and determined grasp. She knows His excellence and worth, and no temptation can lead her to lay her trust elsewhere. Christ Jesus is so delighted with the heavenly gift of faith that He never ceases to strengthen and sustain her with His loving embrace and the all-sufficient support of His eternal arms. Thus is established a living, sensible, and delightful union that sends forth streams of love, confidence, sympathy, fulfillment, and joy from which both the bride and the Bridegroom love to drink. When the soul perceives the reality of this oneness between Christ and itself, the pulse may be felt as beating for both, with the same blood flowing through the veins of each. Only then is one's heart as near to heaven as possible here on earth and fully prepared for the enjoyment of the most glorious and spiritual kind of fellowship.

From the pen of Jim Reimann:

As we have seen today, faith is the first gift of grace. Paul said, "It has been granted to you on behalf of Christ ... to believe on him" (Phil. 1:29). Along with that faith, however, comes the gift of love, for Paul also said, "The grace of our Lord was poured out on me abundantly, along with the faith and love that are in Christ Jesus" (1 Tim. 1:14). And we know that true faith will manifest itself in a deep and abiding love for the Lord. Thus, with that in mind, may this hymn be the prayer of our heart this morning:

> Once earthly joy I craved, sought peace and
> rest;
> Now thee alone I seek, give what is best.
> This all my prayer shall be: More love, O Christ,
> to thee;
> More love to thee, more love to thee!
> Elizabeth P. Prentiss, 1818 – 1878

DECEMBER 29

Samuel took a stone and ... named it Ebenezer, saying,
"Thus far has the LORD helped us."

1 Samuel 7:12

From the pen of Charles Spurgeon:

The words "thus far" appear to be a hand pointing to the past. Whether twenty years (see 1 Sam. 7:2) or seventy — "Thus far has the LORD helped us"! Through poverty and wealth, through sickness and health, at home and abroad, on land and at sea, in honor and dishonor, in difficulty and joy, in trials and triumphs, and in prayer and temptations — "Thus far has the LORD helped us"! Just as we delight looking down a long avenue of trees that forms a lush, green temple, with its branching pillars and arches of leaves, we enjoy looking back on the long aisles of the years of our life. View the green boughs of God's mercy overhead and the strong pillars of His loving-kindness and faithfulness that lift our joys heavenward. Do you see the birds singing in the branches? Surely there are many and they are all singing of the Lord's mercy received "thus far."

But these words also point forward, for when someone marks a certain place, it means he is not yet at the end and there is still some distance to travel. We must cross more temptations and joys, more trials and triumphs, more prayers and answers, more weariness and strength, and more battles and victories. Then will come old age, sickness, disease, and death, but will this be the end? No! We will awaken to much more — the likeness of Jesus, thrones, harps, songs, psalms, robes of righteousness, the face of Jesus, the fellowship of the saints, the glory of God, infinite happiness, and the fullness of eternity.

O believer, be of good courage and, with grateful confidence, set up your Ebenezer stone as Samuel did, for:

The Lord who "thus far" has helped you

Will help you all your journey through.

John Newton, 1725 – 1807

When the words "thus far" are read in heaven's light, what glorious and miraculous prospects they reveal to our grateful eyes!

From the pen of Jim Reimann:

When Samuel "took a stone ... and named it Ebenezer," he was doing what the Israelites often did to commemorate a time of God's blessing. For example, when Israel crossed the Jordan,

> Joshua called together the twelve men he had appointed from the Israelites, one from each tribe, and said to them, "Go over before the ark of the LORD your God into the middle of the Jordan. Each of you is to take up a stone on his shoulder, according to the number of the tribes of the Israelites, to serve as a sign among you. In the future, when your children ask you, 'What do these stones mean?' tell them that the flow of the Jordan was cut off before the ark of the covenant of the LORD. When it crossed the Jordan, the waters of the Jordan were cut off. These stones are to be a memorial to the people of Israel forever."

Joshua 4:4 – 7

Likewise, our lives are to be living memorials to the Lord, for Peter wrote,

> As you come to him, the living Stone — rejected by men but chosen by God and precious to him — you also, like living stones, are being built into a spiritual house to be a holy priesthood.

1 Peter 2:4 – 5

DECEMBER 30

The end of a matter is better than its beginning.

Ecclesiastes 7:8

From the pen of Charles Spurgeon:

Look at our Lord and Master's beginning, for "He was despised and rejected by men, a man of sorrows, and familiar with suffering" (Isa. 53:3). Then look at "the end of the matter," "where Christ is seated at the right hand of God" (Col. 3:1) and "waits for his enemies to be made his footstool" (Heb. 10:13). "In this world we are like him" (1 John 4:17). We must bear a cross or we will never wear a crown; we must wade through mire or we will never walk streets of gold.

Thus, cheer up, sad Christian! "The end of a matter is better than its beginning." Consider the lowly worm and its contemptible appearance, for it is only the beginning of the matter. Then notice the butterfly with its gorgeous wings, playing in the sunbeams and sipping nectar from the blossoms. It is full of happiness and life, but that is "the end of [the] matter." That caterpillar is you until the time you are wrapped in the chrysalis of death. "But ... when he appears, [you] shall be like him, for [you] shall see him as he is" (1 John 3:2).

Thus, be content to "be like him" here on earth — a worm, a no one — that like Him you may be fully satisfied when you wake up in His likeness in glory. Think of that rough-looking diamond placed on the stonecutter's wheel. He cuts it on every side, removing much that the diamond thought was so important for itself. But when the king is crowned, and the crown is placed upon the monarch's head with the joyful fanfare of trumpets, a glittering flash of light beams from that very diamond that not long ago had been so troubled at the hands of the stonecutter.

Go ahead — dare to compare yourself to that diamond, for you are one of God's people and this is the time of the cutting process. Let faith and "perseverance ... finish its work" (James 1:4), for on the day when the crown will be set upon the head of "the King eternal, immortal, invisible" (1 Tim. 1:17), one ray of glory will shine from you. "They shall be mine, saith the LORD of hosts, in that day when I make up my jewels" (Mal. 3:17 KJV).

Truly — "The end of a matter is better than its beginning."

From the pen of Jim Reimann:

Perseverance and endurance are continual themes in God's Word. Life was never meant to be easy but, instead, was meant to conform us to "the likeness of [God's] Son" (Rom. 8:29). Today Spurgeon briefly quotes from James, but here is the verse in its context:

> Consider it pure joy, my brothers, whenever you face trials of many kinds, because you know that the testing of your faith develops perseverance. Perseverance must finish its work so that you may be mature and complete, not lacking anything.
>
> James 1:2 – 4

Paul stressed endurance as well by writing this to the Thessalonians:

> We continually remember before our God and Father your work produced by faith, your labor prompted by love, and your endurance inspired by hope in our Lord Jesus Christ.... You became imitators of us and of the Lord; in spite of severe suffering, you welcomed the message with the joy given by the Holy Spirit. And so you became a model to all the believers.
>
> 1 Thessalonians 1:3, 6 – 7

Father, may we glimpse "the end of the matter," but even now be "the aroma of Christ among those who are being saved" (2 Cor. 2:15).

DECEMBER 31

On the last and greatest day of the Feast, Jesus stood and said in a loud voice,
"If anyone is thirsty, let him come to me and drink."

John 7:37

From the pen of Charles Spurgeon:

"*Perseverance* ... finish[ed] its work" (James 1:4) in Jesus, and through "the last ... day of the Feast" He pleaded with the Jews, just as on this last day of the year He longingly pleads with us. The patience of the Savior year after year is to be admired, especially in light of our times of rebellion and resistance to His Holy Spirit.

"*Pity* expressed itself quite plainly," for Jesus cried out, not just loudly, but tenderly. He pleads with us to be reconciled through the words of Paul: "We implore you ..." (2 Cor. 5:20). How deep must be the love that makes the Lord weep over sinners. Surely our hearts will respond to such a call of love.

"*Provision* is offered plenteously," for Jesus offers all we need to quench our soul's thirst. To our conscience, Christ's atonement brings peace; to our understanding, the gospel brings the richest instruction; and to our heart, Jesus is the highest object of affection. To our entire being, Christ supplies the purest sustenance of all. He can quench the deepest thirst, and fully restore even the most starved of souls.

"*Proclamation* is made freely," for anyone is welcome. Nothing but thirst is required. Whether we suffer from the thirst of greed, ambition, knowledge, or weariness, we are invited to come and drink. Sin seeks deeper and deeper drinks of lust, thus, it is not goodness within us causing the Creator to make His invitation. He offers it freely, for "God does not show favoritism" (Acts 10:34).

"*Personality* is declared fully," for a sinner must come to the Person of Jesus — not to works, laws, or doctrines, but to a personal Redeemer, who "himself bore our sins" (1 Peter 2:24). The bleeding, dying, but rising Savior is our only hope. Oh, that He would grant you the grace to come and drink before the sun sets on this last day of the year!

Notice Jesus' invitation does not mention you having to wait or to prepare yourself to come. He simply says "drink," something anyone can do. No amount of sin can block His invitation to believe. No jewel-covered chalice is required, for the mouth of poverty is welcome to drink of Him. Filthy, blistered, leprous lips may drink from His stream of love, for they will not pollute it, but they themselves will be purified.

Dear reader, hear the Redeemer's loving voice as He cries, "If anyone is thirsty, let him come to me and drink."

From the pen of Jim Reimann:

As we face a new year, it is tempting to once again make a list of resolutions. Yet so often, resolutions are broken within a matter of days. This year may we make a different kind of resolution — one that will pay spiritual dividends for years to come. May we simply resolve to go to Jesus every day of the year — and drink of Him!

May our closing prayer of this year be that of David, who prayed,

"*One thing I ask of the LORD, this is what I seek: that I may dwell in the house of the LORD all the days of my life, to gaze upon the beauty of the LORD and to seek him in his temple*" (Ps. 27:4).

Scripture Index

Subject Index

ABOUT THE AUTHOR

Jim Reimann has more than five million books in print in more than twelve languages, including the updated editions of *Streams in the Desert* and *My Utmost for His Highest*. He is a former retail executive and past chairman of the Christian Booksellers Association. Jim is an ordained minister, Bible teacher, author, and Israel tour host, having lead numerous Bible-teaching tours to Israel and other Bible lands, which he offers through his website *www.JimReimann.com*.

Jim and his wife, Pam, have three married children and six granddaughters. They make their home in Atlanta, Georgia.

The companion volume to *Morning by Morning: The Devotions of Charles Spurgeon* is also available from Zondervan:

Evening by Evening: The Devotions of Charles Spurgeon
Expanded, Indexed, and Updated in Today's Language by Jim Reimann

Other Classic Devotionals Updated by Jim Reimann:

My Utmost for His Highest by Oswald Chambers, Updated Edition
Published by Discovery House Publishers

Streams in the Desert by L. B. Cowman, Updated Edition
Published by Zondervan

Streams for Teens by L. B. Cowman, Updated Edition
Published by Zondervan

Streams in the Desert for Graduates by L. B. Cowman, Updated Edition
Published by Zondervan

Streams in the Desert®

366 Daily Devotional Readings

L. B. Cowman.
Edited by Jim Reimann,
Editor of My Utmost for His Highest, Updated
Edition

For years, the beloved classic devotional *Streams in the Desert* has sustained and replenished God's weary desert travelers. Now, bursting forth like a sparkling clear river of wisdom, encouragement, and inspiration, this updated edition of *Streams in the Desert* promises to revive and refresh today's generation of faithful sojourners, providing daily Scripture passages from the popular, readable New International Version—and modern, easy-to-understand language that beautifully captures the timeless essence of the original devotional. Filled with insight into the richness of God's provision and the purpose of his plan, this enduring classic has encouraged and inspired generations of Christians.

James Reimann, editor of the highly acclaimed, updated edition of *My Utmost for His Highest* by Oswald Chambers, again brings us the wisdom of the past in the language of today by introducing this updated edition of *Streams in the Desert.*

Day by day, *Streams in the Desert* will lead you from life's dry, desolate places to the waters of the River of Life—and beyond, to their very Source.

Evening by Evening
The Devotions of Charles Spurgeon

Jim Reimann,
Editor of the Updated Editions of Streams in
the Desert® and My Utmost for His Highest

What can *Evening by Evening* do for you?

A lot! Especially if you're a serious Christian or a Bible student who wants to be challenged to think differently about how to apply God's Word to your life.

Jim Reimann, inspired interpreter of such classics as *Streams in the Desert* and *My Utmost for His Highest*, gives *Evening by Evening* — the powerful devotions of Charles Spurgeon — a new spin.

Reimann carefully maintains the strength and dignity of the original edition, but broadens the appeal by adding:

- *Updated language and precise NIV text*
- *Contemporary applications and prayers*
- *Scripture references for every Bible quote*
- *Easy-to-use Scripture and subject indexes*
- *Scriptures selected from every book of the Bible*

These additions are designed to make *Evening by Evening* ideal for personal use as well as for sharing in study groups. But it's the author's thoughtful "From the pen of Jim Reimann" segments that really make this devotional shine.

The author's daily commentary complements Spurgeon's writing perfectly. Each day, Reimann includes personal reflections and shares thought-provoking ideas gleaned from his extensive travel and studies in Israel and other Bible lands. The result is a day-by-day opportunity for Christians to pause, reflect, learn, and grow.

Whether you're mature in your faith or new to the journey, this stimulating devotional delivers a daily dose of just what you need.

Available in stores and online!

Share Your Thoughts

With the Author: Your comments will be forwarded to the author when you send them to zauthor@zondervan.com.

With Zondervan: Submit your review of this book by writing to zreview@zondervan.com.

Free Online Resources at

www.zondervan.com

Zondervan AuthorTracker: Be notified whenever your favorite authors publish new books, go on tour, or post an update about what's happening in their lives at www.zondervan.com/authortracker.

Daily Bible Verses and Devotions: Enrich your life with daily Bible verses or devotions that help you start every morning focused on God. Visit www.zondervan.com/newsletters.

Free Email Publications: Sign up for newsletters on Christian living, academic resources, church ministry, fiction, children's resources, and more. Visit www.zondervan.com/newsletters.

Zondervan Bible Search: Find and compare Bible passages in a variety of translations at www.zondervanbiblesearch.com.

Other Benefits: Register yourself to receive online benefits like coupons and special offers, or to participate in research.

ZONDERVAN®

ZONDERVAN.com/
AUTHORTRACKER
follow your favorite authors